NON-STATE ACTORS IN INTERNATIONAL LAW

The role and position of non-state actors in international law is the subject of a long-standing and intensive scholarly debate. This book explores the participation of this new category of actors in an international legal system that has historically been dominated by states. It explores the most important issues, actors and theoretical approaches with respect to these new participants in international law. It provides the reader with a comprehensive and state-of-the-art overview of the most important legal and political developments and perspectives.

Relevant non-state actors discussed in this volume include, in particular, international governmental organisations, international non-governmental organisations, multinational companies, investors and armed opposition groups. Their legal position is considered in relation to specific issue-areas, such as humanitarian law, human rights, the use of force and international responsibility. The main legal theories on non-state actors' position in international law—neo-positivism, the policy-oriented approach and transnational law—are covered at the beginning of the book, and the essential political science perspectives—on non-state actors' role in international politics and globalisation, as well as their soft power—are presented at the end.

Volume 55 in the series Studies in International Law

Studies in International Law

Recent titles in this series

Fighting Corruption in Public Procurement: A Comparative Analysis of Disqualification or Debarment Measures
Sope Williams-Elegbe

The Interception of Vessels on the High Seas: Contemporary Challenges to the Legal Order of the Oceans
Efthymios Papastavridis

Integration at the Border: The Dutch Act on Integration Abroad and International Immigration Law
Karin de Vries

An Equitable Framework for Humanitarian Intervention
Ciarán Burke

Democratic Statehood in International Law: The Emergence of New States in Post-Cold War Practice
Jure Vidmar

International Law and the Construction of the Liberal Peace
Russell Buchan

The OIC, the UN, and Counter-Terrorism Law-Making: Conflicting or Cooperative Legal Orders?
Katja Samuel

Statelessness: The Enigma of the International Community
William E Conklin

The Reception of Asylum Seekers under International Law: Between Sovereignty and Equality
Lieneke Slingenberg

International Law and Child Soldiers
Gus Waschefort

The Contractual Nature of the Optional Clause
Gunnar Törber

For the complete list of titles in this series, see 'Studies in International Law' link at www.hartpub.co.uk/books/series.asp

Non-State Actors in International Law

Edited by
Math Noortmann
August Reinisch
and
Cedric Ryngaert

• HART •
PUBLISHING
OXFORD AND PORTLAND, OREGON
2017

Hart Publishing
An imprint of Bloomsbury Publishing Plc

Hart Publishing Ltd
Kemp House
Chawley Park
Cumnor Hill
Oxford OX2 9PH
UK

Bloomsbury Publishing Plc
50 Bedford Square
London
WC1B 3DP
UK

www.hartpub.co.uk
www.bloomsbury.com

Published in North America (US and Canada) by
Hart Publishing
c/o International Specialized Book Services
920 NE 58th Avenue, Suite 300
Portland, OR 97213-3786
USA

www.isbs.com

First published in hardback, 2015
Paperback edition, 2017

British Library Cataloguing-in-Publication Data
A catalogue record for this book is available from the British Library.

ISBN: PB: 978-1-50991-783-9
HB: 978-1-84946-511-3

Typeset by Compuscript Ltd, Shannon
Printed and bound in Great Britain by
Lightning Source UK Ltd

Contents

List of Contributors

Barrie Axford is Professor in Politics at Oxford Brookes University.

Anna-Luise Chané is Research Fellow and PhD Candidate at the Leuven Centre for Global Governance Studies—Institute for International Law, KU Leuven.

Alan Chong is Associate Professor at the S Rajaratnam School of International Studies.

Jean d'Aspremont is Professor of Public International Law at the University of Manchester and Professor of International Legal Theory at the University of Amsterdam.

Hans Joachim Heintze is a Professor at the Institute for International Law of Peace and Armed Conflict.

Christian Henderson is a Senior Lecturer in Law at the University of Liverpool.

Karolina Miriam Januszewski is a Teaching and Research Assistant in International Law and Human Rights at the University of Vienna.

Markus Kornprobst is a Professor in International Relations at the Vienna School of International Studies.

Charlotte Lülf is a Research Associate at the Institute for International Law of Peace and Armed Conflict.

Math Noortmann is a Professor in Transnational law and Non-State Actors at the Coventry Centre for Trust, Peace and Social Relations.

Manfred Nowak is Professor of International Law and Human Rights at the University of Vienna.

Jordan J Paust is the Mike and Teresa Baker Law Center Professor of International Law at the University of Houston.

August Reinisch is a Professor at the Institute for European Law, International Law and Comparative Law at the University of Vienna.

Cedric Ryngaert is Professor of Public International Law at Utrecht University.

Eisuke Suzuki is Professor of Law at the Ateneo de Manila University Law School, Manila, Philippines.

Ramses A Wessel is Professor of International and European Institutional Law at the University of Twente.

Jan Wouters is Professor of International Law and International Organizations, Jean Monnet Chair *Ad Personam* EU and Global Governance, and Director of the Leuven Centre for Global Governance Studies and of the Institute for International Law, KU Leuven.

1

Introduction

MATH NOORTMANN, CEDRIC RYNGAERT AND
AUGUST REINISCH

NON-STATE ACTORS HAVE added a new dimension of complexity to the study of international law. While the presence of non-state actors in the international realm is widely acknowledged, and consistently growing amongst the students of international law (and international relations), their role and status in that global dominion is equally contested. A wide variety of monographs and edited volumes,[1] chapters and journal articles,[2] thematic conferences[3] and

[1] See, eg, Jean d'Aspremont, 'Non-state Actors from the Perspective of Legal Positivism: the Communitarian Semantics for the Secondary Rules of International Law' in Jean d'Aspremont (ed), *Participants in the International Legal System: Multiple Perspectives on Non-State Actors in International Law* (Abingdon, Routledge, 2011); Math Noortmann, 'Non-State Actors in International Law' in Bas Arts, Math Noortmann and Bob Reinalda (eds), *Non-State Actors in International Relations* (Aldershot, Ashgate, 2001); Math Noortmann and Cedric Ryngaert, *Non-State Actor Dynamics in International Law: From Law-Takers to Law-Makers* (Aldershot, Ashgate, 2010); Philip Alston (ed), *Non-State Actors and Human Rights* (Oxford, Oxford University Press, 2005); Andrea Bianchi (ed), *Non-State Actors and International Law* (Aldershot, Ashgate, 2009); Robert P Barnidge, *Non-State Actors And Terrorism: Applying The Law of State Responsibility and The Due Diligence Principle* (The Hague, TMC Asser Press, 2008); Anne Peters, *Non-State Actors as Standard Setters* (Cambridge, Cambridge University Press, 2009); Rainer Hofmann and Nils Geissler, *Non-State Actors As New Subjects Of International Law: International Law—From The Traditional State Order Towards The Law Of The Global Community* (Berlin, Duncker & Humblot, 1999).

[2] See, eg, Peter Malanczuk, 'Multinational Enterprises and Treaty-Making—A Contribution to the Discussion on Non-State Actors and the 'Subjects' of International Law' in *Multilateral Treaty-Making* (Dordrecht, Springer, 2000); Rebecca J Cook, 'Accountability in International Law for Violations of Women's Rights by Non-State Actors' (1993) 25 *Studies in Transnational Legal Policy* 93; John Cerone, 'Much Ado About Non-State Actors: The Vanishing Relevance of State Affiliation in International Criminal Law' (2008) 10 *San Diego International Law Journal* 335; Hans-Joachim Heintze, 'Do Non-State Actors Challenge International Humanitarian Law?' in *International Humanitarian Law Facing New Challenges* (Berlin, Springer 2007).

[3] See, eg, Hague Joint Conference on Contemporary Issues of International law; *From Government to Governance—The Growing Impact of Non-State Actors on the International and European Legal System*, The Hague, July 2003; Regional Conference of the South African Branch of the ILA on *Good Governance and Non-State Actors in International Law*, Johannesburg, 26–29 August 2007.

research projects[4] on non-state actors provide ample evidence of that state of affairs. The present edited volume reflects and engages the various positions and opinions on non-state actors in international law and international relations. It provides the reader with a general overview of the NSA (non-state actor) discourse in international law, highlighting specific theoretical positions, issues and actors, as well as non-legal perspectives and approaches.[5]

The dazzling confusion that non-state actors have clouded our field of study with must be attributed to a number of eclectic grounds. Non-state actors are not states. This most obvious of statements, however, is not without intrinsic merits. From both a conceptual as well as an analytical perspective, non-state actors do not match the traditional unit of assessment of international law and international relations. Except for some armed opposition groups, non-state actors do not hold or seek governmental control over a territory and population,[6] and they vastly outnumber states, constituting an almost indefinite category of stake-holding participants in international affairs.

Non-state actors cover a broad range of entities, from intergovernmental organisations (IGOs), as bodies composed of states and usually enjoying recognition in the form of international legal personality, to non-governmental organisations (NGOs), multinational corporations (MNCs), and individuals whose status under international law is far more uncertain. Ultimately, the only unifying definitional bond holding them together is the fact that they are not states and that they are still somehow participating in and increasingly shaping the international system originally set up by states.

The existence of non-state actors in itself, however, neither calls for nor vindicates the inclusion of non-state actors in the study of international law per se. The introduction of non-state actors to a discipline that is understood and developed through the (legal personality of the) state has created more ontological and epistemological confusion than it has brought understanding. It is that state of confusion that this publication aims to clarify.

[4] See, eg, European Union (EU) thematic programme, 'Non State Actors and Local Authorities in Development',www.welcomeurope.com/european-funds/non-actors-local-authorities-development-156+56.html#tab=onglet_details. The International Law Association's Committee on Non-State Actors has published three substantial reports on non-state actors since 2008: www.ila-hq.org/en/committees/index.cfm/cid/1023.

[5] The chapters on international relations, soft power and globalisation are included to contextualise the socio-political dimension of the international legal discourse on non-state actors in international law and the paradigmatic connection between international law and international relations/politics.

[6] Outside academia, the qualification 'non-state actors' is generally assigned to armed groups, which (aim at the) control of territory for political and non-political reasons.

The non-state actor/international law relationship is perceived in terms of 'in' and 'and', which signal a fundamentally different perspective and approach. 'Non-state actors in international law' indicates an appreciation of the relationship from the internal perspective of international law. 'Non-state actors and international law' signal a more undetermined socio-legal relationship. Whereas the first analytical interest lies in the determination of the formal legal status and the authorised standing of non-state actors, the second concern is with the direct and indirect influence of non-state actors on the development of international law. It is our understanding that the line between determining and developing international law is inherently fluid. The title of this publication therefore reflects our intention to look at non-state actors from within international law, while being receptive to the socio-legal and political aspects of this relationship. The question whether both approaches are equally relevant for the student of international law is a matter of disciplinary debate and opinion, and informs many of the chapters in this handbook.

In Part I, Jean d'Aspremont, Eisuke Suzuki and Math Noortmann set out and discuss the main 'philosophical' contenders with respect to the status and function of non-state actors in international law: (neo)positivism, the policy-oriented approach and transnational law. While these authors approach non-state actors from different theoretical choices, they seem to agree that we can no longer study international law in a business-as-usual mode of investigation, when it comes to the appreciation of non-state actors' presence in the international realm.

Jean d'Aspremont discusses international law's approach to non-state actors from a (neo-)positivist approach. D'Aspremont argues that the state/non-state distinction is based on a legal conception of order in an international environment. Discussing the nature of the role of non-state actors in the constitution of that order in terms of socio/political and legal practice, he acknowledges the intrinsic socio-legal aspects of non-state actors research, but advocates a clear(er) distinction between social and legal practice.

Eisuke Suzuki starts with the well-known policy-oriented postulation that 'the whole notion of "subjects" and "objects" has no credible reality'. In the typical New Haven tradition, he takes non-state actors 'in context' and demonstrates the complexity that is inherent in a legal process that amounts to authoritative decision-making, rather than the determination of the law by a single body, however defined. Non-state actors in his perspective are perfectly capable of having such an authoritative decision-making capacity. The question of whether they should or should not is not irrelevant. Rather, the questions should focus on the policies for non-state actor participation and functionality. The ultimate aim is to give civil society an authoritative voice in a socio-political and legal decision-making process that sets the markers for a world society based on human dignity.[7]

After a positivist international legal and a non-positivist international legal approach, Math Noortmann posits transnational law as a possible third alternative to bring non-state actors into a legal realm that transcends the nation-state. He does so by first critically reviewing Philip Jessup's *Transnational Law* and using it as a basis for exploring the development of the concept over the last 50 years. He warns of the dangers that linger with the adoption of a modified transnational law concept by 'transnationalised legal traditionalists'. The transnational law concept of the (new) *lex mercatoria* comes closest to Jessup's original idea, but it shares with Jessup the oversight of those non-state actors which are not market- and trade-oriented organisations. To Noortmann, transnational law is a separate legal realm that partly overlaps with public international law and private international law, but constitutes an essentially separate legal space.

Part II deals with specific legal issues that are raised by the activities of non-state actors. Christian Henderson analyses the rules that apply when states use force against non-state actors. Hans-Joachim Heintze and Charlotte Lülf then look beyond the right to use force, into the consequences for international humanitarian law of the presence of humanitarian non-state actors at the new, non-international battlefields. (For armed non-state actors, see Chapter 13.) The issue of human rights and the accountability of non-state actors for its violation is addressed by Manfred Nowak and Karolina Miriam Januszewski. Cedric Ryngaert then looks at the other side of the accountability coin, ie the responsibility of states for non-state behaviour.

The use of force against non-state actors by states has both 'internal' and 'international' dimensions, according to Henderson. The threshold between the two is fluent and the determination of permissible 'internal use of force' (co-) determines the (inter)national status of armed non-state actors. That qualification determines whether the use of force against non-state actors is permitted under the rules of the UN Charter, and whether, consequently, a state is legally responsible for its resort to the use of force. The use of force against terrorists has raised particular questions in international legal literature. Henderson seems to conclude that non-state actors have changed the character of the use of force and so have they affected a change in the application of the rules, in particular proportionality and necessity.

Heintze and Lülf direct our attention to the consequences and role of humanitarian non-state actors in non-international conflicts, in particular

[7] *cf* W Michael Reisman, *The Quest for World Order and Human Dignity in the Twenty-first Century* (Brill, Martinus Nijhoff, 2013). 'Human Dignity', a core concept in the Policy Oriented Approach, has recently been included in the language of 'human security'.

the International Committee of the Red Cross. The latter organisation is responsible for shaping international humanitarian law and has acquired a specific protected role in the implementation of the 'Geneva rules'. That protected role, however, is increasingly contested by the activities of armed non-state actors. The ICRC is no longer the sole humanitarian organisation, and many others have followed in its footsteps. But not all have abided by the rigorous rules of international humanitarian assistance, in particular impartiality, neutrality, and independence. Given the necessity of providing humanitarian assistance in both violent conflict and disasters, and the increased presence of armed non-state actors in these situations, 'adherence to the humanitarian principles [is] even more important' than before.

Nowak and Januszewski's non-state actors are both protectors and violators of human rights. Their respective roles and consequences of their actions are obviously different. The problem revolves around the question whether there exist 'explicit' and 'direct' human rights obligations for non-state actors, which the authors answer in the affirmative, as only on that basis can non-state actors be held responsible. Their line of argument starts with the convincing 'dismantling' of the-state-as-the-only-subject-of-international-law myth and the building of a new 'real life' human rights narrative. The state in their argument is neither the sole threat nor the grand protector anymore and a more horizontal human rights order must be constructed in order to secure human dignity as the accumulated sum of all civil-political, economic, social and cultural rights.

In his chapter, Ryngaert implicitly agrees with Nowak and Januszewski that a state-centred responsibility approach has its limitations. But he submits that the rules of state responsibility on attribution and due diligence have lost little of their significance when it comes to regulating non-state actors. Reviewing the various rules of attribution and analysing the concept of due diligence, Ryngaert points out that the separation between the state and the non-state (the public-private distinction), is not always clear-cut, and that the 'state's capacity to exercise due diligence over non-state actors' should be 'strengthened'.

These substantive issues return in Part III, albeit that they are discussed from the perspective of specific actors. Ramses Wessel analyses international governmental organisations (IGOs) and the legal consequences of their institutional development. Math Noortmann discusses the roles of NGOs and the necessity to find a delicate balance between NGO rights and responsibilities. Jan Wouters and Anna-Luise Chané focus on multinational corporations (MNCs) as clusters of market-oriented non-state actors. August Reinisch focuses on investors as specific stakeholders who have sparked the development of international investment law. In his chapter on armed opposition groups, Jordan Paust focuses on a specific

..on-state actor that is equally diverse as IGOs, NGOs and MNCs, and their legal statuses and effects.

Wessel analyses IGOs from the perspective that these organisations are the most important non-state actor. His argument revolves around the changing nature of IGOs and particularly their trajectory from state to non-state actors. The substantive qualification 'governmental' is contested, as these actors are no longer exclusively 'governmental' in their decision and law-making processes. Since the days of the League of Nations, these organisations have gained a form of autonomy. In significant cases their 'behaviour', as reflected in executive councils and boards, is more than the sum of its constitutive state members. While the road to non-state 'actor-hood' for IGOs is far from clear, states are arguably IGOs' best friends, but no longer their leading lady. IGOs are increasingly becoming more then the sum of their constituent parts, ie they increasingly acquire a separate 'institutional agency' in 'international' affairs.

Non-governmental organisations, Noortmann argues, are distinctively different in their public and private roles which makes them at the same time more vulnerable as well as egotistical. NGOs' societal roles are secured and undermined by politics and law, and depend on political rather than factual recognition by the gatekeepers of the international legal system. A socio-legal/political approach is necessary to determine the specific rights and obligations that NGOs should be granted for specific purposes in specific contexts. NGO responsibility and accountability can be achieved through self-regulation, but this is not always effective, as the cases of the Gaza Flotilla and Christian Solidarity International show.

Wouters and Chané take the globalising business environment as their starting point for arguing that MNCs 'increasingly expand … into traditionally state-run sectors'. In line with the previous chapter, it provides a broad overview of the rights and obligations of MNCs, whereby specific legal fields such as investment, environment, human rights and international criminal law are considered. The legal regulation of the sector is clearly in a state of perplexity, including self-regulation, international regulation and national proceedings. The international trajectory of the role and status of MNCs is as of yet unclear and the effectiveness of international initiatives is still to be seen.

Investors are different in this respect, according to August Reinisch, as they are the 'driving forces of the development of international investment law', which builds on international customary law, investment treaties and arbitral awards. Especially in the specific procedure for settling investment disputes, Reinisch argues that we can observe 'the loss of exclusive state control'. His chapter analyses the developments of investment dispute settlement and the specific influence exerted by investors. Investors, perhaps more than other non-state actors have acted as norm-entrepreneurs in their own interest, through specific legal procedures.

In opposition to the previous non-state actors, armed opposition groups can be divided, according to Jordan Paust, into those organisations who have a recognised status under international law and those groups who have not, such as pirates, terrorists and brigands. These groups also trigger different international legal developments. Paust's chapter analyses the legal position of these various groups in the light of existing international law. It provides a comprehensive (historical) context of the varied developments in the field of regulated armed conflict and illegal violence.

Last but not least, Part IV discusses non-state actors in the international arena from the perspectives of political science and international relations (IR). Markus Kornprobst first of all takes stock of the IR debates, Alan Chong focuses on the specific concept of 'soft power', and Barrie Axford engages the idea of globalisation as a 'paradigm for a decentered world and the role of non-state actors in it.

Kornprobst starts with an introduction of theoretical IR debates to position non-state actors in various IR discourses: war, terrorism, arms control, economy, human rights and environment. He subsequently engages the question whether there is a 'global polity'. In his conclusion, Kornprobst connects his findings to international law and revisits the seminal international law-international relations discourse of the 1990s and the early twenty-first century. He argues that our international world does not distinguish between law and politics when it comes to the engagement of non-state actors, and suggests that a practical approach should be adopted by academia.

Chong introduces the reader to the concept of soft power, its workings, and how non-state actors acquire non-economic, non-military power. In particular, he explores the role of the Internet in increasing non-state actors' soft power, the latter's influence in matters of disaster relief and development, unethical practices and what he calls 'the soft power of legal manoeuvres'. Chong clearly relates the soft power of non-state actors to what he calls 'noble missions' orientation and the linkages between moral and legal considerations. In the end, however, Chong warns for the power of states to use and misuse the (soft) power of non-state actors.

Axford, last but not least, takes us beyond the idea of the 'international' and introduces 'the idea of global governance' as a manner of investigating 'novel versions of governmentality' beyond the state. Setting out 'new geographies of governance', he argues that 'globalisation' is a transformative concept, in which non-state actors stand as 'avatars of different kinds of globalisation', which urge us to reinterpret international law and international relations in manners that are neither fixed nor fluid.

The chapters overlap to some extent with respect to issues and actors. Given the nature of the non-state actor discourse, we are of the view that it is not entirely possible to avoid that overlap. We have decided not to avoid it with rigorous editing as it not only reflects the current state of the art in the non-state actors debate, but also testifies to the variety of opinions held be different authors with respect to various issues and actors.[8]

The different conclusions which different authors draw are symptomatic for the non-state actor discourse in international law and provide the reader an insight in the perspectives and positions that underlie the various arguments. In this respect this handbook facilitates the reading and re-reading of the academic literature and policy documents on non-state actors in/and international law. This will foster the understanding of the variety of approaches and perspectives that has provided the debate with that bewildering confusion. Such understanding is fundamental to the apprehension and appreciation of the diverse nature of non-state actors and the consequences of this diversity for the determination and development of international law.

[8] As an example, we refer to para 11.4.2 on international investment law in Ch 11 and to Ch 12 on investors. The two authors identify different sources as critical in the position of the non-state actor in question, whereby the role of that NSA in international law is different. Wouters and Chané stress the investment treaty as pivotal, whereas Reinisch emphasises the role of investors in arbitral proceedings. The role of MNCs in treaty formation is a socio-legal one, whereas the role of the investor in arbitration is that of a legal/normative entrepreneur.

Part I

2

Non-State Actors and the Social Practice of International Law

JEAN D'ASPREMONT

IT IS TRUISTIC that the role and status of non-state actors in the international legal order is perspective-specific.[1] Each perspective comes with a different paradigmatic framework[2] according to which the role and status of non-state actors is captured, described and reconstructed in a certain way, without any of these different perspectives having any ascendency other than social.[3] Said differently, the role and status of non-state actors is a matter of paradigmatic choice. This choice is being informed by normative preconceptions and agendas as well as the possible awareness of the expectations of the community one seeks to convince.

It is with this platitude in mind that this chapter consciously makes the choice for a certain positivist paradigm choice. It is assumed here that such a paradigm, despite the conspicuous ailment of many of its variants,[4] continues to remain intellectually stimulating to engage with questions pertaining to the role and status of non-state actors in international law. Indeed, it postulates that non-state actors, far from being demoted to factual and irrelevant entities in a dominantly state-centric system,[5] can

[1] Noortmann and Ryngaert, *Non-State Actor Dynamics in International Law: From Law-Takers to Law-Makers* (London, Ashgate, 2010).

[2] MacIntyre, however, argues that all perspectives are anchored in a similar tradition. See Alasdair C MacIntyre, *Whose Justice? Which Rationality?* (Notre Dame, University of Notre Dame Press, 1988).

[3] See generally, Jean d'Aspremont, 'Wording in International Law' (2012) 25 *Leiden Journal of International Law* 575. On the idea of social validation of legal argumentation, see generally Stanley Eugene Fish, *Doing What Comes Naturally: Change, Rhetoric, and the Practice of Theory in Literary and Legal Studies* (Durham NC, Duke University Press, 1989).

[4] For some self-reflective studies on the methodological and conceptual moves of international legal positivism, see Richard Collins, 'Classical Legal Positivism in International Law Revisited' in Jörg Kammerhofer and Jean d'Aspremont (eds), *International Legal Positivism in a Post-Modern World* (Cambridge, Cambridge University Press, 2014).

[5] It has been convincingly demonstrated that this understanding of international law is very much a strawman. See ibid. See also Steve Charnovitz, 'Two centuries of participation: NGOs and international governance' (1997) 18 *Michigan Journal of International Law* 183.

be entrusted with wide-ranging and determinative functions in terms of design (and understanding of the functioning) of the secondary rules of international law pertaining to the sources. In such a perspective, non-state actors can be seen as contributing to the design of the modes of identification of international law and thus the doctrine of sources.[6] In that sense, such a positivist paradigm promotes, rather than demotes, the role and status of non-state actors in international law as it makes them play a very central function in the design of the modes of cognition of the international legal order as a whole.

Needless to say that the choice for such a (variant of the) positivist paradigm is controversial, not because it redeems a role for non-state actors in positivist studies in international law, but because, as has been rightly pointed out in the literature,[7] it rests on empirical frameworks that remain in need of disclosing their underlying theory to avoid self-referencing.[8] This chapter is an attempt to further spell out and refine (the foundations of) such a perspective.

The chapter starts by a few epistemological observations on the idea that international law is, not only a set of rules, but also an argumentative practice between actors that are not necessarily of a non-state character (2.1). Changing the perspective from an argumentative understanding of international law to a rule-based understanding, it then distinguishes between two types of social practices and thus two types of engagement of non-state actors with social practice (2.2). It then exposes the positivistic paradigm whereby the doctrine of sources is itself nourished by a certain type of social practice (2.3) as well as the attempts witnessed in jurisprudence and general legal theory to pluralise such a paradigm as to include the social practice of non-state actors (2.4). Such a pluralistic positivist paradigm is then applied to international law with a view to discussing which non-state actors can potentially nurture the contents of the modes of identification of international law (2.5). The chapter ends with some remarks on the politics of definition (2.6).

2.1 EPISTEMOLOGICAL CONSIDERATIONS: NON-STATE ACTORS AND THE ARGUMENTATIVE PRACTICE OF INTERNATIONAL LAW

International law can be construed as an argumentative practice. So understood, international law boils down to a toolbox elaborated and used by

[6] See d'Aspremont, 'Wording' (n 3).

[7] Sahib Singh, 'International Law as a Technical Discipline: Critical Perspectives on the Narrative Structure of a Theory' in Jean d'Aspremont (ed), *Formalism and the Sources Of International Law: a Theory of the Ascertainment Of Legal Rules* (Oxford, Oxford University Press, 2011).

[8] MacIntyre, *Whose Justice?* (n 2) 333.

actors with or without an affiliation with a state—whether scholars, officials or activists, engaged in the business of persuasion. Put differently, a myriad of actors can be seen as being engaged in an argumentative struggle to secure persuasiveness and argumentative authority, thereby shaping (the discourse of) international law.[9] As Martti Koskenniemi puts it, 'international actors routinely challenge each other by invoking legal rules and principles on which they have projected meanings that support their preferences and counteract those of their opponents'.[10] What is more, this argumentative practice is social because validation of arguments that are thrown around is carried out through a social process involving a whole range of actors. Indeed, international law as argumentative practice remains the product of a community.[11] Arguments are thus created by virtue of communitarian processes where a whole series of actors manoeuvre to secure argumentative authority.

The foregoing means that a whole range of actors, including a string of non-state actors, can be seen as engaged in an argumentative struggle about international law. The argument could even be pushed further. It could be contended that all those actors engaged in the business of persuasion argue with one another irrespective of their official capacity. This point does not imply that the official capacity of an actor is of no relevance if one construes international law as an argumentative practice. Indeed, chances of securing persuasiveness within the interpretive community of international law may be enhanced by the official position the actor concerned is holding, be its membership to the bench of the judicial organ of international organisations, the position of legal adviser of an influential state, or its affiliation to a prestigious research institution. Yet, although constituting a parameter bearing upon the argumentative power of actors, one can say that, from an epistemological point of view, the argumentative practice of international law is that of a myriad of actors for whom the (lack of) affiliation to the state is of no import.

The argumentative practice of international law is not unconstrained. It is subject to all kinds of formal and non-formal structures. Among those structures, rules play a specific constraining role. Those rules, although they are constraining the argumentative practice, are simultaneously constituted by such a practice. More precisely, the rules structuring the argumentative practice are nurtured by the social practice of those actors engaged in legal argumentation. This chapter focuses on that part of the argumentative

[9] See generally, d'Aspremont, 'Wording' (n 3) 25. On the idea of social validation of legal argumentation, see generally Fish, *Doing What Comes Naturally* (n 3) 237.

[10] Martti Koskenniemi, 'International Law and Hegemony: A Reconfiguration' (2004) 17 *Cambridge Review of International Affairs* 197, 199.

[11] Stanley Eugene Fish, *Is there a Text in this Class? The Authority of Interpretive Communities* (Cambridge MA, Harvard University Press, 1980) 13–15.

practice that feeds into the rules of international law, and especially secondary rules pertaining to the sources of international law. This part of the argumentative practice of international law, which this chapter looks at, and that informs the rules constraining argumentative practice, is called here, the *social practice*. The sections that follow are thus devoted to the contribution of non-state actors to the social practice that nurtures the rules constraining the argumentative practice of international law, especially those pertaining to the sources of international law.

2.2 TWO TYPES OF SOCIAL PRACTICE AND TWO TYPES OF ENGAGEMENT BY NON-STATE ACTORS

As was indicated above, this chapter focuses on one aspect of the argumentative practice of international law, namely the social practice that feeds into the rules that constrain international legal argumentation, and especially that informing the secondary rules pertaining to the sources of international law. This specific focus calls for a series of observations on the distinction between two types of social practice nourishing the rules of international law. Indeed, two types of social practice should not be conflated: the social practice revolving around the determination of the content of rules, on the one hand, and that geared toward the identification of these rules as law properly so-called, on the other hand. If one accepts that, from a conceptual point of view, these processes must be distinguished, it follows that the social practices that feed into each of them should not be put on the same footing and hence, non-state actors' social engagement with content-determination and with law-ascertainment should be distinguished.

The distinction between these two types of social practices is supported by the following arguments. From a functional point of view, it can be contended that the content-determination argumentative practice pertains to the substantiation of the normative containers of the international legal order whereas law-ascertainment argumentative practice geared towards the certification of these containers. Put differently, the former is what feeds (and creates) the *negotium*, whilst the latter allows the validation of the *instrumentum*.[12]

Another fundamental distinguishing factor lies with the type of discursive and argumentative constraints these practices generate (and are subject to). The generation of constraints is inherent in any argumentative practice, for, short of constraints, arguments cannot be formed and expressed.

[12] On the distinction between *negotium* and *instrumentum*, see Jean d'Aspremont, 'Softness in international law: a self-serving quest for new legal materials' (2008) 19 *European Journal of International Law* 1075.

Nor can arguments ever gain authority and secure persuasiveness if they are made outside any constraints. Although both social practices nurture (and are subject to) constraints, constraints can also be a factor of differentiation between these two social practices. It is argued here that content-determination practices organise themselves around disciplinary rules.[13] In contrast, law-ascertainment social practices have structured themselves around a tradition. That means that the practice of engagement with law-ascertainment presupposes a belief or a step of faith.[14] It also allows the constraints to be of a dynamic character, in a constant state of composition and adjustment while still preserving some continuity.[15] The best manifestation thereof is also that the social practice of law-ascertainment tolerates a great deal of heterogeneity.[16]

The necessity to distinguish between social practice pertaining to content-determination, and social practice related to law-ascertainment, is further underpinned by the different type of formalisation to which they have been subjected in mainstream international legal thinking. Indeed, international lawyers have tried continuously to stabilise and discipline these practices through forms. The forms they have been resorting to tame some have been very different from those they have used to bridle the others. As far as content-determination is concerned, attempts to check such a process has manifested itself in theories of interpretation. The Vienna Convention on the Law of Treaties can be seen as an attempt to formalise content-determination social practice. As far as rule-ascertainment is concerned, formalisation has materialised in the portrayal of the doctrine of sources as a formal theory despite the contradictory but uncontested resort to intent or state practice as law-ascertainment yardstick.[17] None of the attempts to formalise content-determination have been very successful. Quite the contrary, they have been perceived as a deceitful smokescreen for the above-mentioned power struggles at play behind these social practices. The failure of these two formalist projects is, however, further reason to vindicate the distinction made here. The failure of the formalisation of the constraints on the content-determination social practice can probably be traced back to the fact that formal constraints on interpretation are

[13] Owen M Fiss, 'Objectivity and interpretation' (1982) 34 *Stanford Law Review* 739.

[14] MacIntyre, *Whose Justice?* (n 2) 359: 'At every stage beliefs and judgments will be justified by reference to the beliefs and judgments of the previous stage, and insofar as a tradition has constituted itself as a successful form of enquiry, the claims to truth made within that tradition will always be in some specifiable way less vulnerable to dialectical questioning and objection than were their predecessors.'

[15] Mark T Mitchell, 'Michael Polanyi, Alasdair MacIntyre, and the Role of Tradition' (2006) 19 *Humanitas* 97, 105.

[16] ibid, 106.

[17] This is an argument I have made in d'Aspremont, *Formalism* (n 7).

themselves in need of constraints, to be understood and operable.[18] The failure of the formalisation of the constraints on the law-ascertainment social practice, on the other hand, stems from their being not formal in the first place.[19]

It must be acknowledged that it is not always possible to distinguish *in concreto* these two social practices (and their underlying processes), for they may operate simultaneously in legal reasoning. It can prove difficult to isolate the ascertainment of rules from the determination of their content, as is illustrated by the (application of the) mainstream doctrine of customary law.[20] The difficulty of distinguishing these two types of practice is also frustrated by the unqualified disrepute into which attempts to formalise each of them has fallen. Indeed, the feeling of deceitfulness that has accompanied the formal framing of each of them has provoked a backlash against formalism in all its dimensions that makes no distinction between formal content-determination and formal law-ascertainment. De-formalisation across the board—and generalised loss of faith in the formalisation of the constraints on social argumentative practices—have further obfuscated the differences between these various types of social practice (and attempts to formalise them). Such factors of obfuscation do not, however, suffice to nullify the distinction between these two types of social practice.

It does not seem controversial to claim that each of these two social practices gives rise to distinct types of engagement by non-state actors. The way non-state actors engage with content-determination does not necessarily equate with the way they engage with law-ascertainment. This distinction between the involvement of two types of non-state actors in the social practice that feeds into the rules constraining the argumentative practice of international law is what allows this chapter to restrict its inquiry to one type of social practice, and thus one type of engagement of non-state actors, as is explained by the following section.

2.3 SOCIAL PRACTICE OF NON-STATE ACTORS FOR THE SAKE OF LAW-ASCERTAINMENT

Of the two types of social practice—and thus the two types of non-state actors—depicted above, this chapter will focus on the contribution of non-state actors to the practice of law-ascertainment (and thus the doctrine of sources). It accordingly leaves aside the social practice—and engagement

[18] Stanley Eugene Fish, 'Fish v. Fiss' (1984) 36 *Stanford Law Review* 1325, 1336; see also George Letsas, *A Theory of Interpretation of the European Convention on Human Rights* (Oxford, Oxford University Press, 2007) 534.

[19] This is the argument I have made elsewhere. See d'Aspremont, *Formalism* (n 7) esp ch 7.

[20] ibid.

of non-state actors—pertaining to the determination of the content of rules.[21]

The focus on the engagement of non-state actors in connection with law-ascertainment social practice inevitably calls for some methodological choice as to how such a social practice is understood. In this respect, this chapter embraces another positivistic posture, often associated with the dominant concept of law in British analytical jurisprudence, which must now be spelled out. According to this other positivist premise, the social practice pertaining to law ascertainment is best understood as the use of formal standards to identify rules of international law. According to that blueprint, any norm that meets pre-defined formal standards is a rule of international law. These standards constitute the pedigree of international legal rules. The idea that law is identified by virtue of a standardised pedigree of rules constitutes what is referred to in jurisprudence as the *source thesis*. The 'source thesis' provides that law is determined by its pedigree, and that identifying the law boils down to a pedigree test.[22] Because this pedigree is the object of a prior standardisation, the source thesis is thus synonymous with formal law-ascertainment. The source thesis is often contrasted with models of law-ascertainment based on substantive criteria, like that defended by the classical natural law school. It also is sometimes conceptualised as a rule-approach to law,[23] in contrast to effect-based[24] or process-based[25] definitions of law.

It is important to realise at this stage that the source thesis found in positivism inevitably brings about some indeterminacy.[26] Indeed, because of the indeterminacy of the language with which the standard pedigree of the rules is defined, formalism as a set of standardised criteria of law-identification inevitably fails to produce an autonomous and self-contained linguistic convention for the sake of law-identification. Herbert Hart himself

[21] The importance of that question has been similarly pinpointed (and discussed) by Harlan Cohen, 'Finding International Law: Rethinking the Doctrine of Sources' (2007) 93 *Iowa Law Review* 65; see also Harlan Grant Cohen, 'Finding International Law, Part II: Our Fragmenting Legal Community' (2012) 44 *New York University Journal of International Law and Policy* 1049, 1064.

[22] On the 'source thesis', see generally Joseph Raz, 'Legal Positivism and the Sources of Law' in Joseph Raz (ed), *The Authority of Law: Essays on Law and Morality* (Oxford, Clarendon Press, 1983).

[23] Nigel Purvis, 'Critical legal studies in public international law' (1991) 32 *Harvard International Law Journal* 81, 84.

[24] José E Alvarez, *International Organizations as Law-makers* (Oxford, Oxford University Press, 2005) esp x–xi; David J Bederman, 'The Souls of International Organizations: Legal Personality and the Lighthouse at Cape Spartel' (1996) 36 *Virginia Journal of International Law* 275, 372; Nigel D White, 'Separate but Connected: Inter-Governmental Organizations and International Law' (2008) 5 *International Organizations Law Review* 175, 181–86.

[25] This is classically construed as the 'New Haven approach'.

[26] See Raz, 'Legal Positivism' esp 41–52. See more generally Liam B Murphy, 'The Political Question of the Concept of Law' in Jules L Coleman (ed), *Hart's Postscript: Essays on the Postscript to The Concept of Law* (Oxford, Oxford University Press, 2001) 393.

recognised that law-ascertainment criteria—in his words, the 'rule of recognition'—are vague and open-textured.[27] This point is important, because positivists have devised several conceptual strategies to overcome the non-self-sufficiency of the source thesis. And this is what brings the argument back to the idea of social practice discussed above. Indeed, one of the instruments to address the non-self-sufficiency of the source thesis is the use of social practice by those actors engaged in legal argumentation. Such a particular conception of the foundations of the source thesis has been designated in the literature as the *social thesis*. The archetype social thesis purports to supplement the classical positivist source-based criteria of identification of international law ('the source thesis'), with a view to endowing it with some limited autonomy, by inferring the meaning of the standard pedigree of rules derived from the practice of law-applying authorities.[28]

This positivist conception of the social practice pertaining to law-identification that has been presented here is certainly not new. On the contrary, it is rather traditional. It corresponds with the well-known conception defended by Herbert Hart in the *Concept of Law*.[29] While Hart's theory can prove significantly helpful in sharpening formalism in the context of international law, it can be argued that Hart's insights do not suffice to appraise the place of non-state actors from the perspective of international legal positivism, especially when it comes to the conceptualisation of the law-applying authority capable of generating a meaningful social practice for the sake of international law-ascertainment. Indeed, Hart adopted a very restrictive conception of law-applying authority, which is exclusive of non-state actors. It is this notion of 'law-applying authority' that ought to be discussed now. Indeed, the determination of the actors that contribute to the social practice of law-ascertainment is dependent on how this notion of law-applying authority is understood. It will not come as a surprise that, given its importance in positivist thinking, this notion has been fiercely debated in jurisprudence and legal theory. It is the ambition of the next section to briefly recall such debates.

2.4 THE SOCIAL PRACTICE BY NON-STATE ACTORS IN GENERAL LEGAL THEORY

The positivist construction recalled above makes the production of social practice for the sake of law-ascertainment dependent on the practice of

[27] Herbert LA Hart, *The Concept of Law*, 2nd edn (Oxford, Clarendon Press, 1997) 144–50.

[28] It has also been referred to as the 'exclusive internal point of view'. See George P Fletcher, 'Law as a Discourse' (1991–1992) 13 *Cardozo Law Review* 1631, 1634.

[29] Hart, *The Concept* (n 27) 108–09. For a recent reappraisal of Hart's relevance in international legal scholarship, see d'Aspremont, 'Herbert Hart in Today's International Legal Scholarship' in Jörg Kammerhofer and Jean d'Aspremont (eds), *International Legal Positivism in a Post-Modern World* (Cambridge, Cambridge University Press, 2014) 114–50.

the so-called 'law-applying authorities'. Here too another conceptual and descriptive framework must be chosen to determine those non-state actors, which, in international law, can be held as contributing to the social practice of law-identification. Mention must here be made of the debates by which jurisprudence and legal theory have been riven.

A well-known refinement of the Hartian concept of law-applying authorities—and thus of social practice—has been put forward by Brian Tamanaha. According to the modernisation proposed by Tamanaha, a law-applying authority is 'whomever, as a matter of social practice, members of the group (including legal officials themselves) identify and treat as "legal officials"'.[30] The social practice on which the rule of recognition is based must accordingly not be restricted to strictly defined law-applying officials but must include all social actors.[31] This expansion of the concept of law-applying authority is undoubtedly of great relevance in a legal order—like the international legal order—which lacks any vertical nomenclature or institutional hierarchy. Tamanaha's definition, although proving somewhat all-embracing to a certain extent, can help capture the practice necessary for the establishment of the criteria for the ascertainment of international rules. It surely points to the insufficiency of a too-narrow construction of the Hartian concept of law-applying authority as well as to the necessity not to limit the production of social practice to practice of formal judicial authorities only.

Another refinement of the concept of 'law-applying authority' and of social practice has more recently been offered by Keith Culver and Michael Giudice.[32] These authors espouse a similar anti-state legal pluralism to that of Tamanaha. However, they argue that the latter author surrenders too readily and too much to a kind of scepticism about the possibility of broad and general understanding of legal order applicable across cultures and times.[33] They accordingly propose an inter-institutional theory of legality and strive to build a dynamic theory severed from the state to avoid problem of state officials.[34] Their theory is supposed to make a minimal use of the ideas of legal officials and legal system in providing an explanatory basis for various non-state types of legality.[35]

This chapter is not the place to revisit these jurisprudential debates. Nor would it be appropriate to evaluate the merits of each of these various

[30] Brian Z Tamanaha, *A General Jurisprudence Of Law And Society* (Oxford, Oxford University Press, 2001) 142.

[31] ibid, 159–66.

[32] Keith Charles Culver and Michael Giudice, *Legality's Borders: An Essay In General Jurisprudence* (Oxford, Oxford University Press, 2010).

[33] On the difference with Tamanaha, see ibid, 144–45.

[34] ibid, 115.

[35] ibid, 182.

constructions. For the sake of the argument made here, it is only necessary to recall that, in general jurisprudence and legal theory, the notions of 'law-applying authority' or 'state official' have been subject to pluralist accounts. It is argued here that international lawyers have much to gain from such pluralistic accounts when it comes to describe the social practice that feeds into the doctrine of sources. This is why the following sections adopt the same pluralistic account to describe the way in which non-state actors contribute to the modes of identification of international law. On that basis, the following paragraphs mention those social actors whose practice must be deemed relevant by virtue of the pluralistic positivist understanding of the social practice that has been discussed above. It will be shown that among these various social actors, non-state actors play a significant role when it comes to producing the social practice that nurture the rules about the sources of international law, that in turn constrain international law as an argumentative practice.

2.5 WHICH NON-STATE ACTORS FOR WHICH SOCIAL PRACTICE IN INTERNATIONAL LAW?

From a traditional Hartian perspective that restricts the production of social practice to that of state officials, it seems uncontroversial to hold that international courts and tribunals play the central role when it comes to providing law-ascertainment social practice. Espousing the pluralistic account of the social practice that was discussed in the previous section, it however becomes possible to ascribe a role to a wide array of other (non-state) actors.[36] The following paragraphs elaborate on the contemporary law-ascertaining role of non-state actors, thereby showing that the international courts and tribunals can no longer be seen as being endowed with any kind of monopoly on the definition of the law-ascertainment criteria of the international legal system. Other actors' social practice takes the form of what is called here *communitarian semantics*, that directly inform the content of the doctrine of sources of international law. This section, drawing on the various positivist conceptual choices mentioned in the previous sections, contends that non-state actors are very instrumental in the communitarian semantics necessary to give contents to law-ascertainment criteria, that is the doctrine of the sources of international law.

It must be made very clear, as a preliminary point, that being a 'social actor' whose practice of law-ascertainment informs the formal

[36] For a similar pluralistic posture with respect to the doctrine of sources, see Cohen, 'Finding International Law' and 'Finding International Law, Part II' (n 21) 1064.

criteria of the identification of law does not necessarily elevate that actor to a formal international law-maker. It is true that some of the actors mentioned here may well wield some undeniable law-creating powers—as is illustrated by judges whose role in the development of international law is almost uncontested[37]—or some influence on the making of international law—as exemplified by the influence of non-state actors.[38] However, the potential law-creating/law-making role of these actors as regards the (progressive) development of substantive international legal rules is of no relevance here. Indeed, although law-determination by international courts may sometimes come close to law-creation, and even if law-identification and law-creation may be carried out simultaneously,[39] the practice relevant for the sake of law-ascertainment is alien to any question of a law-making power properly so-called. The communitarian semantics that they generate by identifying international legal rules do not constitute a substantive law-making exercise. The actors mentioned below simply partake in the semantics of the formal criteria of law-ascertainment, which—although they are often captured through the Hartian concept of the rule of recognition—do not constitute legal rules in the same sense as the substantive rules of international law.

There is no doubt that the central law-applying authority whose behaviour is the most instrumental in defining the standard of law-ascertainment is the International Court of Justice (ICJ). Yet, the ICJ is not the only law-applying authority in the international legal order. Arbitral tribunals have

[37] Hans Kelsen, 'La Théorie Pure dans la Pensée Juridique' in Charles Leben and Rene Kolb (eds), *Controverses sur la Théorie Pure du Droit* (Paris, LGDJ, 2005) 173; Hart, *The Concept* (n 27) 136; See also Herbert LA Hart and Tony Honoré, *Causation in the Law*, 2nd edn (Oxford, Clarendon Press, 1985) 5; J Raz, *Authority of Law* (Oxford, Clarendon Press, 1983) 41–52. As regards international law more specifically see Robert Jennings, 'What is International Law and How do we tell it when we see it' (1981) 37 *Annuaire Suisse de Droit International* 37, 77; Hugh Thirlway, 'The Sources of International Law' in Malcolm Evans (ed), *International Law*, 2nd edn (Oxford, Oxford University Press, 2006) 129–30; Hersch Lauterpacht, *The Development of International Law by the International Court*, 2nd edn (New York, Praeger, 1958); Manfred Lachs, 'Some Reflections on the Contribution of the International Court of Justice to the Development of International Law' (1983) 10 *Syracuse Journal of International Law & Commerce* 239; Rosalyn Higgins, *Problems And Process: International Law And How We Use It* (Oxford, Clarendon Press, 1994) 202; Alan E Boyle and Cristine M Chinkin, *The Making Of International Law* (Oxford, Oxford University Press, 2007) 266–69 and 310–11. See however the statement of the International Court of Justice in its advisory opinion on the *Legality of the Threat or Use of Nuclear Weapons* 1996-I ICJ Rep 237 [18] (according to which the Court 'states the existing law and does not legislate' and this is so 'even if in stating and applying the law the Court necessarily has to specify its scope and sometimes not is general trend'). Art 38 of the Statute of the International Court of Justice also seems to lend support to a strictly cognitive task of international courts.

[38] See generally Jean d'Aspremont (ed), *Participants in the International Legal System: Multiple Perspectives On Non-State Actors In International Law* (Abingdon, Routledge, 2011).

[39] See Robert Jennings, 'General Course on Principles of International Law' (1967) 121 *Collected Courses of The Hague Academy of International Law* 341.

also applied international legal rules and thus participated in the elaboration of the linguistic indicators of law-ascertainment.[40] Moreover, and despite the ICJ occasionally still believing in its natural monopoly to set the tone in the international judicial arena,[41] a growing number of international tribunals have been applying international law, thereby participating in the elaboration of the criteria for the ascertainment of international legal rules. Furthermore, all these various tribunals are engaged in an uncontested 'cross-fertilisation' which further shores up the importance of the social practice which they generate.[42]

Even though the contribution of the ICJ in this respect has not always been consistent and fully satisfying—as is illustrated by the fluctuations in its case law regarding the formal evidence of custom, the law-ascertainment criteria of unilateral promises or the evidence of intent to make law for the sake of the identification of international agreements[43]—the practice of the ICJ has nonetheless proved more indicative than that of other tribunals. Indeed, the International Court of Justice has long carried a lot of clout over international judicial proceedings, making its contribution to the practice of law-ascertainment naturally dominant. Whatever the varying weight of each of these tribunals, it is uncontested that the judicial practice of law-ascertainment in the international arena, now emerging from a greater variety of tribunals, is thus far the most generative of communitarian semantics for the sake of law-ascertainment criteria in international law.

[40] For a recent example, see the final award in the Abyei Arbitration *The Government of Sudan/The Sudan People's Liberation Movement/Army* 22 July 2009 [425]–[435] available at www.pca-cpa.org/showpage.asp?pag_id=1306.

[41] See the famous rebuke of the ICTY by the ICJ in its decision on 26 February 2007 in the case of the *Application of the Convention on the Prevention and Punishment of the Crime of Genocide* (*Bosnia and Herzegovina v Serbia and Montenegro*) [2007] ICJ Rep [402]–[407]; See also Report of Stephen M Schwebel President of the International Court of Justice UN GAOR 54th Sess Agenda Item 13 UN Doc A/54/PV 39 (26 October 1999) 3–4; Report of Gilbert Guillaume President of the International Court of Justice UN GAOR 55th Sess Agenda Item 13 UN Doc A/55/PV 42 (26 October 2000) 7; See also Gilbert Guillaume, 'The future of international judicial institutions' (1995) 44 *International and Comparative Law Quarterly* 848, 860–62; Shigeru Oda, 'Dispute settlement prospects in the law of the sea' (1995) 44 *International and Comparative Law Quarterly* 863, 864.

[42] See eg Francis G Jacobs, 'Judicial dialogue and the cross-fertilization of legal systems: The European Court of Justice' (2003) 38 *Texas International Law Journal* 547; Paul Tavernier, 'L'interaction des jurisprudences des tribunaux pénaux internationaux et des cours européennes et interaméricaines des droits de l'homme. Actualité de la jurisprudence internationale: a l'heure de la mise en place de la Cour pénale internationale' (Bruxelles, Bruylant, 2004) 251–61.

[43] See eg as regards the identification of international treaties see ICJ, *Aegean Sea Continental Shelf* (*Greece v Turkey*) Judgment of 19 December 1978 [95]–[107]: emphasis is put on the actual terms and circumstances. Compare *Maritime Delimitation and Territorial Questions between Qatar and Bahrain (Qatar v Bahrain)* Judgment of 1 July 1994. Regarding the identification of unilateral promise, see ICJ, *Nuclear Tests* (*Australia v France*) 20 December 1974 [43]; *Military and Paramilitary Activities in and against Nicaragua* (*Nicaragua v United* (1986). See ICJ, *Frontier Dispute* (*Burkina Faso/Republic of Mali*) 22 December 1986, [1986] ICJ Rep. This case law is analysed in d'Aspremont, *Formalism* (n 7).

International courts and tribunals are not the only judicial authorities, which generate communitarian semantics of law-ascertainment and contribute to the social practice. Indeed, international law has long ceased to exclusively govern inter-state relations and has become more regulatory of internal matters and issues affecting individuals. Compliance with international law has accordingly incrementally required the adoption of domestic rules, thereby increasing the application of international law by domestic courts.[44] Even rules regulating inter-state relations have required domestic implementation. This infiltration by international law into domestic systems is thus a natural consequence of the extension *ratione materiae* of its object.[45] That international law now regulates objects previously deemed of domestic relevance is insufficient, however, to explain the growing application of international law by domestic courts. Because international law only enters domestic legal orders if so allowed, the greater presence of international law in the domestic legal orders of states is also the direct consequence of the growing amenability of states towards international law.[46] In this respect, it is not disputed that states are proving less reluctant to allow international law to enter and even pervade their own legal orders. Incorporation is not the only means by which international law has been applied by domestic courts. Indeed, most states in the world instruct their courts to construe domestic law in a manner that is consistent with their international obligations. If international law is not the 'law of the land' because it has not been incorporated, it may still yield effects in the domestic legal order if domestic judges interpret national law in accordance with international law.[47] The growing effect of

[44] For an analysis of some significant decisions of domestic courts applying international law see A Nollkaemper, *National Courts and the International Rule of Law* (Oxford, Oxford University Press, 2011).

[45] According to Provost and Conforti, 'The truly legal function of international law essentially is found in the internal legal system of States'. See Benedetto Conforti, *International Law And The Role Of Domestic Legal Systems* (Leiden, Martinus Nijhoff, 1993) 8; Joseph HH Weiler, 'The geology of international law–governance, democracy and legitimacy' (2004) 64 *Heidelberg Journal of International Law* 547, 559–61; see also Armin Von Bogdandy, 'Globalization and Europe: How to Square Democracy, Globalization, and International Law' (2004) 15 *European Journal of International Law* 885, 889; Mattias Kumm, 'The legitimacy of international law: a constitutionalist framework of analysis' (2004) 15 *European Journal of International Law* 907; see contra Gaetano Arangio-Ruiz, *Le domaine réservé: l'organisation internationale et le rapport entre droit international et droit interne: cours général de droit international public* (Leiden, Martinus Nijhoff, 1990) 435–79.

[46] See generally André Nollkaemper and Janne Elisabeth Nijman, 'Beyond the Divide' in André Nollkaemper and Janne Elisabeth Nijman (eds), *New Perspectives On The Divide Between National and International Law* (Oxford, Oxford University Press, 2007) 341–60.

[47] This principle of *consistent interpretation* of domestic law is also known as the 'Charming Betsy' principle. See US Supreme Court *Murray v The Schooner Charming Betsy* 6 US (2 Cranch) 64 (1804); see also *Restatement (Third) of Foreign Relations Law* §114 (1987). On the Charming Betsy principle, see RG Steinhardt, 'The Role of International Law as a Canon of Domestic Statutory Construction' (1990) 43 *Vanderbilt Law Review* 1103 or J Turley, 'Dualistic Values in

international law in the domestic legal order through incorporation and consistent interpretation has been accompanied by a general amenability of domestic judges towards international law as a whole, irrespective of whether it is incorporated into national law and binding upon the state.[48] Whether the entry of international law into domestic legal orders takes the path of incorporation, consistent interpretation, or simple persuasiveness and to whomever this entry can be traced back, it is uncontested that international law is becoming more and more present in domestic legal orders and is continuously applied by domestic courts. In applying international law, these domestic courts are thus called upon to ascertain its rules, thereby participating in the general practice of international law-ascertainment. It has thus become undeniable that domestic courts count as actors participating in the generation of the communitarian semantics of law-ascertainment as well.[49]

It goes without saying that, despite the multiplicity of international and domestic judicial authorities engaged in the ascertainment of international legal rules, their practice has remained too scarce to generate sufficient communitarian semantics. After all, these law-applying authorities are limited in number and their case law is proportionally modest, especially if compared to the practice of law-ascertainment of domestic legal rules generated by domestic courts. This is precisely why, in line with Keith Culver and Michael Giudice and Brian Tamanaha's proposition, the practice of other actors engaged in the application of international law should be included in the social practice necessary to establish the social practice at the heart of formal law-ascertainment in international law.

It must be acknowledged that the practice of law-ascertainment generated by states is no longer so central, for international law nowadays has grown beyond its original strictly inter-state configuration. It cannot be

an Age of International Legisprudence' (1993) 44 *Hastings Law Journal* 185. A similar principle is found in regional legal orders as is illustrated by the European legal order where European Law ought to be interpreted in conformity with international law. See Case 41/74 *Van Duyn v Home Office* [1974] ECR 1337; see also *Anklagemyndigheden Poulsen and Diva Navigation Corp* [1992] ECR-I 6019.

[48] See generally Y Shany, *National Courts as International Actors: Jurisdictional Implications* Hebrew University International Law Research Paper No 22-08 (October 2008). See also the remarks by E Benvenisti and GW Downs, 'National Courts Domestic Democracy and the Evolution of International Law' (2009) 20 *European Journal of International Law* 59–72; G Betlem and A Nollkaemper, 'Giving effect to Public International Law' (2003) 14 *European Journal of International Law* 569; see also J d'Aspremont, 'Systemic Integration of International Law by Domestic Courts: Domestic Judges as Architects of the Consistency of the International Legal Order' in A Nollkaemper and OK Fauchald (eds), *Unity or Fragmentation of International Law: The Role of International and National Tribunals* (Oxford, Oxford University Press, 2012) 141–65.

[49] On the application of international law by domestic courts see generally K Knop, 'Here and There: International Law in Domestic Courts' (2000) 32 *New York University Journal of International Law and Politics* 501; A von Bogdandy, 'Pluralism direct effect and the ultimate say: On the relationship between international and domestic constitutional law' (2008) 6 *International Journal of Constitutional Law* 397.

denied that some non-state actors also provide some interesting insights as to the meaning of law-ascertainment criteria. Particular mention should be made here of the International Committee of the Red Cross (ICRC). It is true that the study produced by the ICRC on customary international law[50] can bring about some severe reservations in terms of the consistency of its methodology in the establishment of customary international law[51]—a large part of which can be traced back to the non-formal character of custom-ascertainment, for which the ICRC cannot be blamed. Yet, it cannot be denied that the determination of what is law and what is non-law by the ICRC—as is illustrated by the extent to which states took pains to react to it—constitutes a practice of law-ascertainment that is to be reckoned with. A few other non-state actors are probably also instrumental in the consolidation of a practice of law-ascertainment.[52] It is not my intention to list them all here.[53] It must simply be recalled once again that recognising that law-ascertainment by non-state actors like the ICRC constitutes relevant practice does not amount to saying that these bodies or entities are endowed with law-making authority.[54]

It could be tempting to include the International Law Commission (ILC) among those non-state bodies which engage in a practice of ascertainment of international legal rules. Certainly, the ILC ascertains international

[50] Jean-Marie Henckaerts, 'Study on customary international humanitarian law: A contribution to the understanding and respect for the rule of law in armed conflict' (2005) 87 *International Review of the Red Cross* 175, 175.

[51] See the critique of Boyle and Chinkin, *The Making of International Law*, 36. See also the critique expressed by John B Bellinger III and William J Haynes II, 'A US government response to the International Committee of the red cross study customary international humanitarian law' (2007) 89 *International Review of the Red Cross* 443, 454. See the reaction of Jean-Marie Henckaerts, 'Customary International Humanitarian Law: a response to US comments' (2007) 89 *International Review of the Red Cross* 473.

[52] See eg, the 2004 Report of the UN Secretary General's High Level Panel available at www.un.org/secureworld/. See also the 2001 Report of the independent International Commission on Intervention and State Sovereignty as established by the Government of Canada in September 2000, available at www.iciss.ca/report-en.asp.

[53] On the role of non-state actors in the international legal order, see generally J d'Aspremont (n 38) *Participants*.

[54] Such a perception often permeates the legal scholarship. See generally Caroline Thomas, 'International Financial Institutions and social and economic rights: an exploration' in Tony Evans (ed), *Human Rights Fifty Years On: A Reappraisal* (Manchester, Manchester University Press, 1998) 163; for a mild approach, see Isabelle R Gunning, 'Modernizing Customary International Law: The Challenge of Human Rights' (1991) 31 *Virginia Journal of International Law* 211; Slaughter is not far from recognising such a law-making role for individuals: Anne-Marie Slaughter, 'The real new world order' (1997) *Foreign Affairs* 183. See also Andrea Bianchi, 'Une generation de 'communautaristes' in Emmanuelle Jouannet and Hélène Ruiz-Fabri (eds), *Regards d'une génération sur le droit international public* (Paris, Pedone, 2008) 78. For a criticism of that perception, see Jean d'Aspremont, 'Les travaux de la Commission du droit international relatifs aux actes unilatéraux des Etats' (2005) 109 *Revue Generale de Droit International Public: droit des gens, histoire diplomatique, droit penal, droit fiscal, droit administratif* 163, 297.

legal rules when it codifies international law. In this respect, the codification undertakings of the ILC could potentially yield some relevant social practice for the sake of law-ascertainment. Yet, the Commission is also endowed with the responsibility to propose progressive developments of international law. Whilst these two tasks ought to be clearly distinguished according to its Statute,[55] the practice shows that the Commission carries them out simultaneously and does not deem it necessary to make any distinction in this regard.[56] The final outcome of the work of the ILC, whatever form it may take, will generally fall short of making any distinction between those rules that have been codified and those that originate in a progressive development. It is usually the commentary that will indicate whether a rule must be considered the mere codification of an existing rule, or whether it constitutes a progressive development of international law. But such indications do not always suffice and rules meant by the Commission to be progressive development of international law are sometimes subsequently elevated to codified rules by the judicial bodies applying them.[57] The near impossibility of distinguishing between progressive development and codification explains why the contribution of the International Law Commission to the practice of law-ascertainment ought to be seen as very modest. The same is probably true with respect to the Institut de Droit International (IDI).[58]

Finally, mention must be made of the secondary role played by international legal scholars in the ascertainment of international legal rules. It is argued here that international legal scholars, although they are not at the origin of a practice of law-ascertainment generative of communitarian semantics, undoubtedly participate in the fine-tuning and streamlining of the formal criteria of law-ascertainment which, in turn, are picked up by the above-mentioned social actors involved in the application of international legal rules. In other words, it is submitted here that legal scholars

[55] See, eg, Arts 16–18 of the ILC Statute UN General Assembly Resolution 174 (II). 21 November 1947. The Statute as was subsequently amended is available at www.un.org/law/ilc/.

[56] This is why the Commission suggested that such a distinction be abolished. See the Report of the International Law Commission 48th session (1996) A/51/10 para 147(a) and paras 156–59. On that aspect of the Statute of the ILC, see d'Aspremont, 'Les travaux de la Commission'.

[57] See the famous contention of the International Court of Justice that under Art 16 of the Articles on State Responsibility, a state is responsible for its internationally wrongful acts, which corresponds with a rule of customary international law—a position contrasting with that of the Special Rapporteur of the International Law Commission. *Cp* ICJ *Application of the Convention on the Prevention and Punishment of the Crime of Genocide* (*Bosnia and Herzegovina v Serbia and Montenegro*) 26 February 2007, [2007] ICJ Rep [420] and James Crawford, *The International Law Commission's articles on state responsibility: introduction, text, and commentaries* (Cambridge, Cambridge University Press, 2005) 148.

[58] On the Institut de Droit International see, eg, Francois Rigaux, 'Non-state Actors from the Perspective of the Institut de Droit international' in d'Aspremont, *Participants* (n 38).

come to play the role of grammarians of formal law-ascertainment who systematise the standards of distinction between law and non-law. This can be explained as follows.

It is undeniable that scholars may occasionally be instrumental in the progressive development of primary norms. Indeed, while they certainly are not law-makers,[59] international legal scholars often play a public role or participate in public affairs.[60] Although international legal scholars themselves may be tempted to see their offerings as more influential than they really are[61] and even though their contribution is more modest today than it used to be a century ago—for states have grown wary of the influence that scholars can have[62]—their writings, their opinions and their decisions also influence law-making and international legal adjudication.[63] Article 38 of the Statute of the International Court of Justice has shrouded the influence of scholars and judges upon law-making in a formal veil by elevating them to a 'subsidiary means for the determination of rules of law'. Nothing could be more illusory than the formalisation of their

[59] d'Aspremont, 'Softness'; Jörg Kammerhofer, 'Law-Making by Scholarship? The Dark Side of 21st Century International Legal "Methodology"' in James Crawford and Sarah Nouwen (eds), *Selected Proceedings of the European Society of International Law*, vol 3 (Oxford, Hart Publishing, 2010).

[60] For an illustration of the public role that scholars may play according to the conception submitted here, see Matthew Craven and others, 'We are teachers of International Law' (2004) 17 *Leiden Journal of International Law* 363; see also the letter published in the *Guardian*, 'War Would be Illegal' 7 March 2003 available at www.guardian.co.uk/politics/2003/mar/07/highereducation.iraq/print; see also the 'appel de juristes de droit international concernant le recours à la force contre l'Irak' initiated by the Centre de Droit International of the Free University of Brussels (ULB) in January 2003, reference available at www.ridi.org/adı/specıal/ındex.htm. On the idea that international legal scholars are not immune from the political debates in which they have been claiming a say, see Lauri Mälksoo, 'The Science of International Law and the Concept of Politics: The Arguments and Lives of the International Law Professors at the University of Dorpat/Iur'ev/Tartu 1855–1985' (2005) 76 *British Yearbook of International Law* 383, 499.

[61] For a classical example of this belief, see Oscar Schachter, 'Invisible College of International Lawyers' (1977) 72 *Northwest University Law Review* 217, 217: 'We should be mindful however that international lawyers both individually and as a group play a role in the process of creative new law and in extending existing law to meet emerging needs. This legislative role is carried out principally through multilateral treaties but it may also be accomplished through the evolution of customary international the use of general principles … In all of these processes the professional community may perform a significant function.'

[62] Michel Virally, 'A propos de la "lex ferenda"' in D Bardonnet (ed), *Meélanges offerts à Paul Reuter: le droit international: uniteé et diversiteé* (Paris, Pedone, 1981) 519–33 at 520.

[63] See the famous statement of Justice Gray in the case of *The Paquete Habana and the Lola* in 1920: 'where there is no treaty and no controlling executive or legislative act or judicial decision resort must be made to the customs and usages of civilized nations; and as evidence of these to the works of jurists and commentators who by years of labor research and experience have made themselves peculiarly well acquainted with the subject of which they treat. Such works are resorted to by judicial tribunals not for the speculations of their authors concerning what the law ought to be but for trustworthy evidence of what the law really is' (cited by R Jennings, 'International Law Reform and Progressive Development' in Gerhard Hafner et al (eds), *Liber Amicorum Professor Ignaz Seidl-Hohenveldern; In honour of his 80th birthday* (The Hague, Kluwer, 1998) 333).

influence on law-making which—albeit recognised as secondary—in the making of international law is not tangible, and can hardly be captured in formal terms. The role of legal scholars in the making of substantive rules of international law falls outside the ambit of our inquiry. All that matters is to shed light on their contribution to the practice of law-ascertainment and their corresponding contribution to communitarian semantics.

Clearly legal scholars do not constitute law-applying authorities *sensu stricto*. Nor are they social actors, as was understood by Keith Culver, Michael Giudice or Brian Tamanaha. Indeed, strictly speaking, they do not apply the law but interpret and comment upon it. However, it cannot be denied that international legal scholars have always constituted grammarians of the language of international law.[64] By contrast to domestic law,[65] the systematisation of international law has primarily been an achievement of legal scholarship rather than of legal practice.[66] International law would not have reached, in the consciousness of international lawyers, its current level of systematics without the input of international legal scholarship. One of the paramount tasks undertaken by scholars has been the systematisation and the streamlining of the criteria for the distinction between law and non-law.[67] While their work in

[64] See Pierre-Marie Dupuy, 'L'unitee de l'ordre juridique international' in Hague Academy of International Law (ed), *Collected Courses* vol 297 (Leiden, Martinus Nijhoff, 2002) 205: 'un internationaliste ne devrait jamais prétendre à autre chose que d'être un bon grammarien du language normatif du droit international'. Paul Reuter, 'Principes de droit international public' in Hague Academy of International Law (ed), *Collected Courses* vol 103 (Leiden, Martinus Nijhoff, 1961) 459: 'Le droit n'est pas seulement un produit de la vie sociale il est également le fruit d'un effort de pensée s'efforçant d'agencer les données ainsi recueillies dans un ensemble cohérent et aussi logique que possible. C'est l'aspect systématique du droit international il est à la fois plus important et plus délicat que celui des droits nationaux. Il est plus important parce que les sociétés nationales du fait qu'elles sont profondément centralisées par l'autorité étatique engendrent un droit déjà systématisé par ses conditions d'élaboration. Au contraire la « décentralisation du pouvoir politique » qui règne dans la société internationale rejette sur le juriste un fardeau plus lourd. Il est plus délicat parce que le désordre de la société internationale n'est pas tant désordre de la pensée que désordre du pouvoir; certes le juriste peut se laisser aller à la systématisation mais s'agit-il de systématiser seulement ses pensées ou de systématiser aussi la réalité ? Certes de par sa nature même le droit est avide d'ordre mais à quoi servirait-il par excès de rigueur dans la pensée de poursuivre une systématisation en dehors du cadre des solutions admises'. See also Fried van Hoof, *Rethinking the Sources Of International Law* (The Hague, Kluwer Law and Taxation Publishers, 1983) 291 or Jochen von Bernstorff and Thomas Dunlap, *The Public International Law Theory Of Hans Kelsen: Believing In Universal Law* (Cambridge, Cambridge University Press, 2010) 266.

[65] In this regard, the Code Napoléon has been particular instrumental in the systematisation of continental European domestic orders.

[66] For some general thoughts on the contribution of legal scholars to the systematisation of law see Neil MacCormick, *Institutions of Law: An Essay in Legal Theory* (Oxford, Oxford University Press, 2008) 6.

[67] Anthony D'Amato, 'What "Counts" as Law?' in Nicholas Greenwood Onuf (ed), *Law-making in the Global Community* (Durham NC, Carolina Academic Press, 1982) 106–07; See also Virally, 'A propos' (n 62) 532.

this respect does not constitute, strictly speaking, practice of law-applying authorities, the law-ascertainment criteria carved out and polished by legal scholars have been very conducive to shaping the practice of law-applying authorities. That means that international legal scholars do not themselves yield social practice. Yet, they clearly impact on that practice by contributing to the elaboration of the communitarian semantics of law-ascertainment in international law.

The foregoing has attempted to show that the practice of law-ascertainment generating the criteria of law-ascertainment can be attributed to a diverse set of social actors, among which a few non-state actors play a paramount role. All these actors, although they are not necessarily endowed with a formal status are thus very instrumental in providing meaning to the secondary rules of the international legal system. International legal scholars, while they do not themselves directly yield a practice of law-ascertainment, undoubtedly partake in the shaping of the communitarian semantics necessary to ensure the meaningfulness of formal law-ascertainment criteria. The role played in this regard by domestic courts and non-state actors in generating social practice for the sake of the meaning of the law-ascertainment criteria of the international legal system participates in the reinforcement of the ability of the international legal system to produce a vocabulary enabling the delineation of the rules of which it is composed. This is the reason why, according to positivist account presented here, non-state actors can hardly be ignored by international lawyers, who should take them very seriously.

Whether it would be appropriate to include other non-state actors in the production ot the social practice (communitarian semantics) that feeds into the doctrine of sources (law-ascertainment criteria) remains an open question. It is not the ambition of this chapter to discuss it any further. It raises fundamental and wide-ranging questions of participation and pluralism, which cannot be taken on here. Obviously the determination of which actors are allowed to take part in legal argument on the criteria of ascertainment of legal rules constitutes a huge political debate with which it seems unnecessary to engage here. The ambition of this chapter remains modest. The intention was only to raise some awareness about the political implications of the positivist conceptual choices that have been discussed in the previous sections. There is one aspect of this debate, which, however, deserves a few concluding remarks. The foregoing should have shown the wide extent of the politics of definition inherent in defining the role of non-state actors in the production of those social practices that inform the rules that constrain the argumentative practice of international law. This is the object of the last section of this chapter.

2.6 CONCLUDING REMARKS: THE POLITICS OF DEFINITION AND THE DEFINITION OF POLITICS

Defining a concept or a practice in a universal fashion is inevitably hegemonic. Indeed, defining something that is supposed to be of a universal character is necessarily an attempt to impose a certain view of the world and a certain understanding of the law.[68] What is more, defining is inevitably political. It suffices to take the example of the question of non-state actors that has been grappled with here. It does not seem controversial to say that defining non-state actors as non-state entities is of an excluding nature. By adopting a distinction between 'state' and 'non-state' actors, international lawyers seek to create a certain type of order.[69] It is the realm of the state that is equated with order as it falls under international law. In contrast, disorder is associated with the realm of the non-state, that less easily allows itself to be subjected to international law. In that sense, the definition of order and disorder are not apolitical and objective descriptions. On the contrary, they are normatively motivated. In the case of non-state actors, it cannot be excluded that relegating non-state actors to the realm of the 'non-state' allows one to blame those fringe and unruly creatures and legitimise attempts to regulate their practice.

It is important to stress, at this concluding stage, that the positivist posture adopted in this chapter is no less suspicious of such normative and hegemonic presuppositions. Constructing a legal order that can be defined by law-ascertainment techniques (ie a doctrine of sources), themselves nurtured by the practice of certain non-state actors, inevitably involves a certain vision of order and disorder.[70] Likewise, the positivist paradigms adopted here confront international lawyers with the thorny question of which non-state actors are entitled to contribute to the determination of the law-ascertainment criteria, and thus to the contents of the doctrine of sources. The political dimension—and the risk of a hegemonic approach—are self-evident. The inclusion or exclusion of certain non-state actors as producers of social practice for the sake of the doctrine of sources of international law necessarily determines the type of doctrine of sources international lawyers will base their legal argumentation on. If one embraces such a positivist posture, the determination (and contents) of the criteria by which international law is identified comes to be depend on those non-state actors whose behaviours are allowed to feed into the social practice.

[68] Martti Koskenniemi, 'Hegemonic Regimes' in Margaret A Young (ed), *Regime Interaction in International Law: Facing Fragmentation* (Cambridge, Cambridge University Press, 2012) 311.

[69] On the passion for order of international lawyers, see James Crawford, 'International Law as Discipline and Profession' (2012) 106 *American Society of International Legal Proceedings* 471.

[70] Singh, in d'Aspremont, *Formalism* (n 7).

What is more, the political and hegemonic definition of those non-state actors whose social practice can potentially be determinative of the contents of the doctrine of sources is not only a political question in itself. It also is a question determinative of the politics of definition at work in international law as a whole. Indeed, the politics behind the definition of non-state actors and that of their contribution to the doctrine of sources bears upon how international lawyer define the politics they want to be engaged in. This means that the way the contribution of non-state actors to the identification of international law is defined simultaneously determines the type of politics at work in international law, and which international lawyers should consciously confront. In that sense, the discussion in this chapter on the contribution of non-state actors to the social practice at the heart of the modes of identification of international law has constituted an opportunity to recall that the politics of definition of legal categories are simultaneously determinative of the type of politics international lawyers should be aware of and should consider engaging with.

3

Non-State Actors in International Law in Policy Perspective

EISUKE SUZUKI

3.1 INTRODUCTION

THE NOTION OF non-state actors derives from a dichotomy of states as subjects of international law, and other non-state entities as objects. Rosalyn Higgins's comment is real today: 'the whole notion of "subjects" and "objects" has no credible reality, and, in my view, no functional purpose. We have erected an intellectual prison of our own choosing and then declared it to be an unalterable constraint.'[1] The centrality of the only'states as subjects' approach hinges on the creation of the 'entrance requirements', a technique employed by territorial elites to safeguard their vested interests by setting up a rigid requirement for participation by non-state entities in the organised arenas of formal law-making.[2] In such organised arenas these states represented by their respective governments are gatekeepers. To illustrate, the Preamble of the Charter of the United Nations proclaims at the outset that it is 'We the people' that set out our purposes and designed how to achieve them, but in the end it concludes that it is 'our respective Governments' that agreed to establish the United Nations.

International organisations, though often referred to as non-state actors, play a role as gatekeepers, which are essentially the extension of the state apparatus, distinguished from the rest of the participants in the global decision process which is civil society in Antonio Gramsci's sense, ie, non-state and private entities.[3] In zeroing in the organised arenas of formal

[1] R Higgins, *Problems and Process: International Law And How We Use It* (Oxford, Clarendon Press, 1994) 49.

[2] Myres S McDougal, Harold D Lasswell and W Michael Reisman, 'The World Constitutive Process of Authoritative Decision' (1967) 19 *Journal of Legal Education* 253, 262.

[3] Antonio Gramsci, 'State and Civil Society' in Quintin Hoare and Geoffrey Nowell-Smith (eds), *Selections From The Prison Notebooks of Antonio Gramsci* (London, Lawrence & Wishart, 1971) 127: 'State = political society + civil society.'

law-making, conventional analysis in terms of government organs tends to overlook numerous private initiatives involved in the anterior processes that precede such formal law-making in organised arenas.[4] This is unfortunate because, as Michael Reisman states, '[a] moment's reflection should dispel the notion that legislation originates, transpires and concludes in the legislature.'[5] There is more to this than meets the eye.

A list of 'Major Groups and Stakeholders' recognised by the United Nations Environment Programme (UNEP) is illustrative; it attests to how wide the range of participants in the UNEP decision-making process really is. The concept of the nine 'Major Groups' established by Agenda 21 at the Earth Summit in 1992[6] recognises the following: farmers, women, the scientific and technological community, children and youth, indigenous peoples and their communities, workers and trade unions, business and industry, non-governmental organisations, and local authorities. A group of non-governmental organisations is just one of the nine major groups. The UNEP uses the term 'civil society' as an umbrella term covering all nine Major Groups, whose representatives influence and collaborate with UNEP and participate in the Governing Council/Global Ministerial Environmental Forum and its related meetings.[7]

There are other private entities not included in the definition of UNEP's Major Groups, such as political parties, gangs, and private armies, which also participate in the global decision process. For the purpose of this chapter, I treat international organisations *not* as 'non-state actors', but primarily as decision-making arenas.[8] Although formal and final decisions are made in the name of international organisations, 'the actors that participated in shaping the content of the decisions of these organisations disappear in the shadow of the organizations.'[9] Territorial elites

[4] W Michael Reisman, 'Private International Declaration Initiatives' in *La declaration universelle des droit de l' homme 1948–98: Avenir d' un ideal commun* (Paris, Documentation française, 1999) 79–80.

[5] ibid, 79.

[6] Agenda 21, adopted by the UN Conference on Environment and Development (UNCED); www.unep.org/Documents.Multilingual/Default.asp?documentid=52.

[7] UNEP, The Guidelines for Participation of Major Groups and Stakeholders in Policy Design at UNEP [hereinafter 'the Guidelines for Participation'], para 7; www.unep.org/civil-society/Portals/59/Documents/Guidelines-for-CSO-participation-Aug2609.pdf.

[8] McDougal, Lasswell and Reisman, 'The World Constitutive Process', above n 2, 264: 'International organizations may be either participants or arenas in the constitutive process.' See also Steve Charnovitz, 'The Relevance of Non-State Actors to International Law' in Rüdiger Wolfrum and Volker Röben (eds), *Developments of International Law in Treaty Making* (Heidelberg/New York, Springer, 2005) 543, 545–47.

[9] Mahnoush H Arsanjani, 'The Uses and Abuses of Illusion in International Politics' in Mahnoush H Arsanjani et al (eds), *Looking to the Future: Essays on International Law in Honor of W Michael Reisman* (Leiden/Boston, Martinus Nijhoff Publishers, 2011) 63; Susan Strange, *The Retreat of the State: The Diffusion Of Power In The World Economy* (Cambridge, Cambridge University Press, 1996) xiv: 'The international organization is above all a tool of national government, an instrument for the pursuit of national interest by other means.'

representing the membership of these international organisations are formal and official decision-makers whom various non-official and private entities influence and collaborate with in the decision-making process provided by these international organisations.

3.2 NON-STATE ACTORS IN CONTEXT: MULTIPLE AFFILIATIONS AND COMPLEX LAYERS OF DECISION PROCESSES

As '[n]o dependable relationship exists between a structure that is called "governmental" in a particular body politic and the facts of authority and control',[10] so 'we, the people' of different territorial communities are participating in any international decision process through numerous entities operating in both public and private spheres of different levels of community before that decision process culminates in the making of the final authoritative decision by 'our respective Governments'. Functionally, therefore, states represented by their respective territorial elites are not the sole category of participants in the global decision process, even though they will continue to be primary participants in that process.[11]

When we focus on individual human beings who constitute groups and communities, it becomes evident that individual human beings have their own demands, identifications and expectations. They act on their own behalf or act collectively to maximise values through institutions affecting resources. Groups and different levels of community they choose to join will accordingly be multiple and complex; their affiliation and consociation become transnational, interpenetrating territorial boundaries and cultures. In this global social process, participating individuals and groups in pursuit of their demands compete, coalesce, collaborate and cooperate with each other, taking account of the activities and demands of other participants. Such interaction among participating individuals and groups generates competing claims on the authoritative decision process for response. It is, therefore, ineluctable to see a much wider range of actors other than states participating in the global decision process.[12]

10 McDougal, Lasswell and Reisman, 'The World Constitutive Process', above n 2, 260.

11 W Michael Reisman, 'Designing and Managing the Future of the State' (1997) 8 *European Journal of International Law* 409, 416.

12 See Myres S McDougal, W Michael Reisman and Andrew R Willard, 'The World Community: A Planetary Social Process' (1988) 21 *UC Davis Law Review* 807, 822–26; W Michael Reisman, Mahnoush H Arsanjani, Siegfried Wiessner and Gayl S Westerman, *International Law in Contemporary Perspective* (New York, Foundation Press, 2004); W Michael Riesman, 'The Democratization of Contemporary International Law-Making Processes and the Differentiation of Their Application' in Rüdiger Wolfrum and Volker Röben (eds), *Developments of International Law In Treaty Making* (Heidelberg/New York, Springer, 2005) 262–351 (Establishment of International Actors Other than States). See also Steve Charnovitz, 'Two centuries of participation: NGOs and international governance' (1997) 18 *Michigan Journal of International Law* 183.

To use the New Haven School's terminology, by a participant in the global decision process, 'we mean an individual or an entity which has at least minimum access to the process of authority in the sense that it can make claims or be subjected to claims.'[13] These participants include, apart from states and international organisations, the elites of transnational non-governmental organisations operating in the wide range of value sectors from those concerned with economic development, health, food, and population to those concerned with religious practices and teaching, fraternity, family, and skills and knowledge development, multinational business corporations, transnational professional associations, gangs, terrorist groups, and individuals.[14] As Mahnoush H Arsanjani observes,

> The expansion of the range of relevant actors to include non-state entities has further complicated the dynamics of decision making at the international level. Non-state entities have become more influential in decision-making at international fora through the adroit use of various strategies. Likewise, rapid communications systems, which are not always subject to the control of the state apparatus have required quicker reactions to international events than the organized deliberative multilateral system can supply.[15]

Students of the New Haven School are not so much concerned with making any material distinction between the terms 'participants' and 'actors', as making sure that the accurate and comprehensive framework of inquiry is employed to map social and decision contexts. Math Noortmann, however, argues that '[t]he main difference between the "participants" and "actors" approach is not one of empirical focus but one of concept and theoretical outlook, it is not the unit of reference, but the unit of analysis.'[16] What the New Haven School offers is a conceptual tool with which to accurately describe and assess any social process. We focus on individuals and groups in the first category of a phase analysis by asking who are relevant actors in the situation (participants), followed by what are their subjectivities, their identifications, expectations and demands (perspectives), where they are interacting (situations), what resources are at their disposal (bases of power), how those resources are used (strategies), and with what culminating events (outcomes) or what longer-term consequences (effects).[17]

[13] McDougal, Lasswell and Reisman, 'The World Constitutive Process', above n 2, 262.

[14] W Michael Reisman, Siegfried Wiessner and Andrew R Willard, 'The New Haven School: A Brief Introduction' (2007) 32 *Yale Journal of International Law* 575.

[15] Arsanjani, 'The Uses and Abuses', above n 9, 52.

[16] Math Noortmann, 'Understanding Non-State Actors in the Contemporary World Society: Transcending the International, Mainstreaming the Transnational. Or Bringing the Participants Back In?' in Math Noortmann and Cedric Ryngaert (eds), *Non-State Actor Dynamics In International Law: from Law-Takers To Law-Makers* (Surrey, Ashgate, 2010).

[17] Harold D Lasswell and Myres S McDougal, *Jurisprudence for a Free Society: Studies in Law, Science, and Policy* (Dordrecht/Boston/London, M Nijhoff, 1991) Pt II, The Social Process Context, p 333.

We often use the terms 'actors' and 'participants' interchangeably, as indicated in the fundamental schema for characterising the social process: '*Man* (actors, participants) acts to optimize *values* (preferred events) through *institutions* affecting *resources*.'[18] What is important is 'a comprehensive delineation which permits the observer, with minimal preconception, to identify those who are *in fact* actors in each context.'[19] And the following explanation is given:

> The first step is to provide the observer with a 'checklist' that covers the various conceivable 'form' of interaction in the world community. Otherwise, significant modes of participation may be overlooked. The great variety of practices that comprise the planetary social process, therefore, encourages the responsible observer to use a more general delineation or taxonomy in the initial phase of any survey. Once a provisional list of participants is developed, those who are critical actors can be identified, again on a tentative basis, by their apparent impact on the pattern of value shaping and sharing in the situation under scrutiny.[20]

'[I]n this model', says Higgins, 'there are no "subjects" and "objects", but only participants. Individuals are participants, along with international organizations … multinational corporations, and indeed private and non-governmental groups.'[21]

3.3 NON-STATE ACTORS AND SPECIALISED AGENCIES OF THE UNITED NATIONS

It cannot be denied that the combined effect of the provisions of Article 57 of the United Nations Charter regarding the various specialised agencies brought into relationship with the United Nations[22] and the provisions of Article 71 regarding the Economic and Social Council's (ECOSOC) consultation with non-governmental organisations[23] has contributed to the spawning of non-governmental organisations around the world.

These specialised agencies have 'wide international responsibilities in economic, social, cultural, educational, health, and related fields',[24] and for that reason, they were brought into relationship with the United Nations to undertake international economic and social co-operation

[18] McDougal, Lasswell and Reisman,'The World Constitutive Process', above n 2, 259.
[19] McDougal, Reisman and Willard, 'The World Community', above n 12, 816.
[20] ibid, 816.
[21] Higgins, *Problems and Process*, above n 1, 50.
[22] Art 57 Charter of the United Nations.
[23] ibid, Art 71.
[24] ibid, Art 57(1).

'for the accomplishment of the purposes set forth in Article 55'.[25] That article provides:

> With a view to the creation of conditions of stability and well-being which are necessary for peaceful and friendly relations among nations based on respect for the principle of equal rights and self-determination of peoples, the United Nations shall promote:
>
> a. higher standards of living, full employment, and conditions of economic and social progress and development;
> b. solutions of international economic, social, health, and related problems; and international cultural and educational cooperation; and
> c. universal respect for, and observance of, human rights and fundamental freedoms for all without distinction as to race, sex, language, or religion.[26]

A corollary of the purposes set forth in Article 55 is the promotion and development of various non-governmental organisations, the tasks of each of which are similarly delineated in the corresponding areas of responsibilities of the specialised agencies.

As evidenced in the provisions of Articles 70 and 71, ECOSOC's competence to allow 'representatives of the specialized agencies to participate, without vote, in its deliberations',[27] and for 'consultation' with non-governmental organisations (NGOs), are almost comparable in its essential function. Non-state actors, ie, those entities external to the membership of the United Nations, are allowed thereby to participate in ECOSOC's decision process. Yet, the form and substance of NGOs' relationship with either ECOSOC or any of the specialised agencies are vastly diverse and varied from one NGO to another, reflecting the different 'size, resources, impact, methodology, objectives and approach to international organizations'.[28] By the same token, ECOSOC and the specialised agencies have their own diverse and idiosyncratic ways of dealing with NGOs.[29]

It is the consultative status accorded by ECOSOC that determines which NGOs will be given access to the organised decision arena of ECOSOC.[30] It is essential to bear in mind that ECOSOC is itself an organised decision arena of the most comprehensive universal international

[25] ibid, Art 59.
[26] ibid, Art 55.
[27] ibid, Art 70.
[28] Report of the Secretary-General, Arrangements and practices for the interaction of non-governmental organisations in all activities of the United Nations system, UN Doc A/53/170 (10 July 1998); available at www.un.org/documents/ga/docs/53/plenary/a53-170.htm.
[29] Math Noortmann, 'Who Really Needs Article 71? A Critical Approach to the Relationship between NGOs and the UN' in Wybo P Heere (ed), *From government to governance: the growing impact of non-state actors on the international and European legal system: proceedings of the sixth Hague joint conference held in The Hague, the Netherlands*, 3–5 July 2003 (The Hague, TMC Asser Press, 2004) 113.
[30] ECOSOC Resolution 1996/31 of 25 July 1996; available at www.un.org/documents/ecosoc/res/1996/eres1996-31.htm. See also 'Introduction to ECOSOC Consultative Status', available at http://esango.un.org/paperless/Web?page=static&content=intro.

organisation, and at the same time ECOSOC is the sole 'gatekeeper', and actually shapes 'global civil society'.[31] It declares, 'The granting, suspension and withdrawal of consultative status, as well as the interpretation of norms and decisions relating to this matter, are the prerogative of Member States exercised through the Economic and Social Council and its Committee on Non-Governmental Organizations.'[32] Those NGOs accredited by ECOSOC with consultative status must operate in accordance with the UN Charter and ECOSOC Resolution 1996/31.[33]

3.4 NON-STATE ACTORS AND CIVIL SOCIETY

The non-state actors within the purview of ECOSOC are not concerned, in principle, with the power process per se of any body politic. But there are many private consociations competing with the state. As Max Weber observed,

> The law of the state often tries to obstruct the coercive means of other consociations…
>
> But the state is not always successful. There are groups stronger than the state in this respect … This conflict between the means of coercion of the various corporate groups is as old as the law itself. In the past it has not always ended with the triumph of the coercive means of the political body, and even today this has not always been the outcome.[34]

Where non-state actors such as opposition political parties or armed private groups were involved in seeking to supplant the authority and control of the state, the hitherto monopolised domain of coercive means of the state is breached, and they will start competing with the extant territorial elites for power. Michael Reisman and I called these private groups 'aspirants', which are 'groups which seek to participate in authoritative processes of a community with the aim of achieving influence or lawful control.'[35] They are non-state actors like political parties, pressure/interest groups or citizens' action groups, or even private armies like the

[31] Ngaire Woods, 'Multilateralism and building stronger international institutions' in Alnoor Ebrahim and Edward Weisband (eds), *Global Accountabilities: Participation, Pluralism, and Public Ethics* (Cambridge, Cambridge University Press, 2007) 137.

[32] ECOSOC Resolution 1996/31 of 25 July 1996, (above n 30), Pt II: Principles to be Applied in the Establishment of Consultative Relations, para 15.

[33] ibid. See also Eisuke Suzuki, 'Global Governance and International Financial Institutions' (2011) 19 *Asia Pacific Law Review* 15.

[34] Max Rheinstein (ed), *Max Weber on Law in Economy and Society* (Cambridge MA, Harvard University Press, 1954) 19.

[35] Michael Reisman and Eisuke Suzuki, 'Recognition and Social Change in International Law: A Prologue for Decisionmaking' in W Michael Reisman and Burns H Weston (eds), *Toward World Order and Human Dignity: Essays In Honor of Myres S McDougal* (New York, Free Press, 1976) 242.

Sudan People's Liberation Movement/Army (SPLM/A).[36] The point of emphasis is that the monopolisation of coercive means by the territorial elites to the exclusion of any other entities in a given body politic is the hallmark of the state.[37] Nonetheless, even that power of monopoly of the state becomes liable for erosion by non-state actors within the state when they acquire coercive means. It is not difficult to understand, therefore, that other consociations are more likely to be in a position to complement, compete with, and supplant, the authority and control of the state in any other value processes of a community.

3.5 NON-STATE ACTORS' ACTIVITIES IN THE MAJOR VALUE PROCESSES

Power

Since most non-state entities are seeking to achieve a particular political end, they are seeking some form of power and exercising that power to varying degrees by influencing decision without assuming formal political power. Non-state entities seeking formal power as a scope value within the body politic in which they operate are usually political parties. Should participation in civic arenas be denied, internal political arenas would become irregular, and when such non-state actors acquire significant political strength, they would become liable for suppression by the incumbent territorial elites of the body politic. These aspirants would be more likely to resort to higher levels of coercion with a view to organising a proto-state. The latest non-state actor which organised a proto-state was the SPLM/A, which had negotiated with the government of the Republic of Sudan for a referendum on whether Southern Sudan should be independent by seceding from Sudan proper.[38] Unlike any other non-state actors, those counter-territorial elites who are aspirants are more often than not 'outlawed' by the incumbent territorial elites because they are not only competing with the extant territorial elites in power, but also seeking to replace them—sometimes extra-constitutionally.[39] As HL Nieburg aptly summarises it: 'Every group that acts as a proto-state does

[36] See the Permanent Court of Arbitration case, *The Government of Sudan/The Sudan People's Liberation Movement/Army (Abyei Arbitration)*, which was conducted under the PCA Optional Rules for arbitrating disputes between two parties of which only one is a state. The Final Award was given on 22 July 2009, available at www.pca-cpa.org/showpage.asp?pag_id=1306.

[37] Max Weber, *The Theory of Social and Economic Organization* (Talcott Parsons ed, AM Henderson tr, Martino Publishing, 1947 [2012 reprint]) 154.

[38] See the Comprehensive Peace Agreement between the Government of the Republic of the Sudan and the Sudan People's Liberation Movement/Sudan People's Liberation Army of 9 January 2005, available at www.aec-sudan.org/docs/cpa/cpa-en.pdf.

[39] Eisuke Suzuki, 'Extraconstitutional Change and World Pulic Order: A Prologue to Decision-Making' (1977) 15 *Houston Law Review* 23, 36–40.

not seek to become a revolutionary regime. Yet, in some cases, the process at work produces that result. Violence is the essential cutting edge that creates and maintains ecological separation between integrated social organizations.'[40]

The decolonisation process allowed newly emerging internal elites to set up 'national liberation movements'. Many obtained observer status in the United Nations and its related agencies and/or regional organisations, such as the former Organisation of African Unity (OAU). For those aspirants such as the National Liberation Front (FLN) in Algeria, the South West Africa People's Organisation (SWAPO) in Namibia, various contenders in Angola, the Polisario Front of the Sahrawi people in Western Sahara, and the Palestinian Liberation Organisation (PLO), access to organised international arenas was an important milestone, as was the recognition of representatives prior to their gaining control over territory.[41] Non-state actors seeking some form of 'recognition' are, in turn, subjected to claims by others for conformity to critical international standards of conduct.[42]

Globalisation and the development of communications and information technology have made recognition of aspirants real. Ahead of any other states, France recognised Libya's rebel leadership, the Libyan National Council, as the sole legitimate representative of the Libyan people in March 2011,[43] even though the Libyan National Council had not secured a satisfactory level of territorial control of a portion of Libya, a situation that would traditionally only accord non-state actors the status of insurgents or belligerents.[44] The United States granted Libyan rebel leaders full diplomatic recognition as the governing authority of Libya on 15 July 2011. In the words of Secretary of State Hillary Rodham Clinton, the rebels' Transitional National Council 'has offered important assurances today, including the promise to pursue a process of democratic reform that is inclusive both geographically and politically.'[45]

40 HL Nieburg, *Political Violence: The Behavioral Process 100* (New York, St Martins Press, 1969). See Eisuke Suzuki, 'Self-Determination and World Public Order: Community Response to Territorial Separation' (1976) 16 *Virginia Journal of International Law* 779, 788–89.

41 See Reisman and Suzuki, 'Recognition', above n 35, 424–30.

42 ibid, 442–44.

43 Alan Cowell and Steven Erlanger, 'France Becomes First Country to Recognize Libyan Rebels', *The New York Times* (3 November 2011), available at www.nytimes.com/2011/03/11/world/europe/11france.html; and Stefan Talmon, 'Recognition of the Libyan National Transitional Council' (2011) 15 *ASIL Insights* 13. See W Michael Reisman and Andrew R Willard (eds), *International Incidents: The Law That Counts In World Politics* (Princeton NJ, Princeton University Press, 1988).

44 Reisman and Suzuki, 'Recognition', above n 35, 425–28.

45 William Wan and William Booth, 'United Sates recognizes Libyan rebels as legitimate government', *Washington Post* (15 July 2011), available at http://link.email.washingtonpost.com/r/46MP2V/PRTNUU/CKHD1L/YENMHK/UIROV/PJ/h.

Wealth

There are three categories of non-state actors operating in the global wealth process: (i) transnational business entities whose primary purposes are profit-making, capital accumulation, capital investment, and expansion of business; (ii) labour unions in the sharing of wealth; and (iii) not-for-profit organisations whose primary purposes are to ensure the policies and practices of business entities in the first category are fair, socially responsible, and environmentally sound and sustainable in the long run.

In the wake of the collapse of the Soviet Union, neo-liberalism came to rule the world economy. As the state's responsibility for provision of primary social services was relegated to private entities, even non-governmental organisations (NGOs), not normally considered for-profit entities, have grown 'to a $1 trillion industry, riding the global wave of privatization of services'.[46] Globalisation has reinforced the effective reach of transnational business entities in setting global standards and forms of best practices in their respective areas of business activities such as financial transactions (foreign direct investment, bonds, and insurance), transportation, construction, and so on. In the beginning, these standards were originally introduced by major actors in a particular industry in their business agreements, which have subsequently become common usage and practice among many other entities in the same industry. Such developments can be considered akin to 'adhesion contracts' that cannot be negotiated. 'In the eyes of the community', explained Lasswell and McDougal, 'the power exercised by unofficial organizations may be both controlling and authoritative.'[47]

Just like the tripartite representation of states, workers, and employers of the International Labour Organization (ILO), workers and trade unions as well as business and industry associations play major roles in shaping policy for workers' wages, industrial investment, and so on.

Enlightenment

International professional associations obtain and disseminate information and increase the general level of understanding of particular subject-matters

[46] Siegfried Weissner, 'Legitimacy and Accountability of NGOs: A Policy-Oriented Perspective' in Wybo P Heere (ed), *From Government To Governance: The Growing Impact Of Non-State Actors On The International And European Legal System: Proceedings Of The Sixth Hague Joint Conference held in The Hague, the Netherlands, 3–5 July 2003* (The Hague, TMC Asser Press, 2004).

[47] Lasswell and McDougal, *Jurisprudence for a Free Society*, above n 17, 368.

in which their respective associations have expertise. The role of the Institut de Droit International IDI) and the International Law Association (ILA) in the development of international law is undeniable. Mass communication media and international news agencies and other social networking services, are the principal channels through which public perceptions are shaped about what is happening around the world.

Skills

Increasingly, groups trained in information technology are developing an interactive democracy in which people receive news and respond to it by expressing their views, which in aggregate quickly become public opinion. Recent political changes for democracy which started off as 'the Arab Spring' in Tunis first in January 2011 spread quickly to Cairo, Tripoli, and Bahrain in less than a month, all thanks to the Internet and training provided by a unique transnational skill group called 'the Centre for Applied Non-violent Action and Strategies', based in Belgrade, Serbia.[48]

Affection

Historically, individuals associated themselves in pursuit of their demands on the basis of group identification, be it cultural, ethnic, linguistic, or religious. Minority groups within a body politic often sought to establish an equal political basis with the dominant group of the territorial community. These groups often extend across territorial boundaries into neighbouring states, affecting those states' policy. What are commonly referred to as 'war lords', in Afghanistan, Congo, Somalia, or any other similarly conflict-torn states, are local political families, which enjoy a broad ethnic group's support.

Rectitude

Of all rectitude groups, none is more influential in its reach than the Roman Catholic Church. Its power reflects the cohesiveness of its tenet, the strength of organisational hierarchy, and, above all, an enormous number of its followers around the world. The international legal status of the Vatican as Holy See attests to the unique position enjoyed by the Catholic Church.

[48] Tina Rosenberg, 'Revolution U' *Foreign Policy* (16 February 2011), available at www.foreignpolicy.com/articles/2011/02/16/revolution_u?page=full.

Wellbeing

Private wellbeing groups such as Médecins Sans Frontières (MSF) have been increasingly active in alleviating the suffering of people in natural calamities such as earthquakes, tsunamis, typhoons and other natural disaster situations. The International Committee of the Red Cross (ICRC) plays a special role in humanitarian assistance.[49]

Respect

Many private associations have been major non-state actors in the protection of human rights. As transnational business corporations expand their operational scope across boundaries and cultures, respect deprivations are committed as well. Although in conjunction with activities of the United Nations, the role played by private individuals and groups in the creation of the United Nations Global Compact is noteworthy.[50]

All private groups in the value processes enumerated above complement and, sometimes compete with, programmes of official agencies, while seeking to increase their influence and effectiveness 'by finding niches in critical decision functions which would allow them to shape prescriptions incorporating their preferred policies.'[51]

3.6 POLICY FOR NON-STATE ACTORS' PARTICIPATION IN DECISION-MAKING

It is individual human beings acting collectively as the ultimate actors in all groups (whether they are territorial, functional, organised or unorganised) which comprise participants, including non-state actors. As McDougal, Lasswell, and Lung-chu Chen explained:

> Ours is a world of pluralism and diversity, a global arena in which various participants—groups (territorial and functional, governmental and nongovernmental) and individual human beings—constantly interact under ever-changing conditions. All of the above-mentioned group participants—nation-states, groups, and private associations—are forms of associations *through which individuals cooperate to achieve fulfilment of their demands*.[52]

[49] David P Forsythe, 'International Humanitarian Assistance: The Role of the Red Cross' (1996–97) 3 *Buffalo Journal of International Law* 235.

[50] See the Ten Principles of the UN Global Compact, available at www.unglobalcompact.org/aboutthegc/thetenprinciples/index.html.

[51] Reisman, 'Democratization', above n 12, 15, 21.

[52] Myres S McDougal, Harold D Lasswell and Lung-chu Chen et al, *Human Rights and World Public Order: The Basic Policies of an International Law of Human Dignity* (New Haven CT, Yale University Press, 1980) 179.

The fundamental premise for such diversity is 'the reciprocal honoring of freedom of choice about participation in value processes'.[53] The perspectives and operations of the individual human being are the basic empirical foundation of pluralism and diversity. And the basis of authority of government is the will of the people as expressed in Article 21(3) of the Universal Declaration of Human Rights, now considered customary international law and *jus cogens*.[54]

We no longer consider sovereignty in terms of 'a metaphysical abstraction called the State', but in terms of 'the sovereignty of individuals'.[55] We must accept that the basis of authority expressed in Article 21(3) of the Universal Declaration of Human Rights perforce extends to claims for participation in the global decision process.[56] Authority for such participation is summed up by Article 20 of the same Declaration, which provides: 'Everyone has the right to freedom of peaceful assembly and association.'[57]

Participation by civil society in multiple decision processes of varying territorial compass perforce involves a huge number of private entities across all value processes. Several of these private entities are well organised through their respective systems of representation linking their affiliated organisations from local and national through regional to international membership organisations. The range of participants should be as comprehensive as feasible, but it must be calibrated by the principle of economy to ensure the effectiveness of representation. The principle of effectiveness also requires participants' capacity to enjoy participatory rights to bear their corresponding obligations because participation entails responsibility.

To be responsible participants, they need to meet the requirements of transparency and accountability. They need to disclose to the public at large pertinent information about their organisation, purposes, activities and what their sources of funding are; and they need to be accountable for their actions and conduct.[58]

[53] ibid, 7.

[54] Universal Declaration of Human Rights, GA Res 217(III), UN Doc A/810, art 21(3): 'The will of the people shall be the basis of the authority of government; this will shall be expressed in periodic and genuine elections which shall be by universal and equal suffrage and shall be held by secret vote or by equivalent free voting procedures'; available at www.un.org/en/documents/udhr/index.shtml.

[55] W Michael Reisman, 'Sovereignty and Human Rights in Contemporary International Law' in Gregory H Fox and Brad R Roth (eds), *Democratic Governance and International Law* (Cambridge, Cambridge University Press, 2000).

[56] See Volker Röben, 'Proliferation of Actors' in R Wolfrum and V Röben (eds), *Developments Of International Law In Treaty Making*, above n 8.

[57] Universal Declaration of Human Rights, above n 54, art 20.

[58] M Weber and SN Eisenstadt, *Max Weber on Charisma and Institution Building: Selected Papers* (Chicago IL, University of Chicago Press, 1968).

3.7 RECENT TRENDS OF NON-STATE ACTORS AS AUTHORITATIVE DECISION-MAKERS

3.7.1 General Framework for Participation

Perhaps it is appropriate now to examine the real effect of what is referred to as the clear 'distinction' between participation without vote in the deliberations of ECOSOC for any UN member and representatives of the specialised agencies, under Articles 69 and 70 of the UN Charter, on the one hand, and 'consultation' with NGOs, under Article 71, on the other.[59] Part II of Resolution 1996/31, Principles Governing the Nature of the Consultative Arrangements, further elaborates that distinction by stating that:

> Under Articles 69 and 70, participation is provided for only in the case of States not members of the Council, and of specialized agencies. Article 71, applying to non-governmental organizations, provides for suitable arrangements for consultation. This distinction, deliberately made in the Charter, is fundamental and the arrangements for consultation should not be such as to accord to non-governmental organizations the same rights of participation as are accorded to States not members of the Council and to the specialized agencies brought into relationship with the United Nations.[60]

The distinction underlined by Resolution 1996/31 is formalism in reiterating the states as subjects of international law. In contrast, even though the UNEP Guidelines for Participation of Major Groups and Stakeholders in Policy Design acknowledge that the Rules of Procedures of the Governing Council provide for 'international non-governmental organisations having an interest in the field of the environment' to attend 'as observers at public meetings of the Governing Council and its subsidiary organs, if any',[61] the Guidelines for Participation adopted a more creative approach for the engagement of non-state entities, as follows:

> Subject to approval of the President of the Governing Council, the accredited organisations are allowed, under the coordination of the Major Groups Facilitation Committee (MGFC)
>
> a) To participate in the Ministerial Round Tables of the GMEF [Global Ministerial Environmental Forum];
> b) To have 9 seats in each of the plenary sessions of the meeting (opening, closing, GMEF, Committee of the Whole);

[59] ECOSOC Resolution 1996/31 of 25 July 1996, above n 30, para 18. See text accompanying nn 22–33 above.

[60] ibid.

[61] See UNEP, 'Consultation on Enhancing Major Groups Participation at UNEP's Governance Level', available at www.unep.org/civil-society/About/ConsultationonEnhancing/tabid/2991/language/en-US/Default.aspx; the Guidelines for Participation, above n 7.

c) To have the opportunity to submit their written input to the President;
d) To participate in the open-ended subsidiary organs and bodies of the meeting.[62]

It is a truism to say that there is a gap between what is formally stated in the official pronouncement and how actual practice develops. In the process of the actual implementation of formal statements, somewhat different interpretations and applications will be made by those who are in the 'trade', so to speak. It is the 'operational code'.[63] According to Reisman, 'what is distinctive about the operational code is that it is a private public law in systems in which public is supposed to be public; those authorized to play control functions and those who deal directly with them come to accept procedures that deviate from the myth system as licit.'[64]

It is not helpful, therefore, to become entangled in the semantic and syntactic exercise of the difference between 'participation' and 'consultation'[65] because 'consultation' is only one of the forms of 'participation', and a wide range of participants perform a variety of decision functions in different decision arenas, organised and unorganised. The effectiveness of their participation hinges on how they can make use of access to a particular process of authority; what kind of resources they have at their disposal; what kind of instrument of policy they can employ in the course of performance of their various functions; and what kind of outcome they seek to achieve with what effect.

3.7.2 The Need for Functional Analysis

When we recognise that the reality of globalisation has deconstructed a dichotomy of national and international law, in terms of the relative supremacy of one system of rules or other inter-relations of rules, we can no longer afford to entertain the conventional theory about the states as the only subjects of international law; nor can we subscribe to the common conception of law-making in domestic political systems. Rather, it is more useful to adopt the New Haven School's functional approach to describing the world's different community decision processes in terms of the interpenetration of multiple processes of authoritative decision of varying territorial compass.

62 The Guidelines for Participation, above n 7.

63 W Michael Reisman, *Folded Lies: Bribery, Crusades, And Reforms* (New York, Free Press, 1979); McDougal, Lasswell and Reisman, 'The World Constitutive Process', above n 2, 260: '[I]t is not unusual to discover, for example, that the authority formally provided in a written constitutional charter may be ignored, or totally redefined by unwritten practice.'

64 ibid, 18.

65 Eibe Riedel, 'The Development of International Law: Alternatives to Treaty-Making? International Organizations and Non-State Actors' in R Wolfrum and V Röben (eds), *Developments of International Law In Treaty Making*, above n 8, 305–06.

In these multiple processes of decision-making, people make a decision to maximise their preferred events through institutions affecting resources. The New Haven School has dissected the expression 'decision' in terms of its seven discrete, but interrelated decision functions as: (1) *intelligence*: the gathering, processing, and disseminating of information relevant to the making of choices; (2) *promotion*: the active advocacy of policy alternatives; (3) *prescription*: the fashioning of one of competing policies as 'law' and projecting it as the authoritative policy of the community in question; (4) *invocation*: the provisional characterisation of events of deviation from prescriptions and the invocation of an authoritative response; (5) *application*: the applying of prescriptions to an alleged deviation, with sanction; (6) *termination*: putting an end to existing prescriptions and other arrangements that no longer reflect appropriate public order goals; and (7) *appraisal*: the on-going evaluation of the general performance of the decision process.

All these decision functions are distinct and discrete, and the performance of each decision function affects the performance of every other function. All these decision functions relate to the authoritative response to claims about a set of problems developing in the global social process. For the purpose of this chapter, I will focus on how various non-state entities perform any one of these functions relating to claims for participation in the global constitutive process of decision. All non-state entities are performing any one of these decision functions to varying degrees.

The Intelligence Function

The intelligence function is the starting point for any action; it includes the gathering, processing, and disseminating of information essential to decision-making.[66] The information and data assembled and evaluated clarify conditions that account for the current state of affairs and help direct the necessary action to improve the situation.

As indicated in Agenda 21, non-state entities are actively participating in gathering information, monitoring events in local communities.[67] Most notably, NGOs such as the International Commission of Jurists, Amnesty International (AI) and Human Rights Watch actively perform the intelligence function relating to the protection and development of human rights law. Amnesty International's activities are fact-based and include sending experts to talk with victims; observing trials; interviewing local

[66] McDougal, Lasswell and Reisman, 'The World Constitutive Process', above n 2, 131–54; Myres S McDougal, Harold D Lasswell and W Michael Reisman, 'The Intelligence Function and World Public Order' (1973) 46 *Temple Law Quarterly* 365.

[67] See Agenda 21, above n 6, at Section III, Strengthening the Role of Major Groups, ch 23, available at www.un.org/esa/dsd/agenda21/res_agenda21_23.shtml.

officials; liaising with human rights activists; monitoring global and local media; publishing detailed reports on human rights conditions; informing the news media; and publicising our concerns in documents, leaflets, posters, advertisements, newsletters and websites.[68]

In other value process areas, the World Wide Fund for Nature (WWF), Oxfam International, the Bank Information Center, and so on[69] undertake various intelligence tasks. All these NGOs are better positioned than territorial elites and their functionaries of the state to initiate any effort that may result in either limiting the state power or altering the direction of the extant policy.[70]

Intelligence is the most critical and indispensable initial input to activate the decision process. The quality of intelligence shapes all the subsequent decision functions, but 'the utility of the most accurate and timely intelligence depends upon a decisionmaker capable and willing to use it.'[71]

The Promotion Function

On the basis of the intelligence gathered and processed, the decision phase turns to the promoting function which refers to the advocacy of policy alternatives, including the taking of initiatives which lead to the enactment of prescriptions. For non-state entities, which are mostly denied access to organised arenas of decision because of 'the entrance requirement', the promotion function provides them with opportunity to play a critical role in stimulating demands for the enactment of new prescriptions. Several NGOs are initiating, participating in the decision process or co-opting, incorporating or circumventing the various phases of the global decision process, as analysed by Judge Oda in his dissenting opinion on the *Legality of Nuclear Weapons cases*.[72] 'The idea behind the resolution whereby the UN General Assembly (and also the World Health Organization (WHO)) requested advisory opinions, had previously been advanced by a handful of non-governmental organizations (NGOs) which

[68] Amnesty International, 'How does Amnesty International carry out its work?'; available at www.amnesty.org/en/who-we-are/faq#how-ai-works. Another equally active NGO, Human Rights Watch, 'challenge[s] governments and those who hold power to end abusive practices and respect international human rights law' and 'enlist[s] the public and the international community to support the cause of human rights for all.' Mission statement of Human Rights Watch; available at www.hrw.org/en/about.

[69] See www.worldwildlife.org/home-full.html, www.oxfam.org/, and www.bicusa.org, respectively.

[70] Steve Charnovitz, 'How Nongovernmental Actors Vitalize International Law' in Mahnoush H Arsanjani et al (eds), *Looking to the future*, above n 9, 136: 'an initiative to limit government power is not likely to emanate from governments and is instead more likely to come from interested private actors.'

[71] McDougal, Lasswell and Reisman, 'The Intelligence Function', above n 66, 366.

[72] *Legality of the Threat or Use of Nuclear Weapons, Advisory Opinion* [1996] ICJ Rep (8 July) 226, 330, 335.

initiated a campaign for the total prohibition of nuclear weapons.'[73] The contributions by various NGOs to the conclusion of multilateral conventions cannot be overstated.[74] Notable recent examples include the United Nations Convention on the Rights of the Child,[75] the Rome Statute for the International Criminal Court,[76] and the International Campaign to Ban Landmines, which led to the Mine Ban Treaty[77] and the Cluster Munition Coalition's work for the Convention on Cluster Munitions.[78] Without their advocacy campaign and lobbying around the world, it would not have been possible to have had these treaties concluded. As Stephan Hobe states, 'NGOs do not only participate in state-initiated conferences but have also taken up the role of initiatives of state conferences.'[79]

The Prescribing Function

The prescribing function is communicating people's expectations about policy, authority, and control through reciprocal claims and mutual tolerance in their interactions.[80] Sequentially, the prescriptive function has four distinct phases: the initiation of the process, the evaluation of relevant facts and potential policies; the formulation of the policy to be projected as authoritative for the community; and the communication of the prescriptive content and expectations about authority and control to the target audience. As mentioned in the promotion function above, NGOs play a considerable role in the first two phases.

[73] ibid, [8]. See also Judge Oda's separate opinion in *Legality of the Use by a State of Nuclear Weapons in Armed Conflict*, ibid, 88, 96 [9]: '[I]t also seems to be clear from the records of the Forty-fifth and Forty-sixth World Health Assemblies for1992 and 1993, respectively, that resolution WHA46.40 was initiated by a few NGOs which had apparently failed in an earlier attempt to get the United Nations General Assembly to request an advisory opinion on the subject.'

[74] Stephan Hobe, 'The Role of Non-State Actors, in Particular of NGOs in Non-Contractual Law-Making and the Development of Customary International Law' in R Wolfrum and V Röben (eds), above n 8, 319, 322–24.

[75] UN Doc GA Res 44/25 of 20 Nov 1989; available at www2.ohchr.org/english/law/pdf/crc.pdf.

[76] UN Doc A/CONF 183/9 of 17 July 1998, as corrected; available at http://untreaty.un.org/cod/icc/statute/english/rome_statute(e).pdf.

[77] The Convention on the Prohibition of the Use, Stockpiling, Production and Transfer of Anti-Personnel Mines and on Their Destruction, signed on 3 December 1997 and effective on 1 March 1999, available at www.un.org/Depts/mine/UN Docs/ba_trty.htm. See also www.icbl.org.

[78] Convention on Cluster Munitions, signed on 3 December 2008; available at www.clusterconvention.org/pages/pages_ii/iia_textenglish.html. The Convention enters into force six months after 30 ratifications. Twenty-four states had ratified as of 15 November 2009.

[79] Hobe, 'Non-State Actors', above n 74, 323.

[80] Myres S McDougal and W Michael Reisman, 'The Prescribing Function in World Constitutive Process: How International Law Is Made' (1980) 6 *Yale Studies in World Public Order* 249.

To appreciate the realistic scope and range of the prescribing function that can be performed by non-state actors, the narrow range of the 'sources' of international law as specified in Article 38 of the Statute of the International Court of Justice is far from satisfactory.[81] The stark reality is that no decisions of any of the international organisations operating worldwide today, including the United Nations, have been mentioned in Article 38. Since most decision arenas in which NGOs participate are parliamentary or quasi-parliamentary settings like international conferences, the exclusion of decisions of international organisations would ipso facto preclude a large portion of NGOs' contribution to the prescribing function. Nevertheless, however tenuous its relevance may be, subparagraph (b) of Article 38, 'international custom, as evidence of a general practice accepted as law', may be invoked to recognise a contribution of non-state entities in general, and NGOs in particular, to the prescribing function as the development of customary international law.[82]

The Invoking Function

The invoking function is for claimants who characterise, from their perspective, on-going events in terms of extant prescriptions by asserting a certain set of facts about what has happened, what policies or prescriptions have been violated, and what remedies might be available to rectify the deteriorating conditions. International NGOs, which have networks with national NGOs, which are most knowledgeable in the local conditions of various countries, initiate the invoking function. 'The quality of the process of authoritative decision depends in no small measure upon the ability of individuals and non-state actors to challenge unlawful deprivations.'[83]

Many NGOs are accorded locus standi not only in international human rights fora such as the European Court of Human Rights and the American Commission on Human Rights, but also in the World Trade Organisation's dispute settlement panel and various accountability mechanisms of international financial institutions (IFIs), such as the World Bank and the Asian Development Bank. NGOs are in a position to lodge claims on behalf of victims before these international decision arenas.[84]

[81] The Statute of the International Court of Justice, art 38, available at www.icj-cij.org/documents/index.php?p1=4&p2=2&p3=0.

[82] Hobe, 'Non-State Actors' above n 74, 320.

[83] McDougal, Lasswell and Chen, above n 52, 278–79.

[84] Ruth Wedgwood, 'Legal Personality and the Role of Non-Governmental Organizations and Non-State Political Entities' in Rainer Hofmann and Nils Geissler (eds), *Non-state actors as new subjects of international law: international law—from the traditional state order towards the law of the global community* (Berlin, Duncker & Humblot, 1999). See also Suzuki and Nanwani, 'Responsibility of international organizations: the accountability mechanisms of multilateral development banks' (2005) 27 *Michigan Journal of International Law* 177.

The Application Function

Non-state entities face the perennial barrier, ie, 'the entrance requirement', mentioned at the outset, to the organised arenas of decision as the applying function is the final characterisation of the events alleged by the claimants in terms of extant prescriptions and the management of sanctioning measures to secure enforcement. It is considered the prerogative of the state elites. They undertake various forms of application such as 'investigation', 'fact-finding', 'reporting', 'negotiation', 'good offices', 'mediation', 'commissions of enquiry', 'conciliation', 'arbitration', and 'adjudication'.[85]

Non-state actors' participation in the application function, that had started with the tasks of monitoring compliance with treaty-obligations of human rights instruments, has vastly broadened to include access to judicial bodies, and conversely the ICJ has increasingly become the target of popular appeal that it allow 'more and diverse voices to be heard in addition to those of the States parties to the proceedings, especially those belonging to groups traditionally silenced by the primacy accorded to States' interests.'[86]

Traditionally, the technique to overcome the 'entrance requirement' was for the state of private corporations to espouse its nationals' claims before international tribunals. Today, the proliferation of bilateral investment treaties (BITs) and free trade agreements (FTAs) that have empowered investors to bring their own claims against host states has rendered the *démarche* of diplomatic protection unnecessary for the settlement of investor–state disputes.[87] The investors' right to bring claims against the host state has generated the case law through the investor-state arbitrations, and private attorneys are now making 'global administrative law' in the course of such arbitrations.[88]

Increasingly NGOs are participating in the applying function process by way of filing *amicus curiae* briefs in international tribunals.[89] The adamant refusal by the ICJ of NGOs' *amicus* briefs notwithstanding, NGOs have won partial success in the Appellate Body of the WTO.[90] As indicated by

[85] See McDougal, Lasswell and Reisman, 'The World Constitutive Process', above n 2; see also art 33(1) of the UN Charter.

[86] Christine M Chinkin, 'Presentation' in Connie Peck and Roy SK Lee (eds), *Increasing the effectiveness of the International Court of Justice* (The Hague/Boston/London, M Nijhoff Publishers, 1997). See also Dinah Shelton, 'The Participation of Nongovernmental Organizations in International Judicial Proceedings' (1994) 88 *American Journal of International Law* 611, 641–42.

[87] Jose E Alvarez, 'Are Corporations Subjects of International Law?' (2011) 9 *Santa Clara Journal of International Law* 1.

[88] See Gus Van Harten and Martin Loughlin, 'Investment treaty arbitration as a species of global administrative law' (2006) 17 *European Journal of International Law* 121.

[89] See Shelton, 'Participation' above n 86.

[90] Charnovitz, 'How Nongovernmental Actors' in Arsanjani et al (eds), *Looking to the Future,* above n 9, 135, 151–60.

the North American Free Trade Association's Free Trade Commission,[91] and demonstrated by the *Methanex* Tribunal,[92] a growing trend is to accept NGOs' *amicus* briefs.

The Terminating Function

The termination function sometimes takes place concurrently as the prescribing function is being performed. The former terminates an extant prescription that has become short of meeting demanded public order goals and the termination of a prescription itself often leads to a new prescription. Non-state actors being unofficial, private groups cannot be formal 'terminators', but as in the prescribing function they would be active promoters of new prescriptions. They represent 'affected parties', which are mostly private citizens.

As in the prohibition of child labour, anti-personnel land-mines, and cluster munitions, the termination function is designed to keep prescriptions in line with the goals of world public order. NGOs campaign for the withdrawal of certain incidental benefits of recognition from the target government or terminating obsolete policies for international financial institutions' financial assistance.

The Appraising Function

Various non-state entities of varying degrees of effectiveness perform the intelligence, promotion, law-making or prescription, invocation, and application functions of decision-making and help enormously in the performance of the on-going appraisal function. The core task of appraisal is to identify who is responsible for success or failure, in terms of the policy objectives of the larger community. Non-state actors contributed to ECOSOC's reporting task on the performance of its responsibilities.[93]

3.8 FOR THE FUTURE

Antonio Gramsci's writings suggest 'a sturdy structure of civil society' is in the core of the state, which is 'only an outer ditch', behind which civil society is 'a powerful system of fortresses and earthworks'.[94] I draw upon

91 NAFTA Free Trade Commission, *Statement on Non-Disputing Party Participation* (7 Oct 2003), available at www.international.gc.ca/trade-agreements-accords-commerciaux/dispdiff/nafta_commission.aspx?lang=en.

92 *Methanex Corp v United States* Final Award of the Tribunal on Jurisdiction and Merits, Part II, Chapter C, (2005) 44 *ILM* 1345, 1365 (2005).

93 See UN Charter, arts 62 and 64.

94 Gramsci, above n 3, 238.

Gramsci's ideas about 'a complex and well-articulated civil society' to be constructed 'within the hush of political society' by the initiatives of the private individuals.[95] It is the critical contributing force of private groups and associations that build and re-confirm the hegemony of the governed, ie, the sovereignty of the individuals.

3.8.1 Bridging the Gap Between Vertical Internal Processes of Decision with the Horizontal International Process of Decision

In domestic political arenas, the question of law-making is initiated and addressed systematically in institutionalised and organised settings such as public hearing fora and public opinions surveys, periodical elections, parliamentary deliberations, governments' review boards, and judicial proceedings. In international political arenas, however, no formal process or mechanism exists in which private individuals or groups have access to any organised arena of decision. The commonly held conception of law-making perpetuates this disconnection between the vertical order of the state's domestic arenas and the horizontal order of international arenas. The separation of the international process of the world community and the internal process of the state is thus used as a pretext to rationalise the 'entrance requirements', and vice versa. The combined effect is to buttress and safeguard the power base of territorial elites. Even in modern democracies, ordinary private citizens' participation in decision-making processes on foreign affairs is rarely open unless public hearings are held. It remains entirely within the domain of public officials.[96]

The range of operations undertaken, and decision functions performed, by various non-state actors, however, demonstrates abundantly that non-state actors are now transcending the neat traditional separation of the two processes. 'Hegemony', in Gramsci's sense, must be continuously reconstructed in the context of ongoing social change by educating private individuals and groups for support to a newly emerging social order.

Non-state actors are bridging the gap between the internal vertical processes of bodies politic and the international horizontal process of the world community. As Pascal Lamy, Director-General of the WTO, says, 'the degree of legitimacy decreases with distance from domestic political processes.'[97] For an international decision to be legitimate, the general support of a majority of citizens in their domestic political processes is

[95] ibid, 268.

[96] Robert A Dahl, 'Can international organizations be democratic? A skeptic's view' in Ian Shapiro & Casiano Hacker-Cordón (eds), *Democracy's Edges* (Cambridge, Cambridge University Press, 1999) 19.

[97] Pascal Lamy, 'Statement: Strengthening the WTO as the Global Trade Body' (29 Apr, 2009); available at www.wto.org/english/news_e/news09_e/tnc_chair_report_29apr09_e.htm.

indispensable, as it is the source of authority. Individual members of local NGOs are connected through national NGOs with international NGOs in the decision arenas of international organisations. They are clearly equally legitimate participants in the global process of decision as states represented by their territorial elites. They are all making claims and being subject to claims in the most comprehensive process of decision. Individuals and private groups are making choices about events that will have some effect on the international plane. Individuals who are non-state actors will continue demanding their participation in the global process of decision from local efforts through local institutions in the internal political processes of bodies politic.

3.8.2 Civil Society's Access to Official International Decision-making Processes

What is needed is to connect these two separate processes of decision in terms of discrete transnational functional decision processes as part of global governance. By 'discrete functional transnational decision processes', I refer to a national process of decision that transcends national scope to impact on the international process of decision. For example, local or national chapters of non-state actors will generate their respective claims through national mechanisms, which will eventually culminate in their national decision outcomes. These national decision outcomes will in turn become part of the input to the international decision process. Two separate processes of decision will thus be interlocked. These processes are functional since there is no centralised overall 'political infrastructure' to support oversight of such two discrete processes.

To integrate the artificially segregated processes, we will need the stronger political leadership of territorial elites of states who are supported by the influence and power of the legislature and its relevant political parties in the state concerned. Without the development of open political processes within the state, 'participation' in the international process would become a mere rhetorical exercise.

From the perspectives of the territorial elites, the non-state actors are interlocutors from outside. It is the territorial elites that regulate the non-state actors' access to the organised arenas of international organisations by deciding which non-state actors to consult with. Under these circumstances, non-state actors must not only co-opt, and ride with, the power of the government and the legislature of the country,[98] but must also

[98] But see Noortmann, above n 29, 118: 'Civil society is not served by co-opting NGOs into a bourgeois governmental or State system, but by creating independent opposition to secure the necessary checks and balances to establish a liveable, just, sustainable society.'

stimulate demands and expectations about authority for non-state actors as effective participants in the global constitutive process of decision.[99] Civil society is, after all, part of political society and non-state actors made of private individuals should become 'its normal continuation, its organic complement', rather than entering into conflict with it.[100] Non-state actors, as participants in that global process of decision, must capitalise on the will and capability of local and national institutions such as local courts, local police, civil service, local media and civil society in order to transnationalise the internal decision process of their country and integrate it with the global process of decision.[101]

[99] See Reisman, 'Democratization', above n 12, 21–22.
[100] Gramsci, above n 3, 239.
[101] See Eisuke Suzuki, 'Reconfiguration of Authority and Control of the International Financial Architecture' in MH Arsanjani et al (eds), *Looking to the Future*, above n 9, 271, 296.

4

Transnational Law: Philip Jessup's Legacy and Beyond

MATH NOORTMANN

4.1 INTRODUCTION

TODAY'S TRANSNATIONAL LEGAL discourse is without doubt rooted in Philip Jessup's *Transnational Law*.[1] Jessup's narrative, however, inspired and directed scholars within the two main international legal traditions (both public and private) to understand and (re) conceptualise 'transnational law' differently and appreciate non-state actors accordingly. While *Transnational Law* facilitated the transnationalisation of the international legal traditions, it failed to constitute an intersubjective understanding of transnational law as a separate legal category.

The problem is threefold. First of all, Jessup understood transnational law in the sense that '[b]oth public and private international law are included, as are *other rules which do not wholly fit into such categories*'.[2] These 'other rules', which are genuinely transnational, appear as an oblique non-international residual category. In doing so, Jessup reinforced the traditional comfort zone of international legal scholars—whether public or private—and the *nolens volens* neglect of an existing third legal realm beyond the nation state.

[1] Philip C Jessup, *Transnational Law* (New Haven CT, Yale University Press, 1956). For reference to Jessup's influence, see Math Noortmann, 'Understanding Non-State Actors in the Contemporary World Society: Transcending the International, Mainstreaming the Transnational or Bringing the Participants Back In?' in Math Noortmann and Cedric Ryngaert (eds), *Non-State Actors In International Law, Politics And Governance Series* (Aldershot, Ashgate, 2010; Roger Cotterrell, 'What is Transnational Law?' (2012) 37 *Law & Social Inquiry* 500; Philip C Jessup, 'The Present State of Transnational Law' in Maarten Bos (ed), *The Present State of International Law and Other Essays* (New York, Springer, 1973); Peer Zumbansen, 'Transnational law' (2006) *Encyclopedia of Comparative Law* 738, who advises us to 'reread the slim, but nevertheless immensely rich volume' (ibid, 738); Christian Tietje, Alan Brouder and Karsten Nowrot, *Philip C Jessup's transnational law revisited on the occasion of the 50th anniversary of its publication* (Halle/Saale, Universität Wittenberg, 2006); Craig Scott, 'Transnational Law as Proto-Concept: Three Conceptions' (2009) 10 *German Law Journal* 859.

[2] Jessup, *Transnational Law*.

Secondly, Jessup was concerned with solving 'transnational problems' caused by 'situations and events that transcend national frontiers'.[3] These 'transnational problems' raised three main questions which Jessup framed in terms of 'universality', 'power/jurisdiction' and 'choice of law'.[4] This framing instigated three different conceptualisations,[5] and facilitated the incorporation of those conceptions into the traditional international legal framework.

Last, but for the purpose of this chapter definitely not least, while there is little doubt that Jessup established the intrinsic relationship between non-state actors and transnational law, he unfortunately did not treat non-state actors as a conceptual or defining benchmark. Jessup's non-state actor was (as it often is today) an empirical phenomenon, without the (trans)formative agency of a transnational subject.

As a consequence, the idea of transnational law became amalgamated in the discourses of international law, or co-opted by the treatises of private international law and created what Craig Scott calls a community of 'transnationalised legal traditionalists'.[6] The impact of that transnationalisation on the development of a more comprehensive stand-alone concept of transnational law as a separate legal realm is not constructive. While the ontology of transnationalism is widely accepted, including in the field of international law, the acceptance of a corresponding 'is' in terms of transnational law is subject to mainstream resistance.[7]

This chapter critically reviews the rather paradigmatic transnational legal debate.[8] As a starting point, I have taken the advice to 'reread the

[3] ibid, 2.

[4] See the corresponding chapters in *Transnational Law* on 'The universality of the human problems' (ibid, 1–34); 'power to deal with problems' (ibid, 35–71) and 'The choice of law governing the problems' (ibid 72–111).

[5] Craig Scott, 'Transnational law as a Proto-Concept: Three Conceptions' (2009) 10 *German Law Journal* 859.

[6] ibid. In writing this chapter, I have appreciated Craig Scott's unorthodox conceptualisations: 'Transnationalized Legal Traditionalism', 'Transnationalized Legal Decisionism' and 'Transnational Socio-Legal Pluralism', as an intellectual effort to understand the transnational legal discourse.

[7] This chapter will not discuss the socio-political concept of 'transnationalism' which, although closely related to the development of the legal counterpart, would fall beyond the remit of this chapter. For a better understanding of the relation between transnationalism in the social sciences and in law, see: Noortmann, 'Understanding Non-State Actors'; Ludger Pries, *Rethinking transnationalism: the meso-link of organisations* (Abingdon, Routledge, 2008); Steven Vertovec, *Transnationalism* (Abingdon, Routledge, 2009); Thomas Risse-Kappen, *Bringing transnational relations back in: non-state actors, domestic structures, and international institutions*, Cambridge Studies In International Relations (Cambridge, Cambridge University Press) xvi; Sidney G Tarrow, *The New Transnational Activism* (Cambridge, Cambridge University Press, 2005).

[8] There have been many 'attempts' to add more precision to Jessup's original idea. See eg Harold Hongju Koh, 'Transnational Legal Process' (1996) 75 *Nebraska Law Review* 181; Peer Zumbansen, 'Piercing the Legal Veil: Commercial Arbitration and Transnational Law'

slim, but nevertheless immensely rich volume',[9] as an incentive to make sense of Jessup's original understanding of transnational law and to properly (re)capture his idea that transnational law is more than the sum of public international law and private international law. The ultimate question is not, whether transnational legal scholars can overcome the traditional split of the international legal realm into a public and private one, but whether they can envisage, identify and formulate 'other rules which do not wholly fit into such standard categories'.[10]

It is the purpose of this chapter therefore to critically recollect the concept of a 'transnational law', which according to Craig Scott has not (yet) developed beyond the status of a 'proto-concept',[11] by (a) appraising Jessup's original understanding, (b) elaborating on competing interpretations, and (c) discussing the contours of transnational law and the role of non-state actors in the formation of transnational law.

In the following section, I—first of all—review Jessup's understanding of 'transnational law' and the role of non-state actors in that legal realm. I will, particularly, address Jessup's sympathy for public and private international law and his conception of the character and purpose of both. In section 4.3, I then discuss the concept of 'transnationalised legal traditionalism', in particular the transnational legal process.[12] In section 4.4, I reflect upon the concept of transnational law as an independent legal realm that first of all regulates the behaviour of and relations between transnational non-state actors, rather then the situations and events they create. I will argue that transnational law, like any other proper legal system is grounded in and expressed by: (1) the consent of all participants, whether conceptual, contractual or customary, and/or (2) authoritative decisions and/or (3) specific or general legal dogmata. The (new) *lex mercatoria* school deserves special attention. This concept probably comes closest to the idea of 'other rules' which are neither public nor private international law, and for the sake of argument I suggest disregarding their exclusive focus on economic non-state actors.

(2002) 8 *European Law Journal* 400; Sigrid Quack, 'Legal professionals and transnational law-making: A case of distributed agency' (2007) 14 *Organization* 643; Janet Koven Levit, 'Bottom-Up Lawmaking: The Private Origins of Transnational Law' (2008) 15 *Indiana Journal of Global Legal Studies* 49.

[9] Zumbansen, 'Legal professionals' 738.

[10] Jessup, *Transnational Law.*

[11] Scott, Transnational law as a Proto-Concept

[12] Craig Scott considers the transnational legal process approach to constitute a separate conceptual understanding of Jessup, based on Jessup's chapter on 'Power to deal with Problems'. See hereunder section 4.2.

4.2 JESSUP'S UNDERSTANDING OF TRANSNATIONAL LAW AND THE NON-STATE ACTOR IN IT

Philip Jessup's use of the term 'transnational law' reflected the growing uneasiness in the 1950s with the dominant positivist conceptions of international law.[13] Those conceptions are historically ingrained in the Westphalian political world-view and the legal philosophies of Jeremy Bentham and John Austin.[14] Jessup's transnational endeavour, however, was not meant to engage those conceptions at the philosophical level.

More problematic than the lack of philosophical engagement in understanding *Transnational Law*, however is the apparent absence of concept. To Jessup, the analytical difficulty is caused by the lack of 'appropriate' terminology.[15] The practical problems that Jessup is concerned with 'are in large part those which are *usually* called international.'[16] His suggestion to 'use, *instead* of "international law", the term "transnational law"',[17] is as simple as it is problematic, in particular, because he avoids 'further classification of transnational problems and further definition of transnational law'.[18] In that way *Transnational Law* offers little direct ontological or epistemological guidance and avoids an explicit conceptualisation or theorisation of the idea of transnational law. This is not to say that Jessup's transnational law is void of idea, but that his idea of 'transnational' and 'transnational law' must be derived from an engagement with Jessup's corresponding ideas of international law and non-state actors.

4.2.1 Jessup's Conception of 'International Law'

Essential to Jessup's idea of transnational law is his understanding that

> [T]he *term* 'international' is *misleading* since it suggests that one is concerned only with the relations of one nation (or state) to other nations (or states). Part of the difficulty in analyzing the problems of the world community and the law

[13] Others, like Myres McDougal and Harold Lasswell, had already utilised the term 'transnational' to capture activities of actors that were not states. The idea that Jessup 'coined' the term 'transnational law' is incorrect. (See eg, Harold G Maier, 'Some Implecations of the Term Transanational' (1992) 25 *Vanderbilt Journal of Tranantional Law*. According to Jessup himself, 'the term was not new,—it was not an original creation of the author'. See also Noortmann, 'Understanding Non-State Actors'.

[14] John Austin and Robert Campbell, *Lectures on jurisprudence, or, The philosophy of positive law*, 5th edn (Clark NJ, Lawbook Exchange, 2005); Jeremy Bentham, *An Introduction to the Principles and Morals of Legislation* (Kitchener, Batoche Books, 2000); HLA Hart, *Essays on Bentham: Studies in Jurisprudence and Political Theory* (Oxford, Oxford University Press, 1982).

[15] Jessup, *Transnational Law*, 1.

[16] ibid, 1 (emphasis added).

[17] ibid, 2.

[18] ibid, 7.

regulating them is the lack of an appropriate term for the rules we are discussing. Just as the term 'international' is inadequate to describe the problem, so the *term* 'international law' will not do.[19]

Jessup's uneasiness with existing terminology obscures what seems to be a more fundamental discontent with the development of the *concept* of international law, and in particular the vulgarisation of the idea of the 'international'. In that, he challenges the traditional Benthamite conception of international law, which is based on the international/domestic law dichotomy and the centrality of the state or state-related public authority. But Jessup's discontent with the *term* 'international' was perhaps not wholly justified, and based on a biased reading of Bentham.

Etymologically speaking, there is nothing wrong with the term 'international', nor is there anything misleading in Bentham's conception of 'international' as the space that covers—to use Bentham's expression—'matters betwixt nation and nation'.[20] By turning the law *of* nations into the law *between* nations, Bentham 'merely' changed the inclusive non-state character of that specific field of law into an exclusive undertaking of the (nation) state.

What is generally ignored in Bentham's work, however, is his recognition of a possible third legal space that was neither 'internal law' nor 'international law', and which he called 'the imaginary law of nature'.[21] Jessup's idea of a transnational legal space reflects a similar understanding of the lack of regulatory coverage in the combined national/international space.

Jessup's conceptual distinction between 'international' and transnational', however, is confusing, as he at the same time includes and excludes international law in transnational law.

It is never clear whether and when Jessup 'uses' transnational law as an exclusive concept. The examples given by Jessup are not wholly convincing to this reader, and signal Jessup's own applied struggle with his new concept.[22] It is for example unclear why the situation in which an individual's passport is challenged by border control officials and s/he is subsequently refused to enter the country would be a transnational

[19] ibid, 1.

[20] One could argue that Bentham has interpreted the preposition 'of' in 'the law of nations' as a preposition of belonging, rather then of identity: 'The word *international*, [which] is calculated to express, in a more significant way, the branch of law which goes commonly under the name of the *law of nations*'.

[21] The existence of such a possible third legal realm was merely mentioned in a footnote, without further explanation. One can only speculate as to Bentham's reasons for not elaborating this idea.

[22] Which may explain why Jessup suggests 'for the time being at last [to] avoid further classification of transnational problems and further definition of transnational law': Jessup, *Transnational Law*, 7.

situation. The individual in question is moving 'between' nations in the traditional Benthamian way. The rules that regulate these moves are considered to be international, which allows and requires the individual to exhaust national remedies and could eventually lead to an international case. Whether the situation creates a transnational legal dispute is not merely determined by the situation, but by the inter-subjective understanding that this individual has or should have recourse to a dispute-settlement mechanism that is neither national nor international. In this respect, for example, some human rights mechanisms are national, some are international, others are transnational and some others are hybrid, and it is particularly when the jurisdiction of these mechanisms is not confined to a specific set of rules.[23] Indeed, transnational legal issues might force us to think outside the box 'of any particular forum'.[24] Jessup's distinction between public and private international law, or monistic and dualistic systems is immaterial in this respect as these qualifications are just other significations of the *inter*national vs national debate.

Jessup understood international legal problems as follows:

> In the customary method of the study of international relations and international law, the stress is on the state or nation factor. If the matter does not involve the government of one state in its relation with another government or governments, the matter is said to be 'domestic'. By and large, the orthodox approach precluded international consideration of the problem until at least it had a transnational dimension.[25]

Jessup's historical examples in the field of maritime law (Phoenecian and Rhodean 'sea law'), demonstrates that he considered transnational law (1) to be an a priori concept, preceding the creation of the nation (state) and signifying an area of law that would transcend specific 'grounded' laws, that came with territory, and (2) to be the summation of non-governmental, governmental and intergovernmental regulation.[26]

Being concerned with adequateness and appropriateness of terminology, Jessup never properly discussed the intrinsically conceptual distinction between international law, whether public or private and transnational law. Upon reflection, one cannot avoid the impression that Jessup's transnational situations and events can equally be considered to

[23] See Richard Carver, 'National Human Rights Institutions, Displacement and Human Security' in Cedric Ryngaert and Math Noortmann (eds), *Human Security and International Law: The Challenge of Non-State Actors* (Cambridge, Intersentia, 2014). UN Human Rights Council and human rights treaty committees, which are hybrid because of the international instrument on which these Committees are based and the constitution of the Committees which are non-national.

[24] Jessup, *Transnational Law*, 6

[25] ibid, 11

[26] ibid, 109–12.

be international and subsequently governed by the rules of international law.[27] The latter is, according to Jessup, 'a valuable and valid legal system which on the whole is as well observed as national law'.[28]

4.2.2 Jessup and Non-State Actors

Jessup makes it very clear from the beginning: 'the state, in whatever form, is not the only group with which we are concerned', and more importantly, 'states are not the only subjects of international law'.[29] Jessup's position in this, however does not solve our legal conundrum, for we must still assume that where international law applies to the subjects of international law (whether state or not), our query is about another legal system that may equally apply to the subjects of international law, for nothing prevents the individual or institutional actor to move in and out of the national, international or transnational legal space(s).

Jessup's understanding of transnational law was—as said—problem-oriented, rather than actor-oriented. His identification of involved non-state actors is either hypothetical or empirical, but never conceptual. The question of what, conceptually speaking, constitutes a transnational actor is left wide open by Jessup. He mentions the following non-state actors involved in transnational activities and situations:

> individuals, corporations, states, organizations of states, intergovernmental organizations, nongovernmental organisations, families, clans, tribes, towns, secret societies, dissident group[s], insurgents or belligerents, political parties [and] public and private administrations.[30]

Jessup's 'general problem' is that '[p]eople form groups' of different sizes and with different principles and purposes, and that these groups interact and thus create what Christer Jönsson calls, a 'moving public-private borderline'.[31] More particularly, however, Jessup was concerned with the practical problems of these interactions,[32] which appeared to Jessup as empirical realities that created transnational 'situations' or 'events', rather than with the structural legal mechanism(s) that trigger or generate these

[27] See, eg, ibid, 2–5.
[28] ibid, 36, fn 3.
[29] ibid, 1 and 3 respectively.
[30] ibid, 3, 4 and 8.
[31] Christer Jönsson, 'International Organizations at the Moving Public-Private Borderline' (2013) 19 Global Governance 17.
[32] *Transnational Law's* table of contents prompted the reader to understand Jessup's approach as a practical, problem-oriented one. The chapter titles: 1. 'The Universality of the Human Problems', 2. 'The Power to Deal with the Problems' and 3. 'The Choice of Law Governing the Problems'.

ground level realities.[33] The 'problems in general arise from conflicts of interest or desire, real or imagined',[34] according to Jessup, rather than from a structural deficit in the absence of rules that apply to situations that are neither international nor national.[35] Jessup also does not seem to differentiate between transnational and other non-state actors. With respect to intergovernmental organisations, for example, he states: 'governments have been accustomed to use international or transnational organizations for the solution of transnational problems',[36] without proper indication of the difference between the international and the transnational organisation. Also with respect to 'cases involving administrations, public or private, of different countries',[37] Jessup considered this transnational without explanation.

The question with respect to non-state actors is whether and when we are to qualify non-state actors (NSAs) as transnational for the purpose of transnational law. Adhering to the positivist distinction between actors which have a qualified law-making capacity and those that have not, one could argue that the transnational law-maker should possess that qualifying agency. This is not to say that NSAs do or do not have that quality per se that states possess, of a *qualitate qua* law-making quality in international law. The law-making quality of most entities comes with a temporal/special functionality, not with an absolute status like that of the state in international law.[38]

4.3 'TRANSNATIONALIZED LEGAL TRADITIONALISM'

'"Transnationalized Legal Traditionalism" asks', according to Scott, 'how/where "law" *as we currently know and practice it*, fits into the [transnational] picture'.[39] For the legal traditionalist, 'there is not and is no need for something distinct called transnational law.'[40] The events and situations

[33] I refer here to the distinctive levels domains of reality that critical realists adhere to: empirical, actual, real. See, Roy Bhaskar, *A Realist Theory Of Science* (London, Verso, 2008); Alan W Norrie, *Dialectic and Difference: Dialectical Critical Realism And The Grounds Of Justice* (Abingdon, Routledge, 2010); Berth Danermark, Mark Ekström et al, *Explaining Society: Critical Realism In The Social Sciences* (Abingdon, Routledge, 2002).

[34] Jessup, *Transnational Law*, 11. It is to be noted that Jessup tends to take a rational choice and economic perspective, and implicitely rules out the problem of ideological and socio-cultural conflicts.

[35] ibid, 8.

[36] ibid, 112–13.

[37] ibid, 78.

[38] A classification or categorisation of transnational legal capacity would fall outside the scope of this chapter.

[39] Scott, 'Transnational law as a Proto-Concept', 868.

[40] ibid, 869.

that Jessup labels as transnational can, according to the traditionalist, be captured by either national or international law. The answer to the question asked by Scott's transnationalised legal traditionalist is found in a counter-question: how/where does the transnational picture fit into the law as we know and practise it? The question is for example rephrased as to whether 'current *international* law fully accepts direct participation of non-state actors'.[41] The question reveals the standpoint of the scholar asking the question.

In his chapter on 'the power to deal with the problems', Jessup once more confuses the reader, as he opines that the query as to which 'authorities deal effectively with which transnational situations' is considered to be answered as a 'matter of jurisdiction',[42] which essentially is established according to the rules of international law but doubts whether 'there is fundamentally good reason' for separating criminal and civil jurisdiction in terms of 'international law and conflict of laws'.[43]

Observing non-state actors, situations and activities beyond the state, and which are not by Benthamite definition 'international', has created theoretical discomfort for the positivist international lawyer. International law is exclusively constituted of the states, by the states and through the states. The transnational legal traditionalist is traditional in an (inter)national sense, ie, first and foremost state-centered. S/he recognises the transnational as an *empirical* realm in which activities and actors surpass national frontiers. In the words of the Malcolm Shaw:

> A wide variety of non-subjects exist and contribute to the evolution of the international system. Participation and personality are two concepts, but the general role played in the development of international relations and international law by individuals and entities of various kinds that are not international legal subjects as such needs to be appreciated.[44]

Shaw is an accomplished *international* lawyer. His handbook is written for students of *international* law. As such, he distinguishes correctly between the socio-political development of international law and the legal development of that law. In his appreciation of the potential law-making impact of non-state subjects and the extra-legal development of international law, Shaw may be regarded as a transnationalist, but in his appreciation of international law as a legal system, Shaw is a legal traditionalist.

However, like many other transnationalist legal scholars, Shaw also occasionally creates conceptual and paradigmatic confusion when using terms

[41] Till Müller, 'Customary Transnational Law: Attacking the Last Resort of State Sovereignty' (2008) 15 *Indiana Journal of Global Legal Studies* 19.
[42] Jessup, *Transnational Law*, 36.
[43] ibid, 39.
[44] Malcolm N Shaw, *International Law*, 6th edn (Cambridge, Cambridge University Press, 2009) 264.

like 'international' and 'transnational' and giving them quasi-conceptual meanings.[45] Jessup himself—as argued—was not wholly blameless in creating that confusion. The loose transnational vocabulary that many international legal scholars have adopted lacks the paradigmatic implications that are necessary for the further development of transnational law, ie, we need to know what we are talking about. The mere acknowledgement of the presence of non-state actors on the world scene can become a forceful argument in trumping many of the more theoretical interventions in the legal debate. One easily resorts to a traditional fall-back position, as Jessup does: '[I]f there is any virtue in developing transnational law, much more exploration and analysis would need to procede the ponderous tread of *governmental* action.'[46] That opinion should be restated: if there is any virtue in developing transnational law, much more exploration and analysis would need to procede the ponderous tread of *NON-governmental* action.

4.4 THE TRANSNATIONAL LEGAL PROCESS APPROACH

One such theoretical intervention is the Transnational Legal Process (TLP) approach. The conceptual roots of TLP lie in the narrated efforts of different strands of American international legal thought that where distinctively process-, policy-, and/or problem-oriented.[47] More recently, Harold H Koh has developed the concept further with a view to understanding the critical issues of compliance with international law.[48] According the Koh:

> transnational legal process describes the theory and practice of how public and private actors—nation-states, international organisations, multinational enterprises, non-governmental organizations and private individuals—interact in a variety of public and private, domestic and international fora, to make interpret, enforce and ultimately internalize *rules of transnational law*.[49]

In Koh's conception, transnational law is the generative mechanism and does not qualify as a separate legal system.[50]

[45] Shaw for example states that 'another possible candidate for international personality is the transnational ... company'.

[46] Jessup, *Transnational Law*, 113.

[47] See Koh's reference to A Chayes, T Ehrlich and AF Lowenfeld, *The International Legal Process: Materials for an Introductory Course* (Cambridge MA, Harvard Law School, 1967); MS McDougal, HD Lasswell and WM Reisman, *The World Constitutive Process of Authoritative Decision* (New Haven CT, Association of American Law Schools, 1966); HJ Steiner, *Transnational Legal Problems* (St Paul MN, Foundation Press, 1986). These different orientations shared the socio-political inclination of American legal realism.

[48] Harold Hongju Koh, 'Transnational Legal Process' (1996) 75 *Nebraska Law Review* 181, 183.

[49] ibid, 194.

[50] A comparison with the new transnational legal approach is left out here as such comparison would exceed the objective of this chapter. *Cf* Mary Ellen O'Connell, 'New International Legal Process' (1999) *American Journal of International Law* 334; Mary Ellen

The question to answer was whether the existence and activities of transnational non-state entities and other participants at the global plane could comfortably be incorporated in 'international law'. My answer is no; not without giving up the Benthamite concept of international law, which implicitly or explicitly holds up the notions of and discourses on international law. Jessup was, in my opinion, not so much in need of a new term, as in need of a new concept, in very much the same way as Jeremy Bentham was 175 years earlier when he coined the term 'international'.[51]

Jessup's examples of transnational problems include few that do not refer to economic and/or commercial events and situations. Accordingly, most non-state actors appearing in Jessup's study are companies, and many situations would traditionally be covered by the rules of international private law/conflict of laws.

Jessup's understanding of 'transnational economic relations' involves state and non-state stakeholders. An agreement between the heads of different oil companies is qualified as '"private" or non-governmental', but the involvement of the United Kingdom, as a majority shareholder in one of these companies, turns it into an 'transnational one' as it could not have been an 'international agreement in current terminology'.[52] Here, the private involvement of a state discredits the purity of the non-governmental or private character of the agreement, according to Jessup. But why? The involvement of the British government as shareholder does certainly not constitute an *actum jure imperii*. The differentiation between *imperii* and *gestiones* itself, however, would be governed by an interpretation of public international law,[53] meaning that the state is considered to set the parameters under which it participates as a private party at the transnational stage.

O'Connell, 'New International Legal Process' (2004) 36 *Studies on Transnational Legal Policy* 79. It is to be noted that international legal scholars have equally started to introduce non-state actors in their works. See eg Jordan J Paust, 'The Reality of Private Rights, Duties, and Participation in the International Legal Process' (2003) 25 *Michigan Journal of International Law* 1229; James AR Nafziger, 'Regulation by the International Council of Museums: an example of the role of non-governmental organizations in the transnational legal process' (1972) 2 *Denver Journal of International Law & Policy* 231; Sergei Voitovich, *International economic Organizations in the International legal Process* (Leiden, Martinus Nijhoff Publishers, 1995); Monica Hakimi, 'The Media as Participants in the International Legal Process' (2006) 16 *Duke Journal of Comparative & International Law*.

[51] See Jeremy Bentham, *An Introduction to the Principles and Morals of Legislation* (London, W Pickering, 1789), 'The chancellor D'Aguesseau has already made, I find, a similar remark: he says that what is commonly called *droit* des *gens*, ought rather to be termed *droit* entre *les gens*' (*Œvres*, Vol II, p 337; edit 1773).

[52] Jessup, *Transnational Law*, 13

[53] *Jurisdictional Immunities of the State (Germany v Italy: Greece intervening)*, Judgment [2012] ICJ Rep 99.

4.5 TRANSNATIONAL LAW: WHAT IT IS AND HOW IT WORKS

Transnational law (TL) constitutes an independent legal realm, separated from, but partially overlapping with national law, public international law, and private international law. It neither includes all these legal realms as a kind of all-encompassing legal system, nor does it concur with an exclusive *lex mercatoria*. Conceiving of transnational law as all-inclusive, or specifically exclusive is too limited. Transnational law is the legal realm where all actors meet, but not necessarily all of the time, ie some (like states) can move in an out other legal realms, others are confined to legally engage other transnational actors in this specific realm.

Transnational law distinguishes itself from other legal realms by explicitly not being exclusive, ie all transnational actors, state or non-state, are potential constituents of and participants in transnational law.

If the concept of transnational law is to be understood as a legal system that regulates the legal relations between all kinds of different participants, whose activities transcend the quasi-territorial borders of proxy sovereigns and as such outdo one specific jurisdiction, such a concept has logically existed in space and time and must properly be called an a priori concept, in the Kantian sense of the term.

While the revitalisation of the *lex mercatoria* concept constitutes the most transformative understanding of transnational law, it does not constitute in and of itself a separate transnational legal system. Its exclusive business orientation prevents it from acquiring a wider status. However, it has come closest to the revolutionary potential of the concept of transnational law by deconstructing the 'false dichotomies of the national and the international' and one must add the increasingly false dichotomy between the private and the public.[54] The private dimension of the *lex mercatoria* directly informs that progressive quality of transnational law.[55] According to Peer Zumbansen,

> Transnational law is thus teaching us, while still in the process of emerging something about the necessity and the hard to follow architecture of global law and global governance … More clearly: the study of transnational law cannot be separated from questions of the conditions and possibilities of governance beyond the Nation State.[56]

[54] Ursula Stein, *Lex Mercatoria: Realität und Theorie* (Frankfurt am Main, V Klostermann, 1995); Filip De Ly, *International Business Law and Lex Mercatoria* (The Hague, TMC Asser Instituut, 1992); Klaus Peter Berger, *The Creeping Codification Of The New Lex Mercatoria*, 2nd edn (Leiden, Kluwer Law International, 2010).

[55] Peer Zumbansen, 'Piercing the Legal Veil: Commercial Arbitration and Transnational Law' (2002) 8 *European Law Journal* 400, 427.

[56] ibid, 414 and 429. For another definition of transnational law, see: Carrie Menkel-Meadow, 'Why and How to Study Transnational Law' (2011) 1 *UC Irvine Law Review* 97, 103.

Zumbansen considers the TL and the *lex mercatoria* discourses to be mutually reinforcing, in the sense that both address the political themes of (economic) development and order.[57] In that sense, both TL as well as the *lex mercatoria* constitute a structural challenge to the absolutist position of the state in the domestic and the international legal regime.

As such, the *lex mercatoria* is considered to be 'an autonomous body of regulations created and independently enforced by private economic actors to govern their international trade and financial relations without the involvement of states'.[58] As such, the parallels between this medieval, pre-state normative order and contemporary developments in commerce, trade and finance are easily envisaged. To the extent that the *lex mercatoria* is neither public international (economic) law nor domestic law, and involves all kind of inter-sectorial transactions and regulations, it cannot properly be captured in today's (inter)national legal discourses, which are based on that double private/public and national/international distinction.[59]

One cannot identify the *lex mercatoria* with transnational law. At most, it can help 'to guide the general process' of the formation and identification of transnational law.[60] The political exclusiveness of the transnational merchant law prevents it from setting the standard for a more comprehensive transnational legal system.[61] The *lex mercatoria* is too exclusive in terms of the participants, and that restriction makes its overall legal nature too private. Moreover, the *lex mercatoria* also bears the marks of what Claire Cutler calls 'medieval [and] modern internationalism'.[62]

'The problem of developing transnational law is not actually so difficult as it is sometimes made to appear', according to Jessup.[63] While he provides us with some interesting potential novel sources of transnational law, such as 'the adoption of identical legislation' and

[57] Zumbansen, 'Transnational law', 741.

[58] Tietje, Brouder and Nowrot, *Jessup's Transnational Law*, 20; see also Berger, *The Creeping Codification*; Stein, *Lex Mercatoria*; De Ly, *International Business Law*.

[59] Alex Mills, 'The private history of international law' (2006) 55 *International and Comparative Law Quarterly* 1, 47. On the question of whether the international/national dichotomy is false, see here above.

[60] Jessup, *Transnational Law*, 109.

[61] A Claire Cutler, *Private Power and Global Authority: Transnational Merchant Law In The Global Political Economy* (Cambridge, Cambridge University Press, 2003); A Claire Cutler, Virginia Haufler and Tony Porter, *Private Authority and International Affairs* (New York, State University of New York Press, 1999).

[62] Cutler, *Private Power*, 104. While transnational law's pre-modern history is well recognised (see, eg, Menkel-Meadow), its connection with 'modern internationalism' is less obvious. This chapter does not intend to expound on the relationship between transnationalism and modern internationalism, but suggests that that relationship affects the conceptual understanding of transnational law.

[63] Jessup, *Transnational Law*, 109.

'voluntary private agreement',[64] Jessup also confuses again by listing an international convention, which although negotiated under the auspices of the 'international maritime community' is a genuine international agreement in the sense of the Vienna Convention.[65] The question remains: which agreements, customs and judicial decisions constitute genuine transnational ones?[66]

4.5.1 Transnational Agreements

If agreements fall outside the scope of Article 2.1.a of the Vienna Convention of the Law of Treaties (VCLT), our international law textbooks get vague.[67] Occasional references to the *Anglo Iranian Oil Company Case*,[68] *Texaco v Libya*[69] and the *South-West Africa* cases[70] reflect the contested legal status of agreements between states and non-state actors and the failure to properly qualify them.[71] At most, the hybrid or internationalised character of agreements between states and multinational companies is recognised. More often, however, state/NSA agreements, such as peace and ceasefire agreements, are ignored.

From a legal perspective, however, Article 2.1.a of the 1969 VCLT definition of a treaty can easily be used to cover state/non-state agreements, as demonstrated by the 1986 Vienna Convention on the Law of Treaties between States and International Organizations or between International Organizations. One simply substitutes the term 'international' with 'transnational', and 'international organizations' with 'transnational non-state actors' in articles 1(a) and (b), and 2(1)(a)(i) and (ii).[72]

[64] ibid, 110.
[65] ibid, 111.
[66] As stated above, I adhere to a rather positivist conception of law in the sense that not every agreement, custom or decision by judicial bodies is creating law. Agreements, customs and decisions can be of a political, social, economic or any other non-legal nature. What differentiates the law from non-law in an epistemological sense, however, is mostly a matter of inter-subjective agreement, ie, the cumulative effect of *opinio iuris,* with or without an accompanying practice.
[67] Art 2.1.a of the 1969 Vienna Convention on the Law of Treaties reads: 'For the purpose of the present Convention: Treaty means an international agreement concluded between states in written form and governed by international law, whether embodied in a single instrument or in two or more related instruments and whatever its particular designation.'
[68] [1952] ICJ Rep.
[69] 53 (1979) ILR 389.
[70] [1962] ICJ Rep.
[71] See Art 2 Vienna Convention on the Law of Treaties; see also Anthony Aust, *Modern Treaty Law and Practice* (Cambridge, Cambridge University Press, 2000).
[72] I suggest that this approach is commensurable with the cut-and-paste exercise of the drafters of the 1986 VCLT.

Lacking an overall transnational agreement on transnational agreements,[73] the determination and analysis of related authoritative statements and practices is necessary. Our task is to identify a body of law based on convergent state/non-state practices and opinions that can properly be called transnational law.

4.5.2 Transnational Custom

Transnational law, according to Carrie Menkel-Meadow,

> like formal international law, has customary practices ... of behavioural regulation that are broader than, and perhaps, even more complex then formal law.[74]

Also, the debate on the existence of customary transnational law is subject to confusion as to the concept of transnational law. Till Müller's position is revealing: 'the development of CIL [customary international law], could lead to the emergence of ... transnational law', which in itself is the result of the 'emergence of non-state actors participation in CIL'.[75] As stated above, I consider international law and transnational law to be two separated realms, not as a legal trajectory which predicts the next generation of law. The problem once again is the difference between (1) (non-state) actors *influencing* the legal practices and opinions of states, ie the making or unmaking of customary *international* law, and (2) NSAs actually making law through their own combination of practices and legal opinions.

Much depends on the interpretation of Article 38 of the Statute of the International Court of Justice (ICJ), which—as noted elsewhere—does not refer to state practice. That makes sense with respect to the qualification of custom in the Court Statute as being 'international', ie, between states. In order to constitute *international* custom then, both practice and *opinio juris* must be equally '*international*'. In our quest for transnational customary law, practice and *opinio juris* must ipso facto be transnational, ie, the practice and *opinio juris* must be that of transnational or *non-state* actors.[76]

[73] It goes without saying that such a treaty is open to ratification/accession by non-state actors. The problem here is not the conceptual possibility of such a procedure, but the determination as to which non-state actors can be considered to be transnational. From a practical and political point of view, an independent non-governmental body should be charged with a depositary role—an international chamber of non-state actors, perhaps.

[74] Menkel-Meadow, 'Why and How to Study Transnational Law', 103.

[75] Müller, 'Customary Transnational Law', 21§.

[76] See also Karsten Nowrot, 'Legal consequences of globalization: The status of non-governmental organizations under international law' (1998) 6 *Indiana Journal of Global Legal Studies* 579.

4.5.3 Transnational Jurisprudence

Jessup recognises—as many others do—that '[a]n international court may be authorized to apply other law' or decide *ex aequo et bono* 'if the parties agree hereto'.[77] In the *Delimiting Abyei Area* case, for example, the Permanent Court of Arbitration (PCA) was authorised by Sudan and the Sudan People's Liberation Movement/Armee to apply 'general principles of law and practices as the Tribunal may deem relevant'.[78] These 'general principles of law and practices' must be understood to be principles and practices that are shared by the parties to the dispute, ie state and non-state.

Whether non-state actors are allowed to participate in non-national judicial and arbitral proceedings depends both on the constitutive documents of the particular institution and the willingness of state party. The ICJ Statute's exclusivity does not appear to have a benchmark quality in this respect. Other dispute settlement provisions like the International Tribunal for the Law of the Sea (ITLOS) and the International Centre for Settlement of Investment Disputes (ICSID) are intentionally inclusive.[79]

The participation of non-state actors in transnational judicial proceedings affects the framing of the applicable law. Where it is no longer a matter of forum choice, 'a rule of *lex non conveniens* might well be applied', as Jessup rightly intimates.[80] In the absence of a choice of 'proper' positive law, and in order to avoid a *non liquet*, judges and arbitrators must base their legal arguments on practices, principles and rules common to the parties. Rather then being a 'modern law of nature' this commonality constitutes positive transnational law.[81]

Similarly, disputes between 'international civil servants' and their international governmental employers are governed by transnational law as 'the rules applying between states are not of use', nor is it a 'legal relationship of private law'.[82] Unfortunately, as decisions made by tribunals are hardly consistent, so are decisions that would hypothetically touch

[77] Jessup, *Transnational Law*, 77. That recognition is substantiated in such rules as art 42(1) of the Convention on the Settlement of Disputes between States and nationals of Other States: 'The Tribunal shall decide a dispute in accordance with such rules of law as may be agreed by the parties', and art 38(1) of the Statute of the International Court of Justice.

[78] *Sudan/Sudan Peoples Liberation Movement/Army, Delimiting Abyei Area*, Permanent Court of Arbitration, 22 July 2009, p 153.

[79] See Preamble of the Convention on the Settlement of Disputes between States and nationals of Other States, https://icsid.worldbank.org/ISCID/StaticFiles/basicdoc/CRR_English_final.pdf, p 11 art 20(2) of the ITLOS.

[80] Jessup, *Transnational Law*, 82.

[81] For the idea of a 'modern law of nature' see: *In the Matter of an Arbitration between Petroleum Development (Trucial Coast) Ltd and the Sheikh of Abu Dhabi*, as quoted by Jessup in *Transnational Law*, 81–82.

[82] ibid, 84 and 85 respectively. It can be argued that customary transnational law is codified by states and as such transformed into international law proper. It would be a matter of politics and scholarly appreciation to qualify these rules as either 'international' or 'transnational'.

upon matters of transnational law. In the *Serbian Loans* case the Permanent Court of International Justice (PCIJ) held: 'Any contract which is not a contract between states in their capacity as subject of international law is based on the municipal law of some country.'[83] According to the Court:

> The question as to which this law is forms the subject of that branch of law which is at the present day usually described as private international law or the 'doctrine of the conflict of laws'. The rules thereof may be common to several States and may even be established by international conventions or customs, and in the latter case may possess the character of true international law governing the relations between States. But apart from this, it has to be considered that these rules form part of municipal law.[84]

This clear dichotomy between national and international law, unfortunately, still informs many writings and decisions.

4.6 CONCLUDING REFLECTIONS

Transnational law's *problematique*, is not a terminological one as Jessup suggested in the beginning of his seminal publication, but a disciplinary and socio-political one, as he concludes at the end of *Transnational Law*:

> The difficulty ... [in the creation of new transnational law] lies in the minds of man [which] are trained, or so we fondly believe, in our schools and universities. If those who are trained particularly in our law schools and graduate schools of political science, are nourished on the pap of old dogmas and fictions, it is not to be expected that they will later approach the solution of transnational problems with open-minded intelligence instead of open-mouthed surprise.[85]

Jessup seems to have little doubt as to the superior value of transnational law. Transnational law, however, is not merely an instrument for understanding and explaining international law as Koh does. Rather, one has to agree with Zumbansen that transnational law 'offers itself as a supplementary and challenging category'.[86]

Its legal quality is in its inclusiveness that is capable of transforming the legal activities of and relation between different actors at the world stage. In that respect, transnational law is both 'descriptive' as well as 'evaluative',[87] ie transnational law exists and should exist as a distinctive legal realm.

The Benthamite term 'international' has hijacked the legal and political discourses, and has become the preferred term of art to identify ideas, activities and actors that transcend rather than cross the borders of the

[83] *Case concerning the Payment of Various Serbian Loans issued in France*, Judgment No 14, Publications of the Permanent Court of International Justice, series A Nos 20/21, p 41.

[84] ibid.

[85] Jessup, *Transnational Law*, 109. See also Menkel-Meadow, 'Why and How to Study Transnational Law' 101.

[86] Zumbansen, 'Transnational law' 738.

[87] Scott, *Torture as Tort*.

nation-state. The idea of a legal realm that equally transcends the nation-state and is grounded in and regulates the relation between states and non-state actors and non-state actors inter se has always existed in the minds of legal philosophers. The law that is neither 'national' nor 'international', must properly be called 'transnational', based on its own sources and subjected to its own rules of identification, which as stated above are not wholly different in character from the sources of other legal systems. While the concept of custom, eg, has universal value, the content of that custom is subject of wide global variation. The transnational legal space not only accommodates what Bentham would probably call mutual transactions between sovereigns and non-sovereigns, ie, contractual engagements, but also transnational customs that amount to law and elements of a transnational law of nature and jurisprudence that pronounces on the rights of states and non-state actors alike.

Today's discourse on transnational law in general and the role and position of non-state actors in it is built around a common language that is heavily caveated[88] and lacks conceptual coherence. Transnational socio-legal pluralism captures that separate 'normative sphere' that transnational legal scholarship seeks to identify and establish.[89]

The main question with respect to the existence, making, and explication of transnational law is first of all whether the relations between different actors are exclusively regulated by national, *inter*national or *trans*national rules and regulations. It is neither the forum, nor the actors involved, nor the 'jurisgenerative' result that determines the transnational legal process.

Whether legal fora, courts and tribunals can be qualified as national, international and transnational depends on their constitutional context: who has access, which rules will be applied and what is the relevance of the authoritative outcome. Transnational law's critical potential and its imaginative transnational legal reality is out there.

In order to conceptualise transnational law, we must realise that not every transnational situation gives rise to transnational regulation. Whether or not a situation falls with the remit of the law is a matter of—positively speaking—the applied linking of 'facts' and 'rules'.[90] From a positive perspective, the law ultimately determines whether a situation falls within and is regulated by the law or not. Inasmuch as not every international situation triggers international law, not every transnational situation triggers questions of transnational law.

[88] Scott identifies 'six linguistic caveats', which revolve around the idea of the 'transnational' (see *Torture as Tort*, 864–68). For the purpose of my argument, it is not necessary to assess these caveats and it merely suffices to state that these caveats have an equal bearing upon the conceptualisation of 'transnational law'.

[89] ibid, 873.

[90] I have put these terms in quotation marks, as both facts and rules are not objective parameters, but are subject to interpretation and construction.

Part II

5

Non-State Actors and the Use of Force

CHRISTIAN HENDERSON

5.1 INTRODUCTION

THERE CAN BE no doubt that non-state actors have attained an increasingly prominent role in almost all frameworks of a fragmented international legal system. In this respect the framework governing the use of force is no exception. However, while the law on the use of force *against* non-state actors has, as this chapter will demonstrate, gone through a process of development over the past 20 years, the law governing the use of force *by* non-state actors has not witnessed a similar development. In particular, while the norm prohibiting the threat or use of force, and the contemporary right of self-defence, have birth dates of 1945,[1] their subjects have remained state actors. Although arguments can be made that the rules and norms of the *jus ad bellum* apply to certain non-state actors, perhaps in the context of what we might call 'contested states',[2] it is difficult to find any authority or support for claims that the activities of other non-state actors, such as terrorist groups, are now also regulated by them.[3] As we witness frequently, regulation of the forcible activities of these non-state actors is still through the criminal law, of both a domestic and international nature.[4]

[1] See Arts 2(4) and 51 of the UN Charter (1945) respectively.

[2] See Christian Henderson, 'Contested States and the Rights and Obligations of the *Jus Ad Bellum*' (2013) 21 *Cardozo Journal of International & Comparative Law* 367.

[3] See Nicholas Tsagourias, 'Non-State Actors and the Use of Force' in Jean d'Aspremont (ed), *Participants in the International Legal System: Multiple Perspectives On Non-State Actors In International Law* (Abingdon, Routledge, 2011) 326.

[4] For example, as recently as the end of 2013, the alleged al Qaeda leader, Nazih Abdul-Hamed al-Ruqai, more commonly known by his alias Abu Anas al-Liby, who was wanted by the US for the 1998 bombings of the US embassies in Kenya and Tanzania, appeared before a Federal Court in New York to plead not guilty to the offences with which he was charged, none of which involved a violation of the rule prohibiting the threat or use of force. See BBC News, 'Al-Qaida suspect al-Liby in New York to face charges', 15 October 2013, available at www.bbc.co.uk/news/world-africa-24528600.

This chapter will thus primarily focus upon the law as it applies to the use of force by states against non-state actors, in particular those perceived by the acting states as being of a terrorist nature. In the context of what we might call 'global' terrorism these actors and their bases are rarely found upon the territory of the state against which they target their terrorist activities. In these circumstances it is the response of the victim state upon which international law has most to say and requires an examination of issues such as the gravity of the attacks which have been undertaken by the non-state actor, the location of the non-state actors at the time any response is undertaken, the delay in the response, the responsibility of the host state and whether the acts of the non-state actors can be attributed to it, and the aim and modalities of the resulting forcible actions undertaken by the victim state. However, before examining, and hopefully clarifying, these issues, this chapter will first provide brief treatment of the use of force by and against non-state actors in the domestic context.

5.2 NON-STATE ACTORS AND THE REGULATION OF THE INTERNAL USE OF FORCE

Traditionally, and as an integral element of state sovereignty, matters that occurred within a state were the sole concern of that state. The police or armed forces of a state were in this respect relatively unrestricted in their use of force within the territorial confines of that state. Today, while there is no discrete and independent norm prohibiting a state from using force against individuals located within its territory, international human rights law provides some regulation of the actions of state authorities in peacetime situations. Law enforcement officers, for example, are not able to use force freely, and in particular are not permitted to simply deprive an individual of their life. Indeed, everyone has the right not to be 'arbitrarily deprived of [their] life', as expressly contained within the landmark International Covenant on Civil and Political Rights, adopted in the 1960s.[5] So while the death penalty is not entirely precluded under international human rights law, in the extra-judicial context individuals cannot simply be targeted with lethal force, regardless of the gravity of the crime that they have allegedly committed. Instead, they should be given the right to surrender and/or be arrested. However, this formulation of the right to life suggests that it is not absolute. If an individual poses an imminent threat to the life or safety of others, for example, lethal force may be used against that individual.[6] Furthermore, as witnessed most prominently in

[5] See Art 6(1), International Covenant on Civil and Political Rights (1966).

[6] See Nils Melzer, *Targeted Killing In International Law* (Oxford, Oxford University Press, 2008) 101.

the Arab Spring, internal disturbances that are regulated by international human rights law may reach the intensity of a non-international armed conflict between rebel forces and the armed forces of a state. At this point, international humanitarian law provides an additional form of regulation, and a basis upon which to judge the actions of both the state and non-state actors involved.[7]

A perennial issue that has most recently made an appearance in the context of the Arab Spring is whether, given the disparity in arms between non-state actors within a state and the state's armed forces, outside states may assist the non-state actors in their struggle against the state authorities. Any assistance during peacetime constitutes an infringement of the principle of non-intervention, one that, although not well-defined,[8] is nonetheless now well-established in customary international law.[9] While passing comment upon the affairs of another state is not caught by the principle, interventions that take on a coercive nature are,[10] with the most obvious form of coercion being a use of force which, as the International Court of Justice (ICJ) has attempted to clarify, may take the form of the provision of arms or training or other forms of military assistance.[11] Although some have claimed that during a civil war, where the outcome is not certain, assistance to both the non-state actors *and* the government of the state concerned becomes prohibited,[12] state practice during the Arab Spring indicates that this is not perhaps the case. Indeed, the sale of weapons by Russia to Syria, while condemned by many, was not considered unlawful.[13] Although the non-state actors in the Arab Spring might be

[7] See, in general, Sandesh Sivakumaran, *The Law Of Non-International Armed Conflict* (Oxford, Oxford University Press, 2012); Lindsay Moir, *The Law Of Internal Armed Conflict*, vol 19 (Cambridge, Cambridge University Press, 2002).

[8] In general this principle can be said to 'involve ... the right of every sovereign state to conduct its affairs without outside interference'. See *Case Concerning Military and Paramilitary Activities in and Against Nicaragua (Nicaragua v United States of America) (Merits)* [1968] ICJ Rep 14 [202].

[9] *Nicaragua* case, ibid [246]; Declaration on the Inadmissibility of Intervention in the Domestic Affairs of States and the Protection of their Independence and Sovereignty, GA Resolution 2131 (XX), UN Doc A/RES/20/2131 (21 December 1965), para 1; Declaration on Principles of International Law concerning Friendly Relations and Co-operation among States in accordance with the Charter of the United Nations, GA Resolution 2625 (XXV), UN Doc A/Res/25/2625 (24 October 1970), para 3; Art 19, Charter of the Organization of American States (1948); Malcolm N Shaw, *International Law*, 6th edn (Cambridge, Cambridge University Press 2008) 1147.

[10] *Nicaragua* case, ibid [205].

[11] ibid [228]. The Court stated that while arming and training rebels was an unlawful use of force, the supply of funds was instead an unlawful intervention.

[12] See Louise Doswald-Beck, 'The legal validity of military intervention by invitation of the government' (1985) 56 *British Yearbook of International Law* 189, 251; Christine D Gray, *International Law and the Use of Force*, 3rd edn (Oxford, Oxford University Press, 2008) 92.

[13] Christian Henderson, 'The Provision of Arms and Non-Lethal Assistance to Governmental and Opposition Forces' (2013) 36 *University of New South Wales Law Journal* 642, 669–70.

considered to be struggling to secure their right to self-determination,[14] the elaboration of this right, and the ambiguity as to whether it provided for a right of states to assist through forcible means those fighting for it, emanates from the decolonisation era of the twentieth century. It appears, in this respect, to be limited to national liberation movements battling against colonialism and occupation, as opposed to disgruntled groups seeking to overthrow a government or achieve secession.

However, in the Arab Spring, along with various incidents in the 1990s, the use of force by the state authorities concerned was criticised by other states as excessive.[15] This concern poses the question of whether a customary prohibition upon the use of *internal* force by states might be emerging.[16] Yet, while one cannot rule out the possibility of such a norm emerging in the future, it would be premature to state that one exists *lex lata*. Indeed, examining the condemnation from the international community of the repressive use of force by the Libyan and Syrian authorities against parts of their own populations suggests that this was framed in the context of international human rights law and international criminal law,[17] as opposed to a discrete norm governing the internal use of force.

5.3 THE REGULATION OF THE INTERNATIONAL USE OF FORCE AGAINST NON-STATE ACTORS

An issue that has given rise to particular difficulties in state practice, the jurisprudence of the ICJ, and in scholarship, is the use of force against non-state actors that are located outside of the territory of the victim state. Any forcible action outside of the territory of the state is independently prohibited in Article 2(4) of the United Nations Charter, a prohibition also established as a norm under customary international law:[18]

[14] As the 1970 Declaration on Principles of International Law concerning Friendly Relations and Co-operation among States declared: 'all peoples have the right freely to determine, without external interference, their political status and to pursue their economic, social and cultural development'. See n 9 above, para 5.

[15] On the Syria conflict, see UN Doc A/RES/66/253/B, 7 August 2012, preamble, which expressed '[c]*oncern* … about … the use by the Syrian authorities of *excessive* force' (emphasis added). On the Kosovo conflict, see UN Doc S/RES/1160 (1998), 31 March 1998, preamble, which '[c]ondemn[ed] the use of *excessive* force by Serbian police forces against civilians and peaceful demonstrators in Kosovo' (emphasis added).

[16] See, eg, Jochen Frowein, 'Globale und regionale Friedenssicherung nach 50 Jahren Vereinte Nationen' (1995) *Zeitschrift für Schweizerisches Recht* 269–70.

[17] See, on Libya, UN Doc S/RES/1970 (26 February 2011), preamble; UN Doc S/RES/1973 (17 March 2011), preamble; on Syria, see, for example, UN Doc S/RES/2042 (14 April 2012), preamble; UN Doc S/RES/2043 (21 April 2012), preamble; UN Doc A/67/L63 (8 May 2013), preamble. See, in general, Annyssa Bellal and Louise Doswald-Beck, 'Evaluating the Use of Force During the Arab Spring' (2011) 14 *Yearbook of International Humanitarian Law* 3.

[18] *Nicaragua* case, n 8 above.

> All Members shall refrain in their international relations from the threat or use of force against the territorial integrity or political independence of any state, or in any other manner inconsistent with the Purposes of the United Nations.

One might argue, of course, that a limited use of force to attack non-state actors located upon the territory of a third state would not constitute a violation of the host state's 'territorial integrity or political independence', as it would not be depriving the state of its territory or the independence of its government.[19] Yet, the inclusion of such an—admittedly unnecessary and clumsy—stipulation in Article 2(4) is, nonetheless, a result of the wishes of the drafters to emphasise the protection of these two attributes of statehood, as opposed to intending to provide an additional exception or loophole in the breadth and scope of the prohibition.[20] In this sense, Article 2(4) also does not provide, or allude to, the existence of any exceptions to the prohibition. However, as included elsewhere in the Charter and now well established in customary international law,[21] there are two well-known exceptions to this prohibition, both of which have relevance in the context of forcible measures against non-state actors.

5.3.1 Action Taken or Authorised by the UN Security Council

The threat or use of force may be authorised by the United Nations Security Council (UNSC), an organ which has a central role in the regime governing the use of force.[22] In order for the forcible powers of the UNSC to become available, the Council first needs to identify the existence of either a threat to the peace, breach of the peace or act of aggression.[23] While the identification of the latter two by the Council is relatively rare, it now regularly identifies threats to the peace, as a precursor to measures being taken of both a non-forcible and forcible nature.[24] The UNSC has a wide discretion in determining a threat to the peace,[25] which does not have to be specifically connected with the activities of

[19] See, eg, Derek William Bowett, *Self-Defence in International Law* (Manchester, Manchester University Press, 1958) 152.

[20] See Albrecht Randelshofer, 'Article 2(4)' in Bruno Simma et al (eds), *The Charter of the United Nations: a commentary*, vol 2 (Oxford, Oxford University Press, 2002) paras 37–39.

[21] *Nicaragua* case, n 8 above [34].

[22] See, in general, Christian Henderson, 'The Centrality of the United Nations Security Council in the Legal Regime Governing the Use of Force' in Nigel D White and Christian Henderson (eds), *Research Handbook On International Conflict And Security Law:* Jus Ad Bellum, Jus In Bello *And* Jus Post Bellum (Cheltenham, Edward Elgar, 2013) 120.

[23] Art 39, UN Charter (1945).

[24] See Arts 41 and 42 respectively of the UN Charter (1945).

[25] Hans Kelsen, *The Law of the United Nations: A Critical Analysis of its Fundamental Problems* (London, Stevens, 1950) 727.

a state.[26] There is, as such, no hurdle to the activities of a non-state actor constituting a threat.[27] Indeed, the resolutions adopted by the UNSC in the aftermath of the events of 9/11 identified the existence of a threat to the peace, without simultaneously identifying a state as the perpetrator of the attacks.[28]

With the identification of a threat to the peace, the UNSC is, without having to exhaust non-forcible options first,[29] able to authorise the use of force by states or regional organisations.[30] In this respect it could well be argued that the forcible response to the attacks of 9/11 should have been authorised by the UNSC, given its prior determination of a threat to the peace and the delay between the attacks and the response,[31] rather than taken as a unilateral act of self-defence.[32] There can be no doubt that it would have done so in light of the widespread condemnation of the attacks and the general support for a forcible response.[33] Furthermore, the UNSC can conceivably authorise force not just in response to a prior use of force by non-state actors, but simply because the peace was threatened by their actions or intentions. In this sense, authorisation by the UNSC in response to a threat to the peace has a pre-emptive thrust. However, while the UNSC has been particularly active in taking measures of a non-forcible nature in regards to the activities

[26] See Steve Ratner, 'Self-Defence Against Terrorists: The Meaning Of Armed Attack' and 'The role of the UN Security Council in relation to the use of force against terrorists' in LJ van den Herik and Nico Schrijver (eds), *Counter-Terrorism Strategies In A Fragmented International Legal Order: Meeting The Challenges* (Cambridge, Cambridge University Press, 2013) 317, 322.

[27] See, eg, UNSC Resolution 1438 (2002) (Bali); UNSC Resolution 1530 (2004) (Madrid); UNSC Resolution 1377 (2001) ('Declaration on the Global Effort to Combat Terrorism'); UNSC Resolution 1456 (2003) ('Declaration on the Issue of Combating Terrorism'). As Gazzini notes, 'in a string of resolutions … the Security Council without hesitation declared international terrorism a threat to peace'. See Tarcisio Gazzini, *The Changing Rules on the Use of Force in International Law* (Manchester, Manchester University Press, 2005) 33.

[28] UNSC Resolutions 1368 (2001) and 1373 (2001).

[29] Art 42 of the UN Charter (1945) merely states that the Council should 'consider that measures provided for in Article 41 *would be* inadequate or have proved to be inadequate' (emphasis added).

[30] Tams notes that 'unlike 20 years ago, it is beyond doubt today that the Security Council can authorize military measures against terrorists, and thereby justify the extraterritorial use of force by a state implementing that mandate.' CJ Tams, 'The use of force against terrorists' (2009) 20 *European Journal of International Law* 359, 377.

[31] The delay may provide the action with the look of being taken in retaliation or punishment, rather than defence, and thus constituting an unlawful reprisal. However, as Tams has observed, recent state practice 'seems to suggest that as long as victim states claimed to act defensively, other states are likely to accept their explanation even if the real motive might have been to retaliate or punish.' CJ Tams, 'The necessity and proportionality of anti-terrorist self-defence' in LJ van den Herik and Nico Schrijver (eds), *Counter-Terrorism Strategies In A Fragmented International Legal Order: Meeting The Challenges* (Cambridge, Cambridge University Press, 2013) 401.

[32] For more on which see below, section 5.3.2.

[33] ibid.

of non-state actors,[34] it has only occasionally authorised states to use force within a state in response to attacks by non-state actors, and even then with the consent of the host state.[35] The UNSC has yet to authorise forcible intervention in another state in response to the activities of a non-state actor located there and against the wishes of the host state.

5.3.2 Unilateral Action by States and Regional Organisations

Despite the possibility today of UNSC authorisation, states tend to prefer to take matters into their own hands in responding forcibly to terrorism. In this respect, state action is restricted to that taken in self-defence. The right of self-defence, as contained in Article 51 of the UN Charter,[36] provides that:

> Nothing in the present Charter shall impair the inherent right of individual or collective self-defence if an armed attack occurs against a Member of the United Nations, until the Security Council has taken measures necessary to maintain international peace and security. Measures taken by Members in the exercise of this right of self-defence shall be immediately reported to the Security Council and shall not in any way affect the authority and responsibility of the Security Council under the present Charter to take at any time such action as it deems necessary in order to maintain or restore international peace and security.

While the prohibition of the use of force is firmly placed within the inter-state conception of international law in prohibiting the threat or use of force by states in their 'international relations' and against 'any state',[37] Article 51 merely affirms an inherent right of self-defence 'if an armed attack occurs', without specifying that it must be perpetrated by a

[34] It has, eg, established an anti-terrorism committee and ordered UN member states to freeze the bank accounts of certain individuals suspected of being terrorists. See, respectively, UNSC Resolutions 1267 (1999), 1373 (2001), and 1735 (2006).

[35] See, eg, UNSC Resolution 2085 (2012), paras 7, 9, 11, 13 and 14 in which the UNSC authorised the use of force ('all necessary measures') by an African-led International Support Mission in Mali (AFISMA) while urging all member states, including 'interested bilateral partners', to help the deployment of AFISMA and offer 'any necessary assistance in efforts to reduce the threat posed by terrorist organizations'. There was, however, consent to this authorisation by the Malian authorities. Furthermore, in UNSC Resolution 1851 (2008) the UNSC authorised states and regional organisations 'to undertaken all necessary measures that are appropriate in Somalia, for the purposes of supressing acts of piracy and armed robbery at sea'.

[36] This is also a right of customary international law. See *Nicaragua* case, above n 8, [176]. While the right as found in Art 51 has undoubtedly influenced and informed the customary form of the right, the customary right of self-defence has had an equal impact upon how we read and interpret the treaty form of the right, in particular by requiring that any action in self-defence, whether against a state or non-state actor, must be both necessary and proportionate.

[37] See above section 5.3.

state.[38] Thus, while the ICJ affirmed as recently as 2005 in its *Wall* advisory opinion, in a statement 'startling in its brevity',[39] that 'Article 51 of the Charter ... recognizes the existence of an inherent right of self-defence in the case of armed attack *by one State* against another State',[40] Judge Higgins was correct in pointing out in her separate opinion that '[t]here is, with respect, nothing in the text of Article 51 that ... stipulates that self-defence is available only when an armed attack is made by a State.'[41]

Furthermore, state practice since 9/11 would now seem to suggest that international law has developed to allow for self-defence against 'armed attacks' perpetrated by non-state actors—if indeed it ever was the case that the law required state involvement in an 'armed attack' before self-defence could be invoked.[42] For example, the fact is that al Qaeda was not a wing of the Afghan state when it carried out the 9/11 attacks, and yet the justification of self-defence under Article 51 by the US for the launching of Operation Enduring Freedom in 2001 was overwhelmingly accepted, or at least acquiesced in.[43] Similarly, when Israel launched its operations against

[38] See Noam Lubell, *Extraterritorial Use of Force Against Non-State Actors* (Oxford, Oxford University Press, 2010) 31–32; Elizabeth Wilmshurst, 'The Chatham House Principles of International Law on the Use of Force in Self-Defence' (2006) 55 *International and Comparative Law Quarterly* 963, 969–70 (hereinafter 'Chatham House principles').

[39] Sean D Murphy, 'Self-Defense and the Israeli Wall Advisory Opinion: An Ipse Dixit from the ICJ?' (2005) 99 *American Journal of International Law* 62.

[40] *Legal Consequences of the Construction of a Wall in the Occupied Palestinian Territory*, advisory opinion, [2004] ICJ Rep 135 [139] (emphasis added).

[41] ibid [33], separate opinion of Judge Higgins. See also ibid [35], separate opinion of Judge Kooijmans, and ibid [6], declaration of Judge Buergenthal; and *Armed Activities on the Territory of the Congo (Democratic Republic of the Congo v Uganda)*, merits [2005] ICJ Rep 169 [4]–[15] (separate opinion of Judge Simma), [9] (declaration of Judge Koroma), and [19]–[30] separate opinion of Judge Kooijmans.

[42] There is much academic support for this view. See, eg, Thomas M Franck, 'Terrorism and the Right of Self-Defense' (2001) 95 *American Journal of International Law* 839, 840; Murphy, above n 39, 67–70; Kimberley N Trapp, 'Back to Basics: Necessity, Proportionality, And The Right Of Self-Defence Against Non-State Terrorist Actors' (2007) 56 *International and Comparative Law Quarterly* 141, 147–55; Ruth Wedgwood, 'Responding to terrorism: the strikes against Bin Laden' (1999) 24 *Yale Journal of International Law* 559, 564; and Ruth Wedgwood, 'The ICJ Advisory Opinion on the Israeli Security Fence and the limits of self-defense' (2005) 99 *American Journal of International Law* 52, 57–59; Chatham House principles, above n 38, 970.

[43] Although the support of the international community for the US's forcible response to the horrendous 9/11 attacks may be explained in various ways, and should not be taken in and of itself as representing a shift in international law, Operation Enduring Freedom was nonetheless explicitly condoned in 2001 by Russia, China, Pakistan, Japan, the United Arab Emirates and Saudi Arabia, as well as by 19 NATO states. Offers of direct military assistance to the United States came from the United Kingdom, Australia, Canada, Singapore, Spain, Turkey, Ukraine, Romania, Portugal, New Zealand, the Netherlands, Germany, Italy, Jordan, Belgium, Denmark, France and South Korea (collated by the United States Department of State, www.state.gov/s/ct/rls/fs/2001/5194.htm and the United Kingdom Parliament, www.parliament.uk/commons/lib/research/rp2001/rp01-081.pdf, 31). See also UNSC Res 1368; UNSC Res 1373; Sean D Murphy, 'Contemporary Practice of the United States Relating to International Law' (2001) 95 *American Journal of International Law* 132, 248; and MJ Kelly, 'Understanding September 11th—An International Legal Perspective on the War in Afghanistan' (2002) 35 *Creighton Law Review* 283, 285–86.

Hezbollah in Lebanon in 2006, the justification of self-defence in response to these attacks by this particular group was, in principle, accepted.[44]

Yet while nothing exists conceptually to prevent non-state actors from carrying out an 'armed attack', the question arises as to what constitutes such an attack. Although both were implicitly accepted as armed attacks giving rise to the right of self-defence, the attacks by the non-state actors in the two examples above were of a starkly differing nature, with the attack by al Qaeda in 2001 using aircraft as missiles resulting in the deaths of 3,000 civilians, while the attack by Hezbollah resulted in the death of three military personnel from the use of an anti-tank missile, and the abduction of a further two soldiers. The ICJ has adopted the position that armed attacks (giving rise to the right of self-defence) are to be distinguished from mere uses of force, (which do not), by their 'gravity' and 'scale and effects'.[45] The 9/11 attacks can be clearly distinguished in their 'scale and effects' from the incident in Israel that sparked the war in Lebanon. The Court did not, however, elaborate further on how one is to make this distinction,[46] which has led some, such as Rosalyn Higgins, to argue that it is in practice operationally unworkable and that instead, the legality of a forcible response will depend more upon the proportionality of the response, as opposed to the gravity of the prior attack.[47] The above two examples arguably bear witness to this: whereas the 9/11 attacks, where so many lives were lost, led to the forcible toppling of a governmental regime, the relatively minor attacks by Hezbollah led to more limited strikes within Lebanon. While the latter operation was accepted by the international community as a lawful action in self-defence, when Israel began targeting Lebanese state infrastructure condemnation of this action as disproportionate became widespread.[48]

If one accepts, however, that a certain gravity is necessary before a use of force constitutes an 'armed attack' for the purposes of Article 51 of the Charter,[49] then terrorist attacks may pose a particular problem, in that that the modus operandi of terrorist groups is not, generally speaking,

[44] See UN Doc S/PV 5489 (2006).

[45] *Nicaragua* case, above n 8 [191]; *Case Concerning Oil Platforms (Islamic Republic of Iran v United States of America)*, merits [2003] ICJ Rep 161 [51] and [62]; *Armed Activities* case, above n 41 [147].

[46] A distinction that appears to be no different depending whether the attack is perpetrated by state or non-state actors. See S Ratner, 'Self-defence against terrorists: the meaning of armed attack' in LJ van den Herik and N Schrijver (eds), *Counter-Terrorism Strategies in a Fragmented International Legal Order: Meeting The Challenges* (Cambridge, Cambridge University Press, 2013) 341. *Cf* Chatham House principles, above n 38, 971.

[47] R Higgins, *Problems and Process: International Law And How We Use It* (Oxford, Clarendon Press, 1994) 251.

[48] See UN Doc S/PV.5488.

[49] See, eg, Gray, above n 12, 148.

to launch attacks on the scale of those witnessed on 9/11, which on their own were accepted as having the gravity of an armed attack.[50] Instead, terrorist groups, due often to their size, capabilities and covert nature, launch smaller 'pin prick' attacks on a regular basis.[51] This sort of activity can arguably be witnessed in the missiles that are regularly launched by Hamas-affiliated non-state actors from the Gaza Strip into Israel. In response to these types of pin prick attacks, some maintain that, under what is called the 'accumulation of events' theory, a state is permitted to equate the accumulation of these smaller attacks to an 'armed attack', thus justifying a forcible response in self-defence. Although controversial from many perspectives, Israel's invasion of the Gaza Strip in 2008/09 is an example of this theory in action.[52] Yet, there has been little discernable acceptance of this theory by states, and while the ICJ has (perhaps unwittingly) given a certain nod to it,[53] the UNSC has seemingly rejected it.[54] As such, it remains an element of the law that is unclear.[55]

Discussion of the accumulation of events theory also raises the issue of the temporal nature of an armed attack for the purposes of Article 51, which permits self-defence 'if an armed attack occurs'. While it is conceivable to think of a state responding in self-defence to an 'armed attack' of a non-state actor that is actually in progress, the covert nature of terrorist groups and the surprise element of their attacks, combined with the need to obtain sufficient evidence to identify the perpetrator following one[56] and the various preliminary issues that need to be addressed,[57] dictates

[50] See SD Murphy, 'Terrorism and the Concept of Armed Attack in Article 51 of the UN Charter' (2002) 43 *Harvard International Law Journal* 41, 45–51; and C Constantine Antonopoulos, 'Force by Armed Groups as Armed Attack and the Broadening of Self-Defence' (2008) 55 *Netherlands International Law Review* 159, 169. By recognising the right of self-defence in the aftermath of 11 September 2001, the Security Council appeared to imply that this attack could be viewed as an armed attack in UNSC Resolution 1368 (2001). However, the issue of gravity was not referenced explicitly in the resolution.

[51] Christopher Greenwood, 'International Law and the United States' Air Operation Against Libya' (1987) 89 *West Virginia Law Review* 933, 955–56.

[52] UN Doc S/2006/515.

[53] See, eg, *Oil Platforms* case, above n 45, [64].

[54] Gray, above n 12, 155.

[55] It has been accepted by some authors. See, eg, Theresa Reinold, 'State weakness, irregular warfare, and the right to self-defense post-9/11' (2011) 105 *American Journal of International Law* 244, 271 and 284. However, it has been rejected by many others on the basis that it possibly provides 'an open-ended licence to use force'. See Elizabeth Wilmshurst, 'Anticipatory self-defence against terrorists' in LJ van den Herik and Nico Schrijver (eds), *Counter-Terrorism Strategies In A Fragmented International Legal Order: Meeting The Challenges* (Cambridge, Cambridge University Press, 2013) 368; Nigel D White, *Advanced Introduction to International Conflict and Security Law* (Cheltenham, Edward Elgar, 2014) 43.

[56] See Mary Ellen O'Connell, 'Evidence of Terror' (2002) 7 *Journal of Conflict and Security Law* 19.

[57] Gauging whether the state is willing and able to take action against the terrorist group, for example. See Ashley S Deeks, 'Unwilling or Unable: Toward a Normative Framework for Extraterritorial Self-Defense' (2012) 52 *Virginia Journal of International Law* 483. See below.

that the response is most often likely to occur after the particular attack has come to an end, sometimes by a considerable amount of time. For these reasons the response to the 9/11 attacks, for example, came several weeks after the attacks.[58] While it may be claimed that actions taken ostensibly in self-defence are more akin to actions of reprisal,[59] as long as the response can be seen to have a clear and identifiable defensive element to it, such a distinction has now become blurred to the point of extinction.

Although a response in self-defence may resemble a reprisal action, given the delay between the initial attack and the response, the defensive element to the forcible response is nonetheless often portrayed prospectively. Given the overarching aims of terrorist groups and the likelihood that following one attack plans will be afoot for another, the action will often be taken with the expressed aim of preventing further future attacks. While if no prior attack from the particular terrorist group had been sustained the response would be difficult to reconcile with Article 51's requirement for the 'occurrence' of an armed attack, and in this sense appear to be of a purely anticipatory or pre-emptive nature,[60] such a prospective thrust to the defensive claims of states does not seem to be a bar to acceptance of the legality of the action if the victim state has previously been the victim of an attack from the targeted group. For example, in its justification for Operation Enduring Freedom in 2001 the United States was clear that it was responding to '[t]he attacks on 11 September 2001 and the ongoing threat to the United States and its nationals posed by the al Qaeda organization' and, in doing so, was taking action 'designed to prevent and deter further attacks on the United States.'[61]

However, while states possess a certain freedom to use force against such individuals located on the high seas, albeit with any restraints imposed by international human rights law and international humanitarian law, non-state actors, and in particular terrorists, will normally be located on the territory of another state. In this respect, while this chapter has thus far sought to demonstrate that a use of force in self-defence in response to the actions of a non-state actor is possible in conceptual terms, it is the location of them within the territory of another state, and in this sense whether such action can be justified as necessary

[58] After gathering evidence attributing the attacks to al Qaeda, the US unsuccessfully requested the Taliban to unconditionally close al Qaeda training camps in Afghanistan, surrender Osama bin Laden to the US, and open Afghanistan to inspections. See *Keesing's Record of World Events* (2001) 44337.

[59] For this reason Dinstein employs the term 'defensive armed reprisals' to distinguish between purely punitive actions and those of a defensive nature. Yoram Dinstein, *War, Aggression, and Self-Defence*, 5th edn (Cambridge, Cambridge University Press, 2012) 244–45.

[60] See Niaz A Shah, 'Self-defence, anticipatory self-defence and pre-emption: international law's response to terrorism' (2007) 12 *Journal of Conflict and Security Law* 95.

[61] See UN Doc S/2001/946.

and proportionate,[62] which has arguably created the most problematic issues. Indeed, if the non-state actors are now located in another state, or a manifestation of that state such as an embassy,[63] then that state's sovereignty and territorial integrity provide an initial barrier to the victim state simply being able to launch forcible actions within its territory. In this way, it becomes necessary to examine whether, and if so how, the sovereignty barrier might be overcome.

Overcoming the Sovereignty Barrier: Attribution to the Host State

While, as noted above, the ICJ has taken a rather conservative approach in general to the issue of self-defence against the actions of non-state actors, it did not say that an armed attack must be physically carried out by a state. On the contrary, the ICJ in the *Nicaragua* case of 1986, and in drawing upon paragraph 3(g) of the 1974 Definition of Aggression, took the position that aggression, which it appeared to equate with an armed attack, may take the form of the 'sending by or on behalf of a state of armed bands, groups, irregulars or mercenaries, which carry out acts of armed force against another State of such gravity as to amount to [aggression], or its substantial involvement therein.'[64] Under this definition, the actions of the non-state actors should be 'of such gravity as to amount' to an act of armed force by traditional forces of a state. As noted above, non-state actors have been recognised as capable of carrying out force of the necessary gravity for a response in self-defence.[65] However, under the ICJ's apparent conception of self-defence, before an armed attack which has been perpetrated by non-state actors becomes something against which a state can respond to in self-defence, it has to be shown that the non-state actors concerned have been 'sent by or on behalf' of the state in which they are located, or that the state has been 'substantially involved' in the perpetration of the acts concerned. In other words, the actions of the

[62] While the requirement of an armed attack is to be found in Art 51, these two criteria, which have been hailed by some as being of more relevance and significance than the armed attack criterion, are of a customary international law nature. See James A Green, *The International Court of Justice and Self-Defence in International Law* (Oxford, Hart Publishing, 2009) 108–09. See, in general Judith Gail Gardam, *Necessity, Proportionality and the Use of Force by States*, vol 35 (Cambridge, Cambridge University Press, 2004). For more on their operation in the use of force against non-state actors, see below.

[63] Although Ratner has claimed that whether such a manifestation of a state is covered by the term armed attack in Art 51 is 'contentious'. See Ratner, above n 46, 339.

[64] Although this is a definition of 'aggression' as opposed to 'armed attack' there is nothing to suggest that there is a substantial degree of difference between the two, at least for the purposes of attribution. As Ratner notes, the Definition of Aggression 'does not define armed attack per se, but seems helpful in understanding its contours'. Ratner, n 46, 335.

[65] See above section 5.3.2.

non-state actor must be attributable to a state through the 'effective control' it exerted over them.[66]

Although not specifically confirming or contradicting the ICJ's apparent position in *Nicaragua* that for an armed attack by an non-state actor to give rise to the possibility of self-defence it must be attributed to a state through the 'effective control' standard,[67] the ICJ did endorse in general this standard of attribution in the 2007 *Bosnian Genocide* case and elaborated further upon what is required for this standard to be satisfied:

> it is not necessary to show that the persons who performed the acts alleged to have violated international law were in general in a relationship of 'complete dependence' on the respondent State; it has to be proved that they acted in accordance with the State's instructions or under its 'effective control'. It must however be shown that this 'effective control' was exercised, or that the State's instructions were given, in respect of each operation in which the alleged violations occurred, not generally in respect of the overall actions taken by the persons or groups of persons having committed the violations.[68]

The necessity for the attribution of the actions of non-state actors to the host state through a relationship of 'effective control' accords with the traditional understanding of self-defence as a purely inter-state phenomenon.[69] This is a view that has also been adopted by some writers, so that 'if self-defence is invoked against action by armed groups it must be attributed to another State in the sense of proving the existence of substantial or effective control by that State of the armed group.'[70]

Yet, accepting this high threshold of state involvement for the invocation of the right of self-defence raises various conceptual and practical issues. It is, for example, difficult to find any real examples of such 'effective control' in action.[71] Today, while states are often involved in the terrorist

[66] *Nicaragua* case, above n 8, [115]. See below for an alternative reading of the Court's jurisprudence on this issue.

[67] The effective control standard of attribution was subsequently adopted in Art 8 of the International Law Commissions Articles on the Responsibility of States for Internationally Wrongful Acts (2001).

[68] *Case Concerning Application of the Convention on the Prevention and Punishment of the Crime of Genocide (Bosnia and Herzegovina v Serbia and Montenegro)* [2007] ICJ Rep 43 [400]. However, see the Dissenting Opinion Judge Al-Khasawneh (dissenting opinion, [36]–[39]) and Judge ad hoc Mahiou (dissenting opinion, [113]–[117]). See also *Independent International Fact-Finding Mission on the Conflict in Georgia*, Report, September 2009, vol II, 260: 'In the law governing state responsibility, and arguably also for identifying the responsibility for an armed attack, control means "effective control".'

[69] See, eg, Hans Kelsen, 'Collective security and collective self-defense under the charter of the United Nations' (1948) 42 *American Journal of International Law* 783, 791.

[70] C Antonopoulos, 'Force by Armed Groups as Armed Attack and the Broadening of Self-Defence' (2008) 55 *Netherlands International Law Review* 159, 168; see also Shah, above n 60, 108–11.

[71] Arguably an example of this standard of control in practice can be found in the attempted assassination of former US President George HW Bush in Kuwait in 1993 by Iraq. See Dino Kritsiotis, 'The legality of the 1993 US missile strike on Iraq and the right of self-defence in international law' (1996) 45 *International and Comparative Law Quarterly* 162, 174.

activities of non-state actors, it is almost never the case that they exert such a high degree of control over them. The burden of proof that victim states would need to meet before being able to establish the existence of a right of self-defence renders the very idea of self-defence redundant in most cases. It may also be that the non-state actor is not, or is no longer, located within the territory of the controlling state, but instead within the territory of another state. In this case, while a forcible response may be taken against the controlling state, the non-state actor would be effectively protected from one. There thus exists the potential for terrorist organisations to operate with a degree of impunity from military response, even in relation to actions taken on a massive scale by said group against a state (in a world where traditional 'one state against another'-style conflict is no longer the norm).[72]

Furthermore, under the 'effective control' standard for attributing the acts of non-state actors to states for the purposes of self-defence, the non-state actor concerned in effect becomes a limb of the controlling state, thus making the state fully responsible for its actions. In this case, the victim state may invoke its right of self-defence against both the non-state actors *and* the controlling state. Indeed, regardless of whether the victim state in fact wishes to take defensive measures against both, the only way the sovereignty barrier can be overcome, thus permitting self-defence against either, is by establishing such effective control. Yet given that the armed attack may have been perpetrated by a non-state actor acting entirely without state support, or at least of the state upon whose territory it is located, is the victim state in these situations expected to simply endure the attack without having the possibility of responding forcibly? Or might the victim state have the possibility of taking action only against those who actually physically perpetrated the armed attack, that is, the non-state actors? Perhaps in such cases there might be more flexibility in terms of the sovereignty barrier, given that while force is to be used *within* a state, it is not to be targeted specifically *against* it.

The Sovereignty Barrier and Self-defence Restricted to the Targeting of Non-State Actors Located Upon a Host State's Territory

Some maintain a right to self-defence in the context of attacks by non-state actors may only arise if the actions of the non-state actors have been effectively controlled by a state.[73] Yet others take the polar opposite view that there is now a right of self-defence against attacks by

[72] Murphy, above n 39, 66.

[73] See, eg, A Cassese, 'The International Community's Legal Response to Terrorism' (1989) 38 *International and Comparative Law Quarterly* 589, 596–97.

non-state actors regardless of any state involvement.[74] However, both of these positions throw up problems, in that while the former means that non-state actors can effectively act with impunity, the latter fails to show any respect towards preserving the sovereignty of states. However, the jurisprudence of the ICJ on this issue, which as noted above has been influential in determining and shaping the law in this area, is not as rigid as at first might appear.

In both of the two main contentious cases of the ICJ in which the Court addressed claims to self-defence against attacks undertaken by non-state actors—*Nicaragua* and *Armed Activities*—the state claiming self-defence targeted its defensive actions at least partly against the host state and its associated infrastructure. In the *Nicaragua* case, the US provided support to the *contras* in their operations against the Nicaraguan government and military. It was in this sense unsurprising that the court required attribution of the activities of the non-state actors attacking El Salvador (which the US was acting in collective self-defence of) to Nicaragua before action could be taken against Nicaragua itself, as opposed to taking measures solely against the non-state actors who physically perpetrated the attacks. Similarly, in the *Armed Activities* case, Uganda took action in self-defence against the Democratic Republic of the Congo (DRC), as opposed to limiting its actions to the non-state actors that were carrying out raids within its territory. Given that the conditions for self-defence against the DRC were not satisfied, in that the attacks carried out by rebel groups operating from the DRC's territory against Uganda were 'non-attributable to the DRC', the Court did not address the claims of self-defence by Uganda further and, importantly, expressly left the question open as to 'whether and under what conditions contemporary international law provides for a right of self-defence against large-scale attacks by irregular forces'.[75] As Trapp notes, '[i]t seems far less incredible that the Court required that the armed attacks mounted by non-State actors be attributable to the State in whose territory defensive force was being used when one considers that the territorial State was itself the subject of defensive measures.'[76] In this respect, far from ruling that self-defence can only occur against a state or state controlled armed attack, the Court was, instead, silent as to the possibilities for self-defence if the action taken was restricted to the non-state actors.

Furthermore, state practice does seem to point towards the emergence of a middle ground, in that it appears to bear witness to a shift towards the acceptance of forcible responses in self-defence that are limited to

[74] See, eg, Dieter Janssen, 'International Terrorism and Self-Defence' (2006) 36 *Israel Yearbook of Human Rights* 149, 170–71.
[75] *Armed Activities* case, above n 38, [147].
[76] Trapp, above n 42, 142.

targeting the non-state actors and their bases. Incidences of states restricting their forcible actions in self-defence to the non-state actors located within another state's territory are not a recent phenomenon. For example, following the death of three Israeli citizens in Cyprus in 1985, Israel targeted the Palestinian Liberation Organisation (PLO) headquarters in Tunis, Tunisia.[77] In invoking its right of self-defence, Israel claimed that '[i]t was against [the PLO] that our action was directed, not against their host country.'[78] However, in order to justify its violation of Tunisian territory, Israel nonetheless felt the need to state that 'the host country does bear considerable responsibility'.[79] In particular, 'Tunisia did not show an inkling of a desire or an intention to prevent the PLO from planning and initiating terrorist activities from its soil.'[80] In reaction, states, however, focused upon the fact that Tunisia could not be held responsible for the conduct of the PLO and therefore condemned the actions of Israel. As Trapp notes, '[t]his line of argument is in line with some of the contemporaneous thinking on the right of self-defence',[81] in that it was considered that the right of self-defence could only be invoked in response to an armed attack by a state, with a seeming rejection of the possibility for attribution being found in acquiescence in terrorist activities.

Yet, 20 years later, attitudes apparently began to shift, arguably with the recognition of the emergence of what might be described as 'global' terrorism. In response to the bombing of its embassies in both Kenya and Tanzania in 1998, the US responded by bombing an al Qaeda training camp in Afghanistan and a pharmaceutical plant in Sudan, which it claimed was being used by the terrorist group to manufacture biological weapons.[82] Importantly, echoing Israel's justification in 1985, the US claimed only to be attacking installations of al Qaeda in invoking its right of self-defence, and not the states in which they were located. Furthermore, they were 'carried out only after repeated efforts to convince the Government of the Sudan and the Taliban regime in Afghanistan to shut these terrorist activities down and to cease their cooperation with the Bin Laden organization'.[83] However, on this occasion any condemnation of the response was limited to the attack on the pharmaceutical plant, as there was no evidence to suggest that this had been used for anything other than civilian purposes, with little condemnation of the attack on the training camp or the justification of self-defence in general.

[77] UN Doc A/40/688-S/17502 (1985).
[78] UN Doc S/PV 2611 (1993) 22–25.
[79] ibid.
[80] ibid 26.
[81] Trapp, above n 42, 149.
[82] UN Doc S/1998/780. See, in general, Jules Lobel, 'The Use of Force to Respond to Terrorist Attacks: The Bombing of Sudan and Afghanistan' (1999) 24 *Yale Journal of International Law* 537.
[83] ibid.

While every action in self-defence is different, this general pattern of states limiting their actions to the targeting of non-state actors located in a host state while claiming at least some responsibility of the state for failing to put an end to the activities of the non-state actors can be seen in subsequent state practice. Israel's use of force against Hezbollah in Lebanon in 2006,[84] Russia's use of force against Chechen rebels in Georgia in 2002,[85] Colombia's forcible response against the Revolutionary Armed Forces of Colombia—People's Army (FARC) in Ecuador in 2008,[86] and Turkey's 2008 'Operation Sun' in northern Iraq[87] are all examples of this practice, which represents recognition that 'states can invoke self-defence against terrorist attacks not imputable to another state'.[88] However, perhaps the most prominent example of this practice can be found in the US incursion into Pakistani territory in the raid to apprehend Osama bin Laden in 2011.[89] This general practice does not suggest, however, that it is no longer necessary to establish 'effective control' by a host state over the actions of a non-state actor, for self-defence to extend to taking action directly against the state concerned. An anomaly to this line of state practice is the response taken by the US to the 9/11 attacks, in that while the attacks were undertaken by the al Qaeda group, the US actions in self-defence in Afghanistan were directed against both al Qaeda *and* the de facto government of Afghanistan, the Taliban. Indeed, while only claiming that the attacks had 'been made possible by the decision of the Taliban regime to allow the parts of Afghanistan that it controls to be used by this organisation as a base of operation', the US nonetheless included 'measures against al Qaeda terrorist training camps *and* military installations of the Taliban regime in Afghanistan'.[90] Operation Enduring Freedom was notable for two reasons. First, the 'harbouring' standard of attribution employed by the US on this occasion stood in stark contrast to the 'effective control' standard expressly adopted by the ICJ and seemingly witnessed in state practice.[91] While accepted on this occasion, the harbouring standard of attribution has not been witnessed since, arguably due to an underlying recognition of dangerous consequences that it has the potential for if used

[84] UN Doc S/2006/560.

[85] UN Doc S/2002/854; UN Doc S/2002/1012.

[86] See Comunicado del Ministerio de Relaciones Exteriores de Colombia, 081, Bogota, 2 March 2008, http://web.presidencia.gov.co/comunicados/2008/marzo/81.html for the specifics of this self-defence claim.

[87] UN Doc A/HRC/7/G/15.

[88] Tams, above n 30, 381.

[89] See Meagan S Wong, 'Targeted Killings and the International Legal Framework: With Particular Reference to the US Operation against Osama Bin Laden' (2012) 11 *Chinese Journal of International Law* 127.

[90] UN Doc S/2001/946 (emphasis added).

[91] See Christian Henderson, *The Persistent Advocate and the Use of Force: The Impact of the United States Upon the* Jus Ad Bellum *in the Post-cold War Era* (Farnham, Ashgate Publishing, 2013) 137–70.

in the longer term.[92] Secondly, it was also a notable incident in that the targeting of the non-state actors responsible for the armed attack along with the host state was out of step with the more limited strikes that had become a part of state practice following the US's actions in Afghanistan and Sudan in 1998.

The question remains, however, as to how we legally rationalise this new practice. It has been suggested by some that it represents a lowering of the threshold for attribution. For example, as opposed to the need to demonstrate 'effective control' over the non-state actors, states now only need to act with 'complicity'[93] or 'acquiescence'[94] in the conduct of the non-state actors, or to 'aid and abet' them.[95] Yet it is somewhat artificial to 'attribute' the actions of non-state actors to a state when it may have not taken any positive action itself in connection with their commission, and does give rise to the impression that action may be taken against the host state as well as the non-state actors, which lies in contrast to the recent state practice.[96] Furthermore, while this seems to cover the occasions when a host state is unwilling to take action against the non-state actors, it would seem somewhat unrealistic, not to mention unfair, to attribute the actions of a non-state actor to such a state merely on the basis that it was unable to take, or was unsuccessful in taking, action against the non-state actors upon its territory.[97]

As a response, and while maintaining the necessity for attribution under the effective control standard if the defending state wishes to extend its defensive actions *against*, as opposed to merely *within*, the host state and its infrastructure, another view is that attribution is not necessary if the victim wishes to limit its response solely against the non-state

[92] ibid. Although for a recent argument in favour of it, see Daniel Bethlehem, 'Self-Defense Against an Imminent or Actual Armed Attack by Nonstate Actors' (2012) 106 *American Journal of International Law* 769, principle 11.

[93] Tams, above n 30, 385.

[94] Derek Jinks, 'State responsibility for the acts of private armed groups' (2003) 4 *Chinese Journal of International Law* 83.

[95] Tom Ruys and Sten Verhoeven, 'Attacks by private actors and the right of self-defence' (2005) 10 *Journal of Conflict and Security Law* 289, 315.

[96] Tams notes that 'the underlying legal claim argument—that states aiding and abetting terrorists abuse their sovereignty and *must accept some form of counter-action*—has become a standard formula of modern debates and would probably meet with approval of some and tacit agreement of many states.' Tams, above n 30, 393 (emphasis added). This again gives the impression that the action in self-defence is taken *against* the state itself as opposed to *on* the state's territory.

[97] Tams concedes that the attribution approach has limitations in that 'where a state is unaware of terrorist conduct it will not be exposed to forcible responses', but does not then go on to say whether a victim state must simply sit and do nothing or whether and what sort of action it is able to take should the host state be unable to offer the protection it requires. Ibid 386. Trapp, on the other hand, notes that in this circumstance 'the victim State is left with little choice. Either it respects the host State's territorial integrity at great risk to its own security, or it violates that State's territorial integrity in a limited and targeted fashion, using force against (and only against) the very source of the terrorist attack.' Trapp, above n 42, 147.

actors. However, '[u]sing force against the base of operations of non-State terrorist actors within another State's territory surely amounts to a violation of that State's territorial integrity, even if the use of force is defensive and not targeted at the State's apparatus.'[98] In this sense, it has been suggested that both the jurisprudence of the ICJ and the state practice can be explained upon the basis of the customary law criteria of necessity and proportionality,[99] so that if a host state is unable or simply unwilling to effectively deal with the terrorist group on its territory it then becomes necessary for the victim state to do so itself. However, this does mean that before an action in self-defence can be justified as necessary the possibility of seeking a solution via the territorial state should normally be explored first. This would mean that it should either request the host state to take the appropriate means (not necessarily of a forcible nature) to cease the activities of the non-state actor, or request consent to do so itself. If it transpires that the host state is either unable or unwilling to assist, then a right of self-defence will arise, possibly after (and depending upon the circumstances) the victim state having approached the UNSC to take or authorise appropriate action.[100] For example, while the Somalian authorities were simply unable to halt the activities of al-Shabaab in the border region with Kenya before Kenya invaded Somalian territory in 2011 invoking its right of self-defence under Article 51,[101] the international community appeared to accept that the Taliban regime was unwilling to take action against al Qaeda or permit the US to do so in 2001. Furthermore, the fact that the victim state limits its forcible actions to targeting the non-state actors concerned means that its actions, in principle, can be justified as proportional. The action taken, while in quantitative terms may be

[98] Trapp, ibid 145. See also Dapo Akande, 'Classification of armed conflicts: relevant legal concepts' in Elizabeth Wilmshurst (ed), *International Law and the Classification of Conflicts* (Oxford, Oxford University Press, 2012) 73–74, where it is stated that 'the use of force by [a defending state against non-state actors] on the territory of the territorial State, without the consent of the latter, is a use of force *against* the territorial State. This is so even if the use of force is not directed against the government structures of the territorial State, or the purpose of the use of force is not to coerce the territorial State in any way.' While this view is in some ways appealing, and such uses of force may well give rise to an international armed conflict (legally speaking), it fails to fully engage with the distinctions highlighted in this section regarding actions in self-defence, in particular that of the victim state limiting its actions as far as possible by only taking those necessary to defend itself given that the territorial state has proved to be either unable or unwilling to take action against the non-state actors concerned. For example, when Israel undertook its mission in Lebanon in 2006 in response to the Hezbollah attacks, this was not justified by Israel or perceived by the international community as an action against Lebanon. Indeed, it was only when Israel began targeting Lebanese infrastructure that claims of illegality were available.

[99] See, eg, Trapp, ibid 145–55.

[100] See above, section 5.3.1.

[101] See Vidan Hadzi-Vidanovic, 'Kenya Invades Somalia Invoking the Right of Self-Defence', *EJIL Talk!*, 18 October 2011, available at www.ejiltalk.org/kenya-invades-somalia-invoking-the-right-of-self-defence/.

perceived as disproportionate, as it may well result in greater destruction and loss of life than the attacks it is responding to, the prospective aim of ceasing, or attempting to cease, the activities of the non-state actor will favourably affect the proportionality equation. As Tams has observed, '[w]here there is a well-founded fear of repetition … the international community seems to have accepted that states are entitled to use self-defence as a means of severely weakening the terrorist organisation'.[102] These twin principles of customary international law thus provide a means to overcome the sovereignty barrier while maintaining the inter-state context of the law governing self-defence against armed attacks by non-state actors.

5.4 CONCLUSION

This chapter has attempted to show that while states have not recognised non-state actors as subjects of either the norm prohibiting the use of force or the right of self-defence, these actors have come to play a greater role in the regime governing the use of force. The ICJ has been instrumental in developing and highlighting the rules governing the use of force in the context of non-state actors. Yet, while '[t]he traditional approach requiring "effective state control" may have become accepted over time … it was a standard developed by the Court, not God-given',[103] and 'the Court has yet to engage recent State practice of using defensive force against non-State actors in reliance on Article 51 of the UN Charter'.[104] With the advent, or at least recognition, of global terror networks, it is now safe to say that it has been recognised through state practice that not only can non-state actors be the perpetrators of 'armed attacks' for the purposes of triggering the right of self-defence, but that the relationship that exists between them and their host state does not have the rigid consequence for a victim state that it once did. This should not necessarily be seen as a weakening of the rules—including that of attribution—or the promotion of the use of force globally, but more a recognition of what the twin regulatory norms of necessity and proportionality mean in today's world. Of course, the 'global war on terror' has meant more force being used and, with the use of drones becoming increasingly prevalent, different and often controversial means in its deployment. Yet, with the focus upon these fundamental twin principles of the regime of self-defence, and the further development and refining of sub-tests such as the 'unable or unwilling' standard,[105] not only is the use of force regime still seen through the prism of state sovereignty, but non-state actors are less able to act with impunity.

[102] Tams, above n 31, 413.
[103] Tams, above n 30, 386.
[104] Trapp, above n 42, 150.
[105] In this regard see Deeks, above n 57.

6

Non-State Actors Under International Humanitarian Law

HANS-JOACHIM HEINTZE AND CHARLOTTE LÜLF

6.1 INTRODUCTION

INTERNATIONAL HUMANITARIAN LAW (IHL), or the law of armed conflict, is the field of law applicable upon the first exchange of armed hostilities. In contrast to the *jus ad bellum*, which is concerned with the legitimacy of the use of force, IHL enshrines mainly the protection of persons that are not or are no longer participating in the hostilities (*hors de combat*) and the restriction of methods and means of warfare. Traditionally, and due to the state-centric order of international politics and international law, IHL regulated inter-state wars with states' armed forces facing each other in more or less symmetrical battles.[1] Over recent decades, however, the role of various non-state actors has expanded on the international plane, with international organisations, multinational corporations (MNCs), non-governmental organisations (NGOs), and private individuals claiming their share and strengthening their position in politics and to some extent also in international law. The increasing occurrence of non-international armed conflicts between armed forces of states on the one side and non-state actors on the other, furthermore, has led to a normative change in the application of IHL, which was primarily designed to regulate wars between states with legal personality. A developing body of regulations for non-international armed conflicts, characterised by the participation of non-state armed groups without a legal standing under IHL as factual protagonists, changed its character. Through the introduction of a law of internal armed conflict, in a first step with the incorporation of Common Article 3 of the 1949 Geneva Conventions and later with the entry into force of Additional Protocol II, relations of state authority with the people they are supposed to govern entered

[1] Knut Ipsen et al, *Völkerrecht*, vol 6 (München, Beck Verlag, 2014) 928, 1223ff.

the formerly state-centric international humanitarian law system and thus moved closer to the human rights law arena.[2]

Excluding non-state parties to the conflict, another group of non-state actors are active during armed conflict situations: humanitarian aid organisations. A variety of NGOs with divergent institutional and legal structures are involved in dealing with the consequences of war. Interestingly, and despite the state-centric framework of IHL, this body of law reserves a prominent role for one specific actor, the International Committee of the Red Cross (ICRC). Although not a traditional subject under international law, it has a restricted legal personality to follow its task under the mandate given to it by the Geneva Conventions. In addition to the involvement of the ICRC, there are other non-governmental humanitarian actors, classical NGOs, private organisations engaged in humanitarian assistance during armed conflict.[3]

This chapter will address the status of humanitarian non-state actors under international humanitarian law and discuss whether and how the laws of armed conflict refer to this kind of actor involved, not as conflict but as a third party, in most cases focusing on the protection and delivery of aid to the affected population. The different bodies of the Red Cross movement will be highlighted in a first step due to their prominent role in IHL, to then focus secondly on other humanitarian organisations outside of the Red Cross movement.

6.2 THE RED CROSS AND RED CRESCENT MOVEMENT

6.2.1 The International Committee of the Red Cross

The ICRC was established in 1863 in implementation of a proposal made by Swiss businessman, Henry Dunant, in the aftermath of the Battle of Solferino. Dunant was overwhelmed by the fate of the victims of war and organised the first aid to the wounded combatants with the women of Solferino. This experience was recounted in his book, *A Memory of Solferino*, published in 1862. Inspired by the experiences of his first aid activities to treat wounded soldiers, without distinction, of all parties to the conflict, he issued the momentous proposal for the establishment of national aid NGOs in all countries. The task of these organisations would be the treatment of wounded soldiers. He also urged the establishment of an international treaty to guarantee the immunity and neutrality of the medical entities in the field. Moreover, he argued that these medical activities needed protection by a single emblem, which became later the

[2] Rachel Brett, 'Non-governmental human rights organizations and international humanitarian law' (1998) 38 *International Review of the Red Cross* 531.

[3] Ipsen (n 1) 1242ff.

Swiss flag reversed, ie the red cross on a white ground. Dunant's book led to a heated debate on the fate of the victims of war, and his ideas won the support of prominent and influential citizens of Geneva, among them the lawyer Moynier and the soldier Dufour. Dufour became later the founder of the International Committee for Relief to the Wounded, which became the predecessor of the International Committee of the Red Cross.[4]

In 1864, the Committee persuaded the Swiss government to host a diplomatic conference on issues of the law of warfare. The conference adopted the First Geneva Convention for the Amelioration of the Condition of the Wounded in Armies in the Field, which was signed by 12 states. This marked the birth of a modern law of war, taking into consideration the principles of humanity, neutrality and impartiality. These became the guideline for further action of the Red Cross movement. In 1863, the ICRC replaced the Committee for the Relief of the Wounded and became the most important international non-state actor with a very particular legal status, specifically addressed by IHL.[5]

Status of the International Committee of the Red Cross

The ICRC is an ordinary society under Swiss law, consisting entirely of Swiss citizens. However, it has been assigned tasks by the international community, which are enshrined in legally binding provisions. Therefore, the ICRC is a Swiss private association with public elements. It is generally accepted as a non-governmental organisation with a restricted legal personality under international law to carry out its mandate established under the Geneva Conventions:[6] 'The International Committee of the Red Cross (ICRC) is an impartial, neutral and independent organization whose exclusively humanitarian mission is to protect the lives and dignity of victims of war and other situations of violence and to provide them with assistance.'[7] In order to fulfil its purpose, the ICRC has become a subject of international law. This status is unique, because a mono-national leadership of an NGO deals with international activities, and an organisation that is national by its structure is completely international in its work and staff. This distinguishes the ICRC from every other international governmental or non-governmental organisation.

[4] ICRC *Solferino and the International Committee of the Red Cross. Solferino and Henry Dunant in a Nutshell* (Geneva, ICRC, 2014), available at www.icrc.org/eng/resources/documents/features/2010/solferino-feature-240609.htm.

[5] ICRC *History of the ICRC* (Geneva, ICRC, 2014), available at www.Icrc.org/eng/whowheare/history.htm.

[6] André von Walter, 'Arbitration on Oil Concession Disputes' in Rüdiger Wolfrum (ed), *Max Planck Encyclopedia of International Law* (Oxford, Oxford University Press, 2013).

[7] ICRC, *The Mandate and Mission of the ICRC*, available at www.icrc.org/eng/who-we-are/mandate/.

The legal background of the activities of the ICRC is constituted in the Geneva Conventions and the Additional Protocols (AP). These actions are so-called treaty-based or conventional activities of the Committee. The Statutes of the Red Cross and Red Crescent Movement form the second legal bases for its work. The Statutes are the results of the International Conferences of the Red Cross and Red Crescent. The participants of these conferences represent national Red Cross Societies, their international Federation and all state parties of the Geneva Conventions. The decisions of these conferences lead to so-called 'extra-conventional activities' of the ICRC. However, in practice the ICRC does not refer to its specific legal basis and therewith also avoids any statement on the conflict they are dealing with.[8] The 1997 Seville Agreement is a confirmation of its leading role in times of armed conflict and occupation within the movement: Article 5 paragraph 3 of the Seville Agreement defines the responsibilities of the ICRC for situations requiring a lead agency for 'situations of international and non-international armed conflicts, internal strife and their direct results'.[9]

General Role of the ICRC During Armed Conflicts

In international armed conflicts, the ICRC undertakes tasks according to the Geneva Conventions and AP I. Its general task consists mainly in serving as a neutral intermediary between the parties to the conflict. This enables the ICRC to protect and to assist the victims of the hostilities, irrespective of their affiliation. The ICRC can also act as a substitute for a Protecting Power and can offer its good offices to facilitate the creation of hospital and safe zones. 'If protection cannot be arranged accordingly, the Detaining Power shall request or shall accept, subject to the provisions of this Article, the offer of the services of a humanitarian organization, such as the International Committee of the Red Cross, to assume the humanitarian functions performed by Protecting Powers under the present Convention.'[10] In the event of non-international armed conflicts, the ICRC may offer its services to the parties to the conflict.[11]

Besides these conventional tasks, the ICRC can act as the guardian of the Geneva Conventions, as laid down in the Statutes of the Red Cross and Red Crescent Movement. Therefore, it can take any humanitarian

[8] David P Forsythe, 'International Humanitarian Assistance: The Role of the Red Cross' (1996) 3 *Buffalo Journal of International Law* 235.

[9] Art 5 III of the Agreement on the organisation of the international activities of the components of the International Red Cross and Red Crescent Movement—the Seville Agreement of 25–27 November 1997, (1998) *International Review of the Red Cross* 322.

[10] Art 10 III Common to the Geneva Conventions of 1949, and similarly established by Art 5 IV AP I.

[11] Common Art 3 to the Geneva Conventions of 1949.

initiative, which comes within its role as a specifically neutral and independent institution and intermediate, and may consider any question requiring examination by such an institution. Its prominent role within the IHL framework makes it, furthermore, responsible for certain task outside of armed conflict situations, such as advisory services, dissemination and humanitarian diplomacy.[12]

Special Focus of the ICRC

Respect for International Humanitarian Law

The duty of dissemination of IHL belongs to the obligations of the state parties to the Geneva Conventions. The ICRC supports the states in this field and has undertaken this task in many cases. Therefore, it offers programmes for the main target groups of armed forces and other weapon bearers, political leaders and opinion-makers. Of special importance are programmes for future decision-makers, students and scholars. The ICRC offers also special teaching materials for pupils belonging to different cultural groups. The dissemination of IHL constitutes an obligation, which has to be implemented in peacetime because these rules cannot be taught at the last minute, ie after the outbreak of hostilities. Dissemination work can therefore be considered a preventive effort for the application of IHL.[13]

The development of more and more powerful weapons and new methods und means of warfare involves the devolution of IHL. Thus, the ICRC inspires the improvement of rules concerning the protection of war victims and identifies issues where improvements are needed, in particular with regard to modern weapons technologies. Moreover, it recommends and advises the state parties to the Geneva Conventions to adopt national activities to improve the implementation of the international obligations. Another field of action is the assistance to states concerning the redress of grave breaches or war crimes.

The wording of the Geneva Conventions and the APs is necessarily very general, which makes interpretations of the respective rules indispensible. All codification of IHL took place on the initiative of the ICRC. One brilliant example is the Customary International Humanitarian Law Study, which has been published in 2005.[14] The mandate for this study assigned

[12] Marco Sassòli, Antoine A Bouvier and Anne Quintin, *How Does Law Protect In War?* (Geneva, ICRC, 2011).

[13] ICRC, Advisory Service on International Humanitarian Law, *The Obligation to Disseminate International Humanitarian Law* (Geneva, ICRC, 2003), available at www.icrc.org/eng/assets/files/ither/oligation_to_disseminate.pdf.

[14] J Henckaerts and M Doswald-Beck, *Customary International Humanitarian Law* (Cambridge, Cambridge University Press, 2005).

to the ICRC was given by the 26th International Conference of the Red Cross and Red Crescent, in 1995. This study assists in the interpretation of treaty provisions, as it is a well-established principle that a treaty must be interpreted in good faith and with due regard for all relevant rules of international law. Knowledge of the applicable law is a vital first step towards enhancing the effectiveness of IHL. Against this background, the ICRC takes part in the discussion on the compatibility of certain weapons with IHL. In particular the questions whether the weapons are discriminate enough and whether they cause superfluous injuries or unnecessary suffering constitute the focus of the ICRC approach. Thus, the organisation played a leading role for instance in the adoption of the Ottawa Treaty, banning anti-personnel mines.[15]

The activities assumed by the ICRC relating to situations of armed conflict are inter alia enshrined in Article 81 of AP I, paragraph 1 of which orders all parties to a conflict to grant 'all facilities within their powers so as to enable it to carry out the humanitarian functions assigned to it by the Conventions and this Protocol in order to ensure protection and assistance to the victims of the conflicts'.

Protection in Armed Conflicts and Delivery of Humanitarian Assistance

In the provision regulating occupation, the ICRC is given further rights and duties. The occupying power is under an obligation to ensure and maintain the safety and survival of the civilian population. If the civilian population within an occupied territory lacks supplies in relief items, the occupying power is obliged to agree to humanitarian assistance and, if necessary, grant access to other actors offering assistance from outside (Art 59 I GC IV): 'Such schemes, which may be undertaken either by States or by impartial humanitarian organizations such as the International Committee of the Red Cross, shall consist, in particular, of the provision of consignments of foodstuffs, medical supplies and clothing. All Contracting Parties shall permit the free passage of these consignments and shall guarantee their protection.' To facilitate the delivery of the respective goods and assistance to the relief personnel is, by virtue of Article 59 IV GCIV and Article 71 3 AP I, further enshrined, although the provision of relief goods are controlled by respective rights of the occupying powers, as for instance to influence routes or times of delivery (Art 69 2 AP I, Art 59 IV GC IV).

AP I enshrines the right to free access for relief goods, personnel and equipment also in cases where these items are designated for the civilian

[15] A Parlow, 'Towards a Global Ban on Landmines' (1995) *International Review of the Red Cross* 307.

population of the enemy party, as laid down in Article 70. Having these concrete provisions in mind, the International Court of Justice (ICJ) in its landmark *Nicaragua* case held: 'there can be no doubt that the provision of strictly humanitarian aid to persons or forces in another country, whatever their political affiliations or objectives, cannot be regarded as unlawful interventions, or as in any other way contrary to international law'.[16]

Even in the more limited framework applying to non-international armed conflicts, the special status of the ICRC assigned to it by the Geneva Conventions is upheld, as stated by Common Article 3 II: 'an impartial humanitarian body, such as the International Committee of the Red Cross, may offer its services to the Parties to the conflict'. Not just the state parties involved in the armed conflict, but also non-state conflict parties might receive such assistance. The actual scope of rights however remains unclear from the mere wording of the article. With entry into force of AP II, the regulations of Common Article 3 in relation to humanitarian assistance were put into a broader regime that enshrines the right of 'relief societies located in the territory' to offer assistance (Art 18 1 AP II).

Prisoners of War

Articles 126 GC III and 143 GC IV establish the ICRC delegates' prerogatives to visit prisoners of war camps and civilian detainees to ensure their physical and mental conditions and prevent possible abuses by the detention power, and other rights which delegates are entitled to by law. To conduct private interviews with prisoners without witnesses is another of these rights. One other important task is performed through the Tracing Agency, to inform the other party of the conflict on POWs and civilians in detention and inform the families of dead combatants.[17]

The ICRC is a special actor within the law of armed conflict and is protected by the emblems of the Red Cross, Red Crescent and Red Crystal. The Red Cross is the most prominent symbol for humanitarian assistance, but applies only to a limited category, and is a protection emblem that may not be used by independent humanitarian organisations outside the Red Cross and Red Crescent Movement. The actual use of the emblem is restricted by the Geneva Conventions. Injured or sick civilians and combatants alike enjoy the right to medical care and therefore the IHL framework ensures safe treatment by providing protection for those delivering it. The use of the emblem is controlled by the state parties to the Geneva Conventions. It is assigned to medical services of states' armed forces, but other medical services and personnel, such as national societies that are assigned to

[16] *Military and Paramilitary Activities (Nicaragua v USA)* [1986] ICJ Rep 242.
[17] Arts 16 II GC I, 123 GC III, 140 GC IV and 33 3 AP I.

the state party (Arts 26, 42, 44 Geneva Convention I) if approved by the military authorities, and similarly civilian hospitals, may use the sign. In general, state parties to the Convention can use the emblem, but are under a duty to prevent its misuse (Arts 53 and 54 Geneva Convention I) and therefore permission to use the emblem will probably not be granted to independent organisations that act outside the state's control.

There is one exception to the general rule on its usage, correlating with the leading role of the IRCR within armed conflict situations as assigned by the Geneva Conventions. Its major use is to designate activities of the ICRC and the IFRC.[18] Their usage of the emblem is not restricted to medical services, as laid down by Article 44 GC I: 'The international Red Cross organisations and their duly authorised personnel shall be permitted to make use, at all times, of the emblem of the red cross on a white ground.'

While having a dominant and distinctive role at times of war, the ICRC is very reluctant to become involved in politics surrounding an on-going crisis. The protection of individuals in times of armed conflict can be seen as its major goal and the work of the ICRC can be considered in line with a very traditional approach with regard to state consent when engaging in assistance. The dissemination and promotion of humanitarian law is part of its main political task; however, judgemental 'naming and shaming' is rarely used and only in special cases as a last resort.[19]

6.2.2 The International Federation of the Red Cross

The Red Cross Movement can be considered an institutionally fragmented actor, especially since the end of the First World War with the creation of the International Federation of the Red Cross and Red Crescent (IFRC). While the ICRC fulfils the mandate given to it under international humanitarian law, the IFRC functions as an umbrella organisation and furthers the implementation of humanitarian principles in situations outside of armed conflict. The dilemma to ensure that all National Societies of the Red Cross respect the humanitarian principles such as impartiality and independence could be witnessed in the apartheid regime in South Africa.[20]

The division of labour between the ICRC and the IFRC was settled by the Seville Agreement, making the IFRC the leading agency in times of

[18] Kate Macintosh, 'Beyond the Red Cross: the Protection of Independent Humanitarian Organizations' in H-J Heintze and A Zwitter (eds), *International Law and Humanitarian Assistance: A Crosscut Through Legal Issues Pertaining to Humanitarianism* (Heidelberg, Springer, 2011).

[19] David P Forsythe, 'The International Committee of the Red Cross and humanitarian assistance: A policy analysis' (2003) 36 *International Review of the Red Cross* 512, 84.

[20] ibid, 87.

peace, focused on disaster relief and humanitarian assistance. In contrast to the ICRC, the IFRC is a non-governmental organisation without an international legal personality and therefore is not a subject of international law. Its work is not mandated by international agreements, and with the Seville Agreement, its drive to expand to work in armed conflict situations was resolved.[21] However, the IFRC was granted an official observer status at the General Assembly of the United Nations, one of only three humanitarian NGOs, the others being the ICRC and the Order of Malta.[22]

6.2.3 National Societies of the Red Cross and Red Crescent

With 186 National Societies and over 97 million volunteers, the Red Cross and Red Crescent Movement is present all over the globe. Different from the ICRC and the IFRC, the National Societies play an international role, but are principally national manifestations of the Movement. Nonetheless, and although not being subjects of international law but under the domestic laws of their respective home countries, they are given specific tasks directly under IHL Article 81 2 of the AP enshrines the tasks of the National Societies. Access has to be granted by the conflict parties, as well as 'the facilities necessary for carrying out their humanitarian activities in favour of the victims of the conflict, in accordance with the provisions of the Conventions and this Protocol and the fundamental principles of the Red Cross as formulated by the International Conferences of the Red Cross'. Sanctioned, however, are just those that act in accordance with the fundamental principles of the Red Cross Movement: humanity, impartiality, neutrality and independence. Obligations of the state and conflict parties are further to facilitate the assistance of the organisations and the IFRC in every possible way, as laid down in Article 81 3. The National Societies of the Red Cross and Red Crescent Movement are further explicitly mentioned as conducting assistance that can only be temporarily suspended in cases of urgent reasons of security, by virtue of Article 63 I GC IV.

Common Article 3 II, applying to non-international armed conflict situations, laid the groundwork that was expanded by Additional Protocol II. Article 18 1 AP II enshrines the right of 'relief societies located in the

[21] A von Walter, 'Arbitration on Oil Concession Disputes' in Rüdiger Wolfrum (ed), *Max Planck Encyclopedia of International Law* (Oxford, Oxford University Press, 2013). For a detailed discussion see also Forsythe, 'International Humanitarian Assistance: The Role of the Red Cross' (n 19).

[22] Resolution of the General Assembly, Observer Status of the International Federation of the Red Cross and Red Crescent Societies in the General Assembly, A/RES/49/2 of 19 October 1994.

territory' to offer assistance. The National Societies of the Red Cross and Red Crescent Movement, as auxiliaries to their public authorities, are specifically addressed if they act in accordance with their humanitarian principles.[23] However, the precondition for their assignment is the consent of the state party, and in practice probably also the consent of the non-state actor involved.[24] This approach takes into consideration the very basic international law principle of state sovereignty applicable also in cases of emergency and disasters.

As offering relief was mainly addressed to states by treaty law, considering customary law became of utmost importance. Customary humanitarian law extends to other types of actors as national or international non-governmental organisations. The right to offer assistance can be considered as part of their humanitarian mandate. Against this background, the distinction between treaty law and customary law becomes relevant. A debate has come up especially with regard to the question of whether consent of a party to accept assistance as upheld by treaty law is still necessary or if there is enough state practice and *opinio juris* given to constitute a right to access of customary law nature and if so under which preconditions. So far, however, the majority view among legal scholars as well as comments of states and IOs suggest that such a development has not taken place yet and consent of the sovereign state is still necessary.[25]

6.3 AID OUTSIDE OF THE MOVEMENT—OTHER NON-GOVERNMENTAL ORGANISATIONS AND THEIR STATUS UNDER INTERNATIONAL HUMANITARIAN LAW

6.3.1 Humanitarian Aid Organisations

Humanitarian Aid Organisations and Armed Conflicts

Non-governmental organisations working in the field of humanitarian assistance are in practice implementing the majority of humanitarian operations. However, protection by the respective legal regime is to a great extent denied. NGOs are private entities, restricted and based on domestic laws of their state of origin, and as such their presence in international law in general and humanitarian law specifically is not comparable to that of states or the ICRC. Humanitarian assistance is used in the legal context of

[23] Heike Spieker, 'The Right to Give and Receive Humanitarian Assistance' in Heintze and Zwitter (eds), *International Law and Humanitarian Assistance* (n 18).

[24] Michael Bothe, 'Relief action' in Rudolph Bernardt (ed), *Encyclopaedia of Public International Law* vol 4 (Amsterdam, North-Holland, 2000) 171.

[25] *cf* the International Law Commission's Preliminary report on the protection of individuals in the event of natural disasters, UN doc A/CN.4/598, 5 May 2008.

IHL as the relief provided to the civilian population, including access to a population of an occupied territory. The legal framework as it had been originally established by the respective IHL treaties and rules of customary nature has adapted to the new situations and at least to some extent broadened as regards the scope, content, and what is of most relevance for this chapter, the actors.

Traditionally, as with any other treaty of international law, the main subject of rights and duties were states, and therefore legal regulation of humanitarian assistance has focused on states. However, the growing practice of non-state actors or non-governmental actors providing relief and assistance has made it necessary to adapt the legal framework to a new type of actor as bearer of rights and duties, as was done explicitly in the Geneva Convention IV on the Protection of Civilians and AP I. Especially with the drafting of the APs, the formerly limited duty of states to grant free passage for certain relief items has been expanded into a comprehensive system addressing the parties to the conflict, humanitarian actors as well as the vulnerable population.

The role of the various institutional elements of the Red Cross/Red Crescent Movement, the ICRC, the IFRC and the National Societies, has traditionally been strong, however, one can witness a further increase in the engagement of NGOs in the humanitarian sector.[26] Médecine Sans Frontières (MSF), Care and Amnesty International (AI) are prominent non-governmental organisations that are involved in armed conflict situations, working for the protection of civilians and victims of war. Contrary to the Red Cross approach, very often other NGOs pressure for a revised and less strict understanding of neutrality and impartiality. They use public opinion and the opportunity to pressure parties to the conflict, by naming and shaming them, but also negotiate, for example, access to populations in occupied territories.

Under international law, NGOs have the same legal status as individuals, only a limited form of personality, existing under national laws but with few standing as subjects of international law. In the renowned *Barcelona Traction* case, the International Court of Justice decided that international corporations act under the national laws of their place of incorporation, which can also be applied to the status of NGOs.[27] They must act in compliance with the national laws of their state of nationality as well as the laws of the state where they are active.[28] Under international

[26] Philippe Ryfman, 'Non-governmental organizations: an indispensable player of humanitarian aid' (2007) 89 *International Review of the Red Cross* 21.

[27] *Barcelona Traction, Light and Power Company, Ltd (Belgium v Spain)* (5 February 1970, ICJ), para 42.

[28] Mary Ellen O'Connell, 'Enhancing the status of non-state actors through a global war on terror' (2004) 43 *Columbia Journal of Transnational Law* 435, 437.

law they have certain rights; for example, their property cannot be nationalised without compensation of the NGO. The fact that humanitarian assistance is to a major extent distributed among non-governmental aid organisations stresses the question of right of access to populations in need, also to sovereign states and questionably also without the consent of the respective state. Regarding the role of sovereignty of the state in question, enough incidents have shown that the issue of sovereignty is still very prominent, for example, in the expulsion of Oxfam and Save the Children from Sudan in 2004, a symbolic gesture of the full discretion of the country to act as it might choose. The United Nations Security Council in its Resolution 1265 of 1997 however emphasised 'the importance of safe and unhindered access of humanitarian personnel to civilians in armed conflict, including refugees and internally displaced persons, and the protection of assistance to them', as well as the 'need of combatants to ensure the safety, security, and freedom of movement of … personnel of international humanitarian organizations'.[29]

One can argue that certain rights develop directly under international laws and if violated by states, NGOs can hold them responsible before national and international courts. In 1999 Kofi Annan called the Security Council to strengthen the right of NGOs to 'actively engage the parties to each conflict in a dialogue aimed at sustaining safe access for humanitarian operations, and the demonstrate its willingness to act where such access is denied'.[30] However currently one cannot definitely state that the general trend of an increased NGO involvement is mirrored by the speed or scope of legal standing.

Humanitarian Aid Organisations Under International Humanitarian Law

To a limited extent, independent humanitarian organisations outside of the Red Cross framework are addressed explicitly in the Geneva Conventions. Common Article 3 established the right for impartial humanitarian bodies such as the ICRC to offer services to the parties of a conflict. Similarly Article 9 Geneva Conventions I–III and Article 10 Geneva Convention IV state:

> The provisions of the present Convention constitute no obstacle to the humanitarian activities which the International Committee of the Red Cross or any other impartial, humanitarian organisation may, subject to the consent of the parties to the conflict concerned, undertake for the protection … and relief.

[29] Security Council Resolution 1265, Adopted by the 4046th meeting on 17 September 1999, S/RES/1265 (1999).

[30] Report of the Secretary General, UNGA OR 55th Session, Agenda Item 10, Prevention of Armed Conflict, UN Doc A/55/985-S/2001/574 (1999), Annex I, 16.

Geneva Convention IV holds in Article 59:

> If the whole or part of the population of an occupied territory is inadequately supplied, the Occupying Power shall agree to relief schemes on behalf of the said population, and shall facilitate them by all means as its disposal. Such schemes, *which may be undertaken either by States or by impartial humanitarian organizations such as the International Committee of the Red Cross*, shall consist, in particular, of the provision of foodstuffs, medical supplies, and clothing.

Similarly impartial humanitarian bodies are addressed by Article 61:

> The distribution of the relief consignment referred to in the foregoing articles shall be carried out with the cooperation and under the supervision of the Protecting Power. This duty may also be delegated, by agreement between the Occupying Power and the Protecting Power, to a neutral Power, *to the International Committee of the Red Cross or to any other impartial humanitarian body*.[31]

Reference to the ICRC is made as an example and in comparison to the state parties, which suggests the other impartial humanitarian organisations referred to are also independent and not assigned to the medical services of a state conflict party. One can therefore interpret the provisions regulating assistance as implicating independent humanitarian organisations as addressees next to the ICRC and governmental organisations. Article 81 4 entails the obligation for states and conflict parties to 'make facilities similar to those mentioned in paragraphs 2 and 3 available' to other humanitarian organisations which are authorised by the belligerent parties to 'perform their humanitarian activities in accordance with the provisions of the Conventions and this Protocol'. Humanitarian organisations are entitled to provide assistance under Article 63 I a Geneva Convention IV, as are special organisations of a non-military character for the purpose of ensuring the living conditions of the civilian population (Art 63 II Geneva Convention IV).[32]

What has proved increasingly difficult over the last few years is the protection of relief personnel within the Red Cross movement, but even more so for other humanitarian organisation, whose protection is highly dependent on their implementation of the humanitarian principles, mostly neutrality and independence, as they are excluded from the established protection mechanisms that exist for authorised medical staff. They do not work under the protected emblem of the Red Cross/Crescent/Crystal, and in most cases they are also excluded from the protection offered by the UN Convention on the Safety of United Nations and Associated Personnel.

A minimum standard of protection is granted under international humanitarian law, as personnel of humanitarian agencies falls under the general protection that is assigned to civilians. They have no specific

[31] Emphasis added by authors.
[32] M Bothe, 'Relief action' (n 24).

rights or duties, and enjoy no privileges or immunities. But Articles 69 2 and 71 1 AP I, nonetheless, establish a special status for those people that participate in humanitarian operations. The parties to the conflict are obliged to respect and protect relief personnel (Art 71 2 AP I), who, if necessary must be defended or supported. If their safety is endangered or their actions contravene a military operation, the occupying powers may temporarily restrict their movements, or even terminate their mission, by virtue of Article 71 4 AP I.[33] In practice however, their safety is in most cases dependent on their neutrality, as well as precautionary measures, such as sending nationals of the conflict state as members of the humanitarian operation.

6.3.2 Human Rights Organisations

In particular, NGOs working in the area of human rights rather than humanitarian assistance have for a long time struggled with the nature of IHL towards civilians. The potentially legal infliction of damage upon civilian objects, and injuring or killing of people as collateral damage, if the fundamental principles of military necessity and proportionality hold, contradict a purely human rights perspective. Therefore with the determination of an armed conflict and the application of IHL, human rights NGOs in most cases withdraw, leaving armed conflicts to be handled by the ICRC. The increasing convergence of IHL and human rights law and their parallel application during armed conflict was one major incentive to reconsider this position. Human rights NGOs have increasingly used their techniques and mechanisms to raise awareness of IHL violations, in particular by state actors. This was the case with the Report on Israel's 'Grapes of Wrath' operation in Southern Lebanon by Amnesty International, using IHL provisions to evaluate the operation of the Israeli armed forces.[34] Similarly, the advantages of a co-application of both IHL and human rights law have been emphasised by the Human Rights Watch's report on assessing refugees and internally displaced persons (IDPs) camps in Burundi, with reference to not only human rights law but the more specific provisions of IHL, here in particular Article 17 1 AP II concerning the exact preconditions for displacement of the civilian population.[35]

[33] For further discussion, see H Spieker, 'The Right to Give and Receive Humanitarian Assistance' in Heintze and Zwitter (eds), *International Law and Humanitarian Assistance* (n 18) 11.

[34] Amnesty International, *Israel/Lebanon, Unlawful killings during operation 'Grapes of Wrath'* (London, Amnesty International, 1996).

[35] Human Rights Watch, *Proxy targets: Civilians in the war in Burundi* (New York, Human Rights Watch, 1998).

6.4 CONCLUSION

International humanitarian law governing armed conflicts has traditionally been focused on the exchange of hostilities between states' armed forces. The incorporation of non-state armed groups as conflict parties through a body of law specifically focusing on non-international armed conflict, expanded its application beyond state actors. However, observing its principal object, the protection of victims of war, and its historical development, IHL has always addressed an additional kind of non-state actor, the International Committee of the Red Cross, and in a wider context the Red Cross movement. The ICRC in particular is explicitly mentioned by the Geneva Conventions and the APs, to fulfil its mandate in accordance with the law, and concrete tasks are assigned to it, in times of conflict as well as during peace-time. In close relation with these provisions and incentives of the ICRC, other humanitarian aid organisations are referenced by IHL. However, they are merely mentioned in comparison to the ICRC, and are only given a limited task and protection by concrete provisions. This makes their adherence to the humanitarian principles even more important.

7

Non-State Actors and Human Rights

MANFRED NOWAK AND KAROLINA MIRIAM JANUSZEWSKI

Where, after all, do universal human rights begin? In small places, close to home—so close and so small that they cannot be seen on any maps of the world. Yet they are the world of the individual person; the neighborhood…; the school or college…; the factory, farm, or office … Such are the places where every man, woman, and child seeks equal justice, equal opportunity, equal dignity without discrimination. Unless these rights have meaning there, they have little meaning anywhere.

Eleanor Roosevelt, 'In Our Hands' (1958 speech delivered on the tenth anniversary of the Universal Declaration of Human Rights).

7.1 REASSESSING SOME MYTHS ABOUT INTERNATIONAL LAW AND HUMAN RIGHTS

WHEN DEALING WITH the role of non state actors within the international legal system, it is irremissible to consider the significant impact the human rights movement has had in this regard. It is indisputable that the internationalisation of human rights law, as well as the parallel development of international criminal law, which both were a reaction to the painful experiences of the Holocaust forcing the international community to recognise that an unconditional reliance on the state as the ultimate guarantor and guardian of its population's wellbeing was no longer tenable, reshaped the international legal system dramatically. Although certain regulatory interventions by international law vis-à-vis individuals had already been observed far earlier, the embedding of the human rights project within the architecture of international law elevated the protection of human dignity to a matter of international concern and the individual on the international plane. The individual empowered through the adoption of an impressive body of declarations and treaties enshrining economic, social, cultural, political and civil rights to guarantee the individual's welfare, and at the same time capable of being held accountable internationally for certain gross and systematic human rights violations such as genocide, crimes against humanity and war crimes henceforth appeared to be more than a mere object of international legal regulation.

This 'regulatory turn'[1] caused quite a headache for international lawyers, since traditionally, so the legal literature says, only states were subjects of international law possessing the capacity to bear international rights and obligations. Thus, the question arose of how to fit individuals with their internationally enshrined rights and duties into this state-centric construction of the international legal order.

The realities of international life are relentlessly and persistently challenging to international lawyers. The emergence of potent new players on the international arena, pulling significant strings in international relations, some of them overshadowing states, did not go unnoticed, and triggered a vivid discussion about the role of these non-state actors within the international legal framework and the role of international law with regard to these entities, respectively. This fragmented reality of power structures not only touches upon classic understandings, principles, concepts and categories of international law, but also inevitably bears on the effective protection of human rights with its underlying rationale of curbing abuses of might by empowering the individual.

The issue of non-state actors as potential violators and protectors of human rights is far from being new within the human rights discourse. Yet, the developments observed since the late twentieth century have significantly reinforced the calls for acknowledging what has probably always been trivial for victims of indignities: that the state does not constitute the sole menace to the enjoyment of human rights. On the contrary, if one drew a map depicting the sources of human suffering, it would inevitably be polycentric: a state's homophobic laws or a police officer's overzealous use of the gun; the UN peacekeepers' passivity when a civilian population is attacked, the international community standing by when every 13 minutes a child dies from poverty; a rebel leader's command to recruit child soldiers or loot a neighbouring town; a company's discriminatory hiring methods or reckless exploitation of its workers; as well as the spouse's firm fist against the wife's face all constitute assaults on human dignity and have to be assigned a place in this atlas of injustices.[2] Moreover, when drawing such a map, one observes an essential common feature: the sources of violence keep growing and thriving where power structures remain without restraint.

As centres of power are far more fragmented than they used to be (or used to be perceived), it is undisputed that the oppressive potential is not limited to the state apparatus with its monopoly on the legitimate

[1] Borrowing the phrase from J Katz Cogan, 'The Regulatory Turn in International Law' (2011) 52 *Harvard International Law Journal* 322–72.

[2] For child mortality rates, see for instance UNICEF, www.unicef.org/mdg/index_childmortality.htm

use of force.[3] Some of these imbalances of power can be traced back to enduring patriarchal structures of subordination; others seem to have augmented through recent phenomena such as globalisation, with its concomitants privatisation, out-sourcing and trade liberalisation, or the changing nature of armed conflicts. Finally, the exercise of state-like functions and expansion of activities of international organisations in human-rights sensitive areas, such as the adoption of targeted sanctions and the interim administration of territories, have created new dimensions of power. These novel realities are perceived to have profoundly impaired states' power to control territory and population, thus undermining the significance of the state and causing the state-centric construction of international human rights law to totter.

However, just as with states, the potential of business corporations, interstate and non-governmental organisations or individuals of having a serious impact on an individual's wellbeing is not one-sided and only destructive. The (growing) factual socio-economic and political power of some of these non-state entities can equally be utilised to promote the human rights enterprise.[4]

As the significant role non-state actors de facto play with regard to human rights is incrementally recognised, different endeavours to include them within the international human rights regime have gained momentum correspondingly. The major concern in this respect remains the containment of the undeniably harmful capacities of non-state actors. Due to the polysemous concepts of international law and human rights, different approaches have materialised among international lawyers. On the one hand, international human rights monitoring bodies and legal scholars have devised the notion of the state 'obligation to protect', a concept emphasising the guarding role of the state as well as operating within the established framework of state responsibility. Traditionalists following the state-centric lines of general international and human rights law

[3] A Clapham, *Human Rights in the Private Sphere* (Oxford, Clarendon Press, 1993) 137; W Kälin and J Künzli, *The Law of International Human Rights Protection* (Oxford, Oxford University Press, 2010) 78.

[4] The terms human rights enterprise, movement and project have been consciously used in this contribution to remind the reader that the protection of human rights is a continuing and never-ending process. The enormous progress achieved by now is undeniable, and extremely impressive. One only has to look at the enormous collection of human rights declarations, treaties and voluntary commitments adopted over the last 70 years. The institutionalisation of human rights on the international level reflected in the plethora of different political, judicial and quasi-judicial as well as investigative protection and enforcement mechanisms and the contribution of civil society to the enhancement of the realisation of human rights definitely warrants speaking of the existence of an international human rights regime. Due to the enduring lack of a coherent and effective approach towards non-state actors as violators of human rights, as will be outlined on the following pages, the human rights project can however not be considered as concluded and will realistically never be, as new challenges will continue to arise demanding adequate responses.

appreciate the adherence to the already established human rights system and contend that any other approach will ultimately fail due to conceptual impossibilities as well as political considerations. The idea of making non-state actors accountable for their human rights abuses through the imposition of direct international human rights obligations, which ideally would be accompanied by a corresponding enforcement mechanism, constitutes, according to the orthodox view, precisely such a 'utopian' response with no added value, ridiculing and denaturing human rights.[5] Some exponents of this 'utopian' theory propound that direct obligations on non-state actors, including human rights duties, can be already found in international law and should be further adopted. By complementing the state's primary responsibility, such horizontal obligations close the existing accountability gap.[6] And there are other more radical suggestions demanding a reconceptualisation of the international legal order wherein powerful non-state actors also assume a more leading part, or even directly participate in the international law-making process.[7] Between those three currents one can identify many variations with different shades of grey.[8]

However, until now, despite extensive research and debate on that matter, and a clear tendency among human rights lawyers to demand that certain non-state actors should be subjected to the international human rights regime, international human rights law has very modestly responded to the changing circumstances in the real world with its myriad of potent participants.

This inertia can be traced back to the prevalent traditional school of thought still feeding the state-centric conceptualisation of both human rights law and the international legal order. While international law still very much looks through the Westphalian prism of a 'law of nations', which serves solely and exclusively to regulate and facilitate interstate relations, state-centrism also seems to run like a golden thread through the dominant human rights narrative, according to which human rights were from the very beginning designed for a purely vertical relationship to protect the citizen against the omnipotent state. Hence, the traditional

[5] See for instance Nigel Rodley, 'Non-State Actors and Human Rights' in S Sheeran and N Rodley (eds), *The Routledge Handbook of International Human Rights Law* (Abingdon, Routledge, 2013) 523–44.

[6] A Clapham, *Human Rights Obligations of Non-State Actors* (Oxford, Oxford University Press, 2006) 565f.

[7] G Teubner, '"Global Bukowina": Legal Pluralism in the World Society' in G Teubner (ed), *Global Law Without A State* (Brookfield, Dartmouth, 1997) (available at http://papers.ssrn.com/sol3/papers.cfm?abstract_id=896478); see further Clapham, *Human Rights Obligations of Non-State Actors* (n 6) 25–29.

[8] P Alston, *Non-State Actors and Human Rights* (Oxford, Oxford University Press, 2005); R McCorquodale, 'Non-State Actors and International Human Rights Law' in S Joseph and A McBeth (eds), *International Human Rights Law* (Cheltenham, Edward Elgar Publishing, 2009) 97–114.

legal doctrine relying on this one-dimensional, slimmed-down premise, and seemingly also on the motto 'what presently is, necessarily always has to remain',[9] contends that general international law and international human rights law, due to these conceptual restraints, are simply inappropriate to regulate non-state actors' behaviour directly.

Finding explicit direct human rights obligations for non-state actors within the present human rights landscape, therefore, reminds one of the search for a needle in a haystack; despite the fact that over the last 50 years an impressive and diverse corpus of modern human rights law has developed, this plethora of norms seems, with a few exceptions, to apply only between the individual and the state. The regulation of non-governmental behaviour, in order to curb its detrimental potential, is according to these classical legal approaches considered to be a matter of the sovereign state.

Despite doctrine and jurisprudence having in recent years actively worked on closing this apparent protective lacuna, by developing the theory of a due diligence obligation of states to protect individuals from abuse by private actors, the lack of effective implementation in many states has only contributed to the perception of an accountability gap and an enduring bitter aftertaste. There are well-documented and damning records of indications, carefully collected by intergovernmental and non-governmental human rights organisations or the media, reminding the international community that mere reliance on individual states to hold those non-governmental actors responsible is deficient. All too frequently, (host or home) states are unable or are loth to take appropriate protective measures, due to different reasons, including the dependence of states on willing investors.

Therefore, there is a clear necessity for international human rights law to properly respond to the manifold challenges posed by non-state actors in the real world to the enjoyment of human rights, in order to afford effective protection and still be conceived as a credible and legitimate enterprise. A legal system that is unable to adapt to the needs of society will inevitably lose its relevance.

Much has been written on non-state actor obligations and human rights. This contribution will not reinvent the wheel, but draw from the impressive research already conducted and try to draft a coherent picture of the general approach international human rights law takes with regard to non-state actors, the status quo of the law, and ultimately suggest possible adjustments. In doing so, we will have to confront and dismantle inherited and resilient assumptions of the functioning of international human rights law to remove the apparent obstacles to a reconceptualisation of the human rights regime. Since the issues of subjects of international law and

[9] R Higgins, *Problems and Process: International Law and How We Use It* (Oxford, Clarendon Press, 1994) 49.

international legal personality are dealt with in separate chapters within this book, our discussion with regard to these matters will remain cursory. It aims at reminding the reader that international law is fully capable of imposing obligations on non-state actors, provided that states consent to it.

Essentially, it is suggested that the issue of whether non-state actors can and shall be included in the human rights architecture as duty-bearers, ultimately depends on our general understanding of human rights, rather than on legal impossibilities. Human rights have primarily been looked at through a purely libertarian prism, with the state in its dual role as protector and possible violator in a world divided into 'public' and 'private' spheres. However, without overexerting our imagination and turning the idea of human rights upside down, human rights can be conceived more broadly, as tools for an all-around protection of a dignified life with the basic aim to empower the powerless within any oppressive power structure. If we adopt this more general approach, non-state actors as possible violators of human rights become a logical consequence. As alluded to above, since from the victim's perspective it hardly makes any difference who commits the infringement, the orthodoxly narrow notion of human rights of the state as the only bearer of human rights obligations is no longer appropriate in our present-day world.

7.1.1 Dismantling Obstacle No 1—International Law is All About States—The Subject of International Law as a Haunting Phantom

When trying to fit non-state actors within the realm of international human rights law and placing respective obligations directly on them, one will still be confronted with a well-known spectre of international law, the ominous subject of international law.[10] The familiar mantra goes as

[10] The present description of international law's approach towards non-state actors does not endeavour to analyse the issue exhaustively. For a more elaborate examination, the reader is asked to refer to the respective contributions dealing with the concepts of 'subjects of international law' and 'international legal personality'. Rather, this chapter intends to remind the reader that the traditional legal and political caveats towards a stronger inclusion of non-state actors in international law still commonly rely on the dominant assumption that only subjects of international law with their law-making powers are capable of bearing international obligations. Such a view, however, can be described as being more royalist than the king, and to be honest, outdated. A short inquiry into international law allows concluding that the picture drawn by traditionalists does not reflect the heterogeneous realities of international life and law. The following remarks shall serve to show that international law as every legal system must adapt and indeed has adapted to changing circumstances without losing the essential predictability, in order to ensure that it is able to contribute to the solution of today's problems. See, for a classic treatise of this challenge and the understanding of international law not as a set of rules but as a process, Higgins, *Problems and Process* (n 9).

follows: in order to legitimately be held accountable on the international plane, it is required that the respective entity infringed an international obligation incumbent on it. However, only subjects of international law are endowed with international legal personality necessary to be capable of directly bearing rights and obligations under international law. Everything else is merely an object at the legislative disposal of the subjects. This dichotomy appears to suggest that the starting point of any further examination must be whether non-state actors can be subjects of international law possessing international legal personality. However, if one takes a closer look at international law, the developments in this area clearly show that these compartments of 'subject' and 'object' are not as watertight as they might appear at first sight. In its ground-breaking *Reparations for Injuries* advisory opinion the ICJ rejected the view that subjectivity was only a matter of statehood, leaving room for the reconsideration and expansion of these categories.[11] Moreover, it discarded the claim that the recognition of international legal personality of other international actors would inevitably equate the respective entity to the existing subjects of international law, vesting it with law-making capacity, a privilege states are not inclined to share.[12] The Court emphasised that the needs of the international community as well as the requirements of international life might necessitate the admission of further entities within the exclusive club of subjects and that the rights and duties of these new subjects might differ considerably.

Likewise, a quick survey of the evolution of international law refutes the enduring caveat that the international legal order is not capable of directly, ie, without intervention of state legislation, imposing obligations on non-state actors. On the contrary, it reveals that whenever an issue was in their interest, states were willing to regulate the behaviour of non-state actors by directly imposing obligations on them. In their fight against piracy during the seventeenth and eighteenth centuries, states readily adapted to the jurisdictional challenges posed by pirates acting on the high seas; pirates were declared *hostis humani generis*, enemies of humankind, and their acts were considered violations of the law of nations subject to universal jurisdiction.[13] Through the gradual emergence of the notion of war crimes

[11] *Reparation for Injuries Suffered in the Service of the United Nations*, Advisory Opinion [1949] ICJ Rep 174, 178: 'The subjects of law in any legal system are not necessarily identical in their nature or in the extent of their rights, and their nature depends on the needs of the community. Throughout its history, the development of international law has been influenced by the requirements of international life, and the progressive increase in the collective activities of States has already given rise to instances of action upon the international plane by certain entities which are not States.'

[12] P Alston, 'The "Not A Cat Syndrome": Can the International Human Rights Regime Accommodate Non-State Actors?' in Alston, *Non-State Actors and Human Rights* (n 8) 19; Clapham, *Human Rights Obligations of Non-State Actors* (n 6) 59.

[13] J Crawford, *Brownlie's Principles of Public International Law*, 8th edn (Oxford, Oxford University Press, 2012) 302ff; MN Shaw, *International Law*, 6th edn (Cambridge, Cambridge University Press, 2008) 397ff.

on the international level, starting with the Hague Conventions of 1899 and 1907, individuals were also incrementally obliged by international law to abstain from certain deplorable conduct in the context of war.[14]

The most profound watershed, however, constituted the international communities' legislative activities in reaction to the Second World War and the gruesome experience of the Holocaust. The painful realisation that an unconditional reliance on the state as the ultimate guarantor and guardian of its populations' wellbeing was insufficient, gave impetus to several crucial adjustments of the international legal order which elevated the protection of human dignity to an international concern.[15] The international community recognised that an internationally guaranteed set of rights together with international scrutiny are essential for the protection of human rights as well as international peace. Thus, in order to prevent recurrence of such barbarity and achieve a stable security, states agreed to launch a new human rights project placed within the international legal order. Human rights were not only designated in general terms to be one of the objectives of the United Nations, but step by step proclaimed and firmly enshrined in regional and universal treaties covering a wide range of rights. These international instruments reaffirmed that every individual by virtue of being a human being possesses human rights which are neither dependent on the grace of a government nor at its unlimited disposal.[16] Hence, states by the adoption of treaties or respective custom consciously placed fundamental rights within the international legal order, and once again exposed that international law is capable of directly acting upon non-state actors.[17] Today, these rights of individuals can be seen as having

[14] WA Schabas, *An Introduction to the International Criminal Court*, 4th edn (Cambridge, Cambridge University Press, 2011) 122; A Cassese et al, *Cassese's International Criminal Law*, 3rd edn (Oxford, Oxford University Press, 2013) 63ff.

[15] This attitude has been reiterated in many international documents, from the Charter of the United Nations (Arts 1 and 55) to for example the Vienna Declaration of 1993, para 4, wherein all states have acknowledged that 'the promotion and protection of all human rights is a legitimate concern of the international community'.

[16] See Universal Declaration of Human Rights (adopted 10 December 1948) UNGA Res 217 A(III) [hereinafter 'UDHR'] and the nine UN core human rights conventions on civil, political, economic, social and cultural rights, the elimination of racial discrimination and discrimination against women, the prohibition of torture and other cruel, inhuman or degrading treatment or punishment, the rights of migrant workers, children, and persons with disabilities and the protection from enforced disappearance.

[17] That individuals could have rights under international law was in fact not that much of a novelty. Already in 1928 the Permanent Court of Justice held in the *Courts of Danzig* that '[it] cannot be disputed that the very object of an international agreement, according to the intention of the contracting parties, may be the adoption by the parties of some definite rules creating individual rights and obligations and enforceable by the national courts'; see *Jurisdiction of the Courts of Danzig (Pecuniary Claims of Danzig Railway Officials who have Passed into the Polish Service, against the Polish Railways Administration)*, Advisory Opinion (1928) PCIJ Series B No 15, 17f.

assumed a separate legal existence, to a considerable extent independent of state agreement and control.[18]

Likewise, when codifying international humanitarian law states recognised the realities of war and extended the scope of application to all parties of a conflict, even if they are not parties to the Geneva Conventions; accordingly, the behaviour of and towards individuals and rebel groups is directly regulated by international law.[19] Additionally, it is well-established that certain gross and systematic human rights violations and breaches of humanitarian law categorised as genocide, crimes against humanity and war crimes constitute international crimes entailing individual criminal responsibility, even irrespective of the individual's link to the state.[20] International criminal law thus establishes direct international duties on individuals enforceable by national courts or international institutions.[21] The need to cooperate in the fight against terrorism similarly convinced the international community to adopt several treaties explicitly making specific private conduct an offence.[22]

With regard to other fields of international law, such as international economic law, there was also enough consensus among states to consider non-state actors—in general, foreign corporations—to enjoy rights directly

[18] Many human rights treaties, such as the two UN Covenants, do not provide for a right to withdraw from the treaty. The Human Rights Committee in its General Comment 26 on the continuity of obligations, held that 'once the people are accorded the protection of the rights under the Covenant, such protection ... does not permit a State which has ratified or acceded or succeeded to the Covenant to denounce it or withdraw from it', see UN Doc CCPR/C/21/Rev 1/Add 8/Rev 1 (1997), paras 4 and 5. Likewise, to the extent, human rights norms have achieved *jus cogens* or customary law status, they enjoy an independent status; see R McCorquodale, 'The Individual and the International Legal System' in MD Evans, *International Law*, 3rd edn (Oxford, Oxford University Press, 2010) 291.

[19] See, eg, Common Art 3 to the Geneva Conventions of 1949 as well as Protocol II; Art 5 Geneva Convention I; see D Fleck, *The Handbook of International Law*, 2nd edn (Oxford, Oxford University Press, 2008) 76.

[20] See, eg, Art 4 Convention on the Prevention and Punishment of the Crime of Genocide (adopted on 9 December 1948, entered into force on 12 January 1951), 78 UNTS 277: 'Persons committing genocide or any of the other acts enumerated in Article 3 shall be punished, whether they are constitutionally responsible rulers, public officials or private individuals'. See also Arts 6–7 Statute of the International Criminal Tribunal for the Former Yugoslavia (as amended on 7 July 2009 by Resolution 1877); Arts 6, 7, 8(2) (c–f) and 25–27 Rome Statute of the International Criminal Court (adopted on 17 July 1998, entered into force on 1 July 2002) [hereinafter Rome Statute].

[21] Cassese, *Cassese's International Criminal Law* (n 14) 3ff; see also MC Bassiouni, *International Criminal Law*, vol 1—Sources, Subjects and Contents, 3rd edn (Leiden, Martinus Nijhoff, 2008) 41ff.

[22] See, eg, Convention for the Suppression of Unlawful Seizure of Aircraft (adopted on 16 December 1970, entered into force on 14 October 1971) 860 UNTS 105, and supplemented by the Protocol Supplementary to the Convention for the Suppression of Unlawful Seizure of Aircraft (adopted on 10 September 2010, not yet in force) DCAS Doc No 22; Convention for the Suppression of Unlawful Acts against the Safety of Civil Aviation (adopted on 23 September 1971; entered into force on 26 January 1973) 974 UNTS 178; Convention on the Suppression of Unlawful Acts Relating to International Civil Aviation (adopted on 10 September 2010, not yet in force) DCAS Doc No 21.

under international law. The respective treaties provide for international arbitration in case of dispute directly accessible for non-state actors and foresee that the dispute is to be resolved by a combination of the domestic law of a country chosen by the contracting parties and general international law.[23] Further international duties for corporations can for instance be found in the 1969 Convention on Civil Liability for Oil Pollution Damage or the 1982 UN Convention on the Law of the Sea.[24]

This proliferation of non-state actors' substantive rights and obligations was partially and only incrementally accompanied by the establishment of corresponding monitoring and enforcement mechanisms open for non-state actors. Besides the already mentioned arbitration possibilities, where non-state actors have procedural standing to sue or be sued, states did set up human rights monitoring mechanisms, some of which are of judicial or quasi-judicial nature; others in turn are purely political. Whether the non-state actor has the possibility to file a complaint, however, ultimately depends on the state's consent to such a monitoring mechanism and requires, in addition, the exhaustion of domestic remedies.[25] Within the framework of international criminal law, several decades had to pass by after the Nuremberg and Tokyo trials to motivate the international community to enforce those crimes by international institutions. Once again, tragic events, this time in former Yugoslavia and Rwanda, gave impetus to direct international enforcement. The formation of the ad hoc tribunals in the early 1990s was followed by the establishment of the permanent International Criminal Court in 1998 and several hybrid tribunals prosecuting individual perpetrators on the international plane and under the application of international law. International procedures for disputes

[23] R Dolzer and C Schreuer, *Principles of International Investment Law*, 2nd edn (Oxford, Oxford University Press, 2012) 81ff; Higgins, *Problems and Process* (n 9) 54; A Reinisch, 'The Changing International Legal Framework for Dealing with Non-State Actors' in Alston, *Non-State Actors and Human Rights* (n 8) 85; McCorquodale, *The Individual and the International Legal System* (n 18) 297; D Kinley and J Tadaki, 'From Talk to Walk: The Emergence of Human Rights Responsibilities for Corporations at International Law' (2004) 44 *Virginia Journal of International Law* 931, 946ff.

[24] Art III International Convention on Civil Liability for Oil Pollution Damage (adopted on 27 November 1992; entered into force on 30 May 1996 1992): 'the owner [which according to Art I(2) covers any individual or partnership or any public or private body, whether corporate or not, including a State or any of its constituent subdivisions] of a ship at the time of an incident, or, where the incident consists of a series of occurrences, at the time of the first such occurrence, shall be liable for any pollution damage caused by the ship as a result of the incident'; Art 137(1) UN Convention on the Law of the Sea (adopted on 10 December; entered into force on 16 November 1994) 1833 UNTS 3: 'No State shall claim or exercise sovereignty or sovereign rights over any part of the Area or its resources, nor shall any State or natural or juridical person appropriate any part thereof. No such claim or exercise of sovereignty or sovereign rights nor such appropriation shall be recognized.'

[25] See, eg, Art 5 Optional Protocol to the International Covenant on Civil and Political Rights (adopted on 16 December 1966; entered into force on 23 March 1976) 999 UNTS 302.

purely between non-state actors applying substantive international law are missing, a gap which can be traced back to the state-centric thinking still pervading international relations.

These procedural deficits, as unfortunate as they are, do not affect the existence of the individual's rights and duties under international law. International rights and obligations exist independently from corresponding redress avenues or enforcement mechanism on the international plane.[26] The prohibition of genocide was internationally codified in 1948 whereas the correlative international enforcement mechanisms followed nearly half a century later. Likewise, although some of the UN human rights treaties have reached almost universal ratification, certain states are still reluctant to be subjected to an individual complaints procedure allowing individuals to file applications against them.[27] Nonetheless, these rights exist, even if they cannot be enforced before an international body.

This journey through the vast and varied landscape of international law illustrates quite well that international law has been constantly faced with new challenges and has, sometimes only very slowly, adapted to the requirements of international life. These developments occur, as Rosalyn Higgins aptly noted, 'as much through the force of circumstances as through any conscious intellectual processes',[28] suggesting that whether non-state actors possess rights and duties under international law is less a question of immutable conceptual barriers, but rather an issue of state interest and political will leading to an international normative consensus. Whenever it suited them, states as the ultimate law-makers accorded non-state actors rights and obligations under international law and even granted them direct access to international dispute settlement bodies or subjected them to the jurisdiction of international criminal tribunals.[29]

[26] H Lauterpacht, 'General Laws of the Law of Peace' in E Lauterpacht (ed), *International Law: Being the Collected Papers of Hersch Lauterpacht*, vol 1 The General Works (Cambridge, Cambridge University Press, 1970) 286f; Clapham, *Human Rights Obligations of Non-State Actors* (n 6) 74; Higgins, *Problems and Process* (n 9) 51ff; N Jägers, *Corporate Human Rights Obligations: In Search of Accountability* (Antwerp, Intersentia, 2002) 38.

[27] As of October 2013 an average of 168 states had ratified the ICCPR, ICESCR, CAT, CERD, CEDAW, CRC and CRPD, while an average of 63 states had accepted the respective individual complaints. Within the Council of Europe region, its 47 states were subjected to a mandatory individual complaints procedure before the European Court of Human Rights rendering binding judgments.

[28] Higgins, *Problems and Process* (n 9) 54.

[29] Cogan, 'The Regulatory Turn in International Law' (n 1) 331; Reinisch, 'The Changing International Legal Framework' (n 23) 87; Clapham, *Human Rights Obligations of Non-State Actors* (n 6) 73; R McCorquodale, 'Overlegalizing Silences: Human Rights and Non-State Actors' (2002) 96 *Proceedings of the Annual Meeting (American Society of International Law)* 384–88.

7.1.2 Dismantling Obstacle No 2—The Axiomatic State-Centrism in Human Rights Law

The changed topography of power within the international community, commonly attributed to globalisation and characterised by the eroded almightiness of the state, as well as the mushrooming of new centres of power such as transnational corporations generating sums of money which dwarf the GDPs of some countries, states out-sourcing their competences to private companies, international organisations with expanded fields of activity and influential, internationally active civil society groups, organised crime and global terrorism cells and fragmented armed conflicts, illustrates quite well that the continuing reliance on a wholly state-centric human rights law is untenable.

Human rights law as it exists today, with its strong vertical alignment, is increasingly unfit to provide for an effective protection and promotion of human rights. Although non-state actors are not absolutely out of the realm of international human rights law, as states have the obligation to protect rights-holders against abusive private parties and some isolated cases of direct horizontal obligations exist, international human rights protection relies heavily on a functioning national human rights protection system.[30] Hence, states are assumed to be powerful enough, possessing the necessary resources and political will, to implement the human rights project on their own. Such an assumption, however, seems to ignore the crumbling ability or deficient willingness of states stemming from the growing interdependence and interrelations between all the participants on the international plane, as well as the fact that their transnational activities make it difficult for states to get a grip on them.[31] Moreover, by privatising sectors such as prison administration, health care or education, as well as delegating powers to international organisations, states intentionally transfer governmental tasks to non-state actors in order to absolve themselves from their obligations.

The prevalent muteness in international as well as national human rights law with regard to horizontal obligations is however not immutable. As briefly outlined above, in order to be perceived as a credible and useful tool to safeguard human wellbeing, international human rights law must be conceived as a dynamic and ever-evolving process, rather than a static system resilient to evolution and unable to adapt to new circumstances.[32] Likewise, this predominant legal silence which can be traced

[30] M Nowak, *UN Covenant on Civil and Political Rights—CCPR Commentary*, 2nd edn (Kehl/Strasbourg/Arlington, NP Engel, 2005) 28.

[31] Above all, terrorists, organised crime and transnational corporations operate within many jurisdictions.

[32] On the importance of perceiving international law not merely as a set of rules but a process, see Higgins, *Problems and Process* (n 9).

back to the strong influence of liberalism in Europe and North America in the eighteenth and nineteenth centuries, leading to the bourgeois revolutions and a subsequent wave of constitutional protection of human rights, reducing these all-encompassing rights to mere claims against state interference, does not in itself render private obligations conceptually inconceivable.[33] On the contrary, whether one considers horizontal human rights obligations as conceptually reconcilable or not ultimately depends on one's approach to human rights, ie, how one understands their meaning and purpose.[34] This approach, in turn, will naturally inform human rights practice and the formation of corresponding international human rights law.

7.2 THE SIGNIFICANCE OF HUMAN RIGHTS AS A REACTION TO REAL LIFE CHALLENGES

7.2.1 The Meaning of Human Rights—A Quest for Human Dignity, Equality and Justice

Human rights are commonly understood, and here fortunately there do not seem to be too many voices of dissent, literally, as rights individuals possess by virtue of being human.[35] Many theories and visions exist trying to give human rights a justifying underpinning. Despite some fundamental differences in origin, meaning, purpose or terminology, a common theme can be derived: human beings ought to be protected due to the distinctive human nature, a quality which demands respect of their dignity.[36] For Immanuel Kant, who was the first to formulate the idea of human dignity in such a formative way, this particular characteristic of human beings stems from them being free and rational agents capable of autonomously choosing their ends and taking responsibility for

[33] M Nowak, *Introduction to the Human Rights Regime* (Leiden/Boston, Martinus Nijhoff Publishers, 2003) 51; McCorquodale, 'Overlegalizing Silences' (n 29) 384–88; Clapham, *Human Rights Obligations of Non-State Actors* (n 6) 73; JH Knox, 'Horizontal Human Rights Law' (2008) 102 *American Journal of International Law* 1.

[34] JJ Shestack, 'The Philosophic Foundations of Human Rights' (1998) 20 *Human Rights Quarterly* 201, 202.

[35] Art 1 UDHR: 'All human beings are born free and equal in dignity and rights'; for a good insight into the genealogy and visions of human rights, see PG Lauren, *The Evolution of International Human Rights—Visions Seen* (Philadelphia PA, University of Pennsylvania Press, 2011).

[36] J Donnelly, *Universal Human Rights in Theory and in Practice*, 3rd edn (Ithaca NY, Cornell University, 2013) 28ff; see also M Nowak, 'Progress Report of the Eminent Persons Panel' within the framework of the Swiss Initiative to Commemorate the 60th Anniversary of the UDHR—Protecting Dignity: An Agenda for Human Rights, www.udhr60.ch.

their acts.[37] He conceived dignity as inalienable, 'absolute inner worth'[38] which inheres in all humans qua human beings and requires us to '[a]ct in such a way that you treat humanity, whether in your own person or in the person of any other, never merely as a means to an end, but always at the same time as an end.'[39] Although other philosophical, religious, political and literary contemplations which can even be traced back to antiquity developed different visions of dignity, there seems to be an 'overlapping consensus' to 'allow human dignity to serve as an accepted principle of shared morality',[40] which ultimately found its way into post-World War II national constitutions and modern international human rights law.[41] The adoption of the Universal Declaration of Human Rights, wherein dignity features prominently in the opening sentence as well as the famous first article stating that 'All human beings are born free and equal in dignity and rights',[42] reflects this evolved consensus. Thus, today human dignity is generally understood as the underlying, 'super'[43] value generating and shaping all other human rights.[44] The significance of human dignity and its protection as well as its foundational notion are reiterated in all major human rights instruments, such as in the preambles of the two international Covenants and the Convention against Torture stating that the enshrined 'rights derive from the inherent dignity of the human person'.[45]

[37] Shestack, 'The Philosophic Foundations of Human Rights' (n 34) 216; J Donnelly, 'Human Dignity and Human Rights' (2008) 19 *European Journal of International Law* 20ff.

[38] Immanuel Kant, *The Metaphysics of Morals* (first published 1797; Mary Gregor tr, Cambridge, Cambridge University Press, 1996) 186.

[39] Immanuel Kant, *Grounding for the Metaphysics of Morals*, 3rd edn (first published 1785; James W Ellington tr, Indianapolis, Hackett Publishing, 1993) 30.

[40] See Donnelly, 'Human Dignity and Human Rights' (n 37) 82, who borrowed the phrase of 'overlapping consensus' from Rawls; J Habermas, 'The Concept of Human Dignity and the Realistic Utopia of Human Rights' (2010) 41 *Metaphilosophy* 464, 467.

[41] See C McCrudden, 'Human Dignity and Judicial Interpretation of Human Rights' (2008) 19 *European Journal of International Law* 655, 664: He lists, eg, the three defeated nations of the Second World War, Germany, Japan and Italy, and gives a detailed account of the incorporation of the concept of human dignity and its protection before and after the Second World War in national, regional as well as international human rights instruments; see Art 1 Basic Law for the Federal Republic of Germany or Art 1 Charter of Fundamental Rights of the European Union.

[42] See also preamble of the American Declaration of the Rights and Duties of Man of 1948.

[43] Shestack, 'The Philosophic Foundations of Human Rights' (n 34) 226.

[44] For an excellent account on the concept of dignity and its link to human rights, see the two research projects of June 2009 on human dignity in the framework of the Swiss Initiative to Commemorate the 60th Anniversary of the UDHR—Protecting Dignity: An Agenda for Human Rights, www.udhr60.ch/research.html; J Donnelly, 'Human Dignity and Human Rights' (n 37), and F Mégret and F Hoffmann, 'Dignity: A Special Focus on Vulnerable Groups'; see as well C McCrudden, 'Human Dignity and Judicial Interpretation of Human Rights' (2008) 19 *European Journal of International Law* 655; J Habermas, 'The Concept of Human Dignity and the Realistic Utopia of Human Rights' (2010) 41 *Metaphilosophy* 464.

[45] International Covenant on Economic, Social and Cultural Rights (adopted 16 December, entered into force 3 January 1976) 993 UNTS 3 (hereinafter: ICESCR) and International Covenant on Civil and Political Rights (adopted 16 December 1966, entered into force 23 March 1976) 999 UNTS 171 [hereinafter: ICCPR].

The first chapter of the Charter of Fundamental Rights of the European Union is explicitly devoted to dignity. And as vague as the concept might be, the adoption of international legal instruments referring to human dignity and its protection, above all the rich body of international human rights law, as well as the subsequent judicial interpretations give essential contours and interlining to the notion of human dignity.[46]

Human rights thus centre upon the human being, entitling every individual equally to live a life in dignity. The effective realisation of human rights thus logically implies a broad conception of claims against all actors able to affect the dignity of a human person. As a minimum, these rights thus demand mutual tolerance or, as Kant formulated it, that 'Every human being has a legitimate claim to respect from his fellow human beings and is in turn bound to respect every other'.[47] The relentless beating by the husband or father constitutes as much an affront to human dignity, as does the maltreatment by a police official, school teacher or soldier. Negating this seems cynical and loses sight of the individuals concerned and their experience. Support of such a comprehensive protective effect of human rights can be found in modern moral and political theory. John Rawls, Charles Beitz and Alan Gewirth, to name but a few, base their theories on notions of equal and mutual private rights and/or duties.[48]

Moreover, the genealogy of human rights shows that a common postulate of all the different visions of human rights is their empowering and liberating character. Human rights seek to curb oppression, strengthen the powerless and end inequalities.[49] They do so by allowing the individual to become active. The individual does not have to wait for the realisation. Rights are claims which the individual can exercise to demand respect and, in case of disregard, explanation and accountability.[50] Accordingly,

[46] See for a list of treaties referring to human dignity, Clapham, *Human Rights Obligations of Non-State Actors* (n 6) 537–41.

[47] Immanuel Kant, *The Metaphysics of Morals* (n 38) 209; see for similar reasoning of a broad notion of human rights based on the foundational notion of human dignity, eg, C Jochnick, 'Confronting Impunity of Non-State Actors: New Fields for the Promotion of Human Rights' (1999) 21 *Human Rights Quarterly* 56, 60f; Clapham, *Human Rights Obligations of Non-State Actors* (n 6) 525ff; M Scheinin, 'Characteristics of Human Rights Norms' in C Krause and M Scheinin (eds), *International Protection of Human Rights: A Textbook*, 2nd edn (Turku/Åbo, Institute for Human Rights Åbo Akademi University, 2012) 19, 35ff; BH Weston, 'Human Rights', *Britannica*, Academic Edition, www.britannica.com/EBchecked/topic/275840/human-rights/11717/Additional-Reading; H Steiner, 'Some Characteristics of the Liberal Political Tradition' in H Steiner and P Alston, *International Human Rights in Context: Law, Politics, Morals* (Oxford, Clarendon Press, 1996) 187ff.

[48] A Fagan, *Human Rights—Confronting Myths and Misunderstandings* (Cheltenham, Edward Elgar Publishing, 2009) 136ff; SR Ratner, 'Corporations and Human Rights: A Theory of Legal Responsibility' (2001) 111 *Yale Law Journal* 443, 507ff; Clapham, *Human Rights in the Private Sphere* (n 3) 140ff.

[49] Lauren, *The Evolution of International Human Rights* (n 35).

[50] Jochnick, 'Confronting Impunity' (n 47) 60.

like two sides of the same coin, this right to respect entails the obligation to refrain from prejudicial behaviour. That rights logically implicate corresponding duties is neither new nor controversial. It is common understanding that to enjoy, assert or exercise a right means to have a claim against somebody else, be it a natural or legal person, a public authority or all of them. This logic obviously also applies to human rights.[51] Conceiving human rights as rights to an 'all-around' protection and regulating human relations in social, political, economic or cultural contexts, requires acknowledging that there might be more than just one duty-holder, and that their obligations might be different in scope and content.[52] One right does not necessarily entail one single correlative duty; nor is the rights-bearer necessarily confined to one single duty-holder. The follow-up question is of course, who can be considered to be a duty-bearer, and what is the required behaviour?[53] Since the values, interests and elements human rights seek to protect can be affected by state and non-state actors alike, an individual must thus have claims against all of them. The horizontal right-duty relationship is characterised by a special feature which is inherently lacking in the vertical application of human rights: the state confronted with a human rights claim can only invoke the legitimate exercise of limitation and derogation clauses to justify an interference. If a private party is confronted with a human rights claim, she might be able to counter with a human right herself. Such a clash of rights ultimately requires a balancing of conflicting interests, a task usually done by the legislator when drafting ordinary law.[54]

[51] M Nowak, 'Eight Reasons Why We Need a World Court of Human Rights' in G Alfredsson and others (eds), *International Human Rights Monitoring Mechanisms: Essays in Honour of Jakob TH Möller*, 2nd edn (Leiden/Boston, Martinus Nijhoff Publishers, 2009) 321; Scheinin, 'Characteristics of Human Rights Norms' (n 47) 19, 33ff; Fagan, *Human Rights* (n 48) 117ff; Donnelly, *Universal Human Rights* (n 36) 8.

[52] For the concept of an 'all-round effect' of human rights ('Rundumwirkung der Grundrechte'), see G and E Küchenhoff, *Allgemeine Staatslehre*, 7th edn (Stuttgart, Kohlhammerverlag, 1971) 55; see also M Nowak, *Politische Grundrechte* (Wien/New York, Springer-Verlag, 1988) 195ff.

[53] *cf* Martin Scheinin who conceives human rights as a complex multi-party structure relating to several subjects: 'Hence, any human right consists of a core element that relates to the primary relationship between the right holder and another, the duty-bearer, as well as one or more protective elements regulating the duty of third parties, usually state authorities, to ensure that the core element receives appropriate protection. Human rights are aggregates or bundles of binary relationships that exist as various combinations between at least three parties'; quoted from Scheinin, 'Characteristics of Human Rights Norms' (n 47) 34.

[54] Aharon Barak, 'Constitutional Human Rights and Private Law' in D Friedmann and D Barak-Erez (eds), *Human Rights in Private Law* (Oxford, Hart Publishing, 2001) 13, 17; D Oliver and J Fedtke, 'Human Rights and the Private Sphere—the Scope of the Project' in D Oliver and J Fedtke (eds), *Human Rights and the Private Sphere: A Comparative Study* (Abingdon/New York, Routledge-Cavendish, 2007) 18ff.

7.2.2 Human Rights as 'All-round' Protection

This perception of an 'all-round' effect of human rights is neither far-fetched nor revolutionary, and only requires a return to the very essence extracted from the different philosophical and ideological understandings of human rights, as well as a reconsideration of their origins and casting off of the pure Eurocentric liberal and positivist filters which eventually led to a historic and legal simplification of human rights as mere claims against the state.[55]

This essence, or in other words, the important common denominator of the diverse human rights visions which have evolved over time all around the world, is that these rights, regardless of their justification, are conceived as a means to challenge and tame power, be it political, economic or social, fight repression and reject 'the notion that the strong do what they can and the weak do what they must'.[56] Although the fathers of liberalism in their writings strongly emphasised the state, this logic of an all-round protection of human rights is not alien to European thinking and is reflected in the treatise on deontological ethics and natural law, above all by John Locke (1632–1704) and Immanuel Kant (1724–1804), who arguably played a seminal role for the following human rights movement.[57]

John Locke drew from the idea of a social contract already formulated by Hobbes, but his approach differed fundamentally from his fellow philosopher, who under the impression of the English Civil Wars of the 1640s conceived the state of nature, ie, the situation prior to the establishment of state power, as anarchic and wolfish, characterised by a constant 'war of all against all' where all men are egoistically defending their right to everything. To end this situation people have to unite and by means of a social contract delegate their power to the absolutist rule of the Leviathan which finally establishes peace and tolerance.[58] Locke not only rejected Hobbes' idea of the inherently destructive human nature, but also the totalitarian rule of the great Leviathan. In Locke's opinion, individuals are born equal and free in the pre-governmental state and endowed with natural rights. They are guided by reason which teaches them that 'no one ought to harm another in his life, health, liberty, or possessions.'[59] In the state of nature, 'every man hath a right to punish the

[55] See G Jellinek, *System der subjektiven öffentlichen Rechte*, 2nd edn (Tübingen, Mohr Siebeck, 1905) 94ff. See also Nowak, *Politische Grundrechte* (n 52) 63.
[56] Lauren, *The Evolution of International Human Rights* (n 35) 2.
[57] RG Steinhardt, 'Corporate Responsibility and the International Law of Human Rights: The New Lex Mercatoria' in Alston, *Non-State Actors and Human Rights* (n 8) 214.
[58] Thomas Hobbes, *Leviathan* (first published 1651).
[59] John Locke, *Two Treatises of Government* (first published 1690), book II, ch II.

offender, and be executioner of the law of nature'.[60] The accumulation of property leads to a situation of augmented social injustice which motivates human beings to consensually agree in a social contract to form a community and transfer their executive authority to enforce their natural rights to a newly established body politic. By surrendering this right to enforcement they do not, however, forgo their rights. On the contrary, the state, which now has the monopoly on the use of force, is obliged to protect these rights from any interference.[61] If the government fails to fulfil this contractual duty, it forfeits its legitimacy and may be dissolved by its people.[62] The very rationale behind the conclusion of the social contract thus lies in the realisation that individuals can interfere with the enjoyment of the natural rights of others and need a state to ensure coexistence in peace.[63]

That liberal theory devoted much attention on the risk of abuse of power by the state can be explained by the historical context in which those theories arose. John Locke, Thomas Hobbes (1588–1679), Jean-Jacques Rousseau[64] (1712–78), Immanuel Kant, John Stuart Mill (1806–73) and Montesquieu (1689–1755) were undeniably influenced by the events of their time, the cruel absolutist rule as well as decades of civil and religious wars.[65] Against this backdrop, in their quest for justice and human dignity, they indeed primarily reflected upon state reforms, legitimate rule, its purpose and objectives, and were considerably less attentive in formulating theories concerning the behaviour of non-state entities. However, these aspects did not pass unnoticed. They were well aware that other structures causing human suffering and oppression, such as economic exploitation, social suppression, gender violence, torture or intolerance existed and constituted threats to liberty.[66] Thus, they postulated a freedom of the individual to personal autonomy and self-realisation without any form of interference from outside, above all but not confined to the state, as the church, society and the individual himself can equally pose a threat to the realisation of liberty. Therefore, freedom is not limitless but has its intrinsic boundary which lies in the freedom of others and entitles each

[60] ibid.

[61] 'The great and chief end, therefore, of men's uniting into commonwealths, and putting themselves under government, is the preservation of their property'; see John Locke, *Two Treatises of Government*, book II, ch IX.

[62] ibid, book II, ch XIX.

[63] See also DM Chirwa, 'In Search of Philosophical Justifications and Suitable Models for the Horizontal Application of Human Rights' (2008) 8 *African Human Rights Law Journal* 297ff.

[64] Jean-Jacques Rousseau, *Discourse on Inequality* (first published 1754) and *Of The Social Contract, Or Principles of Political Right* (first published 1762).

[65] Jack Donnelly, *Universal Human Rights* (n 36) 85.

[66] Lauren, *The Evolution of International Human Rights* (n 35) 18.

individual to equal respect.[67] The importance of the state lies in its securing task, in keeping order and ensuring respect between the individuals. For this purpose it is endowed with an executive authority which makes the state not only the essential guardian of human rights responsible for their implementation and enforcement, but at the same time the primary threat.[68] Hence, these rights not only enable the individual to demand respect within private relations, but also shield against threats emanating from the state machinery by limiting governmental power.

In a nutshell, threats to the enjoyment of human rights thus can emanate from many different, not necessarily state, sources. However, the state, accordingly, does play a dual role. On the one hand, it is the original and primary guardian of human rights, as postulated by John Locke. On the other hand, the specific and immense power the modern state enjoys to fulfil its 'human rights preserving' task makes it inevitably also a significant threat to the enjoyment of human rights and fundamental freedoms. In order to contain this threat, the power of the state is constitutionally curbed by requiring it not to interfere arbitrarily with individuals' freedoms.[69] The fear of tyranny by powerful government prompted liberal theorists to emphasise strict limitations on state power, formulating negative rights and freedoms which ultimately found their way into the constitutions. This tendency was reinforced by legal positivism which developed in the eighteenth and nineteenth centuries, especially by the thoughts of Jeremy Bentham (1748–1832) and John Austin (1790–1859). Since the positivist school considers law as human construct, only rules expressly enacted in a state's legal process can be considered law. Thus, the idea of natural law and therewith natural rights was rejected as 'nonsense upon stilts';[70] only human rights explicitly granted by the state were consequently considered real rights. Such way of thought inevitably strengthens the important

[67] See Art IV Déclaration des Droits de l'Homme et du Citoyen 1789: 'La liberté consiste à pouvoir faire tout ce qui ne nuit pas à autrui: ainsi l'exercice des droits naturels de chaque homme n'a de bornes que celles qui assurent aux autres Membres de la Société, la jouissance de ces mêmes droits. Ces bornes ne peuvent être déterminées que par la Loi'; for literature see H Shue, *Basic Rights*, 2nd edn (Princeton NJ, Princeton University Press, 1996) 35ff; D Lubin, 'Just War and Human Rights' in C Beitz and LA Alexander (eds), *International Ethics* (Princeton NJ, Princeton University Press, 1985) 209: 'A human right, then, will be a right whose beneficiaries are all humans and whose obligors are all humans in a position to effect the right'; Nowak, *Introduction* (n 33) 10; Steiner, 'Some Characteristics of the Liberal Political Tradition' (n 47); Weston, 'Human Rights' (n 47).

[68] J Donnelly, *Universal Human Rights* (n 36) 33.

[69] M Goodhart, 'Human Rights and Non State Actors—Theoretical Puzzles' in G Andreopoulos and others (eds), *Non-State Actors in the Human Rights Universe* (Bloomfield CT, Kumarian Press, 2006) 25.

[70] Jeremy Bentham, *The Book of Fallacies* (1824): 'Right is a child of law; from real laws come real rights, but from imaginary laws, from laws of nature, come imaginary rights … Natural rights is simple nonsense: natural and imprescriptible rights, rhetorical nonsense—nonsense upon stilts'.

role of the state with regard to human rights. In this vein, the following wave of constitutionalism, set off by the French and American revolutions of the eighteenth century, as well as the subsequent bourgeois revolutions of the nineteenth century, made human rights legal rights, although under a different label.[71] These 'children of law' were formulated as pure 'hands-off' obligations of states owed to their citizens whose autonomy and liberty is to be shielded from governmental excesses. Hence, legal positivism coupled with a distorted liberal understanding of human rights and an emerging laissez-faire capitalist economy led to the dominant one-dimensional understanding of human rights: the ever-meddling and overbearing state considerably threatens the enjoyment of liberty and property, and thus must be bound to respect human rights. Consequently, since only the state is explicitly obliged to respect the rights of its citizens, only the state apparatus can violate them.[72]

This liberal conception of human rights, revolving around the sacrosanct private autonomy, led to the division of the world in a public sphere and inviolable private realms free from external restraints.[73] What happened within this private domain was considered to be beyond the state's protective reach. Human rights considerations were confined to the public sphere; not allowed to enter the bell jar of the private home. Thus the exploitation of workers and domestic violence as purely private matters warranted state indifference. However, it is obvious that such state abstention concerning family/private life was and is pure fiction. Liberal states, as it is their very purpose to guarantee life in harmony and peace, sought and seek to regulate private relations through family, matrimonial, divorce, custodial, property or inheritance laws, laws which were or still are highly discriminatory against women.[74]

7.3 THE PUBLIC/PRIVATE DIVIDE AS A BÊTE NOIRE

The public/private dichotomy, which as a liberal postulate appertains to the constitutional protection of human rights, and the concomitant exclusion of the non-state actor as human rights addressee, came under heavy fire from many different sides. Marxist and more recently feminist

[71] These 'children of law' were given wonderful names such as 'Grundrechte', civil rights, civil liberties, 'libertés publiques' or 'droits de l'homme et du citoyen'. The English term 'human rights' is far younger, and only since the Second World War has been on everyone's lips.

[72] See for instance Oliver and Fedtke, *The Scope of the Project* (n 54) 10 and 17.

[73] For the philosophical foundation of this strict separation between state and society, see GWF Hegel, 'Grundlinien der Philosophie des Rechts oder Naturrecht und Staatswissenschaft im Grundrisse' published in K Löwith and M Riedel (eds), *Hegel Studienausgabe* vol 2 (Frankfurt am Main/Hamburg, Fischer Bücherei, 1968).

[74] ibid, 21; Goodhart, 'Human Rights and Non State Actors' (n 69) 26.

theories, as well as human rights advocates, pointed out that the liberal conception based on natural law considerations wrongly assumed that all human beings were born free and equal. Reality, however, is characterised by major systemic discrepancies and disparities between the privileged and the underprivileged, between socially, economically and politically powerful men and continuously supressed women.[75]

Similar deliberations led John Stuart Mill, one of the most influential proponents of liberalism, to theorise on the limits of power exercised by the state, society or the individual over other individuals. In *On Liberty*, when elaborating the so-called 'harm principle' as basis for legitimate restrictions of liberty, Mill insisted that the principle is not only to be applied to relations between the government or society and the individual, but also horizontally, in relations among individual themselves, in particular in relationships between 'despotic' husbands and their wives, as well as between parents and their children.[76] His considerations, however, were not reflected in subsequent human rights law. This narrow conception of human rights law revolving around the sanctuary of individual autonomy and demanding a strict public/private divide therefore appears not to be receptive to the 'private' suffering of women, children or (domestic) workers.

Moreover, the dividing line between the public and private realms appears to be constantly shifting, tugged by different ideologies. A significant shift took place with the emergence of the welfare state, wherein the state assumed the main responsibility for the promotion and protection of its citizens' social and economic wellbeing. This development not only led to a strong regulatory authority of the state within the respective spheres; the state step-by-step started to administer sectors which had been in private hand but were now considered to be essential for a well-functioning society. Neoliberalism, as it is understood today, demanding maximum flexibility and zero bureaucracy, called for an extensive reversal of these achievements. The subsequent deregulation and the privatisation of public services and utilities such as roads, 'public' transport, electricity, water, education, health care or the administration of detention facilities caused another shift. These constant changes exemplify quite clearly how arbitrary the lines between public and private realms are, and expose another

[75] See above all C Chinkin, 'A Critique of the Public/Private Dimension' (1999) 10 *European Journal of International Law* 387, 392; H Charlesworth, C Chinkin and S Wright, 'Feminist Approaches to International Law' (1991) 85 *American Journal of International Law* 613; R Copelon, 'Recognizing the Egregious in the Everyday: Domestic Violence as Torture' (1993) 25 *Columbia Human Rights Law Review* 291; C Romany, 'Women as Aliens: A Feminist Critique of The Public/Private Distinction in International Human Rights Law' (1993) 6 *Harvard Human Rights Journal* 87; R Cook (ed), *Human Rights of Women: National and International Perspectives* (Philadelphia PA, University of Pennsylvania Press, 1994).

[76] John Stuart Mill, *On Liberty* (first published 1859), ch V, Applications.

essential issue which is of peculiar relevance with regard to specifically human rights-sensitive matters such as prison administration: that there has been a change in the nature of the service provider, from public to private, must not be paralleled by the loss of an individual's human rights protection.[77] Adherence to the state-centric alignment of human rights law and its enforcement mechanisms, however, significantly obstructs the access to justice for victims of 'privatised' human rights violations. In addition, this deferral of tasks into the private sphere is accompanied by a change in the tripartite obligations of states[78] whereas its obligation to respect appears to cease, its obligation to protect is increased to a more stringent supervisory responsibility over the private provider when executing these human rights sensitive activities.[79] Thus the state cannot fully divest itself of its general positive obligations to protect and progressively work towards a full realisation of human rights.[80]

These considerations by no means aim to question the protection of private life. Its bedrock significance, as guaranteed in major human rights treaties, goes without saying. In a world in which Google, Amazon and Facebook can compile enormous libraries of personal user data, and reproductive rights of women or LGBTI rights are being continually challenged, the right to privacy and individual autonomy are of utmost importance.[81] What must be reconsidered is the distinction between public and private domains, which confines human rights to the relationship between the individual and the state in order to accept private actors as bearers of human rights obligations. The traditional kind of understanding still seems to inform governmental thinking, with the effect that private life, and with it issues such as family violence, femicide in all its forms, including honour

[77] For a good insight in the issue of privatisation from the human rights perspective, see K Feyter and F Gómez Isa (eds), *Privatisation and Human Rights in the Age of Globalisation* (Antwerp/Oxford, Intersentia, 2005).

[78] That states' human rights obligation is of tripartite nature not only encompassing a duty to respect but also an obligation to progressively ensure the full realisation of human rights is well-established in human rights law, confirmed by all relevant treaty monitoring bodies, see General Comment 31 of the Human Rights Committee or diverse General Comments of the ICESCR Committee (see n 124, below). See also A Eide, 'Report on the Right to Adequate Food as a Human Right', UN Doc E/CN 4/Sub 2/1987/23; MM Sepúlveda, *The Nature of the Obligations Under the International Covenant on Economic, Social and Cultural Rights* (Utrecht, Intersentia, 2003); M Ssenyonjo, *Economic, Social and Cultural Rights in International Law* (Oxford, Hart Publishing, 2009) 109ff.

[79] A McBeth, 'Privatising Human Rights: What Happens to the State's Human Rights Duties When Services are Privatised?' (2004) 5 *Melbourne Journal of International Law* 133.

[80] *Costello-Roberts v United Kingdom* App no 13134/87 (ECtHR, 25 March 1993) establishing in para 27 that 'the State cannot absolve itself from responsibility by delegating its obligations to private bodies or individuals'.

[81] Art 12 UDHR; Art 17 ICCPR; Art 11 American Convention on Human Rights (adopted 22 November 1969, entered into force 18 July 1978); Art 8 ECHR; Arts 7 and 8 Charter of Fundamental Rights of the European Union (adopted in Nice in 2000); Data Protection Directive 95/46/EC; Directive on Privacy and Electronic Communications Directive 2002/58/EC (as amended by Directive 2006/24/EC and Directive 2009/136/EC).

killings, forced marriage and female genital mutilation, or domestic workers are excluded from state intervention.[82]

Thus, the public/private divide should, as has been suggested by some scholars, be reduced to a merely 'explanatory' tool to establish whether a right has been violated. Whereas in private relations, two opposite rights might collide, such as the right to information with the right to privacy, in the public sphere, the state will not be able to invoke a human right but merely be able to rely on secrecy due to specific considerations.[83]

7.4 DAVID VS GOLIATH—THE ISSUE OF POWER IMBALANCE AND HUMAN RIGHTS

The struggle against power inequalities runs like a common thread through the history of human rights. These power asymmetries had and have different roots. Whereas in India, until the era of British rule in the nineteenth century, these imbalances stemmed from powerful non-state actors, the bourgeoisie of the eighteenth century revolutions in Europe was in their quest for justice primarily striving for political participation and the containment of state authority. The anti-slavery movements aimed at liberating slaves from their masters, and industrialisation was accompanied by demands of exploited workers for labour rights. Human rights thus always centred on the empowerment of the rights-holder.

Hence the notion of justice underlying the idea of human rights is closely linked to the need to limit power, be it political, legal, social, cultural or economic; thus, the human rights system can be seen as a tool which shall protect the weaker against the strong.[84] Indeed, the supreme power of the state with its legal and political tools, the legislative authority, courts and police force differs from the factual, socio-economic power of non-state actors. This might also explain why at the inception of the international human rights movement, the focus was on the state. International institutions were established to supervise the states and hold them accountable in case of failure to discharge their obligations properly.

[82] Chinkin, *A Critique of the Public/Private Dimension* (n 75) 393; see also thematic reports of the Special Rapporteur on violence against women, for instance: UN Doc A/HRC/20/16 (of 23 May 2012) on gender-related killings as the extreme manifestation of existing forms of violence against women, para 103 identifying 'the blindness to structural inequalities and the complex intersecting relations of power in the public and private spheres' as 'the root causes of sex and gender discrimination'.

[83] This suggestion is borrowed primarily form Andrew Clapham. The state will only be able to invoke the claim of secrecy if provided for by law and justified by a legitimate purpose, such as national security or rights of others. See Clapham, *Human Rights in the Private Sphere* (n 3) 134f.

[84] See in general on centrality of power imbalances F Raday, 'Privatising Human Rights and the Abuse of Power' (2000) 13 *Canadian Journal of Law and Jurisprudence* 103.

It seems that international lawyers assumed that this supervision would be enough to guarantee the wellbeing of individuals.

The significant power imbalances the international community faces today reveal that this old assumption cannot be maintained. The substantial redistribution of power due to the emergence of potent and influential non-state actors able to compete in strength with states or even dwarf them has been carefully observed, and is not a novelty. These developments did not happen overnight and are far more than a simple, accidental by-product of globalisation. Neo-liberal policies questioning the achievements of the welfare state and demanding economic flexibility quite intentionally foresaw deregulation as well as outsourcing of state competencies to non-state entities. With these competencies goes power, and with power goes the ability to control. These developments led some commentators to proclaim the downfall of the sacrosanct Westphalian structures of the international legal order due to the demise of sovereign states or, less dramatic and probably more accurate, the 'medievalisation' of international relations.[85] Accordingly, similar to the feudalist medieval Europe, we are confronted with an order in which power is distributed among various important actors with states having only partial capacity to control.[86] Neither is the realisation that these developments crucially affect the effective protection and realisation of human rights breaking news.

Many factors are said to have contributed to this development, above all the driving forces of globalisation. This highly complex, opaque and elusive/intangible phenomenon of interrelated cross-border processes of integration and growing interdependence might be best described by several of its components, such as privatisation, trade liberalisation and economic deregulation, increasing trans-border transactions as well as sociocultural exchange owing to the technology revolution as well as rising migration and tourism and the mushrooming of potent national and transnational corporations (TNCs) with impressive resources at hand increasingly influencing international and domestic state policies.[87] Each of these aspects, above all the privatisation of sectors such as health, water, education, prison and security services, the explosion of TNCs as well as the liberalisation of trade and the race to attract foreign investment,

[85] *cf* Reinisch, 'The Changing International Legal Framework' (n 23) 74: see literature listed in fn 190; JA Hessbruegge, 'Human Rights Violations Arising From Conduct of Non-State Actors' (2005) 11 *Buffalo Human Rights Law Review* 21.

[86] Hessbruegge, 'Human Rights Violations' (n 85) 21.

[87] For a more detailed description of this global process see D Shelton, 'Protecting Human Rights in a Globalized World' (2002) 25 *Boston College International and Comparative Law Review* 273; see also Reinisch, 'The Changing International Legal Framework' (n 23) 76f; see also IMF, 'Globalization: A Brief Overview' (May 2008), www.imf.org/external/np/exr/ib/2008/053008.htm.

undeniably afflict the dominant conservative premise of international human rights law.[88] Not only are the boundaries between governmental and non-governmental spheres constantly shifting, but new, obscure power relations evolve without a corresponding accountability mechanism. Moreover, the constantly expanding functions of international organisations now covering a wide range of state-like tasks, which encroach into particularly human rights-sensitive areas, and the increase of internal armed conflicts with strong armed rebel groups capable of controlling a considerable part of territory and population as well as committing gross and systematic human rights violations have also been conducive to this new situation of international relations. What is crucial is that these perceived structural changes question the legitimacy of the traditional one-dimensional, state-centric paradigm of international human rights law and dramatically dismantle what essentially might have actually always been a theoretical construction, the omnipotence of states.[89]

7.5 THE RELUCTANCE TO ENFORCE HUMAN RIGHTS AGAINST NON-STATE ACTORS

7.5.1 International Law Addressing Threats to Human Rights from Non-State Actors

Both international law and international human rights law have for quite some time paid attention to the destructive potential of private actors and contemplated, in varying degrees and forms, the regulation of private behaviour. A mixture of humanitarian, political and economic considerations, for instance, motived states to tackle the issue of slavery and serfdom in the late eighteenth century.[90] Already in 1815, at the Vienna Congress,

[88] See for the negative impact of the business sector on human rights J Ruggie, 'Corporations and human rights: a survey of the scope and patterns of alleged corporate-related human rights abuse', UN Doc A/HRC/8/5/Add 2 of 23 May 2008. Pursuant to ILO estimates (see n 100 below), some economic sectors, such as agriculture, construction, manufacturing and domestic work, seem to be particularly susceptible to forced labour practices; Human Rights Watch reports highlight the deplorable situation in the extractive industry: Human Rights Watch, 'Hear No Evil—Forced Labor and Corporate Responsibility in Eritrea's Mining Sector' of 15 January 2013, 'Striking Oil, Striking Workers—Violations of Labor Rights in Kazakhstan's Oil Sector' of 10 September 2012, 'A Poisonous Mix—Child Labor, Mercury, and Artisanal Gold Mining in Mali' of 6 December 2011. The electronics industry and the garment sector are also well-known for their human rights violations, see eg, BBC, 'Foxconn admits labour violation at China factory', www.bbc.co.uk/news/business-24486684; Clean Clothes Campaign (CCC) and the Centre for Research on Multinational Corporations (SOMO), 'Fatal Fashion—Analysis of Recent Factory Fires in Pakistan and Bangladesh', March 2013, www.cleanclothes.org/resources/publications.

[89] Jochnick, 'Confronting Impunity' (n 47) 63.

[90] See F Ermacora, *Menschenrechte in der sich wandelnden Welt*, vol I (Wien, Verlag der Österreichische Akademie der Wissenschaften, 1974) 171–75, 254ff.

a handful of states declared to abolish slavery and slave trade.[91] Many multi- and bilateral initiatives finally led to the adoption of the Slavery Convention of 1926 and its Supplementary Convention of 1956 aiming at the abolition of these most deplorable practices of economic exploitation of human beings by fellow human beings.[92] British anti-slavery efforts even led to the establishment of special international courts to enforce bilateral treaties banning slave trade.[93] Hence, the prohibition of slavery, serfdom and forced labour, which as a classical civil right can be found in all major human rights treaties, was never aimed at restricting the state, but private behaviour, thus having a clear horizontal effect.[94] The language of the two treaties, however, indicates its indirect nature. Whereas the 1926 Slavery Convention requires contracting parties to 'prevent and suppress the slave trade' as well as to 'bring about, progressively and as soon as possible, the complete abolition of slavery in all its forms', the Supplementary Convention adds another state obligation, namely the criminalisation of slave trade and slavery.[95] For private duties to arise, states have to enact corresponding legislation.

Article 3 of the Genocide Convention of 1948 goes further and acknowledges that genocide, as an international crime, can be committed by individuals not affiliated to the state machinery, thus directly imposing on them a private duty to refrain from committing genocide.[96] In the same

[91] Likewise instrumental in the early fight against slave trade and slavery was the Quintuple Treaty (London 1841/42), with 26 states parties.

[92] Convention to Suppress the Slave Trade and Slavery (adopted on 25 September 1926, entered into force on 9 March 1927) and United Nations Supplementary Convention on the Abolition of Slavery, the Slave Trade, and Institutions and Practices Similar to Slavery (adopted on 7 September 1956, entered into force on 30 April 1957) 266 UNTS 3.

[93] See JS Martinez, 'Anti-Slavery Courts and the Dawn of International Human Rights Law' (2008) 117 *Yale Law Journal* 550, 557ff. JS Martinez, *The Slove Trade and the Origins of International Human Rights Law* (Oxford, Oxford University Press, 2012).

[94] As much as slavery was primarily a private phenomenon, facilitated by the state, contemporary forms of slavery, including bonded labour, serfdom, forced marriages, forced prostitution or domestic servitude, trafficking of human beings as well as forced and child labour continue to be predominately deployed by private actors, happening behind closed doors, in the private home or corporations, and thus hard to suppress. According to ILO estimates, almost 19 million victims of modern forms of slavery and forced labour are exploited by private individuals or enterprises, compared to over 2 million by the state or rebel groups; see International Labour Organization, *ILO Global Estimate of Forced Labour 2012: Results and Methodology* (Geneva, ILO, 2012) available online at ilo.org.

[95] See Arts 3(1) and 6(1) stating that slave trade and slavery 'shall be a criminal offence under the laws of the States Parties to this Convention and persons convicted thereof shall be liable to very severe penalties'; Ratner suggests that by authorising state parties to prosecute or punish individuals who have committed egregious abuses such as slavery, torture or enforced disappearances, international law actually directly obliges them to abstain from this internationally condemned conduct; see Ratner, 'Corporations and Human Rights' (n 48) 467.

[96] Convention for the Prevention and Punishment of the Crime of Genocide (adopted on 9 December 1948, entered into force on 12 January 1951) 78 UNTS 277, Art 1: 'The Contracting Parties confirm that genocide, whether committed in time of peace or in time of war, is a crime under international law which they undertake to prevent and to punish' and Art IV: 'Persons committing genocide or any of the other acts enumerated in article III shall be punished, whether they are constitutionally responsible rulers, public officials or private individuals.'

explicit vein, the Apartheid Convention of 1973 declares apartheid practices to constitute international crimes for which individuals, regardless of whether they acted as state agents or not, can be held internationally accountable. As with piracy, however, the enforcement of these crimes was left to states.

Only one day after the adoption of the Genocide Convention, on 10 December 1948, the Universal Declaration of Human Rights was proclaimed 'as a common standard of achievement for all peoples and all nations, to the end that every individual and every organ of society … shall strive by teaching and education to promote respect for these rights and freedoms'. The document contains essentially a long list of civil, political, economic, social and cultural rights without referring to the corresponding duty-bearers explicitly. Such an approach can be explained by the fact that since declarations are of a purely proclamatory nature with no intention of being binding for anyone, a reference to duty bearers was omitted.[97] Then again, this list of entitlements can be understood as providing for claims towards all possible abusers.[98] Article 1, clearly inspired by Kant's notion of human dignity, could support such a reading, as it seems to recognise mutual respect demanding that all human beings 'should act towards one another in a spirit of brotherhood'. The last of the 30 articles stipulates that 'nothing in this Declaration may be interpreted as implying for any State, group or person any right to engage in any activity or to perform any act aimed at the destruction of any of the rights and freedoms set forth herein'.[99] The wording of the Declaration strongly suggests that the drafters drew from moral philosophy with its demand of reciprocal tolerance and forbearance, and were well aware of the dangers coming from the private side, thus accepting the relevance of horizontal duties. Throughout the whole drafting process, the drafting commission of the UN Commission on Human Rights stewed over the inclusion of private duties which, only some months earlier, had been accepted by the Latin American countries and the United States in a

[97] *cf* M Hakimi, 'State Bystander Responsibility' (2010) 21 *European Journal of International Law* 341, 346.

[98] In support of such a view see JJ Paust, 'The Other Side of Right: Private Duties Under Human Rights Law' (1992) 5 *Harvard Human Rights Journal* 51.

[99] See also Art 5 ICCPR and Art 17 ECHR: 'Nothing in this Convention may be interpreted as implying for any State, group or person any right to engage in any activity or perform any act aimed at the destruction of any of the rights and freedoms set forth herein or at their limitation to a greater extent than is provided for in the Convention'. See also Clapham, *Human Rights in the Private Sphere* (n 3) 184ff in favour of the view that Art 17 ECHR provides for private duties to respect the ECHR rights. Likewise, Paust considers both provisions as implicitly providing for correlative duties of non-state actors not to limit the rights of others, see JJ Paust,'Human Rights Responsibilities of Private Corporations' (2002) 35 *Vanderbilt Journal of Transnational Law* 801, 813.

very straightforward way.[100] The American Declaration of the Rights and Duties of Man of May 1948, as the title suggests, not only formulates rights but devotes a whole chapter to duties, some of them demanding respect of human rights of others, whereas another category provides for duties owed by the individual to the community or the state, such as to obey the law.[101] The preamble, like the Universal Declaration, requires individuals to 'conduct themselves as brothers one to another' and in general explains the importance of duties: 'The fulfillment of duty by each individual is a prerequisite to the rights of all. Rights and duties are interrelated in every social and political activity of man. While rights exalt individual liberty, duties express the dignity of that liberty.'

The dangerous potential of private duties owed to the state, giving the government a justification to limit human rights, seems to have convinced the drafting commission of the Universal Declaration to reduce the duty-language to a minimum. Only Article 29(1) UDHR makes an explicit reference by stating that '[e]veryone has duties to the community in which alone the free and full development of his personality is possible'. The imposition of horizontal duties, which the drafters considered essential for the realisation of a peaceful and functioning society, was consequently left to the domestic legislator.[102] Hence, the second paragraph of Article 29 was formulated as follows:

> In the exercise of his rights and freedoms, everyone shall be subject only to such limitations as are determined by law solely for the purpose of securing due recognition and respect for the rights and freedoms of others and of meeting the just requirements of morality, public order and the general welfare in a democratic society.

7.5.2 The State as the Primary Guardian of Human Rights; or How Locke's Wish Came True

When adopting the major human rights treaties, the international community seems, at least to a large extent, to have embraced this approach

[100] On the considerations, negotiations and respective drafts with regard to the inclusion of private duties, see J Morsink, *The Universal Declaration of Human Rights: Origins, Drafting, and Intent* (Philadelphia PA, University of Pennsylvania Press, 1999) 239–80; GS Alfredsson and A Eide, *The Universal Declaration of Human Rights: A Common Standard of Achievement* (Leiden/Boston, Martinus Nijhoff Publishers, 1999); as well as Knox, 'Horizontal Human Rights Law' (n 33) 4ff.

[101] American Declaration of the Rights and Duties of Man (adopted by the Ninth International Conference of American States in 1948 reprinted in Basic Documents Pertaining to Human Rights in the Inter-American System OEA/Ser L V/II 82 Doc 6 Rev 1 at 17 of 1992) ch 2. This concept of rights and duties was also adopted in the African Charter of Human and Peoples' Rights, see nn 140–42 below and accompanying text.

[102] John H Knox aptly uses the label 'converse' duties for vertically aligned private duties, the individual owes to the state and 'correlative' duties for the second category; see Knox, 'Horizontal Human Rights Law' (n 33).

of silence with regard to private duties. Thus international human rights treaty law, having proclaimed an impressive list of human rights in a fairly general manner, strongly relies on the state with regard to their implementation and enforcement, assuming for itself primarily a supervising role.[103] Almost exclusively, international human rights treaties impose obligations on the state to implement and enforce the enshrined human rights norms. This state-centric focus is partially due to the still sacrosanct sovereignty of states which are not yet inclined to transfer their regulating competences to the international community, as well as the persistently lingering narrow conception of human rights as claims against the state, but has also quite pragmatic reasons. States are in principle considered to be better equipped to place, tailor, and enforce these rights and their corresponding private duties; being closer to the people concerned, knowing the economic, social and cultural circumstance within its boundaries, and ideally democratically legitimised as well as politically accountable, the primary reliance on the state is well justified. Moreover, the nation-state usually disposes of resources the international community can only dream of. Therefore, international law leaves this task to states and confines itself to regulate non-state actor behaviour through indirect horizontal obligations requiring the state to intervene, through domestic legislation and other appropriate measures.

That the state draws to a large extent its raison d'être from the 'preservation' of human rights, as a Lockean postulate which pervaded political philosophy, is not new, and today is well-established. The concrete content and scope of the obligation, however, is not unambiguous, since a general comprehensive conception is missing. The fragmented landscape of human rights treaties formulating the obligation to protect in different ways and the treaty monitoring bodies, which further elaborated and specified it, provide for a complex web of measures. Additionally, international legal doctrine seems to be still to some extent split over the question whether such an obligation might be applicable with regard to all human rights or not. Whereas some contend that in principle every right can generate such an obligation, others see inherent limits, as some rights are purely directed against the state, such as the right to fair trial or the right to vote.[104]

103 Nowak, *CCPR Commentary* (n 30) 28.

104 See Human Rights Committee, General Comment 31, para 8 stating that the obligation to protect only exists with regard to the 'Covenant rights in so far as they are amenable to application between private persons or entities'; see Nowak, *CCPR Commentary* (n 30) 39; Hessbruegge, 'Human Rights Violations' (n 85) 71ff; Monica Hakimi argues that the treaty bodies' practice is inconsistent and suggests that '[states] must protect only against conduct that: (1) causes serious physical or psychological harm; or (2) affects people because they belong to a vulnerable group' see Hakimi, 'State Bystander Responsibility' (n 97) 367.

It is safe to assume that the obligation to protect from abuses by private parties in general requires positive action by the state, both preventive and remedial. In other words, the state is made responsible for just standing by if it could intervene. However, the state will not always be required to act, since this would be on the one hand too burdensome for the state, and could on the other hand lead to an over-intrusive state machinery. Hence, this obligation is conceived to be one of conduct rather than of result, requiring the state to discharge it with due diligence.[105] Only if the state knows or ought to have known of a real risk to the enjoyment of a human right, and fails to take all reasonable and appropriate measures, does it violate its obligation to protect.[106]

This due diligence obligation of states to protect human rights against non-governmental threats and abuses thus indicates what positive, regulatory action in the private sphere is required by the state. Many international lawyers loyal to the purely state-centric alignment of international and human rights law contend that private threats to the enjoyment of human rights can only be tackled through the regime of state responsibility, since non-state actors are not and cannot be bound to abide by human rights. Hence, in order to be successful, a human rights claim must prove that the behaviour of the non-state actor can be attributed to the state pursuant to the ILC Articles on State Responsibility. According to this attribution regime, states can only under certain conditions, if exercising governmental power and authority even if the non-state actor exceeds this authority, be held accountable for activities of private actors. Essentially, the attributed conduct is regarded as governmental conduct.[107] In case of purely non-governmental activities, not attributable to the state via the ILC Articles, one will have to show that the state failed to discharge its obligation to protect.

On the other hand, this due diligence doctrine does implicitly recognise that non-state actor behaviour can be detrimental to human rights and must be regulated.[108] To formulate it more strongly, this obligation

[105] *Velásquez Rodríguez v Honduras*, Judgment of 29 July 1988, Inter-American Court of Human Rights, Series C No 4 (1988); see also Hakimi, 'State Bystander Responsibility' (n 97); Kälin and Künzli, *The Law of International Human Rights Protection* (n 3) 106.

[106] *Osman v UK* ECHR 1998–VIII 3124 [116].

[107] International Law Commission, 'Draft Articles on Responsibility of States for Internationally Wrongful Acts' 2001 *Yearbook of the International Law Commission*, vol II, Pt 2, Arts 5, 7, 8, 10 and 11.

[108] 'International human rights law requires a state to take measures—such as by legislation and administrative practices—to control, regulate, investigate and prosecute actions by non-state actors that violate the human rights of those within the territory of that state. These actions by non-state actors do not have to be attributed to the state, rather this responsibility is part of the state's obligation to exercise due diligence to protect the rights of all persons in a state's territory': quote taken from R McCorquodale and P Simons, 'Responsibility Beyond Borders: State Responsibility for Extraterritorial Violations by Corporations of International Human Rights Law' (2007) 70 *Modern Law Review* 599, 618.

presupposes that non-state actors are bound to respect human rights or must be obliged to and sheds light on how the international community expects private actors to interact.[109]

All major human rights treaties endorse the obligation to protect human rights against interference from non-governmental actors in different degrees of specification. Although in their preamble the two International Covenants recognise 'that the individual, having duties to other individuals and to the community to which he belongs, is under a responsibility to strive for the promotion and observance of the rights recognized in the present Covenant',[110] Article 2 of the International Covenant on Civil and Political Rights formulates only obligations for the states parties requiring them 'to respect and to ensure to all individuals within its territory and subject to its jurisdiction the rights recognized in the present Covenant'.[111] This obligation to ensure is generally understood as encompassing positive duties, including the obligation to protect human rights from non-state actors. Interestingly, the third paragraph of the very same article proscribes a right to 'effective remedy, notwithstanding that the violation has been committed by persons acting in an official capacity' and hence seems to recognise that violations can emanate from non-governmental, purely private behaviour.[112]

The importance of the obligation to protect was reaffirmed by the Human Rights Committee stating that

> the positive obligations on States Parties to ensure Covenant rights will only be fully discharged if individuals are protected by the State, not just against violations of Covenant rights by its agents, but also against acts committed by private persons or entities that would impair the enjoyment of Covenant rights in so far as they are amenable to application between private persons or entities. There may be circumstances in which a failure to ensure Covenant rights as required by article 2 [ICCPR] would give rise to violations by States Parties of

109 See Clapham, *Human Rights Obligations of Non-State Actors* (n 6) 347; Nicola Jägers, 'UN Guiding Principles on Business and Human Rights: Making Headway Towards Real Corporate Accountability?' (2011) 29 *Netherlands Quarterly of Human Rights* 159, 161.

110 For Paust, this formulation is understood as an acknowledgement of a private duty to respect the human rights of others, see Paust, 'Human Rights Responsibilities of Private Corporations' (n 99) 813.

111 Art 2(1) ICCPR.

112 See also Art 13 ECHR: 'Everyone whose rights and freedoms as set forth in this Convention are violated shall have an effective remedy before a national authority notwithstanding that the violation has been committed by persons acting in an official capacity.' See Nowak, *CCPR Commentary* (n 30) 40; the UN Basic Principles and Guidelines on the Right to a Remedy and Reparation for Victims of Gross Violations of International Human Rights Law and Serious Violations of International Humanitarian Law adopted by the UN General Assembly in 2005 seem to rely on the same conclusion. Pursuant to para 15, persons, legal persons and other entities can be found liable for reparations for harm suffered; hence, it seems to implicitly accept that non-state entities can violate human rights; see UN Doc A/RES/60/147 (adopted on 16 December 2005) (hereinafter Van Boven/Bassiouni Guidlines).

those rights, as a result of States Parties' permitting or failing to take appropriate measures or to exercise due diligence to prevent, punish, investigate or redress the harm caused by such acts by private persons or entities.[113]

In addition, some specific ICCPR rights explicitly demand for 'the protection of the law'.[114] Similar general obligations are enshrined in the Convention on the Rights of the Child, the European Convention on Human Rights and its American counterpart.[115] The weaker wording employed in the operative article of the International Covenant on Economic, Social and Cultural Rights reminiscent of the deep ideological schism during the Cold War requires states to 'take steps with a view to achieving progressively the full realization of the rights recognized in the present Covenant by all appropriate means, including particularly the adoption of legislative measures' and is generally also considered to generate an obligation to protect.[116] The two UN anti-discrimination conventions address the regulation of private conduct in an even more conscious and confident way. The Convention on the Elimination of All Forms of Racial Discrimination, recognising that discrimination takes place in the 'political, economic, social, cultural or any other field of public life', requires each state party 'to prevent, prohibit and eradicate all practices of this nature in territories under their jurisdiction'.[117] Article 5(b) of the Convention stipulates that the right to security of person demands 'protection by the State against violence or bodily harm, whether inflicted by government officials or by any individual group or institution'. In the same paragraph, the CERD explicitly extends its protective net deep into the private sphere by requiring governments to regulate private behaviour

[113] Human Rights Committee, General Comment 31, 'The Nature of the General Legal Obligation Imposed on States Parties to the Covenant', UN Doc CCPR/21/Rev 1/Add13 (2004), para 8. In the very same paragraph, the Committee held that the ICCPR itself did not impose obligations on non-governmental actors directly without however in any way suggesting that human rights obligations by non-state actor were incompatible with international (human rights) law: 'The article 2, paragraph 1, obligations are binding on States [Parties] and do not, as such, have direct horizontal effect as a matter of international law. The Covenant cannot be viewed as a substitute for domestic criminal or civil law.'

[114] Arts 6 (1), 9(1), 17(2), 23, 24 and 27 ICCPR.

[115] Art 1 ECHR: 'The High Contracting Parties shall secure to everyone within their jurisdiction the rights and freedoms defined in Section I of this Convention'; Art 1(1) American Convention on Human Rights (adopted on 22 November 1969, entered in force on 18 July 1978): 'The States Parties to this Convention undertake to respect the rights and freedoms recognized herein and to ensure to all persons subject to their jurisdiction the free and full exercise of those rights and freedoms'; see also Art 2 Convention on the Rights of the Child (adopted on 20 November 1989, entered into force on 2 September 1990) 1577 UNTS 3.

[116] Art 2 ICESCR; see also the General Comments of the Committee on Economic, Social and Cultural Rights as listed in n 124 below.

[117] International Convention on the Elimination of All Forms of Racial Discrimination (adopted on 21 December 1965, entered into force on 4 January 1969) 660 UNTS 195 [hereinafter CERD].

with regard to 'access to any place or service intended for use by the general public, such as transport, hotels, restaurants, cafes, theatres and parks'. The Convention on the Elimination of All Forms of Discrimination Against Women similarly extends to 'the political, economic, social, cultural, civil or any other field' and elaborates on the measures to be taken by states parties, such as the adoption of appropriate legislative and other measures, prohibiting all discrimination against women, aiming at the elimination of discrimination against women by any person, organisation or enterprise, in general and in more concrete terms.[118] The EU's anti-discrimination directives likewise give some insight into how far private behaviour should be regulated.[119]

In this context of positive obligations, the comprehensive normative framework of labour standards developed by the International Labour Organization (ILO) must also not go unmentioned. The ILO has adopted 189 Conventions prescribing labour standards which cover issues such as forced and child labour, worker's rights, occupational safety and health, and which in a fairly specified manner oblige states to adopt corresponding national legislation.[120] These highly detailed provisions thus show how companies are expected to perform towards their employees.

These provisions are either formulated quite vaguely, giving states a considerable margin of appreciation to implement human rights treaties and establish the essential domestic infrastructure to protect against private threats, or they are already to some extent specified, obliging the state to take particular legislative or other measures to regulate private

[118] International Covenant on Economic, Social and Cultural Rights (adopted on 16 December, entered into force 3 January 1976) 993 UNTS 3 [hereinafter ICESCR]; Convention to Eliminate All Forms of Discrimination Against Women (adopted on 18 December 1979; entered into force on 3 September 1981) 1249 UNTS 13 [hereinafter CEDAW], see eg, Arts 2 (drafted in general terms), 15 (dealing with equality of women with regard to economic and social life requiring states to take all appropriate measures with regard to the rights to bank loans, mortgages and other forms of financial credit or participation in recreational activities, sports and all aspects of cultural life) or 16 (dealing with matters concerning marriage and family life).

[119] See Art 19 Treaty on the Functioning of the European Union granting the EU the power to combat discrimination based on sex, racial or ethnic origin, religion or belief, disability, age or sexual orientation. See Council Directive 2000/43/EC of 29 June 2000 implementing the principle of equal treatment between persons irrespective of racial or ethnic origin; Council Directive 2000/78/EC of 27 November 2000 establishing a general framework for equal treatment in employment and occupation; Council Directive 2004/113/EC of 13 December 2004 implementing the principle of equal treatment between men and women in the access to and supply of goods and services; Directive 2006/54/EC of the European Parliament and of the Council of 5 July 2006 on the implementation of the principle of equal opportunities and equal treatment of men and women in matters of employment and occupation (recast).

[120] See above all the eight 'fundamental conventions' on the freedom of association and the effective recognition of the right to collective bargaining, the elimination of all forms of forced or compulsory labour, the effective abolition of child labour, and the elimination of discrimination in respect of employment and occupation.

behaviour. Moreover, over the years, the treaty-monitoring bodies in their decisions, general comments or recommendations, final views or concluding observations affirm this positive state obligation with its horizontal effect, fleshing it out substantially, and confirm the destructive potential of non-state actors. Accordingly, states in general are required to take appropriate legislative, administrative and other measures to prevent violations and in case of a violation, to investigate promptly, thoroughly, impartially and effectively in order to identify the possible perpetrators and, if appropriate, bring them to justice.[121] Moreover, states have to provide the person claiming to be the victim of the human rights violation with equal access to effective remedies, including adequate reparation.[122] Whereas other treaty bodies have concentrated on the state's obligations to protect, the Committee on Economic, Social and Cultural Rights in its General Comments on a number of occasions went even further and addressed the responsibility of third parties, especially the private business sector, with regard to the effective realisation of socio-economic rights. Recently it has been doing so under the heading 'obligations of actors other than states'.[123] With regard to the right to food, it held that

> [w]hile only States are parties to the Covenant and are thus ultimately accountable for compliance with it, all members of society—individuals, families, local communities, non-governmental organizations, civil society organizations, as

[121] See Art 3 International Convention for the Protection of All Persons from Enforced Disappearance (adopted on 20 December 2006, entered into force on 23 December 2010): 'Each State Party shall take appropriate measures to investigate acts defined in article 2 committed by persons or groups of persons acting without the authorization, support or acquiescence of the State and to bring those responsible to justice'.

[122] The following treaty body documents are just a few among an impressive body of output dealing with the obligation to protect: Human Rights Committee, General Comment Nos 6 (Art 6, right to life), 20 (Art 7, prohibition of torture, cruel, inhuman or degrading treatment or punishment), 21 (Art 10, humane treatment of persons deprived of their liberty) and 16 (Art 17, right to privacy); Human Rights Committee, *Delago Paéz v Colombia* Communication No 195/1985, UN Doc CCPR/C/39/D/195/1985 (1990) (failure to take reasonable and appropriate measures to protect a teacher who had received death threats and been attacked, after a colleague from work had been shot by unknown killers); Inter-American Court of Human Rights, *Velásquez Rodríguez v Honduras* (1988) Series C no 4, judgment of 29 July 1988; European Court of Human Rights: *X and Y v The Netherlands* (1985) Series A no 91; *A v the United Kingdom* ECHR 1998–VI; *Plattform 'Ärzte für das Leben' v Austria* (1988) Series A no 139; *Osman v UK* ECHR 1998–VIII 3124; *Opuz v Turkey* App no 33401/02, judgment of 9 June 2009 (domestic violence case); *Siliadin v France* ECHR 2005–VII (case concerning domestic servitude); *Costello-Roberts v UK* (1993) Series A no 247C (corporal punishment in private schools). For a detailed analysis of the obligation to protect, please see Clapham, *Human Rights Obligations of Non-State Actors* (n 6) 349ff; Künzli and Kälin, *The Law of International Human Rights Protection* (n 3) 103ff, Nowak, *CCPR Commentary* (n 30); A Mowbray, *The Development of Positive Obligations under the European Convention on Human Rights by the European Court of Human Rights* (Oxford, Hart Publishing, 2004).

[123] General Comment 18, Right to Work (Art 6), adopted on 24 November 2005, para 52; General Comment 21, Right of everyone to take part in cultural life (Art 15(1)(a)), adopted on 13 November 2009, para 73.

> well as the private business sector—have responsibilities in the realization of the right to adequate food. The State should provide an environment that facilitates implementation of these responsibilities. The private business sector—national and transnational—should pursue its activities within the framework of a code of conduct conducive to respect of the right to adequate food, agreed upon jointly with the Government and civil society.[124]

Moreover, when it stated that the state's 'failure to regulate activities of individuals or groups so as to prevent them from violating the right to food of others' constitutes a human rights violation, it implicitly asserted that private actors could violate human rights.[125]

7.5.3 Enforcing Human Rights Against Non-State Actors on the National Level

On the domestic level, human rights protection is ideally realised through a complex web of different measures creating an infrastructure essential for an effective enjoyment of human rights. With regard to private duties, the primary source is domestic legislation such as criminal, labour, family, social, corporate, private, environmental as well as administrative laws. These ordinary laws provide for legal rights and obligations which effectively (should) cover the object of human rights as laid out in the respective treaties. Criminal laws, for example, although like other domestic laws usually not explicitly referring to human rights and predating the modern human rights movement, protect some of the values and interests enshrined in human rights instruments, such as life, physical integrity, health, liberty, privacy, reputation or property. Thus, these ordinary laws oblige the individual to act in a certain way and provide for corresponding legal rights, civil, criminal or administrative law procedures and bodies to enforce human rights on a national level.[126]

Furthermore, in a considerable number of countries, protection against private threats has found its way into specific statutory provisions or even the constitution, thus enjoying an enhanced legal status above ordinary law

124 See eg, Committee on Economic, Social and Cultural Rights, General Comment 12, The Right to Adequate Food (Art 11), adopted 12 May 1999, para 20; see very similar statement of the Committee in General Comment 14, The Right to the Highest Attainable Standard of Health (Art 12), adopted on 11 August 2000, para 4; General Comment 15, The Right to Water (Arts 11 and 12), adopted 26 November 2002, paras 23–24; General Comment 18, The Right to Work (Art 6), adopted on 24 November 2005, para 52: Under the heading 'Obligations of Actors Other Than States Parties' the Committee once again confirms responsibilities of non-state actors; General Comment 21, Right of everyone to take part in cultural life (Art 15, para 1(a), of the ICESCR).

125 General Comment 12 (n 124) para 19.

126 Nowak, *Introduction* (n 33) 51ff; Oliver and Fedtke, 'The Scope of the Project' (n 54) 4ff; Donnelly, *Universal Human Rights* (n 36) 32.

and requiring special protection.[127] A comparative examination shows that the conceptualisation and concrete implementation of such an approach varies significantly in the different domestic legal systems, from direct application of human rights in private relations to highly varying indirect forms where judges interpret, apply and develop the law in conformity with constitutional rights and values. Which approach is in fact taken depends on the country's history and legal traditions shaping the national legal architecture.[128] The classic textbook example for the weaker, indirect model is the doctrine of 'third-party effect' (*Drittwirkung*) of human rights. According to this doctrine, which is based on the assumption that fundamental rights are primarily 'defensive' rights of the citizen vis-à-vis the state, the German Basic Law (Grundgesetz of 1949) constitutes a value system permeating the whole legal system. These constitutional values are thus understood to 'radiate' into all areas of private law requiring judges as organs of the state to interpret the law in conformity with the constitution.[129] In France, India, Ireland, Italy, Namibia, South Africa, Spain or Sweden, constitutionally or internationally enshrined human rights are in variable forms and degrees given direct horizontal effect.[130] The fundamental rights landscape of India stands out as it addresses human rights duties of private bodies in an exceptionally clear way. The Constitution of India, which came into force in 1950, foresees fundamental rights which with some exceptions are binding on state and non-state actors alike. The constitution thus recognises that in order to promote welfare for all and overturn inequalities deeply rooted in

[127] There is a vast amount of academic writing on the issue of horizontal application of constitutional rights. This chapter primarily draws from the recent comparative study in Oliver and Fedtke, *Human Rights and the Private Sphere* (n 54) as well as: S Gardbaum, 'The "Horizontal Effect" of Constitutional Rights' (2003) 102 *Michigan Law Review* 387; M Tushnet, 'The Issue of State Action/Horizontal Effect in Comparative Constitutional Law' (2003) 1 *International Journal of Constitutional Law* 79; M Hunt, 'The Horizontal Effect of the Human Rights Act' [1998] *Public Law* 423; D Friedmann and D Barak-Erez, *Human Rights in Private Law* (n 54); A Barak, 'Constitutional Human Rights and Private Law', Faculty Scholarship Series Paper 3698 (1996) http://digitalcommons.law.yale.edu/fss_papers/3698; Clapham, *Human Rights in the Private Sphere* (n 3) 150–77 and 298–342; Clapham, *Human Rights Obligations of Non-State Actors* (n 6) 437–531.

[128] See in general Oliver and Fedtke, *Human Rights and the Private Sphere* (n 54) wherein 14 different domestic legal systems are analysed and compared with regard to private duties.

[129] First formulated by the German Federal Constitutional Court in the *Lüth* judgment, see BVerfGE 7, 198 of 15 January 1958: 'Die Grundrechte sind in erster Linie Abwehrrechte des Bürgers gegen den Staat; in den Grundrechtsbestimmungen des Grundgesetzes verkörpert sich aber auch eine objektive Wertordnung, die als verfassungsrechtliche Grundentscheidung für alle Bereiche des Rechts gilt.' In Art 9(3) the Basic Law exceptionally provides for direct effect, namely with regard to trade unions; for further elaboration see J Fedtke, 'Germany—Drittwirkung in Germany' in Oliver and Fedtke, *Human Rights and the Private Sphere* (n 54) 125; J Schwabe, *Die sogenannte Drittwirkung der Grundrechte* (Munich, Wilhelm Goldmann Verlag, 1971).

[130] See for detailed information on the listed countries the respective chapters in Oliver and Fedtke, *Human Rights and the Private Sphere* (n 54) and Clapham, *Human Rights Obligations of Non-State Actors* (n 6) 437.

socio-cultural traditions and long-standing discrimination practices which are passed on from generation to generation, such as 'untouchability', trafficking in human beings and forced labour, human rights must permeate the private sphere.[131] That the South African Constitution of 1996 expressly provides for the direct and indirect horizontal effect can be explained by the majority's fear of a continuation of apartheid within the private sphere. Accordingly, section 8(2) of the Constitution ties non-state activities to constitutional rights 'if, and to the extent that, [such a right is] applicable, taking into account the nature of the right and the nature of any duty imposed by the right'.[132] In a similarly explicit manner, whenever their acts are not purely private, non-state actors with 'functions of a public nature' are bound to respect the UK Human Rights Act 1998.[133] In Ireland constitutional rights can also directly operate in private relations. The Supreme Court conceptualised a cause of action against non-state actors based on constitutional rights, often referred to as 'constitutional tort', which can be vindicated if no private law remedy exists.[134]

Hence, the picture commonly presented of national human rights protection solely covering the vertical relationship between the individual and the state, does not fully correspond with legal reality. However, one also has to admit, that in many of these countries the extension of constitutionally enshrined rights into the private sphere has set off heated debates. In general, besides the common assumption that private human rights duties constitute an undue interference with the individual's autonomy, the attachment to 'verticalism' seems to be based on several common apprehensions. In general, 'privatising' constitutional rights is considered to have a significantly destabilising effect on the existent order risking legal uncertainty. Above all, entrusting judges with the task of balancing competing human rights, thus transferring this competence from parliament to the courtroom, has evoked much scepticism.[135]

131 MP Singh, 'India—Protection of Human Rights against State and Non-State Action' in Oliver and Fedtke, *Human Rights and the Private Sphere* (n 54) 180; with regard to relevant case law see for instance *Bodhisattwa Gautam v Subhra Chakraborty* AIR 1996 SC 922 (observing that fundamental rights can be enforced against private bodies and rape being a crime against basic human rights); *Vishaka v State of Rajasthan* AIR 1997 SC 3011 (public interest litigation establishing that sexual harassment at the workplace constitutes a violation of gender equality and issuing guidelines directed at public and private employers); *Apparel Export Promotion Council v AK Chopra* AIR 1999 SC 625 (for the first time, the Supreme Court relied on the *Vishaka* Guidelines).

132 See s 8(2) and (3) Constitution of the Republic of South Africa, Act 108 of 1996. In practice the South African Constitutional Court relies on indirect effect; one notable exception of direct applicability is the defamation case *Khumalo v Holomisa* 2002 (5) SA 401 (CC).

133 See s 6 Human Rights Act 1998.

134 C O'Cinneide, 'Irish Constitutional Law and Direct Horizontal Effect—A Successful Experiment?' in Oliver and Fedtke, *Human Rights and the Private Sphere* (n 54) 213.

135 D Oliver and J Fedtke, 'Comparative Analysis' in Oliver and Fedtke, *Human Rights and the Private Sphere* (n 54) 505f; Clapham, *Human Rights Obligations of Non-State Actors* (n 6) 438f.

Another trend to be observed on the national level to counter human rights threats emanating from the private side is to open up the national court's jurisdiction for human rights claims against non-state entities. Since international organisations in general enjoy extensive jurisdictional immunity before national courts, the national legal system can only provide an effective tool of enforcement for other categories of non-state actors.[136] In this respect, the increasing civil litigation for human rights violations, especially against corporate actors, such as Blackwater, Chevron, Coca-Cola, Exxon Mobil, Shell, Texaco and Unocal, before United States courts under the Alien Tort Statute (ATS) of 1789 must not go unmentioned.[137] The landmark judgment *Filártiga v Peña-Irala* of 1980 revived the dormant ATS and for the next 30 years the statute was considered to vest US courts with extraterritorial jurisdiction for international law violations committed all around the world by all kind of non-governmental actors.[138] This understanding, the subject of an ongoing controversy, was reversed by a Supreme Court decision of April 2013 wherein the Court invoked a presumption against extraterritorial application. Henceforth a claim under ATS must show that the matter touches and concerns the United States with 'sufficient force'.[139] Until now, US courts found, inter alia, torture and cruel, inhuman or degrading treatment, war crimes or genocide, slave trade, slavery and forced labour to be actionable, also against corporations, and have thus undeniably contributed to a growing awareness that corporations must abide by human rights.[140]

[136] This immunity is usually provided for in headquarters or host state agreements, the constitutive instrument of the international organisation, multilateral treaties or in domestic laws. See A Reinisch, *International Organizations Before National Courts* (Cambridge, Cambridge University Press, 2000) 127ff.

[137] Alien Tort Statute 28 USC §1350 of 1789, also known as Alien Tort Claims Act (ATCA), providing that '[t]he district courts shall have original jurisdiction of any civil action by an alien for a tort only, committed in violation of the law of nations or a treaty of the United States'; see for more information on the Alien Tort Statute CM Scott (ed), *Torture as Tort* (Oxford, Hart Publishing, 2001).

[138] *Filártiga v Peña-Irala* 630 F 2d 876 (2d Cir 1980). In *Doe v Unocal* 395 F 3d 932 (9th Cir 2002), a US federal district court agreed that lawsuits against private companies were admissible. In *Sosa v Alvarez-Machain et al* the Court held that in order to be accepted as a cause of action the violation of international law must be of a norm that is 'specific, universal, and obligatory'; see 542 US 692 (2004), 732.

[139] *Kiobel v Royal Dutch Petroleum Co* 133 S Ct 1659 (2013).

[140] *Kadić v Karadžić* 70 F 3d 232 (2d Cir 1995) against Radovan Karadžic for genocide, war crimes, and crimes against humanity; Abu Ghraib lawsuits concerning torture in Iraq: *Ibrahim et al v Titan et al; Saleh et al v Titan et al; Doe v Unocal* 395 F 3d 932 (9th Cir 2002) concerning complicity of Unocal in forced labour, murder, rape and torture in Myanmar; *Wiwa v Shell Petroleum (formerly Royal Dutch Petroleum Company) et al* Case No 96 Civ 8386 (1998), concerning Shell's complicity in torture and summary executions in Nigeria; Blackwater USA lawsuit concerning extrajudicial killings and war crimes in Iraq: *Abtan et al v Prince et al* Civil Action Nos 1:09cv615, 1:09cv616, 1:09cv617, 1:09cv618, 1:09cv645, 1:09cv1017, 1:09cv1048.

7.6 THE RARITY OF DIRECT HORIZONTAL HUMAN RIGHTS OBLIGATIONS UNDER INTERNATIONAL LAW

International human rights law, due to the above-mentioned arguments, still tends to address non-state actor behaviour indirectly by obliging states to regulate private actors, instead of imposing direct duties on non-state actors.[141] Horizontal human rights obligations are virtually missing. Efforts to establish explicit horizontal international human rights obligations for non-state actors have until now failed, due to lack of state consent.

The African human rights system constitutes a bit of an outlier in the human rights universe. The African Charter on Human and Peoples' Rights, similarly to the American Declaration of 1948, features a special chapter on private duties towards the family, society, other legally recognised communities and the international community, thus more strongly than any other human rights treaty emphasising the correlation of rights and duties.[142] Article 28 explicitly requires that '[e]very individual shall have the duty to respect and consider his fellow beings without discrimination, and to maintain relations aimed at promoting, safeguarding and reinforcing mutual respect and tolerance'. The African Charter on the Rights and Welfare of the Child likewise directly imposes obligations on parents or other persons responsible for children towards these children and on children towards their parents.[143] Together with the Protocol to the African Charter on Human and Peoples' Rights on the Rights of Women in Africa which, although obliging only states parties, expressly covers threats from the private side or in the private sphere, such as the prohibition of female genital mutilation, forced marriage or violence against women, these documents suggest that the public/private dichotomy as well as the clear rejection of individual duties quintessential in the dominant human rights understanding collide with 'African' human rights theories.[144]

141 In this respect, a trend towards more precise formulations of the obligation to protect seems to crystallise, thus reducing the scope of state discretion to choose the appropriate measures for regulating private relations.

142 Arts 27–29 African (Banjul) Charter on Human and Peoples' Rights, adopted June 27, 1981, OAU Doc CAB/LEG/67/3 rev 5, 21 ILM 58 (1982), entered into force 21 Oct 1986; for more detailed academic elaborations on the African Charter, see M Evans and R Murray (eds), *The African Charter on Human and Peoples' Rights: The System in Practice 1986-2006* (Cambridge, Cambridge University Press, 2008); F Viljoen, *International Human Rights Law in Africa*, 2nd edn (Oxford, Oxford University Press, 2012).

143 Arts 20(1) and 31 African Charter on the Rights and Welfare of the Child, OAU Doc CAB/LEG/24.9/49 (1990), entered into force 29 Nov 1999.

144 Protocol to the African Charter on Human and Peoples' Rights on the Rights of Women in Africa (adopted on 13 September 2000, entered into force 25 November 2005); see further Chirwa, 'In Search of Philosophical Justifications' (n 63) 304f.

Similar to the African Charter on the Rights and Welfare of the Child, the Convention on the Rights of the Child explicitly recalls the responsibilities of parents and legal guardians towards the child.[145] A slightly attenuated and ambiguous formulation with regard to horizontal human rights duties can be found in the Optional Protocol to the Convention on the Rights of the Child on the involvement of children in armed conflict, which stipulates that '[a]rmed groups … should not, under any circumstances, recruit or use in hostilities persons under the age of 18 years'.[146] Whether the use of the word 'should' instead of 'shall' was supposed to provide for a legally binding horizontal human rights obligation is controversial. As has been argued, the humanitarian nature of the treaty, the reference in the preamble to the responsibilities of armed groups as well as the use of the strong phrase 'under any circumstances' can be read as creating a legal obligation.[147]

International criminal law significantly mitigated the dominant lacuna. Similar to the modern international human rights movement, it was a reaction to the Holocaust and the Second World War. These traumatic events exposed the fact that such heinous crimes are committed by individuals against other individuals and not between states.[148] And since these crimes concern the international community as a whole, national prosecution was considered to be not enough and led to the establishment of international tribunals and finally, in 1998 to the set-up of the permanent International Criminal Court in The Hague. Under international criminal law individuals can be held to account, irrespective of whether they acted in an official capacity or not, an approach already adopted in the Genocide Convention.[149] Thus, international criminal law moved away from the state-centric conception predominant in international human rights law.

[145] Art 18(1) CRC: 'Parents or, as the case may be, legal guardians, have the primary responsibility for the upbringing and development of the child. The best interests of the child will be their basic concern'.

[146] Art 4(1) Optional Protocol to the Convention on the Rights of the Child on the involvement of children in armed conflict (adopted on 25 May 2000, entered into force on 12 February 2002) 2173 UNTS 222.

[147] See Clapham, *Human Rights Obligations of Non-State Actors* (n 6) 74f; Hessbruegge, 'Human Rights Violations' (n 85) 31; see Report of the independent international commission of inquiry on the Syrian Arab Republic, UN Doc A/HRC/22/59 (5 February 2013), holding that both the government and the anti-government armed groups violated the Optional Protocol to the CRC; see further concerning the legal nature of the provision UNICEF, *Guide to the Optional Protocol on the Involvement of Children in Armed Conflict* (New York, 2003); International Committee of the Red Cross, 'Optional Protocol to the Convention on the Rights of the Child on the involvement of children in armed conflict, 25 May 2000', www.icrc.org/ihl.nsf/INTRO/595?OpenDocument.

[148] See Judgment of the International Military Tribunal (Nuremberg), 'Judgment and Sentences' (1947) 41 *American Journal of International Law* 172: 'Crimes against international law are committed by men, not by abstract entities, and only by punishing individuals who commit such crimes can the provisions of international law be enforced.'

[149] Art 4 Convention on the Prevention and Punishment of the Crime of Genocide (adopted on 9 December 1948, entered into force 12 January 1951) 78 UNTS 277.

The crime of torture as stipulated in the Rome Statute hence in contrast to the somewhat old-fashioned definition to be found in the Convention against Torture, omitted the 'official capacity' requirement.[150] Moreover, by outlawing certain conduct, it directly places international duties on individuals. International criminal law, however, is confined in its jurisdiction to specific, especially heinous, gross and systematic human rights violations, namely genocide, crimes against humanity and war crimes. Due to this limitation, it cannot serve as a tool to tackle other human rights violations which do not meet the threshold of the three core crimes. Business practices of forced and child labour, sweatshop practices and deplorable working conditions, subversive practices concerning the freedom of association or discrimination, environmental degradation and land grabbing, to name but a few, fall through the cracks. Furthermore, the ICC's mandate is restricted to one category of non-state actors, the individual.[151] That governments decided to leave legal entities outside the jurisdiction of the ICC seems to stem from the fact that in some national legal systems the concept of corporate criminal liability is still unfamiliar, rather than the conviction of states that international law is incapable to directly act upon economic players. Thus, although the suggestions and drafts to include business within the realm of the ICC were finally dropped, international corporate criminal liability is continuously discussed as one possible solution to narrow the existent accountability gap.[152] Furthermore, an

[150] See Art 1 Convention against Torture and Other Cruel, Inhuman or Degrading Treatment or Punishment (adopted on 10 December 1984, entered into force on 26 June 1987) 1465 UNTS 85; Art 7(1)(f) in conjunction with Art 7(2)(e) Rome Statute; Art 8(2)(a)(ii) and Art 8(2)(c)(i) Rome Statute in conjunction with the Elements of Crimes; see also M Nowak, 'Torture and other Cruel, Inhuman or Degrading Treatment or Punishment' in A Clapham and P Gaeta (eds), *The Oxford Handbook on International Law in Armed Conflict* (Oxford, Oxford University Press, 2014); M Nowak and R Janik, 'Torture, Cruel, Inhuman or Degrading Treatment or Punishment' in A Clapham et al (eds), *The 1949 Geneva Conventions: A Commentary* (forthcoming).

[151] The ICC could prosecute individuals acting on behalf of corporations which for instance provide armed groups with weapons or ammunition. Whether its limited resources allow it to indeed deal with such cases is another issue. See R Gallmetzer, 'Prosecuting Persons Doing Business with Armed Groups in Conflict Areas—The Strategy of the Office of the Prosecutor of the International Criminal Court' (2010) 8 *Journal of International Criminal Justice* 947.

[152] See A Clapham, 'The Question of Jurisdiction under International Criminal Law over Legal Persons: Lessons from the Rome Conference on an International Criminal Court' in MT Kamminga and S Zia-Zarifi (eds), *Liability of Multinational Corporations under International Law* (The Hague, Kluwer Law International, 2000) 139; for elaborate discussions concerning corporate criminal responsibility, see the special issue of the *Journal of International Criminal Justice* (2010) vol 8 on 'Transnational Business and International Criminal Law', as well as A Clapham, 'Extending International Criminal Law beyond the Individual to Corporations and Armed Opposition Groups' (2008) 6 *Journal of International Criminal Justice* 899; T Weigend, 'Societas delinquere non potest?—A German Perspective' (2008) 6 *Journal of International Criminal Justice* 927: whereas corporate criminal responsibility is well rooted in common law jurisdictions, it is a relatively new concept in states with continental legal tradition. Weigend observes a growing trend among European countries, such as France, the Netherlands, Switzerland, Austria and Italy, to introduce or expand criminal prosecution to corporations. He also argues that within the European Union, there appears to be an increasing consensus for holding legal entities to account.

essential difference between international criminal law and human rights law must be noted. While criminal law primarily focuses on the perpetrator by requiring criminal prosecution, human rights law is focused on the victim entitling it to demand reparation covering restitution, compensation, rehabilitation as well as satisfaction, a concept of justice which goes significantly beyond the punishment of the offender.[153]

Unmediated human rights duties for non-state actors are primarily taking shape in voluntary, 'soft law' instruments, usually known as codes of conduct. Over the years such non-binding diverse commitments by transnational corporations, international organisations and NGOs have proliferated rapidly due to strong demands for accountability and transparency.[154] These codes establish general guidelines which only to some extent cover the rich array of human rights, and in addition lack proper monitor mechanisms.

7.7 HUMAN RIGHTS IN THE CORPORATE WORLD

Although even in the 1960s the significance of corporations on the international area, including the necessity to regulate their behaviour, was being discussed, international law has until now not adapted to accommodate these powerful participants sufficiently.[155] With regard to the corporate sector the international community relies strongly on soft law instruments, either self-initiated codes of conduct which often are a reaction to consumer

[153] See inter alia Arts 2(3) ICCPR and 13 ECHR; see as well Van Boven/Bassiouni-Guidelines (n 112); Art 75(2) Rome Statute shows a considerable move towards the human rights understanding of justice by allowing the Court to order from the convict 'reparations to, or in respect of, victims, including restitution, compensation and rehabilitation'. See for similar argument Hessbruegge, 'Human Rights Violations' (n 85) 42f; see on the significance of reparations for example D Shelton, *Remedies in International Human Rights Law* (Oxford, Oxford University Press, 2005); International Commission of Jurists, *The Right to a Remedy and to Reparations for Gross Human Rights Violations* (Geneva, December 2006); M Nowak and J Kozma, 'A World Court of Human Rights', Research Project on a World Human Rights Court (June 2009), Swiss Initiative to Commemorate the 60th Anniversary of the UDHR, 'Protecting Dignity: An Agenda for Human Rights', www.udhr60.ch, 23ff. J Kozma et al, *A World Court of Human Rights—Consolidated Statute and Commentary* (Wien, Neuer Wissenschaftlicher Verlag, 2010).

[154] These codes of conduct are usually adopted by the NSA themselves, often as a result of public pressure. With regard to corporate responsibility some codes of conduct have been formulated within international organisations, such as the OECD Guidelines, the ILO Principles or the UN Global Compact encouraging businesses to align their operations and strategies with 10 principles. Under the title 'Observance by United Nations forces of international humanitarian law', the United Nations Secretary-General proclaimed in 1999 a set of 'fundamental principles and rules of international humanitarian law applicable to forces conducting operations under United Nations command and control'; see Secretary General's Bulletin of 6 August 1999.

[155] W Friedmann, *The Changing Structure of International Law* (New York, Columbia University Press, 1964) and W Friedmann, *Law in a Changing Society*, abridged edn (Harmondsworth, Penguin Books, 1964) 213ff.

boycotts, or mobilisations by civil society or international initiatives, such as the OECD Guidelines for Multinational Enterprises, the ILO Tripartite Declaration and the adoption of the UN Global Compact or the Voluntary Principles on Security and Human Rights.[156] These guidelines, which operate on a voluntary basis, remind businesses of their social and moral responsibilities with regard to human rights protection. The *2003 draft UN Norms on the Responsibilities of Transnational Corporations and Other Business Enterprises with Regard to Human Rights* drafted by the UN Sub-commission on the Promotion and Protection of Human Rights tried to go further than these soft law efforts being the 'first non-voluntary initiative'.[157] The 23 articles acknowledged states as the primary duty bearers and supplemented their legal responsibilities with corresponding human rights obligations for corporations within their sphere of influence covering the same range of human rights duties as accepted by states. The *2003 UN draft Norms* which also demanded effective international and national enforcement mechanisms providing for an avenue of redress were understood by their drafters to restate international law.[158] However, this initiative proved extremely divisive and did not find much echo in the corporate world or among governments; thus, the UN Commission on Human Rights finally decided not to adopt the draft norms. John Ruggie, who subsequently was appointed as UN Special Representative of the Secretary General for Business and Human Rights, rejected the 2003 Norms as too far-reaching and not corresponding to the status quo of international law, emphasising that '[t]he international community is still in the early stages of adapting the human rights regime to provide more effective protection to individuals

[156] Organisation for Economic Co-operation and Development, *OECD Guidelines for Multinational Enterprises* (Washington DC, OECD Publishing, 2011), www.oecd.org/dataoecd/43/29/48004323.pdf; International Labour Organization, *ILO Tripartite Declaration of Principles Concerning Multinational Enterprises and Social Policy (1977)*, 4th edn (Geneva, International Labour Office, 2006), www.ilo.org; UN Global Compact (2000), www.unglobalcompact.org; Voluntary Principles on Security and Human Rights (2000), www.voluntaryprinciples.org. The principles are a multi-stakeholder initiative adopted in 2000 by the US, the UK, the Netherlands and Norway, together with the relevant corporations and key NGOs for the extractive sector with the aim to guiding 'companies in maintaining the safety and security of their operations within an operating framework that encourages respect for human rights'.

[157] D Weissbrodt and M Kruger, 'Norms on the Responsibilities of Transnational Corporations and Other Business Enterprises with Regard to Human Rights' (2003) 97 *American Journal of International Law* 901, 903; UN Commission On Human Rights, Sub-Commission on the Promotion and Protection of Human Rights, Norms on the Responsibilities of Transnational Corporations and Other Business Enterprises with Regard to Human Rights, 26 August 2003, UN Doc E/CN 4/Sub 2/2003/12/Rev 2.

[158] Weissbrodt and Kruger, 'Norms on the Responsibilities of Transnational Corporations' (n 157) 913.

and communities against corporate-related human rights harm'.[159] After conducting a thorough multidisciplinary research, Ruggie presented his *Guiding Principles on Business and Human Rights* in 2008, which were endorsed by the Human Rights Council in 2011. His approach contemplates a three-pillared framework resting on 'complementary responsibilities', with the first pillar reiterating the state obligation to protect against human rights abuses by non-state actors, including businesses.[160] The second pillar deals with corporate behaviour, resorting to the language of 'responsibility' of business entities to respect human rights. This responsibility is shaped by the domestic legal framework and social expectations and not only requires companies to act with due diligence to avoid interferences with the human rights of others but also to address adverse impacts that may occur.[161] The third pillar considers the need of victims to have greater access to judicial and non-judicial remedies and the responsibility of states and companies to provide for them. Whether the Guidelines will be successful, especially in evolving a new mind-set among corporate actors to more willingly endorse human rights in their operations, remains to be seen. So far, relying on the state as the sole duty-bearer has proven to be insufficient to counter the human rights harms caused by powerful non-state actors.

7.8 HOLDING INTERNATIONAL ORGANISATIONS ACCOUNTABLE FOR HUMAN RIGHTS VIOLATIONS

Over recent decades, international organisations have proliferated and immensely broadened their scope of activities, reaching far into human rights-sensitive fields directly impacting on the lives of individuals, such as peacekeeping, military actions, administration of territories,[162] and involvement in development projects, adopting targeted sanctions or conducting criminal proceedings, making them not only important protectors and promoters of human rights but also potential perpetrators. This

[159] J Ruggie, 'Protect, Respect and Remedy: a Framework for Business and Human Rights, Report of the Special Representative of the Secretary-General on the issue of human rights and transnational corporations and other business enterprises' UN Doc A/HRC/8/5 of 7 April 2008, para 156; see also J Ruggie, 'Report of the Special Representative of the Secretary General on the issue of human rights and transnational corporations and other business enterprises' UN Doc A/HRC/17/31 of 21 March 2011; see K Lukas and FJ Hutter, *Menschenrechte und Wirtschaft* (Wien/Graz, Neuer Wissenschaftlicher Verlag, 2009) 185ff. Due to the wealth of literature on the issue of business and human rights, the reader is kindly asked to refer to the respective chapter on transnational corporations within this book for further secondary sources.

[160] Ruggie, 'Protect, Respect and Remedy' (n 159) para 9.

[161] ibid, paras 54 and 56.

[162] For an excellent treatise with regard to the human rights accountability of International Organisations, see J Wouters et al (eds), *Accountability for Human Rights Violations by International Organisations* (Antwerp/Oxford/Portland, Intersentia, 2010).

expansion of authority was attentively observed by civil society, policy makers, international institutions and scholars. Both the International Law Association and the International Law Commission have dealt extensively with the issue of accountability. The latter drawing from its draft articles for state responsibility devised 'Draft Articles on the Responsibility of International Organizations', adopted in 2011, which take into account the particularities of these collectives of states. However, although due to their interstate nature, intergovernmental organisations and their undisputed international legal personality assume a special place within the whole 'non-state actors and human rights' discourse, international organisations are rarely parties to human rights treaties. The Convention on the Rights of Persons with Disabilities, including its Optional Protocol, and soon the European Convention on Human Rights, are still more an exception than the rule.[163] As subjects of international law, international organisations are obviously 'bound by any obligations upon them under general rules of international law', ie, custom or general principles of international law.[164] Which human rights have actually achieved the status of international customary international law, is of course another question, and definitely not an uncontroversial one. *Jus cogens* norms such as the prohibitions of genocide, torture, slavery or racial discrimination are undeniably binding upon international organisations.[165] That international organisations have human rights obligations was also affirmed by the UN treaty monitoring bodies in their general comments.[166] Thus, the challenges with regard to the accountability of international organisations for human rights violations are due to the uncertain content and scope of their human rights obligations and, above all, the virtually absent enforcement possibilities. On the national level, international organisations are usually exempted from the domestic legal system enjoying immunity before national courts, thus safeguarding their independent functioning.[167] International courts and human rights monitoring bodies likewise lack jurisdiction to hold intergovernmental organisations to account. International organisations

[163] A Reinisch, 'Securing the Accountability of International Organizations' (2001) 7 *Global Governance* 131, 134ff; A Reinisch, 'Developing Human Rights and Humanitarian Law Accountability of the Security Council for the Imposition of Economic Sanctions' (2001) 95 *American Journal of International Law* 851, 854.

[164] ICJ, Interpretation of the Agreement of 25 March 1991 between the WHO and Egypt, Advisory Opinion [1980] ICJ Rep para 37.

[165] C Chinkin, 'Sources' in D Moeckli et al (eds), *International Human Rights Law* (Oxford, Oxford University Press, 2010) 103, 113.

[166] Under the heading 'obligations of actors other than states' the Committee on Economic, Social and Cultural Rights has also addressed obligations of international organisations, see for the concrete General Comments (n 124). In 2006 for the first time in the framework of the state reporting procedure a UN mission, UNMIK, submitted a report under the ICCPR to the Human Rights Committee, see UN Doc CCPR/C/UNK/CO/1.

[167] A Reinisch, *International Organizations Before National Courts* (n 136).

have incrementally mitigated this lacuna to a certain degree by creating internal monitoring mechanisms, such as the UN Dispute and Appeals Tribunals established by the UN General Assembly, operational since 2009 and competent to hear disputes arising from employment at an international organisation.[168] Beyond staff disputes further significant internal monitoring mechanisms, such as the Inspection Panel of the World Bank, the Kosovo Ombudsperson, the Kosovo Human Rights Advisory Panel or the Office of the Ombudsperson established to deal with claims from blacklisted legal or natural persons according to Security Council Resolution 1267, were created as a response to human rights concerns. The World Bank Inspection Panel, for instance, was set up in 1993 by the Board of Executive Directors as a reaction to growing criticism vis-à-vis certain Bank-financed projects such as the Sardar Sarovar Dam in India.[169] The three-member panel is mandated to carry out independent investigations into allegations of individuals contending to be adversely affected by a World Bank-financed project due to the Bank's failure to adhere to its operational policies and procedures and to subsequently report directly to the Board.[170] The Kosovo Human Rights Advisory Panel of three international human rights experts was established in 2006 to investigate individual complaints of alleged human rights violations committed by or attributable to the United Nations Interim Administration in Kosovo (UNMIK).[171] These internal accountability mechanisms are indeed significant but only half-hearted steps towards closing the accountability gap, as due to their very limited mandate they only issue non-binding opinions and offer only a toothless procedure devoid of any enforcement mechanism.[172]

[168] Similar staff dispute settlement mechanisms can be found within the EU which set up the European Union Civil Service Tribunal or the ILO's Administrative Tribunal.

[169] International Bank for Reconstruction and Development (IBRD) and International Development Agency (IDA), Resolutions, *The World Bank Inspection Panel* No IBRD 93–10 and IDA 93–6 (adopted on 22 September 1993); see further ER Carrasco and AK Guernsey, 'The World Bank's Inspection Panel: Promoting True Accountability through Arbitration' (2008) 41 *Cornell International Law Journal* 3; R Oleschak-Pillai, 'Accountability of International Organisations: An Analysis of the World Bank's Inspection Panel' in Wouters et al, *Accountability for Human Rights Violations* (n 162) 401–28.

[170] ibid.

[171] UNMIK, *On the Establishment of the Human Rights Advisory Panel*, UN Doc UNMIK/REG/2006/12 (23 March 2006).

[172] MA Nowicki, 'The European Convention on Human Rights in the practice of the international Kosovo Ombudsperson' in H Hartig (ed), *Trente ans de droit europeen des droits de l'homme—Etudes a la memoire de Wolfgang Strasser* (Brussels, Bruylant, 2007) 229; M Nowak, 'Enforced Disappearances in Kosovo—Human Rights Advisory Panel Holds UNMIK Accountable' (2013) *European Human Rights Law Review* 275; Chatham House, 'International Law Meeting Summary—The Kosovo Human Rights Advisory Panel' (26 January 2012), www.chathamhouse.org; C Ryngaert, 'The Accountability of International Organizations for Human Rights Violations: The Cases of the UN Mission in Kosovo (UNMIK) and the UN "Terrorism Blacklists"' in M Fitzmaurice and P Merkouris (eds), *The Interpretation and Application of the European Convention of Human Rights* (Leiden/Boston, Martinus Nijhoff Publishers, 2013) 73–91.

7.9 CONCLUSION: HOW CAN NON-STATE ACTORS BE HELD ACCOUNTABLE FOR THEIR VIOLATION OF INTERNATIONAL HUMAN RIGHTS?

If we accept that international human rights law should impose obligations on non-state actors directly, the follow-up question is of course: what is the required behaviour and how can it be enforced? As suggested above, the existent vertical human rights regime is not that easily transposable to the horizontal level. The *2003 draft UN Norms* generously imposed the full range of human rights obligations on corporate entities. Accordingly, corporations would as 'co-equal duty bearers' with states be obliged not only to respect the human rights of others, but to actively ensure them. This approach might indeed be too drastic and far-reaching as '[by] their very nature … corporations do not have a general role in relation to human rights as do States'.[173] That non-state actors, regardless of whether their acts are of private or public nature, have a negative obligation to respect the human rights of others should, however, be undisputable. Since states are under international human rights law obliged to protect human rights from interference by private entities, an obligation which also requires states to proscribe certain private duties or outlaw certain harmful conduct, respectively, international human rights law already contemplates negative obligations for non-state actors. If non-state actors essentially take over governmental functions and exert respective degree of control, such as with regard to private prisons or transitional administration as those established in East Timor and Kosovo, the private positive duties to protect and fulfil should expand correspondingly. These private obligations are not intended to replace but to complement existing state duties. Where states notoriously fail to adequately prevent private human rights violations, either because they are not willing or able, there is a need for international human rights law to step in and close the accountability gap. Human rights by their very nature imply that the duty-holder must have some possibility to hold the duty-bearers to account for their transgression and receive adequate reparation for material and immaterial damages.

There are different possibilities as to how non-state actors can be held accountable under international law. One possibility would be to strengthen the criminal responsibility of non-state actors by extending international criminal law to also cover corporate criminal responsibility, by improving the effectiveness of international criminal tribunals in bringing perpetrators of genocide and crimes against humanity to justice, by extending the scope of human rights crimes subject to universal criminal

[173] Interim report of the Special Representative of the Secretary-General on the issue of human rights and transnational corporations and other business enterprises, John Ruggie, UN Doc E/CN 4/2006/97 of 22 February 2006, paras 66 and 68.

jurisdiction before domestic criminal courts and by strengthening the implementation and enforcement of universal criminal jurisdiction against non-state actors. Another possibility would be to further develop and strengthen the concept of universal civil jurisdiction by introducing respective domestic tort laws similar to the practice under the US Alien Tort Claims Act before *Kiobel*.[174]

The most far-reaching and radical option of holding non-state actors accountable is, however, the proposal to create a World Court of Human Rights with extensive powers vis-à-vis states and other 'entities', as developed in the framework of the Swiss Agenda for Human Rights[175] and the COST Action on the role of the EU in UN Human Rights Reform.[176] In the context of these two projects a consolidated Statute and Commentary for a World Court of Human Rights was drafted.[177] In Article 4 of the draft statute the term 'entity' is defined as 'any inter-governmental organization or non-State actor, including any business corporation, which has recognized the jurisdiction of the Court in accordance with Article 51'. Article 51 provides that any entity may declare that it recognises the competence of the Court to receive and examine complaints from any person, non-governmental organisation or group of individuals claiming to be the victim of a violation by the respective entity of any human rights provided in any human rights treaty listed in Article 5(1), ie, any major UN human rights treaty. The judgments of the future World Court, which is modelled to some extent on the example of the European Court of Human Rights, shall be final and binding under international law. Their implementation by states parties shall be supervised by the UN High Commissioner for Human Rights and, if necessary, enforced by the Human Rights Council or the Security Council. If the Court finds a violation by any state

[174] *cf*, eg, Scott, *Torture as Tort* (n 137); M Nowak, 'Vom Weltstrafrecht zum Weltzivilrecht oder vom Internationalen Strafgerichtshof zum Internationalen Gerichtshof für Menschenrechte? Überlegungen am Beispiel der Folterbekämpfung' in I Buffard et al (eds), *International Law between Universalism and Fragmentation: Festschrift in Honour of Gerhard Hafner* (Leiden, Martinus Nijhoff Publishers, 2008) 667, 686ff.

[175] See Swiss Confederation, Federal Department of Foreign Affairs DFA/Geneva Academy of International Humanitarian Law and Human Rights, *Protecting Dignity: An Agenda for Human Rights* (Geneva, 2008), www.udhr60.ch.

[176] M Nowak et al (eds), *The Role of the EU in UN Human Rights Reform* (Wien/Graz, Neuer Wissenschaftlicher Verlag, 2013).

[177] J Kozma et al, *A World Court of Human Rights—Consolidated Statute and Commentary* (Wien/Graz, Neuer Wissenschaftlicher Verlag, 2010). See also M Nowak, 'Eight Reasons why we need a World Court of Human Rights' in J Grimheden et al (eds), *International Human Rights Monitoring Mechanisms: Essays in Honour of Jacob Th Möller*, 2nd edn (Leiden/Boston, Martinus Nijhoff Publishers, 2009) 697; M Nowak, 'It's Time for a World Court of Human Rights' in MC Bassiouni and WA Schabas (eds), *New Challenges to the UN Human Rights Machinery—What Future for the UN Treaty Body System and the Human Rights Council Procedures?* (Cambridge/Antwerp/Portland, Intersentia, 2011).

party or entity, it shall also order the respondent party, in accordance with Article 17(2), to afford the victim adequate reparation for the harm suffered, including restitution, rehabilitation, compensation, guarantees of non-repetition, or any other form of satisfaction. Although this proposal for establishing a World Court of Human Rights has initially been received with scepticism, it is being seriously considered by an increasing number of states, academics and non-governmental organisations. If adopted by the United Nations, such a future World Court of Human Rights would provide a paradigm shift in present international law by holding inter-governmental organisations, transnational corporations and other non-state actors directly accountable for their violations of international human rights.

8

State Responsibility and Non-State Actors

CEDRIC RYNGAERT

8.1 INTRODUCTION

IT IS A cardinal principle of the law of state responsibility that states are, in principle, not responsible for acts done by private or non-state actors. To hold otherwise would collapse the distinction between the public and the private spheres, and invite—or even require—states to strictly police the behaviour of their citizens (individuals or entities) in order to prevent the international responsibility of the state from being (objectively) engaged.[1] When drafting the Articles on the Responsibility of States for Internationally Wrongful Acts (ARSIWA),[2] the International Law Commission (ILC) initially envisaged enshrining this principle in a separate article, which would read: 'The conduct of a private individual or group of individuals, acting in that capacity, is not considered to be an act of the State in international law.'[3] This idea was abandoned in the final version of the ARSIWA, yet it nevertheless underlies the entire regime of attribution of conduct to states. Only acts of *state organs* can engage the responsibility of the state,[4] even if the act has been done ultra vires.[5]

[1] Djamchid Momtaz, Gérard Cahin and Olivier de Frouville, 'Attribution of Conduct to the State: State Organs and Entities empowered to Exercise Elements of Governmental Authority' in James Crawford et al (eds), *The Law of International Responsibility* (Oxford, Oxford University Press, 2010) 261 (submitting that 'it cannot be required of a State that it is in control of all the events which take place on its territory, short of obliging it to become a totalitarian State').

[2] The final version (2001) is known as Draft Articles on Responsibility of States for Internationally Wrongful Acts, with commentaries. Text adopted by the International Law Commission at its 53rd session, in 2001, and submitted to the General Assembly as a part of the Commission's report covering the work of that session (A/56/10). The report, which also contains commentaries on the draft articles, appears in the *Yearbook of the International Law Commission*, 2001, vol II Pt 2, as corrected.

[3] Robert Ago, 'Fourth Report on State Responsibility', *ILC Yearbook* (1972) vol II 126, para 146.

[4] Art 4 ARSIWA (organic attribution).

[5] Art 7 ARSIWA (excess of authority or contravention of instructions).

In principle, though conduct of non-state actors is not attributed to the state per se, the state may nonetheless entertain a sufficiently strong link to a non-state actor and the non-state actor's conduct to justify the attribution of such conduct to the state. Alternatively, a state may possess the capacity to influence (prevent) wrongful non-state actor conduct, thus justifying holding the state directly responsible for its failure to utilise this influence (due diligence failure). This contribution will address both scenarios.

The ARSIWA contemplate various scenarios of the first sort in Articles 5 and 8–11. Article 5 ARSIWA attributes non-state actor conduct to a state on the basis of a de jure link between the non-state actor and the state, namely the empowerment of the former by the latter to exercise elements of governmental authority. Articles 8–11 ARSIWA, for their part, attribute non-state actor conduct to a state on the basis of a de facto link between the non-state actor and the state, namely direction or control (Article 8), absence or default of official authorities (Article 9), conduct of an insurrectional movement (Article 10), and acknowledgment or adoption (Article 11). The rationale of these principles of attribution of non-state actor conduct to states is to prevent states from evading their responsibility by hiding behind the veil of non-state actors which are in reality doing the bidding of the state. At the same time, for victims, these principles narrow the accountability vacuum that may arise from the absence of direct responsibility by non-state actor. This chapter focuses specifically on attribution on the basis of the exercise of governmental authority (section 8.2), of direction and control (section 8.3), and on attribution of conduct of an insurrectional movement (section 8.4).

States may not only incur responsibility for wrongful non-state actor conduct through general principles of attribution, however; on the basis of discrete international law rules, states may be under a duty to *prevent* wrongful non-state actor conduct. A failure to adequately discharge this duty may result in direct state responsibility, regardless of whether the non-state actor's conduct can be attributed to the state. This duty to prevent, or alternatively, obligation of due diligence, which can be found in specific branches of international law, eg, international human rights law, will be addressed in section 8.5.

This chapter does not satisfy itself with providing an overview of the principles of attribution and due diligence. It will also pinpoint the limitations of the state-centred responsibility approach to wrongful non-state actor conduct, and advocate the development of a separate international responsibility regime for non-state actors, in particular de facto regimes, armed groups, and corporations. However, the emphasis of the contribution lies on state responsibility (and the identification of the problems inherent in the state responsibility approach), so that the conceptualisation of non-state actor obligations and responsibility will necessarily be rudimentary and tentative. Separate contributions to this volume examine more in-depth the obligations and responsibility of such non-state actors as intergovernmental organisations, non-governmental organisations, multinational corporations, and armed opposition groups.

8.2 ATTRIBUTION OF CONDUCT ON THE BASIS OF THE EXERCISE OF ELEMENTS OF GOVERNMENTAL AUTHORITY BY NON-STATE ACTORS

Pursuant to Article 5 of the ARSIWA,

> The conduct of a person or entity which is not an organ of the state under article 4 but which is empowered by the law of that state to exercise elements of the governmental authority shall be considered an act of the state under international law, provided the person or entity is acting in that capacity in the particular instance.

Under this principle of attribution, non-state actor acts are attributed to the state on the basis of a *legal* link which the non-state actor has with the state, namely the exercise of public authority conferred by the state to the non-state actor, short of the latter rising to the level of an organ of the state (Article 4 ARSIWA).

There is limited international case law regarding this mode of attribution, and none from the International Court of Justice (ICJ) for that matter. The leading precedents, cited by the ILC, are a 1985 decision of the Iran-US Claims Tribunal, which attributed the seizure of goods belonging to the US-based Hyatt corporation, by an Iranian charitable foundation to the Iranian state,[6] and a post-World War II Franco-Italian Conciliation Commission which attributed an act of goods confiscation by a Fascist non-state outfit in Italy to the Italian state.[7]

In recent times, attribution of conduct on the basis of the exercise of elements of governmental authority may have become more relevant due to the decentralisation of the state and the privatisation of public tasks. In order to prevent privatisation from giving rise to an accountability vacuum, under this attribution principle, states are not allowed to outsource their responsibility if the corporation to which public tasks have been entrusted violates international law.[8] Thus, in *Gauthier v Canada*, the

[6] *Hyatt International Corporation v Government of the Islamic Republic of Iran* (1985) 9 Iran-USCTR.

[7] *Dame Mossé* (7 January and 6 October 1953) 13 RIAA 486.

[8] State enterprises, ie, corporations fully *owned* by states (and accordingly not privatised) may assume a different position, as such entities may be characterised as organs of the state in the sense of Art 4 ARSIWA. See for a discussion in an investment law context: Abby Cohen Smutny, 'State Responsibility and Attribution: when is a State responsible for the Acts of State Enterprises?: Emilio Agustín Maffezini v the Kingdom of Spain' in Todd Weiler (ed),

Human Rights Committee decided that Canada was responsible for the complainant's 'arbitrary exclusion from access' to Parliamentary media facilities by a private organisation to which the state had delegated responsibilities.[9]

Other examples of corporations exercising such tasks are airline companies exercising functions of immigration control, private companies managing prisons,[10] or private military and security companies engaged in other law-enforcement activities. The Maastricht Principles also attribute non-state actor activities to the state that go beyond just law-enforcement, such as 'the provision of basic infrastructure, certain essential public services such as water and electricity, and traditionally public functions of the state such as education and health'.[11] For attribution purposes, it remains important, however, that the mere exercise of an activity that could be characterised as public or governmental does not suffice: the non-state actor performing such services needs to have been empowered by the state to exercise elements of the governmental authority.

This dual requirement obviously complicates the attribution of non-state actor acts to states. For one thing, it may be unclear whether a certain activity is truly an exercise of governmental authority. For instance, is the provision of water and electricity really to be qualified as an exercise of elements of governmental authority, as the Maastricht Principles want us to believe? It must be noted in this respect that the law of state immunity from jurisdiction would characterise the provision of such services as *acta jure gestionis* (commercial/management acts to which immunity would not be attached) rather than *acta jure imperii* (sovereign acts to which immunity would be attached).[12] Yet possibly, interpretative recourse may be had to the concept of 'inherently governmental functions' in the (domestic) law of public procurement.[13] However, this concept is precisely meant

International Investment Law and Arbitration (London, Cameron May, 2005) 17–45; Kai Hobér, 'State Responsibility and Attribution' in Peter Muchlinski, Federico Ortino and Christoph Schreuer (eds), *The Oxford Handbook of International Investment Law* (Oxford, Oxford University Press, 2008) 549–83.

[9] *Robert W Gauthier v Canada*, Communication No 633/1995, UN Doc CCPR/C/65/D/633/1995 (5 May 1999) 13.6.

[10] See Momtaz, 'Attribution of Conduct to the State', 237 et seq.

[11] Principle 12 of the Maastricht Principles on Extraterritorial Obligations of States in the Area of Economic, Social and Cultural Rights (2012), Commentary (2) applying Art 5 of the ARSIWA. The Principles and the Commentary are published in (2012) 34 *Human Rights Quarterly* 1084–1169.

[12] Art 10 et seq UN Convention on Jurisdictional Immunities of States and their Property (2004). Adopted by the General Assembly of the United Nations on 2 December 2004. Not yet in force. See General Assembly Resolution 59/38, annex, Official Records of the General Assembly, 59th Session, Supplement no 49 (A/59/49).

[13] See, eg, for the US Publication of the Office of Federal Procurement Policy (OFPP) Policy Letter 11–01, Performance of Inherently Governmental and Critical Functions, Federal Register vol 76 no 176 (Monday 12 September 2011) Notices 56227 et seq.

to *exclude* such functions from being performed by private contractors, whereas Article 5 ARSIWA assumes that states do at times outsource such functions to non-state actors (at least if permitted by domestic law), while providing that they are not permitted to outsource their accountability.

Secondly, Article 5 ARSIWA only becomes operational in cases where the state has formally empowered the non-state actor to exercise elements of governmental authority. When the non-state actor just 'happens to' exercise governmental authority without having received an unambiguous mandate to do so, Article 5 ARSIWA will not apply. In such a situation, an alternative attribution principle may apply, laid down in Article 9 ARSIWA, pursuant to which

> The conduct of a person or group of persons shall be considered an act of a State under international law if the person or group of persons is in fact exercising elements of the governmental authority in the absence or default of the official authorities and in circumstances such as to call for the exercise of those elements of authority.

It is particularly ambiguous, however, under what circumstances this principle of attribution will exactly apply. In its Commentary, the ILC does not cite much further practice, satisfying itself with stating that pertinent cases will be 'exceptional' and 'occur only rarely, such as during revolution, armed conflict or foreign occupation, where the regular authorities dissolve, are disintegrating, have been suppressed or are for the time being inoperative'.[14]

It is noteworthy that, for the application of Article 9 ARSIWA, akin to the application of Article 5 ARSIWA, the mere exercise of elements of governmental authority does not suffice for conduct to be attributed to the state: the non-state actor should exercise this authority 'in circumstances such as to call for the exercise of those elements of authority'. For the ILC, it implies that these circumstances 'must have justified the attempt to exercise police or other functions in the absence of any constituted authority'.[15] It may then be in the eye of the beholder whether, in light of the prevailing circumstances, the exercise of elements of governmental authority was really 'called for' or 'justified', although perhaps not—as the ILC held—'necessarily the conduct in question'.[16]

This goes to show that attribution of the exercise of elements of governmental authority by a non-state actor to the state is not automatic; with regard to the application of both Article 5 and Article 9 ARSIWA, additional requirements are imposed. This high threshold may well result in non-attribution of non-state actor conduct to the state, even if the non-state actor

[14] ILC Commentary (1) to Art 9 ARSIWA (n 2) 49.
[15] ILC Commentary (6) to Art 9 ARSIWA (n 2) 49.
[16] ibid.

is exercising elements of governmental authority. This may for instance occur when the non-state actor exercises control over a certain territory without being mandated to do so or without the circumstances being present that call for the exercise of governmental authority. In order to discipline such de facto regimes, a separate responsibility system may well be in order. So far, however, there is little international legal practice with respect to obligations and responsibilities of de facto regimes, or de facto states (these are non-recognised states),[17] although such entities may well violate the human rights of the population under its control, or cause injuries to other subjects of international law, eg, by using (illegal) force.[18]

8.3 ATTRIBUTION OF CONDUCT ON THE BASIS OF INSTRUCTIONS OR CONTROL

The principle of control or instructions has attracted the most scholarly attention within the doctrine of attribution of conduct.[19] Pursuant to this principle, codified in Article 8 ARSIWA, '[t]he conduct of a person or group of persons shall be considered an act of a State under international law if the person or group of persons is in fact acting on the instructions of, or under the direction or control of, that State in carrying out the conduct'. Unlike Articles 4 and 5 ARSIWA, Article 8 governs attribution on the basis of a de facto link: non-state actor acts are attributed to the state

[17] See for some rare studies Michael Schoiswohl, *Status and (Human Rights) Obligations of Non-recognized de Facto Regimes in International Law: The Case of 'Somaliland': the Resurrection of Somaliland Against All International 'odds': State Collapse, Secession, Non-recognition, and Human Rights* (Leiden, Martinus Nijhoff, 2004); Michael Schoiswohl, 'De Facto Regimes and Human Rights Obligations—The Twilight Zone of Public International Law' (2001) 6 *Austrian Review of International & European Law* 45; Jochen Frowein, *Das de facto-Regime im Völkerrecht: Eine Untersuchung zur Rechtsstellung 'nichtanerkannter Staaten' und ähnlicher Gebilde* (Köln, Carl Heymans Verlag, 1968).

[18] See on the undesirability of such a legal vacuum MN Shaw, *International Law*, 4th edn (Cambridge, Cambridge University Press, 1997) 448 (stating: 'if an entity, while meeting the conditions of international law as to statehood, went totally unrecognized, this would undoubtedly hamper the exercise of its rights and duties, especially in view of the absence of diplomatic relations'); James Crawford, 'The criteria for statehood in international law' (1976) 48 *British Yearbook of International Law* 93, 145 (submitting that 'if international law withholds legal status from effective illegal entities, the result is a legal vacuum undesirable both in practice and principle').

[19] Most recently, this has occurred in the context of delineating responsibility between states and international organisations in military or peacekeeping operations. See, eg, Bérénice Boutin, 'Responsibility of the Netherlands for the acts of Dutchbat in Nuhanović and Mustafić: the continuous quest for a tangible meaning for "effective control" in the context of peacekeeping' (2012) 25 *Leiden Journal of International Law* 521; Tom Dannenbaum, 'Translating the Standard of Effective Control into a System of Effective Accountability: How Liability Should be Apportioned for Violations of Human Rights by Member State Troop Contingents Serving as United Nations Peacekeepers' (2010) 51 *Harvard International Law Journal* 113.

not because of an organic link to the state or because of governmental empowerment, but because the non-state actor depends in fact on the state, or is controlled in fact by the state.

The principle underlying Article 8 ARSIWA is typically applied in the context of non-state armed groups (militias) receiving instructions from, or being controlled by the state. It was perhaps most famously applied by the ICJ in the *Nicaragua* case, in which the Court held that acts contrary to human rights and humanitarian law, committed by Nicaraguan contra-revolutionaries assisted by the United States, could *not* be attributed to the latter, as no evidence was adduced that the United States had 'directed or enforced the perpetration of the acts'.[20]

In the *Nicaragua* case, the Court introduced a rather stringent 'effective control' threshold that may often be difficult to satisfy. This standard was confirmed in the Court's 2007 *Bosnia Genocide* judgment, in which the ICJ did not attribute the genocidal acts committed by a Bosnian Serb (non-state) militia to Serbia, as Bosnia (the applicant state) had failed to prove that the militia had acted on the instructions of Serbia, or was effectively controlled by it[21]—although there were clear connections between the Serbian and Bosnian Serb leaderships.[22]

Because the effective control test as devised by the ICJ may often lead to non-attribution of non-state actor acts to the state, alternative standards which would narrow the accountability gap have been proposed; the most renowned being the 'overall control' standard. This looser standard, which considers general control to suffice for attribution, is particularly expounded upon in the judgment of the International Criminal Tribunal for Yugoslavia's Appeals Chamber's decision in the *Tadic* case (1999).[23]

[20] *Military and Paramilitary Activities in and against Nicaragua* (*Nicaragua v United States of America*) (Merits) (Judgment) [1986] ICJ Rep 14, 64 [115]. Note, however, that the Court attributed the attacks perpetrated by the so-called 'Unilaterally Controlled Latino Assets' (UCLAs) in Nicaragua—as opposed to the Contras—to the US. See *Military and Paramilitary Activities Case* 40–41, para 86 ('Although it is not proved that any United States military personnel took a direct part in the operations, agents of the United States participated in the planning, direction, support and execution of the operations. The execution was the task rather of the "UCLAs", while United States nationals participated in the planning, direction and support. The imputability to the United States of these attacks appears therefore to the Court to be established.').

[21] *Application of the Convention on the Prevention and Punishment of the Crime of Genocide (Bosnia and Herzegovina v Serbia and Montenegro)* (Judgment) [2007] ICJ Rep 43 [385]–[415].

[22] On the basis of these connections, the Court proceeded to hold Serbia responsible for violations of *primary* obligations to prevent/punish genocide under the 1948 Genocide Convention. See *Bosnia Genocide* case (n 21) [297] and [376].

[23] *Prosecutor v Tadic* (Appeals Chamber Judgment) IT-94-1-A (15 July 1999) 60-62 [137]–[141]—a standard of 'overall effective control' has also been developed by the European Court of Human Rights, but in respect of delimiting the geographical (territorial/extra-territorial) application of the European Convention of Human Rights, rather than in respect of attributing acts of NSA to States. *Cf Cyprus v Turkey* App no 25781/94 (ECtHR, 10 May 2001) para 76; *Loizidou v Turkey* (preliminary objections) Series A no 310 (1995); *Ilaşcu*

It is of note, however, that in this case, the overall control test was not applied for purposes of state responsibility as the Tribunal only concerned itself with individual responsibility, with the characterisation of a conflict as international or non-international, the exercise of overall control by a state over a non-state armed group embroiled in an armed conflict would suffice for the 'internationalisation' of the armed conflict, which would in turn give rise to the full application of the 1949 Geneva Conventions on the law of war. The overall control test—although not espoused by the ICJ—has nevertheless been supported in the literature.[24] The ARSIWA do not express a preference for either approach (effective or overall control), leaving the exact interpretation of the control standard, at first sight, relatively open. Despite this, the ILC Commentary to Article 8 provides that non-state actor acts will be attributed to the state if the state 'directed or controlled the specific operation and the conduct complained of was an integral part of the operation.'[25] In doing so, the ILC, while perhaps not explicitly supporting an effective control standard as strict as the one applied by the ICJ, appears to have departed from the rather loose standard introduced by the ILC in an earlier version of the ARSIWA (1974), when 'in fact acting on behalf of the State' was held to suffice for attribution,[26] and also departs from the overall control standard, which requires general control over an actor rather than over the actor's specific conduct and operations.

The standard of 'in fact acting on behalf of the State' nevertheless remains in existence in respect of primary rules on the use of force. States are under an obligation not to send their proxies to use force against other states; or as the Definition of Aggression has it, 'the sending by or on behalf of a State of armed bands, groups, irregulars, or mercenaries, which carry out acts of armed force against another State of such gravity as to

and Others v Moldova and Russia App no 48787/99 (ECtHR, 8 July 2004) [311]; *Issa and Others v Turkey* App no 31821/96 (ECtHR, 16 November 2004); *Pad and Others v Turkey* App no 60167/00 (ECtHR, 28 June 2007); *Isaak and Others v Turkey* App no 44587/98 (ECtHR, 28 September 2006).

[24] Antonio Cassese, 'The International Community's "Legal" Response to Terrorism' (2007) 18 *European Journal of International Law* 649; Momtaz, Cahin and de Frouville (n 1) 270 (considering it a 'useful approach to the question'); Kimberley N Trapp, 'Shared Responsibility and Organized Non-State Actors in the Terrorism Context' forthcoming in (2015) 62 *Netherlands International Law Review* (arguing that the 'effective control' standard may be appropriate with respect to paramilitary operations of which humanitarian law violations are a non-inherent feature, but that the 'overall control' standard may be more appropriate in a terrorism context, as the aim of terrorism is precisely to commit international law violations).

[25] ILC Commentary (3) to Art 8 ARSIWA (n 2).

[26] It is nevertheless interesting that Roberto Ago, who was at that time the ILC Rapporteur, supported the application of the stringent effective control standard as a judge in the *Nicaragua* case. See *Military and Paramilitary Activities* (n 20) Separate Opinion Judge Ago 188 [16]. Possibly, in spite of the rather loose wording of the 1974 draft, the ILC had a rather high threshold in mind from the very beginning of its work on state responsibility.

amount to … [invasion, bombardment, blockade, or attack]'[27] qualifies as an act of aggression prohibited by international law. This is not a rule of attribution, however. The state has a direct obligation not to use force, against other states, regardless of utilising non-state actors to carry out its bidding, without the need arising to attribute an unlawful act committed by a non-state actor to the state.

Similarly, the rule that a state may (possibly) exercise its right of self-defence against another state, providing a safe haven to non-state actors carrying out attacks (typically terrorist activities) against the former state, should not be seen as a (secondary) rule of attribution, but rather as a primary rule on the legality of the use of force.[28] Such a principle may rest on the proximity between the non-state actor and the target state, but in no way are the acts of the non-state actor *attributed* to the target state for the purpose of triggering the application of Article 51 of the United Nations Charter. Moreover, this principle does not fall within the ambit of state responsibility. Rather, it is an (alleged) customary international law rule that allows the injured state to use force against another state that has harboured terrorists or tolerated their presence on its territory, without necessarily actively supporting them or endorsing their activities.[29]

There are some technical issues surrounding the application of Article 8 ARSIWA that deserve further scrutiny. A first issue is whether a non-state actor's 'complete dependence' on a state calls for the application of Article 8 ARSIWA or rather Article 4 ARSIWA: does a non-state actor which is completely dependent on a state not become an organ of the state for the purpose of organic attribution, and thus lose its non-state character (Article 4), or should 'complete dependence' be seen as a variation on state control of/instructions to non-state actors (Article 8)?

In the *Nicaragua* case, which predated the adoption of the ARSIWA, the ICJ had referred to this 'complete dependence' test of attribution in the following terms:

> What the Court has to determine at this point is whether or not the relationship of the contras to the United States Government was so much one of dependence on the one side and control on the other that it would be right to equate the

[27] Definition of Aggression, UNGA Res 3314 (XXIX) (14 December 1974) annex, para 3(g). This principle has been applied by the ICJ in *Armed Activities on the Territory of the Congo (Democratic Republic of the Congo v Uganda)* (Judgment) [2005] ICJ Rep 168, paras 131–35, in which it refuted Uganda's allegations that the Democratic Republic of Congo (DRC) had been implicated in attacks perpetrated by DRC-based rebels against Uganda.

[28] See for the connections between primary rules on the use of force and secondary rules on state responsibility André Nollkaemper, 'Attribution of Forcible Acts to States: Connections between the Law on the Use of Force and the Law of State Responsibility' in Niels Blokker and Nico Schrijver (eds), *Legal Aspects of International Organization* (Leiden, Martinus Nijhoff Publishers, 2005) 133–71.

[29] See further Jordan Paust on the right of self-defence and NSA in his contribution to this volume (Ch 13) on armed opposition groups.

contras, for legal purposes, with an organ of the United States Government, or as acting on behalf of that Government.[30]

However, the Court did not fully develop this question, deciding instead to focus on the effective control standard. In the 2007 *Bosnia Genocide* case, however, the ICJ did address the issue and appears to have espoused the former approach, where it held that the acts of de facto organs, such as a non-state militia, could be attributed to the state under Article 4 ARSIWA, provided that 'the persons, groups or entities act in "complete dependence" on the State, of which they are ultimately merely the instrument'.[31] In doing so, the Court may have abandoned the idea that organic attribution requires an institutional link to the state as even acts of non-state actors which are only linked de facto to the state could be attributed to the latter. Griebel and Plücken have rightly considered it 'problematic to regard Article 4 of the ILC Articles as a sufficient basis … for attributing acts of groups one would regard prima facie as private groups',[32] on the ground that 'the complete dependence test focuses on persons which prima facie have nothing in common with *de jure* or … quasi-*de jure* organs',[33] but which are instead de facto organs falling under Article 8 ARSIWA. There is merit in this criticism, as Article 4 ARSIWA, while perhaps not requiring that internal law has determined the status of entities as state organs, at least requires that there is a state practice to determine such status.[34] It is no less true, however, that the ARSIWA are just a codification effort of the rules of state responsibility. The ICJ may sometimes rely on these rules, and their categorisation (eg, de jure vs de facto organs)—as it indeed does—but then again, as Milanovic has usefully reminded us, 'the Court is the authoritative interpreter of its own jurisprudence'.[35]

Another issue with respect to the instructions/control standard of Article 8 ARSIWA concerns the applicability of the rule of ultra vires. Per Article 7 ARSIWA, '[t]he conduct of an organ of a State or of a person or

[30] *Military and Paramilitary Activities* (n 20) [109].

[31] *Bosnia Genocide* case (n 21) para 392. Applying this rule, the Court held that the Bosnian Serbs enjoyed 'some qualified, but real, margin of independence', and thus that they were not completely dependent on Serbia. See for a discussion of the different principles of attribution in *Bosnia Genocide*: Berglind Halldorsdottir Birkland, 'Reining in non-state actors: State responsibility and attribution in cases of genocide' (2009) 84 *New York University Law Review* 1623. See, for an appraisal five years *before* the Court rendered its judgment: André JJ De Hoogh, 'Articles 4 and 8 of the 2001 ILC Articles on State Responsibility, the Tadić Case and Attribution of Acts of Bosnian Serb Authorities to the Federal Republic of Yugoslavia' (2001) 72 *British Yearbook of International Law* 255.

[32] Jörn Griebel and Milan Plücken, 'New Developments Regarding the Rules of Attribution? The International Court of Justice's Decision in Bosnia v Serbia' (2008) 21 *Leiden Journal of International Law* 601, 615.

[33] ibid.

[34] ILC Commentary (11) to Art 4 ARSIWA (n 2)

[35] Marko Milanovic, 'State responsibility for acts of non-state actors: a comment on Griebel and Plücken' (2009) 22 *Leiden Journal of International Law* 307–20.

entity empowered to exercise elements of the governmental authority shall be considered an act of the State under international law if the organ, person or entity acts in that capacity, even if it exceeds its authority or contravenes instructions.' This rule of ultra vires only applies to Articles 4 and 5 ARSIWA, discussed above. The ILC Commentary to Article 8, however, applies it to situations of control as well, but generally not to directions/instructions.[36] This distinction, and the application of ultra vires to situations of control, appears defensible, as the nexus between a non-state actor and the state is stronger in case the latter exercises effective control over the former's acts.[37] Such control comes closer to the 'complete dependence' which the ICJ considered to be covered by the rule on organic attribution (Article 4) to which Article 7 on ultra vires fully applies. Even if the state may not have wanted a specific act to be carried out, as long as it exercises effective control over the general conduct to which a specific act is related, this specific ultra vires act will be attributed to it. The practical relevance of the rule of ultra vires in connection with state control over non-state actor acts is rather limited, however, since—as discussed above—the standard of effective control, at least as applied by the ICJ, is a very strict one that is difficult to satisfy in practice.

The strictness of the effective control standard indeed limits the chances of attributing non-state actor acts to states: even if the latter give 'massive forms of support' to the non-state actor, as happened in the *Nicaragua* case, the non-state actor's acts may not be attributed to the state.[38] As set out above, this has led to calls for a wider 'overall control' standard, but so far this standard has failed to gain currency with the ICJ, possibly on the ground that an overall control standard may collapse the distinction between the private and the public sphere. Inevitably then, the continued applicability of the effective control standard elicits the question as to whether the non-state actor who was supported but not controlled or directed by the state, should not incur responsibility in its own right for violations of international law. Put differently, should the limitations of the state responsibility regime not be remedied by conceptualising direct obligations and responsibility for the non-state actor rather than for the state, which entertains some links with the non-state actor? The same idea also applies in respect of Article 10 ARSIWA, which concerns itself with the attribution of conduct of an insurrectional or other movement to the state, and which is the subject of the next section.

[36] Commentary (8) to Art 8 ARSIWA (n 2) ('In general, a State, in giving lawful instructions to persons who are not its organs, does not assume the risk that the instructions will be carried out in an internationally unlawful way. On the other hand, where persons or groups have committed acts under the effective control of a State, the condition for attribution will still be met even if particular instructions may have been ignored.').

[37] *Contra* Momtaz Cahin and de Frouville (n 1) 271 (characterising the distinction as 'less convincing').

[38] Griebel and Plücken (n 32) 621.

8.4 ATTRIBUTION OF CONDUCT OF AN INSURRECTIONAL OR OTHER MOVEMENT TO THE STATE

Quite a number of principles regarding the attribution of conduct of non-state actor to states have been developed in the context of non-state armed groups committing violations of international law. To provide some examples, private military/security companies interrogating prisoners (non-state armed groups exercising elements of governmental authority, Article 5 ARSIWA), insurrectional movements whose acts are directed or controlled by states (Article 8 ARSIWA, *Nicaragua*-plus scenarios), armed groups carrying out conduct in the absence or default of official authorities (Article 9 ARSIWA),[39] or militias whose acts are acknowledged or adopted by the state as its own (Article 11 ARSIWA).[40] Still, these principles apply, in essence at least, to any non-state actor. One article of the ARSIWA, however, namely Article 10, applies specifically to insurrectional movements (without abrogating the attribution to the state of these movements' conduct on the basis of other attribution principles).[41] Pursuant to this provision, '[t]he conduct of an insurrectional movement which becomes the new government of a State shall be considered an act of that State under international law', and 'the conduct of a movement, insurrectional or other, which succeeds in establishing a new State in part of the territory of a pre-existing State or in a territory under its administration shall be considered an act of the new State under international law'.[42] It is

[39] See notably *Kenneth P Yeager v The Islamic Republic of Iran* (1987) 17 Iran-USCTR 104 [43] (holding that the Islamic Republic of Iran's Revolutionary Guards 'at least exercised elements of governmental authority in the absence of official authorities, in operations of which the new Government must have had knowledge and to which it did not specifically object.').

[40] See in particular the ICJ's attribution to the State of Iran of the seizure of control over the US embassy in Tehran (1979) by armed militants, on which Art 11 ARSIWA was largely based: *United States Diplomatic and Consular Staff in Tehran* (Judgment) [1980] ICJ Rep 3, 35, para 74 ('The policy thus announced by the Ayatollah Khomeini, of maintaining the occupation of the Embassy and the detention of its inmates as hostages for the purpose of exerting pressure on the United States Government was complied with by other Iranian authorities and endorsed by them repeatedly in statements made in various contexts. The result of that policy was fundamentally to transform the legal nature of the situation created by the occupation of the Embassy and the detention of its diplomatic and consular staff as hostages. The approval given to these facts by the Ayatollah Khomeini and other organs of the Iranian State, and the decision to perpetuate them, translated continuing occupation of the Embassy and detention of the hostages into acts of that State.') See also ILC Commentary (4), (6) and (11) to Art 11 ARSIWA (n 2). Going by the examples given by the ILC, this basis of attribution appears to be rather exceptional.

[41] Art 10(3) ARSIWA ('This article is without prejudice to the attribution to a State of any conduct, however related to that of the movement concerned, which is to be considered an act of that State by virtue of Articles 4 to 9.').

[42] Note that the ILC has excluded 'the situation where an insurrectional movement within a territory succeeds in its agitation for union with another State' from the ambit of Art 10, treating this situation as 'essentially a case of succession'. See ILC Commentary (10) to Art 10 ARSIWA (n 2) 51. Contra Patrick Dumberry, 'New state responsibility for internationally wrongful acts by an insurrectional movement' (2006) 17 *European Journal of International Law* 605, 619–20.

immediately apparent that this attribution principle is only of relevance for insurrectional movements which turn out to be *successful* in their struggle against a sitting regime, either by overthrowing the regime and forming the new government, or by seceding from the state with which they are fighting.

In general, for obvious reasons, states do not incur responsibility for the acts of insurrectional movements engaged in armed struggle with them: indeed, given the hostilities between the state and the movement, the connection between them can hardly be more tenuous. Thus, acts of insurrectional movements that are involved in an on-going armed conflict with the state, or acts of such movements that have ultimately been defeated by the state, will not be attributed to the latter. However, when an insurrectional movement is successful in its struggle against the government, and manages to seize the levers of power in the state, according to the ILC, 'it would be anomalous if the new regime or new state could avoid responsibility for conduct earlier committed by it'.[43] Under this principle of attribution, the movement and the eventual (new) Government of the (possibly new) state are seen as continuous, and thus, the movement's acts will *post factum* be attributed to the state. This principle appears to be supported by (somewhat older) practice.[44]

There is no continuity between the insurrectional movement and the state—and attribution of the former's acts to the latter would thus not be appropriate—in case of governments of national reconciliation, however, at least according to the ILC.[45] This appears sensible, as such governments only partly consist of representatives of (former) insurrectional movements, and the continuity is accordingly not complete. Moreover, from a policy perspective, making the state responsible in such a situation would fail to provide an incentive for the incumbent government to open meaningful talks with the insurrectional movement with a view to brokering peace and forming a government of national unity; rather, it would be a recipe for continuous strife. Yet the axiomatic downside of such a solution is represented by the fact that victims of the insurrectional movement's wrongful acts remain in the cold. For this reason, d'Aspremont has attempted to mitigate its consequences by requiring, in addition to a power-sharing agreement, democratic legitimation of such an agreement through elections.[46] However meritorious this attempt, it makes victims of internationally wrongful acts dependent on the contingency of subsequent political processes for accountability to run its course, a scenario which international law, especially international criminal law,

[43] ILC Commentary (4) to Art 10 ARSIWA (n 2) 50.

[44] ILC Commentary (11) to Art 10 ARSIWA (n 2) 51–52.

[45] ILC Commentary (7) to Art 10 ARSIWA (n 2) 51.

[46] Jean d'Aspremont, 'Rebellion and state responsibility: wrongdoing by democratically elected insurgents' (2007) 58 *International and Comparative Law Quarterly* 427, 437–40.

has precisely tended to exclude in the last few decades, by notably outlawing the granting of amnesty for international crimes.[47] What is more, it may offer an insurrectional movement an incentive to carry out even more callous acts, calculating that such acts may give it an entry ticket to a state's government of national unity to which such acts would ultimately not be attributed.[48]

The possibility that non-state armed groups can escape (indirect) accountability by entering into a power-sharing agreement with the government, and even more importantly, the absence of any attribution to the state of acts of insurrectional movements that are not successful in overthrowing the government, or that have no interest in doing so in the first place, may necessitate contemplating the direct responsibility of non-state actors. The ILC explicitly refused to address such responsibility in the ARSIWA (considering it, rather logically in fact, outside the ARSIWA remit), although it did not as such exclude its existence.[49] As we write, it is accepted that armed groups have obligations under international humanitarian law (although the theoretical basis for the latter's binding character remains elusive),[50] but it is less sure whether they have obligations under other rules of public international law (notably international

[47] See, eg, *Prosecutor v Kondewa* case no SCSL-2004-14-AR72 (E) (25 May 2004), Decision on Lack of Jurisdiction/Abuse of Process: Amnesty Provided by the Lomé Accord, Separate Opinion Justice Robertson [48] ('it may therefore be said that State practice is changing to conform to the consistent view that blanket amnesties are, at least in "general", impermissible in international law for international crimes'); *Barrios Altos v Peru* Judgment (Merits) Inter-American Court of Human Rights series C no 75 (14 March 2001) [43] ('Self-amnesty laws lead to the defencelessness of victims and perpetuate impunity; therefore, they are manifestly incompatible with the aims and spirit of the Convention. This type of law precludes the identification of individuals who are responsible for human rights violations, because it obstructs the investigation and access to justice and prevents the victims and their next of kin from knowing the truth and receiving the corresponding reparation.').

[48] See Sten Verhoeven, 'International Responsibility of Armed Opposition Groups: Lessons from State Responsibility for Actions of Armed Opposition Groups' in Noemi Gal-Or, Cedric Ryngaert and Math Noortmann (eds), *Responsibilities of the Non-State Actor in Armed Conflict and the Market Place* (Leiden, Brill, 2015) 285 (arguing that the 'absence of state responsibility might actually cause the insurgent movement to use brute force and to engage in serious violations of international humanitarian law and human rights law in order to secure a place at the bargaining table').

[49] ILC Commentary (16) to Art 10 ARSIWA (n 2) 52 ('A further possibility is that the insurrectional movement may itself be held responsible for its own conduct under international law, for example for a breach of international humanitarian law committed by its forces. The topic of the international responsibility of unsuccessful insurrectional or other movements, however, falls outside the scope of the present articles, which are concerned only with the responsibility of States.').

[50] Raphael van Steenberghe, 'Non-State Actors from the Perspective of the International Committee of the Red Cross' in Jean d'Aspremont (ed), *Participants in the International Legal System: Multiple Perspectives On Non-State Actors In International Law* (Abingdon, Routledge, 2011) 220–24.

human rights law).[51] It is similarly unclear how a responsibility regime for armed groups, in terms of attribution of conduct and consequences of responsibility, should be designed.

8.5 DUE DILIGENCE/FAILURE TO PREVENT

The mechanism of attribution of non-state actor conduct to the state, which has been discussed so far in this contribution, belongs to the realm of *secondary* rules of international law. It is important to distinguish it from the state's failure to prevent certain acts of non-state actor, which under some *primary* rules of international law (notably the law of immunity, international human rights law, and international environmental law) may engage the responsibility of the state. While with respect to both attribution and the state failure to prevent, non-state actor conduct ultimately triggers the responsibility of the state, in the latter instance the state incurs responsibility for its own act—its failure to exercise due diligence—whereas in the case of the former the state incurs responsibility for another actor's act. Failure to prevent/due diligence is not addressed by the ARSIWA, which only contain *secondary* rules of international law, defined as 'the general conditions under international law for the State to be considered responsible for wrongful actions or omissions, and the legal consequences which flow therefrom'.[52] The failure to prevent, in contrast, concerns the extent/content of a primary international obligation.

The principles of due diligence and failure to prevent have been developed in the context of primary norms in the fields of environmental law, human rights, and the law of immunity. This section examines how the principle of due diligence is applied in a human rights context, what its limitations are, and how they could be addressed.

In human rights law, the failure to prevent is known as the state duty to protect or the positive obligations of the state. Notably the European Court of Human Rights (ECtHR), which can hold states responsible for violations of the European Convention on Human Rights (ECHR), has contributed to the development of these principles, particularly in the

[51] See, for a discussion, Jean-Marie Henckaerts and Cornelius Wiesener, 'Human rights obligations of non-state armed groups: A possible contribution from customary international law?' in Robert Kolb and Gloria Gaggioli (eds), *Research Handbook on Human Rights and Humanitarian Law* (Cheltenham, Edward Elgar Publishing, 2013) 146–69; Aristotle Constantinides, 'Human Rights Obligations and Accountability of Armed Opposition Groups: The Practice of the UN Security Council' (2010) 4 *Human Rights & International Legal Discourse* 89–110.

[52] ILC Commentary ARSIWA (n 2) 31.

context of the right to life (Article 2 ECHR). In the seminal case of *Osman v United Kingdom*, the Court held that

> the first sentence of Article 2 §1 enjoins the State not only to refrain from the intentional and unlawful taking of life, but also to take appropriate steps to safeguard the lives of those within its jurisdiction … it is sufficient for an applicant to show that the authorities did not do all that could be reasonably expected of them to avoid a real and immediate risk to life of which they have or ought to have knowledge.[53]

The International Court of Justice has also applied the principle of failure to prevent in a human rights context: in its 2007 judgment in *Application of the Convention on the Prevention and Punishment of the Crime of Genocide*, it cited states' due diligence obligation to prevent and punish under the Genocide Convention,[54] and then went on to find Serbia and Montenegro responsible for failing to prevent the genocidal acts committed by Bosnian Serb militias in Bosnia as well as for failing to punish the responsible persons. The latter judgment offers a fine example of how states can be held responsible for the acts of non-state armed groups not only on the basis of attribution of conduct, but also on the basis of the principle of due diligence and the failure to prevent, prosecute and punish. This may imply that states appear to be under an obligation to provide reparation to victims of atrocities of non-state armed groups which they had the capacity to prevent.[55]

Recently, a number of (soft law) international documents purporting to regulate business actors' adverse effects on the enjoyment of human rights have given pride of place to the principle of state due diligence. Most prominently, the first pillar of the UN Guiding Principles on Business and Human Rights, also known as the 2011 'Ruggie Principles', consists of the state duty to protect. Pursuant to this, 'States must protect against human rights abuse within their territory and/or jurisdiction by third parties, including business enterprises', which 'requires taking appropriate steps to prevent, investigate, punish and redress such abuse through effective policies, legislation, regulations and adjudication.'[56] Principle 24 of the Maastricht Principles on Extraterritorial Obligations of States in the Field of Economic, Social and Cultural Rights (2012) similarly provides that '[a]ll States must take necessary measures to ensure that non-State

[53] *Osman v UK* App no 23452/94 (ECtHR, 28 October 1998) [115]–[116]. See also *Ilascu and others v Moldova and Russia* (n 23) [330]–[331].

[54] See *Bosnia Genocide Case* (n 21) [430].

[55] *The Dust Has Not Yet Settled. Victims' Views on The Right to Remedy and Reparation. A Report from the Greater North of Uganda* (2012) OHCHR 72.

[56] Report of the Special Representative of the Secretary-General on the issue of human rights and transnational corporations and other business enterprises, John Ruggie Guiding Principles on Business and Human Rights: Implementing the United Nations 'Protect, Respect and Remedy' Framework, UN Doc A/HRC/17/31 (2011) Principle 1.

actors which they are in a position to regulate ... such as private individuals and organizations, and transnational corporations and other business enterprises, do not nullify or impair the enjoyment of economic, social and cultural rights.'[57] Additionally, the 'Montreux' document on pertinent international legal obligations and good practices for states related to operations of private military and security companies during armed conflict provides that states have international obligations to regulate the activities of these companies with a view to preventing them from committing violations of international law.[58]

These documents may reserve a prominent place for the state duty to protect, but at the same time, some of them pinpoint the limitations of the state-centred 'indirect responsibility' approach, albeit implicitly. Indeed, the Montreux document has been supplemented by an International Code of Conduct for Private Security Service Providers (ICoC-PSP, 2010),[59] to which these providers may commit themselves voluntarily. Apparently, in and of itself, the state obligations approach of the Montreux document did not suffice. By the same token, after drawing attention to the state duty to protect, the UN Guiding Principles on Business and Human Rights go on to highlight the separate direct (soft) duties of the corporations to respect human rights.[60] This is in line with what the UN Special Representative had earlier flagged as 'governance gaps' regarding business and human rights;[61] governance gaps that may have to be filled by innovative conceptual thinking that widens the circle of international duty-bearers to include corporations.

At any rate, the need for a second pillar of the UN Guiding Principles and a separate code of conduct aimed—only—at corporations demonstrates that reliance on the state, backed up by a state responsibility regime, does not, in itself, guarantee that individuals and communities will be protected from non-state actor activities' adverse effects on human rights. A state responsibility regime may not suffice because states may

[57] Maastricht Principles (n 11).

[58] ICRC, 'The Montreux Document on pertinent international legal obligations and good practices for States related to operations of private military and security companies during armed conflict' (17 September, 2008) accessible at www.icrc.org/eng/assets/files/other/icrc_002_0096.pdf.

[59] The Code is available at www.icoc-psp.org.

[60] UN Guiding Principles (n 56) Principle 11 ('Business enterprises should respect human rights. This means that they should avoid infringing on the human rights of others and should address adverse human rights impacts with which they are involved.').

[61] SRSG, *Protect, Respect and Remedy: a Framework for Business and Human Rights*, UN Doc A/HRC/8/5 (2008) para 3 ('The root cause of the business and human rights predicament today lies in the governance gaps created by globalization—between the scope and impact of economic forces and actors, and the capacity of societies to manage their adverse consequences. These governance gaps provide the permissive environment for wrongful acts by companies of all kinds without adequate sanctioning or reparation. How to narrow and ultimately bridge the gaps in relation to human rights is our fundamental challenge.').

be unwilling to, or incapable of regulating and supervising corporate activities. They may be unwilling because inward corporate investment increases the government's tax base or because officials are bribed, or they may be incapable because they lack resources to police corporate compliance with human rights.[62] The widely publicised collapse of a poorly constructed Bangladeshi garment factory at Rana Plaza on 24 April 2013, a disaster which killed 1,127 people, is a case in point: an official report laid blame partly with local officials for wrongly granting construction approvals after receiving bribes from the building's owner.[63] Given the extent of government negligence and collusion in low-wage countries, the likelihood of the government pressing charges against non-compliant corporations is reduced, and accordingly, a fine case for direct corporate responsibility under international law can be made.

At the same time, however, it remains somewhat unclear how such responsibility can be operationalised, and more particularly, what its added value vis-à-vis domestic regulation would be. Arguably, in the absence of an international court with jurisdiction over corporate misbehaviour, strengthening and enforcing domestic regulation in the home state of the corporation manufacturing or importing constitutes a practically more promising avenue. That being said, the profound transformative power of laying down *international* rather than *domestic* legal obligations for corporations should not be underestimated. For one thing, mention of the term 'international', eg, by corporate social responsibility civil society activists, may make corporations more susceptible to change their ways. For another, the jurisdictional barriers to the exercise of extraterritorial jurisdiction by corporations' home states could more easily be overcome if the applicable liability norms are internationally shared rather than being merely of a—possibly idiosyncratic—domestic nature. Finally, while an international criminal or human rights court with jurisdiction over corporations may, as we write, remain elusive, the promotion of

[62] Eric De Brabandere, 'Human Rights and Transnational Corporations: The Limits of Direct Corporate Responsibility' (2010) 4 *Human Rights & International Legal Discourse* 66, 66–88, believing that the need for direct corporate social responsibility under international law is obviated if State capacity is strengthened. While this position definitely has merit, at the same time, it appears as utopian, given the retreat of the State in many sectors. One of the leading advocates of Third World Approaches to International Law, BS Chimni, has attributed the more limited authority and ability of States belonging to the 'Global South' to the development of international trade and investment regimes over the last decades, regimes that supposedly benefit Western States, corporations, and corrupt officials, rather than citizens of the Global South. See Bhupinder S Chimni, 'Third world approaches to international law: a manifesto' (2006) 8 *International Community Law Review* 3, 7, 10.

[63] Jim Yardley, 'Report on Deadly Factory Collapse in Bangladesh Finds Widespread Blame', *New York Times* (22 May 2013) www.nytimes.com/2013/05/23/world/asia/report-on-bangladesh-building-collapse-finds-widespread-blame.html?_r=0.

corporate legal obligations to the level of international law may precisely create momentum for the establishment of such a court, or the extension of the jurisdiction of an existing court.

8.6 CONCLUDING OBSERVATIONS

While the regime of state responsibility puts a high premium on the separation of the private and the public sphere, under carefully defined circumstances conduct of non-state actors could be attributed to states. Indeed, states and non-state actors do not always operate at arm's length from each other, as states may use non-state actors to do their bidding, support them, or fail to rein them in. The ARSIWA identify a limited number of scenarios of non-state actors acting as agents of the state, which justifies attribution of non-state actor conduct to the state (Articles 5–11 ARSIWA).

Furthermore, even if non-state actors do not serve as state agents, and thus their conduct cannot be attributed to the state, the state can yet, in accordance with specific legal regimes (human rights, environmental), be held responsible for failing to prevent wrongful non-state actor conduct when it had the capacity to influence the non-state actor. In this situation, the state is not so much held responsible for the acts of the non-state actor (through attribution of conduct), but rather for its own failure to exercise due diligence.

From an accountability perspective, these principles are welcome, as they prevent the state from escaping responsibility for the wrongful acts of its proxies, or at least of persons over whom the state was in a position to exercise some form of control or authority. Nevertheless, the criteria for attribution of conduct are rather stringent, and the principle of due diligence does not apply when the state does not have the capacity to influence the non-state actor in the first place. As a result, some non-state actor conduct may fall through the cracks of the state responsibility regime—which may give rise to an undesirable accountability vacuum.

This problem could be remedied by strengthening state capacity to exercise due diligence over conduct by non-state actors, or by lowering the threshold for the application of the attribution principles. However, in the absence of a formidable injection of international funds and forms of capacity-building in low-governance zones or failed states, the former solution might appear utopian.[64] The latter, for its part, may

[64] See on the challenges posed by non-state actor conduct in failed States: Jennifer Moore, 'From Nation State to Failed State: International Protection from Human Rights Abuses by Non-State Actors' (1999) 31 *Columbia Human Rights Law Review* 81.

dangerously conflate the distinction between the public and the private sphere.

Instead, this contribution has favoured the conceptualisation of direct obligations and responsibility of the non-state actors themselves. If non-state actors are exercising real international power and cause harm to third parties, it is only logical that they are held to account on the basis of a separate, tailor-made responsibility regime.

Part III

9

International Governmental Organisations as Non-State Actors

RAMSES A WESSEL

9.1 INTRODUCTION

THIS CHAPTER WILL revisit a classic theme in the law of international organisations and address the development of international organisations as influential non-state actors in global governance. Traditionally, intergovernmental organisations (IGOs) are the most important non-state actors in the international legal order; they clearly outnumber states,[1] and together they have become influential in the process of global law-making.[2] This contribution will address the traditional functions of international organisations, but will above all focus on new functions of international organisations related to their role in global governance. These new functions relate to a number of 'state-like' functions that have been taken up by international organisations—such as law-making and territorial administration. In that respect this contribution will also revisit the distinction between international organisations and their members as to investigate further to which extent international *governmental* organisations can be viewed as *non-state* actors.

The increasing number of competences that are transferred to—or created at the level of—international organisations and the fact that

[1] The 49th edition of the *Yearbook of International Organizations* lists about 5,000 IGOs; Union of International Associations, *Yearbook of International Organizations* (Leiden, Brill, 2012/13), www.uia.be/yearbook. Obviously the number depends on the definition used and most handbooks only count a few hundred major IGOs.

[2] José E Alvarez, *International Organizations as Law-Makers* (Oxford, Oxford University Press, 2005). But see also Ingrid Detter, 'Law making by international organizations' (PhD Thesis, Stockholm University, 1965). See for additional sources also Ramses Wessel, 'Institutional Law-Making: The Development of a Global Normative Web' in Catharina Brölmann and Yannick Radi (eds), *Handbook on the Theory and Practice of International Law-Making* (Cheltenham, Edgar Elgar, 2015).

international decisions[3] are no longer merely directed towards states, but also affect individuals and companies, triggered a debate on their accountability and international responsibility. This is due to the fact that the checks and balances that we are used to at the state level cannot always be found to the same extent at the global level. The emergence of new academic debates (eg, on international constitutional law, constitutional pluralism, global administrative law) can largely be explained on the basis of these developments.

Literature on the law of international organisations and their role in the international legal order is quite extensive,[4] and the field has developed rapidly over the past decade. While this chapter will certainly refer to the main findings of the legal debate on international organisations, its main purpose is to point to the 'autonomous' position international organisations have obtained. There is no doubt that states continue to be influential—and frequently clearly decisive—in relation to the role and function of the international organisations they have created for certain purposes. Yet, as has been noted by many over the past years, the law-making functions of many international organisations made us aware of the existence of—perhaps not the emergence of a world government[5]—but at least of global governance 'beyond the state' in what is sometimes normatively framed as a 'world community'.[6] International organisations have found their place in global governance,[7] and are even considered 'autonomous actors', following an agenda that is no longer fully defined by their member states,[8] which has caused the latter to devote much of

[3] Ramses A Wessel and Ige Dekker, 'Governance by International Organisations: Rethinking the Source and Normative Force of International Decisions' in Ige Dekker and Wouter Werner (eds), *Governance and International Legal Theory* (Leiden, Martinus Nijhoff, 2004) 215–36.

[4] References may be found throughout this chapter.

[5] Yet, see the clear reference to 'global government' in JP Trachtman, *The Future of International Law: Global Government* (Cambridge, Cambridge University Press, 2013). Elsewhere I address the consequences of this line of reasoning for the structure of the international legal order in more detail: Ramses A Wessel, 'Revealing the Publicness of International Law' in Erik Molenaar, André Nollkaemper, Sarah Nouwen, and Cedric Ryngaert (eds), *What's Wrong With International Law?* (Leiden/Boston, Martinus Nijhoff, 2015) 449–66.

[6] But see Martti Koskenniemi, 'The Subjective Dangers of Projects of World Community' in Antonio Cassese (ed), *Realizing Utopia: The Future of International Law* (Oxford, Oxford University Press, 2012) 3–13; as well as the other contributions in Pt I of this volume ('Can the World become a Global Community?').

[7] RA Wessel and I Dekker, 'Governance by International Organisations' (n 3).

[8] Edoardo Chiti and Ramses A Wessel, 'The Emergence of International Agencies in the Global Administrative Space: Autonomous Actors or State Servants' in Richard Collins and Nigel D White (eds), *International organizations and the idea of autonomy* (Abingdon, Routledge, 2011). *Cf* earlier also Lyman C White and Marie Ragonetti Zocca, *International non-governmental organizations; their purposes, methods, and accomplishments* (New Brunswick NJ, Rutgers University Press, 1951) 175.

their time and energy to responding to what has been termed the 'Frankenstein problem'.[9]

Section 9.2 will first of all address the changing nature of international organisations and it will briefly recall the classic debates on their international legal status. Section 9.3 will reflect on one of the most popular themes in the current study of international organisations and address their 'law-making' functions. The autonomy of international organisations vis-à-vis the states that created them will be the topic of Section 9.4. Finally, in Section 9.5, an attempt will be made to answer the question to which extent it makes sense to regard intergovernmental organisations as non-state actors.

9.2 THE CHANGING NATURE OF INTERNATIONAL ORGANISATIONS: FROM STATE ACTORS TO NON-STATE ACTORS?

The international organisations dealt with in this contribution are 'intergovernmental organisations' (IGOs). While this term is still used, the general term 'international organisations' has become more common. This is partly rooted in the idea that international organisations have moved beyond international fora for state cooperation and have partly become international actors in their own right. International organisations can be defined in many ways.[10] We follow Schermers and Blokker: 'international organisations are defined as forms of cooperation (1) founded on an international agreement; (2) having at least one organ with a will of its own; and (3) established under international law.' On the basis of this definition they count somewhere between 500 and 700 international organisations,[11]

[9] Andrew Guzman, 'International Organizations and the Frankenstein Problem' (2014) 24 *European Journal of International Law* 999–1025; *cf* also Jan Klabbers, *An Introduction To International Institutional Law*, 3rd edn (Cambridge, Cambridge University Press, 2015).

[10] The most recent definition laid down in an international legal document may very well be that of the International Law Commission in the 2011 Articles on the Responsibility of International Organizations (see below), which defined an international organisation as 'an organization established by a treaty or other instrument governed by international law and possessing its own international legal personality. International organizations may include as members, in addition to States, other entities.' See more extensively Stephen Bouwhuis, 'The International Law Commission's Definition of International Organizations' (2012) 9 *International Organizations Law Review* 451, 451–65.

[11] Henry G Schermers and Niels Blokker, *International institutional law: unity within diversity*, 5th edn (Leiden, Martinus Nijhoff Publishers, 2011) 37. *Cf* also the Report of the ILA on the Accountability of International Organisations, which mentions the following criteria: (a) the provision (in the constitutive document) of particular powers, either expressly of by way of necessary implication from the grant of functions to the organisation; (b) the possession by the organisation of a certain level of capacity or competence to press its won claims internationally, as distinct from the separate claims from its members; (c) the capacity to enter into international agreements in its own right; and (d) the ability of organs of the organisation to take decisions by majority voting. However, it could be argued that (b) and (c) are consequences of legal personality rather than decisive criteria and that (d) would exclude many well-known organisations (including NATO or the WTO). But see also the *Yearbook of International Organizations*, referred to above, which lists about 5,000 IGOs.

ranging from more general ones such as the United Nations (UN) or the World Trade Organisation (WTO), to organisations in a specific area, such as the International Coffee Organisation (ICO) or the International Network on Bamboo and Rattan (INBR).

Their international legal status is undisputed and is often part of the definition of international organisations.[12] In fact, one may argue that it is in particular the entity's legal personality that distinguishes it from its members.[13] International legal doctrine does not provide a commonly accepted definition of international legal personality, let alone that the criteria for the acquisition of international legal personality are undisputed. For a long time, there were different schools of thought, and since the legal status of international organisations forms one of the central building blocks in our argument, we will briefly revisit this debate. One school of thought held that the attribution of legal personality needed an explicit basis in the constituting treaty of the organisation (the 'will' approach).[14] At the other extreme there those who claimed that the existence of legal personality does not depend on the subjective will of the member states. In this view, international organisations are ipso facto international legal persons; they do not enjoy legal personality because the member states so decided, but because international law so demands (the 'objective' approach).[15]

Both approaches to the legal status of international organisations are flawed. With regard to the 'will theory', Gazzini pointed to two problems:

> First, it postulates that the international organization has been effectively created and is functioning as intended. Second, making the international personality of the organization dependent on the will of he founders is problematic with regard to the relationship between the organization and non-members. Relying on recognition by non-member states would not only contradict the essence of the theory, but also scarcely be useful considering that the shortcomings and

[12] *cf* Tarcisio Gazzini, 'The Relationship between International Legal Personality and the Autonomy of International Organizations' in Richard Collins and Nigel D White (eds) (n 8) 33–55. *Cf* also the Advisory Opinion of the ICJ in *Interpretation of the Agreement of 25 March 1951 between the WHO and Egypt* [1980] ICJ Rep 90: 'international organisations are subjects of international law and, as such, are bound by any obligations incumbent upon the under general rules of international law'. See also the 2011 ILC definition above.

[13] Gazzini ibid, 196–212. See also more extensively Ramses A Wessel, 'Revisiting the international legal status of the EU' (2000) 5 *European Foreign Affairs Review* 507, 507–37.

[14] For instance Grigoriĭ Ivanovich Tunkin, 'The legal nature of the United Nations' in Acedémie de Droit International (ed), *Receuil de Cours*, vol 119 (1966) 2–25.

[15] See most prominently Finn Seyersted, 'Is the International Personality of Intergovernmental Organizations Valid vis-a-vis Non-Members?' (1964) 4 *Indian Journal of International Law* 233, 53. The criteria used by Seyersted are: international organs, which are not all subject to the authority of any other organised community except that of participating communities acting jointly, and which are not authorised by all their acts to assume obligations (merely) on behalf of the several participating communities.

> controversial aspects of recognition of states would only be amplified in the case of recognition of international organizations.[16]

In addition, Klabbers pointed to the fact that 'relatively few constituent treaties explicitly provide for the international legal personality of organizations', because it was not always considered necessary.[17] Moreover, the will theory 'opens up the possibility that the international legal personality of an international organization is an empty concept: what if a number of states decided to create an international organization and endows it with international legal personality, yet no one is willing to enter into engagements with it?'.[18]

While taking 'the objective fact of its existence'[19] as proof of international legal personality would best support the notion of international organisations as 'non-state' actors, it equally meets with some problems. After all, if legal personality implicitly follows the establishment of a legal entity, how do we deal with organisations in which the 'distinct will of its own' is virtually absent because of a largely intergovernmental set-up? And, can we really assume legal personality when the only thing states meant to do was to create a light international framework to facilitate their cooperation (and would this not violate the fundamental rule of international law that states are in principle free to decide what they wish to agree on)?

In practice—and despite their flaws—both theoretical approaches play a role in the establishment of the legal status of an international organisation and a more pragmatic approach seems dominant, phrased by Klabbers in the following way: 'as soon as an organization performs an act which can only be explained on the basis of international legal personality, such an organization will be presumed to be in possession of international legal personality.'[20]

But, what is legal personality?[21] In relation to international organisations, Bekker defined it as 'the concrete exercise of, or at least the potential

[16] Gazzini, *The Relationship between International Legal Personality and the Autonomy of International Organizations* (n 12) 35.

[17] Klabbers, *An Introduction to International Institutional Law* (n 9) 48.

[18] ibid.

[19] Seyersted, 'Is the International Personality of Intergovernmental Organizations Valid (n 15) 30–40. See also Finn Seyersted, 'Objective International Personality of Intergovernmental Organization—Do Their Capacities Really Depend upon the Conventions Establishing Them?' (1964) 34 *Nordisk Tidsskrift International Relations* 3.

[20] Klabbers, *An Introduction to International Institutional Law* (n 9) 50; and more extensively J Jan Klabbers, 'Presumptive Personality: the European Union in International Law' in Martti Koskenniemi (ed), *International law aspects of the European Union* (The Hague, Kluwer Law International, 1998) 231–53.

[21] See for a conceptual analysis Roland Portmann, *Legal Personality in International Law* (Cambridge, Cambridge University Press, 2010); Janne Elizabeth Nijman, *The Concept of International Legal Personality: An Inquiry Into The History And Theory Of International Law* (The Hague, TMC Asser Press, 2004).

ability to exercise, certain rights and the fulfilment of certain obligations'.[22] Earlier, I have argued that it is in particular about the *potential* ability rather than about the concrete exercise of powers.[23] The distinction between *legal personality* and *legal capacity* is illuminating in this respect: the first concerns a *quality*, the second is an *asset*. Where international personality thus means not much more than being a subject of public international law,[24] capacity is concerned with 'what the entity is potentially entitled to *do*'.[25] The rather formal approach is apparent in the work of a number of other authors as well who have stressed that 'the concept of personality does not say anything about the qualities of the person' and that 'it is a mistake to jump to the conclusion that an organization has personality and then to deduce specific capacities from an *a priori* conception of the concomitants of personality'.[26]

The practical value of the possession of legal personality can be found in the fact that the entity has the required status to have certain categories of rights, which enable it to manifest itself on the international plane and to enter into relationships with other subjects of international law.[27] It is the capacities of the entity that ultimately reveal the 'independent' position of a legal person. Thus, international legal persons may have a capacity to bring international claims, they may have international procedural capacity (for instance to start a procedure before an international court), treaty-making capacity, the right to establish diplomatic relations, or the right to recognise other subjects of international law.[28]

[22] Peter HF Bekker, *The Legal Position Of Intergovernmental Organizations: A Functional Necessity Analysis Of Their Legal Status And Immunities* (Leiden, Martinus Nijhoff, 1994) 53.

[23] Wessel, 'Revisiting the Legal Status of the European Union' (n 13).

[24] Or, as nicely put by Gerhard Hafner, 'The Amsterdam Treaty and the Treaty-Making Power of the European Union: Some Critical Comments' in Gerhard Hafner and others (eds), *Liber Amicorum Professor Ignaz Seidl-Hohenveldern; In honour of his 80th birthday* (The Hague, Kluwer, 1998) 259: 'As such, the organization becomes a fundamental structural element of the international order'.

[25] In German: *Rechtsfähigkeit*. Bekker, *The Legal Position Of Intergovernmental Organizations* (n 22) 63. The definition of legal personality as having a standing under international law seems also to have been the basis for the following remarks made by the International Court of Justice in the *Reparation for Injuries* case: 'Has the organization such a nature as involves the capacity to bring an international claim? … In other words, does the Organization possess international personality?' The Court continued: 'what it does mean is that it is a subject of international law and capable of possessing international rights and duties'. *Reparation* case (see below) 179.

[26] Detter, 'Law making by international organizations' (n 2) 21.

[27] *cf* Manuel Rama-Montaldo, 'International legal personality and implied powers of international organisations' (1970) 44 *British Yearbook of International Law* 111, 124 and 134.

[28] While the 'will approach' in particular would stress that the existence of any of these capacities would depend on their express or implied inclusion in the constituting treaty, Rama-Montaldo, 'International legal personality and implied powers' (n 27) 139–40, asserted that some general capacities seem to follow from the entities' recognised standing in international law: the right to express its will through the different legal ways found in the international order for producing legal effects on the international plane; and rights which enable

Very few organisations have been granted an explicit legal personality in their constitutions.[29] At the same time it is difficult to find examples of international organisations which have no (explicit or implied) legal personality and are devoid of legal relations with other subjects of international law. In the *Reparation for Injuries* case the International Court of Justice (ICJ) seemed to hold the same view when it based the international legal personality of the United Nations, inter alia, on an implicit attribution of that personality and because of the fact that 'The Organization is not merely a centre "for harmonizing the actions of nations in the attainment of common ends" (Article 1, para 4)'. It is this classic notion in particular that helps us to understand the separate ('non-state') position of international organisations in international law.

9.3 INTERNATIONAL DECISIONS AND LAW-MAKING

Indeed, while many international organisations were set up as frameworks to allow states to institutionalise cooperation in a specific field, decisions of international organisations are increasingly considered a source of international law.[30] Yet, not each and every decision taken by an international organisation contributes to law-making. Klabbers defined law-making instruments as instruments 'laying down more or less general abstract rules of general application, binding upon all subjects of a given legal system.' These instruments would be different from those that are merely 'applying the law', acts of a 'household nature' and 'acts which [aim] to influence behaviour, but without creating law'.[31] It has even become quite common to regard these types of acts as contributing to the development of 'world legislation'. Over the past decade, the use of the term *legislation*

the organisation to manifest itself as a distinct entity and make possible relations with other international persons. While at first sight these capacities indeed seem necessary to make any sense of the concept of legal personality, the problem is that the categories are so broad that any distinction between personality and capacity would disappear. Therefore, for a theoretical analysis, the more formal approach seems the most helpful, since it enables one to unravel further elements.

[29] Schermers and Blokker, *International institutional law* (n 11) 988. *Cf* Bekker, *The Legal Position Of Intergovernmental Organizations* (n 22) 60: 'Explicit acknowledgement of the possession of international personality is not necessary, at least not for the organisation's Member States and third states that have entered into relations with or have otherwise implicitly recognized the organization concerned, since it is based on the concrete exercise of acts and the objective fact of its existence. In any event, it is rarely found in treaty law'. A recent exception to the rule not to explicitly refer to legal personality in the constituting treaty can be found in the Rome Statute of the International Criminal Court of 17 July 1998, Art 4.

[30] José E Alvarez, 'International Organizations: Then and Now' (2006) 100 *American Journal of International Law* 324, 326–36. For a legal theoretical perspective see also IF Dekker and RA Wessel (n 3).

[31] Klabbers, *An Introduction to International Institutional Law* (n 9) 200. See also below.

in this context was triggered in particular by the adoption of a number of resolutions by the United Nations Security Council (UNSC), which aimed at a certain 'harmonisation' of domestic rules worldwide, rather than at regulating a concrete situation. The idea behind the term 'legislation' is that 'the consent of states need not always be decisive, and may at times be overruled for the sake of the interests of mankind'.[32] Yet, a clear consensus on how to interpret these notions is still lacking.[33] While some are quite generous in granting legislative powers to international organisations,[34] others would stress the idea that in the end it would be the member states that are in charge, which would make the term 'legislation' (as a top-down instrument) inappropriate.

At the same time, it is very difficult to define the broader notion of institutional law-making, as its development differs from one organisation to another and presents itself in various shapes.[35] Moreover—and despite the popularity of the topic today—international lawyers were quite late in recognising an 'emerging reality of global governance' and the 'organization of global rule-making'[36] and only recently started to see and study international organisations as autonomous actors which have as their main objective the crafting of rules for worldwide application.[37]

Indeed, traditionally, law-making is not seen as a key-function of international organisations.[38] The reason is that most international organisations have not been granted the power to issue binding decisions, as states were believed not to have transferred any sovereignty. Nevertheless, these days it is undisputed that many organisations do 'exercise sovereign powers'[39] in the sense that they not only contribute to law-making

[32] ibid, 205.

[33] See the different contributions to the forum on 'World Legislation' in (2011) 1 *International Organizations Law Review*.

[34] Schermers and Blokker, *International institutional law* (n 11) 1066 (para 1657) 'It is submitted that international organizations empowered to issue decisions have legislative capacity'.

[35] As José Alvarez notes, more and more international bodies 'appear to be engaging in legislative or regulatory activity in ways and for reasons that might be more readily explained by students of bureaucracy than by scholars of the traditional forms for making customary law or engaging in treaty-making; [t]hey also often engage in law-making by subterfuge.' Alvarez, 'International Organizations (n 30) 217.

[36] Jonathan GS Koppell, *World rule: accountability, legitimacy, and the design of global governance* (Chicago IL, University of Chicago Press, 2010) 11.

[37] ibid. As well as Kanishka Jayasuriya, 'Globalization, law, and the transformation of sovereignty: the emergence of global regulatory governance' (1999) *Indiana Journal of Global Legal Studies* 425, 425–55.

[38] Not even of the United Nations. See Oscar Schachter, 'The UN Legal Order: An Overview' in Christopher C Joyner (ed), *The United Nations and International Law* (Cambridge, Cambridge University Press, 1997) 3: 'Neither the United Nations nor any of its specialised agencies was conceived as a legislative body'.

[39] Danesh Sarooshi, *International organizations and their exercise of sovereign powers* (Oxford, Oxford University Press 2005). *Cf* also the critical theoretical assessment of (approaches to) the powers of international institutions by Viljam Engström, *Constructing the powers of international institutions* (Leiden, Martinus Nijhoff Publishers, 2012).

by providing a framework for negotiation, but also take decisions that bind their member states. Indeed, the current debates on international law-making to a certain extent mirror the 'governance' debates in other academic disciplines.

It is this dimension of international organisations (and other international bodies) that formed the source of research on global administrative law (GAL), or the exercise of public authority by international institutions.[40] Elsewhere, I referred to this dimension as an 'institutionalised global normative web'.[41] This web not only contains formal international organisations, but also transnational/regulatory bodies. Most bodies in one way or another contribute not only to traditional law-making in the form of international decisions, but also form part of a process of what has been termed 'informal international law-making'.[42] Indeed, a mere focus on traditional organisations would leave us with a very limited picture of the international normative output.[43] Although international networks and informal bodies have existed for a long time,[44] their proliferation and (legal) impact through harmonisation methods (standardisation, certification) has made it impossible for lawyers to disregard them in their analysis of international law-making. In many cases they exercise a public authority, which goes beyond a mere cooperation between public as well as private actors.[45] Obviously, this raises new questions—for instance, related to the constitutionalisation of the international legal order, the legitimacy of the decisions or the accountability of the actors.[46]

[40] See eg, Sabino Cassese et al, *Global Administrative Law: the Casebook* (New York, IRPA-IILJ, 2012); Armin Von Bogdandy et al, *The exercise of public authority by international institutions: advancing international institutional law* (Heidelberg, Springer, 2010).

[41] RA Wessel, 'Institutional Law-Making' (n 2). Some of the arguments used here are dealt with more extensively in that publication.

[42] Joost Pauwelyn, Ramses A Wessel and Jan Wouters, 'When Structures Become Shackles: Stagnation and Dynamics in International Lawmaking' (2014) *European Journal of International Law* 733–63. It may even be argued that informal international law-making (with a focus on non-traditional actors, processes and output) is gradually replacing traditional law-making through treaty-making. See ibid.

[43] See AE Boyle and CM Chinkin, *The making of international law* (Oxford, Oxford University Press, 2007) who accept and describe the role of numerous state and non-state actors in international law-making. It is telling that 'treaties as law-making instruments' is only dealt with marginally (ibid, section 5.4).

[44] *cf* Simeon E Baldwin, 'The International Congresses and Conferences of the Last Century as Forces Working Toward the Solidarity of the World: Appendix' (1907) 1 *The American Journal of International Law* 565, 808; as well as Harold Joseph Laski, *The limitations of the expert* (London, Fabian Society, 1931) (criticising the influence of experts in the making of international public norms).

[45] *cf* Von Bogdandy et al (n 40), *The exercise of public authority.*

[46] See also Jan Klabbers, Anne Peters and Geir Ulfstein, *The constitutionalization of international law* (Oxford, Oxford University Press, 2009) 12, arguing that non-state actors have 'started to compete with states for the scarce resource of politico-legal authority (i.e. the power to set authoritative standards).' In general, the book discusses international constitutionalism as a framework within which further normative debate on a legitimate and

The distinction between formal and informal institutions and networks may have been helpful for lawyers to define their object of study, but no longer does justice to the interconnectedness of the norms they produce. Indeed, as has been observed, the institutions involved in global governance 'interact, formally and informally on a regular basis. In recent years, their programs are more tied together, creating linkages that begin to weave a web of transnational rules and regulations.'[47]

The emerging picture is one of a broad range of international normative fora, from intergovernmental organisations with a broad mandate, treaty-based conferences that do not amount to an international organisation (eg, Conferences of the Parties under the main multilateral environmental agreements, such as the Framework Convention on Climate Change (FCCC) and the Kyoto Protocol, informal intergovernmental cooperative structures (eg, the G20, the Financial Action Task Force on Money Laundering, the Basel Committee on Banking Supervision), and even private organisations that are active in the public domain (eg the International Organisation for Standardisation (ISO), or private regulation of the Internet by the Internet Corporation for Assigned Names and Numbers (ICANN), the Internet Engineering Task Force (IETF) or the Internet Society (ISOC).[48] In addition, normative activities can also be discovered in international bodies that are neither based on a treaty nor on a bottom-up cooperation between national regulators, but on a decision by an international organisation. By delegating or outsourcing some of their tasks, these 'international agencies' as we may perhaps call them,[49] may obtain a role in norm-setting that can be distinguished from the 'parent organisation'.

pluralist constitutional order can occur (Klabbers, at 4, 10). But see also Pauwelyn et al, 'When Structures Become Shackles' (n 42), where we have argued that the effects on legitimacy should not be overestimated as the traditional 'thin state consent' is replace by a 'thick stakeholder consensus'.

[47] Koppell, *World Rule* (n 36) 12.

[48] More extensively on the normative activities of these bodies: Ramses A Wessel, 'Regulating Technological Innovation through Informal International Law: The Exercise of International Public Authority by Transnational Actors' in Michiel A Heldeweg and Evisa Kica (eds), *Regulating technological innovation: A multidisciplinary approach* (Basingstoke, Palgrave Macmillan, 2011).

[49] See more extensively E Chiti and RA Wessel, 'The Emergence of International Agencies in the Global Administrative Space: Autonomous Actors or State Servants' in R Collins and ND White (eds) (n 8) 142–59; as well as Ayelet Berman and Ramses A Wessel, 'The International Legal Status of Informal International Law-making Bodies: Consequences for Accountability' in Joost Pauwelyn, Ramses A Wessel and Jan Wouters (eds), *Informal international lawmaking* (Oxford, Oxford University Press, 2012) 35–62.

9.4 AUTONOMY OF INTERNATIONAL ORGANISATIONS: THE ROLE OF 'INDEPENDENT' ORGANS

This increasing global normative activity by international organisations and other international bodies at the same time led to an increasing autonomy of many of them—perhaps highlighting their 'non-state' dimension. The above-mentioned 'Frankenstein problem' was phrased by Schermers and Blokker in the following terms:

> constitutions of international organizations are Janus-faced. On the one hand, as for their form, they are treaties, covered by the general rules on treaties and the 1969 Vienna Convention on the Law of Treaties. On the other hand, as for their substance, they contain the ground rules for a living body, the practical operation of which may increasingly go beyond the intention of its creators.[50]

The autonomy of international organisations vis-à-vis the states that created them has been noted well in legal analyses.[51] In fact when we accept that international organisations are characterised by 'a will of their own', a certain independence should not come as a surprise. Yet, international organisations will often balance between their managerial tasks (which indeed may imply some autonomy in relation to the member states) and their 'agora' function as a forum for regional or global cooperation.[52] It remains difficult to neglect the Janus-faced nature of international organisations and it has been duly noted by for instance Ryngaert and Freitas de Barros that '[a]lthough the separate personality of an international organization 'establishes the will of the organization as a whole', this does not mean that the various 'member State wills' that led to it lose their relevance.'[53] And we should also keep the warning by Condorelli and Cassese in mind that

> Although the limits to the sovereignty of states are increasingly growing in quantity and depth, partly in consequence of delegations of authority to supranational institutions and agencies, it remains true in substance that those

50 Schermers and Blokker (n 11) 728.

51 See eg, the contributions to Collins and White, *The Relationship between International Legal Personality and the Autonomy of International Organizations* (n 8).

52 J Klabbers, 'Two Concepts of International Organization' (2005) *International Organizations Law Review* 277–93 as well as his 'Contending Approaches to International Organizations: Between Functionalism and Constitutionalism' in Jan Klabbers and Asa Wallendahl (eds), *Research Handbook on the Law of International Organizations* (Cheltenham, Edward Elgar Publishing, 2011) 3–30.

53 Ana Sofia Barros and Cedric Ryngaert, 'The Position of Member States in (Autonomous) Institutional Decision-Making: Implications for the Establishment of Responsibility' (2014) 11 *International Organizations Law Review* 53. *Cf* also J Klabbers, 'Autonomy, constitutionalism and virtue in international institutional law' in Collins and White, *The Relationship between International Legal Personality and the Autonomy of International Organizations* (n 8) 121: 'there is always an element of artificiality in making a distinction between organizations and their members'. See also Niels Blokker, 'International organizations and their members' (2004) 1 *International Organizational Law Review* 139–61.

> growing limits still ultimately arise from the choice of the states: the choice to bind themselves, the sovereign choice to accept limits to their sovereignty.[54]

Thus, as—in turn—rightfully pointed out by Gazzini, 'The question of international legal personality calls for a yes or no answer … The question of the autonomy of international organisations from their membership, on the contrary, is a matter of degree.'[55]

While keeping this in mind, the purpose of the present chapter is to highlight the non-state dimension of international organisations. So-called 'Boards' or 'Councils' perhaps best represent the distinctive position of the organisation vis-à-vis its member states.[56] Alongside a central congress in the form of an 'Assembly' and a Secretariat, the Board completes the 'elementary triad',[57] forming the basis of the institutional structure of most international organisations. Whereas the plenary general congress is usually the reflection of the 'agora' function of an international organisation and the Secretariat has mainly administrative functions, Boards were created to allow organisations to act more effectively through a non-plenary organ that would meet more frequently than the general congress or which would even be in session on a 'permanent' basis. The fact that not all members of the organisation are represented on the Board, and that members may be selected on the basis of the knowledge of the field, turns this organ into a true part of the institutional structure of the organisation. While there are good reasons also to view general congresses as 'true' organs of the organisation (in which the participating states obtain a new identity as 'member state', following the rules and procedures of the organisation and taking decisions that can be accredited to the organisation), the fact that Boards are non-plenary organs strengthens the idea of autonomy.

Most Boards are endowed with executive functions and some even with independent governing functions. It is not unusual for Boards to exercise legislative functions. In fact, due to the increasing activity of international

[54] L Condorelli and Antonio Cassese, 'Is Leviathan Still Holding Sway over International Dealings' in Antonio Cassese (ed), *Realizing utopia: the future of international law* (Oxford, Oxford University Press, 2012) 14; *cf* also in the same volume Jose E Alvarez, 'State Sovereignty is Not Withering Away: A Few Lessons for the Future' in Antonio Cassese (ed), *Realizing utopia: the future of international law* (Oxford, Oxford University Press, 2012) 26–37.

[55] Gazzini, *The Relationship between International Legal Personality and the Autonomy of International Organizations* (n 12) 207–08.

[56] See more extensively RA Wessel, 'Executive Boards and Councils' in J Cogan, I Hurd and I Johnston (eds), *Oxford Handbook of International Organizations* (Oxford, Oxford University Press, 2015) (forthcoming). Parts of this section are based on that contribution.

[57] Schermers and Blokker, *International institutional law* (n 11) 293. Many examples in the present section have been taken from this book as well as from P Sands, P Klein and DW Bowett, *Bowett's law of international institutions*, 5th edn (London, Sweet & Maxwell, 2001); Chittharanjan Felix Amerasinghe, *Principles of the institutional law of international organizations* (Cambridge, Cambridge University Press, 1996); J Klabbers, A Peters and G Ulfstein, *The Constitutionalization Of International Law* (Oxford, Oxford University Press, 2009)

organisations and the need for technical expertise rather than just political input, Boards have obtained a pivotal position and may run the organisation on a daily basis, although in many cases executive tasks have been delegated to the management and staff of the organisation. This is not to say that Boards have the same functions in each and every international organisation. On the contrary: as with other elements of international organisations, it remains difficult to find common denominators. The non-plenary organs we term 'Boards' in this contribution, appear under different names, such as 'Executive Board' (WHO), 'Council' (FAO, OECD), 'Governing Body' (ILO), 'Executive Council' (WMO, OPCW) or 'Council of Administration' (UPU). To complicate things even more, some organisations use the term 'Council' to refer to their plenary central congress (eg the EU or NATO) or even call their plenary organ 'Board' (eg the 'Board of Governors' of the World Bank or the IMF). These organisations use different terms for the Board (eg the 'European Commission' of the EU or the 'Executive Directors' in the case of the World Bank or the IMF). Furthermore, as we will see, the composition differs, both in numbers and in representation.

It is not uncommon for the plenary general congress or assembly to be viewed as representing the more 'intergovernmental' dimension of an international organisation, with the non-plenary board reflecting a 'supranational' element. Political scientists in particular, would perhaps emphasise the 'conference' idea of a plenary organ, in which negotiations take place under the constant shadow of power play. Lawyers would generally have a tendency to point to the rules of the game that have to be followed and underline the fact that even plenary bodies are organs of an international organisation in which states function as 'member states' once they occupy a 'seat'. Indeed, the existence of elements such as 'organ', 'membership' or 'decision' all imply a distinction between the participating states and the international entity. In fact, there is a strong inter-linkage between these elements. Organs act on behalf of the international entity, and are not to be equated with the (collectivity of) the states, in which case the term 'conference' would be more appropriate. The notion of 'membership' (in contrast to 'participation') underlines a similar distinctiveness of the international entity. This seems to allow for the conclusion that for an international entity to be regarded as existing separately from its member states, the entity must have a decision-making organ that is able to produce a 'corporate' will, as opposed to a mere 'aggregate' of the wills of the member states. The outcomes of collective decision-making processes must allow for their ascription to an international organ rather than to the collectivity of the participants.[58]

[58] *cf* J Klabbers, 'Presumptive Personality: The European Union in International Law' (n 20) 243; Rama-Montaldo, 'International legal personality and implied powers' (n 27) 145: 'It is

In the case of non-plenary bodies it may be easier to see the distinction between the organisation and the (collectivity) of its member states. After all, especially because of their non-plenary nature, these Boards rely less on difficult compromises between a large number of member states and are more fit to focus on the institutional objectives rather than on individual national political preferences. At the same time, as we will see below, larger member states will always claim a seat in a Board and national interest may continue to play a (crucial) role even in non-plenary organs (the UNSC forming a prime example). Furthermore, it has been noted that even with regard to non-plenary bodies deciding on behalf of the whole membership, the issue is present. As held by some observers, on the Boards of international financial institutions for instance, the dichotomy inherent in the role of the Executive Directors—the members of these Boards—is clearly noticeable. In a report prepared by the Independent Evaluation Office of the IMF (2008) analysing governance issues in that institution, the self-perception of Board members was described as follows: '[m]ore than half of Board members reported that they occasionally face a conflict between their role as representatives of their authorities and their role in upholding the Fund's institutional interests … while in practice all Directors clearly understand their representational role, their status as officers of the Fund is less clear.'[59] In a similar vein, the famous independence of the members of the EU's Commission must be seen in relative terms. It has been argued that 'Chosen because of distinguished and well-connected prior careers, they have a list of professional and political contacts, with over two-thirds chosen from a party in government at the time of appointment.'[60]

Schermers and Blokker list three reasons why international organisations delegate powers to non-plenary bodies.[61] First, decision-making in a large plenary organ is a slow and cumbersome process. Meetings of more that 12 people rarely work efficiently. Assembling a large number of qualified representatives for a conference is a costly affair, not only financially, but also in irreplaceable personnel. Many states are unable to afford long absences of their top experts. A general congress may save much time by delegating minor decisions and preparatory work for important

the existence of organs which makes it possible to distinguish international organizations from other looser associations of States like, for example the British Commonwealth'. See on the distinction between states and member states and the importance of 'legal personality' in that respect also: RA Wessel, 'Revisiting the International Legal Status of the EU' (n 13).

[59] Barros and Ryngaert (n 53). See Independent Evaluation Office of the IMF Report 'Governance of the IMF: An Evaluation', 2008, p 16, available at: www.ieo-imf.org/ieo/pages/CompletedEvaluation110.aspx.

[60] Arndt Wonka, 'Technocratic and independent? The appointment of European Commissioners and its policy implications' (2007) 14 *Journal of European Public Policy* 169, 178.

[61] Schermers and Blokker, *International institutional law* (n 11) 307–08.

decisions to other organs. It may of then delegate work to the secretariat of the organisation, but some tasks may be too technical or too controversial for a rather small and non-political body. Secondly, some states may be greatly interested in particular decisions that are of lesser or no importance to others. In that case, it might be advisable to grant the interested members a larger share in their preparation. Thirdly, for certain tasks, an organ of government representatives is insufficiently objective. A compromise solution, which is usually the result of bargaining between government representatives, is not always the best. Arbitration and the gathering of expert opinions are traditional examples of functions performed by organs composed of independent persons.

This delegation would result in different roles of Boards: as political counterweight (to the technical decisions made by the organisation's management and staff), as performance police (as monitor and overseer of whether and how management and staff are carrying out the organisation's tasks), as strategic thinker (anticipating how the organisation's goals and instruments will be affected by changes in the external environment) and as democratic forum (giving voice to the individual members).[62] Admittedly, Boards will not always be able to cater for all of these functions, and sometimes the different roles are difficult to combine. 'Trade-offs are inevitable, and therefore organizations trying to balance the effectiveness, efficiency, accountability, and representation must make choices that inevitably strengthen some board roles but weaken others.'[63] In most cases, Boards are composed of government representatives and other commissions or committees can be installed to include the expertise of non-governmental stakeholders. Yet, because of their 'daily' presence in the organisation's institutional machinery, Boards may be in a position to accommodate these needs more easily than a general congress. This does not mean that international organisations need to have a Board. The key example is one of the most important universal international organisations, the World Trade Organization. The WTO found a way to be effective by having decisions taken by plenary organs only: the Ministerial Conference (meeting every two years) and the General Council (meeting regularly in the composition of permanent representatives of all member states). Even the three separate Councils (for goods, services and TRIPs) and the committees are composed of all (currently 159) members and decisions are taken by consensus.[64] Other examples include the Council of Europe, the OECD or NATO.

62 Leonardo Martinez-Diaz, 'Executive Boards in International Organizations: Lessons for Strengthening IMF Governance' Independent Evaluation Office (IEO) Background Paper (BP/08/08) (Washington DC, International Monetary Fund).

63 ibid, 12.

64 See more extensively Peter van den Bossche, *The law and policy of the World Trade Organization: text, cases and materials* (Cambridge, Cambridge University Press, 2005).

Irrespective of their differences, as key organs, Boards form part of the institutional set-up of an international organisation. This implies that—despite their largely intergovernmental set-up—their actions are in principle attributable to the organisation.[65] External legal relations are established on the basis of the legal personality of the organisation. Yet, in exceptional cases Boards may enjoy a separate legal personality. In most cases this personality is functionally limited to practical matters of private law, such as the employment of personnel or the purchase of computers. Doctrine is less clear about the possibility of organs to possess an *international* legal personality as well, for instance allowing them to enter into international agreements. The International Law Commission (ILC) argued on this matter that 'a treaty concluded on behalf of a subsidiary organ should bind the entire organization.'[66] The ILC thus did not rule out the possibility. Examples of organs enjoying a separate legal personality are rare, but include some organs of the European Union (the European Investment Bank (EIB) and the European Central Bank (ECB); the latter even being an 'Institution' of the Union, a principal organ). Subsidiary organs of the UN (including UNICEF, UNITAR, UNRWA, WFP, UNDP, UNTAET and UNMIK) have frequently entered into international agreements with states. Examples of executive boards enjoying a separate international legal personality are hard to find.

The output of the decision-making process differs substantially from one Board to another, and may range for advisory or preparatory work for the general congress to full-fledged legally binding norms that bind all member states directly. In general, the acts by Boards will be subject to the rules of the organisation on the internal hierarchy of norms and their validity depends on following these rules. Most of the work of Boards concerns the 'internal' law of the organisation, in the sense that the acts form part of decision-making procedures that ultimately lead to acts adopted by the general congress. Yet, some Boards do take decisions that arguably go beyond recommendations, irrespective of their 'delegated' powers.[67]

While organs of international organisations are traditionally seen as places where member states meet, the above examples underline the 'autonomous' status that international organisations enjoy through some of their organs. It is in fact this autonomy that forms the source of a 'constitutional' turn in the analyses of international organisations. After all, when powers are transferred from states to international organisations

[65] *cf* Arts 3 and 4 of the Articles on the Responsibility of International Organizations, with Commentaries, in Report of the International Law Commission, 63rd Session, UN doc A/66/10 (2011) 52.

[66] ILC Rep.1982, UN Doc A/37/10, 40.

[67] See further RA Wessel, 'Executive Board and Councils' (n 56).

(or previously not existing powers are created at that level), the call for 'check and balances' becomes louder, in particular when it is not clear whether they have been transferred to the same extent.[68]

9.5 CONCLUSION: FROM 'STATE ACTORS' TO NON-STATE ACTORS?

The above analysis underlines a development that has been acknowledged in the literature on international organisations over the past decade in particular (but which has in fact been present from the outset):[69] international organisations cannot be equated to groups of states but are separate international legal entities which are increasingly involved in international law-making and which—in the exercise of their managerial tasks—have become bureaucracies. These bureaucracies continue to depend on the support of their members, but increasingly rely on internal and external experts to deal with the complex (increasingly technical) questions that formed the reason for their creation in the first place. This allows us to—perhaps ironically—regard intergovernmental organisations as non-state actors. Moreover, it has become well recognised that international rules and standards are increasingly set by other international and transnational bodies, operation at an even larger distance from states.

Yet, we have also noted the continuing governmental influence on the functioning and output of international organisations, even in the non-plenary organs (Boards) that are usually seen as reflecting the 'autonomy' of the organisation best. The main rationale behind the Articles on the Responsibility of International Organizations (ARIO)[70] was the distinction between international organisations and their members (Article 3 provides

[68] This point is addressed more extensively in RA Wessel, 'Revealing the Publicness of International Law' (n 5).

[69] Writing in 1964, Friedmann already noted the change from cooperation to organisation: 'In international law it is today of both theoretical and practical importance to distinguish between the international law of "coexistence", governing essentially diplomatic inter-state relations, and the international law of co-operation, expressed in the growing structure of international organisation and the pursuit of common human interests'. Wolfgang Friedmann, *The Changing Structure of International Law* (London, Stevens & Sons, 1964)

[70] International Law Commission (ILC), 'Draft Arts. on the responsibility of international organisations, with commentaries 2011', Adopted by the ILC at its 63rd session, in 2011, and submitted to the General Assembly as part of the Commission's report covering the work of that session (A/66/10) (2011) *Yearbook of the International Law Commission*, vol II, Pt 2, 5, see in particular Pt 6 where the Commentary refers to Art 57 of the Articles on responsibility of States for internationally wrongful acts. See among the many publications on the responsibility of international organisations the contribution by Wouters, Odermatt, d'Aspremont, Amerasinghe, Nedeski, Nollkaemper, Ahlborn, Von Bogdandy, Steinbrück Platise, Sari, Blokker and Wessel to the Forum on Responsibility of International Organizations (2012) 1 *International Organizations Law Review*.

that 'Every internationally wrongful act of an international organization entails the international responsibility of that organization.').[71]

A classic question addressed in the law of international organisations concerns the role of organs, and in particular the role of member states in those organs. While many have rightfully pointed to the continued and essential role of Member States in influencing the process and the output, it remains equally important to stress the fact that we are indeed dealing with *member* states. Their membership of an international organisation (incidentally underlining the idea that there is something to become a member of) changes the identity of states the moment they participate within the legal/procedural framework of an international organisation. What we look for are the minimum features of an international entity to conclude on some degree of independence *vis-à-vis* its member states.

Earlier, I approached this question by making use of the so-called Institutional Legal Theory.[72] Ruiter's analysis of legal persons and of the elements which then are composed remains helpful in selecting the relevant characteristics of an international entity in order to distinguish it from its members.[73] It is important in this respect to recall the assertion that international legal personality only refers to the legal status of an entity. Three subsystems of legal conditions seem to be relevant:[74]

1. the existence of decision-making processes;
2. the existence of practices that can be conceived of as external behaviour; and
3. the existence of behaviour of others towards the legal person.

Ruiter furthermore pointed to the fact that fictitious entities are incapable of acting and that they depend on other subjects for the performance of their acts. This assertion does not seem too far-fetched. The legal relation between the natural person and the *organ* (mostly by way of a 'seat' in the organ) is referred to as *membership*. The acts of members, though collectively constitutive of acts ascribed to the subject presented by the organ, are not identical with the acts of the latter. The result of acts that are

[71] Other provisions underline the distinct position of an international organisation. In relation to the question of attribution, Art 6(1) ARIO for instance adds that: 'The conduct of an organ or agent of an international organization in the performance of functions of that organ or agent shall be considered an act of that organization under international law, whatever position the organ or agent holds in respect of the organization.' This somewhat obvious rule indicates that conduct by organs and agents can establish the international responsibility of the organisation. According to Art 6(2) ARIO, the 'rules of the organisation' (itself) shall be applied when determining the organs and agents.

[72] RA Wessel, 'Revisiting the International Legal Status of the EU' (n 13).

[73] See in particular Dick Ruiter, *Legal Institutions* (Dordrecht, Kluwer Academic Publishers, 2001); Dick Ruiter, *Institutional legal facts: legal powers and their effects* (Dordrecht, Kluwer Academic Publishers, 1993).

[74] Ruiter, *Legal Institutions* (n 73) 102–03.

ascribed to organs composed of members are termed *decisions*. Since many international organisations have two or more organs, rules are required with a view to a division of powers between the organs as well as to their mutual relations. Not only must the division of powers ensure that the decisions and acts of the different organs can be perceived as originating from one single will (thus requiring authority and accountability rules), this internal practice must also be related to the surrounding societal practice.

Indeed, as we have seen, the existence of these elements (organ, membership and decision) all imply a distinction between the participating states and the international entity and define the extent to which the latter can perform functions as a 'non-state' actor. In relation to the ('realist') criticism that it remains to be about state power, it is important to note that viewing international organisations along these lines renders the question whether decisions are taken unanimously or by a (qualified) majority less relevant. Unanimity does not necessarily mean that decisions are not decisions of an organ, the forming of the 'common will' not being dependent on one Member State.[75] The same line of reasoning would put the relevance of the legal nature of decisions into perspective: 'declaratory' statements do not automatically hint at 'intergovernmental' cooperation, nor do 'imperative' decisions conclusively reveal the legal nature of the entity by which they were adopted. On the other hand, when the term 'decision' is used correctly, it has to be taken by an organ of an international legal entity—otherwise, the term 'agreement' would better suit the outcome of the negotiating process.

Admittedly, taking this line of argument to the extreme would in turn run the risk of ignoring the role of states in intergovernmental organisations all together. Yet, in the current debate on the role of international organisations the distinct position in relation to their Member States has become more prominent. Indeed, it is this position, in combination with the proliferation and increasing interconnectedness of international bodies that has revealed the existence of a global institutional layer in which states play an essential, but perhaps not always the leading role.[76]

[75] *cf* Christian Trüe, 'Verleihung von Rechtspersönlichkeit an die Europäische Union und Verschmelzung zu einer einzigen Organisation—deklaratorisch oder konstitutiv?' (1997) 357 *Vorträge, Reden und Berichte aus dem Europa-Institut* 15.

[76] *cf* Trachtman, *The Future of International Law* (n 5) 3: 'This increasing dense body of law and organizations will be seen to perform governmental functions. It is in this sense that the future of international law is global government.'

10

Non-Governmental Organisations: Recognition, Roles, Rights and Responsibilities

MATH NOORTMANN

10.1 INTRODUCTION

SINCE THE EARLY 1990s, the visibility of non-governmental organisations (NGOs) in international affairs has grown tremendously.[1] Their increased manifestation has not passed unnoticed in international legal discourse. More than any other non-state actor, however, NGOs constitute a conundrum for the students of international law. It is the purpose of this chapter to critically engage the twofold problem that NGOs pose for our discipline.

First of all, the international legal episteme reveals a remarkably persistent refusal to incorporate NGOs in its mainstream discourse. Here, the predominant problem is the paradigmatic preoccupation with the fiction of international legal personality, which emasculates a more pragmatic engagement with the legal aspects and consequences of NGO activities.

Secondly, 'non-governmental organisations'[2] suffer in two important aspects from the same problematic typology as 'non-state actors' (NSAs) do. Both categories are conceptualised as a negation of government or

[1] For an early engagement with NGOs in the international space, see: Lyman Cromwell White, *The structure of private international organizations* (Philadelphia PA, George S Ferguson company, 1933); Lyman Cromwell White, *International non-governmental organizations; their purposes, methods, and accomplishments* (New Brunswick NJ, Rutgers University Press, 1951); Pei-heng Chiang, *Non-governmental organizations at the United Nations: identity, role, and function* (New York, Praeger, 1981).

[2] I will not attempt to provide the reader with a definition of NGO. NGOs—like non-state actors—are qualified by exclusion. It is indeed easier to conceptualise and define NGOs on the basis of what they are not, than trying to seek an understanding that would capture the vast variety of objectives, organisation forms, issue areas and strategies that these organisations have adopted over time. But even the idea that NGOs are *not* governmental, *not* for profit, or *not* public is problematic.

state respectively. Moreover, both labels denominate catch-all categories, which do not lend themselves well to analytical understanding of the different roles, rights, and responsibilities within the NGO community.

The common idea that NGOs *matter* in the international legal system stands in sharp contrast with the widely shared opinion that NGOs have no international legal status.[3] 'Mattering', so it seems, is socio-political rather than legally significant; ie, *for* international law rather than *in* international law. The legal consequences of increased participation in policy-making and implementing practices in a domain that was traditionally reserved for nation states have only reluctantly been accepted. International law's conservative stance with respect to acknowledgement of the subject quality of this particular participant contrasts with the 'agency' status that NGOs have acquired in socio-political research and the early critiques that were uttered in the social and political sciences.[4]

This chapter analyses and conceptualises the legal consequences of the increased NGO participation in global affairs. I do so on the basis of the understanding that paradigmatic thinking about NGOs as subjects of international law is 'not particularly helpful either intellectually or operationally.'[5] A more functional approach would advance the consideration of the International Court of Justice (ICJ) that legal status reflects the needs of the global community.[6] Those needs require a non-governmental involvement that must come with associated rights and responsibilities. Much of the international legal discourse on NGOs, unfortunately, still revolves around an abstract, theoretical idea of legal personality, which is modelled according to the idea of the state.

This chapter argues that NGO rights and responsibilities are interconnected with and co-determined by NGO activities. Some of these activities fall, or ought to fall, outside the ambit of a particular national legal system. It is in this context that we have to discuss the specific consequences of NGO agency and the structure of the *inter*national (legal) system. Critical (realist) legal scholarship would seek to understand and value both the (international legal) structure as well as the agency of NGOs, rather than the practice and opinion of states as the gatekeepers of the system.

[3] Bas Arts, Math Noortmann and Bob Reinalda, *Non-state actors in international relations* (Aldershot, Ashgate, 2001).

[4] It is within the social and political sciences that one encounters a first critical engagement with NGOs and attempts to understand NGOs participation in the 'international' realm in theoretical and conceptual terms. See, eg, James Petras and Henry Veltmeyer, *Globalisation Unmasked; Imperialism in the 21st Century* (Halifax, Zed Books, 2001); Dorothea Hilhorst, 'Being Good or Doing Good: Quality and Accountability of Humanitarian NGOs' (2002) 26 *Disasters* 20; Michael Edwards and David Hulme, *Beyond the magic bullet: NGO performance and accountability in the post-cold war world* (West Hartford CT, Kumarian Press, 1996).

[5] R Higgins, *Problems and process: international law and how we use it* (Oxford, Clarendon Press, 1994).

[6] *Reparations for Injuries Suffered in the Service of the United Nations* [1949] ICJ Rep 174.

After this introduction, the chapter continues with an NGO-informed critique of international legal personality as a concept that limits, rather than facilitates, the understanding of the role of actors in its formative process. That section is based on a review of contemporary debates. Section 10.3 proceeds with a socio-political-legal analysis of the changing global role and function of NGOs and the consequences of those changes for international law's exclusive governmental character. The understanding of qualified roles feeds back into a diversified and gradual understanding of legal personality, and feeds forward into the consideration of rights and responsibilities.

NGO rights and responsibilities constitute the subject matter of sections 10.4 and 10.5. NGOs' international rights spring from both international treaties and institutional arrangements. Whereas the former can be either of a general nature or NGO-specific, the latter set (institutional) rights are generally formulated with NGOs in mind. Where rights often come with corresponding obligations, such obligations tend to signify a particular responsibility and corresponding accountability. In discussing the different literatures on NGO responsibility and accountability, I seek to synthesise socio-political conceptions of responsibility and their accountability mechanisms and more legal/technical ideas and the accompanying legal means of accountability.

10.2 NGOs' INTERNATIONAL LEGAL PERSONALITY: THE POLITICS OF RECOGNITION

> The view that entities other than states can be subject of international law has been denied by many; and although opposition to it has receded under the impact of modern developments it cannot as yet, be said that it has been generally accepted.[7]

Some 45 years after Hersch Lauterpacht's observation (he did not particularly contemplate the possibility of NGOs being subjects of international law), little seems to have changed for NGOs in terms of their subject quality in international law.

The reasons for (non-) acceptance of NGOs' international legal personality vary, but the apparent neglect, significant (qualified) denials and few qualified acceptances, indicate that international law's positivistic stronghold is not faltering.

The logic of denying NGOs international status stands, in the present author's opinion, in sharp contrast with the 1949 Advisory Opinion of the International Court of Justice (ICJ) in the case concerning *Reparation for*

[7] Hersch Lauterpacht, 'The Subject of International Law' in Andrea Bianchi (ed), *Non-State Actors and International Law* (Aldershot, Ashgate, 2009) 3.

Injuries Suffered in the Service of the United Nations. In that decision, the ICJ opined that:

> The subjects of law are not necessarily identical in their nature or in the extent of their rights, and their nature depends on the needs of the community. Throughout its history, the developments of international law have been influenced by the requirements of international life...[8]

In that authoritative opinion, the Court recognised the existence of qualified and varied legal personalities, based on 'the needs of the community [and] the requirements of international life' and provides the basis for a teleological rather then a conservative reading of international law. The main question to be answered seems to be: what is and who determines the 'need of the international community' and 'the requirements of international life'? Can we leave it up to states and governments and their respective organisations and agreements? I suggest that recognition has also lost its constitutive function when it comes to acknowledging NGOs as much as it has lost its function in acknowledging the existence of states.[9] International non-governmental organisations (INGOs), like states, exist on the basis of fulfilling certain (factual) requirements and the simple affirmation that these requirements have been fulfilled. Their legal rights and obligations do not necessarily flow from that affirmation. Legal scholarship plays an important role in establishing the connection between the affirmation of facts and the corresponding entitlements.

International legal literature on NGOs traditionally can be divided in writings that concentrate on NGOs *and* international law and those on NGOs *in* international law. Whereas the former set of publications concentrate on questions concerning the influence and impact of increased participation, the latter set of publications seem to focus more on traditional questions of international legal status. Within both literatures one finds authors concentrating on the relationship between NGOs and intergovernmental organisations (IGOs), or the place of NGOs in specific legal regimes (environment, human rights, (human) security) and those that raise more general and wider questions. The writings in the various sets will be compared over time and in relation to each other.[10]

It is quite remarkable that some publications, such as Dinah Shelton's *The participation of Nongovernmental Organizations in International Judicial*

[8] *Reparations for Injuries Suffered in the Service of the United Nations* (International Court of Justice, 1949). See also Math Noortmann, 'Non-State Actors in International Law' in Bas Arts, Math Noortmann and Bob Reinalda (eds), *Non-state actors in international law, politics, and governance series* (Aldershot, Ashgate, 2001).

[9] For a discussion of recognition in international law see PK Menon, *The law of recognition in international law: basic principles* (Lewiston NY, Edwin Mellen Press, 1994); Stefan Talmon, *Recognition in international law: a bibliography* (The Hague, Martinus Nijhoff Publishers, 2000).

[10] I have not made a methodological distinction between journal articles, chapters in edited volumes and monographs.

Proceedings, do not bother to discuss NGOs' legal personality.[11] Also in publications on the relationship between NGOs and IGOs, no specific attention has been given to the general question of subject quality of NGOs.[12] That abstract legal question was, obviously, irrelevant to the specific question. Legal personality is not required for socio-political activities, which the participation in institutional activities seems to be. One must also conclude that participation in intergovernmental organisations, to the extent that it socio-political in nature, does not entail any form of legal personality.

The specific question on the status of NGOs under general international law began to emerge in the mid-1990s, when NGOs became part of a wider discussion within international law, that dealt more generally with the consequences of the end of the cold war. Within a period of three years, Steve Charnovitz, Stephan Hobe and Karsten Nowrot formulated the different positions that one could take in the debate. Charnovitz—in his widely noted 1997 article on 'NGOs and International Governance'—adopted a rather absolute position with respect to the international legal personality of NGOs. While mentioning 'international personality' as a matter of introduction and, as it seems, rather marginal to the subject matter, he opined that: '[l]eaving aside the Red Cross, NGOs do *not* have international legal personality.'[13] Charnovitz's unqualified assertion was grounded in the noted absence of states' acceptance of the 1923 Institute of International Law (IIL)'s *Projet de convention relative à la condition juridique des associations internationales*.[14]

Hobe, unaware of Charnovitz's position at the moment of writing, argued on the basis of NGO roles, ie, their participation and the acceptance of those roles, that 'the only logical legal conclusion, is the recognition

[11] Dinah Shelton, 'The participation of Nongovernmental Organizations in International Judicial Proceedings' (1994) 88 *American Journal of International Law* 611.

[12] Daniel C Esty, 'Linkages and Governance: NGOs at the World Trade Organization' (1998) 19 *University of Pennsylvania Journal of International Economic Law* 21; Daniel C Esty, 'Non-governmental organizations at the World Trade Organization: cooperation, competition, or exclusion' (1998) 1 *Journal of International Economic Law* 123; Jeffrey Law Dunoff, 'The misguided debate over NGO participation at the WTO' (1998) 1 *Journal of International Economic Law* 433; August Reinisch and Christina Irgel, 'The participation of non-governmental organisations (NGOs) in the WTO dispute settlement system' (2001) 1 *Non-State Actors and International Law* 127; Steve Charnovitz, 'Opening the WTO to Nongovernmental Interests' (2000) 24 *Fordham International Law Journal* 43; Maki Tanaka, 'Bridging the GAP between northern NGOS and southern sovereigns in the trade-environment debate: the pursuit of democratic dispute settlements in the WTO under the Rio Principles' (2003) 30 *Ecology Law Quarterly* 113; Seema Sapra, 'The WTO System of Trade Governance: The Stale NGO Debate and the Approriate Role for Non-State Actors' (2008) 11 *Oregon Review of International Law* 37; Michael Struett, 'NGOs, the International Criminal Court, and the Politics of Writing International Law' in A Bianchi (ed), *Non-State Actors and International Law* (Aldershot, Ashgate, 2009) 187.

[13] Steve Charnovitz, 'Two Centuries of Participation: NGOs and International Governance' (1997) 18 *Michigan Journal of International Law* 103, 188.

[14] ibid. See also www.idi-iil.org/idiF/resolutionsF/1923_brux_02_fr.pdf.

of at least a partial subject quality of international NGOs.'[15] Hobe's 'recognition' I consider to be an ontological one, as it recognises an actuality, ie, partial subject quality that exists in positive international law with or without express state recognition.

Karsten Nowrot, finally, separates 'factual participation' and 'community acceptance' as legal prerequisites and considers the latter (acceptance by states) rather than the former (de facto participation) to be decisive. But in a typical legal circle reasoning, 'community acceptance' is the demonstration of possessing rights or duties under contemporary international law'.[16] Even an elaborate analysis of existing arrangements, rights and duties, does not lead Nowrot to conclude that a more general legal personality for some NGOs exists:

> [T]here is a need to establish an international legal status for NGOs. On one side, the participatory rights of NGOs must be strengthened in order to secure their position in the international decision-making process. On the other side, taking into account the already existing influence of NGOs in the international system, the question arises whether there is a need for a global legal framework in order to set limits on the influence of powerful interest groups like Greenpeace, and to provide some accountability for these organizations for the consequences of their actions.[17]

Nowrot's lengthy quote perfectly reflects the problem of a positivistic understanding of international law and the grounded controversies between scholars who accept qualified and partial international legal personality for NGOs and those who don't.

Today's mainstream arguments have not changed significantly, and revolve around two different positions: (1) whether the role of NGOs and the requirements of the international system determine legal status (as suggested by the ICJ), or (2) whether the recognition of NGOs by states constitutes legal personality. For Steve Charnovitz and many others, '[in] general, a NGO enjoys legal personality, [but] not in international law.'[18] Charnovitz admits that the requirement of recognition is not wholly unproblematic: 'states have worried that granting international recognition to NGOs would reduce governmental control over them'.[19] Recognition is indeed political if it depends on the expressed willingness of states. Precisely for that reason, the declaratory conception of recognition

[15] Stephan Hobe, 'Global Challanges to Statehood: The Increasingly Important role of Nongovernmental Organizations' (1997) 5 *Indiana Journal of Global Legal Studies* 191, 209.

[16] Karsten Nowrot, 'Legal consequences of globalization: The status of non-governmental organizations under international law' (1998) 6 *Indiana Journal of Global Legal Studies* 579.

[17] ibid, 579 (footnotes omitted).

[18] Steve Charnovitz, 'Nongovernmental Organizations and International Law' (2006) 100 *American Journal of International Law* 24, 355.

[19] ibid.

replaced the idea that recognition constituted the state as a subject of international law.

In the same vein, Michael Reisman concluded that the 'granting or withholding of consultative status has become immensely political', which he explains by 'the increasing potential for NGO influence on promotion and prescription'.[20] For understanding policy-oriented scholarship, one needs to recognise that the role of NGOs in the development of international law is a socio-legal one; the making of international law is more of a formal, positive deed of enactment. The policy-oriented approach's concept of (international) law as an 'authoritative decision-making process' requires it to look at all stages and all participants in that formative process. The question, according to Myres McDougal is:

> Who makes effective recommendations to such authoritative prescribers and upon what intelligence, achieved by whom and by what procedures? Who, authorized how, may invoke the application of what prescriptions, with respect to whom, in what arenas? Who, for the promotion of what policies, applies what prescriptions to whom, by what procedures?[21]

There is little doubt nowadays, that the 'who' in McDougal's query is the modern NGO, which as we will see in the next section, has obtained roles that have surpassed the traditional advocacy roles. As service providers, advisors and consultants, mediators, and representatives, new rights and obligations have emerged. On the basis of the extended role of NGOs one cannot but agree with Hobe's 1997 conclusion. On the basis of a proper analysis of the aggregate of the rights and obligations that come with these roles, NGOs must have a legal status under international law that entitles them to operate on an equal footing with other qualified participants in international law.

Whether or not an NGO has an international legal status that is commensurate to its roles and/or activities is neither a matter of 'recognition' nor 'subject' status. The former is wholly political and the latter wholly 'unhelpful'. An international legal status for any participant in international law, whether state or non-state, should be both functional and policy-oriented, ie based on the roles and activities of the NGO in question and the needs and requirements of a legal system that is losing its exclusive national and *inter*national character.

[20] W Michael Reisman and Hague Academy of International Law, *The quest for world order and human dignity in the twenty-first century: constitutive process and individual commitment: general course on public international law* (The Hague, Hague Academy of International Law, 2013) 310.

[21] Myres S McDougal, 'Law as a Process of Decision: A Policy-Oriented Approach to Legal Study' (1956) 1 *Natural Law Forum* 53, 55.

The precise nature and determination of NGO status under international law requires a detailed and robust assessment of what NGO roles, rights and responsibilities are, as well as what they should be.[22]

10.3 NGO ROLES: A SOCIO-POLITICAL-LEGAL APPROACH

> Many textbooks on international law describe the formal and legal role of non-governmental organizations ... as limited, or do not discuss NGOs in legal terms at all. ... it should be noted that the most important role of NGOs at the international level is *probably* outside the strictly legal arena.[23]

While Anna-Karin Lindblom's observation with respect to the descriptive and empirical approach of our episteme is correct, her qualified conjecture, unfortunately, reinforces the memento and the (mis)conception of NGOs *in* international law, that has been so prevalent in our discourses.[24]

Only if we were able to hermetically distinguish between social, political and legal spaces, between non-permeable private and public spaces, or between national, international, transnational and global levels of participation, could we arguably study international law in isolation and exclude all actors that do not sign international treaties as defined by Article 2(1) of the 1968 Vienna Convention on the Law of Treaties (VCLT).[25] In the absence of clear analytical and conceptual distinctions in this respect, we must consider states and non-state actors to straddle different spaces, spheres and levels of participation.

Over recent decades, the number of NGOs has increased and their participation in the social, political and legal space(s) of international affairs has become more visible. Most observers point critically towards (1) the 'increasing popularity of NGOs with governments and official aid agencies' and (2) the 'increasing availability of increased funding'.[26] This popularity, according to Moore, is 'driven by two basic sets of beliefs organised

[22] The absence of enforcement and implementation mechanisms is not significant for the determination of existing rights or obligations. The (potential) gap between determining responsibility and actualising accountability is inherent in (international) law and does not apply exclusively to specific categories of legal person.

[23] Anna-Karin Lindblom, 'Non-Governmental Organizations and Non-State actors in International Law' in Bob Reinalda (ed), *The Ashgate research companion to non-state actors* (Aldershot, Ashgate, 2011) 148 (emphasis added; footnotes omitted). See also Noortmann, 'Non-State Actors in International Law' in B Arts, M Noortmann and B Reinalda (eds), *Non-State Actors in International Relations* (Aldershot, Ashgate, 2001).

[24] Steve Charnovitz's 1997 seminal overview of 'NGOs in international governance' is exemplary of the treatment of NGO by international legal scholarship. Charnovitz, 'Two Centuries of Participation: NGOs and international Governance' (n 13).

[25] See 1155 UNTS 331: '"treaty" means an international agreement concluded between States.'

[26] Edwards and Hulme, *Beyond the magic bullet* (n 4).

around the two poles of neo-liberal economics and liberal theory'.[27] This 'popularity' triggered a multi-disciplinary understanding that their roles have equally transformed and proliferated.[28] The end of the Cold War is generally considered to be the *explanans* of a structural geopolitical development that boosted the transnationalisation of civil society that is generally considered to explain the NGO advancement.[29]

The role(s) that NGOs play in the international space generally reflect their statutory objectives or actual practices. Most typologies differentiate between promotion, advocacy, services, and monitoring roles. Not all organisations perform all roles, but many do perform multiple roles. Most international issues provide room for employing all of the roles mentioned. With respect to the formation of international law, these general roles of NGOs have been investigated in the related and overlapping fields of law-making, law enforcement and dispute settlement.

If the concept of international law-making is taken to be a technical one, ie, international law is made by the ratification of and/or accession to international agreements by states, or the interconnected practices and opinions of those same states, no non-state actor *makes* international law. In that positivistic conception of international law-making NGOs and other non-state actors are excluded from any international law-making activity. That exclusiveness has a doctrinal foundation, but cannot be explained on the basis of international law's internal logic. In other words, there are no reasons on the basis of which NGOs are conceptually excluded from being parties to (international) agreements or from practising behaviour and holding opinions that would constitute proper customary international law. Indeed, Article 2(1) VCLT could have defined 'treaty' less exclusively; states need not be the gatekeepers of the system. Arguments in favour of an inclusive approach are generally more pragmatic than conceptual and infused with considerations of effectiveness and functionality.[30]

[27] ibid.

[28] Steve Charnovitz, 'Two Centuries of Participation: NGOs and international Governance' (n 13); N Arts, RME Keck and K Sikkink, *Activists beyond borders: advocacy networks in international politics* (Ithaca NY, Cornell University Press, 1998); William Korey, *NGOs and the Universal Declaration of Human Rights* (Basingstoke, Palgrave, 1998); Peter Willetts, *'The conscience of the world': the influence of non-governmental organisations in the UN system* (Washington DC, Brookings Institution, 1996); Tarrow, *The new transnational activism* (Cambridge, Cambridge University Press, 2005).

[29] But see Barry Davies, *Modern survival: how to cope when everything falls apart* (New York NY, Skyhorse, 2012). Davies argues that the formation of a transnational civil society is a historical project. He also suggests that the numerical increase does not necessarily constitute prove of a qualitative growth as it may be the result of fragmentation and split-offs (ibid, 1–14).

[30] Jean d'Aspremont, 'Conclusion: Inclusive Law-making and law enforcement processes for an exclusive international legal system' in Jean d'Aspremont (ed), *Participants in the International Legal System: Multiple perpsectives on non-state actors in international law* (Abingdon, Routledge, 2011).

While many international agreements have come into being through the activities of NGOs (lobbying, agenda-setting, consultancy etc), NGOs have never played a formal role in the conclusion of treaties. The four 1949 Geneva Conventions and their protocols, the 1997 Ottawa Convention on the Prohibition of the Use, Stockpiling, Production and Transfer of Anti-Personnel Mines and on their Destruction, the 1998 Rome Statute for the International Criminal Court (ICC Statute) or the 2012 Arms Trade Treaty are well-known examples. The International Committee of the Red Cross (ICRC), the International Campaign to Ban Landmines (ICBL), the Coalition for the International Criminal Court (ICC) or the International Action Network on Small Arms (IANSA) have played crucial roles in promoting and formulating these agreements.[31] The same goes for the roles of professional organisations such as the Institute of International Law (IIL), the International Law Association (ILA) and the International Law Commission (ILC), which are less researched, but given their engagement with *all* international law issues, it would be quite fair to say that international law, as we know it today, would not exist without the intellectual and policy oriented output of these organisations.[32]

Enforcement and implementation are not subject to the same doctrinal restrictions as law-making. Those two attributes of international law can be achieved through socio-political actions that are not governed by the rules of international law.[33] The advocacy and monitoring roles of organisations like Amnesty International and Greenpeace, who speak on behalf of those who cannot, aim at keeping state and non-state organisations' behaviour in line with human rights and environmental agreements. A distinction must be made between solicited and unsolicited NGO roles; ie, roles that NGOs perform upon the invitation of states, often acknowledged in international conventions and those roles that NGOs play, independently of conventional and institutional acknowledgement. Solicited

[31] Tarcisio Gazzini, 'A Unique Non-State Actor: the International Committee of the Red Cross' (2010) 4 *Human Rights & International Legal Discourse* 14; John Washburn, 'Negotiation of the Rome Statute for the International Criminal Court and International Lawmaking in the 21st Century' (1999) 11 *Pace International Law Review* 361; M Struett, 'NGOs, the International Criminal Court, and the Politics of Writing International Law' in A Bianchi (ed), *Non-State Actors and International Law* (n 12) 187; Kenneth Anderson, 'The Ottawa Convention banning landmines, the role of international non-governmental organizations and the idea of international civil society' (2011) 11 *European Journal of International Law* 91.

[32] Gaëlle Breton-le Goff, 'NGO's perspective on non-state actors' in Jean d'Aspremont (ed), *Participants in the International Legal System: Multiple perpsectives on non-state actors in international law* (Abingdon, Routledge, 2011); Math Noortmann, 'The International Law Association and non-state actors: Professional network, public interest group or epistemic community?' in Jean d'Aspremont (ed), *Participants in the International Legal System: Multiple perpsectives on non-state actors in international law* (Abingdon, Routledge, 2011).

[33] This might explain why international legal scholars are generally less interested in the NGO role in implementation and enforcement. Even in the international arena, enforcement and implementation can be achieved through practices that are considered unfriendly, but not illegal.

roles of NGOs range from informative and consultative roles as reflected in articles of the ICC Statute and Article 71 of the United Nations Charter, to participatory and representative roles as laid down in the Aarhus Convention. Where the former are often formulated as an instruction or permission to specific organs (eg, the ICC prosecutor or ECOSOC respectively), the latter are formulated as a right in itself. Where organs act upon such a directive, and invitation may entail rights and specific obligations that lead to responsibility and accountability.

Last but not least, NGOs play a role in dispute settlement procedures. Again, there is no intrinsic reason why NGOs should not participate in international dispute settlement, either as a litigants, witnesses, representatives, advisors, or mediators. We find (hitherto exceptional) examples of all of these roles in the arbitration between Greenpeace and France,[34] in *amicus curiae* roles,[35] as informants to international criminal courts,[36] as representatives and advisors in World Bank Inspection Panel (WBIP) procedures,[37]

[34] Philip Shabecoff, 'France Must Pay Greenpeace $8 Milion in Sinking of Ship', *The New York Times* (New York, 1987), www.nytimes.com/1987/10/03/world/france-must-pay-greenpeace-8-million-in-sinking-of-ship.html. See also Christine Gray and Benedict Kingsbury, 'Developments in Dispute Settlement: Inter-State Arbitration since 1945' (1992) 63(1) *British Yearbook of International Law* 99. They qualify this arbitration as 'unusual'. In accordance with the general rules of (international) arbitration, the award has never (according to my information) been released to the public.

[35] Duncan B Hollis, 'Private Actors in Public International Law: Amicus Curiae and the Case for the Retention of State Sovereignty' (2002) 25 *British Columbia International Competition Law Review* 235; Robert Howse, 'Membership and its privileges: The WTO, civil society, and the amicus brief controversy' (2003) 9 *European Law Journal* 496.

[36] See, eg, Arts 15(2), 18(1) and 17(1) of the Statutes of the International Criminal Court, the International Criminal tribunal for Former Yugoslavia and the International Criminal Tribunal for Rwanda respectively. The 2003 Agreement between the United Nations and Cambodia with respect to the constitution of the Extraordinary Chambers of the Cambodian Courts only provides for a right to access in Art 12(2). The Statutes of the Special tribunals for Sierra Leone (2002) and Lebanon (2007) do not mention NGOs. Whereas the role of NGOs in the establishment of these tribunals has been extensively discussed, their role in the actual proceedings has not attracted a great deal of attention. See eg, Struett, 'NGOs, the International Criminal Court, and the Politics of Writing International Law' (n 12); J Washburn, 'Negotiation of the Rome Statute for the International Criminal Court and International Lawmaking in the 21st Century' (1999) 11 *Pace International Law Review* 361.

[37] In the World Bank's 'Operating Procedures', NGOs are mentioned in Section VII (B) 'Methods of Investigation'. NGOs are not specifically mentioned as an entity that 'Can File A Request' (Section II.A), but the categories mentioned are broad enough to encompass the concept of NGO, both as entities that can file a request as well as entities that can represent requesters:

'(a) any group of two or more people … They may be an organization, association, society or other grouping of individuals; or

(b) a duly appointed local representative acting on explicit instructions as the agent of adversely affected people': http://web.worldbank.org/WBSITE/EXTERNAL/EXTINSPECTIONPANEL/0,,contentMDK:20175161~menuPK:64129254~pagePK:64129751~piPK:64128378~theSitePK:380794,00.html. Jonathan A Fox, 'The World Bank Inspection Panel and the Limits of Accountability' in Jonathan R Pincus and Jeffrey A Winters (eds), *Reinventing the world bank* (Ithaca NY, Cornell University Press, 2002); Gudmundur Alfredsson and Rolf Ring (eds), *The Inspection Panel of the World Bank; A Different Complaints Procedure*, vol 5 (The Hague, Martinus Nijhoff Publishers, 2001).

and as mediators in conflicts between states and armed opposition groups.[38]

While it is clear that, in all of these roles, NGOs' participation may be decisive in the outcome of the procedure, the distinction between more formal and less formal roles is not without consequences. Where NGOs are giving testimony or acting as agents or representatives, that participation may be covered by specific procedural rules and regulation. In their role as informants and 'friends', however, the impact of their roles are less clear and would require clarification as to the possible legal implications.

10.4 INSTITUTIONAL, CONVENTIONAL AND HUMAN RIGHTS

At the global level, NGO entitlements find their basis in different sources.

First of all, international governmental organisations may grant NGOs the right to participate in the organisation. The content and form of that privilege is IGO-specific, and can be based on the organisation's constitution or practice. These institutional rights generally come with corresponding obligations. Secondly, NGO rights may have been constituted in or by specific treaties, in order to facilitate and recognise NGO roles in specific areas. Last but not least, NGO rights may originate from individual human rights, such as the freedom of association or the freedom of expression and opinion, and receive information.

'IGO and INGO foundings are highly correlated', according to John Boli and George Thomas, which might explain early practices of cooperation and debates on institutional rights.[39] Two schemes are particularly interesting in the early years of the INGO-IGO relationship: the informal, open-door policy of the League of Nations and the more formal incorporation of labour and employer organisations into the state delegations of the International Labour Organization (ILO).

The ILO's so-called tripartite system has been both widely praised and widely criticised by those who considered the tripartite system to either include or exclude NGOs.[40] The controversies reflected the different understandings of the private role of labour unions and employers and the more public, altruistic role of the prototypical NGO.[41] According

[38] See eg, Konrad Huber, *'The HDC in Aceh: promises and pitfalls of NGO mediation and implementation'* (Washington DC, East-West Center, 2004) James Larry Taulbee and Marion V Creekmore Jr, 'NGO Mediation: The Carter Center' (2003) 10 *International Peacekeeping* 156.

[39] John Boli and George M Thomas, 'INGOs and the Organization of World Culture' in John Boli and George M Thomas (eds), *Constructing World Culture: International nongovernmental organizations since 1875* (Stanford CA, Stanford University Press, 2003) 28.

[40] Charnovitz, 'Two Centuries of Participation: NGOs and international Governance' (n 13).

[41] J Petras and H Veltmeyer, *Globalisation Unmasked; Imperialism in the 21st Century* (Halifax, Zed Books, 2001).

to Neri Sybesma-Knol, the ILO's NGO policy has primarily been one of rejecting 'infiltration of *other* NGOs'.[42]

The League of Nations' Statute had left open the question of the relation between the League and non-governmental 'International Bureaux' and signalled a rather permissive approach.[43] The logistics of the relationship, however, was the prerogative of the League's Secretariat, which was mounting a bureaucratic concern with the unbridled INGO access to the League's premises. In 1923, the matter was settled by a notable Council Resolution, which read:

> The value set on the collaboration with unofficial organizations in the study of specific questions and its freedom to solicit the opinions of these organizations, without prejudicing their autonomy. [And] It is not desirable to risk diminishing the activities of these organizations, the number of which is fortunately increasing, by even the appearance of an official supervision.[44]

The UN Charter departed from this unofficial and unregulated approach and included a new type of arrangement between non-governmental organisations and (inter) governmental organisation in Article 71.[45] The latter article would become the prototypical provision for the formal regulation of the relation between IGO and INGOs. Article 71 confers so-called 'consultative status' upon NGOs, which is welcomed by most commentators, and critical considerations are few.[46]

---

42 Neri Sybesma-Knol and Paul van der Heijden, *Rol en betekenis van de rechtsontwikkeling in de ILO, serie: Nederlandse Vereniging voor Internationaal Recht* (Deventer, Kluwer, 1999). It wasn't until the end of the 1990s that the ILO started to enter into a consultative relationships with other NGOs. The ILO's list of NGOs having a consultative status with the ILO seems to illustrate Sybesma's point. See www.ilo.org/pardev/civil-society/ngos/WCMS_201411/lang--en/index.htm.

43 The Covenant of the League of Nations merely provided in Art 24 for the possibility to cooperate: '[I]n all matters of international interest which are regulated by general convention but which are not placed under the control of international bureaux or commissions, the Secretariat of the League shall, subject to the consent of the Council and if desired by the parties, collect and distribute all relevant information and shall render any other assistance which may be necessary or desirable.'

In Art 25 the Statute only specified 'co-operation [with] duly authorized voluntary *national* Red Cross organizations, having as purpose the improvement of health, the prevention of disease and the mitigation of suffering throughout the world.' (Emphasis added)

44 See eg, Charnovitz, 'Nongovernmental Organizations and International Law' (n 18); W Korey, *NGOs and the Universal Declaration of Human Rights* (Basingstoke, Palgrave, 1998).

45 Art 71 reads as follows: 'The Economic and Social Council may make suitable arrangements for consultation with nongovernmental organizations which are concerned with matters within its competence. Such arrangements may be made with international organizations and, where appropriate, with national organizations after consultation with the Member of the United Nations concerned.'

46 As an exception to the rule see Noortmann, 'Who Really Needs Article 71? A Critical Approach to the Relationship between NGOs and the UN' in Heere WP (ed), *From government to governance: the growing impact of non-state actors on the international and European legal system: proceedings of the sixth Hague joint conference held in The Hague, the Netherlands, 3–5 July 2003* (The Hague, TMC Asser Press, 2004).

On the basis of this article, NGO participation has been regulated in many ways within the UN. ECOSOC Resolution 1996/31[47] provides the most recent and detailed UN regulation of the rights and duties of NGOs in a consultative arrangement of its kind. In addition to the entitlements stipulated in Resolution 1996/31 NGOs have to demonstrate that they are capable of making 'substantive and substantial contributions ... to the achievement of the objectives of the United Nations'. They also have to declare that '[i]f granted consultative status [the] organisation will act in accordance with the Charter of the United Nations *and* ECOSOC Resolution 1996/31'.[48] On the basis of that unilateral declaration, consultative status can be withdrawn if the NGO 'clearly [*sic*] abuses it status by engaging in a pattern of acts contrary to the purposes and principles of the United Nations including unsubstantiated or politically motivated acts against member states' or, if it 'did not make any positive or effective contribution to the work of the United Nations'.[49] A similar consultative arrangements has been put in place by Article 5(2) of the Agreement establishing the World Trade Organisation[50] and Article 11 of the Treaty on the European Union. The latter provides for a more comprehensive and robust provision, which includes both institutional and more substantial entitlements. Article 11 reads:

1. The institutions shall, by appropriate means, give citizens and representative associations the opportunity to make known and publicly exchange their views in all areas of Union action.
2. The institutions shall maintain an open, transparent and regular dialogue with representative associations and civil society.
3. The European Commission shall carry out broad consultations with parties concerned in order to ensure that the Union's actions are coherent and transparent.

Other organisations like the International Maritime Organisation (IMO) and the World Bank have adopted similar consultative arrangements, without a constitutional basis. These arrangements can be formalised in Guidelines, as in the case of the IMO,[51] or designated as 'partnering

[47] ECOSOC Resolution 1996/31, 49th plenary meeting 25 July 1996.

[48] See Form for Application for Consultative Status with ECOSOC at www.un.org/esa/coordination/ngo/documents.

[49] ECOSOC Resolution 1996/31, Art 57(a) and (c). Press Release ECOSOC 5876, 26 October 1999.

[50] Art 5(2) reads: 'The General Council may make appropriate arrangements for consultation and cooperation with non-governmental organizations concerned with matters related to those of the WTO.' It is implemented through the 'Guidelines for arrangements on Relations with Non-Governmental Organizations', WTO General Council Decision WT/Law/162 of 12 August 1996.

[51] See International Maritime Organization, *Basic Documents*, vol 1 (London, International Maritime organization, 2010); Basic Rules and Guidelines for Consultative Status of Non-Governmental Organizations with the International Maritime Organization.

practices', as in the case of the World Bank. The latter arrangements are perceived with some ambivalence by critical civil society groups and scholarship.[52]

Similar rights are to be found in environmental treaties and statutes of international criminal courts and tribunals. Well-known examples are the Aarhus Convention, which grants the right to information, public participation and access to justice to 'associations, organisations or groups', or the Statute of the International Criminal Court, which allows the Prosecutor to solicit information from NGOs.[53] A second set of substantive NGO rights under international law may flow from specific international conventions, designed to recognise and regulate international NGO activities in that territory of the state parties. The 1986 European Convention on the Regulation of the Legal Personality of Non-Governmental Organisations is the foremost example of such a convention. In its preamble the Convention acknowledges the need of 'laying down the conditions for recognition of the legal personality of [international non-governmental] organizations in order to facilitate their activities at European level'.[54]

Last but not least, NGOs would accumulate a set of human rights that their members would hold individually and which would be crucial for the performance of their public and representative role such as the right to associate, the right to opinion and/or access to information.[55]

10.5 NGO RESPONSIBILITY AND ACCOUNTABILITY

What NGOs are is no longer merely a matter of their intentions and activities. The NGO narrative increasingly is told in the normative rhetoric of responsibility and accountability.[56] The construction of a 'good' NGO

[52] Saladin Al-Jurf, 'Participatory development and NGOs: a look at the World Bank' (1999) 9 *Transnational Law & Contemporary Problems* 175; Christopher Gibbs, Claudia Fumo and Thomas Kuby, *Nongovernmental Organizations in World Bank Supported Projects* (Operation Evaluation Department Series) (Washington DC, Worldbank, 1999).

[53] Arts 2(4) and 3(4) of the Convention On Access To Information, Public Participation In Decision-Making And Access To Justice In Environmental Matters, done at Aarhus, Denmark, on 25 June 1998; Art 15(2) of the Statute of the International Criminal Court, Rome, 17 July 1998.

[54] See http://conventions.coe.int/Treaty/en/Treaties/Html/124.htm. As of 24 April 2014, only 11 European states had ratified the convention.

[55] See eg, *Társágac a Szabadságjogokért v Hungary*, (Application No 37374/05), ECtHR, Judgment 14 April 2009.

[56] The debate on NGO transparency and democracy is and underlying part of this wider accountability discourse. For the purpose of this chapter, I adhere to the following conceptual difference between 'responsibility' and 'accountability': 'responsibility' is an intramural concept, ie, it intrinsically exists *for* something or somebody; 'accountability', on the other hand, is an extramural concept, ie, it exists only on the basis of the potential of being held accountable by somebody or something. In other words, responsibility may exist without accountability, but there can be no accountability without a corresponding responsibility. Jem Bendell, 'Debating NGO Accountability' in Tony Hill (ed), *NGLS Development Dossier* (Geneva, UN-NGLS, 2006).

(image) in terms of performance and accountability is increasingly important. Accountability is considered to be a 'desirable organisational characteristic', to the extent that absence of accountability raises the probability of 'illegality and ineffectiveness' thus referring back to legal and logistical considerations.[57]

In the mid-1990s, a socio-political discourse on NGO accountability[58] emerged parallel to accountability projects and initiatives within the humanitarian and development NGO community.[59] The debates sprang from a general societal critique on NGO performance that came with the proliferation and enhanced visibility of NGOs as service providers and beneficiaries of public funding. The focus on 'accountability' rather than 'responsibility' reflects a biased understanding of the nature of non-governmental activities as inherently good and responsible. That prejudiced understanding, has, until very recently, prevented the NGO community from establishing robust accountability mechanisms.[60]

Michael Edwards and David Hulme were among the first to comprehensively address the complexity of NGO accountability. Accountability, according to the latter scholars is a 'complex and abstract concept', which involves multiple 'functional' and 'strategic' responsibilities and accountabilities, for and towards different stakeholders (beneficiaries, donors public, peers, staff members).[61] Responsibility and accountability differs, furthermore, according to its socio-political *and* legal construction, or the space in which it is applied. Lisa Jordan and Peter Van Tuijl correctly opine that '[a]lthough [accountability] may be grounded in legal obligations, accountability is a normative and socially constructed concept that requires interpretation of particular facts, circumstances, action or inaction.'[62] The opinion of international legal scholarship as reflected

[57] Edwards and Hulme, *Beyond the magic bullet* (n 4) 9.

[58] ibid; Adil Najam, 'NGO Accountability: A Conceptual Framework' (1996) 14 *Development Policy Review* 15; Hilhorst, 'Being Good or Doing Good' (n 4); Margaret P Karns, Timothy J Shaffer, and Richard K Ghere, 'The Challenges of Accountability for International Nongovernmental and Civil Society Organizations' (2012) 3 *Accounting, Auditing & Accountability Journal* 19.

[59] See eg, the SPHERE Project (www.spherehandbook.org/en/what-is-sphere/), the Active Learning Network for Accountability and Performance in Humanitarian Action (www.alnap.org), the Humanitarian Accountability Partnership (www.hapinternational.org) or the INGO Accountability Charter (www.ingoaccountabilitycharter.org). For more recent debates on the accountability of human rights NGOs see Anja Mihr, 'Non-Governmental Organizations in the Human Rights World' in Bob Reinalda (ed), *The Ashgate research companion to non-state actors* (Burlington VT, Ashgate, 2011).

[60] According to Edwards and Hulme, empirical studies indicate that both private and public organisations 'seek to avoid accountability': Edwards and Hulme, *Beyond the magic bullet* (n 4).

[61] ibid.

[62] Lisa Jordan and Peter Van Tuijl, 'Rights and Responsibilities in the Political Landscape of NGO Accountability: Introduction and Overview' in Lisa Jordan and Peter Van Tuijl (eds), *NGO Accountability: Politics Principles and Innovations* (London, Earthscan, 2006).

in Lindblom's reading of NGO accountability as, a 'need to address [that] is usually met outside the scope of formally binding international rules'[63] is defying the interdisciplinary and normative complexity that Edwards and Hulme, and Jordan and Van Tuijl reveal. Lindblom's position explains why issues of NGO responsibility and accountability have not triggered a similar discourse in the field of international law. In our field, there is ample evidence of NGO practices that raise the question as to whether NGOs are or should be responsible and accountable beyond internal and national mechanisms.[64]

There is no reason to assume that NGOs are incapable of violating primary rules that are established by the international community in the same way as states, IGOs, multinational companies (MNCs) or armed opposition groups (AOGs) would be capable of doing so. To the extent that they do, ordinary rules for the establishment of a wrongful act would apply in very much the same way as these apply to states and intergovernmental organisations, including the rules of attribution, circumstances precluding wrongfulness and reparation.[65] These rules are not specific to international law, but are inherent in legal systems. Equally, there is no reason for us to assume that no accountability and dispute resolution mechanisms involving NGOs can be agreed upon and established at the global level.

NGO accountability schemes have been developed along two different routes. First of all, NGOs have started to regulate themselves through organisational standards, code of conducts and certification schemes (which are often coupled with external review and accountancy procedures). Secondly, NGOs have increasingly been subjected to donor and governmental scrutiny.

NGO self-regulation, in particular noticeable in the fields of development and humanitarian aid, has started to develop internal accountability mechanisms, which according to Robert Lloyd is an '*alternative* approach to addressing NGO accountability' in term of law.[66] The Humanitarian Accountability Partnership (HAP) constitutes such an 'alternative approach'.[67] The 2010 HAP Standard in Accountability and

63 A-K Lindblom, 'Non-Governmental Organizations and Non-State actors in International Law' in B Reinalda (ed), *The Ashgate research companion to non-state actors* (Burlington VT, Ashgate, 2011) 155.

64 Like other non-state actors, NGOs do not always operate within the strict boundaries of (international) law. Sea Shepherd and Greenpeace are notorious for seeking the boundaries of international law. In various gradations, the ramming and scuttling of whaling vessels, the interference with oil tanker passage, the demonstrative occupation of oil platforms, and the misrepresentation of facts and data, and criminal actions by sympathisers, pose various degrees of international legal questions. See also section 10.6 below.

65 See the ILC Drafts on State Responsibility and the Responsibility of International Organizations: UNGA Doc A/56/10 and UNGA Doc A66/10.

66 Robert Lloyd, 'The Role of NGO Self-Regulation in Increasing Stakeholder Accountability', www.un-ngls.org/orf/cso/cso9/Self-Regulation.pdf, p 5.

67 www.hapinternational.org.

Performance Quality recognises that accountability mechanisms are extremely important where 'power' is an element in the relationship between stakeholders.[68] For that purpose HAP understands accountability as 'the means through which power is used responsibly. It is a process of taking account of, and being held accountable by, different stakeholders, and primarily those who are affected by the exercise of power.'[69] That understanding is not necessarily shared across the sector. According to the SPHERE Project, '[a]ccountability describes the ways in which organisations … involve different groups in … judging and challenging results'.[70] And Care International questions the value of accountability mechanisms altogether.[71] In the absence of (in)formal accountability procedures and mechanisms, the languages of responsibility and accountability ought to be politically suspect. Where the relationship between NGOs, donors and intended beneficiaries is one of unequal powers, the accountability procedure is likely to be part of that relationship. A robust accountability procedure would allow other stakeholders to raise accountability issues on behalf of vulnerable others. Both problems are particularly apparent in the international legal discourse on responsibility, especially when compared to the legal literature on corporate responsibility.[72]

The political element in the rules and ethics of accountability should not be denied, if it was only for the '[t]he sheer fact of participation in a global campaign embodies a political responsibility toward others engaged in the campaign but operating in a different political arena.'[73] With respect to determining the accountability of NGOs, Edwards and Hulme also observed a trend towards the corruption of NGO information, which tends to become a 'public relations activity', rather then a statement of performance.[74]

The questioning of the politics of self-regulation and internal accountability mechanisms should be matched by an equal questioning of the

[68] Humanitarian Accountability Partnership, *The 2010 HAP Standard in Accountability and Quality Management* (Geneva, HAP International, 2010) 1.

[69] ibid.

[70] The Sphere Project, *Taking the Initiative: Exploring quality and accountability in the humanitarian sector* (GenevaSphere, 2009). The SPHERE Project—in its own words—is 'a voluntary initiative that brings a wide range of humanitarian agencies together around a common aim—to improve the quality of humanitarian assistance and the accountability of humanitarian actors to their constituents, donors and affected populations.' www.sphereproject.org/about/.

[71] Quoted from ibid.

[72] The otherwise excellent edited book by Pierre-Marie Dupuy and Luisa Vierucci, *NGOs in International Law: Efficiency in Flexibility* (Cheltenham, Edgar Elgar, 2008), is illustrative in this respect. Steve Charnovitz's 'Accountability of Public and Private International Organizations' (n 18) is the exception.

[73] Lisa Jordan, 'Mechanisms for NGO Accountability' GPPI Research Paper Series No 3, 20.

[74] Edwards and Hulme, *Beyond the magic bullet* (n 4) 13.

call(s) for external mechanisms for NGO accountability. Lisa Jordan's question: 'Who's Asking And Why Now?'[75] is justified. Where states and corporate actors are being targeted, the danger of national NGO regulatory mechanisms being used for ulterior political purposes is not imaginary. A clear balance has to be struck between the possibility of jeopardising the roles, independence and international civil society function of NGOs and the protection of that same international society against irresponsible practices that disregards the needs and rights of both beneficiaries and targets.[76]

10.6 CONCLUSION

NGO roles in the international space are diverse and varied given the immensity of differences of purposes and activities within the ever-growing global NGO community. Since rights and responsibilities reflect the role and activities of the participants at the global level, the rights and responsibilities of NGOs are equally diverse and varied. Neither the diversity nor the sheer vastness, however, constitutes a valid reason to exclude NGOs from obtaining a legal status that echoes specific entitlements and obligations and that would allow them to perform their (sometimes controversial) roles in the international arena.

Increasing global socio-political and economic interaction between the (inter)governmental and the non-governmental is likely to trigger more rather than less tension and disputes between these actors. The fact that most NGO activities are performed within the jurisdiction of states does not justify national jurisdiction to be exclusively applicable. Nor does the fact that an NGO is constituted according to the laws of a specific state. International legal disputes between NGOs and other global actors ought to be settled within transnationally agreed procedures, and NGO behaviour assessed according to the rules of international and transnational law.

Greenpeace and Sea Shepherd are as much bound by the rules of maritime safety and the entitlements of the coastal state as shipping companies are, and they hold the same rights. The delivering of goods and services by humanitarian and development NGOs like the International Red Cross or Oxfam, should be of a standard that is set and monitored by a transnational community in as much as the activities of internationally operating companies are monitored and scrutinised. The campaigns and actions of such organisations as the Gaza Freedom Flotilla and Christian Solidarity International (CSI) should be judged independently and according to the

[75] L Jordan, 'Mechanisms for NGO Accountability' (n 73) 5.
[76] Noortmann, 'Non-State Actors in International Law' (n 23).

relevant international and transnational standards. Understanding the legal status of internationally operating NGOs in the traditional terms of international legal personality or subjects of international law, obfuscates the need for an inclusive legal system that entitles and obliges states, governments and non-governmental organisations equally.

A possible catalogue of rights and obligations for non-governmental organisations is NGO type-specific for the purpose of determining a legal quality that would permit an NGO in question to perform a specific role, very much like the different consultative status categories. A differentiated perspective would allow us to distinguish between NGOs that do have a law-making capacity, those that merely have participatory rights in law-making and law implementation processes, and those that merely influence the making of international law. Only the first and second roles would create legal entitlements.

The notions of 'international legal personality' and 'subjects of international law' are only useful—to the extent that they are useful at all—as qualified, functional concepts. One cannot take the legal concept of 'the (Westphalian) state' as the ultimate point of reference for assessing the international legal quality of non-state actors in general and non-governmental organisations in particular. In the case of NGOs, the ultimate question is what kind of non-state activity the NGO is engaged in and how these activities would translate into rights and obligations and what kind of international legal standing would flow from the aggregate of rights and obligations.

11

Multinational Corporations in International Law

JAN WOUTERS AND ANNA-LUISE CHANÉ

11.1 INTRODUCTION

THE PAST FOUR decades have witnessed a dramatic rise of globalised business. Today, an estimated 100,000 multinational corporations (MNCs) account for about a quarter of the global gross domestic product (GDP)[1] and generate turnovers which exceed the public budgets of many states.[2] The private sector wields considerable economic and social power and even increasingly expands into traditionally state-run sectors, fulfilling (quasi-) governmental functions by providing infrastructure, housing, and health services or organising elections.[3]

MNCs can thereby contribute to the economic and technological development of societies,[4] but also harm human rights, damage the environment, or even commit crimes. National legislation is often unable to create a stable regulatory environment in which MNCs can operate, as well as to exercise control over the harmful acts of entities which fragment their activities globally, operate in decentralised network structures, and flexibly relocate operations and profits.[5] In addition, economically weaker states depend on the investments of MNCs and may be unwilling to enact

[1] UNCTAD, 'World Investment Report: Non-Equity Modes of International Production and Development' (2011) UN Doc UNCTAD/WIR/2011, 24 and web table 34, http://unctad.org/Sections/dite_dir/docs/WIR11_web%20tab%2034.pdf.

[2] See John Mikler, 'Global Companies as Actors in Global Policy and Governance' in John Mikler (ed), *The Handbook of Global Companies* (Oxford, John Wiley & Sons, 2013) 1, 4 ff.

[3] Alexandra Gatto, *Multinational enterprises and human rights: Obligations under EU law and international law* (Cheltenham, Edward Elgar Publishing, 2011) 4.

[4] Olivier De Schutter et al, 'Foreign Direct Investment, Human Development and Human Rights: Framing the Issues' (2009) 3 *Human Rights & International Legal Discourse* 137, 159.

[5] Gatto, *Multinational enterprises and human rights* (n 3) 14; Nicolás Zambrana Tévar, 'Shortcomings and Disadvantages of Existing Legal Mechanisms to Hold Multinational Corporations Accountable for Human Rights Violations' (2012) 4 *Cuadernos de derecho transnacional* 398, 400.

and enforce demanding human rights and environmental standards in order to enhance their attractiveness to foreign investors.[6]

The perceived inadequacy of domestic legislation to effectively regulate the activities of MNCs has moved the focus to the level of international law. Two dynamics are discernible. First, acknowledging the beneficial effects of international business, efforts have been made to provide companies with a stable environment by granting them rights under international investment and international human rights law. Secondly, reacting to repeated reports about involvement of MNCs in human rights abuses, grave environmental damages and crimes, a number of initiatives have aimed at holding companies accountable under international human rights, environmental and criminal law.

After a short overview of the terminological indeterminacy of the subject matter (section 11.2), this chapter will analyse whether MNCs are subjects of international law (section 11.3) and whether they have rights (section 11.4) and obligations (section 11.5) under international law. The focus will lie on four legal fields whose recent developments have particularly impacted the status of MNCs under international law: human rights protection and responsibilities, investment protection, environmental obligations, and accountability for international crimes.

11.2 DEFINITION

The discussion about MNCs has been characterised by a wealth of different terminologies.[7] In the United Nations (UN) framework the term 'multinational corporations' was originally used and defined as 'enterprises which own or control production or service facilities outside the country in which they are based'.[8] This terminology changed to 'transnational corporation',[9] to emphasise the cross-border operation of the respective company and to distinguish it from such 'multinational corporations'

[6] Jan Wouters and Leen Chanet, 'Corporate Human Rights Responsibility: A European Perspective' (2008) 6 *Northwestern University Journal of International Human Rights* 262; Jan Wouters and Cedric Ryngaert, 'Litigation for Overseas Corporate Human Rights Abuse in the European Union: The Challenge of Jurisdiction' (2009) 40 *George Washington International Law Review* 939.

[7] See, eg, Jan Wouters and Leen Chanet, 'Rechten en plichten van (multinationale) ondernemingen in het internationaal recht' in Robby Houben and Stefan Rutten (eds), *Actuele problemen van financieel, vennootschaps- en fiscaal recht Feestbundel 20 jaar Werkgroep financieel recht* (Antwerp, Intersentia, 2007) 335 ff.

[8] Report of the Group of Eminent Persons to Study the Impact of Multinational Corporations on Development and on International Relations (1974) UN Doc E/5500/Rev.1, ST/ESA/6, 25.

[9] See, eg, UNCHR, *UN Draft Norms on the Responsibilities of Transnational Corporations and Other Business Enterprises with Regard to Human Rights* (Geneva, Sub-Commission on the Promotion and Protection of Human Rights, 2003) UN Doc E/CN.4/Sub.2/2003/12/Rev.2 (Draft Norms).

which are 'owned and controlled by entities from several countries'.[10] However, this distinction was later abandoned and the 2003 *UN Draft Norms on the Responsibilities of Transnational Corporations and Other Business Enterprises with Regard to Human Rights* define the 'transnational corporation' as an 'economic entity operating in more than one country or a cluster of economic entities operating in two or more countries—whatever their legal form, whether in their home country or country of activity, and whether taken individually or collectively'.[11]

OECD and ILO instruments, on the other hand, employ the term 'multinational enterprises'.[12] The *OECD Guidelines for multinational enterprises*—rejecting the need for a precise definition—describe them as follows:

> These enterprises operate in all sectors of the economy. They usually comprise companies or other entities established in more than one country and so linked that they may co-ordinate their operations in various ways. While one or more of these entities may be able to exercise a significant influence over the activities of others, their degree of autonomy within the enterprise may vary widely from one multinational enterprise to another. Ownership may be private, State or mixed.[13]

The terminological confusion is perpetuated in international legal scholarship. Even though scholars have attributed different meanings to the adjectives 'transnational' and 'multinational',[14] and even though 'corporation' can be understood more narrowly, designating a legal entity characterised by 'legal personality, transferable shares, limited liability, centralised management and investor ownership',[15] the terms are generally used synonymously. This terminological indeterminacy results from an inevitable 'degree of arbitrariness',[16] but it also mirrors the existing factual disorder. MNCs today comprise multiple business entities of various legal forms and display diverse forms of integration.[17] As Gatto has observed, MNCs have 'no coherent existence as a legal entity [but are]

10 Peter T Muchlinski, *Multinational enterprises & the law* (Oxford, Oxford University Press, 2007) 6.

11 Draft Norms para 20.

12 See OECD Guidelines for Multinational Enterprises (2011), www.oecd.org/daf/inv/mne/48004323.pdf; ILO, Tripartite Declaration of Principles Concerning Multinational Enterprises and Social Policy, 4th edn (2006) www.ilo.org/wcmsp5/groups/public/---ed_emp/---emp_ent/---multi/documents/publication/wcms_094386.pdf.

13 OECD Guidelines for Multinational Enterprises (n 12), pt I, ch I, para 4; see ILO, Tripartite Declaration of Principles Concerning Multinational Enterprises and Social Policy (n 12) para 6.

14 Andrew Clapham, *Human rights obligations of non-state actors* (Oxford, Oxford University Press, 2006) 199 ff; Gatto, *Multinational enterprises and human rights* (n 3) 38.

15 Peter Muchlinski, 'Corporations in International Law' in Rüdiger Wolfrum (ed), *Max Planck Encyclopedia of Public International Law* (Oxford, Oxford University Press, 2010).

16 Muchlinski, *Multinational enterprises & the law* (n 10) 7.

17 Gralf-Peter Calliess, 'Introduction: Transnational Corporations Revisited' (2011) 18 *Indiana Journal of Global Legal Studies* 601, 604.

a political and economic reality which articulates itself in a confusing variety of legal forms and devices.'[18] It is therefore more helpful to focus on the characteristics that distinguish MNCs from their national counterparts. Other than domestic businesses—even those that operate production facilities abroad, or export goods and know-how—MNCs have the capacity to flexibly move places of production and assets between countries. They structure management units independently of national borders and lose every tie to a nation state except for the formal nexus of incorporation.[19] This operational fluidity and the ensuing detachedness from domestic bonds are one of the main reasons why national legislators fail to put adequate checks on the power of MNCs, and why MNCs have come within the focus of international law.

11.3 INTERNATIONAL LEGAL PERSONALITY

The central debate on MNCs in international law focuses on the question of whether or not they are subjects of international law, that is, whether they are 'capable of possessing international rights and duties, and [have] capacity to maintain [their] rights by bringing international claims'.[20] Traditionally, international law was perceived as governing only the 'mutual transactions between sovereigns'.[21] With the rise of international organisations and international human rights law, however, the small circle of subjects of international law gradually expanded. Positivists assert that states—which remain the primary subjects of international law—can 'upgrade'[22] non-state actors to subjects of international law by endowing them with rights and obligations.[23] Non-state actors thus derive[24] their subjectivity from states and are dependent on their recognition.

Adhering to these formal prerequisites, a large majority of international legal scholars hold that MNCs do not possess international legal personality.[25] It is argued that they have not been granted rights or

[18] Gatto, *Multinational enterprises and human rights* (n 3) 38.

[19] See the detailed juxtaposition of MNCs and domestic enterprises in Muchlinski, *Multinational enterprises & the law* (n 10) 7 f.

[20] *Reparation for Injuries Suffered in the Service of the United Nations* (Advisory Opinion) [1949] ICJ Rep 174, 179.

[21] Jeremy Bentham, *An Introduction to the Principles and Morals of Legislation* (Kitchener ONT, Batoche Books, 1781).

[22] Antonio Cassese, *International Law in a Divided World* (Oxford, Clarendon Press, 1986) 103.

[23] Karsten Nowrot, 'Reconceptualising International Legal Personality of Influential Non-State Actors: Towards a Rebuttable Presumption of Normative Responsibilities' in John Fleurs (ed), *International Legal Personality* (Aldershot, Ashgate, 2010) 372.

[24] Peter Malanczuk, *Akehurst's Modern Introduction to International Law* (Abingdon, Routledge, 1997) 104.

[25] Nowrot, 'Reconceptualising International Legal Personality' (n 23) 372, with further extensive references; Cassese, *International Law in a Divided World* (n 22) 103; Malanczuk, *Akehurst's Modern Introduction to International Law* (n 24) 100; Kay Hailbronner and Marcel Kau,

obligations under international law[26] and that although companies benefit from a range of international law provisions, they do not necessarily enjoy corresponding rights.[27] A few international legal scholars, on the other hand, have recognised MNCs as subjects of international law. Some have adopted a de facto approach based on their significant participation at the level of international law[28] and on the growing privatisation of international law as evidenced by investment law and arbitration.[29] Nowrot has gone further by completely breaking with the positivist view and asserting that a rebuttable presumption exists according to which MNCs are subjects of international law, unless states and international organisations express the contrary in a legally binding form.[30] Others have left the question open,[31] sometimes adding that there is no legal impediment to their ascension in the canon of the subjects of international law.[32]

In an effort to overcome the traditional subject/object dichotomy which has generated extensive 'sterile'[33] debates about the precise scope of the two categories, several legal scholars have advocated alternative approaches. Higgins powerfully described the classification into subjects and objects of international law as an 'intellectual prison' serving no 'functional purpose'.[34] According to her, international law is a dynamic

'Der Staat und der Einzelne als Völkerrechtssubjekte' in Wolfgang Graf Vitzthum (ed), *Völkerrecht* (Berlin, Walter de Gruyter, 2010) 166; Muchlinski, 'Corporations in International Law' (n 15); Eric De Brabandere, 'Human Rights and Transnational Corporations: The Limits of Direct Corporate Responsibility' (2010) 4 *Human Rights & International Legal Discourse* 66, 80; James Crawford, *Brownlie's Principles of Public International Law* (Oxford, Oxford University Press, 2012) 122.

26 Cassese, *International Law in a Divided World* (n 22) 103; Régis Bismuth, 'Mapping a responsibility of corporations for violations of international humanitarian law sailing between international and domestic legal orders' (2009) 38 *Denver Journal of International Law & Policy* 203, 204.

27 See Malanczuk, *Akehurst's Modern Introduction to International Law* (n 24) 100: 'The fact that individuals or companies are the beneficiaries of many rules of international law does not mean that these rules create rights for the individual or companies, in much the same way as laws prohibiting cruelty to animals do not create rights for animals'.

28 See David Adedayo Ijalaye, *The extension of corporate personality in international law* (Leiden, Brill Archive 1978) 244 f; Dominique Carreau and Fabrizio Marrella, *Droit international* (Paris, Pedone, 2012) 66.

29 Zambrana Tévar, 'Shortcomings and Disadvantages of Existing Legal Mechanisms' (n 5) 401.

30 Nowrot, 'Reconceptualising International Legal Personality' (n 23) 379 ff.

31 Malcolm N Shaw, *International Law* (Cambridge, Cambridge University Press, 2014) 182; Katarina Weilert, 'Transnationale Unternehmen im rechtsfreien Raum? Geltung und Reichweite völkerrechtlicher Standards' (2009) 69 *Zeitschrift für ausländisches öffentliches Recht und Völkerrecht* 883, 910.

32 Pierre-Marie Dupuy, *L'unité de l'ordre juridique international: cours général de droit international public (2000)*, vol 297 (The Hague, Martinus Nijhoff Publishers, 2003); Patrick Daillier, Mathias Forteau and Alain Pellet, *Droit international public* (Paris, LGDJ, 2009) 714 f.

33 Simon Chesterman, 'Lawyers, Guns, and Money: The Governance of Business Activities in Conflict Zones' (2011) 11 *Chicago Journal of International Law* 321, 327.

34 Rosalyn Higgins, *Problems and process: international law and how we use it* (Oxford, Clarendon Press, 1994) 49.

decision-making process in which no subjects and objects exist, but only a variety of participants, including MNCs.[35] Clapham focuses on the capacity of non-state actors to have rights and obligations and, affirming both, he consequently attributes limited international personality to MNCs.[36] In a similar vein other scholars measure MNCs based on their roles and duties[37] or rights and responsibilities,[38] instead of concentrating on the 'label'[39] they carry. Klabbers has ascribed a merely descriptive and normatively empty value to the concept of international legal subjectivity. He concludes that 'personality is by no means a threshold which must be crossed before an entity can participate in international legal relations; instead, once an entity does participate, it may be usefully described as having a degree of international legal personality'.[40]

Instead of taking a position in this discussion, the present chapter will follow Alvarez's advice and focus on 'addressing which international rules apply to corporations rather than whether corporations are or are not subjects of international law'.[41]

11.4 RIGHTS UNDER INTERNATIONAL LAW

Notwithstanding the discussion about their international legal subjectivity, it is widely recognised today that MNCs enjoy certain rights under international law, especially in the fields of international human rights law and investment protection.[42]

11.4.1 International Human Rights Law

The European Court of Human Rights (ECtHR) is unparalleled at the international level in granting companies protection under human rights law. Article 34 of the European Convention on Human Rights (ECHR)

[35] ibid, 50.

[36] Clapham, *Human rights obligations of non-state actors* (n 14) 77 f.

[37] See Merja Pentikäinen, 'Changing International "Subjectivity" and Rights and Obligations under International Law—Status of Corporations' (2012) 8 *Utrecht Law Review* 145, 153.

[38] José E Alvarez, 'Are Corporations "Subjects" of International Law?' (2011) 9 *Santa Clara Journal of International Law* 1, 31.

[39] Pentikäinen, 'Changing International "Subjectivity"' (n 37) 153.

[40] Jan Klabbers, *An introduction to international institutional law* (Cambridge, Cambridge University Press, 2009) 52.

[41] Alvarez, 'Are Corporations Subjects of International Law?' (n 38) 31.

[42] Wouters and Chanet, 'Rechten en plichten van (multinationale) ondernemingen in het internationaal recht' (n 7) 342 ff; Clapham, *Human rights obligations of non-state actors* (n 14) 82; Gatto, *Multinational enterprises and human rights* (n 3) 61; Alvarez, 'Are Corporations Subjects of International Law?' (n 38) 31; Pentikäinen, 'Changing International "Subjectivity"' (n 37) 148.

provides that 'any person, non-governmental organisation or group of individuals' with the right to claim a violation of its rights before the Court, including corporations within the scope of 'non-governmental organisation'.[43] Companies have readily made use of this judicial option. Their claims invoke mostly Convention rights that do not necessarily presuppose an individual nexus,[44] especially procedural rights, the right to freedom of expression, and the right to peaceful enjoyment of possessions.

Of these rights, only the latter expressly refers to legal persons (Article 1 of the First Protocol to the ECHR). However, the ECtHR has flexibly granted corporate applicants protection under a range of other Convention rights. Among these are the various due process guarantees of Article 6(1) ECHR.[45] Under the ECHR, companies enjoy a right to a fair and public hearing by an independent and impartial tribunal,[46] access to a court,[47] equality of arms,[48] and reasonable length of the proceedings.[49] Frequently, media companies invoke the Convention on the grounds of alleged violations of the right to freedom of expression (Article 10(1)). The ECtHR readily affirmed the applicability to companies in cases where the expression of opinion contained a political element,[50] reflecting 'controversial opinions pertaining to modern society in general'.[51]

Furthermore, the ECtHR decided in favour of the corporate applicants in three sets of cases which were less clear-cut and engendered significant legal debates: the protection of business premises as 'home', the protection of purely commercial speech under the right to freedom of expression, and the award of monetary compensation for non-pecuniary damages (Article 41 ECHR).

The first of these cases arose under Article 8(1) ECHR, which provides that '[e]veryone has the right to respect for his private and family life, his home and his correspondence'. In *Société Colas Est SA and Others v France* (2002) the claimants sued France over raids on their business premises by investigators acting without a court warrant, arguing that their right to

[43] Winfried HAM van den Muijsenbergh and Sam Rezai, 'Corporations and the European Convention on Human Rights' (2012) 25 *Pacific McGeorge Global Business & Development Law Journal* 43, 48.

[44] A term used by Emberland in the context of ECHR Art 41, see Marius Emberland, *The human rights of companies: exploring the structure of ECHR protection* (Oxford, Oxford University Press, 2006) 125 ff.

[45] ibid 14.

[46] *Sovtransavto Holding v Ukraine* ECHR 2002-VII 95.

[47] *Silvester's Horeca Service v Belgium* App no 47650/99 (ECtHR, 4 March 2004).

[48] *Dombo Beheer BV v The Netherlands* (1993) Series A no 274; *Stran Greek Refineries and Stratis Andreadis v Greece* (1994) Series A no 301-B.

[49] *Unión Alimentaria Sanders SA v Spain* (1989) Series A no 157.

[50] *Sunday Times v The United Kingdom* (1979) Series A no 30.

[51] *VGT Verein gegen Tierfabriken v Switzerland* ECHR 2001-VI 243; see also *Sunday Times v The United Kingdom* (n 50).

respect for their home had been violated. There were weighty arguments against the application of Article 8(1) ECHR to company facilities, including the context of the provision, the drafting history, previous case law, as well as the narrow wording of the English text of the ECHR as opposed to the French term 'domicile'.[52] Notwithstanding this, the ECtHR held that the character of the Convention as a living instrument required a dynamic interpretation of the provision to accommodate for changing conditions. It referred to the fact that companies enjoy a series of rights under the ECHR and concluded that 'the time has come to hold that in certain circumstances the rights guaranteed by Article 8 of the Convention may be construed as including the right to respect for a company's registered office, branches or other business premises'.[53]

Secondly, in *Autronic AG v Switzerland* (1990) the ECtHR held that 'corporate speech'—communication in order to 'incit[e] the public to purchase a particular product'[54]—falls within the scope of Article 10(1) ECHR. According to the Court, it is not necessary to 'ascertain the reason and purpose for which the right is to be exercised'.[55] The prevention of a purely commercial reception of a television programme by Swiss authorities was considered to amount to an interference with the right to freedom of expression.

The third case ensued when corporate applicants requested the payment of monetary compensation for non-pecuniary damages under Article 41 ECHR, which grants successful applicants the entitlement to just satisfaction. In *Comingersoll SA v Portugal* (2001) the applicant had successfully argued that the length of a civil law suit before Portuguese courts constituted a violation of Article 6(1) ECHR. The company claimed monetary compensation for its non-pecuniary damage, arguing that a distinction between natural and legal persons in this respect was unfounded. According to the Portuguese government, on the other hand, monetary compensation should be awarded only for 'anxiety, the mental stress of having to wait for the outcome of the case and uncertainty'—'feelings … peculiar to natural persons'.[56] The ECtHR ruled in favour of the applicant. Adopting a near-'anthropomorphi[c]'[57] approach, it held that companies can suffer non-pecuniary damage such as a loss of 'reputation, uncertainty in decision-planning, disruption in the management of the company …

[52] Emberland, *The human rights of companies* (n 44) 114 f.
[53] *Société Colas Est and Others v France* ECHR 2002-III 105 [41].
[54] *VGT Verein gegen Tierfabriken v Switzerland* (n 51) [57].
[55] *Autronic AG v Switzerland* (1990) Series A no 178 [47].
[56] *Comingersoll SA v Portugal* ECHR 2000-IV 339 [28].
[57] Sébastien van Drooghenbroeck, 'La Convention européenne des droits de l'homme et la matière économique' in Laurence Boy, Jean-Baptiste Racine and Fabrice Siiriainen (eds), *Droit économique et droits de l'Homme* (Brussels, Larcier, 2009) 37.

and ... the anxiety and inconvenience caused to the members of the management team'.[58] The protracted civil proceedings had caused the company, 'its directors and shareholders considerable inconvenience and prolonged uncertainty',[59] justifying the award of monetary compensation.

It has to be noted that the approach of the Court to extend even those provisions of the Convention to corporate applicants that have traditionally been considered to apply only to individuals, is in some instances counterbalanced by a more lenient standard of review.[60] With respect to Article 10(2) ECHR, the ECtHR established in *Markt intern Verlag GmbH and Klaus Beermann v Germany* (1989) that the state's margin of appreciation is 'essential in commercial matters' so that the 'Court must confine its review to the question whether the measures taken on the national level are justifiable in principle and proportionate'.[61] In *Société Colas Est SA and Others v France* (2002) the ECtHR held that the applicant company's rights under Article 8(1) ECHR had been violated, 'even supposing that the entitlement to interfere may be more far-reaching where the business premises of a juristic person are concerned'.[62] Nevertheless, companies enjoy a unique level of protection under the jurisdiction of the ECtHR, which has pioneered the application of human rights to corporate applicants.

Outside the scope of the ECHR, international human rights protection for companies is dim. The UN Human Rights Committee, entrusted with overseeing the implementation of the International Covenant on Civil and Political Rights (ICCPR), has recognised that notwithstanding the lack of explicit wording, legal entities may enjoy certain rights under the Covenant, such as the freedom to manifest one's religion or belief (Article 18) and the freedom of association (Article 22).[63] However, according to Article 1 of the Optional Protocol to the ICCPR, only individuals can claim the violation of their rights before the Human Rights Committee. Companies therefore have to rely on domestic fora in order to obtain protection of their rights. The American Convention on Human Rights on the other hand explicitly accords human rights protection only to human beings.[64]

58 *Comingersoll SA v Portugal* (n 56) [35].

59 ibid [36].

60 Emberland, *The human rights of companies* (n 44) 155 ff.

61 *Markt intern Verlag GmbH and Klaus Beermann v Germany* (1989) Series A no 165 [33]; confirmed eg in *Casado Coca v Spain* (1994) Series A no 285-A [50]; *Krone Verlag GmbH & Co KG v Austria (No 3)* (2003) ECHR 2003-XII 91 [30].

62 *Société Colas Est and Others v France* (n 53) [49].

63 UN Human Rights Committee, General Comment No 31, 'The Nature of the General Legal Obligation Imposed on States Parties to the Covenant' (2004) UN Doc CCPR/C/21/Rev.1/Add.13 para 9.

64 American Convention on Human Rights (entered into force 18 July 1978) OAS Treaty Series No 36 reprinted in Basic Documents Pertaining to Human Rights in the Inter-American System OEA/Ser.L.V/II.82 doc 6 rev 1 at 25 (1992) art 1(2).

Companies can bring petitions before the Inter-American Commission on Human Rights, but only *pro victima* on behalf of a natural person.[65]

11.4.2 International Investment Law

International investment law grants MNCs the most robust rights. Customary international law, bilateral and multilateral investment treaties, as well as agreements between MNCs and host states, have established a set of rules for the protection of foreign direct investment.

For an expropriation to be lawful, customary international law requires that it is undertaken in the public interest, without arbitrariness or discrimination on the basis of nationality, and accompanied by the payment of compensation.[66] The latter has been the subject of protracted disagreements between developed and developing countries, especially in the framework of efforts to establish a New International Economic Order.[67] Developed countries endorse the *Hull* formula, which requires the payment of prompt, adequate, and effective compensation.[68]

The late 1950s saw the conclusion of the first bilateral investment treaties (BITs), designed to extend and protect foreign direct investment. Today, approximately 3,000 BITs are in force, and while no uniform standard exists, a typical BIT contains provisions on the following questions: personal and temporal applicability, definition of investment, treatment of foreign investment, expropriation, currency transfer, and dispute settlement.[69] Furthermore, many BITs include so-called 'umbrella clauses', which oblige the contracting parties to respect any other undertaking they may have entered into with regard to the investment of a national or a company of the other party, thereby elevating the contractual obligation with the investor into an international law obligation.[70]

The contracting parties commit to observing certain standards with regard to foreign investors, such as fair and equitable treatment, full

[65] Inter-American Commission on Human Rights, Rules of Procedure (2009) art 23; see also Julian G Ku, 'The Limits of Corporate Rights under International Law' (2012) 12 *Chicago Journal of International Law* 729, 750 with a reference to the Inter-American Commission on Human Rights' decision in *Tabacalera Boquerón SA v Paraguay*, OEA/Ser.L/V/II.98, doc 6.

[66] Rudolf Dolzer and Christoph Schreuer, *Principles of International Investment Law* (Oxford, Oxford University Press, 2012) 99 f.

[67] ibid 100.

[68] Rudolf Dolzer, 'Wirtschaft und Kultur' in Wolfgang Graf Vitzthum (ed), *Völkerrecht* (Berlin, Walter de Gruyter, 2007) 519.

[69] For an overview of the historical evolution of international investment agreements see Jan Wouters, Philip De Man and Leen Chanet, 'The Long and Winding Road of International Investment Agreements: Toward a Coherent Framework for Reconciling the Interests of Developed and Developing Countries' (2009) 3 *Human Rights & International Legal Discourse* 263.

[70] Prosper Weil, *Problèmes relatifs aux contrats passés entre un État et un particulier*, vol 128 (The Hague, Recueil des Cours, 1969) 130 ff.

protection and security, as well as non-discrimination. The latter requirement means that foreign investors may not be discriminated against, either compared to nationals of the host state (national treatment) or to investors from third countries (most-favoured nation treatment), although BITs can contain exceptions for members of an economic, tariff or monetary union, of a common market, or of a free trade area, as well as exceptions with regard to certain sensitive economic sectors.

Provisions on dispute settlement are the most innovative feature of BITs.[71] They provide investors with the possibility of bringing claims directly against the host state, thereby constituting a powerful enforcement mechanism and contributing to the effective protection of investment. Typically investors can choose between proceedings before a domestic court of the host state or arbitration, either under the Arbitration Rules of the United Nations Commission on International Trade Law (UNCITRAL)[72] or through the International Centre for Settlement of Investment Disputes (ICSID).[73]

BITs have been criticised for restricting the regulatory freedom of the host country and thereby hindering legislation for the protection of human rights or the environment.[74] Recent BITs take these objections into consideration and contain exception clauses to account for the public interest.[75] Other initiatives have aimed at providing policy guidance for sustainable development, such as the UNCTAD Investment Policy Framework for Sustainable Development[76] and the IISD Model International Agreement on Investment for Sustainable Development, which seeks to achieve a balance between the obligations of the host state, the home state and the investor.[77]

[71] See inter alia Jan Wouters and Nicolas Hachez, 'The Institutionalization of Investment Arbitration and Sustainable Development' in Marie-Claire Cordonnier Segger, Markus Gehring and Andrew Newcombe (eds), *Sustainable Development in International Investment Law* (The Hague, Kluwer Law International, 2011) 615; Nicolas Hachez and Jan Wouters, 'International Investment Dispute Settlement in the Twenty-First Century: Does the Preservation of the Public Interest Require an Alternative to the Arbitral Model?' in Freya Baetens (ed), *Investment Law within International Law* (Cambridge, Cambridge University Press, 2013) 417.

[72] UNCITRAL Arbitration Rules (2010) www.uncitral.org/pdf/english/texts/arbitration/arb-rules-revised/arb-rules-revised-2010-e.pdf.

[73] Convention on the Settlement of Investment Disputes between States and Nationals of Other States (adopted 18 March 1965, entered into force 14 October 1966) 575 UNTS 159 (ICSID Convention).

[74] Jan Wouters and Nicolas Hachez, 'When Rules and Values Collide: How Can a Balanced Application of Investor Protection Provisions and Human Rights Be Ensured?' (2009) 3 *Human Rights & International Legal Discourse* 301.

[75] For an analysis of 'new generation' BITs see Jan Wouters, Sanderijn Duquet, Nicolas Hachez, 'International Investment Law: the Perpetual Search for Consensus' in Olivier De Schutter, Johan Swinnen and Jan Wouters (eds), *Foreign Direct Investment and Human Development* (London, Routledge, 2013) 25.

[76] UNCTAD, 'Investment Policy Framework for Sustainable Development', http://unctad.org/en/PublicationsLibrary/diaepcb2012d5_en.pdf.

[77] IISD, Model International Agreement on Investment for Sustainable Development (2005) www.iisd.org/pdf/2005/investment_model_int_agreement.pdf.

A number of multilateral instruments contain similar provisions on investment protection, such as the North American Free Trade Agreement (NAFTA) or the 1994 Energy Charter Treaty. Between 1995 and 1998 the OECD made efforts to draft a Multilateral Agreement on Investment (MAI) in order to replace the multitude of BITs. Strong opposition by NGOs and developing countries, lack of support by the business world, and disagreements between the negotiating parties, particularly about sectoral exceptions as well as social and environmental issues, ultimately led to the abandonment of the project. A subsequent initiative under the auspices of the World Trade Organization (WTO) failed in 2004 due to concerns of the developing world about undue restrictions of their regulatory freedom.[78]

11.5 OBLIGATIONS UNDER INTERNATIONAL LAW

Since the 1970s a range of initiatives has attempted to close the perceived 'governance gap' and to rein in the power of MNCs by subjecting them to binding obligations under international law. Their success has been limited. According to the prevailing view, MNCs have no direct obligations under international law,[79] although there is a growing body of non-binding 'soft law' regulating their conduct.

11.5.1 International Human Rights Law

MNCs can directly impact human rights in the societies they operate in, eg by employing children or forced workers, by operating on the territories of indigenous people without their consent, by using discriminatory recruitment policies, or by damaging the environment and thus endangering the life and health of people. They can also indirectly cause harm if they create incentives for state authorities to violate human rights for business purposes or if they support regimes engaged in human rights violations by providing infrastructure, financial means, or international credibility.

Under current international human rights law, however, states are the primary duty bearers, obliged to respect and fulfil human rights and to ensure their protection against abuses by private actors.[80] While they have

[78] Christoph Schreuer, 'Investments, International Protection' in Rüdiger Wolfrum (ed), *The Max Planck Encyclopedia of Public International Law* (Oxford, Oxford University Press, 2011).

[79] Cassese, *International Law in a Divided World* (n 22) 103; Hailbronner and Kau, 'Der Staat und der Einzelne als Völkerrechtssubjekte' (n 25) 178; De Brabandere, 'Human Rights and Transnational Corporations' (n 25) 80; Crawford (n 25) 122.

[80] For the respective obligations of home and host countries see Olivier De Schutter, 'La responsabilité des États dans le contrôle des sociétés transnationales: vers une convention internationale sur la lutte contre les atteintes aux droits de l'homme commises par les sociétés

enacted domestic legislation to regulate the conduct of companies chartered or operating in their territory, they have not yet imposed directly binding human rights obligations on them under international law.[81]

The Universal Declaration of Human Rights (UDHR) states that 'every organ of society'—a term which possibly includes MNCs[82]—'shall strive by teaching and education to promote respect for these rights and freedoms'. However, this statement is only contained in the preamble, which has not hardened into customary international law.[83] For the ICCPR, the Human Rights Committee has explicitly stated that it does not have direct horizontal effect,[84] while the Committee on Economic, Social and Cultural Rights observed with regard to the International Covenant on Economic, Social and Cultural Rights (ICESCR) that 'private enterprises [are] not bound by the Covenant'.[85] Article 1 of the ECHR binds only the 'high contracting parties [to] secure to everyone within their jurisdiction the rights and freedoms defined in Section I of this Convention'.[86]

The lack of direct binding obligations for MNCs under international human rights law has been the subject of considerable criticism. One of the main causes of concern is a perceived 'protection gap'[87] if the safeguarding of human rights is left entirely to the states: first, because of the uneven status of recognition of human rights instruments in the various jurisdictions; second, because of their disparate enforcement, which is closely connected to the strength of the domestic legal system and the dependence on foreign investment of the respective states.[88] Another

transnationales' in Emmanuel Decaux (ed), *La responsabilité des entreprises multinationales en matière de droits de l'homme* (Brussels, Bruylant, 2010) 19.

[81] See only UNHRC, 'Report of the Special Representative of the Secretary-General on the issue of human rights and transnational corporations and other business enterprises, John Ruggie' (2010) UN Doc A/HRC/14/27 para 55; De Brabandere, 'Human Rights and Transnational Corporations' (n 25) 67.

[82] Muchlinski, 'Corporations in International Law' (n 15).

[83] UNHRC, 'Report of the Special Representative of the Secretary-General on the issue of human rights and transnational corporations and other business enterprises, John Ruggie' (2007) UN Doc A/HRC/4/35 para 38. See Alvarez, 'Are Corporations Subjects of International Law?' (n 38) 5.

[84] UNHRC, General Comment No 31 (n 63) para 8.

[85] CESCR, General Comment No 18, 'The Right to Work—Art 6' (2006) UN Doc E/C 12/GC/18 para 52.

[86] For an analysis of the indirect horizontal effect of the ECHR see Jan Wouters and Leen de Smet, 'Het EVRM, internationale mensenrechtenstandaarden en (multinationale) ondernemingen' in Paul Lemmens (ed), *Uitdagingen door en voor het EVRM* (The Hague, Kluwer, 2005) 68 ff.

[87] UNHRC, 'Report of the Special Representative of the Secretary-General on the issue of human rights and transnational corporations and other business enterprises, John Ruggie' (n 83) para 84.

[88] John Ruggie, 'Prepared Remarks at Clifford Chance' (2007) 4, www.reports-and-materials.org/Ruggie-remarks-Clifford-Chance-19-Feb-2007.pdf.

major ground for criticism is the 'governance gap',[89] which results from the discrepancy between the power of MNCs to severely harm human rights and the inability of domestic legislators to take effective measures in this respect. Some legal scholars have also criticised the one-sidedness of international human rights law, which grants MNCs significant rights and benefits without holding them liable for abuses.[90] There are, however, concerns not only about the effective protection of human rights norms. Commentators have also pointed out that companies suffer significant disadvantages due to the legal uncertainty of the current regime. Companies can incur increased costs and sustain reputational damage when they are measured according to human rights standards by which they are not even legally bound.[91]

Various approaches have been proposed to hold companies accountable under international human rights law. It has been argued that MNCs should incur direct liability for human rights abuses.[92] One of the initiatives to this effect was the drafting of the UN Draft Norms on the responsibilities of transnational corporations and other business enterprises with regard to human rights, which will be treated in more detail below. Fears of diluting the responsibilities of states and undermining their authority, as well as the inapplicability of many human rights norms to private actors, have effectively hindered the success of the Draft Norms, although a recent initiative in the Human Rights Council has re-opened the discussion on a legally binding human rights instrument for MNCs.[93] Others have advocated the imposition of aiding and abetting liability on MNCs for their complicity in human rights violations. The ensuing questions of *mens rea* and attribution have not yet been satisfactorily answered.[94] In light of the considerable resistance at the political, legal, and business levels to impose binding human rights obligations on MNCs, a host of non-binding 'soft law' instruments has seen the light of day, seeking to set certain human rights standards for MNCs. They have been lauded as a 'step in the right direction'[95] and are sometimes regarded as a precursor

[89] UNHRC, 'Report of the Special Representative of the Secretary-General on the issue of human rights and transnational corporations and other business enterprises, John Ruggie' (2008) UN Doc A/HRC/8/5 para 3.

[90] Anna Grear, 'Challenging corporate "humanity": legal disembodiment, embodiment and human rights' (2007) *Human Rights Law Review* 511, 514; Pentikäinen, 'Changing International "Subjectivity"' (n 37) 149.

[91] Ruggie, 'Prepared Remarks at Clifford Chance' (n 88) 4; Adam Walczak, 'Coming to the Table: Why Corporations Should Advocate for Legal Norms for the Protection of Indigenous Rights' (2010) 42 *George Washington International Law Review* 623, 649 ff.

[92] Pentikäinen, 'Changing International "Subjectivity"' (n 37) 149.

[93] UNHRC Res 26/9 (2014) UN Doc A/HRC/RES/26/9.

[94] Jena Martin Amerson, 'What's in a Name? Transnational Corporations as Bystanders under International Law' (2011) 85 *John's Law Review* 1, 36.

[95] Walczak, 'Coming to the Table' (n 91) 643.

for binding rules. Critics, however, consider them inadequate to effectively protect human rights and ensure legal certainty for the private sector.[96] It has been argued that this 'illusion of regulation' may be 'worse than no regulation at all'.[97]

UN Draft Norms on the Responsibilities of Transnational Corporations and Other Business Enterprises With Regard to Human Rights

The Draft Norms on the responsibilities of transnational corporations and other business enterprises with regard to human rights (Draft Norms) were an ambitious attempt to create binding international human rights obligations for MNCs.[98] Drafted by a working group under the UN Sub-Commission on the Promotion and Protection of Human Rights and adopted in 2003 in the form of a resolution by the latter, they were rejected by the United Nations Commission on Human Rights (CHR), which stated in unequivocal terms that the draft had 'not been requested' and had 'no legal standing'.[99]

The Draft Norms were an innovative initiative, insofar as they sought to directly apply human rights rules to MNCs, elevating them to full-fledged duty bearers under international human rights law.[100] Even though the primary responsibility of states was recognised, MNCs were obliged to 'promote, secure the fulfilment of, respect, ensure respect of and protect'[101] a broad range of human rights. Implementation measures included the adoption, dissemination, and implementation of internal rules of operation, periodic reporting duties as well as monitoring and verification by the UN.[102] However, the Draft Norms have been criticised for simply imposing on MNCs human rights instruments which are addressed to states.[103] Apart from the questionable legal basis for this move and ensuing practical difficulties, it was also feared that such an approach might result in a dilution of state responsibility and a weakening of sovereignty.[104] Extensive criticism led to the abandonment of the project and to the readjustment of international efforts.

96 ibid 643 ff.
97 Chesterman, 'Lawyers, Guns, and Money' (n 33) 324.
98 Wouters and Chanet, 'Rechten en plichten van (multinationale) ondernemingen in het internationaal recht' (n 7) 383 ff.
99 UNCHR Res 116 (2004) UN Doc E/CN.4/2004/L.11/Add.7.
100 Amerson, 'What's in a Name' (n 94) 40.
101 Draft Norms para 1.
102 ibid paras 15 and 16.
103 Chesterman, 'Lawyers, Guns, and Money' (n 33) 327.
104 Larry Catá Backer, 'On the Evolution of the United Nations Protect-Respect-Remedy Project: The State, the Corporation and Human Rights in a Global Governance Context' (2011) 9 *Santa Clara Journal of International Law* 37, 46.

Guiding Principles on Business and Human Rights

After the failure of the Draft Norms, the CHR established the mandate of a Special Representative of the UN Secretary-General on the Issue of Human Rights and Transnational Corporations and other Business Enterprises (SRSG), tasked with identifying and clarifying existing standards and practices. The Secretary General appointed John Ruggie, one of the authors of the Global Compact, and influential critic of the Draft Norms.

In the first phase of his mandate (2005–07), the SRSG conducted an extensive mapping of international standards and practices which then served as the basis for the formulation of recommendations during the second phase (2007–08). He developed a three-pillar framework, consisting of (1) the state duty to respect, protect and fulfil human rights, (2) the corporate responsibility to respect human rights, and (3) the need for effective remedy for victims of human rights abuses ('Protect, Respect and Remedy Framework' or 'Ruggie Framework'). In the last phase (2008–11), he elaborated specific recommendations for the implementation of the Framework, resulting in the development of the 'Guiding Principles on Business and Human Rights', which were endorsed by the UN Human Rights Council (UNHRC) on 16 June 2011.

The first pillar of the Ruggie Framework highlights that states are the primary duty bearers under international human rights law. It is their obligation to respect and fulfil human rights and to protect them against abuses, including those committed by MNCs. This requires states among other to enact, assess, and enforce human rights legislation, to ensure policy coherence, to provide guidance on human rights issues to companies—especially to those operating in conflict zones—and to promote respect for human rights by business partners.

The second pillar focuses on the responsibility of business entities to respect all internationally recognised human rights, which requires them to 'avoid causing or contributing to adverse human rights impacts … and address such impacts when they occur' and to 'seek to prevent or mitigate adverse human rights impacts that are directly linked to their operations, products or services by their business relationships'.[105] The responsibility of companies thereby differs significantly from the obligations of states. Whereas states have comprehensive duties to respect, protect and fulfil human rights, companies are merely responsible for ensuring that they do not abuse the human rights of others. The Guiding Principles recommend them to adopt '(a) a policy commitment to meet their responsibility to respect human rights; (b) a human rights due diligence process to

[105] UNHRC, 'Report of the Special Representative of the Secretary-General on the issue of human rights and transnational corporations and other business enterprises, John Ruggie' (2011) UN Doc A/HRC/17/31, para 13.

identify, prevent, mitigate and account for how they address their impacts on human rights; (c) processes to enable the remediation of any adverse human rights impacts they cause or to which they contribute'.[106] Rejecting previous efforts to compile lists of human rights which are applicable to companies, the SRSG stated that 'business enterprises can have an impact on virtually the entire spectrum of internationally recognised human rights' and concluded that their 'responsibility to respect applies to all such rights'.[107]

The third pillar recognises the importance of effective access to remedy for the victims of human rights abuses, identifying responsibilities for both states and businesses. States should ensure the effectiveness of judicial grievance mechanisms and provide access to non-judicial and non-state-based grievance mechanisms. Businesses should establish or participate in the latter and ensure that their collaborative voluntary human rights initiatives provide for dispute settlement procedures.

'Principled pragmatism' is the label that the SRSG has often given to his approach.[108] Opting for a broad and transparent multi-stakeholder process he set out to move beyond the failure of the Draft Norms and to establish an 'authoritative focal point around which actors' expectations could converge'.[109] Rather than laying down principles *de lege ferenda*, he reiterated the existing obligations of states under human rights law and connected them to a voluntary corporate governance framework.[110]

The result has led both to praise and criticism.[111] Supporters have lauded the open consultative process for successfully creating awareness for the problem[112] and appreciated the clear demarcation between state obligations and corporate responsibilities. The business world, which has consistently rallied against the imposition of binding human rights

[106] ibid para 15.
[107] ibid para 12.
[108] UNHRC, 'Report of the Special Representative of the Secretary-General on the issue of human rights and transnational corporations and other business enterprises, John Ruggie' (n 81), para 4 ff.
[109] UNGA Third Committee (65th session) 'Statement by Professor John Ruggie: Mandate of the Special Representative of the Secretary-General on the Issue of Human Rights and Transnational Corporations and Other Business Enterprises' (26 October 2010) 1, www.business-humanrights.org/media/documents/ruggie-statement-to-un-gen-assembly-26-oct-2010.pdf.
[110] Backer, 'On the Evolution of the United Nations Protect-Respect-Remedy Project' (n 104) 43.
[111] See Jan Wouters and Nicolas Hachez, *Business and Human Rights in EU External Relations. Making the EU a Leader at Home and Internationally* (2009) Study for the European Parliament, Directorate-General for External Policies of the Union, Directorate B—Policy Department, EXPO/B/DROI/2009/2, PE407.014, para 29 ff, www.europarl.europa.eu/document/activities/cont/200904/20090430ATT54804/20090430ATT54804EN.pdf.
[112] Susan Ariel Aaronson and Ian Higham, '"Re-righting Business": John Ruggie and the Struggle to Develop International Human Rights Standards for Transnational Firms' (2013) 35 *Human Rights Quarterly* 333, 336.

obligations and was starkly opposed to the Draft Norms, welcomed the Guiding Principles, although a 2013 study by Aaronson and Higham showed little impact on corporate practices.[113] Governments reacted equally favourably, and a number of domestic and regional efforts to implement the Guiding Principles have seen the light of day.[114] NGOs, on the other hand, have generally been more supportive of the Draft Norms and have criticised the 'regressive'[115] approach of the Guidelines to attribute merely non-binding responsibilities to companies. Critics also deplored the preference of process over substance, referring to the failure of the Guiding Principles to establish a clear normative framework as a reference point against which the human rights performance of the business entity can be measured.[116]

Following up on the work of the SRSG, the HRC created a Working Group to promote dissemination and implementation of the Guiding Principles and launched an annual Forum on Business and Human Rights to strengthen dialogue and cooperation.[117] Bringing together participants from governments, businesses and civil society organisations around the world, the annual Forum provides an opportunity to discuss trends and challenges in the implementation of the Guiding Principles.[118] The mandate of the Working Group was extended for another period of three years in 2014.[119]

Human Rights Council Resolution 26/9

Two years after the adoption of the Guiding Principles, the representative of Ecuador delivered a statement during the 24th session of the Human

[113] ibid 355 ff.

[114] See the 2011 revision of the OECD Guidelines for Multinational Enterprises; the three EU Sector Guides on Implementing the UN Guiding Principles on Business and Human Rights (2013) for employment and recruitment agencies (http://ec.europa.eu/enterprise/policies/sustainable-business/files/csr-sme/csr-era-hr-business_en.pdf), for the oil and gas sector (http://ec.europa.eu/enterprise/policies/sustainable-business/files/csr-sme/csr-oag-hr-business_en.pdf) and for the ICT sector (http://ec.europa.eu/enterprise/policies/sustainable-business/files/csr-sme/csr-ict-hr-business_en.pdf); and the national action plans of the UK (September 2013), the Netherlands (December 2013), Italy (March 2014), Denmark (April 2014), Spain (2014), Finland (October 2014) and Lithuania (February 2015), available at www.ohchr.org/EN/Issues/Business/Pages/NationalActionPlans.aspx.

[115] 'Joint Civil Society Statement on the draft Guiding Principles on Business and Human Rights' (2011), www.fidh.org/IMG/pdf/Joint_CSO_Statement_on_GPs.pdf.

[116] Rory Sullivan and Nicolas Hachez, 'Human Rights Norms for Business: The Missing Piece of the Ruggie Jigsaw—The Case of Institutional Investors' in Radu Mares (ed), *The UN Guiding Principles on Business and Human Rights: Foundations and Implementation* (The Hague, Martinus Nijhoff, 2012) 227 ff.

[117] UNHRC Res 17/4 (2011) UN Doc A/HRC/RES/17/4.

[118] OHCHR, 'United Nations Forum on Business and Human Rights', www.ohchr.org/EN/Issues/Business/Forum/Pages/ForumonBusinessandHumanRights.aspx.

[119] UNHRC Res 26/22 (2014) UN Doc A/HRC/RES/26/22.

Rights Council, re-opening the discussion by pushing for a legally binding human rights instrument for MNCs.[120] The statement was supported by a large number of states, including the African Group, the Arab Group, Pakistan, Sri Lanka, Kyrgyzstan and several GRULAC states.

At the 26th session of the Human Rights Council, Ecuador and South Africa jointly tabled a draft resolution which provided for the establishment of an open-ended intergovernmental working group ('IGWG') on transnational corporations and other business enterprises with respect to human rights. The mandate of the IGWG comprises the elaboration of a binding human rights instrument, governing the activities of MNCs and other business enterprises. The draft was co-sponsored by Algeria, Bolivia, Cuba, El Salvador, Nicaragua, Senegal and Venezuela and it was adopted as Resolution 26/9 by 20 votes to 14, with 13 abstentions.[121] Among the no voters were the United States, Japan, South Korea and the EU Member States. The proponents of the resolution argued, that while the Guiding Principles could be considered as a first step, a merely voluntary international framework was ultimately insufficient to provide the victims of corporate human rights abuses with the necessary legal protection, particularly given the often weak level of binding national regulation. The opponents of the resolution referred to the success of the Guiding Principles, the implementation of which would be threatened through the re-opened divisive discussion on a binding instrument. They stressed the importance of national implementation plans and the inappropriateness of a 'one size fits all' approach.[122] The IGWG is scheduled to launch its first deliberations and stakeholder consultations on a potential binding instrument in July 2015.

OECD Guidelines for Multinational Enterprises

The OECD Guidelines for Multinational Enterprises are a set of non-binding recommendations for responsible business conduct that the participating governments address to MNCs which operate in or from their territory. The first Guidelines were adopted in 1976, with the aim to improve the foreign investment climate by strengthening cooperation among OECD Member States and reducing the difficulties arising from the operations of MNCs. A revised version, adopted in 2000, recommended MNCs to 'respect

[120] Statement on behalf of a Group of Countries at the 24th Session of the Human Rights Council, 'Transnational Corporations and Human Rights', General Debate—Item 3, September 2013, http://business-humanrights.org/sites/default/files/media/documents/statement-unhrc-legally-binding.pdf.

[121] UNHRC Res 26/9 (2014) UN Doc A/HRC/RES/26/9.

[122] Human Rights Council, 'Council extends mandates on extreme poverty, international solidarity, independence of judges, and trafficking in persons', 26 June 2014, www.ohchr.org/EN/NewsEvents/Pages/DisplayNews.aspx?NewsID=14785&LangID=E.

the human rights of those affected by their activities'[123] for the first time. The latest revision in 2011 expanded this recommendation by introducing an entire chapter on human rights. Echoing the provisions of the Guiding Principles, it requests MNCs to respect human rights, avoid causing or contributing to adverse human rights impacts, address and seek ways to prevent or mitigate these impacts, have a policy commitment to respect human rights, carry out human rights due diligence, and provide for remediation of adverse human rights impacts. The 2011 revision also introduced a new approach to responsible supply chain management, extending the Guidelines beyond the immediate operations of the MNCs to their relations with, eg, subcontractors or franchisees.

Implementation of the Guidelines lies in the hands of the adhering states, the MNCs, the National Contact Points (NCPs) and the Investment Committee. Each adhering state is required to set up an NCP, tasked with promoting the Guidelines, handling inquiries, and solving disputes. Their role, which has not been uniformly successful,[124] was enhanced by the 2011 revision. If an issue arises under the Guidelines, they will contribute to its solution by making an initial assessment, offering good offices, and publishing the results of the procedure. If necessary, they are assisted by the Investment Committee[125] which also provides advice on the interpretation of the Guidelines. The outcome of these procedures is, however, necessarily non-binding and the names of the companies involved are typically not disclosed in order to protect confidential information.[126] Their effect has thus been characterised as 'commercial rather than legal'.[127]

ILO Tripartite Declaration of Principles Concerning Multinational Enterprises and Social Policy

The ILO Tripartite declaration of principles concerning multinational enterprises and social policy is a non-binding instrument which was

[123] OECD, Guidelines for Multinational Enterprises (2000), www.oecd.org/investment/mne/1922428.pdf, Part I, ch II, para 2.

[124] Wouters and Ryngaert, 'Litigation for Overseas Corporate Human Rights Abuse in the European Union' (n 6) 972 ff; Walczak, 'Coming to the Table' (n 91) 646; Zambrana Tévar, 'Shortcomings and Disadvantages of Existing Legal Mechanisms' (n 5) 404.

[125] The OECD Investment Committee is tasked with the interpretation and implementation of the Guidelines. It monitors the functioning of the Guidelines, provides a forum for discussion as well as for dispute resolution, offers recommendations, and issues reviews and analyses. The Committee was established in 2004, merging the former Committee on International Investment and Multinational Enterprises (CIME) and the former Committee on Capital Movements and Invisible Transactions (CMIT). For more information see the On-Line Guide to OECD Intergovernmental Activity, www2.oecd.org/OECDGROUPS/Bodies/ShowBodyView.aspx?BodyID=7232&Lang=en&Book=True.

[126] OECD Guidelines for Multinational Enterprises (n 12) pt II, Procedural Guidance, para C.3. See Zambrana Tévar, 'Shortcomings and Disadvantages of Existing Legal Mechanisms' (n 5) 404.

[127] De Brabandere, 'Human Rights and Transnational Corporations' (n 25) 82.

adopted after tripartite negotiations between workers' and employers' organisations and state governments in 1977. It has been amended twice, in 2000 and 2006.[128] Reacting to concerns about labour standards and social issues, the Declaration contains principles on employment, training, conditions of work and life, and industrial relations, which 'governments, employers' and workers' organisations and multinational enterprises are recommended to observe on a voluntary basis'.[129] Without providing for a complaints mechanism similar to the one under the OECD Guidelines, the Declaration merely envisages periodic surveys in order to measure its effectiveness and a clarification process, whereby the parties may submit requests for interpretation to the ILO.

Global Compact

The Global Compact is a 'soft law' policy initiative for businesses which voluntarily commit to respect and support 10 principles in the areas of human rights, labour, the environment, and anti-corruption, derived from the UDHR, the ILO's Declaration on Fundamental Principles and Rights at Work, the Rio Declaration on Environment and Development and the UN Convention Against Corruption. The Global Compact was announced by UN Secretary-General Kofi Annan in 1999 and was officially launched in 2000. Today it counts more than 10,000 participants from over 130 countries, making it the largest non-binding corporate responsibility initiative world-wide.[130] Companies must submit an annual report on the implementation of the 10 principles, which, however, is not subject to any review mechanism and has consequently been labelled a mere 'public relations exercise'.[131] Supporters have lauded its contribution to raising awareness for the underlying issues, however, critics decry the lack of monitoring and audit, both for potential and current candidates.[132]

Self-regulation

Rejecting the need for 'hard law', MNCs have frequently opted for voluntary initiatives in which they pledge their respect and support for human

[128] Jernej Letnar Cernic, 'Corporate responsibility for human rights: analyzing the ILO tripartite declaration of principles concerning multinational enterprises and social policy' (2009) 6 *Miskolc Journal of International Law* 24, 26.

[129] ILO, Tripartite declaration of principles concerning multinational enterprises and social policy (n 12) para 7.

[130] 'Overview of the UN Global Compact' (22 April 2013), www.unglobalcompact.org/AboutTheGC/index.html.

[131] Zambrana Tévar, 'Shortcomings and Disadvantages of Existing Legal Mechanisms' (n 5) 405.

[132] Weilert, 'Transnationale Unternehmen im rechtsfreien Raum?' (n 31) 914.

rights.[133] The variety of existing instruments is broad, comprising codes of conduct, transparency initiatives, and social labels. They can have 'soft' positive effects by putting the spotlight on human rights issues and evidencing certain recognition of responsibility by the respective companies, thus possibly preparing the ground for binding regulation.[134] It could also be argued that these voluntary commitments have very tangible legal consequences: failure to comply with a self-imposed code of conduct could amount to deceptive advertisement[135] or evidence a company's violation of its duty of care, entailing liability for damages under tort law.[136]

Nevertheless, the overall merits and legitimacy of corporate human rights self-regulation are disputed. Among the plethora of initiatives, the majority does not provide for independent third-party compliance monitoring or even transparent and accurate self-evaluation and most employ vague and aspirational language instead of making precise and comprehensive human rights commitments.[137] It has been observed that it might be 'inappropriate' to leave human rights questions to corporate self-regulation and unwise to assign companies a role, which they are unable to fulfil.[138] Some authors have even pointed to the danger that self-regulation might 'give the appearance of regulation and thereby ward off criticism and the imposition of external regulation'.[139]

Enforcement

MNCs incur no direct legal obligations under international human rights law and consequently no enforcement mechanism under international law exists. The picture changes, however, if one takes a look at the national level, where MNCs have been sued for human rights abuses before civil and criminal tribunals.[140]

133 In 2008, 86% of the top 200 MNCs had adopted a code of conduct; see Pascale Deumier, 'Les codes de conduite des entreprises et l'effectivité des droits de l'homme' in Laurence Boy, Jean-Baptiste Racine and Fabrice Siiriainen (eds), *Droit économique et droits de l'Homme* (Brussels, Larcier, 2009) 673.

134 Steven R Ratner, 'Corporations and human rights: a theory of legal responsibility' (2001) 111 *Yale Law Journal* 443, 532 f.

135 See Su-Ping Lu, 'Corporate Codes of Conduct and the FTC: Advancing Human Rights Through Deceptive Advertising Law' (2000) 38 *Columbia Journal of Transnational Law* 603.

136 Wouters and Ryngaert, 'Litigation for Overseas Corporate Human Rights Abuse in the European Union' (n 6) 957.

137 Penelope Simons, 'Corporate voluntarism and human rights: The adequacy and effectiveness of voluntary self-regulation regimes' (2004) *Relations Industrielles/Industrial Relations* 101, 106 ff, 113 ff.

138 Muchlinski, *Multinational enterprises & the law* (n 10) 525 f.

139 Gatto, *Multinational enterprises and human rights* (n 3) 22.

140 For an analysis of the justiciability of corporate human rights violations before domestic courts see Katja Sontag, 'La justiciabilité des droits de l'homme à l'égard des sociétés transnationales' in Laurence Boy, Jean-Baptiste Racine and Fabrice Siiriainen (eds), *Droit économique et droits de l'Homme* (Brussels, Larcier, 2009) 569.

The most prominent cases were argued in the United States under the Alien Tort Statute (ATS), which provides district courts with jurisdiction *ratione materiae* for 'any civil action by an alien for a tort only, committed in violation of the law of nations or a treaty of the United States'.[141] Having fallen into oblivion after its adoption in 1789,[142] the statute was rediscovered in the landmark case *Filártiga v Peña-Irala* (1980),[143] where the Second Circuit ruled in favour of two Paraguayan citizens who had sued a fellow countryman over a case of torture that had taken place in Paraguay. The Court assumed subject-matter jurisdiction because 'deliberate torture perpetrated under colour of official authority violates universally accepted norms of the international law of human rights'.[144] In *Sosa v Alvarez-Machain* (2004)[145] the US Supreme Court affirmed jurisdiction for violations of those international norms which are 'specific, universal, and obligatory'.[146]

The ATS quickly became a popular tool for human rights activists to hold perpetrators of human rights abuses accountable. In 1995 the US Court of Appeals for the Second Circuit in *Kadic v Karadzic*[147] opened the door for claims against non-state actors acting without state involvement. Soon, the first successful law suit against a corporate entity, *Doe v Unocal* (1997),[148] followed. However, legal uncertainty about the relationship between domestic US law and international law persisted. Especially the question whether the scope of liability should be governed by international or domestic law remained contentious.

The US Supreme Court commented on this issue in a footnote of the judgment in *Sosa v Alvarez-Machain*, stating that '[a] related consideration is whether international law extends the scope of liability for a violation of a given norm to the perpetrator being sued, if the defendant is a private actor such as a corporation or individual'.[149] Picking up on this, the majority in the Second Circuit decision *Kiobel v Royal Dutch Petroleum* (2010)[150] concluded that the scope of liability—including the question of corporate liability—must be determined by international law instead of domestic

[141] Alien Tort Statute, 28 USC §1350.

[142] Douglas M Branson, 'Holding Multinational Corporations Accountable? Achilles' Heels in Alien Tort Claims Act Litigation' (2011) 9 *Santa Clara Journal of International Law* 227, 230.

[143] *Filártiga v Peña-Irala* 630 F2d 876 (2d Cir 1980).

[144] ibid [2].

[145] *Sosa v Alvarez-Machain* 542 US 692 (2004) 331 F3d 604, reversed.

[146] ibid.

[147] *Kadic v Karadzic* 70 F3rd 232 (2nd Cir 1995), rehearing denied, 74 F3rd 377 (2nd Cir 1996), cert denied 518 US 1005 (1996).

[148] *Doe I v Unocal Corp* 963 F Supp 880 (CD Cal 1997), dismissed in part, 110 F Supp 2d 1294 (CD Cal 2000), aff'd in part, rev'd in part, 395 F3d 932 (9th Cir 2002), vacated, rehearing en banc granted, 395 F3d 978 (9th Cir 2003), dismissed, 403 F3d 708 (9th Cir 2005).

[149] *Sosa v Alvarez-Machain* (n 145), fn 20.

[150] *Kiobel v Royal Dutch Petroleum* 621 F3d 111 (2d Cir 2010), 569 US Docket No 10-1491 (2013).

law. After an analysis of decisions of international tribunals, treaties, and the opinions of international legal scholars, it decided that corporate liability is no 'specific, universal and obligatory' norm of international law, and therefore cannot 'form the basis of a suit under the ATS'—thus sounding the 'death knell'[151] for corporate liability under the ATS. The Supreme Court granted certiorari in 2011 but requested the parties to submit additional briefs on the extraterritorial application of the ATS. Without referring to the issue of corporate liability, the Supreme Court held in April 2013 that 'the presumption against extraterritoriality'—'which provides that when a statute gives no clear indication of an extraterritorial application, it has none'[152]—'applies to claims under the ATS',[153] thereby barring all claims which do not 'touch and concern the territory of the United States … with sufficient force to displace the presumption against extraterritorial application'.[154] This effectively ended the role of the ATS as a 'bonanza'[155] for human rights activists.

It should also be noted that even without legal enforcement mechanisms human rights abuses can be costly for MNCs. Tried in the court of public opinion, they can suffer considerable reputational and financial damage through strikes and boycotts as well as loss of investor and consumer confidence. NGO pressure as illustrated by the 'Green Scissors Campaign' can cost companies substantial sums in incentives and subsidies.[156] These external factors can then translate into internal pressure through shareholder resolutions.[157]

11.5.2 International Environmental Law

Multilateral Environmental Agreements (MEAs) are addressed primarily at states and have at most indirect regulatory implications for MNCs. In accordance with the fundamental 'polluter pays' principle,[158] a few specialised agreements establish civil liability rules for private actors which have the potential to cause particularly grave environmental damage, such as oil spills or nuclear leakages.[159] All of these instruments rely on

[151] Branson, 'Holding Multinational Corporations Accountable' (n 142) 234.
[152] *Morrison v National Australia Bank* 561 US Docket No 08-1191 (2010).
[153] *Kiobel v Royal Dutch Petroleum* (n 150) [III].
[154] ibid [IV].
[155] Branson, 'Holding Multinational Corporations Accountable' (n 142) 228.
[156] Walczak, 'Coming to the Table' (n 91) 644.
[157] ibid 651.
[158] Miriam Mafessanti, 'Responsibility for Environmental Damage under International Law: Can MNCs Bear the Burden? … and How?' (2009) 17 *Buffalo Environmental Law Journal* 87, 90.
[159] See the International Convention on Civil Liability for Oil Pollution Damage (adopted 29 November 1969, entered into force 19 June 1975) 973 UNTS 3; Vienna Convention on Civil Liability for Nuclear Damage (adopted 21 May 1963, entered into force 12 November 1977) 1063 UNTS 265.

domestic implementation, and require the contracting parties to establish the necessary enforcement mechanisms. Noteworthy also are the provisions on sustainable development in the non-binding OECD Guidelines and Agenda 21, last reaffirmed at the Rio+20 conference.[160] Compared to international human rights law, self-regulation by companies through codes of conduct or certification systems, eg, so called eco-labels, is more developed.[161] While the systems' institutional designs vary considerably, many provide for third- or second-party conformity assessments and a few contain dispute settlement or appeal mechanisms.[162]

11.5.3 International Criminal Law

International criminal law does not and has never provided for jurisdiction over legal persons. Already the first international criminal tribunal, the International Military Tribunal in Nuremberg, only exercised jurisdiction over individuals. It famously held: 'Crimes against International Law are committed by men, not by abstract entities, and only by punishing individuals who commit such crimes can the provisions of International Law be enforced.'[163] Neither of the ad hoc international criminal tribunals which were subsequently created by the UN Security Council exercised jurisdiction over corporate entities. The 1998 Draft Statute of the International Criminal Court, on the other hand, provided that 'the Court shall also have jurisdiction over legal persons, with the exception of states, when the crimes committed were committed on behalf of such legal persons or by their agencies or representatives'.[164] This approach was later abandoned, first because corporate criminal accountability is unknown to many domestic legal systems, which would have caused difficulties for the application of the complementarity principle,[165] and secondly because some feared that states might be considered hypocritical if they established criminal responsibility for every entity except for themselves.[166]

160 UNGA, 'The Future We Want' (27 July 2012) UN Doc A/RES/66/288.

161 Muchlinski, *Multinational Enterprises and the Law* (n 10) 546–56.

162 See for an analysis of 400 eco-labels: Axel Marx, 'Varieties of legitimacy: a configurational institutional design analysis of eco-labels' (2013) 26 *Innovation: The European Journal of Social Science Research* 268.

163 'Excerpts from the Judgment of the International Military Tribunal, Nürnberg, 30 September–1 October 1946' (1946–1947) 45 *International Law Studies Series*, US Naval War College 243, 259.

164 Draft Statute for the International Criminal Court (1998) UN Doc A/Conf.183/2/Add.1, art 23.

165 Bismuth, 'Mapping a responsibility of corporations for violations of international humanitarian law' (n 26) 209; Harmen van der Wilt, 'Corporate Criminal Responsibility for International Crimes: Exploring the Possibilities' (2013) 12 *Chinese Journal of International Law* 43, 45.

166 Albin Eser, 'Individual Criminal Responsibility' in Antonio Cassese, Antonio Cassese, Paola Gaeta and John RWD Jones (eds), *The Rome Statute of the International Criminal Court: A Commentary*, vol I (Oxford, Oxford University Press, 2002) 767, 779.

The extension of jurisdiction to corporate entities made it onto the agenda of the 2010 Kampala Review Conference, but received only limited attention due to the strong focus on the crime of aggression.[167] There are, however, several domestic jurisdictions which recognise the criminal liability of legal persons, among them Australia, Belgium, Canada France, India, Japan, the Netherlands, Norway, South Africa the United Kingdom, and the United States.[168]

It is also noteworthy that several international instruments contain criminal liability provisions for legal persons, such as the European Convention on the Protection of the Environment through Criminal Law, the United Nations Convention against Corruption, the United Nations Convention on the Suppression of the Financing of Terrorism and the United Nations Convention against Transnational Organized Crime. All of these conventions oblige the state parties to establish the liability of legal persons for the commission of crimes as defined under the respective instrument. Liability is, however, never reduced to criminal liability alone, but leaves the Member States leeway to adopt administrative or civil measures instead.

11.6 CONCLUSION

It has been argued in this chapter that, on the one hand, MNCs can contribute to economic and technological development, increasing the wealth and the living conditions of society. They therefore merit protection against undue government interference and for the safeguarding of a stable and reliable business environment. On the other hand, MNCs can severely impact human rights or the environment and even commit crimes for which they should be held accountable. Both objectives are insufficiently achieved at the domestic level. MNCs defy concepts of nationality and elude the grip of the—unwilling or incapable—national legislator. But the turn to international law has encountered difficulties as well. Lengthy debates about the international legal subjectivity of MNCs have precluded involvement with the substantive question of the rights and obligations of companies under international law. Subjectivity has been used as a threshold, awaiting the positive granting of rights

[167] van der Wilt, 'Corporate Criminal Responsibility for International Crimes' (n 165) 45.

[168] But not, eg, Argentina, Germany, Indonesia, Spain, Ukraine: see Anita Ramasastry and Robert C Thompson, 'Commerce, Crime and Conflict: Legal Remedies for Private Sector Liability for Grave Breaches of International Law: A Survey of Sixteen Countries' (2006) 536 *Fafo-report* 13; Jan Wouters and Leen De Smet, 'De strafrechtelijke verantwoordelijkheid van rechtspersonen voor ernstige schendingen van het internationaal humanitair recht in het licht van de Belgische Genocidewet' in Eva Brems and Pieter Vanden Heede (eds), *Bedrijven en mensenrechten. Verantwoordelijkheid en aansprakelijkheid* (Antwerp, Maklu, 2003) 309.

and obligations by states. This cannot, however, hide the fact that MNCs already enjoy considerable rights under international investment law and under international human rights law. They can ensure protection of their assets before domestic courts and through arbitration processes and can claim violations of their rights before the ECtHR. Conversely, MNCs do not have binding obligations under international law. Most importantly, they are not bound by international human rights law, notwithstanding a range of initiatives, attempting to create both voluntary and non-voluntary instruments. At most, they bear certain responsibilities not to harm human rights, but implementation and enforcement depend on the respective government authorities.

In light of the ever-growing power of MNCs, and considering ongoing reports about their involvement in human rights abuses and environmental harm, the calls for stronger obligations of MNCs under international law persist. Caution should be exercised, though, since a single-minded focus on MNCs risks distracting from the primary responsibility of states. Here, many instruments are readily available which might benefit from increased attention and achieve similar results. The 'Ruggie Framework' has set in motion a development which provides for heightened MNC responsibility without diluting the primary responsibility of states. Whether the new initiative towards a legally binding human rights instrument will manage to overcome the existing political divisions or share the fate of earlier attempts to move beyond a voluntary framework, remains to be seen.

12

Investors

AUGUST REINISCH

12.1 INTRODUCTION

WHILE THE PREVIOUS chapter focused on private economic actors as potential duty bearers under the business and human rights and corporate responsibility debate,[1] this chapter concentrates on the role of investors, both corporate and individual, as driving forces of the development of international investment law (IIL). IIL builds on the customary international law rules dealing with the treatment of foreigners and is today mainly based on international investment agreements (IIAs). By enabling investors to directly access dispute settlement, mainly in the form of arbitration, modern investment law reflects the emancipation from traditional diplomatic protection paradigms. This has led to rapid development in interpreting and refining mostly treaty-based standards of protection extended to foreign investors, ranging from guarantees against uncompensated expropriations to fair and equitable treatment, full protection and security and the non-discrimination standards of national treatment and most favoured nation (MFN) clauses. Usually, accounts of this development focus on the role of arbitration tribunals in shaping this law. This chapter will aim at unearthing the role of investors and seek to establish whether and how the loss of exclusive state control over dispute settlement—still prevailing in the WTO and other trade dispute settlement systems—has changed the law.

12.2 THE SPECIFIC NATURE OF INVESTMENT ARBITRATION

Stemming from diplomatic protection,[2] as the traditional inter-state paradigm of settling disputes of an economic nature, even if they concern the interests of private traders, investor-state dispute settlement (ISDS) has

[1] J Wouters and A-L Chané, 'Multinational Corporations in International Law', Ch 11 in this volume, 225.

[2] See ILC Draft Articles on Diplomatic Protection with commentaries 2006, available at http://untreaty.un.org/ilc/texts/instruments/english/commentaries/9_8_2006.pdf; see also Chittharanjan Felix Amerasinghe, *Diplomatic Protection* (Oxford, Oxford University

developed into a markedly different type of international dispute settlement. These differences are multi-faceted and affect almost all aspects of the traditional diplomatic protection matrix based on the Vattelian fiction that an injury to foreigners is in fact an injury done to the home state of such foreigners.[3]

12.2.1 Diplomatic Protection

From the viewpoint of this Vattelian premise, many features of diplomatic protection become more easily comprehensible. Individuals have no direct right against the foreign state causing harm to them, and they have no right to the protection of their home state. Rather, it is at the discretion of the home state whether or not to 'espouse' any claim.[4] The home state will decide how to exercise protection (whether through diplomatic pressure, economic or political sanctions—in bygone times even resorting to the use of force, as in the proverbial 'gunboat diplomacy' of European colonial powers in the late nineteenth century[5]—or adjudicatory dispute settlement). The state against which diplomatic protection is exercised

Press, 2008); Malcolm N Shaw, *International Law* 4th edn (Cambridge, Cambridge University Press, 1997) 808 et seq; Ian Brownlie, *Principles of Public International Law*, 7th edn (Oxford, Oxford University Press, 2008) 459 et seq; Annemarieke Vermeer-Künzli, 'A Matter of Interest: Diplomatic Protection and State Responsibility Erga Omnes' (2007) 56(3) *International and Comparative Law Quarterly* 553; Zachary Douglas, *The International Law of Investment Claims* (Cambridge, Cambridge University Press, 2009); Peter Muchlinski, 'The Diplomatic Protection of Foreign Investors: A Tale of Judicial Caution' in Christina Binder et al (eds), *International Investment Law for the 21st Century: Essays in Honour of Christoph Schreuer* (Oxford, Oxford University Press, 2009).

[3] Emmerich De Vattel, *The Law of Nations or the Principles of Natural Law Applied to the Conduct and to the Affairs of Nations and of Sovereigns*, trans CG Fenwick (Washington, DC, Carnegie Institution, 1916) 136 ('whoever ill-treats a citizen indirectly injures the State, which must protect that citizen'). See also *The Mavrommatis Palestine Concessions Case* (1924) PCIJ Ser A, No 2 12 ('by taking up the case of one of its subjects and by resorting to diplomatic action or international judicial proceedings on his behalf, a State is in reality asserting its own right, the right to ensure, in the person of its subjects, respect for the rules of international law').

[4] *Barcelona Traction, Light & Power Co Ltd (Belgium v Spain)*, Second Phase [1970] ICJ Rep 3, 44 ('The State must be viewed as the sole judge to decide whether its protection will be granted, to what extent it is granted, and when it will cease. It retains in this respect a discretionary power the exercise of which may be determined by considerations of a political or other nature, unrelated to the particular case.')

[5] Until it was outlawed by Art 1, Convention between the United States and Other Powers Respecting the Limitation of the Employment of Force for the Recovery of Contract Debts, signed 18 October 1907, entered into force 26 January 1910, 36 Statutes at Large 224 (Drago-Porter Convention) ('The Contracting Powers agree not to have recourse to armed force for the recovery of contract debts claimed from the Government of one country by the Government of another country as being due to its nationals. This undertaking is, however, not applicable when the Debtor State refuses or neglects to reply to an offer of arbitration, or, after accepting the offer, prevents any "compromis" from being agreed on, or, after the arbitration, fails to submit to the award.'). See also James Cable, *Gunboat Diplomacy: Political*

may insist on the exhaustion of local remedies,[6] before which any exercise of such protection might be considered an interference with the internal affairs of the foreign state. Ultimately, the home state finally receiving compensation for the harm done to its nationals is not obliged to hand such compensation over to the victims of the violation.[7] All these elements merely underpin the general assumption that it is the home state that has been wronged in the person of its nationals, and not the nationals themselves. Thus, it is also the home state alone which 'owns' the claim against the foreign injuring state and to decide and act upon it. This latter aspect has been crucial in rejecting any legally binding effect of so-called *Calvo* clauses,[8] by which investors purport to contractually waive diplomatic protection. If it is not the investors' right, but the right of their home state, such attempts would be ineffective.[9]

12.2.2 Investment Disputes Espoused by Home States

Based on such a diplomatic protection paradigm, many investment disputes have been brought to international arbitration or adjudication in the past. On the one hand, states espoused whole groups of similar cases (often concerning claims of expropriation) and brought them before specifically constituted bilateral claims commissions.[10] On the other hand, they approached international courts to litigate what today we would call

Applications of Limited Naval Force (London, Chatto & Windus for the Institute for Strategic Studies, 1971); Luis M Drago, 'State Loans in Their Relation to International Policy' (1907) 1(3) *The American Journal of International Law* 692; Kenneth J Vandevelde, *Bilateral Investment Treaties: History, Policy, and Interpretation* (Oxford, Oxford University Press, 2010).

[6] *Case Concerning Ahmadou Sadio Diallo* (*Republic of Guinea v Democratic Republic of the Congo*), Preliminary Objections, 24 May 2007 [47]; Finnish Ships Arbitration (*Finland v UK*) (1934) 3 RIAA 1479, 1502; Ambatielos Arbitration (*Greece v UK*) (1956) 12 RIAA 83; *Interhandel Case (Switzerland v United States of America)*, Judgment [1959] ICJ Rep 6, 27. See also Art 14(1) ILC Draft Articles on Diplomatic Protection (n 2) ('A State may not present an international claim in respect of an injury to a national … before the injured person has … exhausted all local remedies.').

[7] But see the merely 'recommended practice' contained in Art 19(c) ILC Draft Articles on Diplomatic Protection (n 2) ('A State entitled to exercise diplomatic protection according to the present draft articles, should: … Transfer to the injured person any compensation obtained for the injury from the responsible State subject to any reasonable deductions.').

[8] See Donald Richard Shea, *The Calvo Clause: A Problem of Inter-American and International Law and Diplomacy* (Minneapolis MN, University of Minnesota Press, 1955).

[9] See *North American Dredging Company* (*USA v Mexico)* UNRIAA, vol IV, p 26.

[10] See Abraham Howard Feller, *The Mexican Claims Commissions, 1923–1934: A Study in the Law and Procedure of International Tribunals* (New York, MacMillan, 1935); Bert L Hunt, *American-Turkish Claims Settlement under the Agreement of December 17, 1932* (Washington DC, Government Printing Office, 1934); Jackson Harvey Ralston, *Venezuelan Arbitrations of 1903* (Washington DC, US Government Printing Office, 1904); Jackson Harvey Ralston, *Report of French-Venezuelan Mixed Claims Commission of 1902* (Washington DC, US Government Printing Office, 1906).

investment disputes.[11] The *Chorzow Factory* case,[12] the *Oscar Chinn* case,[13] as well as the *Socobelge* case[14] before the Permanent Court of International Justice (PCIJ) all involved various claims akin to those brought in modern ISDS. Also the International Court of Justice (ICJ) has heard investment disputes in the *Anglo-Iranian Oil Co* case,[15] the *Barcelona Traction* case[16] and the *Diallo* case,[17] or even more pertinently in the *Elettronica Sicula* case.[18] The latter case was not based on customary international law claims, but dealt with alleged breaches of a Treaty of Friendship, Commerce and Navigation between Italy and the United States, which in many ways resembled treaty claims under modern IIAs.

12.2.3 The Evolution of Modern ISDS—From Contract to Treaty Arbitration

In parallel to the evolution of investment disputes being brought before international courts and tribunals through diplomatic protection, the twentieth century saw a development of direct arbitration between states and foreign investors on an ad hoc basis. These first steps leading to direct ISDS were taken by large foreign corporations which had enough bargaining power to insist on an alternative to the domestic courts of the host state. In particular, concession agreements in the field of natural resources exploitation often included not only choice-of-law clauses and the de-nationalising of specific contracts by various forms of internationalisation and stabilisation clauses,[19] but also inserted direct 'international'

[11] See Karel Wellens, *Economic Conflicts and Disputes before the World Court (1922–1995): A Functional Analysis, Studies and Materials on the Settlement of International Disputes* (The Hague, Kluwer Law International, 1996).

[12] *Case Concerning the Factory at Chorzów (Federal Republic of Germany v Poland)*, Judgment, 13 September 1928, 1928 PCIJ Ser A, No 17.

[13] *The Oscar Chinn Case (Belgium v United Kingdom)*, Judgment, 12 December 1934, 1934 PCIJ Ser A/B, No 63.

[14] *Société Commerciale de Belgique*, Judgment, 15 June 1939, 1939 PCIJ Ser A/B, No 78.

[15] *Anglo-Iranian Oil Co* Case (*UK v Iran*), Judgment (Preliminary Objections) [1952] ICJ Rep 93.

[16] *Case Concerning the Barcelona Traction, Light and Power Company, Ltd (Belgium v Spain)* (New Application 1962) [1970] ICJ Rep 3.

[17] *Case Concerning Ahmadou Sadio Diallo (Republic of Guinea v Democratic Republic of Congo)*, Judgment [2010] ICJ Rep 639.

[18] *Case Concerning Elettronica Sicula SpA (ELSI) (United States of America v Italy)* [1989] ICJ Rep 15.

[19] Thomas W Waelde and George Ndi, 'Stabilizing International Investment Commitments: International Law Versus Contract Interpretation' (1996) 31 *Texas International Law Journal* 215; Esa Paasivirta, 'The European Union: From an Aggregate of States to a Legal Person?' (1997) 2 *Hofstra Law & Policy Symposium* 37; AFM Maniruzzaman, 'The Pursuit of Stability in International Energy Investment Contracts: A Critical Appraisal of the Emerging Trends' (2008) 1(2) *Journal of World Energy Law & Business* 121; Joseph Nwaokoro, 'Enforcing Stabilization of International Energy Contracts' (2010) 3(1) *Journal of World Energy Law & Business* 103; Mustafa Erkan, *International Energy Investment Law: Stability through Contractual Clauses, vol 15* (Alphen aan den Rijn, Kluwer Law International, 2011).

arbitration between the concession holder and the concession-granting state as a method of dispute settlement.[20] Examples extend back to the *Lena Goldfields* arbitration[21] and the *RCA v China* case[22] in the 1930s. Most prominent are the ad hoc arbitrations following the Libyan oil concessions expropriation, such as *British Petroleum v Libya*,[23] *Liamco v Libya*[24] and *Texaco/Calasiatic v Libya*.[25] Other oil concession disputes in the Gulf region have also been settled by arbitration.[26]

This contract-based arbitration option is still used in some cases, with investors including in their contracts with host states arbitration clauses referring to the International Chamber of Commerce (ICC), the Arbitration Rules of the United Nations Commission on International Trade Law (UNCITRAL), the International Centre for Settlement of Investment Disputes (ICSID) or other forms of arbitration. Most of the early ICSID cases were in fact based on such contractual stipulations.[27] Today, however, treaty-based arbitration has taken the lead and represents the most frequently used form of ISDS.

The basic premise of treaty arbitration is that the consensual nature of arbitration is sufficiently flexible to encompass an agreement to arbitrate without a direct contractual link between the disputing parties. Rather, the consent to arbitration may be expressed in different instruments as long as they clearly relate to the same potential disputes. What has been aptly characterised as 'arbitration without privity'[28] has become the most

[20] See Stephen John Toope, *Mixed International Arbitration* (Cambridge, Grotius, 1990); Timothy Nelson, '"History Ain't Changed": Why Investor-State Arbitration Will Survive the New Revolution' in Michael Waibel et al (eds), *The Backlash against Investment Arbitration: Perceptions and Reality* (Alphen aan den Rijn, Kluwer Law International, 2010).

[21] *Lena Goldfields Ltd v USSR*, Award, 3 September 1930, reprinted in Arthur Nussbaum, 'The Arbitration between the Lena Goldfields Ltd and the Soviet Government' (1950) *Cornell Law Quarterly* 31.

[22] *Radio Corporation of America v The National Government of the Republic of China*, Award, 13 April 1935, available at www.pca-cpa.org/upload/files/RCA%20v.%20China.pdf.

[23] *British Petroleum v Libya*, 10 October 1973; (1979) 53 ILR 297–388.

[24] *Libyan American Oil Company (Liamco) v Libya*, 12 April 1977; (1981) 20 ILM 1–87.

[25] *Texaco Overseas Petroleum Company/California Asiatic (Calasiatic) Oil Company v Libya*, January 1977, (1978) 17 ILM 1–37.

[26] See, eg, *Elf Aquitaine Iran v National Iranian Oil Company*, Preliminary Award, 14 January 1982; (1994) 96 ILR 251; *National Oil Corporation v Libyan Sun Oil Company*, Award, 31 May 1985; ICC Case No 4462/A5, (1990) 29 ILM 565; *Wintershall AG v Qatar*, Award, 5 February 1988; (1989) 28 ILM 795. For further references see André von Walter, 'Arbitration on Oil Concession Disputes' in Rüdiger Wolfrum (ed), *Max Planck Encyclopedia of International Law* (Oxford, Oxford University Press, 2012).

[27] See, eg, *Holiday Inns SA and others v Morocco*, ICSID Case No ARB/72/1 (settled); *Adriano Gardella SpA v Côte d'Ivoire*, ICSID Case No ARB/74/1, Award, 29 August 1977; *Kaiser Bauxite Company v Jamaica*, ICSID Case No ARB/74/3, Decision on Jurisdiction and Competence, 6 July 1975, (1993) 1 ICSID Rep 296; *AGIP SpA v People's Republic of the Congo*, ICSID Case No ARB/77/1, Award, 30 November 1979, (1993) 1 ICSID Rep 306; *SARL Benvenuti & Bonfant v People's Republic of the Congo*, ICSID Case No ARB/77/2, Award, 8 August 1980, (1984) 67 ILR 345.

[28] Jan Paulsson, 'Arbitration without Privity' (1995) 10 (2) *ICSID Review* 232; see also Stanimir A Alexandrov, 'The "Baby Boom" of Treaty-Based Arbitrations and the Jurisdiction of ICSID Tribunals: Shareholders as "Investors" and Jurisdiction *Ratione Temporis*' (2005) 4(1)

widely used basis for investment arbitration in the last three decades: it is based on the concept that an investor may accept the offer of arbitration by a host state expressed in either the latter's domestic legislation, such as specific investment laws, or in bilateral or multilateral treaties with the home state of the investor. While the host state expresses its consent to arbitration in these instruments, the investor usually expresses its consent by instituting arbitral proceedings. In practice, most investment claims are brought on the basis of investment treaties, hence the term 'treaty arbitration'. This practice started with ICSID cases in the 1990s.[29] Today, most investment disputes are based on host state consent to arbitration expressed in bilateral investment treaties or other IIAs.

12.2.4 Modern ISDS

Modern investment arbitration has radically changed the original dependence of investors on their home states' willingness to espouse their claims. Opening up to direct ISDS in IIAs (as may have partly been the case earlier, in investment contracts between investors and states) meant that investors themselves have taken control of the arbitration process. Most importantly, it is they who decide whether arbitral proceedings are instituted,[30] and what kinds of arguments are brought forward.[31] Indeed, liberating investment disputes from the need to be 'espoused' by investors' home states has been characterised as the crucial virtue of 'depoliticising' them.[32] Indeed, the political overtones of exercises of diplomatic protection, often coupled with power asymmetries between the states involved, frequently meant that an additional harassment factor was part of the game—the

The Law and Practice of International Courts and Tribunals 387; Thomas W Wälde, 'Energy Charter Treaty-Based Investment Arbitration: Controversial Issues' (2004) 5 *Journal of World Investment & Trade* 373.

[29] *AAPL v Sri Lanka*, ICSID Case No ARB/87/3, Award of 27 June 1990, 4 ICSID Reports 246; *Fedax v Venezuela*, ICSID Case No ARB/96/3, ICSID Decision on Jurisdiction of 11 July 1997, (1998) 37 ILM 1378.

[30] Suggestions during the drafting of the ICSID Convention that investors would have to have their home states' authorisation before instituting ICSID proceedings have been rejected: International Centre for the Settlement of Investment Disputes, *Documents Concerning the Origin and Formulation of the Convention History*, vol II Part 2, 982 (Washington DC, 1968).

[31] *Corn Products International, Inc v The United Mexican States*, Decision on Responsibility, ICSID Case No ARB(AF)/04/01 (Additional Facility), 15 January 2008 [173] ('The State of nationality of the Claimant does not control the conduct of the case … The individual may even advance a claim of which the State disapproves or base its case upon a proposition of law with which the State disagrees.').

[32] IFI Shihata, 'Towards a Greater Depoliticization of Investment Disputes: The Roles of ICSID and MIGA' (1986) 1 *ICSID Review* 1.

US intervention in Chile after the sweeping expropriations of the Allende regime[33] or the British/US involvement in toppling Iran's Mossadegh government after the Anglo-Iranian Oil Company was nationalised[34] are only extreme examples of the modern version of gunboat diplomacy.

The shift towards a new form of 'ownership' of investment arbitration by private actors is also clearly evident in the fact that any eventual damages or compensation clearly go to the prevailing investors, and no longer to their home states. Further, the costs of the arbitration are borne by the investors, and not by the home state. One of the few issues where investment arbitration remains ambivalent is the question of the exhaustion of local remedies. While it would appear logical to dispense with this diplomatic protection-inspired requirement[35] and while the ICSID Convention did so,[36] it appears that a number of arbitral tribunals and authors consider this an inherent part of (customary) international law that cannot be simply done away with.[37]

12.3 THE IMPACT OF ISDS ON THE POSITION OF THE INVESTOR IN INTERNATIONAL LAW

The development of ISDS as a system of dispute settlement permitting investors to directly access international arbitration has freed them from the often politically motivated discretion of states whether or not to exercise diplomatic protection.

[33] See Lincoln Gordon and Samuel A Stern, 'The Judicial and Administrative Procedures Involved in the Chilean Copper Expropriations' (1972) 66(4) *The American Journal of International Law* 205; Andreas F Lowenfeld, *International Economic Law* (Oxford, Oxford University Press, 2008) 483.

[34] See Lowenfeld, ibid, 484; W Bishop Jr, 'The Anglo-Iranian Oil Company Case' (1951) 45(4) *The American Journal of International Law* 749; Charles G Fenwick, 'The Order of the International Court of Justice in the Anglo-Iranian Oil Company Case' (1951) 45(4) *The American Journal of International Law* 723.

[35] See Rudolf Dolzer and Christoph Schreuer, *Principles of International Investment Law* (Oxford, Oxford University Press, 2008) 264; Christoph Schreuer, 'Calvo's Grandchildren: The Return of Local Remedies in Investment Arbitration' (2005) 4(1) *The Law and Practice of International Courts and Tribunals* 1; Francesco Francioni, 'Access to Justice, Denial of Justice and International Investment Law' (2009) 20(3) *European Journal of International Law* 729.

[36] Art 26, second sentence Convention on the Settlement of Investment Disputes between States and Nationals of Other States, 18 March 1965, 575 UNTS 159 ('A Contracting State may require the exhaustion of local administrative or judicial remedies as a condition of its consent to arbitration under this Convention.').

[37] See Muchlinski, 'The Diplomatic Protection of Foreign Investors: A Tale of Judicial Caution' (n 2) 344–46. In the context of treaty arbitration, a number of tribunals required the parties to the dispute to resort to local remedies before initiating arbitral proceedings. However, this requirement was not a matter of jurisdiction or admissibility but rather a substantive component of the obligations in question on 'denial of justice'. See Schreuer, 'Calvo's Grandchildren: The Return of Local Remedies in Investment Arbitration' (n 35) 13 et seq; Christoph Liebscher, 'Monitoring Domestic Courts in BIT Arbitrations' in Christina Binder et al (n 2) 117–22.

But this change has also been regarded as having had a more fundamental impact on the legal position of investors. Many scholars see a form of 'emancipation' of the private party from its home state.[38] The fact that investors are now entitled to institute legal proceedings against states is considered by many to have endowed them with at least some degree of international legal personality. The concept of 'partial' international legal personality is sometimes invoked, suggesting that at least with a view to claiming certain substantive investment standards and to accessing ISDS, investors have gained international 'standing'.[39]

An analogy is drawn with the development of human rights where individuals and partly also corporations[40] are allowed to bring direct claims against states before international bodies. In that respect both types of non-state actors are clearly in comparative situations. In human rights discourse, the ability to invoke human rights infringements directly before international bodies is usually seen as evidence of the individual's (at least partial) emancipation from the state.

In spite of the important right to bring investment claims directly before international arbitration tribunals, the view that this circumstance would confer at least partial international legal subjectivity on investors has not gone unchallenged.

It is linked to a heated debate on the true nature of ISDS, often captured by the label 'hybrid nature' of investment arbitration.[41] This stems from the fact that ISDS combines contractual and treaty elements. Linked to this

[38] See also Gerhard Hafner, 'The Emancipation of the Individual from the State under International Law' (2011) 358 *Recueil des cours* 263.

[39] See Tillmann Rudolf Braun, 'Globalization-driven Innovation: The Investor as a Partial Subject in Public International Law—An Inquiry into the Nature and Limits of Investor Rights' (2013) *New York University School of Law—Jean Monnet Working Paper Series* 04/13, 22 et seq; Zachary Douglas, 'The Hybrid Foundations of Investment Treaty Arbitration' (2004) 74(1) *British Yearbook of International Law* 151.

[40] The practice is inconsistent; the European Convention on Human Rights (ECHR; signed 4 November 1950, entered into force 3 September 1953, 213 UNTS 221) remains the only international human rights treaty that has explicitly recognised corporate rights and that permits complaints by corporate entities pursuant to Art 34 ECHR, albeit not with regard to all human rights. See eg, the case of *OAO Neftyanaya Kompaniya Yukos v Russia*, App no 14902/04 (ECtHR, 20 September 2011). By contrast, the International Covenant on Civil and Political Rights, GA Res 2200A (XXI), 21 UN GAOR Supp (No 16) 52, UN Doc A/6316 (1966), 999 UNTS 171, neither specifically refers to legal persons or legal entities in general, nor allows corporations to invoke its system for hearing petitions. See eg UN Human Rights Committee, *A Newspaper Publishing Company v Trinidad and Tobago*, Communication No 360/1989, UN Doc Supp No 40 (44/A/40) (1989), para 3.10. Art 61 of the American Convention on Human Rights, signed 21 November 1969, entered into force 18 July 1978, OAS Treaty Series No 36, 1144 UNTS 123, states that only States and the Inter-American Commission on Human Rights shall have the right to submit a case to the Inter-American Court of Human Rights. See also Julian G Ku, 'The Limits of Corporate Rights under International Law' (2011) 12 *Chicago Journal of International Law* 729; Marius Emberland, *The Human Rights of Companies: Exploring the Structure of ECHR Protection* (Oxford, Oxford University Press, 2006).

[41] Douglas, 'The Hybrid Foundations of Investment Treaty Arbitration' (n 39).

issue is the question of whether investor rights are genuine, direct rights of investors, or derived rights of their home states which investors are permitted to enforce on behalf of their home states.[42]

With regard to the status of investors the fact that investment claims are provided for by states in IIAs, both from a substantive and a procedural perspective, has led to challenges of investors' perceived international status. One can indeed argue that the rights of investors are provided by states, as is the procedural option of enforcing them through ISDS. While such conferment might be seen as a true transfer of substantive and procedural rights,[43] it could also be regarded as a mere technical device allowing investors to invoke and enforce rights of their home states.[44] Where investors are viewed not as subjects vindicating their own rights, but rather as entities having been granted exceptional standing before investment tribunals in order to enforce the inter-state claims of their home states, many traditional inter-state, diplomatic protection paradigms can be maintained. From such a perspective, it is thus understandable to conceive of investors not as partial subjects of international law, but rather as non-state actors without any such status.

It is apparent, however, that most investment tribunals reject the diplomatic protection paradigm.[45] Rather, they have insisted that 'the rules

[42] See Braun, 'Globalization-Driven Innovation: The Investor as a Partial Subject in Public International Law' (n 39) 22 et seq; James Crawford, 'The ILC's Articles on Responsibility of States for Internationally Wrongful Acts: A Retrospect' (2002) 96 *The American Journal of International Law* 874, 888 ('a standard bilateral or regional investment treaty is an interstate agreement, to which individual investors are not privy. It is a matter of interpretation whether the primary obligations (eg, of fair and equitable treatment) created by such treaties are owed to the qualified investors directly, or only to the other contracting state(s). … an interstate treaty may create individual rights, whether or not they are classified as "human rights". … on the other hand, one might argue that bilateral investment treaties in some sense institutionalise and reinforce (rather than replace) the system of diplomatic protection, and that in accordance with the *Mavrommatis* formula, the rights concerned are those of the state, not the investor.')

[43] See eg, *Occidental Exploration and Production Co v Republic of Ecuador*, English Court of Appeal (2005), 12 ICSID Rep 129, 137–38/20, 147–48/37 ('[T]he fundamental assumption underlying the investment treaty regime is clearly that the investor is bringing a cause of action based upon the vindication of its own rights rather than those of its national state.… The case is not concerned with an attempt to invoke at a national legal level a Treaty, which operates only at the international level. It concerns a Treaty intended by its signatories to give rise to rights in favour of private investors capable of enforcement, to an extent specified by the Treaty wording, in consensual arbitration against one or other of its signatory States.… both artificial and wrong in principle to suggest that the investor is in reality pursuing a claim vested in his or its home State.').

[44] See eg, *The Loewen Group Inc v United States*, ICSID Case No ARB(AF)/98/3, Award, 26 June 2003 [233] ('There is no warrant for transferring rules derived from private law into a field of international law where claimants are permitted for convenience to enforce what are in origin the rights of Party states.').

[45] *El Paso v Argentine Republic*, ICSID Case No ARB/03/05, Award, 31 October 2011 [213] ('BITs do not concern situations such as that addressed in *Barcelona Traction:* they do not pertain to diplomatic protection, nor do they reflect the rules of general international law in matters of investment protection.').

of customary international law applicable in the context of diplomatic protection do not apply as such to investor-State arbitrations.'[46]

Ultimately, the question whether investors are partial subjects of international law or not retains an artificial flavour. What is undeniable is the fact that they have gained the very important option of enforcing their rights through ISDS. This has allowed them to act largely independently of their home states, and it has led to an enormous increase in investment cases through which investors have effectively guarded their rights under IIAs and, to a lesser extent, also under customary international law, the law of host states and contractual stipulations.

In addition, investors may have had a considerable impact on the process of solidifying and making more precise international investment law and, partially, even general international law.

12.4 THE CONTRIBUTION OF INVESTORS TO THE DEVELOPMENT OF GENERAL INTERNATIONAL LAW AND OF INTERNATIONAL INVESTMENT LAW IN PARTICULAR

Probably one of the most interesting aspects of the rise of investors as non-state actors in international law is the fact that they are not only permitted to directly vindicate rights, but that they also contribute to the larger process of shaping international (investment) law.

This phenomenon is linked to another 'hybrid' aspect of investment arbitration. ISDS serves not only the enforcement of investor rights, but also as a system of quasi-judicial review of state legislation and regulation. Measures of general application are regularly subjected to international scrutiny by investment tribunals. The yardstick of assessing their legality under expropriation or fair and equitable treatment claims is often comparable to that under domestic constitutional review cases. It is thus no wonder that some features of investment arbitration have been claimed as elements of the 'constitutionalisation' of international law.[47] This has triggered a lively debate about the legitimacy of the whole system of investment arbitration, which is felt to exert too much power over

[46] *Saba Fakes v Turkey*, ICSID Case No ARB/07/20, Award, 14 July 2010 [68] et seq; see also *Siag v Egypt*, ICSID Case No ARB/05/15, Decision on Jurisdiction, 11 April 2007 [198]; *Champion Trading v Egypt*, ICSID Case No ARB/02/9, Decision on Jurisdiction, 21 October 2003, p 16.

[47] See Armin von Bogdandy, 'Constitutionalism in International Law: Comment on a Proposal from Germany' (2006) 47 *Harvard International Law Journal* 223; Mattias Kumm, 'The Legitimacy of International Law: A Constitutionalist Framework of Analysis' (2004) 15 (5) *European Journal of International Law* 931; Armin von Bogdandy, Philipp Dann and Matthias Goldmann, *The Exercise of Public Authority by International Institutions* (Berlin/Heidelberg, Springer, 2010); Jan Klabbers, Anne Peters, and Geir Ulfstein, *The Constitutionalization of International Law* (Oxford, Oxford University Press, 2009).

sovereign decision-making by some.[48] Other commentators have stressed the functional equivalent of investment arbitration to administrative review. Thus, IIL has been claimed by global administrative law as well.[49]

In the present context, however, it is important to note that investors fulfil a dual role in ISDS: they enforce their own rights and they also serve as 'private attorneys general'[50] subjecting regulatory measures of host states to judicial review. Coupled with increased transparency this will often lead to states changing their law if held in violation of investment standards in order to avoid follow-up law suits. Thus, investors also contribute to the decentralised enforcement of the law.

Of course, this role of investors should not be overstated, and it must be recognised that investors are only part of a triad of actors shaping international investment law. Primarily, this is done by states entering into and thus determining the substance of IIAs. Because IIAs are often very vague and indeterminate, the adjudicators, investment arbitration tribunals have a considerable role, not only in applying IIA standards in specific cases, but also interpreting and shaping the often vague standards into more precise ones. It is in this adjudicatory process that investors contribute to the formation of international investment law by making relevant submissions and shaping the arguments ultimately taken up or dismissed by tribunals.

While treaty-makers may emphasise certain standards of investment protection in the IIAs they negotiate and conclude, the 'users' of IIAs, ie, primarily the claimants under the ISDS system, that is, investors, will determine which standards are actually interpreted and thus specified through their application of IIAs by arbitration tribunals.

48 Gus Van Harten, *Investment Arbitration and Public Law* (Oxford, Oxford University Press, 2007); Olivia Chung, 'The Lopsided International Investment Law Regime and Its Effect on the Future of Investor-State Arbitration' (2007) 47 *Virginia Journal of International Law* 953; see also Susan D Franck, 'The Legitimacy Crisis in Investment Treaty Arbitration: Privatizing Public International Law Through Inconsistent Decisions' (2005) 73(4) *Fordham Law Review* 1521; Charles N Brower and Stephan W Schill, 'Is Arbitration a Threat or a Boon to the Legitimacy of International Investment Law', (2009) 9 *Chinese Journal of International Law* 471.

49 See Benedict Kingsbury, Nico Krisch and Richard B Stewart, 'The Emergence of Global Administrative Law' (2005) 62 *Law and contemporary problems* 15; Nico Krisch and Benedict Kingsbury, 'Introduction: Global Governance and Global Administrative Law in the International Legal Order' (2006) 17(1) *European Journal of International Law*; Gus Van Harten and Martin Loughlin, 'Investment Treaty Arbitration as a Species of Global Administrative Law' (2006) 17 *European Journal of International Law* 121.

50 See also José E Alvarez, 'Contemporary Foreign Investment Law: An Empire of Law or the Law of Empire' (2008) 60 *Alabama Law Review* 943; Anne Van Aaken, 'Effectuating Public International Law through Market Mechanisms?' (2009) 165 (1) *Journal of Institutional and Theoretical Economics* 33. An instructive parallel can also be drawn to the 'private attorney general role' of individual litigants before the ECJ, which has been acknowledged by the Court in the *Van Gend* case, *NV Algemene Transport- en Expeditie Onderneming Van Gend & Loos v Nederlandse administratie der belastingen* (Netherlands Inland Revenue Administration), Case 26/62, [1963] ECR 13 ('The vigilance of individuals concerned to protect their rights amounts to an effective supervision in addition to the supervision entrusted by Articles 169 and 170 to the diligence of the Commission and of the Member States.').

If one is willing to regard law-making as a broad notion encompassing both the quasi-legislative task of formulating treaties and the specification of rules by adjudicatory bodies entrusted to interpret and apply such treaties, it is clear that investment law-making does not stop with the conclusion of IIAs. Rather, treaty standards very often become meaningful and applicable only as a result of the interpretation given to them in a line of more or less consistent jurisprudence. This 'concretising' or 'specifying' role given to investment tribunals is particularly evident as a result of the highly indeterminate form of the applicable standards of treatment contained in IIAs.

12.4.1 Investors as Driving Forces of the Shaping of Investment Law

While the role of arbitration tribunals in shaping the content of investment law has often been described,[51] this chapter highlights the crucially important part of investors as drivers of that law-forming role. Since in treaty arbitration it is mostly investors who institute investment arbitration they can thus determine which standards are invoked and how they are used to serve their legal claims. Thus, investors have adopted a 'jurisgenerative' role in investment law.[52]

In addition, the arbitration nature of dispute settlement under IIAs adds to the influence investors have on the process. Arbitration is much more party-driven than adjudication. The adversarial principle of arbitration implies that the arguments are much more shaped by the claims of

[51] Essentially, this role results from the authority of 'precedents'. In *Saipem v Bangladesh*, the tribunal noted that 'it is not bound by previous decisions'. However, it also conceded that it must pay 'due consideration to earlier decisions of international tribunals' and that it has a duty to 'seek to contribute to the harmonious development of investment law and thereby to meet the legitimate expectations of the community of States and investors towards certainty of the rule of law.' *Saipem SpA v The People's Republic of Bangladesh*, ICSID Case No ARB/05/07, Decision on Jurisdiction, 21 March 2007 [67]. An almost identical statement was made by *Bayindir v Pakistan*, ICSID Case No ARB/03/29, Award, 27 August 2009 [145]. On the precedential effect of ICSID decisions, see Gabrielle Kaufmann-Kohler, 'Arbitral Precedent: Dream, Necessity or Excuse?, The 2006 Freshfields Lecture' (2007) 23 *Arbitration International* 357; Generally on the actors shaping international investment law, see Anthea Roberts, 'Clash of Paradigms: Actors and Analogies Shaping the Investment Treaty System' (2013) 107(1) *The American Journal of International Law* 45.

[52] See the critical remarks by Jose E Alvarez, 'Are Corporations Subjects of International Law?' (2011) 9 *Santa Clara Journal of International Law* 1, 11: ('Under investor-state arbitration, therefore, states are mostly passive participants in a game controlled by corporate plaintiffs in which the latter play the jurisgenerative role that in the WTO and throughout much of international law is formally reserved to states. As students of the burgeoning investor-state arbitral case law attest, states have in effect delegated the making of international investment law to third party private attorney's generals, namely the wealthy multinationals that can afford to bring the cases and generate the case law.').

the disputing parties than in a continental law based adjudicatory system operating on the basis of the assumption that the court knows the law (*iura novit curia*).

This implies that arbitration largely relies on the elaborate submissions of the parties to a dispute. Voluminous submissions are more often the rule than the exception and the thoroughness with which often minute details are argued and contested in ISDS is remarkable.

In this exercise, the role of both parties and in particular their counsel is important. It is their submissions that normally shape the line of argumentation analysed by investment tribunals. While it may be difficult to empirically assess the precise impact of party pleadings on a tribunal's decisions, it appears that in general such influence should not be underestimated.

As parties to the ISDS process investors are in full control of the legal arguments which gives them a clear advantage over the merely indirect influence of traders whose interests are defended in World Trade Organization (WTO) dispute settlement by their home states or *amici curiae* who might be permitted at the panels'/tribunals' discretion to file their own briefs on matters relevant in a particular dispute.

Actually, many developments of investment law can be traced back to investors as 'norm entrepreneurs'.[53] Investors usually propose a certain interpretation of IIA provisions which, if convincing, may be adopted by arbitration tribunals. Examples reach from the famous *Maffezini* doctrine,[54]

[53] See Cass R Sunstein, 'Social Norms and Social Roles' (1996) 96 *Columbia Law Review* 903.

[54] See Stephen Fietta, 'Most Favoured Nation Treatment and Dispute Resolution under Bilateral Investment Treaties: A Turning Point?' (2005) 8(4) *International Arbitration Law Review* 131; Jürgen Kurtz, 'The Delicate Extension of Most-Favoured-Nation Treatment to Foreign Investors: Maffezini v Kingdom of Spain' in Todd Weiler (ed), *International Investment Law and Arbitration: Leading Cases from the ICSID, NAFTA, Bilateral Treaties and Customary International Law* (London, Cameron May, 2005); Brigitte Stern, 'ICSID Arbitration and the State's increasingly Remote Consent: apropos the Maffezini Case' in Steve Charnovitz, Debra P Steger and Peter van den Bossche (eds), *Law in the Service of Human Dignity: Essays in Honour of Florentino Feliciano* (Cambridge, Cambridge University Press, 2005); Ruth Teitelbaum, 'Who's Afraid of Maffezini? Recent Developments in the Interpretation of Most Favored Nation Clauses' (2005) 22 *Journal of International Arbitration* 225; Mara Valentini, 'The Most Favoured Nations Clause as a Basis for Jurisdiction in Foreign Investor-Host State Arbitration' (2008) 24 *Arbitration International* 447; Zachary Douglas, 'The MFN Clause in Investment Arbitration: Treaty Interpretation Off the Rails' (2011) 2(1) *Journal of International Dispute Settlement* 97; Stephan Schill, 'Allocating Adjudicatory Authority: Most-Favoured-Nation Clauses as a Basis of Jurisdiction—A Reply to Zachary Douglas' (2011) 2(2) *Journal of International Dispute Settlement* 353; Julie Maupin, 'MFN-Based Jurisdiction in Investor-State Arbitration: Is There any Hope for a Consistent Approach?' (2011) 14(1) *Journal of International Economic Law* 157; Martins Paparinskis, 'MFN Clauses and International Dispute Settlement: Moving Beyond Maffezini and Plama' (2011) 26 *ICSID Review* 14; August Reinisch, 'Maffezini v. Spain Case' in *Max Planck Encyclopedia of Public International Law* (2012); Francisco Orrego Vicuña, 'Reports of [Maffezini's] Demise Have Been Greatly Exaggerated' (2012) 3 *Journal of International Dispute Settlement* 299.

to disregarding waiting periods in IIAs,[55] and broadly interpreting the notion of indirect expropriation.[56]

In *Maffezini v Spain*[57] the Argentine investor managed to persuade an ICSID tribunal that he could rely on the Argentina-Spain BIT's MFN clause in order to access ISDS without awaiting the expiration of that treaty's waiting period by relying on another Spanish BIT (that did not provide for such a waiting period).[58] After an elaborate reasoning on the functioning and effect of MFN clauses, the tribunal adopted the claimant's position.[59] Since then many tribunals have followed this approach,[60] one

[55] See Christoph Schreuer, 'Travelling the BIT Route' (2004) 5 *The Journal of World Investment*; August Reinisch, 'From Rediscovered Waiting Periods to Ever More Activist Annulment Committees—ICSID Arbitration in 2010' (2012) 11 *Global Community Yearbook of International Law and Jurisprudence* 933.

[56] Thomas Waelde and Abba Kolo, 'Environmental Regulation, Investment Protection and "Regulatory Taking" in International Law' (2001) 50(4) *International and Comparative Law Quarterly* 811; Rudolf Dolzer, 'Indirect Expropriations: New Developments' (2002) 11 *New York University Environmental Law Journal* 64; W Michael Reisman and Robert D Sloane, 'Indirect Expropriation and Its Valuation in the BIT Generation' (2003) 74 *British Yearbook of International Law* 115; Jan Paulsson and Zachary Douglas, 'Indirect Expropriation in Investment Treaty Arbitrations' in Norbert Horn (ed), *Arbitrating Foreign Investment Disputes* (The Hague, Kluwer International, 2004); L Yves Fortier and Stephen L Drymer, 'Indirect Expropriation in the Law of International Investment: I Know It When I See It, or Caveat Investor' (2004) 19(2) *ICSID Review* 293; Catherine Yannaca-Small, '"Indirect Expropriation" and the "Right to Regulate" in International Investment Law' in OECD (ed), *International Investment Law. A Changing Landscape* (Washington DC, OECD, 2004); Veijo Heiskanen, 'The Doctrine of Indirect Expropriation in Light of the Practice of the Iran-United States Claims Tribunal' (2007) 8 *The Journal of World Investment and Trade* 215; August Reinisch, 'Expropriation' in Peter Muchlinski, Federico Ortino, and Christoph Schreuer (eds), *The Oxford Handbook of International Investment Law* (Oxford, Oxford University Press, 2008); Anne Hoffmann, 'Indirect Expropriation' in August Reinisch (ed), *Standards of Investment Protection* (Oxford, Oxford University Press, 2008); Caroline Henckels, 'Indirect Expropriation and the Right to Regulate: Revisiting Proportionality Analysis and the Standard of Review in Investor-State Arbitration' (2012) 15(1) *Journal of International Economic Law* 223; Sebastian López Escarcena, *Indirect Expropriation In International Law* (Cheltenham, Edward Elgar Publishing, 2014).

[57] *Emilio Agustín Maffezini v Kingdom of Spain*, ICSID Case No ARB/97/7, ICSID Decision on Jurisdiction of 25 January 2000.

[58] ibid, [40] ('Claimant contends, consequently, that Chilean investors in Spain are treated more favorably than Argentine investors in Spain. He argues, accordingly, that the most favored nation clause in the Argentine-Spain BIT gives him the option to submit the dispute to arbitration without prior referral to domestic courts. Claimant submits, in this connection, that although the Argentine-Spain BIT provides for exceptions to the most favored nation treatment, none of these apply to the dispute settlement provisions at issue in the instant case.').

[59] ibid, [64] ('In light of the above considerations, the Tribunal is satisfied that the Claimant has convincingly demonstrated that the most favored nation clause included in the Argentine-Spain BIT embraces the dispute settlement provisions of this treaty.').

[60] *Siemens AG v The Argentine Republic*, Decision on Jurisdiction of 3 August 2004, ICSID Case No ARB/02/8; *Gas Natural SDG, SA v The Argentine Republic*, ICSID Case No ARB/03/10, Decision of the Tribunal on Preliminary Questions on Jurisdiction, 17 June 2005; *Suez, Sociedad General de Aguas de Barcelona SA and Interagua Servicios Integrales de Agua SA v Argentine Republic*, ICSID Case No ARB/03/17, Decision on Jurisdiction of 16 May 2006. The approach furnished in *Maffezini*, however, was not followed by the tribunals in *Salini Costruttori SpA and Italstrade SpA v Hashemite Kingdom of Jordan*, ICSID Case No ARB/02/13, Decision on

even permitting an investor to rely on an MFN clause in order to invoke an investment tribunal's jurisdiction only provided for in another BIT,[61] though some tribunals had misgivings about the implicit broad reach of MFN treatment, and attempted to confine it to so-called substantive treatment.[62]

Also with regard to waiting periods, routinely included in many dispute settlement clauses of BITs and other IIAs, and normally requiring investors to engage in consultations before instituting investment arbitration, investors have managed to convince tribunals that non-compliance with such requirements would not deprive them of their jurisdiction, regarding such 'consultation periods as directory and procedural rather than as mandatory and jurisdictional in nature.'[63] This often meant that claims could go forward or were simply suspended for a certain time to allow the parties to reach an amicable settlement.[64]

Examples from the area of substantive investment protection abound where investors have been crucial in shaping the law. Their arguments have advanced the meaning of 'fair and equitable treatment', indirect expropriation, the umbrella clause, etc. It is impossible to address this influence in detail; however, one minor aspect should be addressed, because it serves as an example of tribunals being exposed to highly antagonistic views of opposing 'norm entrepreneurs' and having to adjust an early consensus largely shaped by investor-driven arguments, that is the law of indirect expropriation.

Based on customary international law and, in particular, the rich case law of the Iran-US Claims Tribunal, investors were initially successful in

Jurisdiction, 9 November 2004, and *Plama Consortium Limited v Republic of Bulgaria*, ICSID Case No ARB/03/24, Decision on Jurisdiction, 8 February 2005. Most recently, a tribunal refused to let the investor use MFN in order to avoid a 'legality clause', in *Metal-Tech Ltd v Republic of Uzbekistan*, ICSID Case No ARB/10/3 Award of 4 October 2013. See also below, text at n 68.

61 *RosInvest Co UK Ltd v The Russian Federation*, Award on Jurisdiction 2007, SCC Case No Arb V079/2005.

62 See below, text at n 69.

63 *SGS Société Générale de Surveillance SA v Islamic Republic of Pakistan*, ICSID Case No ARB/01/13, Decision on Jurisdiction, 6 August 2003 [184]. See also *Ronald S Lauder v The Czech Republic*, UNCITRAL, Final Award, 3 September 2001 [190] ('To insist that the arbitration proceedings cannot be commenced until 6 months after the 19 August 1999 Notice of Arbitration would, in the circumstances of this case, amount to an unnecessary, overly formalistic approach which would not serve to protect any legitimate interests of the Parties'); *Bayindir Insaat Turizm Ticaret Ve Sanayi AS v Pakistan*, ICSID Case No ARB/03/29, Decision on Jurisdiction, 14 November 2005 [100] ('The Tribunal agrees with the view that the notice requirement does not constitute a prerequisite to jurisdiction. Contrary to Pakistan's position, the non-fulfilment of this requirement is not "fatal to the case of the claimant" … As Bayindir pointed out, to require a formal notice would simply mean that Bayindir would have to file a new request for arbitration and restart the whole proceeding, which would be to no-one's advantage.').

64 See, eg, *Western NIS Enterprise Fund v Ukraine*, ICSID Case No ARB/04/2, Order, 16 March 2006.

arguing that investment tribunals should adopt a broad notion of indirect expropriation according to the so-called sole effect doctrine.[65] According to this approach, tribunals would only look at the intensity of the interference in order to ascertain whether an indirect expropriation has taken place; if so, compensation would be due, even though the measure in question satisfied the legality criteria of expropriation clauses.[66]

The importance of the investors' contribution to such adjudicatory law-making by investment tribunals is probably best reflected in the intense efforts of respondent states to counter such 'investor-friendly' interpretations.

12.4.2 States Reshaping Investment Law

Indeed, states have been seen to 'strike back'. They have used their procedural position as respondents in investment arbitration in order to convince tribunals of their, often more narrow, reading of procedural and substantive investment law rules. In addition, states have relied on their specific sovereign status in order to reshape IIL.[67]

With regard to using their position as litigants, states have been successful in correcting some of the above-described investor-driven interpretations (and, of course, others). Concerning the wide scope of application of MFN clauses, heralded by the *Maffezini* decision, since the *Plama* case states have been successful in casting doubt on such a broad interpretation.[68] In a number of cases, tribunals have resorted to a more limited interpretation of MFN clauses, allowing only the 'importation' of substantive treatment, not of jurisdictional or even merely procedural advantages.[69]

[65] See George C Christie, 'What Constitutes a Taking of Property under International Law' (1962) 38 *British Yearbook of International Law* 307; Rudolf Dolzer, 'Indirect Expropriation of Alien Property' (1986) 1(1) *ICSID Review* 41; Rudolf Dolzer, 'Indirect Expropriations: New Developments?' (2002) 11 *NYU Environmental Law Journal* 64; Yves Fortier and Stephen Drymer, 'Indirect Expropriation in the Law of International Investment: I know It When I See It, or Caveat Investor' (n 56); Newcombe, 'The Boundaries of Regulatory Expropriation in International Law' (2004) 20 *ICSID Review—FILJ* 1; August Reinisch, 'Expropriation' (n 56); UNCTAD, *Taking of Property*, available at http://unctad.org/en/docs/psiteiitd15.en.pdf, 11 et seq (2000).

[66] August Reinisch, 'Legality of Expropriations' in August Reinisch (ed), *Standards of Investment Protection* (Oxford, Oxford University Press, 2008).

[67] See below, text at n 71.

[68] *Plama Consortium Ltd v Republic of Bulgaria*, ICSID Case No ARB/03/24, Decision on Jurisdiction, 8 February 2005 [223] ('an MFN provision in a basic treaty does not incorporate by reference dispute settlement provisions in whole or in part set forth in another treaty, unless the MFN provision in the basic treaty leaves no doubt that the Contracting Parties intended to incorporate them.').

[69] *Wintershall Aktiengesellschaft v Argentine Republic*, ICSID Case No ARB/04/14, Award, 8 December 2008 [168] ('In the absence of language or context to suggest the contrary, the ordinary meaning of "investments shall be accorded treatment no less favourable than that

Also with regard to waiting periods, states have successfully convinced tribunals that non-compliance may not only be a procedural defect that could be cured by lapse of time, but constituted a jurisdictional defect leading to the dismissal of investment claims.[70]

The case of the proper interpretation of what constitutes an indirect expropriation has witnessed the most diverse reaction of states, demonstrating also that states—as opposed to the non-state actors—may have resort to additional (sovereign) means to influence the formation of IIL that investors do not possess.

One the one hand, states have been successfully pushing for a more limited notion of indirect expropriation. The police powers doctrine,[71] adopted by the tribunals in *Saluka*[72] and *Methanex*,[73] had the effect of carving out bona fide regulatory measures from the notion of indirect expropriation, even if such action constituted a substantial interference in the sense of the sole effect doctrine.[74]

accorded to investments made by investors of any third State" is that the investor's substantive rights in respect to the investments are to be treated no less favourable than under a BIT between the host State and a third State. It is one thing to stipulate that the investor is to have the benefit of MFN treatment but quite another to use a MFN clause in a BIT to bypass a limitation in the settlement resolution clause of the very same BIT when the Parties have not chosen language in the MFN clause showing an intention to do this.').

[70] See *Burlington Resources Inc v Republic of Ecuador and Empresa Estatal Petróleos del Ecuador (PetroEcuador)*, ICSID Case No ARB/08/5, Decision on Jurisdiction, 2 June 2010; *Impreglio SpA v Argentine Republic*, ICSID Case No ARB/07/17, Award, 21 June 2011; *Murphy Exploration and Prod Co Int'l v Republic of Ecuador*, ICSID Case No ARB/08/4, Award on Jurisdiction (15 December 2010), para 149 ('the requirement that the parties should seek to resolve their dispute through consultation and negotiation for a six-month period does not constitute, as Claimant and some arbitral tribunals have stated, "a procedural rule" or a "directory and procedural" rule which can or cannot be satisfied by the concerned party. To the contrary, it constitutes a fundamental requirement that Claimant must comply with, compulsorily, before submitting a request for arbitration under the ICSID rules.').

[71] See American Law Institute (ed), *Restatement (Third) of the Foreign Relations Law of the United States* §712 (1987) 201 ('A state is not responsible for loss of property or for other economic disadvantage resulting from bona fide general taxation, regulation, forfeiture for crime, or other action of the kind that is commonly accepted as within the police power of states….').

[72] *Saluka Investments BV (The Netherlands) v The Czech Republic*, UNCITRAL Partial Award, 17 March 2006.

[73] *Methanex Corporation v United States of America*, NAFTA Arbitral Tribunal, Final Award on Jurisdiction and Merits, 3 August 2005.

[74] *Saluka*, above n 72 [255] ('States are not liable to pay compensation to a foreign investor when, in the normal exercise of their regulatory powers, they adopt in a non-discriminatory manner bona fide regulations that are aimed at the general welfare'); *Methanex*, above n 73, IV D para 7 ('as a matter of general international law, a non-discriminatory regulation for a public purpose, which is enacted in accordance with due process and, which affects, inter alios, a foreign investor or investment is not deemed expropriatory and compensable unless specific commitments had been given by the regulating government to the then putative foreign investor contemplating investment that the government would refrain from such regulation.').

On the other hand, and this demonstrates the ongoing imbalance between investors and states, respondent states have resorted to various techniques open to them as contracting parties of the underlying IIAs and not only as disputing parties before an investment tribunal in order to reshape the law.

In a number of instances, states have used the authoritative interpretation option provided to them in IIAs. For instance, Canada, Mexico, and the United States have agreed in the framework of the NAFTA Free Trade Commission that the 'fair and equitable treatment' as well as the 'full protection and security' standards do not go beyond the customary international law minimum standard.[75]

Finally, states have gone beyond their treaty interpretation role and used their treaty-making role, when 'correcting' overly investor-friendly interpretations of IIL. The most prominent example is the trend discernible in recent IIA practice to 'codify' the police powers doctrine to ensure broad host states' discretion in using their regulatory powers. Since their prominent use in the 2004 Canada[76] und US[77] Model BITs, many IIAs have contained a regulatory measures carve-out, aimed at ensuring that such measures are not viewed as indirect expropriation.

These corrective tools employed by states as treaty interpreters and treaty makers demonstrate the limits of the impact of investors as non-state actors forming IIL. Although states have given important substantive protection rights to investors as well as the power to vindicate these rights directly before international investment tribunals, it is clear that states ultimately retain the power to shape and even abolish such a system. While they have not done so on a general level, individual host states

[75] NAFTA Free Trade Commission Clarifications Related to NAFTA Chapter 11, Decision of 31 July 2001, available at www.ustr.gov/regions/whemisphere/nafta-chapter11.PDF ('1. Article 1105(1) prescribes the customary international law minimum standard of treatment of aliens as the minimum standard of treatment to be afforded to investments of investors of another Party. 2. The concepts of "fair and equitable treatment" and "full protection and security" do not require treatment in addition to or beyond that which is required by the customary international law minimum standard of treatment of aliens.').

[76] Annex B 134 (1)(c) Foreign Investment Protection and Promotion Agreement 2004 (Canadian Model BIT), available at www.naftaclaims.com/files/Canada_Model_BIT.pdf ('Except in rare circumstances, such as when a measure or series of measures are so severe in the light of their purpose that they cannot be reasonably viewed as having been adopted and applied in good faith, non-discriminatory measures of a Party that are designed and applied to protect legitimate public welfare objectives, such as health, safety and the environment, do not constitute indirect expropriation.').

[77] Annex B(4) on Expropriation Model Treaty Between the United States and [Country] Concerning the Encouragement and Reciprocal Protection of Investment (US Model BIT), November 2004, available at www.naftaclaims.com/files/US_Model_BIT.pdf ('(b) Except in rare circumstances, non-discriminatory regulatory actions by a Party that are designed and applied to protect legitimate public welfare objectives, such as public health, safety, and the environment, do not constitute indirect expropriations.').

have taken the political decision to 'exit' the investment system, eg by terminating BITs and/or denunciating the ICSID Convention.[78] This should serve as a reminder that the special legal position of investors, which in many respects resembles that of individuals entitled to raise human rights complaints against states before international bodies, is not an unalterable given.

12.5 CONCLUSION

Investors, as a subgroup of non-state actors, have gradually emancipated themselves from the usual diplomatic protection paradigm prevailing in international law. Partly through contractual stipulations by host states, and in recent years more significantly through IIAs concluded between their home states and countries in which they invest, investors have gained access to ISDS, allowing them to initiate direct arbitration against states. This development has been conceptualised as the acquisition of a partial legal personality of investors under international law. Following the old principle of 'no rights without remedies', it would indeed appear that investors, whether large transnational corporations or individual natural persons, have now acquired real international rights which they are able to enforce directly before international tribunals. However, it is also clear that such special rights may be taken away by states just as they were initially conferred, eg, by limiting future IIAs or refraining from contractual promises. The recent, highly politicised debate about the legitimacy and usefulness of ISDS has served as a clear reminder in that respect, casting doubt on the truly independent partial international legal personality of investors.

The special position of investors is not limited to status-relevant issues. Through the instrument of ISDS, investors have also been able to act as norm entrepreneurs, contributing considerable to the shaping of IIL. In conjunction with states, as usual respondents in ISDS, investors have considerably influenced the content of modern IIL, as a hybrid body of treaty and customary international law, national law and general principles as well as jurisprudentially shaped precisions in the form of investment awards.

[78] See, eg, Emmanuel Gaillard, 'Anti-Arbitration Trends in Latin America' (2008) 239 *The New York Law Journal* 239; Julien Fouret, 'Denunciation of the Washington Convention and Non-Contractual Investment Arbitration: "Manufacturing Consent" to ICSID Arbitration?' (2008) 25(1) *Journal of International Arbitration* 71; Oscar M Garibaldi, 'On the Denunciation of the ICSID Convention, Consent to ICSID Jurisdiction, and the Limits of the Contract Analogy' in Christina Binder et al (n 2); Christopher Schreuer, 'Denunciation of the ICSID Convention and Consent to Arbitration' in Michael Waibel et al (eds), *The Backlash against Investment Arbitration: Perception and Reality* (Alphen aan den Rijn, Kluwer Law International, 2010); UNCTAD, Denunciation of the ICSID Convention and BITs: Impact on Investor State Claims, IIA Issues Note No 2, December 2010.

13

Armed Opposition Groups

JORDAN J PAUST

13.1 INTRODUCTION

NUMEROUS NON-STATE ACTORS have had formal or informal participatory roles in the international legal process overthe last few centuries. Among them have been various armed opposition groups that have engaged in armed violence during times both of war and of relative peace against the power and/or authority of states and other non-state actors. Some non-state armed opposition groups have had a formal status under international law, especially under the laws of war. Others have had only an informal or non-recognised status under international law, whether or not their forms of participation were direct and significant, or indirect and of little significance.

Section 13.2 of this chapter identifies certain types of formally recognised non-state armed opposition groups, such as those with the status of a nation, people, tribe, belligerent or insurgent. Necessarily, these formal forms of participation in armed violence must also be addressed in terms of the two general types of armed conflict that exist under the international laws of war—first, whether their participation in armed violence against a state and/or other non-state actors constitutes an international armed conflict, and secondly, whether it constitutes an armed conflict not of an international character. Critical appraisal of claims to change the reach of each form of armed conflict will also be addressed.

Section 13.3 identifies certain non-state armed opposition groups that lack a formal status under international law but recognisably participate in armed violence, whether or not such forms of participation are unlawful under international law or merely without validity. Examples of the latter include so-called non-state terrorists, mercenaries, pirates, brigands and banditti who may or may not also use armed violence in opposition to the power or authority of states and other non-state entities in time of armed conflict or relative peace. Various legal consequences of formal status, orlack of formal status, unlawfulness, and the lack of validity are also explored, as well as certain recent claims to change status and possible consequences if change occurs under international law. In section 13.4, the chapter also addresses the fact that armed attacks on a state by various types of non-state actors maytrigger the right of a state to use armed force in self-defence against such attacks, as well as against states in certain contexts when they are complicit in non-state actor armed attacks.

13.2 NON-STATE ARMED OPPOSITION GROUPS WITH FORMAL STATUS

For the last 250 years, international law has never been merely state-to-state, as if states are the only actors with formal participatory roles and formal rights, duties and competencies.[1] As noted in an earlier study, formal participants in the international legal process have included 'nations' composed of identifiable people with or without a territorial base (such as the Navajo nation and many others, in the Americas, New Zealand, the Pacific and Africa), 'tribes', 'indigenous peoples', free cities, and 'belligerents'.[2] At various times in human history, these types of non-state actors have engaged in violence against a state or against other non-state actors with formal participatory roles. As such, they are recognisably among armed opposition groups that have used violence against other actors.

13.2.1 Types of Status

Nation

A 'nation' is composed of a recognised group of people that may or may not have a governmental process or a formal territorial base. A nation may or may not share a common religious preference, culture, language, or racial or ethnic background. No single criterion is determinative with respect to the existence of a nation, although there will be some form of recognition of its status by other actors in the international community. Further, there is no predetermined number of other actors that must recognise that a nation exists.

[1] See, eg, Jordan J Paust, 'Nonstate Actor Participation in International Law and the Pretense of Exclusion' (2011) 51 *Virginia Journal of International Law* 977; Lung-chu Chen and Longzhi Chen, *An Introduction To Contemporary International Law: A Policy-Oriented Perspective* (New Haven CT, Yale University Press, 2000); Eisuke Suzuki, 'The New Haven School of Jurisprudence and Non-State Actors in International Law in Policy Perspective' (2012) 42 *Journal of Policy Studies* 41. State-oriented British positivism preferred by Oppenheim in the early twentieth century was especially unreal. See Paust, ibid 986–87, 992. Although corporations and companies can have duties and rights under international law (see Paust, ibid 986–89), and some have been complicit with armed opposition groups, they are not highlighted in this chapter.

[2] See Paust, n 1, 979–82, 994–97, 1004.

As Brierly noted, a nation is different from a state and 'a single state, like the British Empire, may include many nations, or a single nation may be dispersed among many states, as the Poles were before 1919.'[3] It is possible to be a member of a nation as well as a citizen of a state. For example, members of the Navajo nation are also citizens of the United States, and a few members of the Palestinian nation are citizens of Israel.

States like Austria-Hungary, Belgium, Canada, Denmark, France, Germany, Great Britain, Italy, Japan, Mexico, the Netherlands, New Zealand, Portugal, Russia, Spain, Sweden, Switzerland and the United States have had treaties with 'Indian' and other indigenous nations,[4] some of which had engaged in violence and even war against states or other non-state actors.[5] In 1818, two Englishmen, Alexander Arbuthnot and Robert Ambrister, were convicted for conduct as accomplices of Creek Indians in carrying on war against the United States in violation of the laws of war: Arbuthnot was found guilty of exciting the Creek Indians to war, while Ambrister was found guilty of levying war by commanding Creek Indians.[6]

During the anti-colonial struggles of the early 1800s in the Americas, the United States Supreme Court noted that

> The government of the United States has recognised the existence of a civil war between Spain and her colonies ... Each party is, therefore, deemed by us a belligerent nation ... [and w]hether Buenos Aires be a state or not, if she is in a condition to make war, and to claim the character and rights of a belligerent, she is bound to respect the laws of war.[7]

Still today, when a nation is at war with a state, all of the customary laws of war are applicable and there is no need to change such a result.

Peoples

Like a nation, peoples with formal status need not have a governmental process or formal territorial base, and may or may not share a number of common characteristics. They may also be found within a single state, or dispersed among a number of states. They are, however, recognised by other members of the international community as a 'people' or an 'indigenous people'. As noted elsewhere, 'Jews are known as "the Jewish people", European Gypsies comprise the bulk of "the Romani people",

[3] James Leslie Brierly, *The Law of Nations* (Oxford, Clarendon Press, 1955) 119.

[4] See Paust, n 1, 979–81 and fns 4, 7, 996–97 and fns 61–62. Other non-state actors also had treaties with such nations. Ibid 979–80 fn 4, 982 fn 7, 984 fn 22, 997 fn 62.

[5] ibid, 982 fns 7–8.

[6] See, eg, Jordan L Paust et al, *International Criminal Law* (Durham NC, Carolina Academic Press, 2000) 335.

[7] *The Santissima Trinidad*, 20 US (7 Wheat) 283, 337 (1822).

and Palestinian Arabs [are] called "the Palestinian people".'[8] In fact, some recognised people also comprise a nation. An example would be the Palestinian people and nation.

An important recognition of the legal status of peoples in the United Nations Charter is expressed in connection with one of the primary purposes and principles of the Charter, which is '[t]o develop friendly relations among nations based on respect of the principle of equal rights and self-determination of peoples.'[9] The UN Charter also recognises that there are 'conditions of stability and well-being which are necessary for peaceful and friendly relations among nations based on respect for the principle of equal rights and self-determination of peoples' and that, in view of such a need, the United Nations shall promote various social and economic standards and outcomes as well as 'universal respect for, and observance of, human rights and fundamental freedoms for all without distinction as to race, sex, language, or religion.'[10] Prominent in human rights law is the right of '[a]ll peoples ... [to] self-determination' and, '[b]y virtue of that right ... [to] freely determine their political status and freely pursue their economic, social and cultural development.'[11] Enjoyment of a process of self-determination can be relative and complex, as in the case of the modern Navajo nation (with its own government and a territorial base within the United States) whose members participate in a process of relative Navajo self-determination as well as in US self-determination.

With respect to armed violence, there has been recognition that a people can be entitled to engage in armed resistance to governmental oppression and criminal acts of violence, and to receive outside assistance during a self-determination struggle.[12] The 1970 Declaration on Principles of International Law affirms that self-determination assistance can be permissible under the United Nations Charter when recognising that '[e]very State has the duty to refrain from any forcible action which deprives peoples ... of their right to self-determination' and '[i]n their actions against, and resistance to, such forcible action in pursuit of the exercise of their right to self-determination, such peoples are entitled to seek and to receive support in

[8] 'People', in Wikipedia, http://en.wikipedia.org/wiki/People. See also Paust, n 1, 981 fn 6, and references cited there.

[9] UN Charter, art 1(2).

[10] ibid, art 55.

[11] Eg, International Covenant on Civil and Political Rights, art 1(1), 999 UNTS 171 (9 December 1966) [hereinafter ICCPR]; International Covenant on Economic, Social, and Cultural Rights, art 1(1), 993 UNTS 3 (9 December 1966). See also Chen and Chen (n 1) 30–38, 123–26; Paust (n 1) 1000.

[12] See, eg, Jordan J Paust, 'International Law, Dignity, Democracy, and the Arab Spring' (2012) 46 *Cornell International Law Journal* 1, 4–12, 17–18; Jordan J Paust, 'Use of armed force against terrorists in Afghanistan, Iraq, and Beyond' (2002) 35 *Cornell International Law Journal* 533, 547–48.

accordance with the purposes and principles of the Charter.'[13] Moreover, as the 1970 Declaration implicitly affirms, the territorial integrity of states can be disrupted and changed if they are not 'conducting themselves in compliance with the principle of equal rights and self-determination of peoples.'[14]

The 1974 Declaration on the Definition of Aggression also recognises the right of a people to self-determination assistance when declaring that '[n]othing in this definition ... could in any way prejudice the right to self-determination ... of peoples forcibly deprived of that right...; nor the right of these peoples to struggle to that end and to seek and receive support, in accordance with the principles of the Charter.'[15] When a people are under armed attack by their government, they might also claim a right to engage in measures of self-defence under customary international law against governmental aggression and to receive outside support as measures of collective self-defence.[16]

In 1984, the UN General Assembly responded to the illegal regime in South Africa and its oppression of the majority of the people of South Africa by affirming the permissibility of self-determination assistance and

> recognizing the legitimacy of ... [the] struggle [of the people of South Africa] to eliminate apartheid and establish a society based on majority rule with equal participation by all the people of South Africa ... [urging] all Governments and organizations ... to assist the oppressed people of South Africa in their legitimate struggle for national liberation ... [and condemning] the South African racist regime for ... persisting with the further entrenchment of apartheid, a system declared a crime against humanity and a threat to international peace and security.[17]

With respect to Africa, the African Charter on Human and Peoples' Rights provides additional support for some forms of self-determination assistance. As the African Charter affirms, 'oppressed peoples shall have the right to free themselves from the bonds of domination by resorting to

[13] Declaration on Principles of International Law Concerning Friendly Relations and Co-Operation Among States in Accordance with the Charter of the United Nations, UN GA Res 2625, 25 UN GAOR, Supp No 28, 121, UN Doc A/8028 (1970).

[14] See, eg, Declaration on the Principles of International Law (n 13); Jordan J Paust and Albert P Blaustein, 'War Crimes Jurisdiction and Due Process: The Bangladesh Experience' (1978) 11 *Vanderbilt Journal of Transnational Law* 1, 18–19, 20 fn 69.

[15] Definition of Aggression, GA Res 3314, Annex, art 7, 29 UN GAOR, Supp No 31, 142, UN Doc A/9631 (1975). Concerning early recognition that private individuals can be criminally sanctioned for acts of aggression and other offences against peace, see, eg, *Henfield's Case*, 11 F Cas 1099, 1108–15, 1117 (CCD Pa 1793) (No 6, 360) (Wilson, J, charge to grand jury) (regarding a relevant 'duty of humanity', 'acts of hostility' and 'aggression', and crimes against 'peace'); 1 Op Att'y Gen 68, 69 (US 1797) ('an offence against the law of nations' and 'the peace of Mankind'); 1 Op Att'y Gen 57, 58 (US 1795) (offence 'against the public peace').

[16] See, eg, Paust, Arab Spring (n 12) 10–12, 17; Paust and Blaustein (n 14) 11 fn 39, 20 fn 69.

[17] UN GA Res 39/2 (28 Sept 1984).

any means recognised by the international community,'[18] which would include rebellion or revolution, and '[a]ll peoples shall have the right to assistance of the States parties to the present Charter in their liberation struggle against foreign domination.'[19]

Tribe

A tribe is an association of people, and one that is normally more closely connected than a nation or people as such. A tribe will usually be smaller than a nation or people and, like each, may be found within a particular state, or dispersed among various states. A number of states have had formal treaty relations with certain Indian or indigenous tribes,[20] and states have been in armed conflicts with certain tribes.[21] Moreover, during such armed violence in the past the United States had granted belligerent rights and treatment as prisoners of war to captured members of Indian tribes that had been at war with the United States.[22] The United States has also prosecuted some members of Indian tribes for violations of the laws of war,[23] and has recognised that the killing of a US military officer by a tribal member during a conflict with a tribe was a legitimate act of war and, therefore, that the tribal member was entitled to immunity from prosecution.[24]

As noted in a prior study,[25]

> [i]t is not clear whether the groups along the 'Barbary coast' in the late 1700s and early 1800s were tribes, cities, Sultanates, or 'states' as such, but the United States had treaties with Algiers in 1795 (wherein Algiers was referred to as a Regency),[26] Tripoli in 1805,[27] and Tunis in 1799 (wherein reference was made to 'Emperor' Selim Kahn, the victorious son of the Sultan Moustafa' and 'Bey Hamouda Pacha').[28] These treaties were addressed by the US Supreme Court in *The Amistad*,[29] and by the US Court of Claims in *Love v United States*.[30]

[18] African [Banjul] Charter of Human and Peoples' Rights, art 20(2), 1520 UNTS 217 (1981).
[19] ibid, art 20(3).
[20] See Paust (n 1) 979–80 fn 4, 982–83 fns 8–9.
[21] ibid, 982, fn 8.
[22] ibid.
[23] ibid.
[24] ibid.
[25] Paust (n 1) 983–84.
[26] Treaty of Peace and Amity, 8 Stat 133 (1795).
[27] Treaty of Peace and Amity Between the United States of America and the Bashaw, Bay, and Subjects of Tripoli, 8 Stat 214 (1805). See Roger S Clark, 'Steven Spielberg's Amistad and Other Things I Have Thought About in the Past Forty Years: International (Criminal) Law, Conflict of Laws, Insurance and Slavery' (1999) 30 *Rutgers Law Journal* 371, 384 fn 34.
[28] Treaty of Peace and Friendship, 8 Stat 157 (1799).
[29] *The Amistad* 40 US (15 Pet) 518, 557–58 (1841).
[30] *Love v United States* 29 Ct Cl 332 (1894).

France, Great Britain, and Spain also had treaties with Algiers, Tripoli, and Tunis,[31] and the United States had a treaty with the Sultanate Muscat in 1833.[32]

Although some of the armed violence engaged in by armed groups at the time was referred to as piracy, it was also recognised that war had existed between certain states like the United States and local armed groups along the Barbary Coast with whom the United States had international agreements.[33]

Belligerent

A belligerent has a technical status under the laws of war. Under traditional customary legal criteria used to determine whether a state of belligerency exists, the putative belligerent group would need to: (1) represent an identifiable group of people or have a relatively stable base of support within a given population, (2) have the semblance of a government, (3) have an organised military force and to be able to field its military units in sustained hostilities, (4) control significant portions of territory as its own, and (5) have outside recognition as a belligerent, nation, or state by a state that it is engaged in an armed conflict with or by other states in the international community.[34] As noted in a US military publication, '[i]f the rebellious side conducts its war by guerrilla tactics it seldom achieves the status of a belligerent because it does not hold territory and it has no semblance of a government.'[35] A well-known example of a belligerent engaged in an armed conflict to which all of the customary laws of war applied was the Confederate States of America during the US Civil War. It met the four customary legal criteria and also had recognition as a 'belligerent' by the United States as well as by Great Britain and a few other European states.[36]

31 See, eg, Clark (n 27) 384 and fn 34 (addressing an England-Tripoli treaty of 18 October 1662, 7 Consol TS 253); Bernard G Heinzen, 'The Three-Mile Limit: Preserving the Freedom of the Seas' (1959) *Stanford Law Review* 597, 603 fn 22 (addressing treaties of Spain-Algiers, 14 June 1786; Great Britain-Algiers, 14 May, 1762; Great Britain-Tunis, 22 June 1762).

32 Treaty of Amity and Commerce, 21 September 1833, 8 Stat 458.

33 In 1801, President Thomas Jefferson dispatched a naval force with Marines to defend US vessels attacked by Barbary 'pirates', but the armed hostilities mostly involved a defensive partial war against Tripoli (1801–05) and Algiers (1815) after their breach of treaties with the United States that had provided immunity from attack for US vessels. President Jefferson sent a message to Congress concerning the defensive response. See President Thomas Jefferson, First Message to Congress (8 December 1801), in 1 *A Compilation of the Messages and Papers of the Presidents 1789–1897*, 314–15; (1801) 7 *Annals of Cong* 11.

34 See, eg, Paust, Bassiouni, et al (n 6) 678, 682, 685; Jordan J Paust, 'War and Enemy Status After 9/11: Attacks on the Laws of War' (2003) 28 *Yale Journal of International Law* 325, 326 and fn 6. No magic number or percentage of states is necessary for such status to berecognised.

35 US Dep't of Army, Pamphlet No 27-161-2, 2 *International Law* (1962) p 27.

36 See, eg, The Prize Cases, 67 US (2 Black) 635, 666–67, 669 (1862) (addressing criteria for belligerent status which include the need to 'occupy and hold in a hostile manner a certain

Under the customary laws of war, a belligerent fighter who is a member of the armed forces of the belligerent has combatant status, combatant immunity for lawful acts of war, and prisoner of war status when captured.[37] Membership is the test for both combatant and prisoner of war status under the customary laws of war,[38] as it is for members of the armed forces of a state or nation engaged in an international armed conflict. Such a recognition dates back to the famous and influential 1863 Lieber Code developed by the United States to reflect customary laws of war applicable during the US Civil War. For example, as the Code recognised, '[s]o soon as a man is armed by a sovereign government and takes the soldier's oath of fidelity, he is a belligerent; his killing, wounding, or other warlike acts are not individual crimes or offenses.'[39] Therefore, the Lieber Code reflected both the membership test for what today is referred to as 'combatant' status, and the fact that a combatant has what is termed 'combatant immunity' for lawful acts of war. There is no need to change the laws of war in this regard. In particular, it is not preferable to change the membership test by requiring members of the armed forces of a belligerent, or those of a state or nation, to wear a uniform or fixed distinctive insignia that is recognisable at a distance, which is a criterion under the 1949 Geneva Conventions that is applicable only for certain militia and volunteer corps who participate in fighting during an international armed conflict.[40]

Insurgent

Being an insurgent is also a technical status under the laws of war, and an insurgency is the lowest level of warfare or armed conflict under international law. Customary and traditional legal criteria for the existence of an insurgency involve the first four criteria required for the existence of a belligerency, noted above.[41] What is missing with respect to an insurgency

portion of territory; have declared their independence; … have organized armies; have commenced hostilities … [and] the world acknowledges them as belligerents'); Nils Melzer, *Targeted Killing in International Law* (Oxford Monographs in International Law 2008) 248–49; US Dep't of Army, Field Manual 27-10, *The Law of Land Warfare* (1956) 9, para 11(a) ('The customary law of war becomes applicable to civil war upon recognition of the rebels as belligerents'); Paust (n 1) 981 fn 7. The Civil War between the United States and the Confederate States of America is an example of a classic civil war between a state and a 'belligerent' which also has the status of an armed conflict of an international character to which all of the laws of war apply.

[37] See, eg, Paust, Bassiouni, et al (n 6) 686, 694, 709.

[38] ibid, 686, 694.

[39] Instructions for the Government of Armies of the United States in the Field, General Orders No 100, art 57 (War Dep't, April 24, 1863) [hereinafter Lieber Code].

[40] See, eg, Geneva Convention Relative to the Treatment of Prisoners of War of 12 August 1949, art 4(A)(1)-(6), 75 UNTS 135; Paust et al (n 6) 694–95; Paust (n 34) 329–30, 333–34.

[41] Paust et al (n 6) 685; Paust (n 34) 326.

is outside recognition of the insurgent as a belligerent or an entity with a higher status under international law, such as a state or nation. One set of treaty-based legal criteria for the application of certain laws of war to an insurgency is slightly different, that reflected in the Additional Protocol to the Geneva Conventions of 12 August 1949, and Relating to the Protection of Victims of Non-International Armed Conflicts.[42] Article 1(1) of the Geneva Protocol requires that there be an 'armed conflict'[43] between a state's armed forces and, at least, a particular type of 'organised armed group'—one that is 'under responsible command' and that 'exercise[s] such control over a part of … [a state's] territory as to enable them to carry out sustained and concerted military operations and to implement the Protocol.'[44]

In 1995, an opinion of the Appeals Chamber of the International Criminal Tribunal for Former Yugoslavia (ICTY) chose a much lower threshold, preferring that 'an armed conflict exists whenever there is resort to armed force between states or protracted armed violence between a governmental authority and organised armed groups or between such groups within a state'.[45] This preference has been shared by some writers, but it is generally without support in continual practice and generally shared patterns of legal expectation or *opinio juris*—two elements needed for the formation of a norm of customary international law[46]—and it has no direct support in treaty law. Responding to such a preference, other text writers, including

[42] Protocol Additional to the Geneva Conventions of 12 August 1949, and Relating to the Protection of Victims of Non-International Armed Conflicts (Protocol II), 1125 UNTS 609 (8 June 1977) [hereinafter Geneva Protocol II].

[43] This is an important qualifying phrase that must be interpreted with reference to any relevant international law, which includes the customary legal criteria needed for the existence of an insurgency (as the lowest level of 'armed conflict'), noted above. Concerning the need to interpret a treaty with reference to relevant international law, see, eg, Vienna Convention on the Law of Treaties, art 31(3)(c), 1155 UNTS 331 (1969).

[44] Geneva Protocol II (n 42) art 1(1).

[45] *The Prosecutor v Dusko Tadic*, IT-94-1-AR72 (Appeals Chamber, 2 October 1995) [70]. See also ibid (Trial Chamber, Judgment, 17 May 1997) [562] ('terrorist activities … are not subject to international humanitarian law'); *The Prosecutor v Boskoski & Tareulovski*, IT-04-82-T (Trial Chamber, Judgment, 10 July 2008) [175], [177]–[178] ('the Trial Chamber in *Tadic* interpreted this test … as consisting of two criteria, namely (i) the intensity of the conflict, and (ii) the organization of the parties to the conflict' and 'care is needed not to lose sight of the requirement for protracted armed violence … when assessing the intensity of the conflict. The criteria are closely related'), [185] (regarding 'protracted' violence, what matters is whether the acts are perpetrated in isolation or as part of a protracted campaign that entails the engagement of both parties in hostilities,' and quoting *The Prosecutor v Kordic*: '[t]he requirement of protracted fighting is significant'), [199]–[203] (identifying various other factors); *The Prosecutor v Musema*, ICTR-96-13-T (Trial Chamber, Judgment, 27 January 2000) [248] ('The expression "armed conflicts" introduces a material criterion: the existence of open hostilities between armed forces which are organized to a greater or lesser degree'); Rome Statute of the International Criminal Court, art 8(2)(d) ('isolated and sporadic acts of violence' are not 'armed conflict'), 2187 UNTS 90.

[46] See, eg, Paust et al (n 6) 6–9.

those who participated in a report for the International Law Association (ILA), have underscored that the required criterion of protracted armed violence will exist only where there is intense fighting.[47] In the author's opinion, there is no need to lower the threshold for the existence of an insurgency under customary international law reflected in the customary criteria noted above and reflected partly in Protocol II to the Geneva Conventions.

As noted in a prior study, 'with respect to insurgents, as opposed to belligerents, there was scant recognition of their status and rights and liabilities until the mid-twentieth century, while today, insurgents clearly can have rights and duties under international law.'[48] Also noted was the fact that during the nineteenth century, US courts declared that insurgents had no lawful status until they were recognised as belligerents.[49]

At least by 1949, insurgents had certain rights and duties under the laws of war, although application of such rights and duties was not meant to affect their legal status.[50] In fact, insurgents are not entitled to combatant status, combatant immunity for lawful acts of war, or prisoner of war status when captured.[51] Therefore, an insurgent fighter is not a 'combatant' but an unprivileged fighter, and can be prosecuted for murder with respect to what would otherwise be the permissible killing of an enemy combatant during an international armed conflict.[52] However, mere participation of an insurgent in unprivileged fighting is not a war crime.[53]

[47] See, eg, Claus Kreß, 'Some reflections on the international legal framework governing transnational armed conflicts' (2010) 15 *Journal of Conflict and Security Law* 245, 261 (the threshold 'requires the insistence on a degree of quasi-military organization of the non-State party that enables it to carry out large-scale armed violence in a coordinated manner', and such does not pertain, at least after 'Al Qaeda's subsequent transformation into a rather loosely connected network of terrorist cells'); Mary Ellen O'Connell, 'Remarks: The Resort to Drones Under International Law' (2011) 39 *Denver Journal of International Law & Policy* 585, 596–97, citing Use of Force Committee of the International Law Association, 'Final Report on the Meaning of Armed Conflict in International Law' 1 (2010), available at www.ila-hq.org/en/committees/index.cfm/cid/1022 (click on 'Conference Report The Hague (2010)' hyperlink); Mary Ellen O'Connell, 'The Choice of Law Against Terrorism' (2010) 4 *Journal of National Security Law & Policy* 343, 355–57.

[48] See Paust (n 1) 983. Concerning international agreements with 'insurgents', see, eg, Ian Brownlie, *Public International Law*, 5th edn (Oxford, Oxford University Press, 1998) 609; Antonio Cassese, *International Law*, 2nd edn (Oxford, Oxford University Press, 2005) 127; Antonio Cassese, 'The Special Court and International Law—The Decision Concerning the Lome Agreement Amnesty' (2004) 2 *Journal of International Criminal Justice* 1130, 1134 fn 3; Camille A Nelson, 'Lyrical Assault: Dancehall Versus the Cultural Imperialism of the North-West (2008) 17 *Southern California Interdisciplinary Law Journal* 231, 240 fn 38 (insurgent Maroons had a treaty with Jamaican colonial overlords).

[49] Paust (n 1) 983, citing *US v The Itata* 56 F 505, 510 (9th Cir 1893); *The Ambrose Light* 25 F 408, 412 (DCNY 1885); *The William Arthur* 28 F Cas 624, 626 (DC Me 1861) (No 16, 702).

[50] See Geneva Convention Relative to the Protection of Civilian Persons in Time of War of August 12, 1949, art 3, 75 UNTS 287, 6 UST 3516 [hereinafter GC].

[51] Eg, Paust et al (n 6) 685–86.

[52] ibid.

[53] ibid.

Nonetheless, insurgents, like ordinary civilians in the theatre of an insurgency or armed conflict not of an international character, are bound by the laws of war applicable during an insurgency and can be convicted for having authorised, perpetrated, or abetted war crimes. Moreover, cases have recognised civil liability of insurgents for war crime activity.[54]

Importantly, insurgents remain bound, as any citizen (natural or juridical, and regardless of what type of group they associate with), by the treaty law that is binding on the state of their nationality and that reaches individuals, and customary international law is applicable universally and can be binding on all state and non-state actors and individuals.[55] Insurgents, when detained, benefit from relevant treaty-based and customary human rights law, as any person who is detained would be in any given social context.[56] There is no evident need to change the status of the insurgent as a non-state actor or the matrix of legal duties, rights, and consequences that presently pertain.

13.3 TYPES OF ARMED CONFLICT IN WHICH THEY PARTICIPATE

13.3.1 Armed Conflicts of an International Character

Armed conflicts of an international character to which all of the customary laws of war apply include those between a state and another state, nation, or belligerent.[57] Depending on the circumstances, an armed conflict between a state and a people or tribe can also be of an international character where, for example, an opposition government of a people is recognised as the legitimate representative of the people during an armed conflict with remnants of a prior government whether or not a belligerency

[54] Eg, *Linder v Portocarrero* 963 F 2d 332, 336–37 (11th Cir 1992) (torture and unlawful killing by the Contras in violation of customary law reflected in common art 3 of the 1949 Geneva Conventions).

[55] See, eg, Paust et al (n 6) 6, 685. See also ibid, 674, 687–88 (human rights law continues to apply during any armed conflict); Jordan J Paust, 'The Other Side of Right: Private Duties under Human Rights Law' (1992) 5 *Harvard Human Rights Journal* 51 (regarding private duties under human rights law); Paust (n 1) 987–88 fn 38 (regarding cases recognising violations of human rights by corporations).

[56] See, eg, Paust et al (n 6) 505–06, 687–88, 691–92, 731–32, 855 passim; Jordan J Paust, 'Judicial Power to Determine the Status and Rights of Persons Detained Without Trial' (2003) 44 *Harvard International Law Journal* 503, 505–10.

[57] See Paust et al (n 6) 678, 682, 685, 697–98. See also Additional Protocol I to the Geneva Conventions of 12 August 1949, and Relating to the Protection of Victims of International Armed Conflicts, art 1(4), 1125 UNTS 3 (1977) [hereinafter Geneva Protocol I]. Treaty law binding these actors will also apply and it is likely that individual members of non-state actor groups will be citizens of a state and, therefore, will be bound by treaties of the state of their nationality that reach individuals. Customary and treaty-based human rights law will also apply. See n 55 above.

exists. Such a circumstance arose in 2011 during the armed conflict in Libya[58] and since 2013 during the armed conflict in Syria.[59]

Earlier, it was recognised that, if a foreign state participated in fighting with insurgents against a recognised government of a state, the armed conflict was internationalised and became an armed conflict of an international character to which all of the customary laws of war applied.[60] However, if a foreign state aided the recognised government against insurgents, the conflict remained an insurgency.[61] Today, the better view is that any participation in the fighting by outside formal actors or the transnational spread of fighting will internationalise the armed conflict.[62] Common article 2 of the 1949 Geneva Conventions also affirms that an armed conflict of an international character can occur between a state party to the Conventions and a 'Power',[63] which can include a nation, people, tribe, or belligerent. It is important for every state to recognise that whenever members of its armed forces are sent abroad to fight that the conflict is recognised as an armed conflict of an international character, so that members of its armed forces can have combatant status and combatant immunity for lawful acts of war as well as prisoner of war (POW) status if captured.[64]

13.3.2 Armed Conflicts not of an International Character

The Nature of Such an Armed Conflict

Armed conflicts not of an international character are insurgencies that take place within a state. They are the lowest level of armed conflict or war, and whether an insurgency exists must be tested by the legal criteria noted above. It should be noted that, contrary to the preference of a few modern writers, there is no such thing as a transnational non-international armed conflict under customary or treaty-based international law. If an insurgency becomes transnational in scope, it is de facto internationalised and should be recognised as an armed conflict of an international character. Moreover, as noted above, if there is outside intervention or participation

[58] See Paust, 'Arab Spring' (n 12) 16–18.

[59] See Jordan J Paust, 'Use of Military Force in Syria by Turkey, NATO, and the United State' (2013) 34 *University of Pennsylvania Journal of International Law* 431, 445–46.

[60] See Paust et al (n 6) 697.

[61] ibid.

[62] ibid, 697–98.

[63] See GC (n 50) art 2. The word 'Power' should also be interpreted with reference to customary international law, which recognises a formal status for a number of non-state actors. Recall n 43 above.

[64] See, eg, Paust et al (n 6) 685–86, 698; Jordan J Paust, 'Propriety of Self-Defense Targetings of Members of al Qaeda and Applicable Principles of Distinction and Proportionality' (2012) 18 *ILSA Journal of International & Comparative Law* 565, 573 fn 23.

in the fighting by armed forces of another state, nation, or people, the conflict has de facto been internationalised.

War Against al Qaeda as Such is not Legally Possible

Notwithstanding the insistence to the contrary by the Obama Administration,[65] the United States cannot be at war or in an armed conflict with al Qaeda as such, even though the United States remains engagedin a real war in Afghanistan, within which certain members of al Qaeda have participated. As noted elsewhere,

> [u]nder traditional international law, it is obvious that al Qaeda is not a state, nation, belligerent, or insurgent group. Indeed, al Qaeda is not known to have even purported to have the characteristics of a state, nation, belligerent, or insurgent ... al Qaeda has never met the legal criteria for insurgent status and has certainly lacked any outside recognition as a belligerent, nation, or state. In particular, al Qaeda does not have the semblance of a government, does not have an organized military force, does not field military units in sustained hostilities, and does not control significant portions of territory as its own. In view of the above, any fighting between the United States and al Qaeda as such cannot amount to war or an armed conflict and, therefore, cannot trigger application of the laws of war for such purposes as targeting, capture, status, detention, treatment, [and] prosecution.[66]

Also of note is the fact that most writers agree that the United States cannot be at war or in an armed conflict with al Qaeda as such.[67]

With respect to criteria addressed in Geneva Protocol II noted above, it is evident that outside the theatre of an actual war in Afghanistan and parts of Pakistan, al Qaeda is not engaged in an 'armed conflict' with military forces of the United States, is not more generally an 'organised armed group', is not under a 'responsible' command, does not 'exercise such control over a part' of territory of a state as to enable al Qaeda 'to carry out sustained and concerted military operations', and certainly does not intend to implement the Geneva Protocol. In fact, al Qaeda does not carry out 'sustained and concerted military operations' anywhere around the globe. Further, under the Geneva Protocol, 'isolated and sporadic acts of violence' are not 'armed conflicts' of any sort.[68] Sporadic acts of terroristic violence comprise the bulk of al Qaeda tactics and, as such, al Qaeda is not

[65] See, eg, President Barak Obama, Remarks, National Defense University, Fort McNair, Washington DC, 23 May 2013 ('the war against al Qaeda', '[u]nder domestic law, and international law, the United States is at war with al Qaeda'), available at www.whitehouse.gov/the-press-office/2013/05/23/remarks-president-national-defense-university.

[66] Paust (n 64) 567–68.

[67] ibid, 568–69 fn 10.

[68] Geneva Protocol II (n 42) art 1(2).

an insurgent but is a terrorist group. There is no need to change the laws of war in this regard.

13.4 NON-STATE ARMED OPPOSITION GROUPS LACKING FORMAL ACCEPTABLE STATUS

13.4.1 Terrorist Groups

Terrorist groups are defined by their choice to use terrorism as a tactic or strategy.[69] As noted above, al Qaeda is such a group. Any actor, state or non-state, group or individual, might use a tactic of terrorism for a political, ideological, religious, or other purpose in opposition to power and/or authority of a state or other actor. At least since 1985, the UN General Assembly has consistently and '[u]nequivocally' condemned 'as criminal, all acts, methods and practices of terrorism wherever and by whomever committed.'[70] The UN Security Council has often passed similar condemnatory resolutions against terrorism,[71] there are express prohibitions of terrorism in certain treaties,[72] and it is widely accepted that terrorism is criminal under customary international law[73] and that it is often in violation of human rights law.[74]

Despite the resolute, persistent, and unequivocal condemnation of terrorism in all its forms, one difficulty has been that the international community has been generally unable to define 'terrorism'. Nonetheless, an objective definition of terrorism is at hand. For example, an objective definition (1) would not exclude any type of actor, (2) would include the element of an intent to produce terror or intense fear and anxiety, and (3) would include the element of a terror outcome.[75] Terrorism is an intentional crime and must necessarily involve the creation of terror. Any new convention on 'terrorism' as such should contain an objective definition of terrorism, and not something unrealistic and manipulated.

[69] If not, they are falsely defined.

[70] See, eg, UN GA Res 40/61) 309, Supp No 53, UN Doc A/RES/40/61 (9 Dec 1985); Paust et al (n 6) 873; Jordan J Paust, 'Terrorism's Proscription and Core Elements of an Objective Definition' (2010) 8 *Santa Clara Journal of International Law* 51, 53 fn 6; Beth Van Schaack, 'Finding the Tort of Terrorism in International Law' (2009) 28 *Review of Litigation* 381, 408–28.

[71] See, eg, UN SC Res 1989 (17 June 2011) (also condemning al Qaeda); UN SC Res 1822 (30 June 2008); UN SC Res 1617 (29 July 2005); UN SC Res 1566 (8 Oct 2004); UN SC Res 1526 (30 Jan 2004); Paust et al (n 6) 873–74; Paust, 'Terrorism' (n 70) 53 fns 6–7.

[72] See Geneva Protocol I (n 57) art 51(2); Geneva Protocol II (n 42) arts 4(2), 13(2); GC (n 50) art 33; Paust, 'Terrorism' (n 70) 55–56.

[73] See, eg, Paust et al (n 6) 873–74; Paust, 'Terrorism' (n 70) 53–54.

[74] See, eg, *Ireland v United Kingdom* 25 (1977) ECtHR (Ser A) No 25, para 149 ('terrorist activities … of individuals or groups … are in clear disregard of human rights'); Paust et al (n 6) 884; Paust, 'Terrorism' (n 70) 51 fn 3. Concerning private duties under human rights law, see n 55 above.

[75] See, eg, Paust et al (n 6) 887–88; Paust, 'Terrorism' (n 70) 58–59.

13.4.2 Mercenaries

Under international criminal law, among the relevant definitional criteria with respect to who is a mercenary are the requirements that the person be 'specially recruited locally or abroad in order to fight in an armed conflict', does 'take a direct part in the hostilities', is not a national or member of the armed forces of a party to the conflict, 'has not been sent by a State which is not a Party to the conflict on official duty as a member of its armed forces', and 'is motivated to take part in hostilities essentially by the desire for private gain'.[76] As such, a group of mercenaries is an armed group fighting in an armed conflict and, therefore, in opposition to some other party to the armed conflict, such as a state, nation, people, tribe, belligerent, or insurgent.

A mercenary 'who participates directly in hostilities or in a concerted act of violence ... commits an offence.'[77] Additionally, '[a]ny person who recruits, uses, finances or trains mercenaries ... commits an offence.[78] Moreover, states are forbidden to 'recruit, use, finance or train mercenaries,' especially 'for the purpose of opposing the legitimate exercise of the inalienable right of peoples to self-determination.'[79]

The growing use of private security contractors during armed conflicts may not cross the line into outlawed mercenarism, because they might not 'take a direct part in hostilities' in many instances and because some might be 'on official duty', but the line can easily be crossed. It is not always clear what supportive conduct constitutes direct participation in hostilities, and it is not clear whether private contractors under contract with a government are necessarily 'on official duty.' Moreover, there have been cases where contractors have used armed violence with impunity, and questions have been raised with respect to adequate training and supervision.[80]

[76] See, eg, Geneva Protocol I (n 56) art 47(2); International Convention Against the Recruitment, Use, Financing and Training of Mercenaries, 2163 UNTS 75 (1989) [hereinafter Mercenaries Convention]; Paust et al (n 6) 604–07. With respect to 'an official duty' limitation, the Mercenaries Convention's limit covers any sort of sending by a state 'on official duty'. Mercenaries Convention, art 1(2)(d).

[77] Mercenaries Convention (n 76) art 3.

[78] ibid, art 2.

[79] ibid, art 5(1)–(2). See also Declaration on Principles of International Law (n 13) ('duty to refrain from organizing or encouraging the organization of irregular forces or armed bands, including mercenaries, for incursion' into another state); Definition of Aggression (n 15) art 3(g) ('sending by or on behalf of a state ... mercenaries, which carry out [certain] acts of armed force ... or its substantial involvement therein').

[80] See, eg, John R Crook, 'UN Human Rights Officials Berate US Human Rights Policies and Practices' (2009) 103 *American Journal of International Law* 594; EL Gaston, 'Mercenarism 2.0—The Rise of the Modern Private Security Industry and Its Implications for International Humanitarian Law Enforcement' (2008) 49 *Harvard International Law Journal* 221; Oliver R Jones, 'Implausible deniability: state responsibility for the actions of private military firms' (2009) 24 *Connecticut Journal of International Law* 239; André M Penalver, 'Corporate Disconnect: The Blackwater Problem and the FCPA Solution' (2010) 19 *Cornell Journal of Law & Public Policy* 459.

13.4.3 Pirates

Pirates are primarily motivated by a desire to acquire wealth from forcible robbery and plunder on the high seas. The common definition of the international crime of piracy requires that perpetrators engage in 'any illegal acts of violence or detention, or any act of depredation, committed for private ends … directed on the high seas.'[81] There have also been references to acts of piratical aggression.[82] In view of the accepted definition, organised armed groups who engage in unlawful acts of violence or detention or forcible robbery on the high seas primarily for a political purpose are not pirates.[83] However, some pirates meet the general definition but also have a purpose to oppose the power or authority of a state or other non-state actors.

In 1817, the United States used military force partly in self-defence to clear islands off the coast of Florida from non-state actor pirates, smugglers, and privateers, and to temporarily occupy Amelia Island, where the non-state actors had created a constitution and allegedly set up a government. The United States relied partly on Spain's inability to control misuse of its islands to prevent armed attacks on US territory and shipping from emanating from the islands and assured Spain that even the temporary control of Amelia Island was not a threat to its sovereignty.[84] The United States had not been at war with the pirates and privateers or with Spain.

Today, pirates operating off the coast of Somalia appear to have an additional purpose of opposing state authority and power. They are, in that sense, armed opposition and piratical groups. In either case, there is no need to change international law with respect to their status and the criminality of piratical conduct.

13.4.4 Brigands and Banditti

Brigands, banditti, and marauders have had a criminal status under customary international law, and are rather like pirates on land in that they

[81] See, eg, United Nations Convention on the Law of the Sea, art 101(a)(i), 1833 UNTS 3 (1982); *Re Piracy Jure Gentium* [1934] AC 586; *The Magellan Pirates* (1853) 1 Sp Ecc & Ad 81; *United States v Palmer* 16 US (3 Wheat) 610, 642–43 (1818).

[82] *The Marianna Flora* 24 US (11 Wheat) 1, 39–41 (1825) (referring to 'a piratical aggression by an armed vessel sailing under the regular flag of any nation').

[83] See, eg, *Republic of Bolivia v Indemnity Mutual Marine Assurance Co* [1909] 1 KB 785 ('not persons who simply operate against the property of a particular state for a public political end'); Jordan J Paust, 'Extradition and United States Prosecution of the Achille Lauro Hostage-Takers: Navigating the Hazards' (1987) 20 *Vanderbilt Journal of Transnational Law* 235.

[84] See, eg, James W Garner, 'Some questions of international law in the European war' (1915) 9 *American Journal of International Law* 818, 878; Abraham D Sofaer, 'Power over War' (1995) 50 *University of Miami Law Review* 33. Some of the pirates had been involved with privateer Jean Lafitte, and others who had formed a town on Galveston Island (now in Texas) that became a base for piracy and slave trading. See Amelia Island Affair, Wikipedia, http://efnwikipedia.org/wiki/Amelia_Island_Affair.

are often primarily motivated to engage in violence in order to rob and plunder.[85] However, some such organised armed groups may also be motivated to obtain independent power, if merely anarchic or in opposition to that of any state. In a given context, they may also associate with other types of non-state actors in violent opposition to state power or authority.

As noted elsewhere,

> 'brigands' had been outlawed at least since the time of Hugo Grotius (1612), Albertico Gentili (1620), and Samuel von Pufendorf (1688). Earlier, Balthazar Ayala (1582) stated that the old jurists assimilated the brigand with the pirate and that both were regarded as the 'common enemy of all', and were subject to punishment by any sovereign. Gentili reiterated these views and stated that brigands have 'broken the treaty of the human race.'[86]

In 1863, Lieber Code also affirmed that during an armed conflict,

> [a]rmed prowlers, by whatever names they may be called, or persons of the enemy's territory, who steal within the lines of the hostile army for the purpose of robbing, killing, or of destroying bridges, roads, or canals, or of robbing or destroying the mail, or of cutting the telegraph wires, are not entitled to the privileges of the prisoner of war.[87]

Additionally, 'men or squads of men, who commit hostilities … without commission, without being part and portion of the organized hostile army, and without sharing continuously in the war … are not entitled to the privileges of prisoners of war, but shall be treated summarily as highway robbers or pirates.'[88] Today, no one can lawfully be 'treated summarily', in view of the right of any captured person of any status to a fair trial under treaty-based and customary human rights law.[89] In any event, there is no need to change customary international law with respect to the criminal status of organised armed groups that are rightly labelled banditti, brigands, or marauders.

13.4.5 Organised Criminal Groups

Some of the groups noted above can fit within the category of organised criminal groups, but there are others known more generally as groups

[85] See Banditry, Wikipedia, http://en/wikipedia.org/wiki/Banditry ('A bandit is "one who is proscribed or outlawed; hence, a lawless desperate marauder, a brigand: usually applied to members of the organized gangs which infest the mountainous districts of Italy, Sicily, Spain, Greece, and Turkey."'); Banditti of the Prairie, Wikipedia, http://en/wikipedia.org/wiki/Banditti_of_the_Prairie.

[86] Paust et al (n 6) 182. See also 11 Op Att'y Gen 297, 305-07 (US 1865).

[87] Lieber Code (n 39) art 84.

[88] ibid, art 82.

[89] See, eg, ICCPR (n 11) art 14; Paust et al (n 6) 505–09.

involved with organised crime, such as drug trafficking, human trafficking, slavery, smuggling, transnational theft and fraud through the Internet, money laundering, counterfeiting, piracy, extortion, bribery of officials, kidnaping, hostage-taking, assassination, bombing, arson, and domestic and transnational terrorism.[90] Several of these activities are proscribed under international criminal law, regardless of the status of the perpetrator or abettor of the crime. Organised crime groups can also engage in core international crimes, such as crimes against humanity.[91]

Some organised criminal groups also engage in armed violence in opposition to the power and authority of the state and/or other formal actors. Some engage in 'gang warfare' in competition with other organised crime groups for power and territorial control. Their criminal bribery and terroristic threats and murder of public officials, including law enforcement and intelligence officials, are especially notorious and threaten the existence of democratic processes, including processes of self-determination, related human rights, and the rule of law. Current examples include Mexican drug cartels, some of which effectively control most of northern Mexico, in opposition to Mexican state and federal power and authority; their criminal violence has spilled over into the United States.[92] Another example involves several interconnected armed criminal groups that participate in trafficking of opiates from Afghanistan, the world's main source of opium, through Russia and other Eastern European states into Western Europe, with a remarkable and suspicious surge in production since the US occupation and war in Afghanistan.[93] In order to protect democratic processes and human rights, it is evident that far more must be done by the international community and regional communities to eradicate armed organised criminal groups.[94] In some circumstances, their armed terroristic attacks

[90] See Organized Crime, Wikipedia, http://enwikipedia.org/wiki/Organized_crime.

[91] See, eg, Paust et al (n 6) 813.

[92] See, eg, Craig A Bloom, 'Square Pegs and Round Holes: Mexico, Drugs, and International Law' (2012) 35 *Houston Journal of International Law* 345; Nagesh Chelluri, 'New War on America's Old Frontier: Mexico's Drug Cartel Insurgency' (2011) 210 *Military Law Review* 51; Carrie Cordero, 'Breaking the Mexican Cartels: A Key Homeland Security Challenge for the Next Four Years' (2012) 81 *University of Missouri-Kansas City Law Review* 289; Callin Kerr, 'Mexico's Drug War: Is It Really a War?' (2012) 54 *South Texas Law Review* 193.

[93] See, eg, John Jupp, 'Legal Transplants as Solutions for Post-Intervention Criminal Law Reform: Afghanistan's Interim Criminal Procedure Code 2004' (2013) 61 *American Journal of ComparativeLaw* 51, 59; Daniel Heilmann, 'The international control of illegal drugs and the UN treaty regime: Preventing or causing human rights violations?' (2011) 19 *Cardozo Journal of International and Comparative Law* 237, 252, 259; Opium Production in Afghanistan, Wikipedia, http://en wikipedia.org/Opium_Production-in-Afghanistan#Drug_trafficking_and_impact_around_the_world.

[94] *cf* UN Convention Against Transnational Organized Crime, 2225 UNTS 209 (2000); Protocol to Suppress and Punish Trafficking in Persons, Especially Women and Children, 2237 UNTS 319 (2000); UN GA Res 46/152 (1991); Susan W Tiefenbrun, 'Sex Slavery in the United States and the Law Enacted to Stop it Here and Abroad' (2005) 11 *William & Mary Journal of Women & Law* 317.

across borders should be increasingly met with selective measures of self-defence and collective self-defence.

13.4.6 Self-Defence and Organised Armed Groups

Defence Against Non-State Actor Armed Attacks

A 2010 study of self-defence targeting of non-state actors,[95] and documented writings of the vast majority of text writers,[96] demonstrate that the use of measures of self-defence against armed attacks by non-state actors is permissible under Article 51 of the United Nations Charter and relevant customary international law, even though the direct effects of responsive force will most often occur in a foreign country.[97] The study also demonstrates that nothing in Article 51 of the Charter or in general patterns of pre- and post-Charter state practice and *opinio juris* requires special express consent of the state from which non-state actor armed attacks emanate and on whose territory a self-defence action takes place against the non-state actor.[98] Additionally, it would be demonstrably incorrect to claim that a state has no right to defend itself outside its own territory, absent (1) express foreign state consent, (2) attribution or imputation of non-state actor attacks to the foreign state when the foreign state is in control of non-state actor attacks, or (3) the existence of a relevant international or non-international armed conflict.[99]

With respect to the need to serve various policies at stake in the context of continual non-state actor armed attacks, including peace, security, human rights, and effective opposition to international crime, it is important to note that state sovereignty is not absolute under international law or impervious to its reach, territorial integrity of the state is merely one of the values preferred in the UN Charter, and permissible measures of

[95] Jordan J Paust, 'Self-defense targetings of non-state actors and permissibility of US use of drones in Pakistan' (2010) 19 *Journal of Transnational Law & Policy* 237.

[96] ibid, 239–41 fn 3.

[97] See, eg, ibid 238–49, 279–80. If responsive force is directed merely against the non-state actors who are perpetrating ongoing armed attacks, the use of force against them in a foreign state in compliance with Art 51 of the UN Charter is not a use of force against the foreign state, against its territory, or in violation of its territorial 'integrity' within the meaning of Article 2(4) of the Charter. Ibid 256, 258–59, 279. Importantly, there are no geographic limits with respect to armed attacks that trigger the inherent right of self-defence. For example, an armed attack by a group that initiates a war between a nation or people and a state, a belligerency, or an insurgency within a single state can justify use of responsive armed force in self-defence. See also Paust (n 12) 534 ('nothing in the language of Article 51 requires that such an armed attack be carried out by another state, nation, or belligerent, as opposed to armed attacks by various other non-state actors').

[98] Paust (n 95) 249–58, 279.

[99] ibid, 249–58, 279–80.

self-defence under Article 51 of the Charter that are reasonably necessary and proportionate against actual armed violence must necessarily override the general impermissibility that attaches to armed intervention.[100]

One should also note that the self-defence paradigm is different from both a mere law of war or law enforcement paradigm, and that self-defence targeting and capture can occur with respect to those who are direct participants in armed attacks, whether or not an armed conflict exists that would also allow the targeting and capture of persons who are combatants, civilians who are direct participants in hostilities, or civilians who are unprivileged fighters engaged in a continuous combat function.[101]

Defence Against State Complicitors in Non-State Actor Armed Attacks

In certain contexts, state complicity in non-state actor armed attacks against another state will allow the state that is attacked to respond in self-defence against the state that is directly complicit in the armed attacks. Under the law of self-defence, this can occur where non-state actor conduct is imputed to the complicit state when, for example, the complicit state sent the armed group that carried out the attacks or had 'substantial involvement therein'.[102] The complicit state does not need to effectively control the non-state armed attacker, but it is not certain exactly what is covered under the 'effective control' test.

13.5 CONCLUSION

As noted in this chapter, there have been many non-state actors engaged in violence against and in opposition to power and authority of states and other actors. Some have had formal participatory roles in the international legal process while others have had informal roles and have even had an illegal nature or status. Some engage in legitimate activity, such as permissible revolution, self-determination, and self-defence. Others have participated in violations of treaty-based and customary international law, including relevant laws of war and human rights law. Of course, individual participants in such groups remain bound by treaty obligations of their state of nationality that reach individuals and relevant customary international law regardless of the nature or status of the group.

[100] See, eg, ibid, 256–57 and fns 47–48, and references cited.

[101] See ibid, 260–69, 271–73, 275, 279–80; Paust (n 64) 574–75, 578; Geneva Protocol I (n 56) art 51(3).

[102] *Case Concerning Military and Paramilitary Activities in and Against Nicaragua (Nicaragua v United States)* [1986] ICJ Rep 14 [195] (quoting the Definition of Aggression (n 15) art 3(g)).

Part IV

14

Non-State Actors in International Relations: Actors, Processes, and an Agenda for Multifaceted Dialogue

MARKUS KORNPROBST

14.1 INTRODUCTION

THE PURPOSE OF this chapter is to review the literature on non-state actors in International Relations. It takes stock, and proposes an interdisciplinary agenda for research that builds on the many insights that this literature has generated over recent decades.

Three decades ago, it would have been rather meaningless to have written such a review. There would not have been much to review. By the 1970s, the Realist paradigm had established itself as the dominant lens through which to look at world politics.[1] Realism does not leave much room for non-state actors. States are taken to be the actors in international politics. These states are assumed to be operating in an anarchic environment, in which only policies of self-help can safeguard the survival of the state. To be sure, not all Realist approaches are the same. Some strands of thought cast doubt on some of these assumptions. For instance, there is some debate across Realist approaches to what extent anarchy really always constitutes that threatening an environment that states are forced to embark on self-help policies.[2] There is also some debate about the extent to which analysts have to look inside the state in order to make sense of a state's behaviour.[3] But Realists shy away from questioning the statism and

[1] Hans Morgenthau, *Politics among nations*, 5th edn (New York, Alfred A Knopf, 1948); Kenneth Neal Waltz, *Theory of international politics* (New York, Addison-Wesley, 1979).

[2] Stephen Walt, *The Origins of Alliances* (Ithaca NY, Cornell University Press, 1987); J Mearsheimer, *The Tragedy of Great Power Politics* (New York, Norton, 2001).

[3] Proponents of Neoclassical Realism open up the black box of the state in order to explain the conditions under which a state balances against other states. See, eg, Randall L Schweller, *Unanswered threats: political constraints on the balance of power* (Princeton NJ, Princeton University Press, 2010).

anarchy assumptions. These assumptions are two sides of the same coin. States are sovereign; there is no common power (such as a world government) that impedes on this sovereignty. This leaves very little room for actors other than states, no matter whether these are non-state actors or international organisations.

It was only in the 1970s that work on non-state actors started to leave its mark in the discipline. Keohane and Nye argued that there is not just a Realist side to world politics, but also another, much more benign one, in which sustained patterns of cooperation mitigate anarchy. They labelled these patterns 'complex interdependence'. Non-state actors were very much part of these patterns.[4] Yet research on non-state actors only gained momentum about two decades later when the so-called 'third debate' came to undermine the dominance of Realism.[5]

During this debate, international relations moved from a discipline in which one paradigm reigned supreme to a field in which multiple perspectives contend for scholarly attention. Within the mainstream of international relations, Liberalism and Constructivism became competitors of Realism. Additionally, Critical Theory and Post-structuralism made significant inroads into the discipline. There are important ontological and epistemological differences among these perspectives. Contemporary Liberalism emphasises material forces over ideational ones. Most importantly, it embraces utilitarian micro-foundations. Politics is about actors trying to maximise their expected utility. Constructivism, as well as Critical Theory and Post-structuralism, situate themselves much further towards the ideational end of the ontological spectrum. The world is socially constructed; politics, ultimately, is about processes through which actors attach meaning to the world. Liberals and some Constructivist schools of thought (eg Conventional Constructivism) embrace similar sets of epistemological assumptions, ie positivism broadly speaking. Other Constructivists (eg Interpretivist Constructivists), by contrast, subscribe to hermeneutics. Critical Theorists and Poststructuralists are not content with explaining or understanding the world but seek to change it; the former by conceiving of different political orders, and the latter primarily by letting multiple—and otherwise suppressed—voices come to the fore.[6]

There is no need to elaborate on these meta-theoretical contestations much further. For one, international relations has left the times of paradigm

[4] Joseph S Nye and Robert O Keohane (eds), *Transnational relations and world* (Boston MA, Harvard University Press, 1971); Robert O Keohane and Joseph S Nye, *Power and interdependence: world politics in transition* (Boston MA, Little, Brown, 1977).

[5] On the Third Debate, see Yosef Lapid, 'The third debate: On the prospects of international theory in a post-positivist era' (1989) 33 *International Studies Quarterly* 235.

[6] For a detailed overview of these paradigms and approaches, as well as their relationships to one another, see Markus Kornprobst, 'International Relations as Rhetorical Discipline: Toward (Re-)Newing Horizons' (2009) 11 *International Studies Review* 87.

wars behind and increasingly embraces eclectic theorising that borrows from various approaches within international relations and beyond. Additionally, and of key importance for this chapter, the contenders of Realism widely agree upon the significance of non-state actors in world politics. Liberal and Constructivist research frequently highlights the role of non-state actors. Critical theorists and Post-structuralists frequently critique non-state actors but, at the same time, they are also seen as important agents able to bring about a different international order.

Reviewing the burgeoning literature on non-state actors, I develop a three-fold contention. First, the literature shows that there is a proliferation of different kinds of non-state actor. There are not just transnational corporations (TNCs) and international non-governmental organisations (INGOs); there are also rebels and terrorists, celebrity diplomats and elder statesmen, cities and cosmopolitan citizens, scientists and journalists, and many more. Second, the literature provides convincing evidence for three important sets of causal processes linking non-state actors to other non-state actors as well as to state actors. Broadly speaking, these processes may be referred to as coercion, incentives, and persuasion. Third, the literature is struggling to see beyond the multiplicities of actors and causal processes. There are a number of useful metaphors suggesting how the actors and process hang together, such as governance, network, regime, complex and bloc. But, ultimately, usage of such metaphors tends to privilege certain actors and certain causal processes. The metaphors, too, tend to be better at zooming in than zooming out.

Given the growing spirit of eclecticism in international relations, this chapter is not organised according to schools of thought. Instead, it addresses the main issue areas identified by the literature on non-state actors, one by one. During this discussion, the meta-theoretical divergences briefly discussed above become apparent. But the discussion also uncovers many convergences and complementarities. The chapter consists of three parts: first, I discuss three issue areas that are located in the discipline's sub-field of International Security (IS): intra-state war, terrorism, and arms control. Second, I proceed with three issue areas that are associated with the sub-field of International Political Economy (IPE): global economy, human rights and environment. Third, I address arguments on how non-state actors reconstitute the global polity. Finally, the conclusion summarises my main findings and outlines an interdisciplinary agenda for further research.

14.2 INTRA-STATE WAR

At first glance, intra-state war has little to do with non-state actors in world politics. After all, intra-state wars occur within the borders of a state. Yet the dynamics of most of these conflicts cannot be understood without taking the international dimension into account. At least one party to an intra-state war is a non-state actor, and these non-state actors are usually very well connected internationally, making it possible for them to challenge the existing government.[7]

Literature on intra-state wars analyses the dynamics of intra-state conflicts, either by trying to discover a causal effect or proposing a more elaborate generative mechanism. As far as the former is concerned, explanations often focus on grievances and greed.[8] Groups are hypothesised to rebel if they are discriminated against by the state,[9] or if their leaders perceive an opportunity to enrich themselves by going to war.[10] As far as the latter is concerned, scholars put under scrutiny an array of social and material forces. They ask questions about how insurgents become socialised into fighting as a way of life,[11] how they create popular support,[12] how they come to embrace the beliefs that motivate their insurgency,[13] and how they finance their insurgency.[14] It is especially with regard to the last

[7] Michael Edward Brown, 'Internal Conflict and International Action' in Michael Edward Brown (ed), *The international dimensions of internal conflict* (Cambridge MA, MIT Press, 1996).

[8] Mats R Berdal and David Malone, *Greed & grievance: Economic agendas in civil wars* (Boulder CO, Lynne Rienner Publishers, 2000).

[9] Donald L Horowitz, *Ethnic groups in conflict* (Berkeley CA, University of California Press, 1985); Ted Robert Gurr, 'Why minorities rebel: A global analysis of communal mobilization and conflict since 1945' (1993) 14 *International Political Science Review* 161; Håvard Hegre and Nicholas Sambanis, 'Sensitivity analysis of empirical results on civil war onset' (2006) 50 *Journal of Conflict Resolution* 508; D Horowitz, *Ethnic Groups in Conflict* (Berkeley CA, University of California Press, 1985); TR Gurr, 'Why Minorities Rebel: A Global Analysis of Communal Mobilization and Conflict Since 1945' (1993) 14 *International Political Science Review* 161; H Hegre and N Sambanis, 'Sensitivity Analysis of Empirical Results on Civil War Onset' (2006) 50 *Journal of Conflict Resolution* 508.

[10] Jack Hirshleifer, 'The technology of conflict as an economic activity' (1991) *The American Economic Review* 130; Paul Collier, *Economic causes of civil conflict and their implications for policy* (Washington DC, World Bank, 2000); Paul Collier and Anke Hoeffler, 'Civil War' in Keith Hartley and Todd Sandler (eds), *Handbook of Defense Economics*, vol 2 (London, Elsevier, 2007); Terrence Lyons, *Demilitarizing Politics: Elections on the Uncertain Road to Peace* (Boulder CO, Lynne Rienner, 2005); Terrence Lyons, 'Peacebuilding, Democratization, and Transforming the Institutions of War' in Bruce W Dayton and Louis Kriesberg (eds), *Conflict transformation and peacebuilding: moving from violence to sustainable peace* (Abingdon, Routledge, 2009).

[11] And also how they become de-socialised from this way of life: Lyons, *Demilitarizing Politics: Elections on the Uncertain Road to Peace;* Lyons, 'Peacebuilding, Democratization, and Transforming the Institutions of War'.

[12] Scott Gates, 'Recruitment and Allegiance The Microfoundations of Rebellion' (2002) 46 *Journal of Conflict Resolution* 111; Macartan Humphreys and Jeremy M Weinstein, 'Who fights? The determinants of participation in civil war' (2008) 52 *American Journal of Political Science* 436; Jeremy M Weinstein, 'Resources and the Information Problem in Rebel Recruitment' (2005) 49 *Journal of Conflict Resolution* 598.

[13] Forrest D Colburn, *The vogue of revolution in poor countries* (Princeton NJ, Princeton University Press, 1994); Mark N Katz, *Revolutions and revolutionary waves* (New York, St Martin's Press, 1997); Fred Halliday, *Revolution and world politics: The rise and fall of the sixth great power* (Durham NC, Duke University Press, 1999)

[14] Karen Ballentine and Jake Sherman, *The political economy of armed conflict: Beyond greed and grievance* (Boulder CO, Lynne Rienner Publishers, 2003); Indra de Soysa and Eric Neumayer,

two questions that students of international politics explore the linkages between these domestically situated non-state actors on the one hand and internationally positioned non-state and state actors on the other hand.

There is empirical evidence for the transnational diffusion of ideas. Ideologies have always spread across state boundaries, motivating people to take up arms against a regime. It is not a coincidence that there are several waves of revolutions in world history. To name but a few, in the late eighteenth century there were anti-monarchical revolutions in the United States, the Netherlands and France In the mid-nineteenth century, a number of short-lived liberal revolutions occurred in Europe. In the mid-twentieth century, anti-colonial revolutions put an end to European empires. In the late twentieth century, communist regimes in Central and Eastern Europe (CEE) collapsed.[15] More recently, the so-called Arab Spring ousted a number of authoritarian regimes in the Middle East and North Africa. What made these waves possible is that ideologies spread. Sometimes they do so very quickly. The Arab Spring, facilitated by a host of new communicative means to spread ideas across state borders, is a dramatic example in this respect.

There is also empirical evidence for the significance of material forces. Few insurgencies are able to finance their campaign entirely on their own. They tend to be, to varying degrees, dependent on outside funding. Outside patrons include sympathetic states, and also non-state actors such as diaspora groups or NGOs. Outside funding efforts tend to be much more deliberate interventions into a domestic conflict than the contagion effect by the spread of ideas described above. Focusing on state behaviour, international relations Theory addresses the causes of such interventions. They are often explained in terms of balancing behaviour. During the Cold War, the superpowers engaged in costly 'signalling'—ie waged limited wars in the periphery—in order to show their resolve to deter the opponent.[16] Addressing the balancing behaviour of third-world states, Steven Davids coined the concept of 'omnibalancing'. Regimes try to balance against other regimes by aligning themselves not only with other states but also with particular rebel groups operating in other states.[17] Other arguments explaining outside funding and other support

'Resource wealth and the risk of civil war onset: results from a new dataset of natural resource rents, 1970–1999' (2007) 24 *Conflict Management and Peace Science* 201; Elisabeth Gilmore and others, 'Conflict diamonds: A new dataset' (2005) 22 *Conflict Management and Peace Science* 257; M Humphreys, 'Natural resources, conflict, and conflict resolution uncovering the mechanisms' (2005) 49 *Journal of Conflict Resolution* 508.

[15] Jack A Goldstone, 'Toward a fourth generation of revolutionary theory' (2001) 4 *Annual Review of Political Science* 139, 145.

[16] Thomas C Schelling, 'Bargaining, communication, and limited war' (1957) *Conflict Resolution* 19; Thomas C Schelling, *Arms and influence* (New Haven CT, Yale University Press, 1966).

[17] Steven R David, 'Explaining third world alignment' (1991) 43 *World Politics* 233.

foreground non-material motivations, such as ethnic kinship or ideological affiliations.[18]

Yet there are not only outside actors who try to fuel war. There are also outside actors who try to de-escalate and put an end to war. Humanitarian INGOs, for instance, try to reach out to rebel groups and persuade them to abide by *jus in bello* principles. A key finding of the literature is that opportunities to engage rebel groups in this manner depend on the 'organisational capacity and centralisation' of these groups. If they have 'state-like characteristics', persuasion efforts are more likely to yield success. A reason for this may be that these groups tend to seek some measure of external recognition.[19]

Many outside actors want to accomplish more than that. They wish to put an end to war. In recent years, scholars and practitioners alike have put more and more emphasis on the concept of peace-building. One of the key findings of the peace-building literature is that external peace-building efforts—state and non-state—only have a chance to succeed if external peace-builders work closely with local actors. Simply linking up to the government of a peace-building state does not suffice. Local actors, including many non-state actors, are of key importance. It is precisely these local actors that are crucial for building peace. The Democratic Republic of the Congo (DRC) is a frequently cited example of this crucial insight.[20]

There are, of course, many situations in which peace-building efforts yield very little success, and outside actors resort to try to enforce peace. It took a US-led force a little more than a month to occupy Afghanistan. But building a stable and democratic Afghanistan proved to be a much more difficult endeavour. The International Security Assistance Force (ISAF) experienced many drawbacks. Taliban and al Qaeda attacks continue to destabilise the country. US-led peace enforcement in Iraq encountered major problems as well. The country is de facto split into three parts; re-establishing state authority has proven to be very difficult.[21] In other words,

[18] For an interesting debate on these issues, see Stuart J Kaufman, *Modern hatreds: The symbolic politics of ethnic war* (Ithaca NY, Cornell University Press, 2001); Stephen M Saideman, 'Discrimination in International Relations: Analyzing External Support for Ethnic Groups' (2002) 39 *Journal of Peace Research* 27; Kristian Skrede Gleditsch, 'Transnational dimensions of civil war' (2007) 44 *Journal of Peace Research* 293.

[19] Hyeran Io and Katherine Bryant, 'Taming of the Warlords. Commitment and Compliance by Armed Opposition Groups in Civil Wars' in Thomas Risse, Stephen C Ropp and Kathryn Sikkink (eds), *The persistent power of human rights: from commitment to compliance*, vol 126 (Cambridge, Cambridge University Press, 2013) 257.

[20] Stein Sundstøl Eriksen, 'The Liberal Peace Is Neither: Peacebuilding, State building and the Reproduction of Conflict in the Democratic Republic of Congo' (2009) 16 *International Peacekeeping* 652; Séverine Autesserre, *The Trouble with the Congo: Local violence and the failure of international Peacebuilding*, vol 115 (Cambridge, Cambridge University Press, 2010); Charles T Call, *Why peace fails: the causes and prevention of civil war recurrence* (Washington DC, Georgetown University Press, 2012).

[21] Frank Ledwidge, *Losing small wars: British military failure in Iraq and Afghanistan* (New Haven CT, Yale University Press, 2011).

encounters between non-state actors and states—even the most powerful ones among them—do not necessarily end the way they might be expected to. This is partly due to the interconnectedness of like-minded non-state groupings across state borders. In Afghanistan, for instance, Taliban and al Qaeda can rely on firm linkages reaching across the border, most importantly to Pakistan. This has greatly hindered ISAF's attempts to stabilise Afghanistan.[22] The next section, addressing international terrorism, will deal with these issues in more depth.

14.3 INTERNATIONAL TERRORISM

International terrorists are non-state actors, too. Since 9/11, international relations has paid more and more attention to this violent dimension of transnationalism. Scholars agree widely upon key features of terrorism. Most importantly, terrorists pursue a goal; violence is a tactic to move closer to this goal. Terrorists do not use violence randomly (although it may often appear as if they did), but pursue political and/or social objectives. Compared to other forms of violence, the key distinguishing feature of terrorist tactics is that terrorists seek 'to intimidate a population that is larger than the direct victims of the attack.'[23]

Scholars find it much more difficult to agree on the causes of international terrorism. Some explanations focus on the regime type of the target state. A number of students argue that states experiencing a democratic transition are more likely to experience terrorist attacks than authoritarian or democratically consolidated states,[24] especially since 9/11.[25] There is the contention that states scoring low in measurements of political freedom are more likely to experience terrorist attacks.[26] A number of authors submit that states experiencing foreign occupation are more likely targets for

[22] More and more detailed accounts of the mechanisms driving the counterinsurgency are available. See, eg, Antonio Giustozzi, *Koran, Kalashnikov, and laptop: the neo-Taliban insurgency in Afghanistan* (New York, Columbia University Press, 2008); Eli Berman and others, 'Do working men rebel? Insurgency and unemployment in Afghanistan, Iraq, and the Philippines' (2011) 55 *Journal of Conflict Resolution* 496.

[23] Ethan Bueno de Mesquita, 'Terrorism and Counterterrorism' in Walter Carlsnaes, Thomas Risse and Beth A Simmons (eds), *Handbook of International Relations* (London, Sage, 2013).

[24] Joe Eyerman, 'Terrorism and democratic states: Soft targets or accessible systems' (1998) 24 *International Interactions* 151; Alberto Abadie, 'Poverty, political freedom, and the roots of terrorism' (2006) 96 *American Economic Review* 50; Peter Kurrild-Klitgaard, Mogens K Justesen and Robert Klemmensen, 'The political economy of freedom, democracy and transnational terrorism' (2006) 128 *Public Choice* 289.

[25] Erica Chenoweth, 'Terrorism and Democracy' (2013) 16 *Annual Review of Political Science* 355.

[26] Abadie Alan Krueger and David Laitin, 'Kto Kogo? A Cross-Country Study of the Origins and Targets of Terrorism' in Philip Keefer and Norman Loayza (eds), *Terrorism, Economic Development, and Political Openness* (Cambridge, Cambridge University Press, 2008).

terrorism.[27] Yet it is important to note that these studies, mostly conducted quantitatively, have tended to select their observations largely from post-9/11 world politics, and, more precisely, terrorist dynamics in (and associated with) the conflicts in Afghanistan and Iraq. It is questionable to what extent the findings of these studies are generalisable. Studies on the *longue durée* of terrorism cast serious doubt on this generalisability.[28]

Other explanations focus on the socio-economic relations that give rise to terrorism. Addressing the macro-level, there is some evidence for relationships between economic deprivation and terrorism.[29] This argument is fully compatible with the grievances hypothesis discussed above. Authors are very careful about explanations focusing on religion. Religious differences are seen as a factor contributing to suicide terrorism, but only in interaction with other ones.[30] The reason for these cautionary arguments is obvious. The Tamil Tigers, a secular movement, committed an extraordinarily high number of suicide attacks and were major innovators of suicide terrorist techniques. This serves as a reminder that simple causal arrows between religion and suicide terrorism, or Islam and suicide terrorism are highly misleading. Dealing with the micro-level, there is empirical evidence suggesting that terrorist operatives tend to reflect the average of the level of education of the societies they come from. They are neither better-educated, nor worse.[31] Yet better-educated ones may be more successful in accomplishing their missions.[32]

How do governments counter terrorism? What makes counterterrorism succeed or fail? Since 9/11, more and more authors have addressed these questions. On the one hand, there are authors suggesting that successful counterterrorism presupposes a determined government response. 'Proactive' strategies such as pre-emption are hypothesised to work better than 'defensive' ones such as deterrence.[33] Government concessions are hypothesised to lead to an escalation of terrorist violence because radicals within terrorist organisations feel cornered by the rapprochement between moderate terrorists and government.[34]

[27] Robert Pape, *Dying to win: The strategic logic of suicide terrorism* (New York, Random House LLC, 2005); E Chenoweth, 'Terrorism and Democracy' (n 25).

[28] Martin A Miller, *The Foundations of Modern Terrorism: State, Society and the Dynamics of Political Violence* (Cambridge, Cambridge University Press, 2013).

[29] Bueno de Mesquita, 'Terrorism and Counterterrorism' (n 23) 638–39.

[30] ibid.

[31] Alan B Krueger and Jitka Malečková, 'Education, poverty and terrorism: Is there a causal connection?' (2003) 17 *The Journal of Economic Perspectives* 119.

[32] Efraim Benmelech and Claude Berrebi, 'Human capital and the productivity of suicide bombers' (2007) 21 *The Journal of Economic Perspectives* 223; Bueno de Mesquita, 'Terrorism and Counterterrorism' (n 23) 638–39.

[33] Todd Sandler, 'Counterterrorism a game-theoretic analysis' (2005) 49 *Journal of Conflict Resolution* 183.

[34] Ethan Bueno De Mesquita, 'Conciliation, counterterrorism, and patterns of terrorist violence' (2005) 59 *International Organization* 145.

On the other hand, there are many studies which argue for a more cautious approach to counterterrorism. They point to the importance of the struggle for hearts and minds. Heavy-handed counterterrorism measures, alienating people and causing suffering, increase the popular support for terrorism. Abrahms even argues that terrorists are 'social solidarity maximisers'. Their strategies are all about seizing opportunities provided by government overreaction.[35] This general insight in how government overreaction actually fuels terrorism has sparked a number of more nuanced inquires. There is, for instance, the claim that heavy-handed government action radicalises the moderates, and, therefore, leads to more violence.[36] There is also the argument that scholars ought to analyse popular perceptions of government responses rather than understand these responses as mere material facts.[37]

Recent studies also address consequences of counterterrorism other than the strengthening or weakening of terrorist networks. On the domestic level, there is research suggesting that counterterrorism may end up undermining what a democratic target state vows to protect. Investing heavily into surveillance and security infrastructure, it may end up sacrificing some of its most crucial liberal achievements.[38] Addressing the international level, studies show how counterterrorism has put a strain on transatlantic relations. There are very notable tensions on how to deal with international terrorism in general and al Qaeda in particular.[39]

14.4 ARMS CONTROL

This section resembles those above. It addresses international security. However, the actors discussed in this section are worlds apart from the ones dealt with above. While the latter kill in order to reach their objectives, the former dedicate their work to help bring about a more peaceful world.

Such work, done primarily by INGOs and advocacy networks composed of INGOs and social movements, will be a recurring theme in the

[35] Max Abrahms, 'What terrorists really want: Terrorist motives and counterterrorism strategy' (2008) 32 *International Security* 78, 104.

[36] B Peter Rosendorff and Todd Sandler, 'Too much of a good thing? The proactive response dilemma' (2004) 48 *Journal of Conflict Resolution* 657.

[37] Ethan Bueno de Mesquita and Eric S Dickson, 'The propaganda of the deed: Terrorism, counterterrorism, and mobilization' (2007) 51 *American Journal of Political Science* 364.

[38] Laura K Donohue, *The cost of counterterrorism: power, politics, and liberty* (Cambridge, Cambridge University Press, 2008).

[39] Wyn YN Rees and Richard J Aldrich, 'Contending cultures of counterterrorism: transatlantic divergence or convergence?' (2005) 81 *International Affairs* 905; Corneliu Bjola and Markus Kornprobst, 'Understanding dissonance in a security community: Germany and the United States on Iraq' (2007) 33 *Review of International Studies* 285.

remainder of this chapter. Yet what is remarkable is that these transnational actors have succeeded in making inroads into what Realists label 'high politics'. They have shaped discussions about what kinds of military capabilities are legitimate and what kinds are not. In doing so, they have critically influenced the making of a number of arms control agreements in the last two decades, most importantly the 1997 Ban on Anti-Personnel Mines (Ottawa Convention), the 2001 Programme of Action on Small Arms and Light Weapons (PoA), and the 2008 Convention on Cluster Munitions.[40]

Scholarly work on advocacy networks puts strong emphasis on the power of the word. Research on the campaign to ban landmines is very telling about this power. In the early 1990s, an advocacy network—composed of about a thousand INGOs and social movements from more than 60 states—started an information campaign to put the issue of landmines on the global agenda. With the diffusion of shocking images and statistics into world opinion, the network increasingly tied its advocacy for banning landmines to existing international norms. It emphasised that while existing *jus in bello* principles are all about protecting civilians, it is precisely these civilians that are killed and maimed by landmines.[41] The message proved to be successful on two fronts. It resonated with more and more actors, enlarging the advocacy network. Most importantly, like-minded states such as Belgium, Canada and Germany joined the advocacy. Furthermore, the network gained more and more communicative authority. In 1997, the International Campaign to Ban Landmines (ICBL) received the Nobel Peace Prize. This, in turn, added further to the momentum of the campaign.

There is evidence that advocacy movements even shape debates about the ultimate weapons, ie nuclear weapons. As Jayantha Dhanapala, the highly respected President of the 1995 Review Conference of the Nuclear Non-proliferation Treaty (NPT), puts it, 'the past, present, and future of the NPT simply cannot be adequately understood when viewed exclusively through the lens of the state alone'.[42] Scholarship echoes this insight, for instance when addressing the disarmament provisions in the 2010 Review Conference of the Nuclear Non-proliferation Treaty.[43]

[40] Simone Wisotzki, 'Between Morality and Military Interests: Norm Setting in Humanitarian Arms Control' *PRIF-Report* No 92 (Frankfurt am Main, Peace Research Institute, 2010).

[41] Richard Price, 'Reversing the Gun Sights: Transnational Civil Society Targets Land Mines' (1998) *International Organization* 613. Corneliu Bjola and Markus Kornprobst, 'Introduction: The argumentative deontology of global governance' in Bjola and Kornprobst (eds), *Arguing Global Governance: Agency, Lifeworld, and Shared Reasoning* (London, Routledge, 2013) 84.

[42] Jayantha Dhanapala and Randy Rydell, *Multilateral Diplomacy and the NPT; An Insider Account* (New York, United Nations, 2005) 29.

[43] Rebecca Johnson, 'Assessing the 2010 NPT review conference' (2010) 66 *Bulletin of the Atomic Scientists* 1, 9.

Current debates about nuclear disarmament underline the role of advocacy networks. In April 2010, Jakob Kellenberger, the President of the International Committee of the Red Cross (ICRC), addressed the diplomatic corps in Geneva, advocating for a humanitarian paradigm. He postulated that talk about nuclear weapons should address the humanitarian consequences of nuclear weapons as opposed to being couched in strategic language borrowed from the Cold War.[44] This postulate, supported by many other non-state actors, such as the International Campaign to Abolish Nuclear Weapons (ICAN) made it—via sympathetic states such as Switzerland and Austria—into the Final Document of the Final Document of the 2010 Review Conference.[45] By the end of 2013, over 120 states had joined the campaign for the humanitarian initiative. The 2013 Oslo Conference and the 2014 Nayarit Conference institutionalise this initiative.[46]

While both examples—the ban on landmines and nuclear disarmament—show that civil society advocates can be important actors, there are also non-state actors that do not fit easily into the literature on civil society. Among these are 'knowledge actors'.[47] Academic institutions, for instance, belong to this category. In the end, what really made it possible for the ICBL to make a difference was that Lloyd Axworthy, Canadian foreign minister, advocated vigorously for the ban on landmines in traditional (state-dominated) diplomatic fora. Some years before assuming office, Axworthy wrote his doctoral dissertation under the supervision of Richard Falk. The latter, turning to international relations after receiving his law doctorate, has always been an outspoken proponent for strengthening international institutions and disarmament.[48]

Think tanks, too, are important knowledge actors. The humanitarian initiative opened up a new branch of the nuclear non-proliferation regime. The other branch, nurtured by Barack Obama, is the nuclear security initiative. Since 2010, regular summits take place in which states debate about action to enhance nuclear security, in particular to prevent nuclear devices from falling into the hands of terrorists. There is very little mention of the humanitarian paradigm in this branch of the regime. Indeed, the two branches evolve in considerable tension to one another. Explaining the origins of the nuclear security summits requires a close analysis of the

[44] Jakob Kellenberger, 'Bringing the Era of Nuclear Weapons to an End'. Statement by the President of the ICRC to the Geneva Diplomatic Corps, Geneva, 20 April 2010.

[45] Action Plan, Action no 1, 2010 Rev Con Final Document.

[46] Markus Kornprobst and Martin Senn, 'Deep Ideational Change: Strategy, Humanitarianism, and Nuclear Weapons' (Toronto, ISA Catalytic Workshop, 25 March 2014).

[47] Diane Stone, 'Learning Lessons, Policy Transfer and the International Diffusion of Policy Ideas' *CSGR Working Paper* No 69 (2001).

[48] Falk has embraced this normative commitment since the very beginning of his long publishing career. See, eg, Richard A Falk and Richard J Barnet, *Security in Disarmament* (Princeton NJ, Princeton University Press, 1965); Richard A Falk, *Legal order in a violent world* (Princeton NJ, Princeton University Press, 1968).

influence of think tanks. There is a plausible argument in the literature that a series of publications and networking endeavours by think tanks, for instance Harvard University's Center for Science and International Affairs, made possible the evolution of the security branch of the non-proliferation regime.[49] The messages reached the halls of government, which, in turn, took action.

The literature on epistemic communities highlights the importance of knowledge actors. Epistemic communities are held together by a stock of shared knowledge. Actors that are part of the network look at the world through the same lens. This lens is, among other things, a product of the dissemination of knowledge from academia and think tanks. The epistemic community literature featured research on arms control from the very beginning.[50]

14.5 GLOBAL ECONOMY

In the past, IPE has been something like the 'engine' of research on non-state actors. Indeed, the concepts of transnational actor and transnational relations originate in this sub-field.[51] Transnational actors may be distinguished according to the motives on the basis of which they engage in transnational politics. For-profit actors such as TNCs are self-interested. Not-for-profit actors such as INGOs and social movements, by contrast, are principled actors; they believe in the cause for which they stand.[52] INGOs are professional organisations who 'engage in routine transactions with the same kinds of actors and provide services to citizens of other states'. Transnational social movements are organised somewhat more loosely and they do not provide services. Instead they 'engage in sustained contentious interaction with states, multinational actors, or international institutions.'[53] There is also the important concept of transnational advocacy network. Such networks are ad hoc and more heterogeneous. They are composed of INGOs and social movements but also of government officials and agents of international institutions.'[54]

[49] Campbell Craig and Jan Ruzicka, 'The Nonproliferation Complex' (2013) 27 *Ethics & International Affairs* 329, 335.

[50] Emanuel Adler and Peter M Haas, 'Conclusion: epistemic communities, world order, and the creation of a reflective research program' (1992) 46 *International Organization* 367. On nuclear arms control, see Emanuel Adler, 'The emergence of cooperation: national epistemic communities and the international evolution of the idea of nuclear arms control' (1992) 46 *International Organization* 101, 101.

[51] Nye and Keohane (eds), *Transnational relations and world* (Cambridge MA, Harvard University Press, 1971) 329.

[52] Thomas Risse, 'Transnational Actors and World Politics' in Walter Carlsnaes, Thomas Risse and Beth A Simmons (eds), *Handbook of international relations* (London, Sage, 2002) 428.

[53] Tarrow, *The New Transnational Activism* (Cambridge, Cambridge University Press, 2005) 12.

[54] ibid 13.

Some time ago, Robert Cox made an influential distinction between problem-solving and critical theories.[55] This distinction is useful for addressing contending understandings of the role of non-state actors in IPE. Most authors writing on the global economy are, in Cox's terminology, problem-solvers. They accept the existing order as a given, try to explain its key dynamics, and, based on this, propose avenues to make it work more smoothly. Their work deals with a great variety of actors and causal relationships. Depending on what actors and what directions of causal linkages between them authors address, their work may be grouped into one of three clusters of research: from non-state to non-state actors, from non-state to state actors, and from state to non-state actors.

Non-state actors shape non-state actors. Many authors are concerned with the issue of how TNCs can be kept in check. A sizeable literature shows that advocacy networks sometimes succeed in making private actors agree to 'principles and practices of corporate social responsibility' (CSR).[56] A key mechanism by which they succeed in doing so revolves around the strategy of shaming. Advocates bring malpractices by private actors to the attention of the public, for instance through demonstrations, boycotts, and by informing the media. Private actors, intent on protecting their reputation, may bend to this pressure.[57]

Non-state actors affect what states do. Literature on the impact of TNCs on development belongs to this category. Over recent years, its analyses have become more and more detailed. There are different kinds of TNCs and there are different domestic contexts in which they are active. The impact of a TNC on a developing state's economy depends on these variables. Related to the debate regarding whether TNCs help a state to develop or not is the debate as to whether TNCs contribute to lower regulatory standards (for example, worker rights) or even higher ones.[58] Judging by the literature, it may be difficult to come up with bold generalisations on this question, too. But it is very clear that the power of TNCs cannot be discarded. Non-state actors can leave their mark on states and their policies. This is not confined to TNCs. Advocacy networks and actors who are now often referred to as 'celebrity diplomats' also belong to the category

[55] Robert W Cox, 'Social Forces, States and World Orders: Beyond International Relations Theory' (1981) 10 *Millennium* 126–55.

[56] David Vogel, 'Private global business regulation' (2008) 11 *Annual Review of Political Science* 261, 262.

[57] For an excellent review, see ibid. For detailed studies, see Tim Bartley, 'Certifying forests and factories: States, social movements, and the rise of private regulation in the apparel and forest products fields' (2003) 31 *Politics & Society* 433; Tim Bartley, 'Corporate accountability and the privatization of labor standards: struggles over codes of conduct in the apparel industry' (2005) 14 *Research in Political Sociology* 211.

[58] For a concise review of these debates, see T Risse, 'Transnational Actors and World Politics' in Carlsnaes W, Risse T and Simmons BA (eds), *Handbook of international relations* (London, Sage, 2002) 431.

of non-state actors able to affect state policies. U2 musician Bono's media-savvy campaigns for third-world debt relief and eradication of poverty raised awareness and did seem to leave an impact on decision-makers, including George W Bush.[59]

For all the power and influence of non-state actors, research on the global economy does not suggest that the state is on its way out. There are many studies that provide convincing empirical evidence that states may be in a rather strong position to assert themselves vis-à-vis non-state actors, even in a globalising age. Studies on migration, for example, argue that states do not necessarily have any qualms in making non-state actors do some of the 'dirty' work for them. If carried out by the state, many discriminatory immigration practices such as racial profiling could cause trouble for state authorities, for instance in court proceedings or in the media. 'Outsourcing' these practices to non-state actors, for example airlines and travel companies, but also employers, hospitals etc, shelters state authorities from such scrutiny.[60] Donor states channel a lot of their funding to the developing world via NGOs. Yet these NGOs are anything but independent. They are vehicles for their states' development policies, with often not a lot of room for manoeuvre.[61] Research on the Global Compact sketches state influence in more subtle terms but also highlights the power of governmental organisations. States and international organisations do not give orders to TNCs. But the latter agree to be part of a 'learning network' in which they guarantee to uphold a normative order whose key principles, ultimately, have been put into place by states.[62]

Media research echoes the influence of states on non-state actors. Research on the Internet—long heralded as an island protected from state intervention—proposes that the state may be staging a major comeback in terms of regulating communication flows.[63] Studies on mainstream media, such as television and newspaper, look at a great variety of actors, such as multinational corporations, journalists, interest groups, government officials, parliamentary committees etc. They make a convincing case that there is a transnational media regime,[64] but they also tend to emphasise the strong role played by the government elites in shaping news coverage.

[59] Andrew Fenton Cooper, *Celebrity Diplomacy* (Boulder CO, Paradigm Publishers, 2008).

[60] Gallya Lahav and Sandra Lavenex, 'International Migration' in Walter Carlsnaes, Thomas Risse and Beth A Simmons (eds), *Handbook of international relations* (London, Sage, 2002).

[61] Clark C Gibson, 'Of waves and ripples: Democracy and political change in Africa in the 1990s' (2002) 5 *Annual Review of Political Science* 201, 213.

[62] John Gerard Ruggie, 'global_governance. net: The Global Compact as learning network' (2001) 7 *Global Governance* 371.

[63] Henry Farrell, 'Regulating Information Flows: States, Private Actors and E-Commerce' (2006) 9 *Annual Review of Political Science* 353.

[64] W Lance Bennett, 'Global media and politics: Transnational communication regimes and civic cultures' (2004) 7 *Annual Review of Political Science* 125.

The media are hypothesised merely to 'index' messages originating from government.[65] Only under certain conditions do media succeed in shaping government decisions; usually the causal arrow goes from the government via other political elites to the media.[66] In other words, the media are often conceptualised as transporters as opposed to being actors in their own right.[67]

Yet not all authors writing on the global economy are problem-solvers. There are also critical writers who postulate an entirely different global order. They fundamentally criticise the injustices of the current order, and embrace a role of an intellectual vanguard for a revolutionary change of global politics. Research borrowing from Karl Marx and Antonio Gramsci belongs to this category. Drawing from Marx, Claire Cutler (2003) juxtaposes domestic and global politics. She contends that profit-oriented private actors such as TNCs have seized the opportunities that globalisation offers to them, and evade the rules and norms that keep these actors in check in domestic settings. They develop their own transnational system of governance, tailor-made to increase their profit, and located beyond the reach of state governments.[68]

Research borrowing from Gramsci also criticises the inequalities of the current international system but adds the ideational underpinnings of exploitation to its research agenda. Stephen Gill concurs with Cutler's analysis that networks of transnational private actors are of key importance. Encouraged by states, these networks form a 'historic bloc'. Yet this bloc does not only consist of material forces, such as capital, but also taken-for-granted ideas that make the acceptance of the 'historic bloc' by others possible, such as liberalisation. Following this diagnosis of existing forms of exploitation, the authors proceed in proposing avenues for how to topple the existing order. Intellectuals, scholars included, are taken to play a key role in this emancipating process. They ought to 'generate alternative ways of thinking';[69] at the core of this thinking ought to be attempts

[65] W Lance Bennett, 'Toward a theory of press—state relations in the United States' (1990) 40 *Journal of Communication* 103; W Lance Bennett, Regina G Lawrence and Steven Livingston, 'None dare call it torture: Indexing and the limits of press independence in the Abu Ghraib scandal' (2006) 56 *Journal of Communication* 467.

[66] Robert M Entman, *Projections of power: Framing news, public opinion, and US foreign policy* (Chicago IL, University of Chicago Press, 2004).

[67] For a critical discussion of this view, see Matthew A Baum and Philip BK Potter, 'The relationships between mass media, public opinion, and foreign policy: Toward a theoretical synthesis' (2008) 11 *Annual Review of Political Science* 39.

[68] A Claire Cutler, *Private power and global authority: transnational merchant law in the global political economy* (Cambridge, Cambridge University Press, 2003).

[69] Stephen Gill, 'Introduction: Global Crises and the Crisis of Global Leadership' in Stephen Gill (ed), *Global crises and the crisis of global leadership* (Cambridge, Cambridge University Press, 2011) 24. On agency, see also Andreas Bieler and Adam David Morton, 'The Gordian knot of agency—Structure in international relations: A Neo-Gramscian perspective' (2001) 7 *European Journal of International Relations* 5.

to 'minimize hierarchical forms of political organisation, as in the World Social Forum.'[70]

No matter whether their research tends more towards problem-solving or critical theory, authors writing on the global economy generate convincing evidence that the economic dimension is of crucial importance in global politics. The economic dimension shapes other issue areas, including those located in the sub-field of international security. Literature on the military-industrial complex, for instance, draws a causal arrow from economics (non-state actors) to security (state actors). There are numerous studies on the military-industrial complex of major powers,[71] but also of middle powers.[72] The concept of 'complex' used in this literature bears some resemblance with the concepts of community or network used in other literatures on non-state actors. It suggests that there are close interactions between state and non-state actors, which enable the latter to influence the former in its decision-making. The arms industry, pursuing its selfish interests to sell arms, makes arms control much more difficult. Many studies on the military-industrial complex are inspired by Marxism, but it is important to note that many people far removed from Marxism have expressed concern about the military-industrial complex as well. They include President Eisenhower, who cautioned against the influence of the military-industrial complex in the United States in his 1961 farewell address.[73]

In a similar vein, research on transnational organised crime transgresses the sub-fields of IS and IPE. Again, the causal arrow that many authors draw runs from economics to security. This is most clearly formulated in research on the linkages between transnational organised crime and international terrorism.[74] Research on transnational organised crime is firmly embedded in the literature on globalisation. Some aspects of the globalising world provide opportunities to criminal networks that did not exist before. The globalisation of the market, along with easier access to travel and communication, is hypothesised to go a long way in explaining the growth of

[70] Gill, 'Introduction: Global Crises and the Crisis of Global Leadership' in S Gill (ed), *Global Crises and the Crisis of Global Leadership* (Cambridge, Cambridge University Press, 2011) 19.

[71] For recent discussions, see Charles J Dunlap Jr, 'The Military-Industrial Complex' (2011) 140 *Daedalus* 135; Steven Rosefielde, 'Economies of the Military-Industrial Complex' in Michael Alexeev and Shlomo Weber (eds), *The Oxford Handbook of the Russian Economy* (Oxford, Oxford University Press, 2013).

[72] Masako Ikegami-Andersson, *The military-industrial complex: the cases of Sweden and Japan* (Aldershot, Dartmouth, 1992).

[73] DD Eisenhower, 'Military-Industrial Complex Speech', 17 January 1961, quoted in Dunlap Jr (n 71).

[74] The scholarly literature wrote about this link well before 9/11. See, for instance, Alex P Schmid, 'The links between transnational organized crime and terrorist crimes' (1996) 2 *Transnational Organized Crime* 40.

transnational organised crime in recent decades.[75] Most authors suggest that effective countermeasures presuppose a strong role for the state.[76]

The economic dimension also plays a crucial role in the issue areas of human rights and environment, reviewed below. Research on these issue areas has been theoretically innovative in many ways. This very much includes our understanding of the politics of non-state actors.

14.6 HUMAN RIGHTS

Research on non-state actors and human rights starts with an important observation. The making of many important human rights treaties cannot be explained without taking non-state actors seriously. These include the Convention on the Rights of the Child (1990), Rome Statute of the International Criminal Court (1997), Optional Protocol on the Involvement of Children in Armed Conflict (2000), Kimberly Agreement on Conflict Diamonds (2002) and 'a whole set of women's rights that were added across the United Nations system'.[77] Researchers try to explain these successes by putting the role of advocacy networks under scrutiny.

The literature points to two general tendencies that facilitate successful advocacies. First, there is the ongoing professionalisation of INGOs, NGOs, social movements and transnational advocacy networks. They employ not only highly motivated volunteers but also professional staff who are experts on the issue areas to be dealt with, and know how to run a successful campaign.[78] Second, the number of what the *Yearbook of International Organizations* labels 'international nongovernmental social change organizations' has increased enormously in the last half century. Margaret Keck and Kathryn Sikkink compare this increase according to issue areas. In what they delineate as the human rights area, they find that these organisations increased from 33 in 1953 to 168 in 1993. This makes human rights rank number one among issue areas dealt with by social change organisations.[79]

[75] Ian Taylor, 'Liberal Markets and the Republic of Europe: Contextualizing the Growth of Transnational Organized Crime' in Mats R Berdal and Mónica Serrano (eds), *Transnational organized crime and international security* (Boulder CO, Lynne Rienner Publishers, 2002).

[76] Peter Lupsha, 'Transnational organized crime versus the nation-state' (1996) 2 *Transnational Organized Crime* 21; Monique de Boer, 'Law Enforcement Cooperation and Transnational Organized Crime in Europe' in Mats R Berdal and Mónica Serrano (eds), *Transnational organized crime and international security* (n 75).

[77] Hans Peter Schmitz and Kathryn Sikkink, 'Human Rights' in Walter Carlsnaes, Thomas Risse and Beth A Simmons (eds), *Handbook of international relations* (London, Sage, 2002).

[78] Risse, 'Transnational Actors and World Politics' (n 58).

[79] Margaret E Keck and Kathryn Sikkink, *Activists beyond borders: advocacy networks in international politics* (Ithaca NY, Cornell University Press, 1998) 11.

Yet the literature goes much beyond correlations between levels of professionalisation and numbers of advocacy organisations. It attempts to trace the processes in detail through which advocates are able to affect the making of international norms. A frequently used concept is framing, which is borrowed from the social movement literature in Sociology.[80] Advocates link the ideas they advocate to already widely established norms. They aim at making the advocated idea resonate with a broader audience by trying to persuade this audience that taking already established norms seriously requires embracing the advocated norm. Research on argumentation and rhetoric echoes this general mechanism.[81]

In the last two decades, scholars have tried to specify processes of framing, argumentation and rhetoric further and embed these processes in a greater context. This contributes to a better understanding of communicative encounters. There is, for instance, Keck and Sikkink's often-cited research on the life cycle of norms. In their view, norm selection proceeds through three stages, ie emergence, norm cascades, and internalisation. They also coined the concept of boomerang effect, which is meant to help explain how a state's recalcitrance to embrace a certain norm may be overcome through transnational pressures.[82] Building on work on the boomerang effect, Thomas Risse, Steve Ropp and Sikkink (1999) proposed a 'spiral model',[83] on which they further elaborated 14 years later.[84]

This elaboration puts much more emphasis on political struggles, strategy and tactics of advocates and counter-advocates, including counter-advocates located on the state level. This analytical move is important because it helps students of human rights advocacies not just to improve

[80] David A Snow and others, 'Frame alignment processes, micromobilization, and movement participation' (1986) *American Sociological Review* 464.

[81] See Corneliu Bjola and Markus Kornprobst, 'Introduction: The argumentative deontology of global governance' in Bjola and Kornprobst (eds), *Arguing Global Governance: Agency, Lifeworld, and Shared Reasoning* (London, Routledge, 2013) 1.

[82] Keck and Sikkink (n 79) 13.

[83] Thomas Risse and Kathryn Sikkink, 'The Socialization of International Human Rights Norms into Domestic Practices: Introduction' in Thomas Risse-Kappen, Steve C Ropp and Kathryn Sikkink (eds), *The power of human rights: international norms and domestic change* (Cambridge, Cambridge University Press, 1999).

[84] Thomas Risse-Kappen and Kathryn Sikkink, 'Conclusions' in Thomas Risse-Kappen, Stephen C Ropp and Kathryn Sikkink (eds), *The persistent power of human rights: from commitment to compliance* (Cambridge, Cambridge University Press 2013); Thomas Risse-Kappen and Stephen C Ropp, 'Introduction and Overview' in Thomas Risse-Kappen, Stephen C Ropp and Kathryn Sikkink (eds), *The persistent power of human rights: from commitment to compliance* (Cambridge, Cambridge University Press, 2013); Thomas Risse-Kappen and Kathryn Sikkink, 'Conclusions' in Thomas Risse-Kappen, Stephen C Ropp and Kathryn Sikkink (eds), *The persistent power of human rights: from commitment to compliance* (Cambridge, Cambridge University Press, 2013); Thomas Risse-Kappen and Stephen C Ropp, 'Introduction and Overview' in Thomas Risse-Kappen, Stephen C Ropp and Kathryn Sikkink (eds), *The persistent power of human rights: from commitment to compliance* (Cambridge, Cambridge University Press, 2013).

their understandings about the conditions under which these advocacies succeed, but also of those under which they fail.

It is difficult to brush off the nexus of advocacy networks and human rights. Indeed, the literature demonstrates that these networks have the potential to affect even the most taken-for-granted pillar of international order, ie, sovereignty.[85] Research on the making of the responsibility to protect, a nascent norm qualifying state sovereignty, shows quite clearly that advocacy networks can leave a major mark. From the mid-1990s onwards, an international network of state and non-state advocates formed, determined to make a repetition of humanitarian catastrophes such as the Rwandan Genocide impossible. In 2000, the Canadian government provided an umbrella for these advocates when it created the International Commission on Intervention and State Sovereignty (ICISS). A year later, ICISS coined the expression 'responsibility to protect'. It is telling who suggested the term: Gareth Evans, an elder statesman (previous Australian foreign minister), Mohamed Sahnoun (former Algerian career diplomat) and Michael Ignatieff (Canadian academic at Harvard University).[86] The advocacy network was composed of a number of different actors, ranging from states to international bureaucracies, from civil society to knowledge actors, and from elder statesmen to political leaders.[87] The advocacy framed the responsibility to protect idea by linking it to the existing body of humanitarian principles, such as the Convention on the Prevention and Punishment of the Crime of Genocide and the Universal Declaration of Human Rights. The idea of human security, becoming more and more accepted from the mid-1990s onwards, also provided a salient anchor for the advocacy. In the early 2000s, the advocacy resonated with more and more states. The responsibility to protect made it into the 2005 World Summit Declaration and was mentioned in UNSC 1973 (2011), imposing enforcement measures against the Gadaffi regime. The principle, however, never became consensual, and there are indications that it may have already weakened again.

[85] There are, of course, many other issue areas where advocacy networks made themselves felt. But, given space constraints, I elaborate more on those issue areas that qualify the principle of sovereignty. For public health, see, for instance, Marco Schäferhoff, Sabine Campe and Christopher Kaan, 'Transnational Public–Private Partnerships in International Relations: Making Sense of Concepts, Research Frameworks, and Results' (2009) 11 *International Studies Review* 451. For an excellent overview of literature on humanitarian governance, see Michael N Barnett, 'Humanitarian Governance' (2013) 16 *Annual Review of Political Science* 379.

[86] Steven Haines, 'Humanitarian Intervention: Genocide, Crimes Against Humanity and the Use of Force' in George Kassimeris and John D Buckley (eds), *The Ashgate research companion to modern warfare* (Burlington VT, Ashgate Publishing, 2010).

[87] Thomas George Weiss, 'The Responsibility to Protect (R2P) and Modern Diplomacy' in Andrew F Cooper, Jorge Heine and Ramesh Thakur (eds), *The Oxford handbook of modern diplomacy* (Oxford, Oxford University Press, 2013).

The making of the International Criminal Court (ICC) is another example where advocacy successfully institutionalised a mechanism that qualifies state sovereignty. As Benjamin Schiff puts it, 'non-governmental organisations have played an important role in generating ideas and political and operational support for the ICC.'[88] Again, existing norms, including the above-mentioned anti-genocide convention, the human rights convention, and the move towards human security, served as a frame for making the big idea to create an ICC and the many small ideas for how to make the ICC work resonate with an audience that went beyond the advocates. The NGO Coalition for the ICC, linking up with state actors, played an important role. The CICC campaign also demonstrates how important leadership is. The head of CICC, William Pace succeeded in accumulating a degree of authority that he 'became an actor at least on a par with representatives of major states'.[89] This is an important insight. Communicative authority is not a given; it is linked to communicative performance. Depending on this performance, it waxes and wanes. Representatives of non-state actors are no exception in this regard.[90]

14.7 GLOBAL ENVIRONMENT

If human rights is the one issue area in which the number of non-state actors, especially INGOs and transnational social movements, has increased markedly in recent decades, the environment is the other. Scholars draw many linkages and parallels between the issue areas of global economy, human rights, and environment. They address the political processes through which TNCs—and the industry in general—advocacy networks, and states interact with one another.[91] Reminiscent of debates on the global economy, there are discussions about how the industry can be made to accept regulations rather than engage in a 'race to the bottom'.[92] Similarly to the literature on the global economy and human rights, scholars foreground the concept of framing when they seek to make sense of the impact of advocacy networks[93] and tend to

[88] Benjamin Schiff, 'Diplomacy and the International Criminal Court' in Andrew F Cooper, Jorge Heine and Ramesh Thakur (eds), *The Oxford handbook of modern diplomacy* (Oxford, Oxford University Press, 2013) 753.

[89] ibid, 754

[90] Markus Kornprobst, 'From Political Judgments to Public Justifications (and Vice Versa): How Communities Generate Reasons Upon Which to Act' (2013) online first *European Journal of International Relations*.

[91] Robert Falkner, 'Private Environmental Governance and International Relations: Exploring the Links' (2003) 3 *Global Environmental Politics* 3.

[92] Thomas Risse, 'Transnational Actors and World Politics' in Walter Carlsnaes, Thomas Risse and Beth A Simmons (eds), *Handbook of International Relations* (London, Sage, 2013) 432.

[93] Richard Alexander, *Framing Discourse on the Environment: A Critical Discourse Approach* (London, Routledge, 2009).

emphasise calculations of costs and benefits when they put for-profit corporations under scrutiny.[94]

Yet there are also at least three directions of research that are more pronounced in studies on the environment than in research on other issues. First, research on the environment puts more emphasis on subnational actors. Subnational actors include NGOs, social movements, cities and, most of all, for-profit corporations. These actors may or may not engage in transnational relations. Cities for Climate Protection (CCP), for example, is a transnational network.[95] But subnational actors can be very powerful even if they focus much more on domestic than transnational politics. LLewelyn Hughes and Philip Lipscy, writing about the power of the private sector to resist the making of new environmental regulation, even argue that 'the literature's emphasis on multilateral climate change agreements may be somewhat misplaced. The more important action is often at the domestic level…'[96]

Second, knowledge actors feature very prominently in research on the environment, especially on climate change. Ronald Mitchell distinguishes three kinds of ignorance: total ignorance, causal ignorance and effect ignorance. For most environmental problems, climate change very much included, scientific knowledge is needed to move beyond these forms of ignorance. These problems start of as 'unknown unknowns', ie they are not even recognised as issues to be addressed by politics.[97] Young puts strong emphasis on scientific knowledge in making states do something about environmental problems. He contends that governments are highly unlikely to address these problems unless uncertainty about them is reduced. Knowledge actors are of key importance for this process of reducing uncertainty.[98]

Third, literature on non-state actors and the environment add to our understanding of the interaction patterns across different actors. There are, for instance, convincing arguments about the role of stunts staged by non-profit actors, especially INGOs. Stunts, such as Greenpeace's 1995 occupation of the Brent Spar, a Shell-owned oil storage buoy, attract media attention, mobilise public opinion, and, thus, put pressure on governments and for-profit actors. In the case of the Brent Spar, Shell succumbed to the pressure and reversed its original decision to dispose the buoy in

[94] Peter M Haas, Robert Owen Keohane and Marc A Levy, *Institutions for the Earth: Sources of Effective International Environmental Protection* (Cambridge MA, MIT Press, 1993).

[95] Michele Merrill Betsill and Elisabeth Corell, 'Cities and the Multilevel Governance of Global Climate Change' (2006) 2 *Global Governance* 141.

[96] Llewelyn Hughes and Phillip Y Lipscy, 'The Politics of Energy' 16 (2013) *Annual Review of Political Science*.

[97] Ronald Mitchell, 'International Enviornmental Politics' in Walter Carlsnaes, Thomas Risse, Beth A Simmons (eds), *Handbook of International Relations* (London Sage, 2002).

[98] Oran R Young, 'The Architecture of Global Environmental Governance: Bringing Science to Bear on Policy' (2008) 8 *Global Environmental Politics*.

the Atlantic Ocean. In other cases, there may be no immediate success for the non-profit actor. But the images diffused globally help their cause in the medium and long run. When Greenpeace activists positioned themselves in between the Vlastny, a Soviet whaling ship, and a whale in 1975, the whalers simply fired their harpoon over the Greenpeace ship and the whale died. But the image—similar ones were added in subsequent years—stayed on. This facilitated subsequent campaigns against whaling and contributed to establishing Greenpeace's reputation as determined and trusted proponent of the environmental cause.[99] Another interesting interaction pattern discussed in the environment literature revolves around NGOs and INGOs that do not use the power of the word (eg framing) to get a convincing message across but use financial incentives instead. Conservation International, for instance, buys land to preserve it. The literature has coined a term for such initiatives: 'free-market environmentalism'.[100] Finally, there are interesting institutionalised arrangements for co-operation among non-state actors, for-profit actors very much included. The International Organization of Standardization (ISO) is one of them.[101]

In recent years, more and more authors express their skepticism about the influence of non-profit actors on environmental politics. In a comprehensive, 27-pages-long review of the literature, Thomas Bernauer dedicates a mere twelve lines to literature on non-profit actors, and criticises it for not providing 'systematic answers to some fundamental questions.'[102] While Bernauer risks throwing the baby out with the bathwater, his criticism cannot be entirely dismissed. There are many incidences where non-profit actors played important roles in bringing about international environmental agreements. This includes the 1982 moratorium on commercial whaling by the International Whaling Commission (IWC), the 1985 Montreal Protocol and Vienna Convention for the Protection of the Ozone Layer, and the 1992 Framework Convention on Climate Change as well as the 1997 Kyoto Protocol. Yet successes, especially in the area of climate change, have been far and few in between in the last decade. This puts the onus on the literature on non-profit actors to explain not just successes but also failures.

[99] On the linkages between stunts and media on the one hand, and government and corporate reactions on the other, see Paul Wapner, 'Politics Beyond the State Environmental Activism and World Civic Politics' (1995) 47 *World Politics* 320–26; Kevin Michael DeLuca, *Image Politics: The New Rhetoric of Environmental Activism* (New York, Guildford Press, 1999).

[100] Collette Ridgeway, quoted in Elizabeth R DeSombre, *The Global Environment and World Politics* (London, Continuum, 2007) 88.

[101] Aseem Prakash and Matthew Potoski, 'The International Organization of Standardization as a Global Governor. A Club Theory Perspective' in Deborah D Avant, Martha Finnemore, and Susan K Sell (eds), *Who Governs the Globe?* (Cambridge, Cambridge University Press, 2010).

[102] Thomas Bernauer, 'Climate Change Politics' (2013) 16 *Annual Review of Political Science* 437.

14.8 GLOBAL POLITY

The proliferation of transnational actors and relations has sparked debates about transformations of global politics. Does this proliferation change the way global politics is done? If so, does it move political processes into warranted directions or not?

The most fundamental debate among these is about how to assess the proliferation of actors and relations. The first wave of arguments, focusing on non-profit civil society organisations, welcomed this proliferation. Authors argued that these organisations counter the exclusivity of inter-state decision-making, and provide opportunities for a more just as well as more peaceful global polity.[103] The second wave of arguments was much more sceptical. Advocacy networks were criticised for being dominated by the global north, and, thus, unrepresentative.[104] They were dismissed as simply yet another facet of the 'historic bloc' ruling the world.[105] They were also criticised for being mere channels through which states exert power.[106] While many critical arguments persist, there is also a third wave of literature on the normative repercussions of a global civil society. This third wave is more nuanced, discussing the processes through which deliberation among civil society actors and between civil society actors and state actors can be expected to generate warranted political outcomes.[107]

Studying 'modern mass democracies' (ie domestic settings), Jürgen Habermas coined the concept of public sphere (*Öffentlichkeit*) in the 1960s.[108] It is defined as 'a theater in modern societies in which political participation is enacted through the medium of talk. It is the space in

[103] Ronnie D Lipschutz, 'Reconstructing World Politics: The Emergence of Global Civil Society,' (1992) 21 *Millennium-Journal of International Studies* 389; Paul Wapner, *Politics Beyond the State Environmental Activism and World Civic Politics* (Albany, State University of New York Press, 1996); John Boli and George M Thomas (eds), *Constructing World Culture* (Stanford CA, Stanford University Press, 1999). David Held, *Global Transformations: Politics, Economics and Culture* (Stanford CA, Stanford University Press, 1999); Mary Kaldor, *Global Civil Society; an Answer to War* (Cambridge, Polity Press, 2003).

[104] Kenneth Anderson and David Rieff, 'Global Civil Society: A Sceptical View' in Helmut Anheier, Marlies Glasius, Mary Kaldor (eds), *Global Civil Society* (London, Sage Publications, 2005); Volker Heins, 'Global Civil Society as Politics of Faith' in Gideon Baker and David Chandler (eds), *Global Civil Society: Contested Futures* (London, Routledge, 2005). Hans-Martin Jäger, 'Global Civil Society and the Political Depoliticization of Global Governance' (2007) 1 *International Political Sociology*.

[105] Stephen Gill, 'Globalization, Market Civilization, and Disciplinary Neoliberalism' (1995) 24 *Millenium* 399.

[106] Ole Jacob Sending and Iver B Neumann, 'Governance to Governmentality: Analyzing Ngos, States, and Power' (2006) 50 *International Studies Quarterly* 651.

[107] John S Dryzek, *Deliberative Global Politics: Discourse and Democracy in a Divided World* (Cambridge, Cambridge University Press, 2006); Corneliu Bjola and Markus Kornprobst, 'Introduction: The Argumentative Deontology of Global Governance' in Corneliu Bjola and Markus Kornprobst (eds), *Arguing Global Governance* (London, Routledge, 2013).

[108] Jürgen Habermas, *Strukturwandel Der Öffentlichkeit: Untersuchungen Zu Einer Kategorie Der Bürgerlichen Gesellschaft* (Frankfurt am Main, Suhrkamp, 1990).

which citizens deliberate about their common affairs, hence an institutionalized arena of discursive interaction.'[109] By the 1990s, a debate had evolved in international relations whether there is such a thing as a global public sphere. Originating in research on domestic politics, the concept had made it into studies on global politics. This was prompted, to a considerable extent, by the telecommunications revolution that came into full swing in the 1990s. The rapid development of transnational news channels such as CNN International, Al Jazeera and many others, as well as the rise of the Internet prompted scholars to ask whether the arena of talk was still confined to the borders of the nation-state or whether it had overcome this confinement.[110]

The exact configuration of this global public sphere is a matter of debate. Manuel Castells' seminal work argues boldly that globalisation pressures transform the state into a networked state that no longer has full sovereignty. At the same time, a global public sphere emerges.[111] Other authors are more cautious and write about an 'ensemble of overlapping (national/sectoral) public communication about the same (sometimes very specific) issue or problem.'[112] There are also voices that are more sceptical about such a global public sphere constituted by transnational civil society actors. Jennifer Mitzen, for instance, fully embraces the concept of global public spheres but the actors she identifies as doing the talking are states.[113]

There is more and more research on configurations of a European public sphere as well. The results converge around an interesting observation. National public spheres are still important. But, being interconnected, they are becoming increasingly Europeanised.[114] In-depth cases studies, on the 1999 Kosovo intervention for example, provide empirical evidence for this claim. There is a synchronisation of the debate. European publics discuss the same issues. National publics also discuss debates happening

[109] Nancy Fraser, 'Rethinking the Public Sphere: A Contribution to the Critique of Actually Existing Democracy' (1990) 25/26 *Social Text* 57.

[110] Rudolf Stichweh, '*Die Weltgesellschaft: Soziologische Analysen* (Frankfurt am Main, Suhrkamp, 2000); Rudolf Stichweh 'The Genesis of a Global Public Sphere' (2003) 46 *Development*; Ingrid Volkmer, 'The Global Network Society and the Global Public Sphere' (2003) 46 *Development* 9; Manuel Castells, 'The New Public Sphere: Global Civil Society, Communication Networks, and Global Governance' (2008) 626 *The ANNALS of the American Academy of Political and Social Science*.

[111] Manual Castells, 'The New Public Sphere: Global Civil Society, Communication Networks, and Global Governance' (2008) 616 *Annals of the American Academy of Political and Social Science* 78–93.

[112] Patricia Nanz and Jens Steffek, 'Global Governance, Participation and the Public Sphere' (2005) 99 *American Political Science Review* 401.

[113] Jennifer Mitzen, 'Reading Habermas in Anarchy: Multilateral Diplomacy and Global Public Spheres' (2005) 3 *American Political Science Review* 99.

[114] Thomas Risse, *A Community of Europeans?: Transnational Identities and Public Spheres* (Ithaca NY, Cornell University Press, 2010).

in other national publics on the same topic. But the nation-state setting remains a key arena for these debates.[115] Civil society actors are very much aware of this and, for strategic purposes, often stage interventions into the 'national public sphere' rather than the more complex configuration of European public spheres.[116]

Another concept used to discuss key transformations of the global polity is citizenship. It is related to debates about a global civil society and public sphere but goes beyond it.[117] Authors formulate the postulate that individuals ought to make use of the transnational communicative space and understand themselves as global citizens,[118] world citizens[119], or at least 'globally oriented citizen[s]'.[120] This discourse about global citizenship is by no means confined to academia. INGOs such as Oxfam and agencies such as the United Nations Environment Programme (UNEP) endorse the term as well.[121] It may serve, among other things, as a mobilising frame, encouraging individuals to address global problems.

Scholarly debates about global citizenship resemble debates about civil society. On the one hand, writers caution against self-appointed global citizens. Doubting their expertise and representativeness, they criticise them as 'dangerous global citizen[s]'.[122] Emphasising the continuing salience of the nation-state, they reject diluting the concept of citizenship by extending it beyond the borders of the nation-state.[123] Invoking international law, they dismiss talk about citizenship beyond the confines of sovereign

[115] Reiner Grundmann, Dennis Smith, and Sue Wright, 'National Elites and Transnational Discourses in the Balkan War a Comparison between the French, German and British Establishment Press' (2000) 15 *European Journal of Communication*.

[116] Hanspeter Kriesi, Anke Tresch, and Margit Jochum, 'Going Public in the European Union Action Repertoires of Western European Collective Political Actors' (2007) 40 *Comparative Political Studies* 243.

[117] Jonathan Fox, 'Unpacking Transnational Citizenship' (2005) 8 *Annual review of political science* 178.

[118] Richard A Falk, 'The Making of Global Citizenship' in Jeremy Brecher, John Brown Childs, and Jill Cutler (eds), *Global Visions: Beyond the New World Order* (Boston, South End Press, 1993); Gerard Delanty, *Citizenship in a Global Age: Society, Culture, Politics* (Buckingham, Open University Press, 2000).

[119] Derek Heater, '*World Citizenship: Cosmopolitan Thinking and Its Opponents* (London, Continuum, 2002). N Yuval-Davis, 'The "Multi-layered Citizen" Citizenship in the Age of Globalization' (1999) 1 *International Feminist Journal of Politics* 119. For a historical overview of the evolution of the idea, see Derek Benjamin Heater, *World Citizenship and Government: Cosmopolitan Ideas in the History of Western Political Thought* (Basingstoke, Macmillan, 1996); Derek Heater, '*Citizenship: The Civic Ideal in World History, Politics and Education*' (Manchester, Manchester University Press, 2004).

[120] Bhikhu Parekh, 'Cosmopolitanism and Global Citizenship' (2003) 29 *Review of International Studies* 12.

[121] Christopher L Pallas, 'Identity, Individualism, and Activism Beyond the State: Examining the Impacts of Global Citizenship' (2012) 26 *Global Society* 172–73.

[122] ibid, 186.

[123] David Miller, 'Bounded Citizenship' in Kimberly Hutchings and Roland Dannreuther (eds), *Cosmopolitan Citizenship* (London, Macmillan, 1999).

states.[124] On the other hand, authors present empirical evidence that cosmopolitans are not as unrepresentative of global society as they are often made out to be,[125] and, focusing on the aspirations and intentions of actors, further specify what a global citizen ought to be.[126] Again, it is not surprising that the issue of transnational citizenship is discussed in literature on Europe and the European Union in considerable detail. With European institutions playing a major role in political decision-making processes, there are many arguments postulating an idea of European citizenship that is *en par* with the Europe's integrated political institutions. Indeed, no other literature has generated more far-reaching calls for transnational—or postnational—citizenship as the EU literature.[127]

14.9 CONCLUSION

The purpose of this chapter was to review the burgeoning literature on non-state actors in International Relations. The discussion suggests a three-fold assessment of the findings that the literature has generated: first, the literature demonstrates that there are more and more different kinds of non-state actors who make a difference in global politics. Early literature on non-state actors focused heavily on three types of transnational actors: TNCs, INGOs and social movements. In recent years—partly due to world political events and partly due to scholarly scrutiny—many actors were added to the research agenda. Some of these actors, such as celebrity diplomats and elder statesmen, have the potential to be forces 'for the good'. Others, by contrast, kill in order to overthrow the current world order (international terrorism) or to reap enormous profits (organised crime).

Second, there are various causal processes linking non-state actors to other non-state actors and state actors. At the risk of oversimplification, the literature suggests three kinds of processes. One revolves around

[124] Stephen Neff, 'International Law and the Critique of Cosmopolitan Citizenship' in Kimberly Hutchings and Roland Dannreuther (eds), *Cosmopolitan Citizenship* (London, Macmillan, 1999).

[125] Peter A Furia, 'Global Citizenship, Anyone? Cosmopolitanism, Privilege and Public Opinion' (2005) 19 *Global Society*.

[126] Nigel Dower, 'The Idea of Global Citizenship-a Sympathetic Assessment' (2000) 14 *Global Society*.

[127] Jürgen Habermas, *Die Postnationale Konstellation: Politische Essays* (Frankfurt am Main, Suhrkamp, 1998); Rainer Bauböck, 'Towards a Political Theory of Migrant Transnationalism' (2003) 37 *International Migration Review* 37; Etienne Balibar, *We, the People of Europe?: Reflections on Transnational Citizenship* (Princeton NJ, Princeton University Press, 2009). For an overview of current debates, see Paolo Foradori, Simona Piattoni and Riccardo Scartezzini (eds), *European Citizenship: Theories, Arenas, Levels* (Baden-Baden, Nomos, 2007).

coercion. Research on intra-state war and international terrorism provides ample evidence for the salience of threats and uses of force. Another process is, ultimately, all about providing incentives. Such incentives are not only important as motivating force for TNCs. They also make a difference, for instance, for an INGO's attempts to preserve land. Yet another set of processes may be captured by the concept of persuasion. Literature on advocacy networks finds convincing evidence for the salience of frames and resonances. Words can be quite powerful; they can even make states embark on arms control measures that they otherwise would not have considered.

Third, the double complexity sketched above—multiplication of actors and causal processes—makes it very difficult for authors to zoom out their area of expertise and provide a more holistic picture of current world politics. When faced with complexity they have difficulties to grasp, scholars have a tendency to experiment with metaphors. The latter make the intangible intelligible in light of the tangible, ie something that has already been authoritatively interpreted. Literature on non-state actors and world politics abounds with such metaphors: network, governance, complex, bloc, and many others. Scholarly interpretations of these metaphors tend to privilege certain types of actors and certain types of causal processes rather than others. Research on transnational criminal networks, for instance, is all about coercion and incentives. Research on transnational advocacy networks focuses on persuasion. In principle, the metaphorisation in studying global politics is to be welcomed. Metaphors have the potential to add to our understandings of the world. In general, there is nothing wrong with privileging certain types of actors and certain types of causal processes. Alongside detailed studies on particular networks and governance processes, however, more research would be warranted that aims for a more holistic scrutiny of global political processes.

Current moves towards eclectic research in international relations are very useful for working towards such a more holistic scrutiny. So is interdisciplinary research. International relations is an 'inter-discipline'. It has a long history of borrowing from history and law, economics and sociology, communications and philosophy, and so on. Crisscrossing research between international relations and international law is very promising in order to further elaborate on the makings and unmakings of normativities in global politics. These are omnipresent in global political processes. Studying them provides opportunities to zoom out and appreciate the multiplicities of global politics.

What is needed is a multifaceted dialogue between International Relations and International Law. Multifaceted means that interdisciplinary encounters ought to appreciate the whole range of formalised and non-formalised norms, their interpretations, and the ideational anchors to which they are tied. All too often, interdisciplinary research between international relations and international law is confined to the question of how incentives make actors comply with formalised legal norms.[128] Yet there is much more to the interdisciplinary borderlands between International Relations and International Law. Informal legal norms as well as the ideas in which they are embedded, such as customs and practices, are highly salient in global politics. These constitutive elements of normativity ought to be studied, too.[129] Dialogue means more than simply talking to one another. At a minimum, it requires approaching communicative encounters with an open mind, committing to inclusive encounters across paradigmatic differences, engaging with one another's arguments, and embracing the open-ended nature of dialogue. Communication practiced as such may very well change our most cherished understandings of global politics. It is precisely because of this potential that we ought to embrace it.[130]

[128] Oona A Hathaway, 'Between Power and Principle: An Integrated Theory of International Law' (2005) 72 *The University of Chicago Law Review* 469; Anne-Marie Slaughter Burley, 'International Law and International Relations Theory: A Dual Agenda' (1993) 87 *American Journal of International Law*. The concept of legalization moves beyond compliance but confines itself to formalised legal norms and incentives: Kenneth W Abbott, Robert O Keohane, Andrew Moravcsik, Anne-Marie Slaughter and Duncan Snidal, 'The Concept of Legalization' (2000) 54 *International Organization* 401.

[129] Martha Finnemore and Stephen J Toope, 'Alternatives to "Legalization": Richer Views of Law and Politics' (2001) 55 *International Organization*.

[130] M Kornprobst, 'International Relations as Rhetorical Discipline: Toward (Re-)Newing Horizons' (2009) 11 *International Studies Review* 87.

15

Non-State Actors and Soft Power

ALAN CHONG

15.1 INTRODUCTION

THE QUESTION OF the power of non-state actors is both mystifying and controversial, in terms of defining their scope as actors. On the one hand, the disinterested observer of world affairs can always rhetorically ask: how can one know if the status of non-state actor produces any tangible outcome? Secondly, one can ask whether non-state actors are simply futile since they operate, seemingly, in the shadows and margins of international politics. It is rarely the case that a nation-state openly acknowledges the force of a non-state actor in the shaping of its official policies. Occasionally, a non-state actor may file a lawsuit that culminates in a change to the policy of a government. It is also becoming increasingly frequent, in the twenty-first century context of global terrorism, for violent non-state actors to determine the national security priorities of sovereign nation-states, by selectively attacking civilian targets of disproportionately large symbolic value. Witness the events of 9/11, or the bombings of tourist bars, passenger trains, residential condominiums, commuter buses and luxury hotels in Bali, Madrid, London, Jakarta and Mumbai.

On the other hand, there are many scholars who argue that non-state actors make an impact through the powers of persuasion and demonstration of principled behaviour. These powers are in turn derived from knowledge bases that are collaboratively built up over time through their networks of information. These networks may be constituted by other non-state actors, ordinary members of the public, or more directly from the victims of injustice. These bases may be supplemented through the tapping of expertise supplied by think-tanks, university professors and laboratories. Consequently, knowledge serves as a platform from which non-state actors argue that they possess superior situational awareness over sovereign national authorities. This knowledge/power nexus enables the non-state actor to hold states to account through publicity through the mainstream media of newspapers, radio and television. The advent of the Internet has augmented non-state media reach immeasurably by reconstituting the meaning of 'going global' in the direction of a parallel information space that operates 24 hours a day all year round, penetrating everywhere, as far as physical cables, wireless satellite and terrestrial radio beacons allow.

This chapter will proceed to examine non-state soft power in terms of its employment of the publicity of unethical practices, legal manoeuvres and grassroots-initiated developmental and disaster relief. These dimensions are justified in terms of the actual reported praxis of non-state activities. But in order to appreciate fully the ramifications of non-state soft power employment, a few definitional controversies need to be discussed in relation to the very notion of soft power. The latter term is borrowed ostensibly from Joseph Nye's conceptualisation of the intangible power of the United States at the beginning of the 1990s. One also needs to establish the premises of non-state soft power through the notional dissociation of the non-state actor from the nation-state, while engaging with the irony that non-state actors may well have to emulate the state's power in order to make an impact in world politics. It follows logically too that in even discussing soft power, one needs to account for the reasons why one large subset of non-state actors, the non-governmental organisation, or NGO, has a distinct preference for soft power over their more violent rivals, the terrorists. Finally, soft power achieves its efficacy within the context of late twentieth century technological and political developments labelled by some scholars as the arrival of global information space.[1]

15.2 NON-STATE ACTORS VIS-À-VIS THE NATION-STATE

Most accounts of the presence of non-state actors in world politics trace their origins in the rise and decline of the modern and European nation-state. Even in the pre-modern Greco-Roman and medieval periods, the precursors of the non-state actor operated under a proto-sovereign order. The Ancient Greeks and Romans shared beliefs about inhabiting a common intellectual and political world, regardless of whether soldiers, traders or ordinary citizens were interacting with one another across a vast and often decentralised empire. Some historians have preferred to label Greek civilisation a commonwealth instead.[2] In any case, certain normative standards were expected of social entities operating under a common civilisation. It is not surprising that International Relations scholarship has revived the term 'imperium' in contemporary scholarship, to refer to

[1] Alan Chong, *Foreign Policy in Global information Space; Actualizing Soft Power* (Basingstoke, Palgrave-Macmillan, 2007).

[2] Alfred Eckhard Zimmern, *The Greek Commonwealth. Politics and Economics in fifth-century Athens* (Oxford, Clarendon Press, 1911).

holistic mentalities pervading nation-states and their subjects. One reads of the 'empire of civil society', the 'empire of safety', the 'cultural imperialism' and Orientalism, and even Liberal Imperialism under post-Cold War *Pax Americana*.[3] The interruption by 'barbarians' of the ideological continuity of Greece and Rome in the European mind did not ultimately scuttle the idea of a common intellectual aspiration towards a unified European world. As Daphne Josselin and William Wallace point out, Hanseatic merchants, religious orders and even mercenaries all dabbled in their respective cross-border ventures under the widely accepted assumption that they were subjects of a singular Christendom.[4] This view was finally disrupted by the Reformation of Christianity.

The Peace of Westphalia, as International Relations legend would have it, ushered in a definitive secular, polycentric framework, invoked as the international society of sovereign statehood. Sovereign states acknowledged no constitutional authority higher than their respective monarchs. It was not until the American and French Revolutions in the late eighteenth century that sovereignty was shifted from the monarch to 'the People'. Nationalism seemed a fitting successor to monarchy, in terms of its zealous guarding of sovereignty. But nationalism, alloyed to a concern for the state, generated also a boom in private ventures undertaken to advance the interests of the nation-state. The unity of the 'diverse many' acknowledging their solidarity to one nation sanctioned private commerce, commissioned piracy against rival nation-states, as well as missionary societies dedicated to the spread of Christianity. Unsurprisingly, the spread of Christianity carried with it the seeds of European values to far-flung colonies as well as to pre-existing self-governing non-European entities in the Americas, Africa and Asia.

While it may be said that colonialism fostered a plethora of non-state agents despatched to secure the national interest of the coloniser, non-state actors have subsequently evolved independently of the western nation-state. From the mid-nineteenth century onwards, peace societies, professional associations, and exile groups promoting ethnic solidarity and collective self-determination started to make an appearance on the international stage, even if they were largely ignored by the governments whose attention they were seeking. The formation of the International Committee of the Red Cross[5] by a Swiss national, Henri Dunant, following his appalling experience tending the battlefield casualties at the Battle of Solferino in 1859 signalled the shape of things to come.

[3] William Bain, *The Empire of Security and the Safety of the People* (Abingdon, Routledge, 2006).

[4] Daphne Josselin and Wiulliam Wallace, 'Non-State Actors in World Politics: a Framework' in Daphne Josselin and William Wallace (eds), *Non-state actors in world politics* (Basingstoke, Palgrave, 2001) 5.

[5] See also Ch 6.

Non-state actors heralded a humanistic front of groups willing to transact with one another across sovereign borders precisely in those issue areas where sovereign authorities failed in their duty to humankind.[6] This trend of pursuing causes of conscience through societal channels was predicated on sharing the Kantian vision of building a cosmopolitan world order through rendering governments accountable. A democratisation of international causes had to be set in motion, in spite of the zealous monopoly of international relations by sovereign powers. While these constellations of peaceful non-state actors were going about their lobbying campaigns, underground revolutionary organisations, dedicated to the overthrow of capitalism, were being inspired by the writings of Karl Marx and Friedrich Engels to strive for a new worldwide social order by terrorising the state and its supporters.

By the turn of the twentieth century, the political estrangement between conscientious non-state actors and states was complete. These movements of conscience gladly embraced the label NGO to distinguish their causes openly. Hence, the late twentieth-century NGO would be typified by the likes of Amnesty International, Human Rights Watch, Greenpeace, Oxfam and Friends of the Earth. While there is no denying that the NGOs relied heavily on the system of international law put in place by states, as well as the states' local provision of basic law and order where possible, NGOs envisioned their roles as filling lacunae in the international society. Ultimately, a mixed actor global society should evolve where states do not automatically enjoy *primus inter pares* in determining the direction of political order; political order in global society should be skewed to serve the widest possible section of a global humanity. The raison d'être of Amnesty International and Greenpeace, as stated on their websites, exemplifies this mission. NGOs see themselves as helping states govern better in their capacities as independent guardians.

The final, and perhaps most psychologically disturbing manifestation of non-state actordom, is perhaps the category of the vigilante and terrorist. Vigilantes aim to take the law into their own hands as an expression of disdain for the policing functions of sovereign states. Terrorists employ violence targeting either third parties in a political quarrel, or directly against states perceived to be oppressive; their aim is to communicate political demands through the language of death and destruction. Terrorists have grown very sophisticated over the years in ratcheting up their scale of violence according to whether direct or indirect pain inflicted in front of globe-straddling media would be sufficient to convince their adversaries to yield. More often than not, it is the sovereign state that is the adversary

[6] Bill Seary, 'The Early History: From the Congress of Vienna to the San Francisco Conference' in Peter Willetts (ed), *The Consciousness of the World: The Influence of non-governmental organisations in the UN System* (London, C Hurst and Company, 1996) 17–19.

of the terrorist. In this regard, the Irish Republican Army (IRA) and Al Qaeda share a great deal in common in terms of the acts of violent communication towards states. Vigilantes are only a shade more accommodative towards states, if only because they seek sovereign authority to act for their cause.

Therefore, the idea of non-state actordom exhibits a chameleon-like relationship towards sovereign nation-states across history. Non-state actors desire to part company from states over rival political visions. But this chequered history also shows that like all actors in politics, non-state actors of both the NGO and violent varieties also act strategically in selectively campaigning with and chastising their state partners. They do so with a choice of soft and hard power. This choice of tools for political action hinges on the efficacy of violence in relation to their cause.

15.3 NON-STATE ACTORS LEAN TOWARDS SOFT POWER

The evolution of non-state actors has clearly demonstrated a trajectory of defining their missions in distinction from the *modus operandi* of states. The peace societies of the late nineteenth century consciously steered a pacifist, disarmament-oriented agenda away from the nationalistic jingoism of the European powers of the day. Moreover, they preferred to stir the voices of conscience through the mobilisation of public opinion, rather than concede the momentum of international politics to trigger-happy politicians and generals. The development-oriented NGO of the late twentieth century deliberately distanced itself from the Cold War and other statist *realpolitik* simply because the constructive possibilities of philanthropic neutrality could not be seen or heard above the loud propaganda of planning for war against a nationalistic enemy state. In actualising Joseph Nye's formulation of soft power, non-state actors employed tools that aimed to 'get others to want what you want' through co-optive strategies of visual and philosophical persuasion. In various books and articles, Nye argued that the bases of soft power lay in a national culture, a nation-state's political values, and its foreign policies.[7] He clearly had the United States in mind as his inspiration. Moreover, Nye kept reiterating that values and foreign policy required positive affirmation by their originator. Haunted by the foreign policies and right-wing orientation of the George W Bush Administration in the shadow of Operation Iraqi Freedom, Nye was conscious that American soft power was being undermined by the wanton use of its superior military strength and its widely perceived hypocrisy in

[7] Joseph S Nye, *Soft power: The means to success in world politics* (New York, Public Affairs, 2004) 11.

preaching human rights and democracy abroad while violating the same in executing the so-called 'War on Terror' against al Qaeda.[8]

I subsequently added the quality of credibility and communitarian bases to the formulation of soft power. It is the idea of attracting 'others' into a common political community favoured by an initially select few that lies at the heart of soft power. Chong, in extrapolating from Nye, rearticulates soft power as

> the long term propaganda of community discourse. The nation-state as a community unto itself, escaping an ungovernable state of nature, generates its own system of collective meaning in the Foucaultian sense. This discourse is propaganda defined as the short-term and specific influencing of social action through affecting the decision processes of men by manipulating and presenting information.[9]

I attribute the projection of political community through soft power in three ways. First, the projection of soft power has to 'package' a way of life in the most attractive way possible while minimising its inconsistencies. Secondly, the appeal of a political community must operate on the assumption that there exists 'the public omnidirectionality of audiences'.)[10] There is no hiding any inconsistencies or contradictions that may skew the showcasing of a community—everyone on Earth will have access to information flows concerning the communitarian model promoted. Thirdly, projecting community effectively requires projecting the model consistently and credibly. The ideal for propagandists of community is to ensure that they 'speak and act with "one voice and one action"'.[11] These attributes apply to non-state actors as well—except for the idea of national community. Unless the non-state actor violates its very essence by acting in the nineteenth century neo-colonial mode of serving as a proxy for national interest, most non-state actors feature goals that transcend any existing nationalism. Even non-state actors such as ethnic solidarity groups and territorial liberation movements tend to appeal to universal humanitarian standards to mobilise sympathy from others. It is of course a different form of communitarian appeal that is mounted once these groups achieve a territorial homeland sanctioned under international law. They may then behave just like any conventional national soft power.

Nonetheless, non-state actors can be argued to lean towards soft power because they are intrinsically concerned with both demonstrating their visions of alternative political community, as well as manifesting an active community of believers through their very existence as an organisation. Amnesty International, for instance, was founded by a handful of human

[8] ibid 55–65.
[9] Chong (n 1) 54.
[10] ibid 55–56.
[11] ibid 56.

rights idealists who were angered by the Portuguese military dictatorship's arbitrary arrest of dissidents in 1961. Likewise, the story of Peter Eigen's spiritual awakening to the evils of official corruption in the Third World during his personal travels led to the formation of Transparency International. There is a thread that runs back in time that links the anti-slavery movement and assorted liberal causes in western imperial capitals that sought to enhance the ethical dimension of colonial policies. All these were initiated by personalities who were affronted by unconscionable acts, or who were victims directly of those acts. The whole purpose of becoming a non-state actor is to improve governance within national societies, and certainly within the international society of states, through the advocacy of peaceful and more harmonious alternatives.

An objection might be raised by critics of non-state soft power, posing the counter-examples of Marxists, vigilantes and terrorists. It is widely and erroneously assumed that these groups espouse pure violence and nothing more. These violent non-state actors will deploy violence along the same spectrum as non-violent means to achieve a singular objective of transforming society. The choice of means across time is dependent on the philosophical arguments of efficacy and the political conditions of the moment. Marx has for instance articulated a propagandistic form of violence—a revolution of awakening—that precedes physical revolution, in his famous 1848 Manifesto of the Communist Party.

Vladimir Illyich Lenin, who subsequently argued that the concrete implementation of Marxist revolution required the formation of a revolutionary party dedicated to the instruments of violence, acknowledged the importance of propaganda in spreading and consolidating the Bolshevik Revolution of 1917. Osama bin Laden was in his turn quite obsessed with expanding al Qaeda's ideology.[12] One of bin Laden's standard propaganda refrains was to supply elaborate justifications, derived from a didactic reading of contemporary world history, to indict the US and its politico-cultural influence for corrupting Arab rulers and young people. Conveniently, bin Laden prefaced his call to arms by addressing Muslims worldwide with a fairly extensive discussion of conducting 'proper relations' towards non-Muslims across the centuries.[13] Bin Laden had clearly hoped to augment his terrorist forces by appealing to a collective transnational Islamic outrage against American power wherever it might be encountered—from tourist destinations in third world countries, to military garrisons in the Middle East, and to merchant vessels in neutral harbours. In the strategy of suicide terrorism, leaders of their

[12] Peter L Bergen, *Holy war, inc.: Inside the secret world of Osama bin Laden* (London, Simon & Schuster, 2002) 19–21.

[13] ibid 103.

networks clearly intend to conquer minds, before turning them into physical explosive instruments. The thoughts of Marx and bin Laden seem to supply the coda that hard power grows out of the psychological conquest of soft power.

15.4 NON-STATE ACTORS OPERATE WITHIN GLOBAL INFORMATION SPACE

The post-Cold War international order that coincided with the information and communication technology revolution produced an environment ready-made for non-state actors to level their power deficiencies vis-à-vis nation-states. The ending of ideological bipolarity meant that multiple philosophies could re-enter the debate about designs for the new world order. The arrival of portable digital cameras and video recorders facilitated micro-reporting by actors of virtually all sizes focused upon political concerns that cross sovereign borders. The establishment of global satellite television systems ensured that non-state voices could enjoy circulation through mainstream media channels, regardless of sovereign approval. The Internet has produced a culmination of these open communication trends by liberating multiple communication channels from the clutches of state-controlled media organisations.

While Joseph Nye concurs that the early history of the non-state actor showed that its transnational influence grew in spite of the deeply entrenched status of the nation-state as the ultimate arbiter of 'international order', he argues that 'the information revolution has led to a dramatic increase in scale in recent years, with the number of NGOs increasing from 6,000 to approximate 26,000 during the 1990s alone.'[14] Corporate branding over time, well-placed citizens, hardcore devotees of causes of conscience, all provide sources of soft power that can penetrate sovereign borders or transcend them at will via electronic channels. Nye was particularly concerned that America's chief non-state enemy in the 2000s, al Qaeda, was proving to be more adept than both the US State Department and the US military in attracting both Muslim and non-Muslim populations to their respective causes. With very little effort, Osama bin Laden was acquiring the aura of a 'Robin Hood' across vast numbers of the economically depressed populations of the Islamic world, from Africa to Pakistan.[15] Nye consigned his treatment of non-state soft power to just eight pages of his book *Soft Power: the means to success in world politics*, and left a suggestion at the end of it that al Qaeda's soft power was best tackled by calling on moderate non-state actors to

[14] Nye (n 7) 90.
[15] ibid 97.

support an 'Abrahamic dialogue among Muslims, Christians and Jews' and hopefully 'create bridges of understanding'.[16] By framing his most recent reflections on non-state soft power in this way, Nye was following up on his collaborative work with Robert Keohane some three decades earlier on the attitudinal changes that could be brought about by the very existence of transnational interactions between citizens of different states, with or without the approval of their sovereign governments.[17]

My conceptualisation of the global information space as 'a product of late twentieth-century technology, economics and politics, which cumulatively produce multilevel globe-extensive space for ideational political struggle' responds to the need to conceptualise more accurately the terrain on which non-state soft power operates.[18] It is a terrain of 'hearts and minds', to use a stock phrase from the practice of propaganda. I defined that global information space as one that 'is constituted primarily by practices (rather than physical geography), and the exchange of symbolic designs (eg ideologies, reports, opinions) preceding action', hence within that space 'discursive power matters in the way it is used by parties engaged in political struggle to react to and construct the parameters of definable social order favouring their particularistic existence.'[19] This is effectively a polycentric space open to all who have a point of view and the capability for expressing it through a personalised electronic access to the Internet and satellite television. This communication commons carries with it the implication that the many views expressed will definitely be hotly contested by their rivals. It can be said that on the plane of discursive rivalry, nation-states and non-state actors are on the same playing field. This playing field cannot be described as an international stage privileging nation-states as *primus inter pares*. It has been transformed by the processes of globalisation into the arena of polycentric global politics.

15.5 THE SOFT POWER OF PUBLICISING UNETHICAL PRACTICES

Scholars of both Political Science and International Relations have grappled with ethical issues in international society from a position of weakness. The bounded political and constitutional natures of nation-states have ensured that every sovereignty can claim unto itself a territorial insulation against the moral authority of supranational organisations, other sovereignties and non-state others.[20] It is in this sense that ethical issues

[16] JS Nye and RO Keohane, 'An Introduction' in Nye JS and Keohane RO (eds), *Transnational relations and world* (Cambridge MA, Harvard University Press, 1971) 97.
[17] ibid xvii.
[18] Chong (n 1) 37.
[19] ibid 37.
[20] Charles R Beitz, *Political theory and international relations* (Cambridge, Cambridge University Press, 1979).

are often marginalised in the daily routines of diplomatic intercourse and treated at the margins of most schools of international relations thought. Yet, the international legal legacies of putting entire sovereignties on trial for both their domestic and international conduct during the First and Second World Wars have set a precedent for the 'intrusion' of moral issues onto the international stage. Moreover, most international legal scholars and liberals have attributed the genocides in former-Yugoslavia, following the retreat of neo-Stalinist communism across Central and Eastern Europe in the early 1990s, as a highly regrettable recurrence of barbarism in international society. Farther away from the television cameras and eyewitness accounts of battlefield inhumanity, there also exists a plethora of harms perpetrated directly and indirectly by sovereign states and non-state actors in the name of economic efficiency: environmental harms; the suppression of labour rights in the name of profit motivation; predatory behaviour by sovereign authorities against their own citizens' human rights; and the neglect of the welfare needs of minorities. All these hitherto invisible harms have been rendered visible through non-state campaigning.

Geoff Gordon and Roland Pierik have suggested that non-state actors could be comprehended from the theoretical angle of having their missions informed by liberal political philosophy. As vehicles of 'figures engaging the public sphere in their private capacity', non-state actors fulfil crucial parts of the prescriptions of John Locke, David Hume and Immanuel Kant with respect to the working of democratic and representative political systems.[21] The basic premise of all three lies in their belief that the individual can and must check the prerogatives of government, insofar as the latter enact arbitrary decisions that go against the spirit of public reasoning and democratic mandate. Gordon and Pierik also draw lessons from Jürgen Habermas's genealogical work on the emergence of democratic civil society in Western Europe during the eighteenth and the nineteenth centuries, namely that it is the non-state actor that disseminates the democratic spirit and prods governments into the democratisation of policy-making. Taking this trajectory forward, one ought not to be dismissive of the non-state actor in furthering John Rawls's *Theory of Justice* among and beyond the nation-state in a globalising world. Other cosmopolitans inspired by Rawlsian ideas, such as Thomas Pogge and Richard Falk, suggest implicitly a role for non-state actors to mediate the widening chasm between what developed nation-states practice in sustaining their affluent lifestyles through international trade, finance and aid policies,

[21] Geoff Gordon and Roland Pierik, 'Liberal Political Philosophy: The Role of Non-State Actors and Considerations of Global Justice' in Bob Reinalda (ed), *The Ashgate research companion to non-state actors* (Farnham, Ashgate, 2010) 133.

and the neglect of supporting thorough socio-economic restructuring of impoverished peoples in the non-west.

In these dual senses, through serving as the sentinel of publicity against humanitarian abuses, and in caring for the transnational downtrodden sectors of the world's population, non-state actors actualise the communitarian bases of their actions. In this regard, one can appraise Margaret Keck and Kathryn Sikkink's book *Activists Beyond Borders: Advocacy Networks in International Politics* as a major work explaining the moralising behaviour of non-state actors.[22] The idea of advocacy for morally guided behaviour by individuals in positions of authority, entire government bureaucracies, military and police forces, as well as multinational corporations, is necessarily domestic and global in strategic terms. This list of targets for non-state actors comprises, first, the bureaucratic exercisers of sovereignty, or governments in short, and their constitutional and political monopoly of violence; and secondly, multinational corporations that represent the hierarchical commanding heights of the global capitalist economy. All these targets possess formal structured power under their direct control, whether in the form of guns, truncheons, imprisonment and the writ of law, or in the case of corporate power, control over the supply of industrial and consumer goods, incomes, liquid investments and raw materials. Non-state actors surmount these constraints by pooling human resources across borders in lobbying governments and other civil society groups into transforming their mindsets towards a specific set of goals. Leaving aside the violent strategies of transnational terrorist groups, the conscience-driven NGOs amplify their soft power of peaceful persuasion by making 'international resources available to new actors in domestic political and social struggles' and 'blurring the boundaries between a state's relations with its own nationals [i.e. state-society relations] and the recourse both citizens and states have to the international system'.[23] Keck and Sikkink label these forms of non-state strategy advocacy networks. Networks are 'forms of organization characterized by voluntary, reciprocal, and horizontal patterns of communication and exchange'.[24] Hence advocacy networks exist to 'plead the causes of others or defend a cause or proposition.[25] These causes and propositions cannot be reduced to rational notions of 'interests' in the way governments and corporations perceive them for policy-making, NGOs would rather promote causes and propositions as principled ideas and norms. Therefore, NGOs tend to behave as political entrepreneurs and friendly contacts taking it upon themselves,

[22] ME Keck and K Sikkink, *Activists beyond borders: advocacy networks in international politics* (Ithaca NY, Cornell University Press, 1998).
[23] ibid 1.
[24] ibid 8.
[25] ibid 8.

first, to practise 'information and symbolic politics' to disseminate awareness of just and unjust actions and attitudes; secondly, to invoke 'leverage politics' by calling upon the more powerful actors in their campaign to compensate for the shortfall in influence by their weaker members; and thirdly, to practise 'accountability politics' as an effort to measure powerful sovereign and corporate actors to the latter's own publicly declared principles or benchmarks.[26] Other scholarship also tends to describe such exercises of moral soft power by NGOs as 'moral entrepreneurship' or 'transnational social experience' arising from contact between persons of differing value environments.[27]

There are plenty of case studies accumulated over some three decades of scholarship that attest to the enduring pattern of NGO moral soft power exercised through mostly interpersonal contact. Keck and Sikkink have documented in a chapter the significant influences of prominent 'abolitionists' on both sides of the Atlantic in the anti-slavery movement. These included William Wilberforce, a member of the British Parliament in the early 1800s, and John Quincy Adams, who acted as the American equivalent of a prominent advocate sitting in Congress in the 1830s; in addition, Harriet Beecher Stowe published the well-known literary classic *Uncle Tom's Cabin* which awakened the collective social conscience in 1852.[28] Of equal importance was the case of the twin movements, the Mothers and Grandmothers of Plaza Mayor of Argentina, who established themselves through the grassroots initiative of the mothers and grandmothers of victims 'disappeared' by the military junta that ruled Argentina from 1976 to 1983.[29] These groups predated the Occupy Wall Street movement of 2011–12 in deliberately monopolising public spaces within town squares to continuously organise banners, exhibits and voices to denounce human rights abuses and call for accountability for the 'disappeared'. In these ways, such local advocacy groups attracted the attention of Amnesty International, Human Rights Watch, the American Association for the Advancement of Science, and other foreign NGOs to their cause. A parallel movement sprung up in neighbouring Chile when General Augusto Pinochet and his junta seized power in 1973 by assassinating an elected socialist president, triggering a networked Chilean diaspora of anti-regime opponents working closely with Amnesty International, Human Rights Watch, and the International Council of Jurists to meticulously

[26] ibid 16.

[27] Donald P Warwick, 'Transnational Participation and International Peace' in Joseph S Nye and Robert O Keohane (eds), *Transnational relations and world* (Cambridge MA, Harvard University Press, 1971); Ariel Colonomos, 'Non-State Actors as Moral Entrepreneurs: a Transnational Perspective on Ethics Networks' in Daphne Josselin and William Wallace (eds), *Non-state actors in world politics* (Basingstoke, Palgrave, 2001).

[28] Keck and Sikkink (n 22) 47.

[29] ibid 90–116.

document the Pinochet regime's abuses for a day of reckoning either in Chile or abroad in a court of law. This is a case that will be referred to also under the category of the soft power of legal manoeuvres. In both the Argentinean and Chilean cases, prosecutions were finally enabled under assorted international and national laws from the early 2000s, drawing heavily upon the evidence marshalled over three to four decades. This is consistent with many scholars' prognoses of soft power as an incremental instrument that culminates very slowly in a far-reaching outcome.[30] The same might be concluded of the Free South Africa Movement, based in the United States in the mid-1980s, which had evolved and shared images of injustice, from continuous domestic campaigns against comparable apartheid conditions in some southern states of the United States in the 1960s.[31] One might also add that the long-term campaign against nuclear energy plants by Greenpeace gained its strongest momentum only following the Japanese earthquake and nuclear plant disaster at Fukushima, in March 2011. The 2012 NGO campaign to reform labour conditions at Apple Computer's subcontracted assembly plants operated by Taiwan-based Foxconn in China has drawn the curtain on the complex, sustained campaigning needed to transform inhumane factory conditions. The labour exploitation stemmed from structural causes involving Chinese school culture in the city of Huai'an and Foxconn's goodwill offerings of internships to those students at its plant near the distant city of Zhengzhou. According to Li Qiang, the founder of China Labour Watch, an advocacy organisation and critic of Foxconn's labour practices,

> They [the students] said they are forced to work by their teachers … They don't want to work there—they want to learn. But if they don't work, they are told they will not graduate, because it is a very busy time with the new iPhone coming, and Foxconn does not have enough workers without the students.[32]

Practising cosmopolitan ethics requires NGOs to indict the moral rapaciousness of capitalism once more, some centuries after the anti-slavery movement first started. But there is a twist to this logic. Just like the remedial measures following the 2013 Rana Plaza garment factory collapse in Bangladesh, reining in multinational corporations and their Global South host companies on the enforcement of labour protections for shopfloor employees is proving to be an existential balancing act. The local garment manufacturers in Bangladesh urged global fashion brands not to

[30] Chong (n 1) and Nye (n 7).

[31] Evalyn W Tennant, 'Locating Transnational Activists: The United States Anti-Apartheid Movement and the Confines of the National' in Saskia Sassen (ed), *Deciphering the global: its scales, spaces and subjects* (Abingdon, Routledge, 2007).

[32] David Barboza and Charles Duhigg, 'Apple Supplier Criticized Over "Interns"', *International Herald Tribune* (12 September 2012) p 17.

abandon 14 million families that depended on their outsourcing plans.[33] In this regard, NGOs' ethical campaigns will increasingly be strung out on the proverbial horns of moral utilitarianism: which is the greater good—sustaining employment for the poorest populations or securing their workplace welfare to the point where it becomes uneconomical to hire them?[34]

15.6 THE SOFT POWER OF LEGAL MANOEUVRES

The realm of international law is closely allied to the mobilisation of moral considerations in humanising international politics. To understand non-state actors' soft power in this realm, it would behove us to consider the social progress of the observance of international law within the international society of states. International law, unlike domestic law, operates amongst abstract, large-scale entities known as sovereign states acknowledging in principle no higher authority than each of their individual 'selves'.[35] These collective selves are unlike individual human selves, in the sense that the former cannot be awed by a Leviathan-like government. Sovereign states may 'contract' themselves into international law, but observe their provisions only according to fleeting understandings of whether their respective national interests require them to honour international law. International law therefore exists and operates according to the default mode of 'constantly flexible adjustment', as Percy Corbett put it elegantly.[36] Moreover, Max Sorensen's study of the International Court of Justice noted that some sovereign states argue that they are reluctant to abide by the Court's decisions because of structural injustices built into it.[37] One major complaint is that the process of authoring the laws setting up the Court has been insufficiently consultative or democratically derived. Moreover, the vast majority of the UN's members were developing and small states and were admitted into the Court's 'jurisdiction' without due consideration of their particular needs. Finally, unequal power relations between great powers and small states bedevilled every prospect of internationally binding legal settlements.[38] Yet objective scholarly and policymakers' analyses may also argue that international law may, in the long

[33] Steven Greenhouse, 'Bangladesh urges brands not to leave', *International Herald Tribune* (4–5 May 2013) p 4.

[34] Stephanie Clifford and Steven Greenhouse, 'Noble goals prove elusive in factory inspections', *International Herald Tribune* (3 September 2013) pp 1 and 16.

[35] Percy Ellwood Corbett, *The study of international law*, vol 1 (Garden City NY, Doubleday, 1955) 46.

[36] ibid 46.

[37] Max Sorensen, 'The International Court of Justice: Its Role in Contemporary International Relations' (1960) 14(2) *International Organization* 261–76.

[38] ibid 272–74.

term, serve as a risk-sharing scheme navigating the uncertainties between war and peace among sovereignties. International law may also serve as a low-cost insurance policy against predatory behaviour by strong states against weak ones. International humanitarian law, erected in reaction against mass unconscionable acts such as the Holocaust, cruelties meted out against prisoners of war in both World Wars, or in reactions against the genocides of the 1990s, involve comparable considerations among sovereign states since they involve indicting public servants, soldiers acting under orders, and even sitting heads of state. In this atmosphere, where the principal subjects of the so-called 'public international law' are sovereign states who are ambivalent towards advancing international law, non-state actors, especially NGOs, can play catalytic and remedial roles in generating a culture of legal observance. This passage from Amnesty International's Operational Handbook states this best:

> National borders are no barrier to helping others … International human rights law is the code of conduct of governments around the world. AI [Amnesty International]'s demands spring from this body of law. AI can point to international standards adopted by the United Nations and it can say, 'Not only has your own government endorsed these rules—so has the whole world.' … Furthermore, international human rights law has an international application. It sets out that governments have promised to uphold certain rights not just for their own citizens, but also for people in other countries as well … Under the Charter of the United Nations, member states pledge to cooperate—internationally—to promote and encourage respect for human rights and fundamental freedoms for everyone … AI affirms fully the commitment of the United Nations to the shared protection of human rights. This is why AI does not accept the argument, used by some governments when they find it convenient, that questions of human rights are the business of the nation concerned, or that AI is 'interfering in the internal affairs of states'.[39]

Amnesty International, in tandem with Human Rights Watch, the International Council of Jurists, an intrepid Spanish prosecutor, Baltazar Garcon, and Chilean NGOs such as the Association of the Relatives of the Detained and Disappeared (AFDD), Corporation for the Promotion and Defence of the Rights of the People (CODEPU) and Chile Democrático, advanced international humanitarian law considerably through their landmark participation in the *Pinochet* case of 1998–2000. General Pinochet had eluded prosecution both at home and abroad since he 'peacefully' stepped down as the President of Chile in 1988, following unprecedented popular elections since he seized power in a military coup in 1973. Before

[39] Amnesty International, *Handbook* (New York, Amnesty International Publications, 1991) 11–12. The AI Handbook has been updated almost every few years since its first appearance in 1962 but its basic approach to the employment of international law has remained consistent.

leaving the presidency, he had engineered for himself a strategic position as the head of the Armed Forces, and subsequently the position of Senator for Life. These positions ensured that no political force at home could jeopardise his legacy and prosecute him and his political allies for human rights abuses committed during his regime from 1973 to 1988. Moreover, the governments in Washington DC and London had acquiesced in Pinochet's transition plans and lauded his assistance in protecting the Latin American southern cone states from communist penetration during the Cold War. The NGO coalition had not given up in the meantime. A series of lawsuits had been prepared based upon the painstaking work of documenting Pinochet's abuses over the 25-year tenure of his regime. By 1998, the end of the Cold War favoured a renewed emphasis on observing international humanitarian standards. The genocides in former Yugoslavia, Rwanda and Chad spurred tremendous NGO pressures upon western governments to act against abusers in positions of high authority. As a result, when Pinochet visited London in 1998 for the twin purposes of inspecting armaments for possible acquisition by Chile and for a chiropractic operation, the anti-Pinochet coalition of NGOs launched a series of lawsuits first from Spain, then on British soil, that kept Pinochet holed up in London as he battled lawsuits requesting his extradition to Madrid for trial for his abuses under the International Convention against Torture. Although the twists and turns of the case need not concern us here, the fact of the matter was that NGO lawsuits ensured that the various international human rights treaties against torture and genocide were given an airing in the British House of Lords, and a landmark precedent was set for trying former heads of state for crimes against their own citizens and other nationalities. Pinochet's guilt was confirmed in the course of the successful extradition hearings. Pinochet was only saved from extradition to Spain by the constitutional authority of the British Home Secretary, who exercised his discretion to avoid political entanglements with both the sovereign authorities in Santiago and Madrid.[40]

Nonetheless, the *Pinochet* case established a benchmark for subsequently trying Chadian president Hissene Habre, President Milosevic of Serbia, and more recently, in 2009, Sudan's sitting President Omar Hassan Ahmad Al-Bashir. Curiously, there were even outlandish attempts (which came to nought) to file third country lawsuits to try former US Secretary of State Henry Kissinger for complicity in Pinochet's abuses. Although Slobodan Milosevic died in the midst of legal proceedings at the International Tribunal for Former Yugoslavia (ICTY) at The Hague, the other two remain very much on the radar of prosecutorial efforts by NGOs in alliance with like-minded states. A check with Amnesty International's website shows

[40] Chong (n 1).

that attempts to drive international law forward in prosecuting human rights violators worldwide remain unrelenting in progress, regardless of sovereign resistance on many occasions.

15.7 THE SOFT POWER OF DEVELOPMENTAL AND GRASSROOTS DISASTER RELIEF

For most scholars and activists, the very existence of an NGO is bound up with its idealistic spirit of wanting to alleviate the material inequalities amongst the world's population. This inequality is rationalised as the root of the misery and shortened life expectancy of more than two-thirds of the world's population. Some of it is structural, in the sense that it emanates from discriminatory trade and industrial policies pursued by the developed economies, and some of it derives from short-sighted economic planning and corrupt behaviour by some Third World political elites. Just as frequently, material inequalities are triggered by large-scale natural calamities, such as droughts, earthquakes, tsunamis, abnormal rainfall volumes, tropical storms and cyclones. Calamities capable of producing mass human misery could also emerge as side-effects of man-made wars, fossil fuel consumption, nuclear energy production, or corrupt governing practices leading to food diversion and inefficient use of factors of production. Governments could be expected to ameliorate these crises with the full capabilities attendant upon their sovereign powers, but more frequently than not, governments demonstrate to their populations that they either constitute part of the developmental problem (such as corruption and the lack of rehearsed and specialist knowledge of coping with emergencies), manifest their culpability in man-made disasters, or compound the misery of a natural calamity through the shortage of resources and bureaucratic ineptitude. Therefore, many scholars and activists claim that it is the NGO that has historically served as the pioneer in delivering aid and reconstructing shattered homes and lives at the appropriate local scale in the territories of the Global South.[41]

From a Global South perspective, Moushumi Basu has identified three specific types of developmental aid that NGOs provide. First, there is relief in terms of the provision of durable consumer goods that mitigate the immediate suffering of victims suffering structural poverty or in the aftermath of a natural disaster: tents, blankets, tinned food and clean water etc. Secondly, there is reconstruction in terms of the repair of bridges, houses and restoration of water and electricity in the aftermath of a natural

[41] Barbara Rugendyke, 'Lilliputians or Leviathans? NGOs as Advocates' in Barbara Rugendyke (ed), *NGOs as advocates for development in a globalising world* (Abingdon, Routledge, 2007) 1–2.

disaster or war. Thirdly, there is development aid 'in the form of investable resources for specific programmes and projects as given out by Oxfam or CARE International.'[42] NGOs essentially prove themselves to be the proverbial noble fools who rush in to assist where the sovereign 'angels', that governments claim to be, fear to tread. For instance, in 2012, Oxfam's roles in Ghana ranged from helping rural female agricultural workers learn to process their harvested rice through more reliable methods, to training maternal care assistants in hospitals, to assisting rural farmers negotiate for compensation from the Ghana Manganese Company over the latter's plans to acquire farmland for gold mining.[43] In 2015, Oxfam also helped local farming communities facing similar circumstances in both Prei Preal Khor, Cambodia and the Char Islands in Bangladesh, to adapt and thrive in spite of capricious weather and general poverty.[44]

Other scholars have noted that the NGO is increasingly broadening into practising 'humanitarian government' and developmental advocacy patterned after interest groups on a national level. The concept of humanitarian government has been defined by French sociologist Didier Fassin as 'the administration of human collectivities in the name of a higher moral principle that sees the preservation of life and the alleviation of suffering as the highest value of action.'[45] This definition is not necessarily exclusive to NGOs, or governments, it could well encompass NGO-government partnerships, where conditions permit.[46] The point about humanitarian government as an operating principle is that nation-state driven power politics is set aside amidst the urgency of saving human lives and averting greater calamities to humanity. Fassin takes that view that the operational precedent for humanitarian government began with the work of the International Committee of the Red Cross (ICRC). This was subsequently diversified in the 1970s when other humanitarian NGOs such as Médecins Sans Frontières (MSF) and[47] Médecins du Monde (MDM), along with Oxfam, Christian Aid and others like it, began to provide relief aid where the ICRC once enjoyed a monopoly at the behest of governments. At some point, the NGOs would even hazard assuming, albeit temporarily,

[42] Moushumi Basu, 'Non-State Actors in the Development Aid World as Seen from the South' in Bob Reinalda (ed), *The Ashgate Research Companion to Non-State Actors* (Surrey, Ashgate Publishing, 2011) 407.

[43] Oxfam, 'Snapshot of Oxfam in Ghana. 2012': www.oxfam.org.uk/what-we-do/countries-we-work-in/ghana (accessed October 7, 2012).

[44] Oxfam, 'How Oxfam is helping communities adapt and thrive': www.oxfam.org.uk/get-involved/campaign-with-us/our-campaigns/food-and-climate (accessed 24 April 2015).

[45] Didier Fassin, 'A Spontaneous Caravan of Relief' in Michel Feher (ed), *Nongovernmental politics* (New York, Zone Books, 2007) 151.

[46] Kendall W Stiles, 'States, Non-State Actors and Global Policy Formulation' in Richard A Higgott, Geoffrey RD Underhill and Andreas Bieler (eds), *Non-State Actors and Authority in the Global System* (Abingdon, Routledge, 2000).

[47] Fassin (n 45) 149–55.

governing functions for the purpose of delivering relief, reconstruction and developmental aid. All these aid and governing functions overlap as realities unfold on any pocket of disaster ground and call for philanthropic initiative and charity in emergency mode. These actions may well prove sovereign authorities inept in the eyes of both their own citizens as well as world opinion. Understandably, the space that humanitarian government occupies is likely to prove highly contested on the ground, such as in the cases of Lebanon, Congo and Pakistan, where aid workers were often confronted and intimidated by soldiers and local militias who had calculated that a show of force might well induce the NGOs to submit to their Machiavellian political manoeuvres to acquire political capital upon the return to normalcy.

Nonetheless, spontaneous grassroots NGO work is thriving even in some authoritarian contexts where government relief agencies are stunned by the scale of the humanitarian tragedy. For instance, in August 2012, following a double earthquake that struck northern Iran, a group of young Iranians in their twenties and thirties, mostly a mixture of hip socialites, private motor club members and children of affluent families, took the initiative to organise a charity effort via Facebook, text messaging and old-fashioned telephone campaigns. They were angered, like so many ordinary Iranians, that the official relief agencies were slow in responding to the scale of the tragedy.[48] Overseas relief efforts donated huge amounts of money but official agencies scandalously channelled the funds 'into the wrong pockets'. There was no better alternative than to organise a citizens' convoy to buy necessities with the money collected and to personally hand deliver the relief materiel to the victims directly, despite the physical hardships involved. The *New York Times* journalist Thomas Erdbrink reported it thus:

> Pouria said he felt pride for his age group, often referred to as the 'burnt generation', because they have few opportunities and are faced with international sanctions on Iran and the increasingly strict rules imposed by the state. 'By organizing our own aid convoy, we showed that we can manage ourselves', he said. 'We don't need others to tell us what to do.'[49]

This anecdote, along with countless other examples of post-disaster grassroots 'crowdsourcing' initiatives in southern Russia, the central Philippines and in the suburbs of New Orleans in recent years, attest to the fact that individual pride projected through collective exercises in goodwill serves as a veritable form of NGO developmental soft power that acts independently to supplement state-led efforts.

[48] Thomas Erdbrink, 'A Spontaneous Caravan of Relief', *International Herald Tribune* (22 August 2012) p 2.

[49] ibid.

NGO advocacy, in the early twenty-first century, has emerged in a distinct developmental role on its own. Advocacy for sovereign attention and transnational civil society involvement is sometimes the more potent aid lever than helping out on the ground might be. Oxfam, for instance, appeals for campaigners to join its staff through this mission description: 'As campaigners, we stand with people who struggle to be heard. When we all speak with one determined voice, it sends a powerful message that people in power can't ignore.'[50] For instance, on its website in 2012, Oxfam was urging its friends and staff to stop land grabs in the developing economies by calling on the World Bank to freeze loans for land deals that leave people living on those lands homeless and hungry.[51] This publicity-driven action is significant since land grabs are particularly notorious for their invisibility in the way Global South states ruthlessly prepare the ground for spectacular projects that ironically become showcases of 'successful development'. For a number of years afterward, Oxfam's website lauded attempts by the band Coldplay, the Coca Cola company and young citizen journalists to up the ante against land grabs in many Global South contexts. Oxfam also called on all its volunteers to monitor the British government's pledge to generously aid some of the world's most heavily indebted states and to highlight omissions in that regard. The G8 summit was also reminded by Oxfam volunteers to honour their pledges to reduce income inequality in the developing world. In this light, some scholars argue that advocacy work beneficially transforms NGOs into actors on a par with national interest groups: they can enjoy direct access to policymakers in exchange for supplying the latter with information to make their agendas and positions heard and advanced; they can establish long-term relationships with parliamentarians and civil servants as part of their campaign; and NGOs can attain organisational efficiency and financial leanness when they compete with all other interest groups for prioritising the attention of sovereign authorities at home and abroad.[52] Ultimately, even NGO advocacy for developmental causes is faithful to the spirit of non-state soft power as a projection of ideal transnational community.

15.8 CONCLUSION: NON-STATE ACTOR SOFT POWER, ITS FOIBLES, AND ACTING IN SPITE OF THE NATION-STATE

Non-state soft power is inherently linked to projecting community. It is ideally a community showcasing the best of humanity. In this regard, the

[50] Oxfam, 'Campaign with Us. October 2012': www.oxfam.org.uk/get-involved/campaign-with-us (accessed October 8, 2012).

[51] ibid.

[52] Elizabeth A Bloodgood, 'The interest group analogy: international non-governmental advocacy organisations in international politics' (2011) 37 *Review of International Studies* 93.

entire paradigm of non-state operation ought to exhibit the ideal of good governance. The above three dimensions of non-state soft power demonstrate an exemplary concern with promoting ethics across all borders in the spirit of global governance. Closely associated with this is the campaign for the advancement of international law through holding sovereign nation-states to the higher standards of civilised behaviour that care for humanity and the sanctity of life. This extends easily into the NGO missions in development aid and humanitarian relief. Non-state actors, by the very nature of their existence, fill the lacunae ignored by national governments and intergovernmental organisations.

Having articulated the ways and means of non-state soft power, one must also acknowledge that all organisations, including those oriented towards noble missions, may also suffer from organisational drift, occasional corruption and interference from politicisation by other non-state actors and sovereign authorities. There *should* be efficiency, professional attention, the spirit of sincere care towards one's target wards, along with organisational accountability.[53] Although it has been widely argued that non-state actors enjoy the benefits of organisational efficiency without having to satisfy the friction-laden processes of having to stand for national elections on a regular basis and consulting public opinion for a stronger mandate on key issues, similar arguments may occasionally be turned against them. Non-state actors cannot be construed to enjoy democratic legitimacy of the form that most governments try to base their decision-making authority on. Non-state actors can only claim a democratic aura insofar as they represent marginalised voices at all levels of global society and promote visions of inclusive and equitable future social orders that politicians cannot contemplate within the horizons of their constitutional mandates. Like all political entities captained by human agents, non-state actors are also vulnerable to the usual range of political vices spanning corruption, arrogance of power, financial dependence upon funders and overstretch of resources.[54]

Ultimately, non-state actors derive their most potent appeal through the power of example and the proverbial 'helping hand'. After all, their action orientation is towards a humane global society. Physical violence is to be shunned as far as possible, since it contaminates the vision of the good world order. Non-state actors oriented wholly towards acts of terrorism, sabotage and armed confrontation with nation-states are a clear minority in the coverage of this chapter. This is necessarily so, since the era of Cold War revolutionary upheaval sponsored by Marxist parties is behind us,

[53] William F Fisher, 'DOING GOOD? The Politics and Antipolitics of NGO Practices' (1997) 26 *Annual Review of Anthropology* 439–64.
[54] ibid 454–58.

and al Qaeda and its ilk seem to have lost their command of the political terrain in the Middle East due to the interruption of the nationally based Arab Spring movements for political change. Although in 2015, the resurrection of al Qaeda's ferocity has manifested in the violent insurrection of ISIS (The Islamic State of Iraq and Syria) in the borderlands of Iraq, Syria and in Libya, their repeated production of videos of beheading their prisoners and other massacres of non-Muslims and 'enemy' Arab combatants have galvanised an armed international coalition comprising the United States, the EU and conservative Arab governments against them. ISIS claims to have set up pockets of a functioning state in Syria and Iraq, but these are likely to be tenuous given the intensity of coalition military operations against their fighters. The problem with the repeated use of physical violence lies in its disproportionate costs to innocent third parties caught up in the conflict, as well as the long-term damage to one's cause in both field support and advocacy in 'peacetime'. Amnesty International, Oxfam and Greenpeace sponsor visions of sustainable humane globalisation, and physical violence undercuts all that they stand for. Symbolic violence is, on the other hand, a legitimate instrument to further humane causes: shaming by naming, staging street demonstrations, web-based campaigning and public speeches by NGO leaders. These are tantamount to being the sermons of a global-scale religion marked by a consciousness of common humanity living on a common planet marked by sociocultural diversities that require democratic respect.

16

Non-State Actors and Globalisation: A Paradigm for a Decentred World?

BARRIE AXFORD

16.1 INTRODUCTION

ONE OF THE key issues for globalisation theory has always been how to transcend methodological nationalism without completely jettisoning the state as a crucial part of the ontology of a globalised world. More prosaically, this involves interrogating its changing role as an instrument of government, a player in complex networks of governance, a focus for allegiance and the frame for defining and delimiting society. State centrism, in whatever form, still bedevils much globalisation theory, but breaking out of that mould is not easy. Nor should the baby be thrown out with the bath water, because states remain crucial to international order and to the conduct of international law; as well as to any science of how these subsist. Yet the idea of global governance leads us to acknowledge the existence of, or potential for, novel versions of governmentality. Even when used purely descriptively, the idea of global governance embraces all actors that order some common aspects of world affairs without state control, or, more accurately, without direct and routine control.

Perhaps more significantly, and certainly more contentiously, global governance is also a normative concept, both in terms of the implied prescription to transcend, if not to abrogate, sovereign power, and because it invests in a world order built around the idea of universals. Less demanding is the claim that the challenges of a globalised world are spawning new forms of non-state and/or beyond-state governance, delivered through a catholic array of sub-state and non-state actors. Inevitably there is a good deal of categorical imprecision and debate about what actors to include under the rubric 'non-state'. And in some ways, caution is appropriate, since the more inclusive the definition, the more untameable the category becomes. At one remove the realm of non-state actors includes those who are (mainly) adjuncts to the business of state-centred governance, or whose actions simply smoothe out tensions in the liberal international order of states. Thus international governmental organisations (IGOs) muster as brokers of national policy differences; while international non-governmental organisations (INGOs) and non-governmental organisations (NGOs) rehearse the politics of insiders and outsiders in their dealings with each other and with various governmental and intergovernmental agencies.[1] Even this modest appraisal might still constitute a 'denationalisation' of governance functions, contributing to the emergence of a multi-layered, multi-scalar regulatory ensemble, much less trammelled by boundaries and jurisdictions than past wisdom—and certainly varieties of realist theory—allowed.[2]

At another remove we begin to shuffle towards the wilder shores of both political theory and practice; albeit crabwise. A denationalised model of governmentality is hardly nation state-centred, but comprises a 'dispersed collection of identities' including states, inter- and supra-national organisations, transnational and proto-global firms, NGOs and INGOs, professional associations, more-or-less formal voluntary associations, as well as individuals.[3] In this model, state sovereignty is not abrogated entirely, but it is increasingly difficult to correlate strongly what is taking place with the nation-state. Whether in security arrangements, aspects of criminal law and policing, or the rules governing trade, there is seldom a single 'locus of coordination'.[4] Rather—and here we do begin to intimate more radical positions about the impact of globalisation and emergent globalities—this kind of governance regime tends to govern at a distance, through 'flexible, fluctuating networks that transcend structured institutional sites'.[5] In some instances, networks have achieved what John Ruggie calls 'genuine political activity at the global level *apart* from the system of states'.[6]

16.2 EXEMPLIFYING 'NEW' GEOGRAPHIES OF GOVERNANCE

Radical or not, there is still a bloodless quality about these images of the new geographies of governance. But in Arjun Appadurai's critique of Huntington's jeremiad on the prospects for civilisational conflict,

[1] John Boli and George M Thomas (eds), *Constructing World Culture* (Stanford CA, Stanford University Press, 1999); Rhiannon Morgan, *Transforming Law and Institution: Indigenous Peoples, the United Nations and Human Rights* (Farnham, Ashgate Publishing, 2013).

[2] Saskia Sassen, *Sociology of Globalization* (New York, WW Norton, 2006).

[3] Nancy Fraser, 'From discipline to flexibilization? Rereading Foucault in the shadow of globalization' (2003) 10 *Constellations* 160, 168.

[4] ibid, 167.

[5] ibid; Iver B Neumann and Ole Jacob Sending, *Governing the Global Polity: Practice, Mentality, Rationality* (Chicago IL, University of Michigan Press, 2010).

[6] John Gerard Ruggie, 'Reconstituting the global public domain—issues, actors, and practices' (2004) 10 *European Journal of International Relations* 4995.

non-state protagonists are much more visceral and oppositional in their demeanour and intent. States and states in concert vie with new forms of connection, solidarity and organisation to shape their own destiny and that of others.[7] Examples of non-state actors that are both oppositional and display network ontologies abound. In his survey of violent non-state-actors (NSAs), Phil Williams opines that they 'have become a pervasive challenge to nation-states'.[8] The variety of these entities is as striking as their recent proliferation. They encompass purely local manifestations (ie, within the territorial state), such as occur in the favelas of Rio de Janeiro and Sao Paulo, where drug traffickers and, more recently, militias provide rudimentary forms of governance in urban areas where the state is weak or absent, along with cross-national networks of jihadists in the Middle East region.[9] Of the latter, Karin Knorr-Cetina says that they have avoided institutional complexity but retained or achieved a degree of purpose and identity that goes beyond solidarity and borders on the spiritual.[10] Economic globalisation too entails a set of practices that, in markets and some epistemic communities, discommodes those rules constituting and sustaining the nation-state. The rhetoric, perhaps the logic, of hyper-globalist and neo-liberal theory underpins some such arguments. Thus forms of 'illicit' globalisation in the shape of criminal gangs and some kinds of piracy offer a pathological version of neo-liberal globalisation, where, increasingly, markets or proto-markets not only operate regardless of national jurisdictions, but in direct contravention of the rules governing international trade, finance and movement of people.[11] They practise a brand of extra-territoriality or trans-territoriality that is as corrosive of the traditional territorial underpinnings of legal jurisdiction as the more direct and obvious transgressions of state sovereignty and norm-making authority seen in martial interventions in states by IGOs and third-party states.

While this is intuitively obvious, it is still a very general claim. Moreover, it is one that lends itself too easily to the sterile debate over whether states are in demise as a result of globalisation and cognate processes in the guise of regionalisation and advanced multilateralism. The more nuanced and

[7] Arjun Appadurai, *Fear of Small Numbers: An Essay on The Geography of Anger* (Durham NC, Duke University Press, 2006); Samuel P Huntington, *The Clash of Civilizations and the Remaking of World Order* (Dehli, Penguin Books India, 1996).

[8] Phil Williams, *Violent Non-State Actors and National and International Security* (Washington DC, International Relations and Security Network, 2008) 1.

[9] ibid, 1.

[10] Karin Knorr-Cetina, 'Microglobalization' in Ino Rossi (ed), *Frontiers of Globalization Research: Theoretical and Methodological Approaches* (New York, Springer, 2007); Manfred Steger, 'Globalism' in Roland Robertson and Jan Aart Scholte (eds), *Encyclopedia of Globalization* (New York, Routledge, 2007).

[11] Peter Andreas, 'Illicit globalization: myths, misconceptions, and historical lessons' (2011) 126 *Political Science Quarterly* 403.

empirically retrievable question is the extent to which NSAs have assumed or can achieve rule-making and norm-producing status, and how far this modifies or even nullifies the competence of territorial states, providing new sources of international law and new kinds of subjects for it.

Insights into the inter-relationships between states and NSAs that produce networks of global governance and even forms of systemic global alterity (for example, a cosmopolitan world order or jihadist globality) remain allusive or incompletely developed; which may enhance their plausibility, but certainly raises questions about the robustness of the empirical research underlying the claims. At the same time, network approaches to understanding the problems of governance and organisational change, as well as fuzzier notions such as global society, are widely bruited. Linked to the theme of democratising world politics through the trope of 'global civil society', network interaction bears directly on the changing nature of governance, politics and sociality in the millennial period of globalisation. Against the still relatively stable configuration of the state and the (liberal) international order of states, network models of global governance and sociality look decidedly volatile. Obviously, they speak to a powerfully transformationalist strain in global theory involving an array of non-state actors.

These observations resonate within and across those disciplines exercised by the nature and quality of governance and the ontologies of the global. Whether or not you admit globalisation as a new paradigm, a game-changer in how to describe and understand world (dis)order, it is clear that the role of non-state actors is integral to any such constitution. Indeed, unless one remains a diehard realist—in which case any study of non-state actors is a mere gloss on the received ontology of international politics with its logic of anarchy—then non-state actors are avatars of a more complex and fluid structuration and perhaps a mixed constitution. A new ontology, as Arjun Appadurai opines, is emerging from the confrontation between, but also the intersection of, two different world geographies. He names these as the 'vertebrate' and the 'cellular' geographies of the world post-9/11.[12] Both systems are global in scope.

The vertebrate system is predicated on generalised norms of conduct, conjoint institutions such as the United Nations and, of course, the international system of states and discrete sovereignties. The cellular system embraces 'disorganised' virtual capitalism, terrorist networks and emergent, sometimes utopian forms of grassroots networking across borders.[13] Cellular forms demonstrate key features of network morphology—being connected but not vertically managed, coordinated yet independent, and

[12] Appadurai (n 7).
[13] ibid, 25.

hazy as regards organisational features. But it is it not necessary, as Saskia Sassen tells us, for such actors simply to 'confront' states or the vertebrate order of states and IGOs for their existence to be very discommoding for usual politics.[14] Indeed, great potential resides in the routine encounters between vertebrate and cellular systems to 'transform the morphology of global economy and politics'.[15] And to complicate matters further, many spatial-temporal forms and orders do not fit neatly into either of Appadurai's categories. For example, global firms and markets 'display a split or mixed personality that resembles and relies on the vertebrate features of the nation-state system, but is also the laboratory for new forms of cellularity, de-linkage and local autonomy'.[16] To accommodate observed overlaps between actors and systems, in what follows I also refer to an in-between or mixed global system.

Appadurai is particularly exercised by recent manifestation of new 'geographies of anger' in the guise of fundamentalist and terrorist networks. But Sassen's less visceral take on a more catholic range of NSAs as networks is that they constitute 'new geographies of power'. The emergence of new geographies as elemental features of globalisation processes is transforming the modern doctrine and practices of state sovereignty, because globalisation brings about new spatial and cultural economies beyond the regulatory capacity of any one state.[17] Taken in the round, they are part of the new sociological realities of a globalised world.

From the perspective of globalisation scholarship, competing/intersecting, geographies offer real insights into the extension of social relations across world space, while still letting us consider and reconsider the obdurate, though changing, nature of existing modalities, most obviously the state and the state system. Using NSAs as the focus of inquiry affords a rich empirical basis for investigating these complex topologies. So, the rest of this chapter is framed by the tensions and intersections between the global vertebrate, mixed and cellular systems and will examine the degree to which different ecologies of NSA behaviour underwrite or transform those systems. This approach allows us to identify either continuity in matters of governance and political engagement, or reveals at least embryonic new worlds. Building on Appadurai's schema for categorical purposes, I distinguish between vertebrate, mixed/in-between and cellular systems, and between the demeanour of NSAs as underwriters of the vertebrate system, as agonistic, but not necessarily antithetical to that system, and as transformative in intent, if not always in effect. Clearly there are problems

[14] Saskia Sassen, *Territory, Authority, Rights: From Medieval to Global Assemblages* (Princeton NJ, Princeton University Press, 2006).

[15] Appadurai (n 7) 29.

[16] ibid, 28.

[17] ibid.

in locating some actors in one category rather than another. It may be the case that too glib, or too inclusive, a reading of the transformative impact of, for example, networked entities wrongly conflates actors with quite different ontologies and normative goals simply on the basis that they all display network features seen as discommoding to the vertebrate order.

I will exemplify the categorisation by reference to the classificatory scheme set out above. This task will involve canvassing the demeanour of NSAs as underwriting usual politics, as agonistic—albeit not necessarily anti-systemic—and as transformative—or potentially so—in relation to the three kinds of global system identified. As I cannot hope to canvass the full NSA universe, my address is illustrative only and my examples do not extend to in-depth case studies. To begin, I want to talk about the concept of globalisation and how NSAs inform that concept.

16.3 GLOBALISATION AS A TRANSFORMATIVE MOTIF

Globalisation as a concept entails two key processes that are sometimes, although not always, related. These processes are interconnectivity and institutionalisation. There is also the matter of consciousness—the awareness by actors of global constraints, along with their variable propensity to 'identify with' the global condition.[18] In all such accounts globalisation appears as a form of intensified and increasingly extensive exchange, and/or a process involving the diffusion of worldwide institutional rules and standards or cultural scripts. Much of the discussion of globalisation has concentrated upon connection and exchange, both said to deliver powerful integrative dynamics. Indeed, the very idea of globalisation presumes integration, and this motif is especially visible in so-called hyperglobalist accounts and in some of those conveniently summarised as transformationalist.[19] Sceptical opinion remains doubtful about the world-integrative power of globalising forces, even in the economic realm,[20] and since the financial and trading crisis of 2008 there has been much talk of de-globalisation, as global capitalism continues to be assailed by economic misfortunes. At the same time, or as a corollary, states have been resuscitated as the defenders of national integrity in areas such as immigration control, food and energy safety and welfare provision, thus contributing

[18] Roland Robertson, *Globalization: Social Theory and Global Culture*, vol 16 (London, Sage, 1992); Barrie Axford, 'Global civil society or "networked globality": beyond the territorialist and societalist paradigm' (2004) 1 *Globalizations* 249.

[19] See D Held, *Global Transformations: Politics, Economics and Culture* (Stanford CA, Stanford University Press, 1999).

[20] Paul Q Hirst et al, *Globalization in Question* (Cambridge, Polity Press, 2009).

to a more profound securitisation and, for some observers, a seeming re-territorialisation of many aspects of everyday life and governance.

But these days, no one takes too seriously the idea that the processes of global integration constitute a neat teleology whereby borders and the identities tied to them have become nugatory and territoriality as the organisational basis for much political and economic life is in demise. At the same time, students of globalisation still have trouble with the intuitively implausible notion that it is a contradictory process, one that does not even imply, let alone require, 'uniformisation', in Francois Bayart's clumsy, but very expressive coining.[21] The balance of research findings tends to the counter-intuitive and vaguely unsatisfactory conclusion that globalisation implies and delivers the simultaneous production of sameness and difference.[22] In other words, globalisation comprises elements of the vertebrate and cellular systems referred to above and, insofar as these features may be taken to express an immanent tension in the nature and direction of change in the global system, what they reveal is its contested and contradictory ontology.

In truth, NSAs stand as avatars of different kinds of globalisation, presenting different constellations of the relationships between infrastructural power (states and national societies) and global process.[23] In some constellations sovereign power is attenuated, in others global and national networks of interaction are mutually constituted and not parasitic on each other or competing for the same interaction space. Because of all this, we should be cautious about claiming irrevocable changes in the character of global governance and politics. Most accounts of international society and some versions of emergent globality still cleave to highly ascetic models of governance beyond the state, rooted in multilateral institutions and reliant on cooperation between states and a tranche of more-or-less incorporated interests. In this scenario, third sector bodies and (transnational) social movements either rehearse the usual politics of interest mediation, though some, as noted earlier, provide increasingly convincing evidence of potent activity at the global level not predicated on and, in some cases, not even reliant on the existence of states.

There are also less modest claims. As a trope for a global system, Michael Hardt and Antonio Negri's postmodern cultural and political economy of *Empire* reduces globalisation to an elemental struggle between NSAs in the guise of networked corporations and networked protestors/global

[21] Jean-François Bayart, *Global Subjects: A Political Critique of Globalization* (Cambridge, Polity Press, 2007).

[22] Barrie Axford, 'Editorial to the special issue on Borders and Networks in the Global System' (2007) 4 *Globalizations*.

[23] Michael Mann, 'Has globalization ended the rise and rise of the nation-state?' (1997) 4 *Review of International Political Economy* 472.

citizens. The real analytical, though also polemical, charge claimed for the idea of *Multitude* in their work is that it is not prefigured in any social theory or in line of descent from earlier kinds of political mediation.[24]

The gamut of categorical and analytical positions on whether or how studying NSAs helps us understand processes of globalisation and emergent globalities is revealed in the journey from Barry Buzan's nuanced, but still quite modest theoretical framework that addresses globalisation as a complex political interplay among state and non-state actors (2004).[25] In his work this interplay reveals two forms of logic at work. The first, pluralist logic, comprises the international system of states, sovereignty, territory, nationalism and even great power politics. The second, or solidaristic logic, is much less ordered, displaying elements of transnationalism, global markets and universalistic values. Much like Appadurai's two systems the two logics coexist in the contemporary world. Moving on, we have John Ruggie's grounded attempts to keep pace with 'actual practices' in world politics, where these refer to the interactions of transnational civic organisations and corporate actors disported across borders.[26] Clearly there is a transformative ethos about such work and in similar vein Saskia Sassen is moved to depict foundational changes in the matrix comprised of territory, authority and rights to produce 'mixed assemblages' of action and power.[27]

These assemblages are enacted through various agencies—such as networks of financial centres and glocal activists—as well as being visible in new jurisdictional geographies only partly embedded in national legal systems.[28] Like the distinction between vertebrate and cellular systems, such dynamics point to an elemental and continuing dialectic between borders and networks, each serving as avatars for quite different orders of governance and constructions of time and space. In this antinomy, borders betoken territoriality, fixity and ontological thickness; while networks speak of fluidity and, to reiterate, enable social relations that cross-space at all scales.[29] Such imagery is potent, but now we have to look more closely at the direction of travel, bearing in mind that the gradations between one global system and another are often quite fine, perhaps

[24] Michael Hardt and Antonio Negri, *Empire* (Cambridge MA, Harvard University Press, 2001); Michael Hardt and Antonio Negri, *Multitude: War and Democracy in the Age of Empire* (London, The Penguin Press, 2004); Michael Hardtand Antonio Negri, *Commonwealth* (Cambridge MA, Belknap Press of Harvard University Press, 2009).

[25] Barry Buzan, *From International to World Society?: English School Theory and the Social Structure of Globalisation*, vol 95 (Cambridge, Cambridge University Press, 2004).

[26] Ruggie, 'Reconstituting the global public domain—issues, actors, and practices' (n 6).

[27] Sassen, *Territory, Authority, Rights: From Medieval to Global Assemblages* (n 14) 267.

[28] Giorgio Agamben, *State of Exception* (Kevin Attell tr, Chicago IL, University of Chicago Press, 2005) 36.

[29] Axford, 'Editorial to the special issue on Borders and Networks in the Global System' (n 22).

seamless; while the character or demeanour adopted by NSAs may not be exclusive or unimodal, and their potential or impact not always extant or easily assessed.

On this much we might agree. Notions such as sovereignty and territoriality are no longer adequate markers for the way in which the allocation of value and competence among states is accorded, or for denoting the proper scope of state power when set alongside the growth in (legitimate) private norm-creation and enforcement in the twenty-first century. Globalisation—expanding and deepening the interdependence of states and societies across economic, social, environmental and geo-military spheres—has wrought a major shift in the traditional meaning of the two concepts and weakened their relevance as contemporary benchmarks for assessing states' basic capacities. Yet ideas such as international society are still largely predicated on a central role for the state. Examples of the continued potency of states include their roles in implementing the rules and standards laid down in international law and the significance of state compliance for the legitimacy and effectiveness of regime-governed behaviour in a host of policy and issue-areas. Global constraints, forms of quite advanced multilateralism, as well the staple of bilateralism are all visible in these undertakings and they are often reliant on the agency of individual states, often preponderant states, to make them work.[30]

Relationships between states and globalisation are complex and, as I have noted, admit a range of possibilities that are not always mutually exclusive. Literature on globalisation as a process that is redefining or repositioning the state focuses on different aspects of the relationships, some of which intimate the secular attenuation of infrastructural power, while others are much more cautious about any such trend. Empirically contested, claims about the transformation of statist governance under globalisation are also normatively charged. If the state is under challenge, how should we assess the consequences for the architectures and conduct of governance, for the emergence and shape of non-state governance and for the location and character of political community and of society? For Max Weber, the sphere of action of any state is territorially bounded and nation, state and territory in turn define the limits of society.[31] But if power and norm-making capacity reside increasingly in institutions and social relationships that are outside the national frame of reference and are, as Manuel Castells says, 'global and local at the same

[30] Ian Clark, *Hegemony in International Society* (Oxford, Oxford University Press 2011).

[31] Max Weber, *Economy and Society: An Outline of Interpretative Sociology* (Günther Roth and Claus Wittich trs, New York, Bedminster, 1968).

time', not only the boundaries, but the very idea of what constitutes society either has to change, or we dispense with the notion of society as a stable form of social organisation.[32] Where globalisation is concerned, the nub of debate turns on the extent to which states and other actors should be considered now primarily as nodes in political, institutional, military and economic interaction networks that may, or may not, be global.[33] Just how power is crystallised along such networks is also a key issue for globalisation research. A focus on the demeanour of NSAs in each of the global system types I have identified provides clues to the nature and direction of travel.

16.4 NSAs IN THE VERTEBRATE GLOBAL SYSTEM

When discussing NSAs and globalisation, an important theme is the durability of the liberal international order of states and of cooperative, but still state-centred, institutions of international governance. In Michael Mann's work we are afforded sources of threat to this system; threats that reside in environmental dangers, identity politics and what he calls 'post-nuclear' geo-politics. Ulrich Beck and his collaborators also point to the transformative effects of a tranche of 'interdependency crises' that challenge—at least—the capacity for effective governance at and beyond the state level of competence.[34] While there is an irreducibly normative content to Beck's cosmopolitan thesis, neither author sees a necessary attenuation of infrastructural power, while both recognise the scope for the repositioning or 'unbundling' of the state as an autonomous collective actor.[35]

In large measure their caution turns on the extent to which non-state actors continue to *underwrite* the vertebrate order and contribute to both complex interdependence and those 'diffuse reciprocities' that, in the form of international regimes, are the hallmark of the liberal international system.[36] This is a long way from all hyperglobalist cant with its stark imagery of a global political economy configured largely through markets and cross-border networks, leaving states only as bit players. Rather than immanent fragility, it is the resilience and adaptability of the liberal order that remains striking to many commentators. Indeed, John Ikenberry

[32] Manuel Castells, *Communication Power* (Oxford, Oxford University Press, 2009) 18.

[33] Michael Mann, *The Sources of Social Power*, vol 1 A History of Power (Cambridge, Cambridge University Press, 1986); Mann, 'Has globalization ended the rise and rise of the nation-state?' (n 23); George Lawson et al, 'Millennium special forum on the Work of Michael Mann' (2006) 48 *Millennium—Journal of International Studies* 261.

[34] Ulrich Beck, *Cosmopolitan Vision* (Cambridge, Polity Press, 2006); Ulrich Beck, *World at Risk* (Cambridge, Polity Press, 2008).

[35] John Gerard Ruggie, 'Territoriality and beyond: problematizing modernity in international relations' (1993) 47 *International Organization* 139–47.

[36] ibid, 58.

looks to further instantiation of that order, to more rather than less liberalism as a system of 'rule-based relations organized around expanding forms of institutional cooperation'.[37]

But how close grained is that judgment and how secure is the vertebrate system? Far from being an obvious and continuing threat to the state system, NSAs are a key feature of the many regulatory functions of governance required to sustain such a system; albeit that the 'unbundling' of national competence is producing ever more disaggregated and rescaled topologies of governance. As Bridget Hutter opines, 'The regulatory capacities of non-governmental actors are increasingly recognised and, on occasions, formally co-opted by the state'.[38] This trend is observable within states and beyond them and, in itself, is hardly novel. Philip Alston reminds us that prior to the current phase of globalisation, as well as by way of early global institutions such as the World Trade Organization (WTO), transnational trade regulation has never been the exclusive competence of states.[39] But such developments clearly point up what he calls a pluralisation of the sources of international law, in which there are diverse sources of authority and enforcement—public certainly, but increasingly private. Some might suggest that this is a rather anodyne account of what is taking place with regard to the widening of the constituency of actors deemed legitimate providers and enforcers of law, especially public international law. Are such judgments better located under a transformative motif?

For now, it is important to underline the extent to which the engagement of states with NSAs *underwrites* the vertebrate system of globality. In fields as various as labour practices, standardisation and stewardship of the natural environment, regulatory provision is reliant on, or makes extensive use of NSAs for a variety of resources and for capacities not available, or available only at greater cost, to states as allocators and regulators of value. These resources include expertise as well as goodwill or support (maybe just acquiescence). In a standard categorisation of functions provided by NSAs in matters of regulatory control, Hood et al cite information-gathering, standard-setting and behaviour-modification.[40] Following Hutter, information-gathering involves the collation and communication of information about policy issues and problem areas, standard-setting comprises the process of setting goals through standards and targets, and behaviour-modification

[37] G John Ikenberry, 'The liberal international order and its discontents' (2010) *Millennium—Journal of International Studies* 173.

[38] Bridget M Hutter, *The Role of Non-State Actors in Regulation* (London, Centre for Analysis of Risk and Regulation, London School of Economics and Political Science, 2006) 1.

[39] P Alston (ed), *Non-state Actors and Human Rights* (Oxford, Oxford University Press, 2005); Sassen, *Sociology of Globalization* (n 23).

[40] Christopher Hood, Henry Rothstein and Robert Baldwin, *The Government of Risk: Understanding Risk Regulation Regimes* (Oxford, Oxford University Press, 2001); Hutter (n 38).

to changing individual or organisational behaviour, for example, through compliance, deterrence or enforcement.[41]

Embracing a very wide constituency of NSAs—TNCs, trade associations, NGOs, INGOs and standards organisations—and applied to a variety of regimes of regulation, these three functions are actually quite loaded concepts because they bear directly on the distribution of power and influence in domestic and international systems, most notably where the displacement of sovereign power is concerned. Writing as early as 2000, Brunsson et al argue that the activities of NSAs, such as international standards bodies, are not only responses to globalisation—mechanisms to alleviate the problems of governance overload visited on states through the trammels of an interconnected world—but evidence of globalisation in process, and thus a form of globalisation.[42] This is still not a very radical claim, but attests to the visible, if modest, impact of global processes and constraints as these denationalise or attenuate state power, rather than proscribe it wholesale. Similar arguments are found in work that finds institutional syncretism typical of global structures or that depicts globalisation as a reflexive process involving elements of centralisation and decentralisation, homogeneity and heterogeneity and relativism and essentialism.[43]

Loaded too, because another kind of power is either apparent or implicit here; the power of co-optation or incorporation. Nowhere is this clearer than in the global human rights regime centred on the United Nations, (global) civil society organisations or movements and states.[44] In some respects their interplay is just another rehearsal of the familiar politics of interest mediation, of insiders and outsiders, albeit in an exotic setting. In other respects, as Rhiannon Morgan notes of the global indigenous peoples' movement, the relationships are much more dialectical than the first scenario might suggest, not least because how one assesses the impact of various actors on the engagement requires attention to 'input' considerations—resources available, including expertise, quality and ease of access—and to 'output' factors such as implementation.

If this dialectic is understood as an elemental contest between subaltern forces and the institutions of authoritative resource allocation, the question of power and changes in power relationships is appropriate. The difficulty is that outcomes are often obscure or irresolute and the systemic direction of travel, to which I referred above, is unclear. Indeed, there may

[41] Hutter (n 38); Hood, Rothstein and Baldwin, ibid.

[42] Nils Brunsson and Bengt Jacobsson, *A World of Standards* (New York, Oxford University Press, 2002).

[43] Robertson Ulf Hannerz, *Transnational Connections: Culture, People, Places* (London, Psychology Press, 1996).

[44] Morgan (n 1).

be no uniform direction of travel at all. The 'blunting' and 'channelling'—or taming—of the demands of NSAs when co-opted into the UN regime is one side of a coin, the flip-side of which may be the effective colonisation or capture of regulatory institutions by the most strategically placed, resourceful and effectively mobilised of NSAs, notably, but not exclusively, in the regulation of economic activity.[45]

Thus, the question of *agonistic* relations between NSAs and states turns out to be very complicated when broached in relation to the vertebrate global order. Relationships between organised interests and institutions of governance (including governments) turn on many factors; not least on the kind of demands articulated by those interests. The ascribed 'helpful' or 'unhelpful' demeanour of different interests will extend beyond the *manner* in which they articulate claims to more fundamental calculations about the *nature* of such claims and the degree to which these validate or challenge organisational principles and the model of resource allocation favoured by the authority in question.

Which is why the role of global civil society carries such a potent charge in these discussions. Imbued with a powerful romantic quality, the notion of civil society—certainly global civil society—hints at, sometimes actually claims, a shift in the locus of power away from states and IGOs.[46] Indeed, in a growing body of literature on global governance and world society formation, subaltern forces are increasingly referenced; their interventions often bruited as new forms of global governance from below. Here the likelihood of progressive globalisation is said to reside in the ability to challenge, subvert, bypass or reform the institutions of usual politics and the interests tied to them.[47] The romantic gloss that often attaches to discussions of this sort of politics is a feature of globalisation debates, but it is not always helpful in formulating sound theory about the emerging ontologies of the global system and it is wise to be more cautious.[48]

Raymond Vernon's seminal *Sovereignty at Bay*[49] was among the first work to advert the importance of transnational corporations (TNCs) as non-state players with clout, while in the 1980s international regime theory began to explore the role of other non-state transnational actors—epistemic

[45] Jeff Corntassel, 'Towards a New Partnership? Indigenous Political Mobilization and Co-optation During the First UN Indigenous Decade (1995–2004)' (2007) 29 *Human Rights Quarterly* 137.

[46] Axford, 'Global civil society or "networked globality": beyond the territorialist and societalist paradigm' (n 18).

[47] Hans-Martin Jäger, '"Global civil society" and the political depoliticization of global governance' (2007) 1 *International Political Sociology* 257.

[48] Ruggie, 'Reconstituting the global public domain—issues, actors, and practices' (n 6); Joseph S Nye and Robert O Keohane (eds), *Transnational Relations and World* (Cambridge MA, Harvard University Press, 1971).

[49] Raymond Vernon, *Sovereignty at Bay: The Multinational Spread of US Enterprises* (New York, Basic Books, 1971).

communities, business or industry peak associations and the like—in various governance regimes, for example in environmental pollution control and financial regulation.[50] In political science it was not until the 1990s that the study of transnational civil society organisations was married to still novel conceptions of global governance. At that point, Margaret Keck and Kathryn Sikkink's pioneering work on transnational advocacy networks and human rights politics extended the study of interest group mediation—the classic politics of influence—to the transnational arena.[51]

Seeing transnational civil society organisations as interest groups still leaves states at the centre of analytical attention. And Sidney Tarrow's extensive body of work on transnational activism reminds us that Western states in particular are 'deeply implicated in the funding and promotion of transnational actors'.[52] Moreover, state policies trigger activism because they remain the 'prime targets and fulcra of political exchange' and thus of oppositional politics.[53] This remains a usefully sceptical view of the actual prospects for what Tarrow defines as *real* transnational action that scales beyond the state and is not predicated on its centrality. His caution underlines the need for careful typology and even more careful inference. Despite its progressive and transformative connotations, global civil society does not stand apart from, nor should it be seen as necessarily in opposition to, the architectures of usual government and governance.

Yet the potential for *transformation* in these architectures and organisational forms remains vivid. Global civil society is held to ameliorate the excess of markets, of globalisation from above; while on the other hand it compensates for the systemic anarchy of states and the weak performance of the institutions of global governance, especially where justice is concerned.[54] It also rounds out eminently respectable and 'thin' liberal assumptions about the character of the global polity and the role of citizens in it.

The ideal version also offers hope for those who aspire to thicker cross border ties of solidarity, and who see in global civil society the possibility

[50] Stephen D Krasner, *International Regimes* (Ithaca NY, Cornell University Press, 1983); Friedrich Kratochwil and John Gerard Ruggie, 'International Organization: A State of the Art on an Art of the State' (1986) 40 *International Organization* 753.

[51] Margaret E Keck and Kathryn Sikkink, *Activists Beyond Borders: Advocacy Networks in International Politics* (Ithaca NY, Cornell University Press, 1998).

[52] Sidney G Tarrow, 'From Lumping to Splitting: Inside "Globalization" and "Resistance"' in Jacky Smith and Hank Johnston (eds), *Globalization and Resistance* (New York, Rowman and Littlefield, 2002) 18.

[53] ibid; Alberto Melucci, *Challenging Codes: Collective Action in the Information Age* (Cambridge, Cambridge University Press, 1996); Tarrow (n 52) 3.

[54] Michael Edwards and John Gaventa (eds), *Global Citizen Action* (Boulder CO, Lynne Reiner, 2001).

for democratic renewal and the creation of strong global publics.[55] In that regard I have already canvassed Hardt and Negri's incurably romantic gloss on the 'multitude' and that subset of NGOs and INGOs that 'represents the least among us'.[56] Both the exotic and the quotidian—the latter in the shape of NGOs and INGOs that act in a consultative role inside the UN, the International Monetary Fund (IMF) or the Association of Southeast Asian Nations (ASEAN)—are features of global civil society and, on some accounts, are contributing to a shift in the nature of governance and the balance of power in world society.[57]

Inevitably there are cautionary voices as well as outright dissent. In world-systems analysis, 'anti-systemic' forces kicking against the pricks of a systemic global geo-culture of neo-liberalism are seen as heroic, but poor drivers of revolutionary change, except in times of acute crisis when they can assume world-historical significance.[58] Even in accounts not mired in theoretical pessimism, globalisation from below in the shape of transnational social movements is still seen as a weak, though welcome, countervailing force to globalisation from above. Thus Richard Falk's *Predatory Globalization*[59] depicts global civil society as a means of offsetting the tendency for national governments to be co-opted by top-down market forces. Transnational social forces represent an innovative and variegated type of politics, one that increases the number and range of interests contesting the way global public goods are managed.

A more systemic version of the transformative motif can be found in the writings of the World Polity School, rooted in sociological institutionalism.[60] The world polity approach to world order is premised on evidence of widespread and still growing cultural consciousness of what John Meyer calls 'civic virtue' on a world scale. This consciousness springs from an awareness of interdependence and shared risk, and thus

[55] Manuel Castells, 'The new public sphere: Global civil society, communication networks, and global governance' (2008) 616 *The Annals of the American Academy of Political and Social Science* 78; Ruggie, 'Reconstituting the global public domain—issues, actors, and practices' (n 6).

[56] Hardt and Negri, *Empire* (n 24) 13. See also Hardt and Negri, *Multitude: War and Democracy in the Age of Empire* (n 24).

[57] Frank J Lechner and John Boli, *The Globalization Reader*, 2nd edn (Oxford, Blackwell, 2004); Jan Aart Scholte, *Globalization: A Critical Introduction* (Basingstoke, Palgrave Macmillan, 2005).

[58] Immanuel Maurice Wallerstein, *Unthinking Social Science: The Limits of Nineteenth Century Paradigms* (Cambridge, Polity Press, 1991).

[59] Richard A Falk, *Predatory Globalization: A Critique* (Cambridge, Polity Press, 1999).

[60] John W Meyer,'Globalization theory and trends' (2007) 48 *International Journal of Comparative Sociology* 261; Didem Buhari-Gulmez,'Stanford School on Sociological Institutionalism: A Global Cultural Approach'(2010) 4 *International Political Sociology* 253; Boli and Thomas, *Constructing World Culture* (n 1); Gili S Drori et al, *Science in the modern world polity: Institutionalization and globalization* (Palo Alto CA, Stanford University Press, 2003).

vulnerability, when faced with the potential for further outbreaks of 'destructive inhumanity' of the kind that disfigured the past century.[61]

By the end of the twentieth century, runs the argument, cultural consciousness translated into a rationalised world institutional and cultural order through the diffusion of universally acceptable models or standards of behaviour in fields such as schooling, accounting, population policy and human rights. Adoption by nation-states has led to global institutional *isomorphism* in a world still characterised by political and cultural *diversity* as well as by material inequalities across states and regions. In other words, world models now greatly influence national and local policies and practices regardless of the type and history of the regime in which they are adopted. Meyer also says that adoption of these models as features of a global cultural script impels nation-states and societies to define themselves, and to be seen by others, as 'virtuous'.[62]

While this shift in global consciousness has firm roots in Western and particularly Enlightenment traditions, cultural scripts for what define the good or virtuous society are no longer the preserve of the West, but have become institutionalised across the globe. For example, national education systems espouse common models of enrolment, curriculum development and organisation, while common notions of citizenship and individual rights also spread across jurisdictional borders and cultural divides. At the core of this model is the idea of global standards enacted by a growing range of actors across an increasingly wide canvas of policy and issue-areas. It is most evident in the globalised politics of rights, where this notion has been extended to health, education, work, welfare and nutritional standards as well as to political equality. The idea of world culture or global standardisation suggests a 'thin', but still compelling, source of legitimacy and motivation whereby, increasingly, people believe they live in one world under universally valid and applicable standards or norms. The world-wide impact of such norms is contagious, not only in the sense that more and more actors are constrained to acknowledge their force, but because the culture of world polity and society also encourages the discovery of new common issues which, in turn, are deemed solvable only through the adoption and application of global standards. In other words, the culture of the world polity provides common models for thinking about the world and for acting on its problems, whether we are talking about global warming or unprotected labour.

From many published accounts, it is clear that NSAs of various hues are key actors in initiating and implementing norms; as well as in contesting them.[63] Writing in 1997, Jessica Matthews opined: 'in numbers and

[61] Meyer (n 60) 233.
[62] ibid, 264.
[63] Frank J Lechner, *Globalization: The Making of World Society* (Chichester, John Wiley & Sons, 2009).

in impact, non state actors have never before approached their current strength'.[64] But, even if correct, does that amount to a power shift? Frank Lechner argues that for all its oppositional qualities, global civil society does not act apart from the state system and the new public spaces opened up by the activities of its denizens are better understood as complementing rather than replacing that system, at least wholesale. Which is much in line with the sense imparted by world polity theory. The presumed structuration is compelling: while actors and actions are institutionally anchored, institutional orders are also socially constructed and thus are capable of being changed through strategic interventions by actors—always allowing for contingency and the ability of actors to mobilise appropriate resources. So the scope for transformation is immanent, and to that point I will return below.

16.5 NSAs IN THE MIXED GLOBAL SYSTEM: A PAUSE FOR BREATH

On the one hand, the idea of a mixed or in-between global system can be taken either as a statement of fact, with the imbrication of statist and non-statist architectures and actions just another messy feature of social life. On the other hand it could be viewed as a transitional phase between resolute state-centrism and one-or-other version of a de-centred, de-territorialised, networked and increasingly privatised biopolitics. In the latter version, even if the shift is incremental, it may be secular and thus profound in its implications for the Westphalian system of public international law and international legal theory, as well as for the kind of politics in which these are couched. In other words, the in-between character of this order should not lead us to dismiss it as a residual category.

As I have noted, Appadurai's reference to the 'split personality' of some global firms and markets is testimony to the importance of the in-between category for describing and understanding the dynamics of the global capitalist system and the complexities of its governance.[65] The system of capitalism is clearly vertebrate, relying on the modal reach of certain legal protocols, accounting standards and treaty structures to subsist and expand and also to manage the immanent logic of the system to accumulate. In this system global firms often have a strong legal nationality and a particular cultural imprint, even as they espouse the language of global brands and global marketing strategies. At the same time, capitalism is a decidedly mobile (Appadurai says 'portable') phenomenon and, notably since the late 1970s, this mobility has enhanced its cellular features. This

[64] Jessica T Mathews, 'Power shift' (1997) 50 *Foreign Affairs* 123. See also Helmut K Anheier, Mary Kaldor and Marlies Glasius, *Global Civil Society 2005/6* (London, Sage, 2005).
[65] Appadurai (n 7).

period is often described as the third wave of globalisation and there is no doubt that over the period the world economy exhibited powerfully integrative tendencies around key institutional clusters and also underwent marked changes.

These tendencies include the shift from 'organised capitalism', in which production, consumption, money and labour circulate nationally, to 'disorganised capitalism' where circuits became increasingly global.[66] Disorganised capitalism is a spatial shift in the key circuits of capitalist accumulation. This spatial shift has been accompanied by changes in the nature and meaning of work, in the creation of a much expanded service economy increasingly based on the 'knowledge' and 'culture' industries and in patterns of consumption especially, though by no means exclusively, in the global north. Usually these changes are understood as the transition from a Fordist to a post-Fordist political economy and as well as having economic significance they have triggered enormous shifts in the organisation and conduct of social and cultural life.

Finally, the trends have forced us to modify rather simplistic models of autonomous, national economies and of centre/periphery models of the economic, political and cultural geography of the world. The upshot is that in the economic realm (but also elsewhere) such practices and forms have produced distinctive and complex spatialities that cannot be subsumed under either the national or the global.[67] Yet the careful inference must be that a world previously made up of unified temporal-spatial units (nation-states) has not been completely overlaid or rendered nugatory by the activities of networks and flows. Rather, network links across (or regardless) of borders are more likely to create 'qualitative disjunctures' between different regulatory and socio-cultural environments.[68] The bridging of these disjunctures, even by way of loose coupling, lies at the heart of the challenge to effect good global governance.

In these global shifts the room for organisational and institutional innovation is pronounced. Organisations diverge from the more conventional decisional models of hierarchy and market, while network forms of coordination have assumed greater prominence in many areas of governance.[69] Sometimes it is tempting to read the changes as no more than organisational adjustments, rather than a transformation in the guise

[66] Paul Andrew Roth, *Meaning and Method in the Social Sciences: A Case for Methodological Pluralism* (Ithaca NY, Cornell University Press, 1987); Scott M Lash and John Urry, *Economies of Signs and Space*, vol 26 (London, Sage, 1994) 322–23.

[67] Sassen, *Sociology of Globalization* (n 2).

[68] Peter Dicken and others, 'Chains and networks, territories and scales: towards a relational framework for analysing the global economy' (2001) 1 *Global Networks* 89, 96.

[69] Grahame Thompson, *Between Hierarchies and Markets: The Logic and Limits of Network Forms of Organization* (Oxford, Oxford University Press, 2003); Robert J Holton, *Global Networks* (London, Palgrave Macmillan, 2007).

and conduct of governance. While this is properly cautious social science, it may hide the transformative potential carried in such changes.

Although much of the commentary on organisational innovation takes place around quite modest ventures and engagements, on an altogether more epic scale is the exercise of advanced multilateralism seen in the European Union. All multilateral regimes, whether the North Atlantic Treaty Organisation (NATO), the World Bank or the International Monetary Fund (IMF) imply a great deal of complex interdependence, and this extends to the European Union (EU). While the EU institutional complex is also described in quite different ways—as supranational, perhaps as a network state—at the least it stands as a highly sophisticated form of non-state governance and the most developed attempt to achieve a transnational community of affect using methods for integrating societal entities that lack a common culture but display ever more functional interconnections.

Writing in 1993, just after the formal completion of the single internal market process in Europe, John Ruggie talked about the potential in a model of governance whereby 'the sovereign importance of place gives way to the sovereign importance of movement'.[70] But with appropriate caution he also referred to the continued centrality of member states in the Union's decision-making arenas. Some 20 years on, and after protracted debates about a constitution for the EU, its autonomous governance role in some areas of post-conflict reconstruction, its piecemeal attempts to solve financial crisis and the difficulties of mounting a common response to naked aggression near to its external land border, similar questions of institutional balance and competence still hold sway.

16.6 NSAs IN THE CELLULAR GLOBAL SYSTEM

While it is sensible not to overdo claims about the direction of travel in the institutional ensemble that constitutes global governance, there is no doubt that a globalised or globalising pattern of regulation is bringing about what Nancy Fraser calls 'a considerable dispersion of governmentality', one that is multi-level and increasingly networked; both rule-governed and dispersed at the same time.[71] Indeed, the idea of global cellularity expresses the emergent qualities of the strong globalisation thesis more readily than any other designation. In reality, as I have noted, the cellular system in Appadurai's schema embraces many forms of non-state

[70] Ruggie, 'Territoriality and beyond: problematizing modernity in international relations' (n 35) 173.
[71] Fraser, 'From discipline to flexibilization? Rereading Foucault in the shadow of globalization' (n 3) 197.

cellularity and admits states as actors or nodes in circuits and networks of interaction. Saskia Sassen too discerns, not all-out de-territorialisation (as a synonym for globalisation), but new versions of territoriality in which there are, or may be, 'foundational' changes in the historical relationships between territory, authority and rights that define how we signify bordered states and societies.[72] To reiterate: these changes are being constituted through various agencies, for example, networks of financial centres and transnational activists, as well as being visible in the emergence of 'new jurisdictional geographies', like refugee camps or Guantanamo, only partly embedded in and subject to national legal systems.[73]

At its most radical or transformational, the notion of a cellular global system has all the attributes of a networked globality, exemplifying social process at odds with the organisational practices of boundary maintenance and the hierarchical decision rules through which such practices have been sustained. But such recognition still need not prescribe an either/or model in which territory and scale no longer matter.[74] Rather, it involves 'rejecting the notion of scale as a bounded, territorially complete concept and of any notion that social relations are, or have to be, contained at particular scales'.[75]

As Neil Brenner argues: 'scales evolve relationally within tangled hierarchies and dispersed inter-scalar networks' and 'the very intelligibility of each scalar articulation of a social process hinges crucially upon its embeddedness within dense webs of relations to other scales and spaces'.[76] Thus it is possible to think of networks—in trade, finance, diaspora, even terrorism, as 'significantly de-territorialised',[77] but also inserted into territories at, as well as across, all scales.[78] In Sassen's account of the reworking of territory and authority the dynamics—they include cross-border networks of activists fighting eminently local struggles and the use made by national courts of international law and conventions—reveal that as a process, globalisation 'inhabits' and relies on the national and yet challenges the received wisdom that the nation-state is the natural container of all social process. Earlier in this chapter I adverted Sassen's use of the expression 'new geographies of power', and it is now apposite to expand on this a little.

[72] Sassen, *Sociology of Globalization* (n 2); Saskia Sassen, *Deciphering the Global: Its Scales, Spaces and Subjects* (Abingdon, Routledge, 2007).

[73] Sassen, *Sociology of Globalization* (n 2) 386–88. See also Agamben, *State of Exception* (n 28).

[74] Harriet Bulkeley, 'Reconfiguring environmental governance: towards a politics of scales and networks' (2005) 24 *Political Geography* 875.

[75] ibid, 884.

[76] Neil Brenner, 'The limits to scale? Methodological reflections on scalar structuration' (2001) 25 *Progress in Human Geography* 591, 605–06.

[77] John Urry, *Global Complexities* (Cambridge, Polity Press, 2003) 58.

[78] Axford, 'Global civil society or "networked globality": beyond the territorialist and societalist paradigm' (n 18).

Four components make up the new geographies of power. The first component is the 'footloose' nature of both contemporary capital and of business. This rootlessness appears in, for example, collaborative business models in activities such as trans-border outsourcing and global supply chains; while new digital architectures affect the very geography of capital accumulation so that 'many of the newer objects of capital accumulation flow through spaces'.[79] The second feature is a novel kind of territoriality best described as 'extraterritoriality', which affects a state's sovereignty by diluting its capacity to regulate various institutions and activities. Free trade zones are an obvious example because many of their activities are not subject to local rules. But the clearest illustration is the phenomenon of global cities, which are the territorial embodiment of global processes. As Bill Robinson has it, 'The global financial, stock, foreign exchange and other markets in these cities constitute de-territorialised activities that do not fall under the regulatory umbrella of the states in which such cities are located.'[80]

The third component is the emergence of a new legal regime for governing mainly economic relations and transactions and which bypasses national legal systems. International credit rating agencies that adjudicate on the debt security and credit worthiness of national governments fall into this category and their power to parlay investment into or away from particular countries renders them a crucial element in the growth of (private) global economic governance.[81] Finally, Sassen refers to the 'virtualization of economic activity'[82] and cites the instance of currency markets which trade without much let or hindrance from national regulators, including central banks. In later work, she also discusses the part being played by the Internet and mobile telephony in the creation of networks of political activists who are players in a novel kind of transnational politics and are contributing to new forms of citizenship; perhaps world citizenship.[83]

Taken together these are powerful emergent properties of a cellular global system, though also of a transitional mixed regime. In terms of changing patterns and structures of governance a powerful tension, even dialectic, is being played out. On the one hand economic globalisation

[79] Scholte, *Globalization* (n 57) 398.

[80] William I Robinson, 'Saskia Sassen and the sociology of globalization: A critical appraisal' (2009) 3(1) *Sociological Analysis* 20.

[81] A Claire Cutler, 'Private Authority in International Trade Relations: The Case of Maritime Transport' in A Claire Cutler, Virginia Haufler and Tony Porter (eds), *Private Authority and International Affairs* (Abingdon, Routledge, 1999); Ruggie, 'Reconstituting the global public domain—issues, actors, and practices' (n 6).

[82] Sassen, *Sociology of Globalization* (n 2) 22.

[83] Sassen, *Territory, Authority, Rights: From Medieval to Global Assemblages* (n 14); Manuel Castells, *Networks of Outrage and Hope: Social Movements in the Age of the Internet* (Cambridge, Polity Press, 2012).

de-nationalises domestic economies and economic governance; while on the other, states struggle to re-nationalise aspects of, for example, immigration policy, either under the guise of controlling labour market supply, or as a component of enhanced and politically charged policy on homeland security. Of course, the existence and visibility of a global human rights regime complicates matters where the management of immigration is concerned, because it reveals that what is often presented as an administrative/rational procedure over allowable numbers is actually a more expressive issue about the nature of citizenship in a 'borderless' world.

16.7 CONCLUSION

In terms of a grand narrative of social change all the instances and practices canvassed above can be seen as the increasingly contested playing out of the major drivers of material and intellectual modernity—secularism, rationality and territoriality. In some measure they still endorse a state-centric (and Westernised) model of world order and display elements of institutional continuity underpinned, possibly strengthened, by routine and incremental adjustments to changing circumstances. Globalisation then subsists as a facet of modernity and in some ideologies of the process, is part of its unfolding teleology of progress.

But such a complacent reading of current trends in global governance and politics cannot be countenanced in a world where global alterities are widely bruited and, even if just in subaltern form, there is a countervailing politics available to pursue them. In this regard we should advert the potential for 'power-shift' seen in the kinds of agonistic politics now visible across global civil society—for example in Castells' 'networks of outrage'—where the goal of systemic change, as well as more modest local resolutions, may be the motivating factors.[84] Yet when recognising the potential for systemic change contained in this politics, we must not underestimate the less agonistic demeanour of a host of NSAs that are contributing to change through routine behaviour, where they supplement or enhance the actions of states and, as Ruggie argues, contribute to the instantiation of a new global public domain.[85] Building on Wapner's sense of 'world civic politics'[86] and Claire Cutler's concept of 'private

[84] Paolo Gerbaudo, *Tweets and the Streets: Social Media and Contemporary Activism* (London, Pluto Press, 2012); Anna Feigenbaum, Fabian Frenzel and Patrick McCurdy, *Protest Camps* (London, Zed Books, 2013).

[85] Ruggie, 'Reconstituting the global public domain—issues, actors, and practices' (n 6).

[86] Paul Wapner, 'Politics beyond the state environmental activism and world civic politics' (1995) 47 *World Politics* 311.

governance'[87] the idea of a global public domain is at once transformative, secular and inclusive. It consists of an increasingly institutionalised transnational realm of 'discourse, contestation and action' on the part of private and public actors to produce global public goods. Critically, even in its non-agonistic guise, it conjures novel opportunities for, as well as constraints on, global and national governance. And as Boli and Thomas observe, a surprisingly large number of international non-governmental organisations extant in the last 50 years or so have been dedicated to sustaining, improving and expanding these global public goods.[88]

Globalisation is a transformative dynamic. When discussing the part played by NSAs in the conduct of global governance and politics, at the very least its use points to a reinterpretation of international society as just the society of states and of international law. In the longer term it is probably useful to identify secular trends that suggest a modal consciousness and institutionalisation, as well as a practical orientation beyond state and society to hint at, and in some respects to instantiate, what John Meyer calls 'a supra-societal or transcendental cosmos'.[89] That process is ongoing.

[87] A Claire Cutler, *Private Power and Global Authority: Transnational Merchant Law in the Global Political Economy* (Cambridge, Cambridge University Press, 2003).
[88] Boli and Thomas, *Constructing World Culture* (n 1).
[89] Meyer (n 60) 11.

17

Concluding Observations

CEDRIC RYNGAERT, MATH NOORTMANN
AND AUGUST REINISCH

NON-STATE ACTORS ARE characterised negatively as, indeed, actors that are not states. This characterisation is normatively charged, as it presupposes that *states* are the dominant and paradigmatic actors in international relations and international law, and that *non-state* actors are *Fremdkörper* that are at best not easily accommodated by extant conceptual frameworks, and at worst irrelevant to the disciplinary analysis. Indeed, in the realist and rational choice strands of international relations that have dominated discussions of international power and normativity, non-state actors are typically left out of the equation.[1] These strands view international law as a set of normative expectations which states have vis-à-vis each other, or as unstable enunciations of converging strategic interests of, again, states. Also doctrinally, non-state actors have been relegated to the margins of international law. They have no role in the process of ascertaining international legal norms, and thus cannot formally contribute to the formation of international law. Where the existence of non-state actors is recognised by international law, it is mainly in their capacity as addressees or objects of regulation. In short, classic international law does not consider non-state actors to be true subjects of international law who can participate in the formation of the collective will to which they are subject.

Classic international law and international relations may—purposively or inadvertently—have turned a blind eye to the phenomenon of non-state actors, but globalisation and world society theories have increasingly recognised the influence of such actors on the international community's constitution. They have drawn attention to the factual and normative power of a panoply of organised transnational entities, such as intergovernmental organisations, multinational corporations, non-governmental

[1] Jack L Goldsmith and Eric A Posner, *The Limits of International Law* (Oxford, Oxford University Press, 2005); Andrew T Guzman, *How International Law Works: A Rational Choice Theory* (Oxford, Oxford University Press, 2008).

organisations, armed opposition groups, terrorists, indigenous peoples, religious movements, etc., whose activities affect people's lives in at times more incisive ways than those of states.

The accumulation of power by these non-state actors can be the result of a formal transfer of competences by states (eg, to international organisations), of a conscious governmental choice to empower private entities to deliver goods or further ideals (eg, corporations respectively civil society groups), or of—sometimes violent—challenges to a state-based order (eg, armed opposition groups). This categorisation, which is based on non-state actors' mode of genesis, shows that non-state actors, or the environment in which they operate, are not created *ex nihilo*. In fact, states could be seen as the very *creators* of non-state actors, either by formal act, or by factual oppressive policies that inevitably engender opposition. After all, states set up international organisations[2] and incorporate private entities. And where they have not formally created non-state actors, they may at least have facilitated their rise. There is no denying that liberal states have encouraged the ascendancy of non-state for-profit actors by establishing a favourable regulatory framework that allowed them to develop lucrative financial centres, to transfer capital worldwide, and to set up production facilities at reduced cost. Moreover, states may support non-state armed groups intent on overthrowing foreign (hostile) regimes, either by actively assisting them or condoning their territorial presence, or they may have contributed to the rise of these groups by oppressive and discriminatory policies antagonising crucial segments of the population.

In international law, this proximity of—at least a number of—non-state actors to the state has invited the question whether the latter could be held responsible for abuses committed by the former, or whether instead a 'private' veil is drawn that insulates states from responsibility for the acts of non-state actors.[3] With a view to providing a modicum of accountability, but also to discourage the kind of totalitarianism in which overly broad rules of state responsibility could result, the law of responsibility has drawn up rather arcane rules of attribution of conduct and responsibility.

[2] Understood as *intergovernmental organizations with a separate international legal personality*. Note that, obviously, individuals can set up *non-governmental organizations*—but such organisations will be organised under the domestic laws of states.

[3] See Arts 4–11 of the International Law Commission's (ILC) Draft Articles on the Responsibility of States for Internationally Wrongful Acts (2001) on the attribution of conduct of non-state actors to states. See also Part V of the ILC's Articles on the Responsibility of International Organizations for Internationally Wrongful Acts (2011), on the responsibility of member states in connection with acts of international organisations. See on states' responsibility for the acts of non-state actors, the contribution by Ryngaert to the present volume (ch 8). Obviously, states and non-state actors may *both* be held responsible for jointly contributing to the same harmful outcome. See on shared responsibility: André Nollkaemper and Dov Jacobs, 'Shared Responsibility in International Law: A Conceptual Framework' (2013) 34 *Michigan Journal of International Law* 360.

These rules are formulated so strictly that only in a handful of cases will states be held responsible for the acts of private actors or international organisations.[4] Indeed, in most scenarios, non-state actors, even if initially created by states or even as state proxies, have sufficiently emancipated themselves from their state creators to be taken seriously as actors who participate in international affairs in their own right.[5]

The participation of autonomously operating non-state actors in international decision-making has drawn the attention of scholars since the early post-war years, when the policy-oriented New Haven School posited that international normativity does not come into being on the basis of decisions taken by states, but rather as a consequence of value- or welfare-maximising actions taken at different levels by a panoply of actors, including non-state ones (policy-oriented research used the term 'participants' for all those actors, in order to reflect the equality of states and non-state actors).[6] Given the diversity of actors participating in the formulation of an international collective will, the question was concomitantly raised, at about the same time, whether the term 'international', with its inevitable 'national' or 'state' connotation, is an appropriate term to characterise the said decision-making process. Philip Jessup has famously suggested using 'transnational law' in this respect, a law that would encompass public and private regulation in which both states and non-state actors participate.[7]

While policy-oriented approaches and transnational law have captured the imagination of scholars, they have not led to an epochal epistemic transformation of how we conceive of international regulation. Nevertheless, in more recent times, which have seen increased privatisation of governance and regulatory functions, the moniker 'transnational law' has staged a remarkable comeback in both practice and scholarship in the guise of 'transnational private regulation' by—in particular—corporate actors. It is probably no exaggeration to say that this scholarship, pioneered by private lawyers and regulation theorists, advances more innovative ideas on the

[4] See notably the strict 'effective control' standard required for the attribution of acts of private actors—armed groups in particular—to states: *Military and Paramilitary Activities in and against Nicaragua (Nicaragua v United States of America)* (Merits) (Judgment) [1986] ICJ Rep 14, 64 [115]; *Application of the Convention on the Prevention and Punishment of the Crime of Genocide (Bosnia and Herzegovina v Serbia and Montenegro)* (Judgment) [2007] ICJ Rep 43 [385]–[415].

[5] See on the independence of international organisations from their member states the contribution by Wessel (ch 9).

[6] See the seminal piece by Myres S McDougal, 'The Law School of the Future: From Legal Realism to Policy Science' (1946–47) 56 *Yale Law Journal* 1345. See also the contribution by Suzuki (ch 3). The term 'participants' for non-state actors has proved influential in international legal scholarship. See Rosalyn Higgins, *Problems and Process: International Law and How We Use It* (Oxford, Oxford University Press, 1995) ch 3; Jean d'Aspremont (ed), *Participants in the International Legal System: Multiple Perspectives on Non-State Actors in International Law* (London, Routledge, 2011).

[7] Philip C Jessup, *Transnational Law* (New Haven CT, Yale University Press, 1956). See also the contribution by Noortmann (ch 4).

role of non-state actors in global governance than public international law and international relations scholarship combined.[8] It is observed, however, that this private regulation scholarship, unlike Jessup's writings on transnationalism, analyses not just a particular state of affairs. Their flag-bearers may not shy away from making the normative claim that private regulation is a more efficient and more legitimate form of global regulation than classic state- or international organisation-based command and control mechanisms. A concern here is how to ensure that such regulation sufficiently accounts for the externalities of corporate action, and thus safeguards public values. It is this concern that has informed the lively and ongoing debate on the international obligations of multinational corporations.[9]

Advocates of transnational private regulation ultimately envision a 'brave new world' where borderless communities live under their own laws without state intervention. With this eschatological, post-geographic vision,[10] they most radically challenge the time-honoured Westphalian system of world order dominated by states. This radical challenge should however not obfuscate the increased profile which non-state actors have *already* acquired in discrete traditional international norm-making, norm-application, and norm-enforcement processes. Human rights treaties[11] and investment agreements[12] have conferred substantive and procedural rights on individuals and other non-state entities. International humanitarian law treaties have recognised rights of non-state humanitarian actors and have imposed obligations on non-state armed groups.[13] The *jus ad bellum*, for its part, appears to be in the process of allowing the exercise of self-defence against non-state actors.[14] Yet it would be mistaken to characterise these normative evolutions within the 'vertebrate system'[15] as creeping

[8] See, eg, Gralf-Peter Calliess and Peer Zumbansen, *Rough Consensus and Running Code: a Theory of Transnational Private Law* (Oxford, Hart Publishing, 2010).

[9] See contribution by Wouters and Chané. This debate has not been terminated by the adoption of the UN Guiding Principles (2011), which affirmed transnational corporations' non-legal duties to respect human rights in their operations. Indeed, civil society organisations, and even some states, have continued to favor the imposition of direct international human rights obligations on corporations.

[10] See also Daniel Bethlehem, 'The End of Geography: The Changing Nature of the International System and the Challenge to International Law' (2014) 25 *European Journal of International Law* 9.

[11] See the contribution by Nowak and Januszewski (ch 7).

[12] See the contribution by Reinisch (ch 12).

[13] See the contributions by Heintze and Lülf (ch 6), as well as Paust (ch 13).

[14] See the contributions by Henderson (ch 5) and Paust (ch 13).

[15] See the contribution by Axford (ch 16), drawing on Arjun Appadurai, *Fear of Small Numbers: An Essay on the Geography of Anger* (New York, Columbia University Press, 2006) 25 (defining the vertebrate system as a system 'predicated on generalized norms of conduct, conjoint institutions such as the UN and, of course, the international system of states and discrete sovereignties', and contrasting it with the 'cellular system', which 'embraces "dis-organized" virtual capitalism, terrorist networks and emergent, sometimes utopian forms of grassroots networking across borders').

inroads that are made by non-state actors. In fact, they are inroads made by *states themselves*, who, as gatekeepers of the international system, have conferred (limited) rights and obligations on non-state actors, largely to suit their own needs. To name just a few examples, armed groups have been burdened with obligations under humanitarian law so as to ensure reciprocity in the conduct of hostilities, terrorists, pirates and transnational criminals have been outlawed so as to protect states' trading and security interests, and non-state actors have been made legitimate targets of the right to self-defence to expand states' options to use force against outside threats. Even where rights have been granted to non-state actors, these may in fact serve *state* interests, eg, the rights conferred on investors further the economic interests of their home states—a notion that formed the original underpinnings of diplomatic protection.

Only when it comes to human rights and human security[16] does it appear that no state interest is served; on the contrary, human rights constitute fundamental constraints on the behaviour of states towards non-state actors. Therefore, the recognition of human rights can be seen as an historical victory of non-state actors over state power, a victory which has been further cemented by the emergence of a global civil society that has relentlessly named and shamed state abusers of human rights, and has accordingly been instrumental in enhancing state compliance with international human rights law.[17] Still, one cannot fail to note that states may well be inclined to abuse the discourse of human rights to bring others into disrepute, and even to pave the way for military intervention to protect non-state actors allegedly suffering at the hands of hostile states. When thus used, human rights are the modern-day equivalent of the crusades or the civilising mission, and amount to no more than a hegemonic instrument in the hand of dominant states.[18]

Leaving possible instrumentalisation of human rights aside, their enduring attractiveness for a theory of non-state actors lies in their considering *the individual*, the non-organised non-state actor *par excellence*, as the primary unit of analysis. The autonomy or—one could even say—'sovereignty' accruing to individuals pursuant to human rights theory allows them, by dint of their freedom of assembly and association, to bond together in communities of solidarity or purpose that coalesce as organised collectivities that are not necessarily states. It is recalled that long before the rise of human rights, and even before the entrenchment of states as the units of world public order, individuals did just that: in an era of powerless or even entirely absent territorial sovereigns, they formed

[16] Cedric Ryngaert and Math Noortmann (eds), *Human Security and International Law: the Challenge of Non-State* Actors (Antwerp, Intersentia, 2014).

[17] See also the contribution by Kornprobst (ch 14).

[18] See for a critique of the Western human rights discourse: Immanuel Wallerstein, *European Universalism: The Rhetoric of Power* (New York, New Press, 2010).

non-territorial communities, often of a tribal nature. To be true, joining such a community was not always a voluntary process and cannot properly be seen as an exercise of human rights. But the point should nevertheless be clear: the system of territorially delimited states—Westphalia's progeny—need not be the natural global order. Especially in times like ours, times of heightened individualism, choice, and autonomy, one can surely imagine that individuals may identify more with self-chosen communities than with their state of nationality,[19] an imagined and involuntary community forced on them by mere birth, which its members often cannot even escape through migration. Should one not respect a group of individuals' choice to self-identify with a particular community—of value, purpose, or profit—as much as individuals' choice to join a state? And if the answer is in the affirmative—which *arguendo* it should, if one takes freedom seriously—should one not accord these communities a legal status on a par with the status of states?

One is obviously tempted to again answer in the affirmative what appears to be just a rhetorical question. Nevertheless, one should not overlook that a qualitative difference remains between a community and a state The variegated communities we currently know are functionally differentiated and cater to different, and often quite circumscribed wishes and needs of individuals: individuals may at the same time join Greenpeace, the Catholic Church, and an e-gaming community, without these memberships being mutually exclusive. States, in contrast, may lay, to a larger extent than non-state actors, totalising claims on individuals, purporting to regulate all, or at least significant aspects of individuals' lives. Such regulation can be freedom-restricting, eg, when autocratic states manage to limit individuals' membership of competing communities of choice. It can however be freedom-enhancing where states provide physical protection against inside and outside threats (ie, the Hobbesian construction to escape the state of nature) or where modern welfare states ensure a fair distribution of resources. This safety net thrown by states may constitute their enduring appeal and legitimacy.

But when states fail in their protective mission, one can expect individuals to turn for relief to non-state actors, who use their soft, and sometimes hard power to attract members.[20] When states oppress them, they might join armed opposition groups bent on the regime's overthrow. When states fail to stand up for public goods, they might join non-governmental organisations defending a conception of global justice.[21] When states fail

[19] See at length Paul Schiff Berman, *Global Legal Pluralism: a Jurisprudence of Law Beyond Borders* (Cambridge, Cambridge University Press, 2012).

[20] See on soft power of non-state actors the contribution by Chong (ch 15).

[21] See for the international legal status of such organisations, or rather the absence of such status, the contribution by Noortmann (ch 10).

to provide work or develop industries, individuals are driven toward self-employment or the formation of corporations. And when the fervour of state ideologies has ebbed, individuals may look for salvation in preachers or entertainers. This is a stylised account, of course, since in reality, as indicated above, states may accommodate non-state actors' demands for limited autonomy. But it remains no less true that the current ascendancy of, and societal/scholarly interest in non-state actors can largely be attributed to the latter's role as a filler of gaps deliberately or accidentally left by a retreating state—for better or worse. It is this de facto gap-filling role that has led to calls for a more secure legal status of non-state actors, with properly delineated rights of participation in national and global governance, and with clear accountability rules in case their factual participation turns awry.

Confronted with the growth of intergovernmental organisations after the Second World War, and attendant calls for the recognition of their legal capacity, the International Court of Justice held, in its advisory opinion in *Reparation for Injuries* (1949) in respect of the United Nations 'that the Organization was intended to exercise and enjoy, and is in fact exercising and enjoying, functions and rights which can only be explained on the basis of the possession of a large measure of international personality and the capacity to operate upon an international plane.'[22] It is posited that this functional approach is also appropriate to determine the international legal personality of other non-state actors. As functional differentiation is a hallmark of the phenomenon of non-state actors—which indeed distinguishes them from states—a conferral of legal personality need not involve the allocation of the bundle of all possible international rights and obligations. Such capacities should be contingent on the actual functions and powers exercised. This suggestion may appear to amount to a paradigm shift, as it allows sociological changes to affect the law without legislative intervention, thereby challenging the supremacy of state consent, and of state gatekeeping of the international legal system. Still, even positivists have admitted that at the level of deciding what international law is and what it is not, non-state actors do and should play a role in determining the criteria for international law-ascertainment. As d'Aspremont observes in this volume, given the meagre social practice of law-applying bodies with respect to such criteria, so as to generate sufficient 'communitarian semantics' 'the practice of other [non-state] actors engaged in the application of international law should be included in the social practice … at the heart of formal law-ascertainment in international law'.[23] Or, put differently, non-state actors, even apart from their actual contribution to the content-determination of substantive legal norms, may have a key role

[22] *Reparation for Injuries suffered in the service of the Nations, Advisory Opinion* [1949] ICJ Rep 79.
[23] See ch 2.

to play in developing criteria that allow us to separate international law from other forms of normativity. That being said, one should not force non-state actors into the straitjacket of international law where this would require such far-reaching adjustments to the primary and secondary rules of international legal process,[24] that international law loses its social validity. This does not equal regulatory defeat, however. After all, internationally active non-state actors may not only be regulated by international law, but also by other forms of regulation that are transnational in nature. Such regulation may perhaps lack the formal binding character reserved for classic public international law, but may nevertheless command legitimacy and compliance at a level only aspired to by international law.[25] The normative expectations generated by novel forms of regulation—through 'soft law', private regulation, or hybrid state/non-state arrangements—may harden into forms and shades of law, if we understand law as a set of normative commands steering human behaviour. The landscape of transnational regulation and governance may thus become a polycentric or pluralistic one, with commands and expectations emanating from various sources without any one source dominating, or aspiring to dominate, another. State-based regulation may not disappear, but be repositioned by the development of transnational networks, or in the words of Saskia Sassen, 'global assemblages', which imbricate the territorial infrastructure of the state to project global power.[26] What we ultimately envision here is a new ontology of global public order that is partly 'beyond territoriality',[27] where new non-state geographies of power, regulation and responsibility, shaped by a variety of actors, emerge which supplement, rival, and replace the apparatus of the territorially delimited nation-state.

[24] The primary rules of international law can be defined as those rules containing substantive commands addressed at subjects of the law. The secondary rules are 'rules of recognition' in a Hartian sense; they set forth the—procedural—criteria, which have to be met for a norm to be considered as a norm of international law.

[25] In fact, studying such regulation presents a window that allows us to bridge the gap between international law and international relations, the two disciplines at the heart of this Handbook. See the contribution by Kornprobst (ch 14) ('All too often, interdisciplinary research between International Relations and International Law is confined to the question of how incentives make actors comply with formalised legal norms. Yet there is much more to the interdisciplinary borderlands between International Relations and International Law. Informal legal norms as well as the ideas in which they are embedded, such as customs and practices, are highly salient in global politics. These constitutive elements of normativity ought to be studied, too') (footnote omitted).

[26] Saskia Sassen, *Territory, Authority, Rights: From Medieval to Global Assemblages* (Princeton NJ, Princeton University Press, 2006). See also the contribution by Axford (ch 16).

[27] Günther Handl, Joachim Zekoll, Peer Zumbansen (eds), *Beyond Territoriality. Transnational Legal Authority in an Age of Globalization* (The Hague, Brill/Nijhoff, 2012).

Select Bibliography

Aaronson SA and Higham I, '"Re-righting Business": John Ruggie and the Struggle to Develop International Human Rights Standards for Transnational Firms' (2013) 35 *Human Rights Quarterly* 333.

Abrahms M, 'What terrorists really want: Terrorist Motives and Counterterrorism Strategy' (2008) 32 *International Security* 78.

Adler E, 'The emergence of cooperation: national epistemic communities and the international evolution of the idea of nuclear arms control' (1992) 46 *International Organization* 101.

—— and Haas PM, 'Conclusion: epistemic communities, world order, and the creation of a reflective research program' (1992) 46 *International Organization* 367.

Al-Jurf S, 'Participatory development and NGOs: a look at the World Bank' (1999) 9 *Transnational Law & Contemporary Problems* 175.

Alexandrov SA, 'The "Baby Boom" of Treaty-Based Arbitrations and the Jurisdiction of ICSID Tribunals: Shareholders as "Investors" and Jurisdiction Ratione Temporis' (2005) 4 *The Law and Practice of International Courts and Tribunals* 19.

Alfredsson G and Eide A, *The Universal Declaration of Human Rights: A Common Standard of Achievement* (The Hague, Kluwer, 1999).

Alfredsson G and Ring R (eds), *The Inspection Panel of the World Bank; A Different Complaints Procedure*, vol 5 (Dordrecht, Martinus Nijhoff Publishers, 2001).

Alston P, 'The "Not-a-Cat" Syndrom: Can the International Human Rights Regime Accommodate Non-State Actors?' in Alston P (ed), *Non-state Actors and Human Rights* (Oxford, Oxford University Press, 2005).

—— (ed), *Non-state Actors and Human Rights* (Oxford, Oxford University Press, 2005).

Alvarez JE, *International organizations as Law-makers* (Oxford, Oxford University Press, 2005).

——, 'Are Corporations Subjects of International Law' (2011) 9 *Santa Clara Journal of International Law* 1.

——, 'State Sovereignty is Not Withering Away: A Few Lessons for the Future' in Cassese A (ed), *Realizing utopia: the future of international law* (Oxford, Oxford University Press, 2012).

Amerson JM, 'What's in a Name—Transnational Corporations as Bystanders under International Law' (2011) 85 *John's Law Review* 1.

Anderson K, 'The Ottawa Convention banning landmines, the role of international non-governmental organizations and the idea of international civil society' (2000) 11 *European Journal of International Law* 91.

—— and Rieff D, ''Global civil society': a sceptical view' in Helmut Anheier, Marlies Glasius, Mary Kaldor (eds), *Global Civil Society* (London, Sage Publications, 2008).

Antonopoulos C, 'Force by Armed Groups as Armed Attack and the Broadening of Self-Defence' (2008) 55 *Netherlands International Law Review* 159.

Arts B, Noortmann M and Reinalda B, *Non-state Actors in International Relations* (Aldershot, Ashgate, 2001).
Axford B, 'Global civil society or 'networked globality': beyond the territorialist and societalist paradigm' (2004) 1 *Globalizations* 249.
——, 'Editorial to the special issue on Borders and Networks in the Global System' (2007) 4 *Globalizations*.
Backer LC, 'On the Evolution of the United Nations Protect-Respect-Remedy Project: The State, the Corporation and Human Rights in a Global Governance Context' (2011) 9 *Santa Clara Journal of International Law* 37.
Baldwin SE, 'The International Congresses and Conferences of the Last Century as Forces Working Toward the Solidarity of the World: Appendix' (1907) 1 *American Journal of International Law* 808.
Barnidge RP, *Non-state Actors and Terrorism: Applying the Law of State Responsibility and the Due Diligence Principle* (The Hague, TMC Asser Press, 2008).
Barros AS and Ryngaert C, 'The Position of Member States in (Autonomous) Institutional Decision-Making: Implications for the Establishment of Responsibility' (2014) 11 *International Organizations Law Review* 53.
Bartley T, 'Certifying forests and factories: States, social movements, and the rise of private regulation in the apparel and forest products fields' (2003) 31 *Politics & Society* 433.
——, 'Corporate accountability and the privatization of labor standards: struggles over codes of conduct in the apparel industry' (2005) 14 *Research in Political Sociology* 211.
Bauböck R, 'Towards a political theory of migrant transnationalism' (2003) 37 *International Migration Review* 700.
Baum MA and Potter PB, 'The relationships between mass media, public opinion, and foreign policy: Toward a theoretical synthesis' (2008) 11 *Annual Review of Political Science* 39.
Bayart J-F, *Global Subjects: A Political Critique of Globalization* (Cambridge, Polity Press, 2007).
Bederman DJ, 'The Souls of International Organizations: Legal Personality and the Lighthouse at Cape Spartel' (1995) 36 *Virginia Journal of International Law* 275.
Bekker PHF, *The Legal Position of Intergovernmental Organizations: A Functional Necessity Analysis of their Legal Status and Immunities* (Dordrecht, Martinus Nijhoff, 1994).
Bellinger III JB and Haynes II WJ, 'A US government response to the International Committee of the red cross study customary international humanitarian law' (2007) 89 *International Review of the Red Cross* 443.
Bendell J, *Debating NGO Accountability* (Hill T ed, UN-NGLS, 2006).
Berger KP, *The Creeping Codification of the New Lex Mercatoria*, 2nd edn (The Hague, Kluwer Law International, 2010).
Berman A and Wessel R, 'The International Legal Status of Informal International Law-making Bodies: Consequences for Accountability' in Pauwelyn J, Wessel RA and Wouters J (eds), *Informal International Lawmaking* (Oxford, Oxford University Press, 2012).
Berman E and others, 'Do working men rebel? Insurgency and unemployment in Afghanistan, Iraq, and the Philippines' (2011) 55 *Journal of Conflict Resolution* 496.

Bethlehem D, 'Self-Defense Against an Imminent or Actual Armed Attack by Non-state Actors' (2012) 106 *American Journal of International Law* 769.

Betsill MM and Corell E, *NGO Diplomacy: The Influence of Nongovernmental Organizations in International Environmental Negotiations* (Cambridge MA, MIT Press, 2008) xvii.

Bianchi A (ed), *Non-state Actors and International Law* (Aldershot, Ashgate, 2009).

Birkland BH, 'Reining in non-state actors: State responsibility and attribution in cases of genocide' (2009) 84 *NYU Law Review* 1623.

Bishop Jr WW, 'The Anglo-Iranian Oil Company Case' (1951) *American Journal of International Law* 749.

Bismuth R, 'Mapping a responsibility of corporations for violations of international humanitarian law sailing between international and domestic legal orders' (2009) 38 *Denver Journal of International Law & Policy* 203.

Bjola C and Kornprobst M, 'Understanding dissonance in a security community: Germany and the United States on Iraq' (2007) 33 *Review of International Studies* 285.

——, 'Introduction: The argumentative deontology of global governance' in Bjola and Kornprobst (eds), *Arguing Global Governance: Agency, Lifeworld, and Shared Reasoning* (London, Routledge, 2011) 1.

Blokker N, 'International organizations and their members' (2004) 1 *International Organizations Law Review* 139.

Bloodgood EA, 'The interest group analogy: international non-governmental advocacy organisations in international politics' (2011) 37 *Review of International Studies* 93.

Boli J and Thomas GM, 'INGOs and the Organization of World Culture' in Boli J and Thomas GM (eds), *Constructing World Culture: International nongovernmental organizations since 1875* (Stanford CA, Stanford University Press, 1999).

Bouwhuis S, 'The International Law Commission's Definition of International Organizations' (2012) 9 *International Organizations Law Review* 451.

Boyle AE and Chinkin CM, *The Making of International Law* (Oxford, Oxford University Press, 2007).

Branson DM, 'Holding Multinational Corporations Accountable-Achilles' Heels in Alien Tort Claims Act Litigation' (2011) 9 *Santa Clara Journal of International Law* 227.

Braun TR, 'Globalization-Driven Innovation: The Investor as a Partial Subject in Public International Law' (2014) 15 *The Journal of World Investment & Trade* 73.

Breton-le Goff G, 'NGO's perspective on non-state actors' in d'Aspremont J (ed), *Participants in the International Legal System: Multiple perpsectives on non-state actors in international law* (Abingdon, Routledge, 2011).

Brett R, 'Non-govemmental human rights organizations and international humanitarian law' (1998) 38 *International Review of the Red Cross* 531.

Brunsson N and Jacobsson B, *A World of Standards* (Oxford, Oxford University Press, 2002).

Bulkeley H, 'Reconfiguring environmental governance: towards a politics of scales and networks' (2005) 24 *Political Geography* 875.

Call CT, *Why Peace Fails: The Causes and Prevention of Civil War Recurrence* (Washington DC, Georgetown University Press, 2012).

Calliess G-P, 'Introduction: Transnational Corporations Revisited' (2011) 18 *Indiana Journal of Global Legal Studies* 601.
Carrasco E and Guernsey AK, 'The World Bank's Inspection Panel: Promoting True Accountability Through Arbitration' (2008) 41 *Cornell International Law Journal* 577.
Castells M, 'The new public sphere: Global civil society, communication networks, and global governance' (2008) 616 *The Annals of the American Academy of Political and Social Science* 78.
——, *Networks of Outrage and Hope: Social Movements in the Age of the Internet* (Cambridge, Polity Press, Cambridge 2012).
Cernic JL, 'Corporate responsibility for human rights: analyzing the ILO tripartite declaration of principles concerning multinational enterprises and social policy' (2009) 6 *Miskolc Journal of International Law* 24.
Cerone J, 'Much Ado About Non-State Actors: The Vanishing Relevance of State Affiliation in International Criminal Law' (2008) 10 *San Diego International Law Journal* 335.
Charlesworth H, Chinkin C and Wright S, 'Feminist approaches to international law' (1991) 85 *American Journal of International Law* 613.
Charnovitz S, 'Two centuries of participation: NGOs and international governance' (1997) 18 *Michigan Journal of International Law* 183.
——, 'Opening the WTO to Nongovernmental Interests' (2000) 24 *Fordham International Law Journal* 43.
——, 'The Relevance of Non-State Actors to International Law' in Wolfrum R and Röben V (eds), *Developments of international law in treaty making* (Berlin, Springer, 2005).
——, 'Nongovernmental Organizations and International Law' (2006) 100 *American Journal of International Law* 24.
Chen L-C and Chen L, *An introduction to Contemporary International Law: A Policy-oriented Perspective* (New Haven CT, Yale University Press, 2000).
Chesterman S, 'Lawyers, Guns, and Money: The Governance of Business Activities in Conflict Zones' (2010) 11 *Chinese Journal of International Law* 321.
Chiang P-H, *Non-governmental Organizations at the United Nations: Identity, Role, and Function* (New York, Praeger, 1981).
Chimni BS, 'Third world approaches to international law: a manifesto' (2006) 8 *International Communication Law Review* 3.
Chinkin C, 'A critique of the Public/Private Dimension' (1999) 10 *European Journal of International Law* 387.
Chiti E and Wessel R, *The Emergence of International Agencies in the Global Administrative Space: Autonomous Actors or State Servants* (Collins R and White ND (eds), Abingdon, Routledge, 2011).
Chong A, *Foreign Policy in Global information Space; Actualizing Soft Power* (Basingstoke, Palgrave-Macmillan 2007).
Clapham A, *Human Rights Obligations of Non-state Actors* (Oxford, Oxford University Press, 2006).
——, 'Extending international criminal law beyond the individual to corporations and armed opposition groups' (2008) 6 *Journal of International Criminal Justice* 899.

Cohen Smutny A, 'State Responsibility and Attribution: when is a State responsible for the Acts of State Enterprises?: Emilio Agustín Maffezini v the Kingdom of Spain' in Weiler T (ed), *International Investment Law and Arbitration: Leading cases from the ISCID, NAFTA, Bilateral Treaties and Customary International Law* (London, Cameron May, 2005).

Colonomos A, 'Non-State Actors as Moral Entrepreneurs: a Transnational Perspective on Ethics Networks' in Josselin D and Wallace W (eds), *Non-state Actors in World Politics* (Basingstoke, Palgrave 2001).

Constantinides A, 'Human Rights Obligations and Accountability of Armed Opposition Groups: The Practice of the UN Security Council' (2011) 4 *Human Rights & International Legal Discourse* 89.

Cook RJ, 'Accountability in International Law for Violations of Women's Rights by Non-State Actors' (1993) 25 *Studies in Transnational Legal Policy* 93.

Corntassel J, 'Towards a New Partnership? Indigenous Political Mobilization and Co-optation During the First UN Indigenous Decade (1995-2004)' (2007) 29 *Human Rights Quarterly* 137.

Cotterrell R, 'What is Transnational Law?' (2012) 37 *Law & Social Inquiry* 500.

Cowell A and Erlanger S, 'France Becomes First Country to Recognize Libyan Rebels' (2011) *The New York Times*.

Cox RW, 'Social forces, states and world orders: beyond international relations theory' (1981) 10 *Millennium: Journal Of International Studies* 126.

Craig C and Ruzicka J, 'The Nonproliferation Complex' (2013) 27 *Ethics & International Affairs* 329.

Craven M and others, 'We are teachers of International Law' (2004) 17 *Leiden Journal of International Law* 363.

Crawford J, *The International Law Commission's Articles on State Responsibility: Introduction, Text, and Commentaries* (Cambridge, Cambridge University Press, 2005).

Cutler AC, *Private Power and Global Authority: Transnational Merchant Law in the Global Political Economy* (Cambridge, Cambridge University Press, 2003).

——, Haufler V and Porter T, *Private Authority and International Affairs* (New York, State University of New York Press, 1999).

D'Amato A, 'What "Counts" as Law?' in Onuf NG (ed), *Law-making in the Global Community* (Durham NC, Carolina Academic Press, 1982).

d'Aspremont J, 'Les travaux de la Commission du droit international relatifs aux actes unilatéraux des Etats' (2005) *Revue Generale de Droit International Public: droit des gens, histoire diplomatique, droit penal, droit fiscal, droit administratif* 163.

——, 'Softness in international law: a self-serving quest for new legal materials' (2008) 19 *European Journal of International Law* 1075.

——, 'Rebellion and state responsibility: wrongdoing by democratically elected insurgents' (2009) 58 *International and Comparative Law Quarterly* 427.

——, 'Conclusion: Inclusive Law-making and law enforcement processes for an exclusive international legal system' in d'Aspremont J (ed), *Participants in the International Legal System: Multiple perpsectives on non-state actors in international law* (Abingdon, Routledge, 2011).

——, 'Non-state Actors from the Perspective of Legal Positivism: the Communitarian Semantics for the Secondary Rules of International Law' in d'Aspremont J (ed), *Participants in the International Legal System: Multiple Perspectives on Non-state Actors in International Law* (Abingdon, Routledge, 2011).

——, 'Wording in International Law' (2012) 25 *Leiden Journal of International Law* 575.

Dahl RA, 'Can international organizations be democratic? A skeptic's view' (1999) *Democracy's Edges* 19.

Dannenbaum T, 'Translating the Standard of Effective Control into a System of Effective Accountability: How Liability Should be Apportioned for Violations of Human Rights by Member State Troop Contingents Serving as United Nations Peacekeepers' (2010) 51 *Harvard International Law Journal* 113.

de Boer M, 'Law Enforcement Cooperation and Transnational Organized Crime in Europe' in Berdal MR and Serrano M (eds), *Transnational Organized Crime and International Security* (Boulder CO, Lynne Rienner Publishers, 2002).

De Brabandere E, 'Human Rights and Transnational Corporations: The Limits of Direct Corporate Responsibility' (2010) 4 *Human Rights & International Legal Discourse* 66.

De Ly F, *International Business Law and Lex Mercatoria* (The Hague, TMC Asser Instituut, 1992).

De Schutter O and others, 'Foreign Direct Investment, Human Development and Human Rights: Framing the Issues' (2009) 3 *Human Rights & International Legal Discourse* 137.

DeLuca KM, *Image politics: The New Rhetoric of Environmental Activism* (Abingdon, Psychology Press, 2005).

Detter I, 'Law making by international organizations' (PhD Thesis, Stockholm, 1965).

Deumier P, 'Les codes de conduite des entreprises et l'effectivité des droits de l'homme' in Boy L, Racine J-B and Siiriainen F (eds), *Droit économique et droits de l'Homme* (Paris, Larcier, 2009).

Dicken P and others, 'Chains and networks, territories and scales: towards a relational framework for analysing the global economy' (2001) 1 *Global Networks* 89.

Dolzer R, 'Indirect expropriation of alien property' (1986) 1 *ICSID review* 41.

——, 'Indirect Expropriations: New Developments' (2002) 11 *NYU Environmental Law Journal* 64.

Douglas Z, 'The hybrid foundations of investment treaty arbitration' (2004) 74 *British Yearbook of International Law* 151.

——, *The International Law of Investment Claims* (Cambridge, Cambridge University Press, 2009).

Dumberry P, 'New state responsibility for internationally wrongful acts by an insurrectional movement' (2006) 17 *European Journal of International Law* 605.

Dunlap Jr CJ, 'The Military-Industrial Complex' (2011) 140 *Daedalus* 135.

Dunoff JL, 'The misguided debate over NGO participation at the WTO' 1998) 1 *Journal of International Economic Law* 433.

Edwards M and Hulme D, *Beyond the Magic Bullet: NGO Performance and Accountability in the Post-cold War World* (West Hartford CT, Kumarian Press, 1996).

Emberland M, *The human rights of companies: exploring the structure of ECHR protection* (Oxford, Oxford University Press, 2006).

Esty DC, 'Linkages and Governance: NGOs at the World Trade Organization' (1998) 19 *University of Pennsylvania Journal of International Economic Law* 21.

——, 'Non-governmental organizations at the World Trade Organization: cooperation, competition, or exclusion' (1998) 1 *Journal of International Economic Law* 123.

Falkner R, 'Private environmental governance and international relations: exploring the links' (2003) 3 *Global Environmental Politics* 72.
Farrell H, 'Regulating Information Flows: States, Private Actors and E-Commerce' (2006) *Annual Review of Political Science* 353
Fassin D, 'A Spontaneous Caravan of Relief' in Feher M (ed), *Nongovernmental Politics* (New York, Zone Books, 2007).
Fedtke J and Oliver D, *Human Rights and the Private Sphere: A Comparative Study* (Abingdon, Routledge-Cavendish, 2007).
Feyter Kd and Gómez Isa F, *Privatisation and Human Rights in the Age of Globalisation* (Antwerp, Intersentia 2005).
Fietta S, 'Most Favoured Nation Treatment and Dispute Resolution Under Bilateral Investment Treaties: A Turning Point?' (2005) 8 *International Arbitration Law Review* 136.
Forsythe DP, 'The International Committee of the Red Cross and humanitarian assistance: A policy analysis' (1996) 36 *International Review of the Red Cross* 512.
Fox J, 'Unpacking transnational citizenship' (2005) 8 *Annual review of political science*.
Fox JA, 'The World Bank Inspection Panel and the Limits of Accountability' in Pincus JR and Winters JA (eds), *Reinventing the World Bank* (Ithaca NY, Cornell University Press, 2002).
Franck TM, 'Terrorism and the Right of Self-defense' (2001) *American Journal of International Law* 839.
Friedmann D and Barak-Erez D, *Human Rights in Private Law* (Oxford, Hart Publishing, 2001).
Frowein J, *Das de facto-Regime im Völkerrecht: Eine Untersuchung zur Rechtsstellung 'nichtanerkannter Staaten' und ähnlicher Gebilde* (Cologne, Carl Heymans Verlag, 1968).
Gallmetzer R, 'Prosecuting Persons Doing Business with Armed Groups in Conflict Areas: The Strategy of the Office of the Prosecutor of the International Criminal Court' (2010) 8 *Journal of International Criminal Justice* 947.
Gaston E, 'Mercenarism 2.0—The Rise of the Modern Private Security Industry and Its Implications for International Humanitarian Law Enforcement' (2008) 49 *Harvard International Law Journal* 221.
Gates S, 'Recruitment and Allegiance The Microfoundations of Rebellion' (2002) 46 *Journal of Conflict Resolution* 111.
Gatto A, *Multinational Enterprises and Human Rights: Obligations under EU Law and International Law* (Cheltenham, Edward Elgar Publishing, 2011).
Gazzini T, 'A Unique Non-State Actor: the International Committee of the Red Cross' (2010) 4 *Human Rights & International Legal Discourse* 14.
——, *The Relationship between International Legal Personality and the Autonomy of International Organizations* (Abingdon, Routledge, 2011).
Gibbs C, Fumo C and Kuby T, *Nongovernmental Organizations in World Bank Supported Projects* (Operation Evaluation Department Series, 1999).
Giustozzi A, *Koran, Kalashnikov, and Laptop: The Neo-Taliban Insurgency in Afghanistan* (New York, Columbia University Press, 2008).
Gleditsch KS, 'Transnational dimensions of civil war' (2007) 44 *Journal of Peace Research* 293.

Goodhart M, 'Human Rights and Non State Actors—Theoretical Puzzles' in Andreopoulos GJ, Kabasakal Arat ZF and Juviler PH (eds), *Non-state Actors in the Human Rights Universe* (Bloomfield CT, Kumarian Press, 2006).

Gordon G and Pierik R, 'Liberal Political Philosophy: The Role of Non-State Actors and Considerations of Global Justice' in Reinalda B (ed), *The Ashgate Research Companion to Non-state Actors* (Aldershot, Ashgate, 2010).

Gurr TR, 'Why minorities rebel: A global analysis of communal mobilization and conflict since 1945' (1993) 14 *International Political Science Review* 161.

Hailbronner K, 'Der Staat und der Einzelne als Völkerrechtssubjekte' in Vitzthum W and Bothe M (eds), *Völkerrecht* (Berlin, Walter de Gruyter, 2004).

Hakimi M, 'The Media as Participants in the International Legal Process' (2006) 16 *Duke Journal of Comparative & International Law*.

Hegel GWF, *Grundlinien der Philisophie des Rechts* (Ditzingen, Reclam, 1970).

Heintze H-J, 'Do Non-State Actors Challenge International Humanitarian Law?' in *International Humanitarian Law Facing New Challenges* (Berlin, Springer, 2007).

Henckaerts J-M, 'Study on customary international humanitarian law: A contribution to the understanding and respect for the rule of law in armed conflict' (2005) 87 *International Review of the Red Cross* 175.

——, 'Customary International Humanitarian Law: a response to US comments' (2007) 89 *International Review of the Red Cross* 473.

—— and Wiesener C, 'Human rights obligations of non-state armed groups: A possible contribution from customary international law?' in Kolb R and Gaggioli G (eds), *Research Handbook on Human Rights and Humanitarian Law* (Cheltenham, Edward Elgar Publishing, 2013).

Henderson C, 'The Centrality of the United Nations Security Council in the Legal Regime Governing the Use of Force' in White ND and Henderson C (eds), *Research Handbook on International Conflict and Security Law: Jus ad bellum, jus in bello and jus post bellum* (Cheltenham, Edward Elgar, 2013).

——, 'Contested States and the Rights and Obligations of the Jus Ad Bellum' (2013) *Cardozo Journal of International & Competition Law*.

——, *The Persistent Advocate and the Use of Force: The Impact of the United States Upon the Jus Ad Bellum in the Post-cold War Era* (Aldershot, Ashgate, 2013).

——, 'Provision of Arms and Non-Lethal Assistance to Governmental and Opposition Forces' (2013) 36 *University of New South Wales Law Journal* 642.

Hessbrügge J, 'Human rights violations arising from conduct of non-state actors' (2005) 11 *Buffalo Human Rights Law Review*.

Higgins R, *Problems and Process: International Law and How We Use It* (Oxford, Clarendon Press, 1994).

Hilhorst D, 'Being Good or Doing Good Quality and Accountability of Humanitarian NGOs' (2002) 26 *Disasters* 20.

Hobe S, 'Global Challanges to statehood: The Increasingly Important role of Nongovernmental Organizations' (1997) 5 *Indiana Journal of Global Legal Studies* 191.

Hobér K, 'State Responsibility and Attribution' in Muchlinski P, Ortino F and Schreuer C (eds), *The Oxford Handbook of International Investment Law* (Oxford, Oxford University Press, 2008).

Hofmann R and Geissler N, *Non-state Actors as New Subjects of International Law: International Law—From the Traditional State Order Towards the Law of the Global Community* (Berlin, Duncker & Humblot, 1999).

Hollis DB, 'Private Actors in Public International Law: Amicus Curiae and the Case for the Retention of State Sovereignty' (2002) 25 *British Columbia International Competition Law Review* 235.
Howse R, 'Membership and its privileges: The WTO, civil society, and the amicus brief controversy' (2003) 9 *European Law Journal* 496.
Huber K, *The HDC in Aceh: Promises and Pitfalls of NGO Mediation and Implementation* (Washington DC, East-West Center, 2004).
Humphreys M and Weinstein JM, 'Who fights? The determinants of participation in civil war' (2008) 52 *American Journal of Political Science* 436.
Hutter BM, *The Role of Non-state Actors in Regulation* (Centre for Analysis of Risk and Regulation, London School of Economics and Political Science, 2006).
Ijalaye DA, *The Extension of Corporate Personality in International Law* (Brill Archive, 1978).
Io H and Bryant K, 'Taming of the Warlords. Commitment and Compliance by Armed Opposition Groups in Civil Wars' in Risse T, Ropp SC and Sikkink K (eds), *The Persistent Power of Human Rights: From Commitment to Compliance*, vol 126 (Cambridge, Cambridge University Press, 2013).
Jägers N, 'UN guiding principles on business and human rights: making headway towards real corporate accountability' (2011) 29 *Netherlands Quarterly on Human Rights* 159.
——, *Corporate Human Rights Obligations: in Search of Accountability*, vol 17 (Antwerp, Intersentia, 2002).
Janssen D, 'International Terrorism and Self-Defence' (2006) 36 *Israel Yearbook of Human Rights* 149.
Jayasuriya K, 'Globalization, law, and the transformation of sovereignty: the emergence of global regulatory governance' (1999) 6 *Indiana Journal of Global Legal Studies* 425.
Jessup PC, *Transnational Law* (New Haven CT, Yale University Press, 1956).
, 'The Present State of Transnational Law' in Bios M (ed), *The Present State of International Law and Other Essays: Written in Honour of the Centenary Celebration of the International Law Association 1873-1973* (Berlin, Springer, 1973).
Jinks D, 'State responsibility for the acts of private armed groups' (2003) 4 *Chinese Journal of International Law* 83.
Jochnick C, 'Confronting the impunity of non-state actors: new fields for the promotion of human rights' (1999) 21 *Human Rights Quarterly* 56.
Jones OR, 'Implausible deniability: state responsibility for the actions of private military firms' (2008) 24 *Connecticut Journal of International Law* 239.
Jönsson C, 'International Organizations at the Moving Public-Private Borderline' (2013) 19 *Global Governance* 17.
Jordan L, 'Mechanisms for NGO Accountability' GPPI Research Paper Series No 3 20.
—— and Van Tuijl P, 'Rights and Responsibilities in the Political Landscape of NGO Accountability: Introduction and Overview' in Jordan L and Van Tuijl P (eds), *NGO Accountability: Politics Principles and Innovations* (London, Earthscan, 2006).
Josselin D and Wallace W, 'Non-State Actors in World Politics: a Framework' in Josselin D and Wallace W (eds), *Non-state Actors in World Politics* (Basingstoke, Palgrave, 2001).

Jupp J, 'Legal Transplants as Solutions for Post-Intervention Criminal Law Reform: Afghanistan's Interim Criminal Procedure Code 2004' (2013) 61 *American Journal of Comparative Law* 51.

Keck ME and Sikkink K, *Activists Beyond Borders: Advocacy Networks in International Politics* (Ithaca NY, Cornell University Press, 1998).

Kelly MJ, 'Understanding September 11th-An International Legal Perspective on the War in Afghanistan' (2002) 35 *Creighton Law Review*.

Kerr C, 'Mexico's Drug War: Is It Really a War' (2012) 54 *South Texas Law Review* 193.

Kinley D and Tadaki J, 'From talk to walk: The emergence of human rights responsibilities for corporations at international law' (2004) 44 *Virginia Journal of International Law* 931.

Klabbers J, 'Presumptive Personality: the European Union in International Law' in Koskenniemi M (ed), *International law aspects of the European Union* (The Hague, Kluwer Law International, 1998).

Koh HH, 'Transnational Legal Process' (1996) 75 *Nebraska Law Review* 181.

Koppell JGS, *World Rule: Accountability, Legitimacy, and the Design of Global Governance* (Chicago IL, University of Chicago Press, 2010).

Korey W, *NGOs and the Universal Declaration of Human Rights* (Basingstoke, Palgrave, 1998).

Kornprobst M, 'International Relations as Rhetorical Discipline: Toward (Re-) Newing Horizons' (2009) 11 *International Studies Review* 87.

—— and Senn M, 'Deep Ideational Change: Strategy, Humanitarianism, and Nuclear Weapons' (*ISA Catalytic Workshop*, Toronto 25 March 2014).

Koskenniemi M, 'International law and hegemony: a reconfiguration' (2004) 17 *Cambridge Review of International Affairs* 197.

——, 'The Subjective Dangers of Projects of World Community' in Cassese A (ed), *Realizing Utopia: The future of International Law* (Oxford, Oxford University Press, 2012).

Kozma J, Nowak M and Scheinin M (eds), *A World Court of Human Rights—Consolidated Statute and Commentary* (Vienna, Neuer Wissenschaftlicher Verlag, 2011).

Krasner SD, *International Regimes* (Ithaca NY, Cornell University Press, 1983).

Kratochwil F and Ruggie JG, 'International Organization: A State of the Art on an Art of the State' (1986) 40 *International Organization* 753.

Krisch N and Kingsbury B, 'Introduction: global governance and global administrative law in the international legal order' (2006) 17 *European Journal of International Law* 1.

Ku JG, 'The Limits of Corporate Rights under International Law' (2011) 12 *Chinese Journal of International Law* 729.

Lapid Y, 'The third debate: On the prospects of international theory in a post-positivist era' (1989) *International Studies Quarterly* 235.

Lasswell HD and McDougal MS, *Jurisprudence for a Free Society: Studies in Law, Science, and Policy* (Dordrecht, Martinus Nijhoff, 1991).

Lauterpacht H, 'The Subject of International Law' in Bianchi A (ed), *Non-State Actors and International Law* (Aldershot, Ashgate, 1977).

Levit JK, 'Bottom-Up Lawmaking: The Private Origins of Transnational Law' (2007) 15 *Indiana Journal of Global Legal Studies* 49.

Lindblom A-K, 'Non-Governmental Organizations and Non-State actors in International Law' in Reinalda B (ed), *The Ashgate Research Companion to Non-state Actors* (Aldershot, Ashgate, 2011).

Lipschutz RD, 'Reconstructing World Politics: The Emergence of Global Civil Society' (1992) 21 *Millennium-Journal of International Studies* 389.

Lloyd R, 'The Role of NGO Self-Regulation in Increasing Stakeholder Accountability' available at www.un-ngls.org/orf/cso/cso9/Self-Regulation.pdf.

Lobel J, 'Use of Force to Respond to Terrorist Attacks: The Bombing of Sudan and Afghanistan' (1999) 24 *Yale Journal of International Law* 537.

Lu S-P, 'Corporate Codes of Conduct and the FTC: Advancing Human Rights Through Deceptive Advertising Law' (1999) 38 *Columbia Journal of Transnational Law* 603.

Lubell N, *Extraterritorial Use of Force against Non-state Actors* (Oxford, Oxford University Press, 2010).

Lupsha P, 'Transnational organized crime versus the nation-state' (1996) 2 *Transnational Organized Crime* 21.

Macintosh K, 'Beyond the Red Cross: the Protection of Independent Humanitarian Organizations' in Heintze H-J, Zwitter, Andrej (ed), *International Law and Humanitarian Assistance: A Crosscut Through Legal Issues Pertaining to Humanitarianism* (Heidelberg, Springer, 2011).

Mafessanti M, 'Responsibility for Environmental Damage under International Law: Can MNCs Bear the Burden … and How' (2009) 17 *Buffalo Environmental Law Journal* 87.

Maier HG, 'Some Implecations of the Term Transanational' (1992) 25 *Vanderbilt Journal of Tranantional Law*.

Malanczuk P, 'Multinational Enterprises and Treaty-Making—A Contribution to the Discussion on Non-State Actors and the "Subjects" of International Law' in *Multilateral Treaty-Making* (Heidelberg, Springer, 2000).

Mann M, 'Has globalization ended the rise and rise of the nation-state?' (1997) 4 *Review of International Political Economy* 472.

Martinez-Diaz L, 'Executive Boards in International Organizations: Lessons for Strengthening IMF Governance', Independent Evaluation Office (IEO) Background Paper (BP/08/08), (Washington DC, International Monetary Fund, 2008).

McBeth A, 'Privatising Human Rights: What Happens to the State's Human Rights Duties When Services are Privatised' (2004) 5 *Melbourne Journal of International Law* 133.

McCorquodale R, 'Overlegalizing Silences: Human Rights and Nonstate Actors' (2002) *Proceedings of the Annual Meeting (American Society of International Law)* 384.

——, 'The Individual and the International Legal System' in Evans MD (ed), *International Law*, 3rd edn (Oxford, Oxford University Press, 2010).

——, 'Non-State Actors and International Human Rights Law' in Joseph S and McBeth A (eds), *Research Handbook on International Human Rights Law* (Cheltenham, Edward Elgar, 2010).

—— and Simons P, 'Responsibility beyond borders: State responsibility for extraterritorial violations by corporations of international human rights law' (2007) 70 *The Modern Law Review* 598.

McCrudden C, 'Human dignity and judicial interpretation of human rights' (2008) 19 *European Journal of International Law* 655.

McDougal MS, 'Law as a Process of Decision: A Policy-Oriented Approach to Legal Study' (1956) 1 *National Law Forum* 53.

—— and others, *Human Rights and World Public Order: The Basic Policies of an International Law of Human Dignity* (New Haven CT, Yale University Press, 1980).

——, Lasswell HD and Reisman WM, 'The World Constitutive Process of Authoritative Decision' (1966) 19 *Journal of Legal Education* 253.

——, 'The Intelligence Function and World Public Order' (1972) 46 *Temple Law Quarterly* 365.

—— and Reisman WM, 'The Prescribing Function in World Constitutive Process: How International Law Is Made' (1979) 6 *Yale Studies in World Public Order* 249.

—— and Willard AR, 'The World Community: A Planetary Social Process' (1987) 21 *UC Davis Law Review* 807.

Menkel-Meadow C, 'Why and How to Study Transnational Law' (2011) 1 *UC Irvine Law Review* 97.

Menon PK, *The law of recognition in international law: basic principles* (Lewiston NJ, Edwin Mellen Press, 1994).

Meyer JW, 'Globalization theory and trends' (2007) 48 *International Journal of Comparative Sociology* 261.

Mihr A, 'Non-Governmental Organizations in the Human Rights World' in Reinalda B (ed), *The Ashgate Research Companion to Non-state Actors* (Aldershot, Ashgate, 2011).

Mikler J, *The Handbook of Global Companies* (Chichester, John Wiley & Sons, 2013).

Milanovic M, 'State responsibility for acts of non-state actors: a comment on Griebel and Plücken' (2009) 22 *Leiden Journal of International Law* 307.

Miller MA, *The Foundations of Modern Terrorism: State, Society and the Dynamics of Political Violence* (Cambridge, Cambridge University Press, 2013).

Mills A, 'The private history of international law' (2006) 55 *International and Comparative Law Quarterly* 1.

Momtaz D, 'Attribution of Conduct to the State: State Organs and Entities empowered to Exercise Elements of Governmental Authority' in Crawford J and others (eds), *The Law of International Responsibility* (Oxford, Oxford University Press, 2010).

Morgan R, *Transforming Law and Institution: Indigenous Peoples, the United Nations and Human Rights* (Aldershot, Ashgate, 2013).

Muchlinski PT, *Multinational enterprises & the law* (Oxford, Oxford University Press, 2007).

Müller T, 'Customary Transnational Law: Attacking the Last Resort of State Sovereignty' (2008) 15 *Indiana Journal of Global Legal Studies* 19.

Nafziger JA, 'Regulation by the International Council of Museums: an example of the role of non-governmental organizations in the transnational legal process' (1972) 2 *Denver Journal of International Law & Policy* 231.

Najam A, 'NGO Accountability: A Conceptual Framework' (1996) 14 *Development Policy Review* 15.

Neff S, 'International Law and the Critique of Cosmopolitan Citizenship' in Hutchings K and Dannreuther R (eds), *Cosmopolitan Citizenship* (Basingstoke, Macmillan Press, 1999).

Nieburg HL, *Political Violence: The Behavioral Process* (New York, St Martin's Press, 1969).

Nijman JE, *The Concept of International Legal Personality: An Inquiry into the History and Theory of International Law* (The Hague, TMC Asser Press, 2004).

Noortmann M, 'Non-State Actors in International Law' in Arts B, Noortmann M and Reinalda B (eds), *Non-State Actors in International Relations* (Aldershot, Ashgate, 2001).

——, 'Who Really Needs Article 71? A Critical Approach to the Relationship between NGOs and the UN' in Heere WP (ed), *From Government to Governance: The Growing Impact of Non-state Actors on the International and European legal system: Proceedings of the Sixth Hague Joint Conference Held in The Hague, the Netherlands, 3-5 July 2003* (The Hague, TMC Asser Press, 2004).

——, 'Understanding Non-State Actors in the Contemporary World Society: Transcending the International, Mainstreaming the Transnational or Bringing the Participants Back In?' in Noortmann M and Ryngaert C (eds), *Non-state Actors in International Law, Politics and Governance Series* (Aldershot, Ashgate, 2010).

——, 'The International Law Association and non-state actors: Professional network, public interest group or epistemic community?' in d'Aspremont J (ed), *Participants in the International Legal System: Multiple Perpsectives on Non-state Actors in International Law* (Abingdon, Routledge, 2011).

—— and Ryngaert C, *Non-state Actor Dynamics in International Law: From Law-takers to Law-makers* (Aldershot, Ashgate, 2010).

Norrie AW, *Dialectic and Difference: Dialectical Critical Realism and the Grounds of Justice* (Abingdon, Routledge, 2010).

Nowak M, *Politische Grundrechte* (Heidelberg, Springer-Verlag, 1988).

——, *U.N. Covenant on Civil and Political Rights: CCPR Commentary* (NP Engel, 1993).

——, *Introduction to the International Human Rights Regime* (Dordrecht, Martinus Nijhoff, 2003).

——, 'Progress Report of the Eminent Persons Panel' Part of the framework of the Swiss Initiative to Commemorate the 60th Anniversary of the UDHR–*Protecting Dignity: An Agenda for Human Rights.*

——, 'Eight Reasons Why We Need a World Court of Human Rights' in Alfredsson G (ed), *International Human Rights Monitoring Mechanisms: Essays in Honour of Jakob Th Moller* 2nd edn (Dordrecht, Martinus Nijhoff Publishers, 2009).

——, 'It's Time for a World Court of Human Rights' in Bassiouni MC and Schabas WA (eds), *New Challenges to the UN Human Rights Machinery—What Future for the UN Treaty Body System and the Human Rights Council Procedures?* (Antwerp, Intersentia, 2011).

——, 'Torture and other Cruel, Inhuman or Degrading Treatment or Punishment' in Clapham A and Gaeta P (eds), *The Oxford handbook of international law in armed conflict* (Oxford, Oxford University Press, 2014).

——, Hofstätter T and Hofbauer J (eds), *The Role of the EU in UN Human Rights Reform* (Vienna, Neuer Wissenschaftlicher Verlag, 2013).

Nowrot K, 'Legal consequences of globalization: The status of non-governmental organizations under international law' (1998) 6 *Indiana Journal of Global Legal Studies* 579.

——, 'Reconceptualising International Legal Personality of Influential Non-State Actors: Towards a Rebuttable Presumption of Normative Responsibilities' in Fleurs J (ed), *International Legal Personality* (Aldershot, Ashgate, 2010).

Nye JS, *Soft power: The Means to Success in World Politics* (New York, Public Affairs, 2004).

—— and Keohane RO, 'An Introduction' in Nye JS and Keohane RO (eds), *Transnational Relations and World Politics* (Cambridge MA, Harvard University Press, 1971).

O'Connell ME, 'New International Legal Process' (1999) *American Journal of International Law* 334.

——, 'Enhancing the status of non-state actors through a global war on terror' (2004) 43 *Columbia Journal of Transnational Law* 435.

Oleschak-Pillai R, 'Accountability of International Organisations: An Analysis of the World Bank's Inspection Panel' in Wouters J and others (eds), *Accountability for Human Rights Violations by International Organisations* (Antwerp, Intersentia, 2010).

Paasivirta E, *The European Union: From an Aggregate of States to a Legal Person?* (1997) 2 *Hofstra Law and Policy Symposium* 37.

Paulsson J, 'Arbitration without privity' (1995) 10 *ICSID Review* 232.

Paust J, 'Human rights responsibilities of private corporations' (2002) 35 *Vanderbilt Journal of Transnational Law* 801.

——, 'Use of armed force against terrorists in Afghanistan, Iraq, and Beyond' (2001) 35 *Cornell International Law Journal* 533.

——, 'Reality of Private Rights, Duties, and Participation in the International Legal Process' (2003) 25 *Michigan Journal of International Law* 1229.

——, 'Self-defense targetings of non-state actors and permissibility of US use of drones in Pakistan' (2009) 19 *Journal of Transnational Law & Policy* 237.

——, 'Nonstate Actor Participation in International Law and the Pretense of Exclusion' (2010) 51 *Virginia Journal of International Law* 977.

——, 'Terrorism's Proscription and Core Elements of an Objective Definition' (2010) 8 *Santa Clara Journal of International Law* 51.

——, 'Propriety of Self-Defense Targetings of Members of al Qaeda and Applicable Principles of Distinction and Proportionality' (2012) 18 *ILSA Journal of International & Comparative Law.*

Pauwelyn J, Wessel RA and Wouters J, 'When Structures Become Shackles: Stagnation and Dynamics in International Lawmaking' Forthcoming in *European Journal of International Law.*

Penalver AM, 'Corporate Disconnect: The Blackwater Problem and the FCPA Solution' (2009) 19 *Cornell Journal of Law & Public Policy* 459.

Pentikainen M, 'Changing International Subjectivity and Rights and Obligations under International Law-Status of Corporations' (2012) 8 *Utrecht Law Review* 145.

Peters A, *Non-state Actors as Standard Setters* (Cambridge, Cambridge University Press, 2009).

Petras J and Veltmeyer H, *Globalisation Unmasked; Imperialism in the 21st Century* (Halifax, Zed Books, 2001).

Portmann R, *Legal Personality in International Law* (Cambridge, Cambridge University Press, 2010).
Prakash A and Potoski M, 'The International Organization of Standardization as a Global Governor. A Club Theory Perspective' in Avant DD, Finnemore M and Sell SK (eds), *Who Governs the Globe?* vol 114 (Cambridge, Cambridge University Press, 2010).
Pries L, *Rethinking Transnationalism: The Meso-link of Organisations* (Abingdon, Routledge, 2008).
Quack S, 'Legal professionals and transnational law-making: A case of distributed agency' (2007) 14 *Organization* 643.
Raday F, 'Privatising Human Rights and the Abuse of Power' (2000) 13 *Canadian Journal of Law & Jurisprudence* 103.
Rama-Montaldo M, 'International legal personality and implied powers of international organizations' (1970) 44 *British Yearbook of International Law* 111.
Ratner S, 'Corporations and human rights: a theory of legal responsibility' (2001) 111 *Yale Law Journal* 443.
Reinisch A, *International Organizations before National Courts* (Cambridge, Cambridge University Press, 2000).
——, 'Developing Human Rights and Humanitarian Law Accountability of the Security Council for the Imposition of Economic Sanctions' (2001) *American Journal of International Law* 851.
——, 'Securing the accountability of international organizations' (2001) 7 *Global Governance* 131.
——, 'The Changing International Legal Framework for Dealing with Non-State Actors' in Alston P (ed), *Non-state Actors and Human Rights* (Oxford, Oxford University Press, 2005).
——, 'Expropriation' in Muchlinski P, Ortino F and Schreuer C (eds), *The Oxford Handbook of International Investment Law* (Oxford, Oxford University Press, 2008).
——, 'Legality of Expropriations' in Reinisch A and Schreuer C (eds), *Standards of Investment Protection* (Oxford, Oxford University Press, 2008).
——, 'From Rediscovered Waiting Periods to Ever More Activist Annulment Committees—ICSID Arbitration in 2010' (2012) 11 *Global Community YILJ* 933.
—— and Irgel C, 'The participation of non-governmental organisations (NGOs) in the WTO dispute settlement system' (2001) 1 *Non-State Actors and International Law* 127.
Reisman WM, *Folded Lies: Bribery, Crusades, and Reforms* (New York, Free Press, 1979).
—— *The Quest for World Order and Human Dignity in the Twenty-first Century: Constitutive Process and Individual Commitment: General Course on Public International Law* (The Hague, Hague Academy of International Law, 2013).
—— and Suzuki E, 'Recognition and Social Change in International Law: A Prologue for Decisionmaking' in McDougal MS, Reisman WM and Weston BH (eds), *Toward World Order and Human Dignity: Essays in Honor of Myres S McDougal* (New York, Free Press, 1976).
——, Wiessner S and Willard AR, 'The New Haven School: A Brief Introduction' (2007) 32 *Yale Journal of International Law* 575.
Riedel E, 'The Development of International Law: Alternatives to Treaty-Making? International Organizations and Non-State Actors' in Wolfrum R and Röben V

(eds), *Developments of International Law in Treaty Making* (Heidelberg, Springer, 2005).
Rigaux F, 'Non-state Actors from the Perspective of the Institut de Droit international' in d'Aspremont J (ed), *Participants in the International LegalSystem: Multiple Perspectives on Non-state Actors in International Law* (Abingdon, Routledge, 2011).
Risse T, 'Transnational Actors and World Politics' in Carlsnaes W, Risse T and Simmons BA (eds), *Handbook of International Relations* (London, Sage, 2002).
Risse-Kappen T, *Bringing Transnational Relations Back In: Non-state Actors, Domestic Structures, and International Institutions* Cambridge Studies in International Relations (Cambridge, Cambridge University Press, 1995).
Röben V, 'Proliferation of Actors' in Wolfrum R and Röben V (eds), *Developments of international Law in Treaty Making* (Heidelberg, Springer, 2005).
Roberts A, 'Clash of paradigms: actors and analogies shaping the investment treaty system' (2013) 107 *American Journal of International Law* 45.
Rosefielde S, 'Economies of the Military-Industrial Complex' in Alexeev M and Weber S (eds), *The Oxford Handbook of the Russian Economy* (Oxford, Oxford University Press, 2013).
Rugendyke B, 'Lilliputians or Leviathans? NGOs as Advocates' in Rugendyke B (ed), *NGOs as Advocates for Development in a Globalising World* (Abingdon, Routledge, 2007).
Ruggie JG, 'Reconstituting the global public domain—issues, actors, and practices' (2004) 10 *European Journal Of International Relations* 499.
Ruys T and Verhoeven S, 'Attacks by private actors and the right of self-defence' (2005) 10 *Journal of Conflict and Security Law* 289.
Ryfman P, 'Non-governmental organizations: an indispensable player of humanitarian aid' (2007) 89 *International Review of the Red Cross* 21.
Saideman SM, 'Discrimination in International Relations: Analyzing External Support for Ethnic Groups' (2002) 39 *Journal of Peace Research* 27.
Sapra S, 'The WTO System of Trade Governance: The Stale NGO Debate and the Approriate Role for Non-State Actors' (2008) 11 *Oregon Review of International Law* 37.
Sarooshi D, *International Organizations and their Exercise of Sovereign Powers* (Oxford, Oxford University Press, 2005).
Sassen S, *Sociology of Globalization* (New York, WW Norton, 2006).
Schäferhoff M, Campe S and Kaan C, 'Transnational Public–Private Partnerships in International Relations: Making Sense of Concepts, Research Frameworks, and Results' (2009) 11 *International Studies Review* 451.
Schmid AP, 'The links between transnational organized crime and terrorist crimes' (1996) 2 *Transnational Organized Crime* 40.
Schoiswohl M, 'De Facto Regimes and Human Rights Obligations-The Twilight Zone of Public International Law' (2001) 6 *Austrian Review of International & European Law* 45.
——, *Status and (human Rights) Obligations of Non-recognized de Facto Regimes in International Law: The Case of 'Somaliland': The Resurrection of Somaliland Against All International 'Odds': State Collapse, Secession, Non-recognition, and Human Rights* (Dordrecht, Martinus Nijhoff, 2004).
Scholte JA, *Globalization: A Critical Introduction* (Basingstoke, Palgrave Macmillan, 2005).

Scott C, *Torture as Tort: Comparative Perspectives on the Development of Transnational Human Rights Litigation* (Oxford, Hart Publishing, 2001).

——, 'Transnational Law as Proto-Concept: Three Conceptions' (2009) 10 *German Law Journal* 859.

Seary B, 'The Early History: From the Congress of Vienna to the San Francisco Conference' in Willetts P (ed), *The Consciousness of the World: The Influence of non-governmental organisations in the UN System* (Washington DC, Brookings, 1996).

Segerlund L, *Making Corporate Social Responsibility a Global Concern: Norm Construction in a Globalizing World* (Aldershot, Ashgate, 2010).

Sending OJ and Neumann IB, 'Governance to governmentality: analyzing NGOs, states, and power' (2006) 50 *International Studies Quarterly* 651.

Seyersted F, 'Is the International Personality of Intergovernmental Organizations Valid vis-a-vis Non-Members?' (1964) 4 *Indian Journal of International Law* 233.

——, 'Objective International Personality of Intergovernmental Organizations-Do Their Capacities Really Depend upon the Conventions Establishing Them' (1964) 34 *Nordisk Tidsskrift International Ret* 3.

Shabecoff P, 'France Must Pay Greenpeace $8 Milion in Sinking of Ship', *The New York Times* (New York), available at www.nytimes.com/1987/10/03/world/france-must-pay-greenpeace-8-million-in-sinking-of-ship.html.

Shah NA, 'Self-defence, anticipatory self-defence and pre-emption: international law's response to terrorism' (2007) 12 *Journal of Conflict and Security Law* 95.

Shelton D, 'The Participation of Nongovernmental Organizations in International Judicial Proceedings' (1994) 88 *American Journal of International Law* 611.

Simons P, 'Corporate voluntarism and human rights: The adequacy and effectiveness of voluntary self-regulation regimes' (2004) *Relations Industrielles/Industrial Relations* 101.

Singh MP, 'India—Protection of Human Rights against State and Non-State Action' in Fedtke J and Oliver D (eds), *Human rights and the Private Sphere: A Comparative Study* (Abingdon, Routledge-Cavendish, 2007).

Spieker H, 'The Right to Give and Receive Humanitarian Assistance' in Heintze H-J, Zwitter, Andrej (ed), *International Law and Humanitarian Assistance: A Crosscut Through Legal Issues Pertaining to Humanitarianism* (Heidelberg, Springer, 2011).

Ssenyonjo M, *Economic, Social and Cultural Rights in International Law* (Oxford, Hart Publishing, 2009).

Steffek J, Kissling C and Nanz P, *Civil Society Participation in European and Global Governance: A Cure for the Democratic Deficit?* (Basingstoke, Palgrave Macmillan 2008).

Stein U, *Lex mercatoria: Realität und Theorie* (Frankfurt a M, V Klostermann, 1995).

Steiner HJ, *Transnational Legal Problems* (Eagan MN, Foundation Press, 1986).

Steinhardt R, 'Corporate Responsibility and the International Law of Human Rights: The New Lex Mercatoria' in Alston P (ed), *Non-state Actors and Human Rights* (Oxford, Oxford University Press, 2005).

Stiles KW, 'States, Non-State Actors and Global Policy Formulation' in Higgott RA, Underhill GRD and Bieler A (eds), *Non-State Actors and Authority in the Global System* (Abingdon, Routledge, 2000).

Stone D, 'Learning lessons, policy transfer and the international diffusion of policy ideas'. (2001) 69/1 CSGR Working Paper.

Strange S, *The Retreat of the State: The Diffusion of Power in the World Economy* (Cambridge, Cambridge University Press, 1996).

Struett M, 'NGOs, the International Criminal Court, and the Politics of Writing International Law' in Dekker IF et al, *Governance and International Legal Theory* (Dordrecht, Springer, 2004).

Sullivan R and Hachez N, 'Human Rights Norms for Business: The Missing Piece of the Ruggie Jigsaw-The Case of Institutional Investors' in Mares R (ed), *The UN Guiding Principles on Business and Human Rights: Foundations and Implementation* (Dordrecht, Martinus Nijhoff, 2012).

Suzuki E, 'Self-Determination and World Public Order: Community Response to Territorial Separation' (1975) 16 *Virginia Journal of International Law* 779.

——, 'Extraconstitutional Change and World Pulic Order: A Prologue to Decision-Making' (1977) 15 *Houston Law Review* 23.

——, 'The New Haven School of Jurisprudence and Non-State Actors in International Law in Policy Perspective' (2012) 42 *Journal of Policy Studies* 41.

—— and Nanwani S, 'Responsibility of international organizations: the accountability mechanisms of multilateral development banks' (2005) 27 *Michigan Journal of International Law* 177.

Sybesma-Knol N and van der Heijden P, *Rol en betekenis van de rechtsontwikkeling in de ILO, serie: Nederlandse Vereniging voor Internationaal Recht* (Deventer, Kluwer, 1999).

Talmon S, *Recognition in International Law: A Bibliography* (Dordrecht, Martinus Nijhoff Publishers, 2000).

——, 'Recognition of the Libyan National Transitional Council' (2011) 15 *ASIL Insights* 13.

Tams C, 'The necessity and proportionality of anti-terrorist self-defence' in Herik LJ vd and Schrijver N (eds), *Counter-terrorism Strategies in a Fragmented International Legal Order: Meeting the Challenges* (Cambridge, Cambridge University Press, 2013).

Tams CJ, 'The use of force against terrorists' (2009) 20 *European Journal of International Law* 359.

Tanaka M, 'Bridging the GAP between northern NGOS and southern sovereigns in the trade-environment debate: the pursuit of democratic dispute settlements in the WTO under the Rio Principles' (2003) 30 *Ecology Law Quarterly* 113.

Tarrow SG, *The New Transnational Activism* (Cambridge, Cambridge University Press, 2005).

Taulbee JL and Creekmore Jr MV, 'NGO Mediation: The Carter Center' (2003) 10 *International Peacekeeping* 156.

Taylor I, 'Liberal Markets and the Republic of Europe: Contextualizing the Growth of Transnational Organized Crime' in Berdal MR and Serrano M (eds), *Transnational organized crime and international security* (Boulder CO, Lynne Rienner Publishers, 2002).

Tennant EW, 'Locating Transnational Activists: The United States Anti-Apartheid Movement and the Confines of the National' in Sassen S (ed), *Deciphering the Global: Its Scales, Spaces and Subjects* (Abingdon, Routledge, 2007).

Teubner G, '"Global Bukowina": Legal Pluralism in the World Society' in Teubner G (ed), *Global Law Without A State* (Brookfield, Dartmouth, 1997).

Thompson G, *Between Hierarchies and Markets: The Logic and Limits of Network Forms of Organization* (Oxford, Oxford University Press, 2003).

Tiefenbrun SW, 'Sex Slavery in the United States and the Law Enacted to Stop it Here and Abroad' (2005) 11 *William & Mary Journal of Women & Law* 317.

Tietje C, Brouder A and Nowrot K, *Philip C. Jessup's Transnational Law Revisited on the Occasion of the 50th anniversary of its Publication* (Halle/Saale, Universität Wittenberg, 2006).

Toope SJ, *Mixed International Arbitration* (Cambridge, Cambridge University Press,1990).

Trapp KN, 'Back to basics: necessity, proportionality, and the right of self-defence against non-state terrorist actors' (2007) 56 *International and Comparative Law Quarterly* 141.

——, 'Shared Responsibility and Organized Non-State Actors in the Terrorism Context' (2015) 63 Shares Research Paper.

Tsagourias N, 'Non-State Actors and the Use of Force' in d'Aspremont J (ed), *Participants in the international legal system: multiple perspectives on non-state actors in international law* (Abingdon, Routledge, 2011).

Tunkin GI, 'The legal nature of the United Nations' in International AdD (ed), *Receuil de Cours*, vol 119 (Dordrecht, Martinus Nijhoff Publishers, 1966).

Tushnet M, 'The issue of state action/horizontal effect in comparative constitutional law' (2003) 1 *International Journal of Constitutional Law* 79.

Urry J, *Global Complexities* (Cambridge, Polity Press, 2003).

Van Aaken A, 'Effectuating Public International Law through Market Mechanisms?' (Year) 165 *Journal of Institutional and Theoretical Economics* 33.

van den Muijsenbergh WH and Rezai S, 'Corporations and the European Convention on Human Rights' (2012) 25 *Pacific McGeorge Global Business & Development Law Journal* 43.

van der Wilt H, 'Corporate Criminal Responsibility for International Crimes: Exploring the Possibilities' (2013) 12 *Chinese Journal of International Law* 43.

Van Schaack B, 'Finding the Tort of Terrorism in International Law' (2009) 28 *Review of Litigation* 381.

van Steenberghe R, 'Non-State Actors from the Perspective of the International Committee of the Red Cross' in d'Aspremont J (ed), *Participants in the International Legal System: Multiple Perspectives on Non-state Actors in International Law* (Abingdon, Routledge, 2011).

Verhoeven S, 'International Responsibility of Armed Opposition Groups: Lessons from State Responsibility for Actions of Armed Opposition Groups' in Gal-Or N, Noortmann M and Ryngaert C (eds), *Conflicts and Markets: the Responsibility of Non-State Actors* (Boston MA, Brill, 2015).

Vermeer-Künzli A, 'A Matter of Interest: Diplomatic Protection and State Responsibility Erga Omnes' (2007) 56 *International and Comparative Law Quarterly* 553.

Vernon R, *Sovereignty at Bay: The multinational Spread of U.S Enterprises* (New York, Basic Books, 1971).

Vertovec S, *Transnationalism* (Abingdon, Routledge, 2009).

Vogel D, 'Private global business regulation' (2008) 11 *Annual Review of Political Science* 261.

Voitovich S, *International economic Organizations in the International legal Process* (Dordrecht, Martinus Nijhoff Publishers, 1995).

Von Bogdandy A and others, *The Exercise of Public Authority by International Institutions: Advancing International Institutional Law*, vol 210 (Heidelberg, Springer, 2010).

von Walter A, 'Arbitration on Oil Concession Disputes' in Wolfrum R (ed), *Max Planck Encyclopedia of International Law* (Oxford, Oxford University Press, 2013).

Waelde T and Kolo A, 'Environmental regulation, investment protection and 'regulatory taking 'in international law' (2001) 50 *International and Comparative Law Quarterly* 811.

Waelde TW and Ndi G, 'Stabilizing International Investment Commitments: International Law Versus Contract Interpretation' (1996) 31 *Texas International Law Journal* 215.

Walczak A, 'Coming to the Table: Why Corporations Should Advocate for Legal Norms for the Protection of Indigenous Rights' (2010) 42 *George Washington International Law Review* 623.

Waltz KN, *Theory of international politics* (Reading Mass, Addison-Wesley, 1979).

Wapner P, 'Politics beyond the state environmental activism and world civic politics' (1995) 47 *World Politics* 311.

Warwick DP, 'Transnational Participation and International Peace' in Nye JS and Keohane RO (eds), *Transnational Relations and World Politics* (Cambridge MA, Harvard University Press, 1971).

Washburn J, 'Negotiation of the Rome Statute for the International Criminal Court and International Lawmaking in the 21st Century' (1999) 11 *Pace International Law Review* 361.

Wedgwood R, 'Legal Personality and the Role of Non-Governmental Organizations and Non-State Political Entities' in Hofmann R and Geissler N (eds), *Non-state Actors as New Subjects of International Law: International Law from the Traditional State Order Towards the Law of the Global Community* (Berlin, Duncker & Humblot, 1999).

Weiler JH, 'The geology of international law–governance, democracy and legitimacy' (2004) 64 *Heidelberg Journal of International Law* 547.

Weilert K, 'Transnationale Unternehmen im rechtsfreien Raum? Geltung und Reichweite völkerrechtlicher Standards' (2009) 69 *Zeitschrift für ausländisches öffentliches Recht und Völkerrecht* 883.

Weissbrodt D and Kruger M, 'Norms on the responsibilities of transnational corporations and other business enterprises with regard to human rights' (2003) 97 *American Journal of International Law* 901.

Weissner S, 'Legitimacy and Accountability of NGOs: A Policy-Oriented Perspective' in Heere WP (ed), *From government to Governance: The Growing Impact of Non-state Actors on the International and European Legal System: Proceedings of the Sixth Hague Joint Conference Held in The Hague, the Netherlands, 3–5 July 2003* (The Hague, TMC Asser Press, 2004).

Wessel R, 'Regulating Technological Innovation through Informal International Law: The Exercise of International Public Authority by Transnational Actors' in Heldeweg MA and Kica E (eds), *Regulating Technological Innovation: A Multidisciplinary Approach* (Basingstoke, Palgrave Macmillan, 2011).

——, 'Institutional Law-Making: The Development of a Global Normative Web' in Brölmann C and Radi Y (eds), *Handbook on the Theory and Practice of International Law-Making* (Cheltenham, Edward Elgar, 2014).
——, 'What's Wrong with International Law? Revealing the Publicness of International Law' in Nollkaemper A, Ryngaert C and Molenaar E (eds), *What's Wrong With International Law?* (Dordrecht, Martinus Nijhoff, 2015).
—— and Dekker I, 'Governance by International Organisations: Rethinking the Source and Normative Force of International Decisions' in Dekker I and Werner W (eds), *Governance and International Legal Theory* (Dordrecht, Martinus Nijhoff, 2004).
Wessel RA, 'Revisiting the international legal status of the EU' (2000) 5 *European Foreign Affairs Review* 507.
White LC, *The Structure of Private International Organizations* (Philadelphia PA, George S Ferguson Co, 1933).
——, *International Non-governmental Organizations; Their Purposes, Methods, and Accomplishments* (New Brunswick NJ, Rutgers University Press, 1951).
White ND, 'Separate but Connected: Inter-Governmental Organizations and International Law' (2008) 5 *International Organization Law Review* 175.
Willetts P, *'The conscience of the world': the influence of non-governmental organisations in the UN system* (New York, Brookings Institution, 1996).
Williams P, *Violent Non-State Actors and National and International Security* (International Relations and Security Network 2008).
Wisotzki S, 'Between Morality and Military Interests: Norm Setting in Humanitarian Arms Control' (2009) 92 *Peace Research Institute Frankfurt Reports* http://edoc.vifapol.de/opus/volltexte/2011/2733/pdf/PRIF_NO_92hp.pdf
Woods N, 'Multilateralism and building stronger international institutions' in Ebrahim A and Weisband E (eds), *Global Accountabilities: Participation, Pluralism, and Public Ethics* (Cambridge, Cambridge University Press, 2007).
Wouters J and others, *Accountability for Human Rights Violations by International Organisations* (Antwerp, Intersentia, 2010).
—— and Chanet L, 'Corporate Human Rights Responsibility: A European Perspective' (2007) 6 *Northwest University Journal of International Human Rights* 262.
——, 'Rechten en plichten van (multinationale) ondernemingen in het internationaal recht' in Houben R and Rutten S (eds), *Actuele problemen van financieel, vennootschaps—en fiscaal recht Feestbundel 20 jaar Werkgroep financieel recht* (Antwerp, Intersentia, 2007).
——, De Man P and Chanet L, 'Long and Winding Road of International Investment Agreements: Toward a Coherent Framework for Reconciling the Interests of Developed and Developing Countries' (2009) 3 *Human Rights & International Legal Discourse* 263.
—— and de Smet L, 'Het E.V.R.M., internationale mensenrechtenstandaarden en (multinationale) ondernemingen' in Lemmens P (ed), *Uitdagingen door en voor het EVRM* (Alphen a/d Rijn, Kluwer 2005).
—— and Hachez N, 'When Rules and Values Collide: How Can a Balanced Application of Investor Protection Provisions and Human Rights Be Ensured' (2009) 3 *Human Rights & International Legal Discourse* 301.
—— and Ryngaert C, 'Litigation for Overseas Corporate Human Rights Abuse in the European Union: The Challenge of Jurisdiction' (2008) 40 *George Washington International Law Review* 939.

Zambrana Tévar N, 'Shortcomings and Disadvantages of Existing Legal Mechanisms to Hold Multinational Corporations Accountable for Human Rights Violations' (2012) 4 *Cuadernos de derecho transnacional* 397.

Zumbansen P, 'Piercing the Legal Veil: Commercial Arbitration and Transnational Law' (2002) 8 *European Law Journal* 400.

——, 'Transnational law' (2006) *Encyclopedia of Comparative Law* 738.

Index

www.ingramcontent.com/pod-product-compliance
Lightning Source LLC
Chambersburg PA
CBHW051150180926
51611CB00001B/7
9781509917839